HUNG OUT TO DIE:
American Wars And Defense Politics

Hung Out To Die: American Wars and Defense Politics
is the first book of the projected *VMS Trilogy*, to include
Why Economics Doesn't Work
and
a third volume as yet untitled

HUNG OUT TO DIE:
American Wars And Defense Politics

by Mark Dennis Greenfield

UNHERD Opinions
New York, New York
1994

HUNG OUT TO DIE:
American Wars And Defense Politics

is dedicated to:

Lord Chancellor William Greenfield, later Archbishop of York, First Collector of English Judicial Decisions, Originator of the "Spendthrift" Trust and Possible Assassin of Pope Boniface VIII, Defender of Carlisle

Sir Richard Greenfield, Baronet, Failed Regicide (Charles I), Thirty Years' War

Lt. Col. Robert Greenfield, New York Volunteers, American Civil War

General Wesley Merritt, Captor of Manila, 1898

Cataloging Data:

Greenfield, Mark Dennis (1953 -)
        Hung out to die : american wars and defense politics.

Library of Congress Card Catalog Number – 94-60199;
ISBN – 0-9641115-0-0.

Printed in the USA.

HUNG OUT TO DIE:
American Wars And Defense Politics

Preface

In its first half, this book clarifies the large issues of war and peace, primarily in the American context, and in its second half the somewhat more specialized issues of the organization -- institutional and technological -- of that force. Such clarification is necessary not simply to overcome simple ignorance and naiveté, although those are present at times, but mainly to oppose patterned ignorance and willful obfuscation. On military and defense issues, it is not merely trite to refer to hindsight as peculiarly accurate, it is incorrect; hindsight exists only in our minds, and is as subject to nonfunction as any other mental -- and therefore complex -- function. Accepted misinterpretations distort our appreciation of the present and its prospects, as indeed they are meant to. Such patterns are frequently alluded to that they may be more widely recognized and compensated for or dispensed with. Variously, such patterns may be technological or institutional, but the main bevy is ideological, and that from liberals and those farther left. Put simply, these patterns tend to be either anti-American, in intent or effect, or anti-military, in intent or effect. A minor paradox is the bad faith of the people spinning the intentional patterns, who frequently affect patriotism or interest in a strong defense; more sincere enemies could undoubtedly make more accurate charges.

Foreign examples are used when important to the U.S., familiar or especially instructive. Probably the most celebrated example of military incompetence of all is the "Charge of the Light Brigade" in the Crimean War Battle of Balaklava. Yet the battle was a British victory, as the Russian line was broken by the Charge of the Heavy Brigade while the enemy concentrated upon the unfortunate Light Brigade. Victory was forgotten for four reasons: British politics had become a fountain of agitation, the high commanders were rather anonymous, Tennyson memorialized the dead with aplomb and the British had disastrously wintered at isolated and unsheltered Balaklava. Strangely enough, while the Charge of the Light Brigade was used as a metaphor for bumbling brasshats, Balaklava was commemorated as a name for a helmet.

Would such cavilry have flown in a simpler time? At Waterloo, the already lustrous repute of Wellington was embellished by a brilliant defensive stand, albeit one stained by the impetuous charge of Ponsonby's Unionist Brigade (Heavy and over-strength), slaughtered by the French center. Not part of a strategy, and unsupported by infantry, artillery or any of the dozen or so other cavalry units under Wellington's control, Ponsonby's defeat merely put fresh courage into the flagging French. But British victory at Waterloo is mainly what is remembered, and Ponsonby, if at all, for gallantry rather than for foolhardiness.

On the large issues of war and peace, the shifting goals of American liberals lead to various fundamental contradictions. But liberal and leftist icons, even the kind that waffled, are always to be respected. Whether Henry David Thoreau the pacifist or Henry David Thoreau the apostle of armed insurrection, it is always Henry David Thoreau the icon, whose versatility actually enhances his value (there is even Henry David Thoreau the environmentalist -- hey, he **doesn't** slice vegetables). Leftists love to moon about "endless cycles of violence" when some leftist aggression is threatened with counter-action, but generally they're busy tossing gasoline on the flames they have themselves set. The immediate spark which set off the U.S. Civil War was the bombardment of Fort Sumter, a bloodbath in no sense whatsoever. Remarkably, violence had been subsiding for years, as hundreds of dead in Bleeding Kansas Territory were followed by the lesser tragedy of the little village at Harpers Ferry, ghoulishly cheered by the "anti-war" Thoreau, and then by the nearly bloodless denting of Fort Sumter's masonry walls on its little island in Charleston's harbor. The cycle of violence was accelerated not by violence itself, but by the fanaticism and opportunism which had caused it in the first place. Political factionalism elected Lincoln to the constitutional office of President, responsible for enforcing a document he had frequently denounced with noisome vitriol. His enforcement would be somewhat selective, quashing the rebellion of his enemies while promoting his own subversions. But in our time, the spectacle of constitutional forms for unconstitutional government has become so chronic that the rituals of denial have even been neglected.

And denial is hardly possible with such blatant two-steps as Woodrow Wilson's neutral in thought, word and deed and Woodrow Wilson's Arsenal of Democracy or Franklin Roosevelt's Neutrality Acts and Franklin Roosevelt's Lend-Lease. The moral compass of liberals consists of the smug assumption that whichever way they happen to be facing at the moment is forward, and that the world should forthwith re-order itself to that meridian of the minute. Describing Lend-Lease with the homey metaphor of lending a neighbor a garden hose so that he might save his burning house was a particular whopper. The multi-billion dollar garden hose was in fact used by that neighbor to spray burning gasoline on the house of a third neighbor, and, like most things lent to neighbors, was only slowly, grudgingly and partially returned to the Arson of Democracy. The belief that we should have less to do with such neighbors is too sane for liberals, who denounce it as isolationism.

Of late, American liberals, frustrated by the failure of their own isolationism in preventing American victory in the Gulf War, have been snuffling furiously for phantom sales of American weapons to Iraq. One would think, from blurbs in *THE NEWSPAPER OF RECORD*, that atomic bombs were made out of computer chips, a later innovation than fission bombs, and severely extraneous to them. Of course, Iraq had been an Israeli bogeyman for some time, and hence deserving American censure through yet another of those "special relationships", wherein the U.S. truckles to dubious foreign regimes. But another country manifestly hostile to the U.S. (and, among others, to Israel), Libya, has indeed received large quantities of several American-pattern weapons, Sparrow missiles, M-113 armored personnel carriers and homing torpedoes. The reason is that the government, little interested in American jobs in arms exports, has actively encouraged production abroad for diplomatic purposes. So Italy builds "American" weapons, and sells them to our enemy Libya, for Italian jobs and export earnings.

But when Italy tried to sell some such to Iraq, at a time when Iraq was not hostile toward the U.S. but Israel was hostile to Iraq, the U.S. dutifully pressured the Italians out of the sale. With their signature inaccuracy, American liberals have since scapegoated the U.S. for "permitting" the financing transactions (by the U.S. branch of an Italian bank with establishment liberal Brent Scowcroft on the board of directors) for the very weapons whose actual sale the U.S. blocked. For the unquestionably patriotic, their country is always wrong, even when it's right.

The trade in weapons is but one aspect of the weapons themselves, which have a plethora of concepts rattling around in the more technical areas of defense. These include the arms race, disarmament, obsolescence, roles and missions, the possibility, impossibility or desirability of air defense, the nature of so-called break-throughs, the constraints of a mobile weapon's medium, guided weapons, comparable costs, service re-organizations, political influence, the economic structure of the arms industry (the so-called war economy), the information boom (in the military sense, the fetish of reconnaissance, predating those modern electronic computers), etc. etc. Usually, these weapons concepts are deployed more according to ideological or other fashions than according to merit, more as weapons than as concepts.

In more technical matters, anti-military agitators themselves seek out comparisons, although their purpose is finding ground to deploy advantageous jargon. For example, those who oppose a technology for fashion's sake characterize it as obsolete. Questions of cost and effectiveness -- appropriateness for some range of useful tasks -- are thereby put out of bounds for the moment (to be nominally resurrected when ideologically opportune), in favor of mere novelty, however tastefully disguised. As with the semantic counter-marches of war and peace -- usually peace or a crusade, seldom actually an acknowledgment of war -- military issues are usually paired into opposed fetishes, with fashion or ideological needs dictating the favored pair of the moment. Thus, during the Cold War Liberal era (1948-1968), Robert McNamara and company advocated cost-benefit analysis (in theory anyway; in practice, the specific calculations were usually bungled) and massive retaliation. During the Modern Liberal era, however, McNamara moved to the left, reflecting his movement to the World Bank and liberalism's movement from titularly favoring a strong defense to opposing defense, and has of late been more an advocate of disarmament. Unlike the left-liberal perspectives of changing jobs or ideologies, and their assiduous reflection by the media, the actual real-world determinants of weapons pursued have been technology and its institutionalization.

Since 1984, the U.S. has spent 10 billion dollars buying Apache attack helicopters, and further billions to run dozens of Apache battalions. The Apache is an extremely refined helicopter, too refined for hard use, but the bad news is that attack helicopters are intrinsically stupid. Bombing and strafing do not require vertical take-off and landing and hovering and all of the expenses that go with them. The Army uses helicopters for attack and other roles largely because of Air Force jealousy of more valuable weapons -- missiles and fixed-wing aircraft -- as institutionalized 35 years ago and left in place through inertia and preoccupation of the civilian authorities with more pressing or politically profitable "issues". Army helicopters are the primary American example of a weapon over-used for entirely **institutional** reasons.

To a lesser degree, the Navy uses helicopters for the reason that they are more "modern" or convenient than older technologies, even though the calculus is defective. For somewhat weightier reasons, the Navy's submarine branch has flourished, first as an expansion from small "coastal defense" submarines to larger and ludicrously named "fleet boats" to the twin tasks of missile battery carriage and anti-submarine submarines. The submarine, largely developed by Americans, was pursued as a technology despite its limited usefulness in wars. The main spur to this early weapons system was the need to deliver an actual weapon, the "automobile" torpedo (automobile soon came to mean a contemporary sensation, the horseless carriage). Enthusiasts for the possibility of the submarine itself (predating the mobile torpedo) had long searched for a crucial role appropriate to its developing capability. Torpedoes made the submarine viable, but for what? The focus moved from coastal defense in the days of limited range, to use as a terror weapon of attrition against merchant ships, to substantial failure for fleet patrol (Japanese), to carriage of seaborne missile silos. In the last case, the over-valuation of the submarine, for **technological** rather than for military reasons, has led, through institutionalization of that technological drive, to hunter-killer submarines. After all, the reasoning goes, if the submarine is top dog (at what, no one has explained), then it must take other submarines to kill it -- find a dog who will eat a dog. Don't shoot a rabid dog, send out the family dog to chew it up.

And if the atomic-powered submarine is the primary example of procurement overkill, including its frequent endorsement by titular opponents of nuclear power (Bill Clinton, for example), the scandalous gutting of atomic power for surface warships has been the primary example of pseudo-economizing. Democrats moan about oil imports and American vulnerability, and promote "high-tech" and imaginary savings on defense through bogus standardization. Yet the two starts on surface atomic power by the Eisenhower and Nixon administrations were aborted by the Whiz Kid advents under Kennedy and Carter, the second abortion sustained by the Reagan-Weinberger and Bush-Cheney teams. And this despite the design of nuclear reactors adaptable for either submarine or surface use, standardization that has long eluded U.S. civilian nuclear power, but which has been foisted upon the nation for such doomed fiascos as the TFX. It might shock some that modern battleships, aircraft and submarines all debuted in significant service in World War I, that the technologies were more simultaneous than successive (when the battleship is labelled peculiarly obsolete, the concept, not the artifact, is an anachronism). The first collisions between such battleships and the submarine and the aircraft carrier were historic but obscure precisely because they refuted fashionable opinion. Truth is strange when pundits have distorted our expectations.

The chapter on the arms trade begins with two pages on guns and their sexual symbolism to troubled liberal minds. Some people may find this offensive, just as others may find the pages on Lincoln the man and Lincoln the commander offensive, or others might find three paragraphs, on Seymour Melman (page 78), on Lyndon Johnson's electioneering (124) and on proposed Israeli submarine production (318), as anti-Semitic. In each case, the problem is that a higher ration of truth is presented here than most people are permitted, by themselves or by the media. Lies help someone; that's why they're manufactured, and why there are so many of them around. If you aren't stepping on some, you aren't covering any real ground. The people singled out for special attention herein are notoriously public figures -- journalists, politicians and tenured, usually chaired, academics, people whom someone has seen fit to provide with soapboxes.

This book is the author's own soapbox, and he is responsible for any errors in it, although he cannot accept any responsibility for the hypersensitivities of others to imagined wrongs. They have their own apparently limitless supply of soapboxes. There may be an attempt to indict the author for political bias (and he has plenty of that in the original sense of skepticism), but the treatment herein of Wm. F. Buckley, Pat Buchanan, Emmett Tyrrell, Evans & Novak, Jeanne Kirkpatrick, Dorothy Rabinowitz, Mendell Rivers, Henry Jackson and Admiral Halsey is a product of their records, just as the treatment of icons more to the left is merited by their records. Others may quibble at the amount of detail, but exposing previous error on a subject requires it. The proper refutation of never is a recitation of whens; anything else is an exchange of tis and tisn't, and there an easy lie will always beat a more complex truth. There are no footnotes to detract from narrative flow;

what some might regard as digressions are relevant to concepts treated within the text. There are also no cross-references within the text, and no index to avoid tempting people to quote from isolated text. The proper way of reading a book is to read a book.

Among the views challenged in the text are those of such icons as Samuel Eliot Morison, Allan Nevins and Walter Millis. Journals, especially those of New York, get occasional mention for their more egregious distortions; three excerpts -- from Pete Hamill, Mary McGrory and a Lockheed company sheet -- are dealt with at length. Reality checks on works of varying value from three recent years appear in the notes.

A rough outline of American dead -- battle, exposure and prisoners (100,000+) -- from its wars:

War	U.S. Dead	Liberal Crusades (The Draft Wars)		Toll
Civil	600,000	First, Domestic		600,000
World War I	100,000	Second	100,000	
World War II	400,000	Third	400,000	
Korea	50,000	First Cold War	50,000	
Vietnam	50,000	Second Cold War	50,000	
The Rest	50,000	Total Foreign Crusades		600,000
Total:	1,250,000	Total Liberal Crusades(96%):		1,200,000

On occasion, some campaigns or battles are examined for their contribution to a war, or to its toll. For example, about 13,500 Union prisoners are thought to have died at the Confederate prison camp at Andersonville, Georgia. About 55,000 Americans died, mostly en route or in Japanese prison camps, from the fall of the Philippines in 1941-42. About 50,000 Americans died in the 8th Air Force, the main arm of American strategic bombing in World War II Europe. The reasons, or rationales, for these wars, and many of the larger episodes, are the main theme of the first half and an important theme of the second. Although some material presented might seem extraneous to American concerns, so might some of the wars. Where appropriate, the author so notes.

The main title, *Hung Out To Die*, is from the expression hung out to dry, now figuratively meant to strand or abandon. The old literal meaning for this term was a punishment for naughty children; the offender was dressed in sturdy clothes, dowsed with water and pinned up on a clothesline. Some overly empathic people view such punishment as having warped young Adolf Hitler; others may opine that his old man may have been ahead of his time or too lenient. In this country, wrapping in wet sheets was long used to treat spasming lunatics by physically exhausting them; nowadays we use chemicals or outdoor exposure. The points of the punishment/treatment reference are that the wrong people have been punished (see death toll chart above), and that some of our iconized leaders should have been.

HUNG OUT TO DIE:
American Wars and Defense Politics

Table of Contents

Table of Contents (continued)

Table of Charts

Table of Maps

HUNG OUT TO DIE:
American Wars and Defense Politics

Chapter 1 - **Introduction and Typology of American Wars**

Defense, apart from meaning the opposite of offense, is the preparation, maintenance and use of military force to advance a nation's interests. Military force is the reformation, by drill and other means, of individuals into coherent units, which act in violent unison to destroy the cohesion of the similarly constituted units of an enemy. Walter Millis fatuously described close-order drill as springing from 17th century musketry, but military discipline is a sign of advanced civilization long predating gunpowder. Spears and swords early gave military drill an advantage in most battles; better drilled men could stay out of the way of their friends' weapons while maintaining a mutually supportive formation to defeat the usual tactics of the less well organized -- ambush and shock attacks. Substituting greater organization for mere numbers, including developing the collateral organizational skills of logistics and engineering, made possible the survival of smaller political units and the virtues they subsumed. Instead of huge hordes run by despots, small cities -- Greek, Rome, Carthage, Renaissance Italian -- could maintain their independence and their cultures as long as their societies could field disciplined forces. This more or less voluntary innate tendency to identify with a larger group is a sort of natural socialism which should be welcome to Modern Liberals. But, in the context of national defense or any other endeavor unrelated to a left-wing cause-of-the-moment, such activity, although uniquely human, is stigmatized as "dehumanizing". Liberalism, a movement in lock step and not much else, despises any useful efforts similarly organized.

Despite ideological distortion, the "essence of defense" is the organization of ready force for co-ordinated application, placing a premium on the tractability to command of those occupying the military pyramid's lowest levels. Unlike many similarly structured social organizations, the military at least has a reason: one brain to command, the few to co-ordinate the action, and the mass to actually strike, where their numbers can be made to count through efficient command of the fruits of organization. War is not a sporting event and dilettantes who criticize actions as not being fair or balanced would only prolong war and increase its costs; given the vituperative sadism of most pacifists, such is probably their wish. The sporting analogy, usually brought up by America's enemies when applied to specifics, often incorporates massive quantities of defective hindsight. The U.S. may indeed have won most of its wars, but it tended to enter them unprepared, substantially without a standing army in several instances. When victories happened, it was supposedly because the other side was weak, or because the U.S. was a bully, or both, never because Americans were doing something right that they believed in, at threat to their lives. The only real heroes of the left are from the Spanish Civil War, or civil rights marches.

For the left, war must either be bloody and bootless, a war they oppose, or a heroic crusade, a war they endorse. One can judge the principles of the left through such exemplars as Henry David Thoreau. Opposed to a war (the Mexican War), Thoreau preached non-violence and refused to pay taxes; favoring an American civil war, he promptly began raving about "Sharps rifles" as "tools" for achieving justice. In this century, the primary lodestone of the American left was Soviet Russia. Take Pete Seeger, so-called folk singer and Communist for Dukakis in 1988, for example. When the U.S. had opposed Nazi Germany when it was at war with Britain and allied with Soviet Russia, Seeger dusted off the old pacifistic dirge "I Didn't Raise My Boy to be a Soldier" for the eclectic mob against British war-mongering -- pacifists, Communists, Nazi sympathizers, the professional Irish and isolationists. But when Germany invaded holy Soviet Russia, the continued American baiting of Germany, by then costing American lives, got Seeger's sudden blessing, including that "good ship *Reuben James*", sunk by a U-boat it was attacking. It is amazing how cheering it is for the "unquestionably patriotic" left when Americans die in bunches.

Leftists make hay by stressing the bloodiness of conflicts they oppose, and by urging more bloodiness where there is some leftist stake. The left accordingly actually opposes most measures to limit the bloodiness of wars, although it will make lip-service in that direction. War-crimes tribunals of the left, official or otherwise, tend toward the selective. The leftist IRA, for example, car-bombers, bar-bombers, kidnappers and assassins, will be supported in part by an insistence of the legitimacy of both its cause and methods, as well as by opposition to measures that might defeat them. Sadly, some will fall for the two-step where the IRA and organizations like it are described as legitimately military, and then excused from the standards expected of a real military. This goes back mainly to World War II, when the Allies fomented disorder behind German lines by encouraging the war crime of partisanship, earlier internationally acknowledged as unnecessarily bloody and militarily ineffective, and therefore titularly banned, at least until someone found it prospectively advantageous. The Allies' goal was precisely a bloodbath, partisan terrorism and escalating German countermeasures. With any legitimate military action, civilians may get in the way, but that is unavoidable; as Eisenhower said, there are civilians everywhere. But assuming the burden of moral fine-tuning always gives the advantage to the evil, because they don't do it. Part of the moral squalor of the left is that it is deeply aware of the moral burden, but uses it only for propaganda and as something to handicap its opponents.

War is not a method of settling disputes, it **is** a dispute, a violent and often large one. Although affected to be despised, it is a definitive human activity, conscious and steeped in the sort of arcane social rituals liberals dote upon when they involve the religious, kinship or puberty rites of distant minor societies too incompetent to defend themselves. Military activity linked to a large people's national security and integrity is to be piously deplored, however. Whether the active pursuit is defensive, political or conquest for the sustenance of a people is irrelevant to liberals. What is important to them is how such realities can be twisted to fit liberal myths and the goals that those myths generate. Eventually, of course, real victims resembling some of the demons generated by liberal myth must be warred upon; the pacifistic gabble is temporarily laid aside. To abolish war, start by killing the liberals.

War is a political activity which primarily utilizes the narrow technical specialty of military science as its "other means". (Liberals may gag at Clausewitz or blanch at his applicability to modern times -- temporal prejudice -- but they are usually all for the older doctrines of one Adam Smith -- except when they are against them.) The first half of this book is devoted to the complex question of why wars are fought in the American political context, and how that context determines both how and how well they are fought. Allowing for the changing valences of the left, the "Modern" (from the election of Richard Nixon) Liberal fog on this issue is that "the Pentagon" starts wars that liberals don't like, or grow to dislike. That of course begs the question of how and why the Pentagon came to be; it did not conjure itself into being. The second half of this work focuses on narrower issues -- locations of military bases, organization of military services, technical limits of ships, tanks, missiles and aircraft and American participation in the international arms trade -- which have technological and professional aspects in addition to the usual left-wing pitfalls.

Government, whether as the military, law and order, or taxation, is force, and war is government at work. To obscure these truths is to misgovern. Fashionable as it may be, blaming militarism for wars makes about as much sense as blaming fire departments for fires. Wars are political decisions, and when a military is to blame for starting one, as occasionally happens, it is virtually always the case that that military has usurped political power and thus become the political structure -- by making such decisions, the military merely ceases to function as a purely military entity. But even in most military coups, the military-dominated government is not usually notable as a breaker of international peace, the most notable exceptions being in the Near East, modern left-wing military regimes in Egypt, Iraq, Syria and Libya, as well as the ancient Diadochi, whose unifying political entity had expired of a fever.

When a military is consulted on questions of war and peace, those asked are virtually always the highest ranking, usually elderly men snug and smug in secure positions only capable of being threatened by inefficiency or defeat in war, but not notably capable of enhancement by victory. Only in dire national emergencies will such bureaucracies support active measures. Generals have it made; it is junior officers worried about promotion who are usually disagreeable. And it is they who are tapped for quick promotion when a political leadership decides upon war, as in the sacking of senior brass by Hitler and Roosevelt preparatory to the commencement of active policies, and their replacement by younger men (Hitler, undesirous of general war, merely picked younger generals; the more sanguine Roosevelt dipped into the pool of American colonels to come up with the ambitious Marshall and Eisenhower).

In the case of 1930s' Japan, however, the initial emergency was the threat of assassinations and civil war by the younger officers, disgruntled and adventurous; the resulting political decision was for war with China, and the possibility of national aggrandizement, rather than the national humiliation, and physical danger to the politicians, of war upon the insubordinate fanatics. And in the war that did ensue, despite *bushido* bravado, then and since, about respecting those who fought, the Japanese in practice were most vicious toward those who resisted the best, as of the massacre of the Chinese at Nanking after weeks of Chinese resistance and Japanese casualties, courtesy of Chiang Kai-shek's troops, the ones who would not fight. That pattern continued later, when after their humiliating loss of four old destroyers at Wake, the Japanese massacred 100 American civilians on the island as well as beheaded captured Marines on the trip to Japan, or after the long drawn-out battle for Bataan, when the Japanese put the survivors through a Death March much ghastlier than the early treatment of prisoners from the much more quickly surrendered Singapore.

Even as the war with China had been forced by upstart military officers, the choice of national humiliation or the chance of victory was forced upon Japan by Roosevelt's policies. The Imperial Navy, a force in Japan's by-then completely militarized government, approved war on America on that basis. The Emperor evidently did not, awarding no medals in the American war, despite profuse early Japanese victories and later desperate heroics.

Military governments are in a sense as regressive as religious governments, because both represent a return to older times, when both spheres were more closely integrated with, or even within, governments. Rome's was structurally representative, as well as important in itself, widespread both geographically and temporally. Those who are today regarded as military chiefs -- Sulla, Marius, Caesar, Crassus and Pompey -- were simply the political figures in a turbulent and overgrown garrison state, at a time when military affairs were less technologically demanding, and more explicable to the average politician. Specialization, with its costs and benefits, was to come later. There were also traditions that demanded that politicians should have military experience, as times were too harsh to permit tyros to run affairs; politicians fought and led armies as matters of civic duty, among other things. The religious duties of such politicians are among the least regarded by moderns, whose usual interpretation of the movement of Lepidus from Triumvir to Pontifex Maximus is that it was a demotion (Lepidus thought so), a view that perhaps would have struck his predecessor Caesar and his successors, from Augustus through the medieval Popes, as insane. "How many divisions has the Pope?" quipped Napoleon (and later Stalin), a man who emphasized a different sort of moral aspect; the Pope, it turns out, has two divisions, and four limbs.

Much later, the instructive lesson of Caesarism was reinforced by the example of Napoleon and the "Napoleonic" Wars. The French Revolution had terrified other European leaders, who saw it as a standing threat to their legitimacy -- their power, wealth and lives. Even as it unfolded, the French Revolution was the target of successive attack coalitions by the arthritic military leaders charged with its suppression by legitimatists. The national energy released by the French Revolution, casting aside such old war-horses of birth, yielded youthful energy and innovation; French power expanded by beating back the attacks upon it.

One beneficiary was the young professional officer Bonaparte. Starting as a pamphleteer against a fellow Corsican, one Buttafuoco, Napoleon was quickly promoted into political responsibilities as a Commissar of the Committee of Public Safety (*i.e.*, a local franchisee of the Reign of Terror), in addition to his military duties of defending Toulon against an English invasion. After re-establishing Caesar's pattern of "great" revolutionaries first briefly becoming political prisoners (followed by Genghis, Timurlame, Marx, Lenin, Stalin, Trotsky, Mussolini, Hitler, Franco, Mao, Ho and Castro as beneficiaries of an unorganized "amnesty international" for political prisoners), Napoleon, by dint of intrigue, opportunity and ability, and the previous revolutionary sweeping-away of the establishment (in the name of "the career open to talent"), soon became supreme leader of the French Revolution. As he was not legitimate, but simply the chief usurper, the foreign attacks continued, as did their defeat and French expansion. Even as Napoleon became more self-consciously legitimate in his trappings and aspirations, seeking to stabilize his position within the French realm and to placate his external enemies from their continued onslaughts, the coalitions were themselves energized by their own separate national awakenings, as their defeats and the example of the French Revolution brought fresh blood to the fore and energized opponents of that French rule which had sprung from the exuberantly successful defenses of the French Revolution. Although the main outbreak had finally been contained, the medics had themselves been infected, and many later developed the disease.

The modern consequence of the Caesar and Napoleon legends, or, less sentimentally, their vulgar simplifications and distortions, is that they are inspirations to aspiring *juntaistas* and bogeymen that liberal ignorati use to frighten other simpletons. Neither man was a cause of the disruption of his time; rather, both were products of societies in decay, where political breakdown, of the Roman Republic and the French Monarchy, had put society into extended civil wars, situations where the martial virtues of the men, part of the make-up of any superior being, were utilized to their maximum. The relevance of such rises to a functioning political system is minimal, but then, a liberal political system can hardly be called functional. In fact, used sparingly by liberal ideology and propaganda, the Roman Republic and the French Monarchy were themselves victims of intrigue which smacks of modern liberalism. The Roman Civil Wars were started by the demagogic Gracchi brothers, successive popular tribunes seeking to aggrandize their power by expanding their office beyond its lawful bounds. Tribunes had only one power, vetoing the Roman Senate's actions, and were ineligible for reelection. One Gracchi tried to get another term, and the other tried to assume the power to legislate. They succeeded only in causing their followers and opponents to embark on a series of long and bloody civil wars, which killed most of the participants and long outlasted the lucky ones. The French Monarchy was undermined by the kind of alliance which Modern Liberalism itself is built around, the classic bond between the ambitious and willful rich and those at the bottom of society, in the French case between the idle salon wits and the brutes, against the King and his ministers. Many of the wits were killed or had to flee the country, many of the brutes were killed in the wars which soon followed, and very few were better off. The choices of Napoleon and Caesar in their careers were set by their opponents, often former friends grown ambitious or leery. Caesar could fight or submit, possibly with his life, to an ultimatum, something you get from enemies, not from friends. Caesar's erstwhile associates, previously conniving at his unconstitutional five-year and absentee consulships, outlawed him by driving out the vetoing tribunes. Why did Caesar cross the Rubicon? To get to the other side.

While liberals oscillate dramatically on war -- stridently "anti-war", playing up the gore, between bouts of playing up the next liberal war -- they dislike defense for itself, although definitely not as part of typically wasteful big government. Liberal criticisms of military waste are merely propaganda formalities, with the merits never really well thought-out. After all, wasteful big government is the primary means and goal of Modern Liberalism, and its principal side-effect. What liberals do find galling about the goal of defense, or the military structure used to achieve it, is that it is a legitimate constitutional goal, with virtues predating and morally overshadowing shabby liberal dogmas. Loyalty, bravery and technical proficiency in national service intrinsically outweigh liberal shenanigans, necessitating a continuing make-weight of liberal propaganda to offset the moral disadvantage with a blizzard of billingsgate. The anti-military twaddle churned out, in addition to polluting public discourse generally, not only further di-minishes liberal capacity to understand defense reasonings and means, it also reinforces and refuels liberalism's dominant emotional and antago-nistic element. Reinforced irrationality means more frequent, incompe-tent and prolonged use of international force; hysterical denunciations of violence warp the often necessary use of force in the real world, just as eliminating "barbarous" capital punishment destroys a means of making civilization possible, making society a victim of more barbarism, not less.

Contemptuous of generals they presume are preparing to fight the last war, liberals are busy trying to prevent it. And while affecting to prevent war, liberal actions help start future wars. Harry Truman lame-ly justified his China policy as seeking to avoid having the U.S. fight a land war in Asia; technically, he succeeded: the U.S. fought two land wars in Asia as a result of his buffoonery. And liberal disability extends from international politics, where wars start, to the nuts-and-bolts of military management, which liberals also sneer at, between spasms of putative reform.

Once a new war occurs, Modern Liberals are too pre-occupied with prophecising an outcome, through offerings to the great god of ne-gotiations, to win the war, and make the negotiations quick and defini-tive rather than protracted and bootless. Dominating force, frequently sudden and harsh, wins wars; sponge-trousered diplomacy does not, al-though it can recruit allies or discourage potential opponents (the "striped-pants set" is an outsider's perspective on diplomats, usually of people who still prefer them to military "brass-hats"). In war, victory, properly defined, should be the top priority; making "peace" a priority in war-time merely prolongs war, and delays the achievement of peace. Peace comes quickest when wars are won, not negotiated.

The success or failure of American policy operating at any time is mediated by the broad realities of war and peace and military organ-ization, as well as by the gradual unfolding of technological change and its effects on given physical realities. But policy is irrelevant when the U.S. is out-led by people who realize that "making a revolution is not a dinner party", even as America's liberals are busy planning a menu and guest list for the "peace talks". There are people with other priorities than peace, just as there are people, American liberals, with priorities other than the efficient organization of American defense. And, of course, liberalism always implies some sort of wool-gathering, a loss of focus that, in military matters of life and death, gets people killed pointlessly. Such distractions have included Lincoln's fruitless gambles at quick bloody victories to sell war-bonds; Wilson's tinkering with the map of Europe; Roosevelt's back-and-forth shifting of the U.S. Navy between Atlantic and Pacific to alternately bait Japan and Germany, and ending up at war with both; Truman's substantial disarming of the U.S., his renunciation of the defense of Korea and his pursuit of the racial integration of the remnant of the armed forces, all either directly antithetical to or separate from military effectiveness, simply ensuring that hastily rebuilt American units would not fight as well as they had before; and Lyndon Johnson's "management" of the Vietnam War.

Military force, for most societies, is a necessary corequisite for existence, if not from moment to moment, at least sporadically, historically or prospectively, and, if not on their own part, at least on the part of some protector, by agreement or in fact. A society's workings depend upon its security, a military matter against outside threats, and a law and order matter against domestic entropy. The third function of government is another coercive power, taxation, the actual or implied threat of caging people for not parting with a portion of their livelihoods. Taxation, besides being involuntary, is also not ordinarily a military function; it is the core function of government which the military is least capable of efficiently managing (the military is capable of some law and order role, but its modern utilization for such is usually a sign of a society in chaos, having lost its ability to defend itself internally by internal means).

Liberalism's fetish is to utilize such a public power not for a public purpose, but for flipperies like parking subsidies for the Kennedy Center, for junk sculpture to pollute public places, for payments to people for not growing wheat in their ponds, or for gifts to foreign and domestic ne'er-do-wells. The expansive yet contradictory public sector is definitive liberalism, much as abortion becomes first defensible as a private matter, yet instantly worthy of public subsidy.

A modern military is dependent upon its political system because it cannot support itself, financially or otherwise. It needs a civilian commissary, and accepts in turn a civilian commissarship. Competition between nations simply increases the dependence, as military equipment has grown more costly than a sword, shield and sandals. Defense is primarily a military matter, but, as with diplomacy, decisions regarding military force are constrained by more generic politics, to the frequent dismay of the specialists concerned, brass-hatted or sponge-trousered.

Prior to the Gulf War with Iraq, American wars were divisible into four sharp categories. First, there were the colonial wars, primarily countless Indian wars and the four French and Indian Wars, and early post-colonial wars, the American Revolution, the undeclared naval war with France, the Barbary wars and the War of 1812. These established the nation, and are therefore somewhat questionable to the "unquestionably patriotic".

Next, there were the three big Liberal Crusades, the American Civil War, World War I and World War II. These were expensive, prolonged and America's three bloodiest wars, eventually military successes but ultimately failures in the aims of their wagers. The American Civil War was fought to preserve the Union and to end slavery, but was quickly followed by the disenfranchisement of southern Whites in favor of southern Blacks, and then by a reversal of that situation; Whites dragged back into the Union had been disenfranchised, and Blacks pulled out of slavery re-oppressed. American military participation in World War I was boomed by Woodrow Wilson as The War To End All Wars, but was quickly followed by more wars, most auspiciously World War II. Despite its general reputation as a bloody fiasco, American military accomplishment in World War I was superb if later denigrated; what seduced liberals was the government running the war economy, a typical case of liberals imitating failure. In World War II, the integrity of Poland and China was putatively the issue, but both were shorted to mollify Soviet Russia. The loss of Poland and the rest of Eastern Europe rang in the Cold War, and Cold War Liberalism, and the loss of China rang in chaos in Asia.

That chaos, the loss of China (with its effect on the Communist effort in North Vietnam) and the previous signing-away of North Korea to the Soviets, led to the third category of American wars, the two Cold War Liberal Crusades of Korea and Vietnam. Both were bloody, politically bungled, unpopular with the left and unsatisfactory in dénouement, with an American garrison necessary in South Korea for decades and South Vietnam, Cambodia and Laos lost following an American pull-out and the achievement of "peace". Both Cold War Crusades were fought by "accidental" presidents desperately seeking election in their own right, with each adopting Lincolnesque expedients of civil rights, massive corruption and bungled war as their meal-tickets for office. Both were also products of New Deal diplomacy, America effectively exporting its political confusion, by other means.

The fourth category of American wars is the least bloody, the shortest and most salutary for the U.S., and hence the wars most vociferously opposed by liberals past and present. These were the Latin wars, the Mexican War and the Spanish-American War (which dragged on somewhat into the Filipino Insurrection). Liberal opposition to these Latin wars led to a hysterical gabble of pacifism, an emotional upsurge that was soon tapped for the big Liberal Crusades which followed. World War II had no Latin prelude, but should have; Mexico confiscated billions in American oil investments, with a token payment of about 18 million dollars (less than one-tenth of a cent on the dollar), but Franklin Roosevelt, previously embarrassed by his own swaggering imperialist rhetoric during his first national political campaign, was indisposed to do anything about Americans' being plundered by such foreign piracy.

Both Latin wars started with American military disasters, the slaughter of a surrendered American military patrol north of the Rio Grande and the blowing-up of the battleship *Maine* in 1898. But those incidents merely illustrate the fragility of hypothesizing military init- iation of American wars. Mexico initiated hostilities by invading the U.S., and the sinking of the *Maine* led to a Spanish declaration of war first. When militarily provoked, the U.S. usually bides its time, waiting for an opportunity to fight when it wants to and whom it wants to. The British attack on the *Chesapeake* in 1809 did not in itself lead immedi- ately to war (although it was definitively an act of war), nor did the U.S. accept the Japanese bombing of the *Panay* in 1937 as a *casus belli*, nor did the U.S immediately retaliate for Iraq's missiling of an American frigate; nor did the U.S. directly retaliate for the mining of yet another frigate by Iran; those obstreperous regimes could be relied upon for fur- ther provocations. On a different wavelength, the U.S. swore off retali- ation for other dastardly attacks upon the American military, North Ko- rea's capture of the spy ship *Pueblo* or its shooting-down of an American spy plane, both in international waters, or the similar previous Israeli sinking of the American spy ship *Liberty*. The North Koreans were ig- nored while the U.S. concentrated on the Vietnam War, and the Israeli attack was pooh-poohed on account of Lyndon Johnson's frantic court- ship of the American Jewish vote, the attack leading not to retaliation but to the on-going Niagara of American largess.

The colonial aspect of the American military tradition was formed mostly from collisions with the Indians and the French. Colo- nies which were unprepared for Indian hostility -- Roanoke and Massa- chusetts -- disappeared entirely or lost scores of villages in King Philip's War. The distant British Army was of little use in battling the Indians, and so all of the colonies had a militia tradition. As the first opponents of America, the Indians naturally have a cozy spot in liberal ideology, roughly worth a warm grate for a tramp. Indian treachery and brutality gets the amnesty of amnesia, Indian reactionaries get dutifully paraded in archaic costumes, as contemporary as tri-cornered hats, and the mass of unassimilated Indians gets segregated in tribal homelands, America's *apartheid* for nostalgic Stone Agers. Of course, people did not originate in America, and the ancestors of the Indians were merely part of the first six waves of colonists from across the Bering land-bridge, during its existence (followed by the seventh Asian wave, the Eskimos, as later by the Columbian waves, Europeans, Africans and lastly Asians). For those who decry nativism, imperialism, militarism and "rape of the en- vironment", Indians are peculiar heroes, given their old habits of doing each other in (individually and tribally), to the extent of driving the oldest Americans down to the tip of South America, and of doing a simi- lar job upon North America's Pleistocene mammals (killing off horses, camels, rhinos, giant sloths, mammoths, mastodons, dire wolves and sabre-toothed tigers) much more thoroughly than did the stay-at-home Old Worlders (among the last archaic animals to go were the giant Irish elk and the European cave bear, but camels, horse, rhinos, elephants and tigers survived in the Old World). Although Indians did a good job of domesticating New World plants, the idea probably came with the middle group of Asian arrivals, given the similarity of "*mai*" (rice) and "*maize*" (corn). But of all of the slaughter and diseases passed back and forth (and the Indians gave some to the more populous Old World), the great equalizer has been the Indian tobacco habit.

In the four wars with France that played a colonial counterpoint to European politics, American militias were drawn upon by the British but scorned by British officers of the British troops tardily sent in to protect British interests. The militia and their leaders performed well, whether in the capture of St. Augustine, the two captures each of Port Royal and Louisbourg, the exploits of Rogers' Rangers, or the superior leadership of Washington before Fort Duquesne and the ambush of Braddock. British haughtiness accounted for the reciprocal colonial contempt for regular troops, for standing armies, and for the British government which had bartered away the initial colonial gains of St. Augustine, Port Royal and Louisbourg, three enemy bastions, for gains elsewhere in the world (including for the East India Company, making that company a focus of Massachusetts enmity long before the Boston Tea Party). British fear of colonial capabilities accounted for their pre-Revolutionary exactions.

Fearing further growth and rambunctiousness, Britain in 1763 tried to limit westward expansion to the Appalachian Mountains, after having lured people to settle America on the strength of grants extending clear to the Pacific. With the French threat at an all-time low, more British garrison troops were sent in peace-time than had been sent in hot war, ostensibly to protect the colonists, but really to keep them under tighter control. Taxes to support the occupation were levied, adding a third colonial grievance, and war ensued. Critical to the subsequent British defeat was neglect of the Royal Navy, the target of foolish economies while the British Army had been so bootlessly expanded and deployed. Liberals usually denigrate, or deny, the justification for the American Revolution (our country, always wrong), but robust colonial achievements despite British neglect had frightened British conservatives, who were also nettled at the popularity of Whiggery and religious dissent in America. British Tories had long been out of power, having started as minions of the ousted Catholic Stuarts, and later intriguing with the French as earlier British traitors had intrigued with then-powerful Spain. At the end of the French and Indian Wars, the slow Tory ooze toward respectability made a forced march with the accession of George III, a foe of Whigs and religious dissenters, and keen on the Tories and their parvenu embrace of the Anglican church and the Hanoverians. Inflicting this propriety upon the colonies was the goal of King and those who wanted royal favor, first pliable Whig figureheads and later Tories.

With American victory came the problem of foreign relations in a context more complex than soliciting aid from Britain's old colonial rivals. France soon became Revolutionary France in its passing seasons, and began attracting some Americans -- Paine (not really an American, but an itineranter) and Jefferson -- and repulsing others -- Washington and the Federalists. The Federalist Navy soon proved capable of dealing with the French, however. Despite Jeffersonian pacifism and military conservatism, British actions continued to nettle the U.S. long after the French had lost offensive power. British troops held forts on American soil, the British encouraged Indian hostility to America, and the Royal Navy kidnapped thousands of American sailors for extended British duty (at a time when ordinary British sailors were cooped up on ship for more than a decade, with no shore leave). American desire for Canada, the focal point of the British garrisons and Indian-riling, was also important, but, absent a large U.S. Navy, Canada was the only place where America could threaten the British. The War of 1812 saw America re-assert its independence, although it proved as incapable of conquering Canada as it had in 1775. The British, pre-occupied in Europe, proved unable to mount a creditable threat to the five American Atlantic cities, due to their fortification in previous years. Although the new little village of Washington was burned, the nearby city of Baltimore was saved by its stout Fort McHenry. On the seas, the Federalist frigates and new privateers troubled Britain for awhile, but it mastered those threats with its huge navy. More serious for the British war effort was the American preponderance on the northern lakes, with smashing American victories on isolated Lakes Champlain and Lake Erie, and a successful defense of the U.S. Lake Ontario base, building a huge sailing battleship able to dominate that lake against any possible Canadian construction or British ships small enough to pass up the St. Lawrence narrows from the sea.

The British, aside from negotiating, used troops freed up from the end of war in Europe to attack strategic New Orleans, gateway to the Mississippi, newer in American hands and therefore not well fortified. Liberals hoot that the American victory there occurred after the negotiation of a peace treaty between the U.S. and Britain, which attacked anyway. Liberals assume that victorious Britain, possessing the gateway to the Mississippi, would have kept its new treaty obligations (and it had been welshing on its old treaty obligations for a generation) as it did after being routed by Jackson's defenders at the cotton-bale wall. As usual, America's attacker gets a free pass from the liberals, and America gets censured for defending itself. That pattern was to be repeated in the war with Mexico.

Chapter 2 - **Prelude and Mr. Lincoln's War**

The post-colonial era saw the Federalist Party supplanted by the Democratic Party (initially the Anti-Federalists, or opponents of the Constitution, then the Democratic-Republicans, then simply the Demo-crats), who favored a weak federal government. John Quincy Adams, son of the only fully Federalist President, got a term over a divided opposition through the short-lived National Republican label, but that soon wilted against the re-unified Democrats under Andrew Jackson. The next opposition to the Democrats was the Whig Party, an alliance of northern high-tariff advocates and southern and western politicians seek-ing to by-pass incipient local Democratic machines; traditional rabble-rousers, anti-Masonic and anti-slavery fanatics, as well as a new group, the anti-immigrationists, sought in turn to supplant the Whigs. It was the most active measure of Jefferson's caretaker terms, the Louisiana Purchase which he had brooded over the legality of, whose long-term effects doomed the Whigs, and paved the way for their successors. Whatever the moral dimensions of the slavery question, severely a mat-ter of perception and dogma, such moral issues were resolutely old hat. But national expansion gave anti-slavery agitators the long-term advan-tage, because each new accession of territory, or organization of terri-tories into states, re-put the live political question of whether slavery would spread to the new areas. Other firebrand issues -- taxation, immigration and conspiracies -- did not have such an opportunity, al-though they were certainly as susceptible of being swaddled in moralistic flannel as abolitionism. New England, which had led the American Revolution and then the Federalist Party, saw itself playing a shrinking role in an expanding nation, something that did not sit well with local throbbing consciences too sensitive to be sublimated in the prevalent money-milling. Fervor which had gone into nationalism, or before that into witch-hunting or opposing "Godless" vaccinations (the "liberal" Quakers), soon found a new outlet in agitation for various "social" causes, with the territorial question giving the advantage to anti-slavers. Other busybodies, with the usual mangy grab-bag of concerns, had enough functional shrewdness to go with the main chance of abolitionism.

The first Louisiana Purchase fall-out on slavery had been occa-sioned partly by the acquisition of Florida, giving northern Nervous Nellies a severe case of The Fear (an anxiety attack) lest the new area soon become one or more slave states. Although that anxiety was some-what assuaged by the next year's Missouri Compromise, which extended the old Northwest Ordinance's bar to slavery in the Old Northwest to the New Northwest, the issue kept re-occurring, in large part because of chaos along America's southern border, part of the chaos being where that border was: both Spain and the U.S. attempted to renege on the Florida-for-Texas swap. Northerners feared that such land was only suitable for plantation crops, and therefore amenable to the spread of America's slave-holding domain.

The Louisiana Purchase had of course been engineered by France, which had obtained from Spain the rights to a tract which extended as far south as Tampico, Mexico (about halfway from the Rio Grande to Mexico City). The Spaniards, after in one year giving up their rights to Florida in favor of America's, in return in part for a renunciation of American rights to Texas (and by extension further south to Tampico), had overthrown their government making the deal, and its successor immediately demanded Florida back, but also demanded to keep Texas, which it proved incapable of doing anyway. (Spain had, of course, originally gained control of both Florida and Texas by ejecting the French (Huguenots and Royalists, respectively) from each.)

An early abolitionist, John Quincy Adams, soon sought, as Monroe's Secretary of State and the architect of the failed deals with Royal Spain, a more unilateral renunciation of the Louisiana Purchase's huge southwestern chunk, to restrict it to its present size on the maps of liberal educators. Adams' purpose was twofold: to curry favor with newly independent Mexico, and to rid the nation of further possible slave territory. The Senate refused to consent to such a blatant give-away of the taxpayers' money, an episode of economy and freedom from liberal guilt that would be astounding in our time. The land, including Texas, remained legally American, purchased at arms'-length from a willing buyer, but the Mexicans were pleased to regard the land as theirs, and subsequent America-haters, liberal politicians and historians, were prone to humor that absurd imposture. Adams' lack of sincerity was proven by one of his last secretarial gestures, the "Monroe Doctrine", which purported to deprive newly re-Royalist Spain of land it had lost, including the very Texas which Adams had shortly before tried to give it.

The last gesture assured Adams of a brief image as a man in favor of standing up to the Europeans, much as his political rival Andrew Jackson had gotten by invading Spanish Florida, and helped to scrape away a bit of the stigmata which Adams had sprouted by his foolish attempt to get rid of Texas. However, by putting Texas' ownership back into play in the first place, he had sown the seeds of three wars -- Texan, Mexican and American Civil -- to spite some Americans and to shore up New England support for his presidential bid. Adams' attempt to curry Mexican favor had been foreshadowed by his earlier obsequious deferral to the new Argentine Republic, apologizing for a U.S. Navy officer's expulsion of an Argentine officer from the Falkland Islands (the Argentine and his associates had driven out the only locals, American seal-hunters, to set up a base for piracy). After the American disavowal, the British moved into the vacated isles, making the later Falklands War possible. Power, like any other force of nature, abhors a vacuum.

Mexico, with "its" northeast next to an expanding U.S., sought security through the dubious device of inviting in American settlers, some of whom had previously cleared their land acquisitions with the overthrown Spaniards. This was really the third wave of Latin settlement of the West, albeit with non-Spaniards this time. The first Spanish wave had forestalled France by destroying its fort in Texas and later settling the upper Rio Grande -- Santa Fe, away from the French Navy. Although Santa Fe was abandoned to Pueblo Indian attack from 1680 to 1692, British politics changed that. In 1688, the Stuarts, Spain's allies against France, were overthrown and the anti-Spanish Dutch Orange dynasty took their place. New Mexico again became a desirable colonial bulwark, this time against the Orange King and his Whiggish backers, and Santa Fe was re-established. Although France quickly became Spain's main nemesis again and the main target of Britain, a later temporary advent of anti-Spanish Tories -- cryptic Stuart supporters whose cause had been aided by France -- mandated the establishment of Albuquerque in that strange litmus of European politics, New Mexico. The second Spanish wave, mission/fortifications on the West Coast, was to forestall American Revolutionary expansionism. The third "Spanish" wave peopled Texas with American expatriates, picked up by independent Mexico.

Mexico soon won some liberal American friends, as one of its rapidly changing governments "abolished" slavery. Of course, the pronouncer was soon assassinated, and slavery was not really abolished in Mexico for another century, surviving under the rubric of peonage, or hereditary serfdom for debt. For its own national part, Mexico was soon on a merry Latin path of dishonoring its debts, as the debts of overthrown governments, and seizing the property of anyone foolish enough to invest in such a benighted country. As with the other Latin countries whose shabby buffoonery extends in a straight line from the fall of Indian barbarisms to and beyond the conquistadors and their even more authoritarian opponents, the U.S. is somehow responsible, under the peculiar lights of liberalism, anyway.

Having been persuaded to move under one regime, Americans in Texas were no more willing than their forebears had been to see a distant government attempt to alter the terms of their settlements, such as bringing them under the more direct control of the central government of the moment. The Texans revolted, but, after the bloody but unsuccessful defense of the Alamo, their Goliad garrison surrendered to a Mexican promise of safe conduct. Hundreds were slaughtered by the treacherous Mexicans, who thoughtfully castrated each prisoner and suffocated him by shoving his genitals down his throat. If that is what Mexicans characterize as safe conduct, one wonders what they consider barbarity. Following that episode, long bowdlerized and now frequently totally omitted from our schools' history books, the Texans still at large rather unsurprisingly declared their independence, which they won at San Jacinto. Mexican prisoners, released with that understanding, of course soon treacherously recanted.

Texan independence made re-annexation of the territory a big American issue. Martin Van Buren was soon too weak politically, from a financial panic, and the Whig ticket which succeeded him was too cautious for such a move, fearing it would wreck northern support for their fragile coalition. The election of Polk, with his campaign pledge to get Texas back, changed the situation; before he took office Congress authorized re-annexation and re-occupation, the latter not really having originally occurred, except in the northwestern part of Texas by Pike's western expedition to the source of the Rio Grande. Getting the agreement of the Texans, Polk sent troops in to take possession, much as Jefferson had sent a regiment to New Orleans and explorers to other parts of the Louisiana Purchase (Louis & Clark to the far northwest, and Pike to Minnesota and Colorado). North of the Rio Grande, a patrol foolishly surrendered to Mexican invaders.

After a repetition of the Goliad protocol upon several dozen more hapless Americans, the commander of the larger American force, General Zachary Taylor, defeated the Mexicans twice north of the Rio Grande, and pursued them south across that river. "The [Mexican War] was provoked by a Tonkin Gulf-style incident [which, according to Mr. Hamill's other diatribes, never occurred or, if it did occur, blah, blah, blah] in April 1846. Three thousand American troops were sent across the Rio Grande at Matamoros, plunging some distance into Mexican territory. The Mexicans then had the gall to shoot at them.... and the war was begun." As Mr. Hamill's purpose in this pseudo-reminiscence was to show the U.S. bullying Latins, well then, the initial Mexican invasion, massacre and defeats had to be ignored, as was the fact that the American force was heavily out-numbered by the much larger Mexican force, which just happened to be concentrated at that country's northeastern extremity for that invasion of the U.S. which Zachary Taylor crushed. The innocence of the Mexicans was quickly taken up as a theme by the Whigs, who saw no partisan advantage in heaping abuse upon the Mexicans, but plenty in attacking the Democrat Polk, the dark horse who had defeated their Kentucky horse in 1844. Former House Speaker Polk had defeated the more well known Henry Clay by advocating definite policies, while Clay had trimmed his hedges; the man who stood for something positive had defeated the better known figure who positively stood for everything, and for his third different party. The Whigs, a coalition with little in common besides a lust for office and no coalescence on any issues save torchlight parades and abusing the Democrats, reached the negative campaigning landmark of Polk-in-a-Pig, a porcelain knick-knack with a push-button that caused a facsimile of

Polk's head to emerge from the pig's backside. Liberals always recycle ancient guff, which resembles the feeding of cattle on modern lots; they are fed a mixture of feed 30% diluted with their own droppings. Academic and media swill is of the same grade, and people receiving their "history" or "current events" from liberal troughs are more blinkered than was the *Volkische Beobachter*'s readership.

Following Taylor's pursuit of the defeated Mexicans south of the Rio Grande, for which liberals blame him and the U.S. for "starting" the war, distant Washington did indeed declare war. Defenders of the Mexicans, habitual anti-Americans in disguise, usually point out that the Mexicans considered the Nueces River, north of the Rio Grande, as Texas' proper southern border. That is severely beside the point, and not just the atrocity point; Mexico did not recognize Texan independence, although its Mexican War leader had temporarily professed recognition after being captured at San Jacinto. There were a number of more extreme Mexican positions, from holding the Red River as Mexico's proper northern border, to holding the Mississippi as Mexico's border (arguing that the French had tricked Spain out of Louisiana before selling it to the U.S.), to holding the entire eastern U.S. as part of Mexico's Spanish patrimony, courtesy of the papal grant overrun by the British, French, Dutch, Swedes and Americans. By that same level of analysis, of course, most of Texas and the later Mexican Cession had been part of the southern thirteen American colonies, courtesy of their continental slices chartered by the English crown, and then unsuccessfully limited in 1763.

Ever unquestionably patriotic, contemporary liberals, in company with other America-haters, were speedily cheering for a Mexican victory. As Mexico, unlike the United States, possessed a large standing army, well trained and experienced, expert opinion thought the Mexicans would win. That fact also gets omitted from the textbooks, because the liberal mindset needs to see a weak victim set upon, not a conflict which was forced upon an unprepared U.S. by the surprise invasion of its territory and the treacherous seizure and slaughter of its citizens.

There are several reasons for supposing that President Polk did not seek war with Mexico in obtaining Texas. First, there is no proof that he sought war, other than the fact that war happened; the fighting was at Mexican initiative, and would not have occurred had the Mexicans stayed south of the Rio Grande. Polk can hardly be faulted for defective mind-reading from two thousand miles away. Second, in addition to obtaining Texas, Polk had campaigned for office with the intention of lowering tariffs, the U.S. government's chief source of revenue until the 20th century, and of annexing Oregon, all of which pledges he kept. Aside from bearing witness that Polk was a man of his word, the kept pledge to cut governmental revenues is hardly the type of thing a government does before embarking on a war, nor was it likely

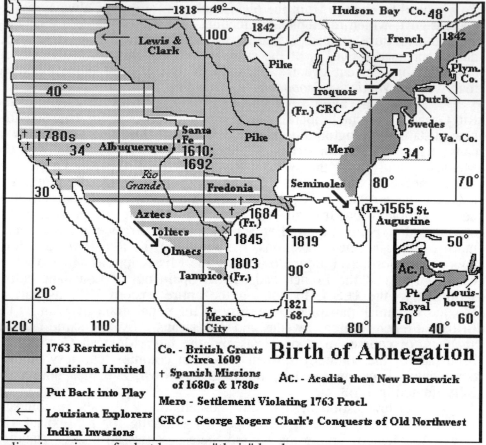

Birth of Abnegation

Legend:
- 1763 Restriction
- Louisiana Limited
- Put Back into Play
- ← Louisiana Explorers
- → Indian Invasions

- Co. - British Grants Circa 1609
- + Spanish Missions of 1680s & 1780s
- Mero - Settlement Violating 1763 Procl.
- GRC - George Rogers Clark's Conquests of Old Northwest
- Ac. - Acadia, then New Brunswick

Indian invasions of what became "their" land.

Colonial British Grants and Foreign Interference, including with each other (French and Spanish in Florida and Texas).

1763 British Limits negated their own (frequently contradictory) grants.

Mero was one of three competing Tennessee governments, each casting one electoral vote for Washington in 1796.

Jefferson's expeditions laid basis for Oregon and Lake Superior claims.

Louisinana Purchase limited by John Quincy Adams' diplomacy of 1818 and 1819, just before Missouri Compromise (1820). Texan, Mexican and Civil Wars followed.

Fredonia was an 1827 flop at Texan independence.

After Civil War, US troops persuaded French to pull their troops out of Mexico, abandoning Mexico to deadbeats under Juarez. Mexicans used opportunity to annex Yucatan, ending its independence.

that Polk wanted to forfeit leverage by being in a war with Mexico before entering negotiations with the other Oregon claimant, Great Britain. Third, Polk had seen his Democratic Party go up twice against Whig war-hero William Henry Harrison, and was in no hurry to create another such hero for the opposition, whether in the form of his personal enemy Zachary Taylor, the commander of the Texas expedition, or in the form of the Army's senior officer, Winfield Scott, the natural choice to lead the expedition to defeat the Mexicans definitively. Both men ran for president as Whigs, while Polk was reduced to trying to slide a few Democrats into subordinate positions. While some of these were duds, some were competent, and Franklin Pierce did become President, defeating his old commander Winfield Scott (Scott, prone to political gaffes, had written a letter about having "a hasty plate of soup", which phrase led Washington wags to dub him "Marshal Tureen"). But at least in spite of his anxiety, Polk let his political opponents fight the war without hindrance or his amateur interference, trusting that their abilities would prevail, and that, if anything, their selfish ambition would motivate them to victory. For having that mass of good faith, competence and discernment, and for leading the nation in a war won with a succession of victories, Polk is despised by liberal historians. Well, he was no Lincoln.

Lincoln gained his first national notice during his congressional term, when at the Mexican War's end he denounced Polk, and the U.S., in a rancid speech riddled with the most tawdry lies in the history of any parliamentary body, including even the pre-Nazi *Reichstag*. Lincoln compared Polk's call for a declaration of war, after the massacre of Americans and two large battles north of the Rio Grande, to "the half-insane mumblings of a fever dream"; later scholars were persuaded that it was Lincoln who was a psychotic (manic-depressive; of course, as with any term denoting an incapacity, the terminology goes in and out of liberal fashion, as new euphemisms are sought to convey the same meaning, albeit trimmed to keep ahead of the public). Ironically, that made him more acceptable to the loonies of the anti-slavery effort, a college of droolers fated to die in diverse asylums. Ever flexible of principle, Lincoln moved from attacking the Democrat Polk's purported war-mongering along the Rio Grande in favor of the extension of slavery to the endorsement of the presidential candidacy of Zachary Taylor, the slave-holder turned Whig who had led Polk's troops. How Polk could have been guilty and his instrument Taylor innocent is one of those mysteries that Lincoln cultists acknowledge only by dismissal. After all, Lincoln is a cult-figure, so such warts only advance his culthood; if he had massively helped precipitate civil war, the division of the Union, well, he had "saved" the Union, primarily from himself. In bringing himself to the would-be liberal establishment's attention as a soulmate, however, Lincoln also prejudiced his short-term political career, because, besides the nation, his Illinois district took notice. He failed of re-election to the House, in two races for the Senate (in the first, as ostensible campaign manager for Lyman Trumbull, Lincoln tried to subvert Trumbull's slate of pledged state legislative candidates) and in a try for the new "Liberal Republican" Party's first vice-presidential nomination, before the nation's rising temperature, a product of his strange type of statesmanship, made him, and civil war, acceptable.

Deputized by a railroad, on a generous commission-basis, to get land grants from local land-owners along the proposed right-of-way, Lincoln had achieved notable success in Illinois, where the spirit of development, then not anathema to liberalism, prevailed. Lincoln made big bucks in Illinois, becoming rich enough that buying three $5,000 carriages in a year, for a sum that a half-dozen average men of the time would have to work their lifetimes to make, was not a large expenditure in comparison to his means. But the grabby always want more, and the proposed extension of the railroad through Mississippi sent Lincoln on a bootless errand there. Slavery made labor-intensive cotton cultivation profitable, and such a bulky commodity was more suited to available waterways than to rail traffic. Planters proved unwilling to give away their land to Lincoln and the railroad, and he returned North for once not a noticeably richer man, but certainly a bitter one. Before Lincoln became a fervent opponent of slavery, he had tried to deal with it; his animus, aside from the growing usefulness of anti-slavery politics, was that he himself had made no money out of the peculiar institution.

Lincoln proved his legal mettle to the first liberal alliance, the fusion of corporations and fanaticism that became the Republicans, by his defense of the railroad's exemption from taxes; for his client, equality would have been a demotion. Years later, the so-called 14th Amendment would be interpreted by the Supreme Court as making corporations citizens, with the privileges of citizens to legal remedies (but not to vote, strangely enough), and that decision would be attacking by angry liberals as an abomination. Evidently, Mr. Lincoln would have also thought so, not from principle, but as a professional opportunist who realized that cases, not principles, make profits.

As the organization of the country proceeded, the slavery issue in the states-to-be arose again and again, with each ratchet-turn of pressure making extremism more profitable North and South. Lincoln attempted to unseat moderate Democrat Stephen Douglas from the Senate, re-advertising his credentials with his combination of stage wit, of the type later possessed by such specimens as Herman Goering and John Lindsay, and homey religious metaphor. One of his grabbers was the "house divided" piece, which was to reverberate within the consciousness of left-wingers past and present; Ramsay Clark's string tie positively writhes in ecstasy whenever he stops heaping scorn upon the U.S. long enough to reminisce about Lincoln's Cooper Union version of the house divided theme. The nation which originally heard those speeches had different ears and resonances than the generally more secular and less literate nation of today. Lincoln's theme was drawn from the Christian Bible, and the house divided, to which he likened the United States, was an echo of Satan's house, as described by Jesus. Lincoln thereby further endeared himself to the unquestionably patriotic crowd, to whom the American Constitution was "the Compact with Hell", because it had dealt with slavery and improved the world, rather than waited upon the slowest, the sure way of accomplishing nothing. Lincoln was of course ever modestly offering himself as the Messiah, with the same quiet good taste that had gotten him defeated in state, congressional and senatorial races. Lest anyone miss the Satanic reference, Lincoln also added the venomous snake metaphor to describe his fellow citizens that same year.

The year before, Lincoln's "Last Speech" for his second unsuccessful Senatorial run had called for a return to the Missouri Compromise. Republicans complained that Douglas' Kansas-Nebraska Act was a usurpation of national power in favor of local democracy, although like-minded Republicans and pre-Republicans had previously been active in state subversion of the federal Fugitive Slave Law, an 1850 legal codification of an express constitutional provision. It was the same federal/state shell-game later liberals would play with abortion and gun-control, making a matter a federal case when that forum was favorable, resorting to state action when the federal forum was hostile to them. The Missouri Compromise had succeeded, Maine being balanced by Missouri and the prohibition on other slavery north of Missouri's southern border, but the Northern wish for California, with its southern extension, as a non-slave state led to its throwing-over in favor of the 1850 Compromise. Radical sabotage of the 1850 Compromise's new Fugitive Slave Law inflamed Southern opinion and led to the Kansas-Nebraska Act. For all of the furor over "Bleeding Kansas", largely a product of abolitionistic fanaticism, Kansas became a "free" state, as did, much more quietly, Oregon, Minnesota and Nebraska. Fanatics gave us bleeding Kansas and a few hundred dead while Douglas's work consolidated the West; Lincoln's position, expediently embracing fanaticism, would give us Bleeding America, and 600,000 dead.

Lincoln's pose of moderation had not gotten him a Senate seat, so it was time again for a pose of extremism. 1859 saw the eastern tour, the house dividing and the venomous snake encountered (safely in New England). That got him a presidential nomination and, in a four-way race, the presidency itself. Extremism having profited him politically, President-elect Lincoln greeted Southern proposals for a return to the Missouri Compromise with the contemptuous silence of a politician already made, and so not needing any further dissembling. As a man of probity and general worth, Lincoln was solidly in line with fellow Republican presidential nominees Frémont and Grant, capable in a few

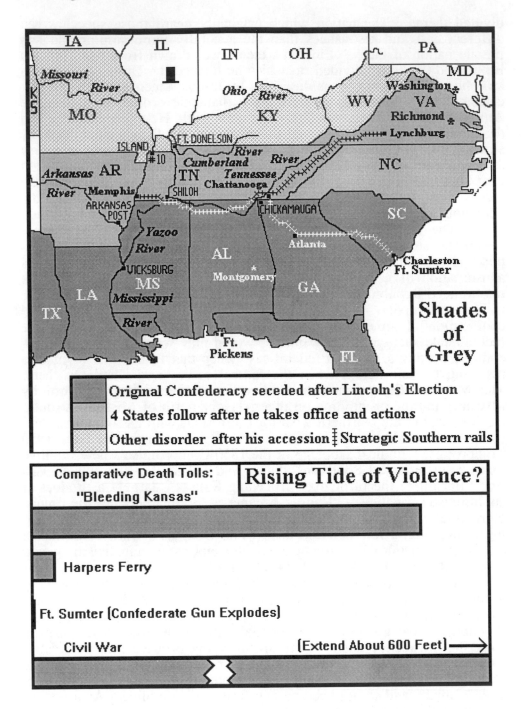

Shades of Grey

Original Confederacy seceded after Lincoln's Election

4 States follow after he takes office and actions

Other disorder after his accession ‡ Strategic Southern rails

Comparative Death Tolls:

"Bleeding Kansas"

Rising Tide of Violence?

Harpers Ferry

Ft. Sumter (Confederate Gun Explodes)

Civil War   (Extend About 600 Feet)⟶

respects, massively incapable in others. It was precisely because Lincoln was such a low-grade politician that his appeals to abolitionists were so miscast, if effective. He had not the excuse of his own fanaticism; his unpatriotism was frustrated greed and miscalculating ambition. The old rail-splitter had swung too hard, cleaving not just the Democrats, but the nation. Modern Liberals moan about expensive elections, someone cutting into their media monopoly with money, but Lincoln's election was most expensive, costing the nation, in battle, from wounds, in camp and in prison camps, 600,000 dead.

That cost was not inevitable. That any of it was paid was due in large part to three Lincoln decisions, the decision to appeal to the radicals (his main Republican rival had been Seward, another opportunist whose anti-slavery principles had not prevented him from an embrace of slave-owner Zachary Taylor, even closer than Lincoln's, seeking to crowd out Taylor's Vice President, New York rival Millard Fillmore), the decision to say nothing about future policies after his election (including the Missouri Compromise revival), letting the nation split in expectation of his own radicalism, and the decision to maintain forts in the Confederacy. Once the Confederates had taken the first shots, the resulting death toll was driven up and up by Lincoln's military policies. Although he had striven successfully to make himself commander-in-chief, at the cost of civil war in fact, Lincoln had not bothered to learn anything important about military matters, and never did. The politician in a hurry mutated into the commander-in-chief in a hurry, promoting haste, casualties and political preference for Republicans into a gigantic death list.

Lincoln's first stroke of buffoonery was to make an immediate descent onto Richmond, which with the rest of Virginia and a few other states had seceded after it became clear that Lincoln's policy was war. The result was a Rebel victory, the defense of their northern railhead in the direction of Washington, and a crisis of confidence in the young Union Army. One bright spot was the conquest of trans-Appalachian Virginia, and the officer most responsible, George McClellan, was put in charge of the Union Army of the Potomac, in spite of being a Democrat. McClellan's thoroughness in training and organizing the Army enraged Lincoln, who demanded an offensive. At last, McClellan moved his available troops by sea to menace Richmond from the coast, avoiding land maneuvering in northern Virginia (where the Rebels had the rail advantage, better cavalry to threaten Union overland supply lines, and a position from which they could easily threaten movements into the Shenandoah Valley or directly upon Washington), in favor of safer sea movement and supply. Despite being deprived of large numbers of troops to allay Lincoln's fears about a Rebel attack upon Washington, probably the most fortified spot in the world by that time and already with its own massive garrison, McClellan's army fought its way forward, nearer

Richmond, tying down the bulk of Rebel forces in the East. Then, the desperate Rebels continually counterattacked, driving McClellan slowly backward, although at disproportionate Rebel loss, something their lower White population could not long sustain. With McClellan's lines daily shorter, easier to defend, and closer to the supporting Union fleet's artillery, but still threatening Richmond, Lincoln hamstrung McClellan; his Peninsula campaign stagnated and the Rebels gained the initiative.

That initiative wisely consisted in letting Lincoln run the Union war-effort into the ground, primarily that of northern Virginia. Lincoln deputized another general, the victorious Republican Pope from the Mississippi Valley, to lead the mass of troops near Washington, that had been withheld from McClellan, in another direct thrust toward Richmond. In one of his peculiarly homey metaphors, the President took his image from butchery, arguing that Pope and McClellan could co-operate, one holding the carcass and the other skinning; but the President had been too long a lawyer in courts where skinning the living was easily accomplished. The Rebel army, although somewhat bled against McClellan, was still alive, not a carcass, and moving up the Union detachment to conveniently near the Rebel railhead put new life into it. With McClellan finally sacked, the Rebels moved upon Pope's army, shattering it before capturing another smaller Union army of recruits at the north end of the Shenandoah Valley (originally posted there by McClellan in the then-confident expectation that he would tie down most of the Rebels at Richmond). As the Rebels, only a few months before desperately worried about Richmond, invaded the North, McClellan was called back to command their repulse. As with their next invasion of the North, the Rebels forfeited their home rail advantage and were defeated, at South Mountain and "Bloody Antietam", by McClellan. The victor was cashiered, for the last time, for not taking enough casualties, and for not promptly re-assuming the futile overland offensive. The cause of Lincoln's haste, aside from bloodthirst and intellectual laziness, was the perceived need to sell war-bonds, leading to a quick-fix policy, offensives to get quick victories, and resultant bloody defeats leading to more pressures for further bloody precipitous folly.

With McClellan out of the way again, Lincoln resumed his policy of the suicidally direct approach, overland assaults upon Richmond that wasted time and lives. The President's much over-praised bookishness had not included the Latin history so familiar to others of his time -- since abandoned in favor of Greek philosophizing or more current manias -- with its military background, such as the importance of encampment over rapid advances, and the limitations in numbers for overland advances over rough roads and tracks (why most consular campaigns were conducted with only two legions). Massive Union columns bogged down and blocked each other's progress, while time and again smaller

Rebel forces took the only good roads in America, the railroads, to arrive organized, concentrated and as supplied as their means permitted. The Civil War was one of modern transportation and communications -- telegraphs, railways and steamships -- things well familiar to Lincoln in themselves, but not in their effect upon the first modern war. Poorer in such modern resources, the South better used what it had; for the North, misdirected riches proved the worst sort of poverty.

The North unambiguously dominated water, whether the great Mississippi Valley or the coasts, with the huge Navy its industry was able to build. The Union's attacks upon the South's ports were generally successful, tying down disproportionate numbers of Rebel soldiers, artillery and engineers, as was McClellan's Peninsula campaign. In the Mississippi Valley, naval support made possible all of the great victories, exhausting the gunpowder of Fort Donelson for Grant's attack, providing gun support and ferrying reinforcements from Buell to Grant's defense of Pittsburg Landing after Shiloh, helping Pope conquer the Confederate fort of Island Number 10, helping McClernand overrun Arkansas Post and helping Grant try a little daring (he had tried everything else, and Lincoln was getting impatient) by ferrying his troops south of Vicksburg. The South's advantage was two-fold in defense: first, its cavalry was far more skillful than the Union cavalry, until the last year of the war, anyway, so that it could always disrupt Union supply lines on Southern land, whether rail or wagon, while at the same time protecting the South's meager railroads, its second defensive advantage away from navigable waters.

In the West, the Union twice forfeited its water advantages while the South still had enough resources to take advantage; the results were bloody battles at Shiloh and Chickamauga. In both battles, Rebel concentrations were effected by rail against Union troops ordered by Lincoln to move overland in difficult country, away from their water communications, and with railheads as their very objectives. It was like a boxer trying to win by putting his chin in the path of his opponent's most powerful blows. Grant's men were strung out on the south bank of the Tennessee River, west and south of Pittsburg Landing, with the advanced elements echeloned inland as far south as Shiloh Church in the hills toward Lincoln's fatuous goal, the Confederate railroad station at Corinth, Mississippi on the Charleston-Memphis line, at the direction of the inimitable General Sherman. Formerly head of a military school, and with no excuse for such indefensible encampment, Sherman's other eccentric escapades, two more involving large death tolls, got him the original title of the man with loose screws. On the first day, the Rebel advance from easily reinforced Corinth shattered several Union divisions, driving the surviving units back to Pittsburg Landing. But the Union Army managed to fall back upon its communications, and the Union flotilla -- gunboats and ferries bringing reinforcements from

Buell's Union Army of the Tennessee -- negated an otherwise explicable Confederate attempt to achieve the textbook victory of defeating an army with its back to the water.

Later, at the Chickamauga, Rebel reinforcements arrived from Virginia via the Lynchburg rail-line to defeat Rosecrans' Union Army, ordered by Lincoln to advance over difficult terrain against a railroad, with the initial Confederate impetus again shattering several Union divisions. But further back of the Chickamauga, General Thomas' rear-guard action saved the rest of that Union Army, bottling up the Confederate advance in narrow passes while the flight took place. Later in the war, Thomas stood at Nashville against a weaker Confederate Army, seeking only a thaw or snow to negate the glare ice that would've hampered his attack. Lincoln had actually fired Thomas when the ground became passable and he won a huge victory. Lincoln's was the mentality that liberals project upon World War I generals, the straight-ahead attack, no matter what the obstacles, no matter what the cost. It pays to understand what drives such a "general", even when it is some civic idol like Lincoln.

The South forfeited its rails on the attack, as when it invaded the North, and lost both times. As with Lincoln's politicized bond drives on Richmond and other points, the Rebel defeats at Antietam and Gettysburg were political campaigns, designed to impress Europe, and failing for the reason that there was no clear way of attaining that goal other than invasion for its own sake, military bootlessness. But, with the South weaker and defensive, Jefferson Davis' own politicized military bankruptcy could only flower twice, but each time galvanizing the Union by handing it victories its own foolish initiatives had been unable to achieve.

Lincoln, on the other hand, pushed forward five invasions of northern Virginia, first forfeiting his advantage to bloody defeat at Bull Run and Second Bull Run (both just forward of the Confederate rail junction at Manassas, where Confederate reinforcements from the central Shenandoah Valley and its railroad to Manassas could join with Confederates from the southern Shenandoah line, from the Richmond line and from the main line of the Orange & Alexandria Railroad, whose northern part to the Potomac had been torn up to handicap Northern attackers). Later, Lincoln dimly perceived that attacking Manassas had been bad, although he did not abstract a reason, but rather shifted to another railhead. Fredericksburg and nearby Chancellorsville, scene of the next two Union disasters in the East, were both on the main line from Richmond, the Richmond, Fredericksburg and Potomac Railroad, with its Potomac extension also de-activated, and connected with both Shenandoah lines at Hanover Junction. The message this time to Lincoln was that his commanders lacked perseverance in carrying out his insane ideas, so he found a serviceable villain in Grant, whom he had toyed

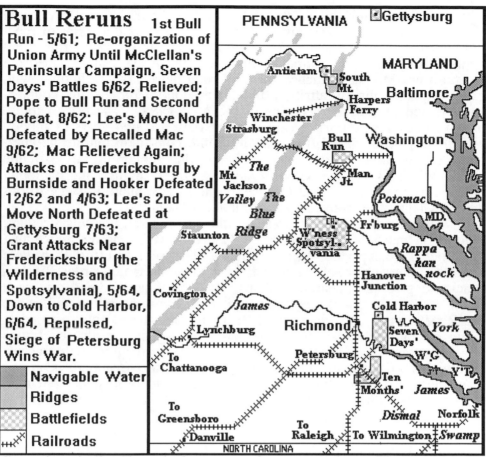

Bull Reruns 1st Bull Run - 5/61; Re-organization of Union Army Until McClellan's Peninsular Campaign, Seven Days' Battles 6/62, Relieved; Pope to Bull Run and Second Defeat, 8/62; Lee's Move North Defeated by Recalled Mac 9/62; Mac Relieved Again; Attacks on Fredericksburg by Burnside and Hooker Defeated 12/62 and 4/63; Lee's 2nd Move North Defeated at Gettysburg 7/63; Grant Attacks Near Fredericksburg (the Wilderness and Spotsylvania), 5/64, Down to Cold Harbor, 6/64, Repulsed, Siege of Petersburg Wins War.

- Navigable Water
- Ridges
- Battlefields
- Railroads

Campaigns in the Shenadoah were too frequent to show. They were generally successful for the Confederacy, and a source of quick rail reinforcements for the Army of Northern Virginia, but "the Valley" was devastated. With railroads and cavalry, the Confederates were superior on their own land. McClellan's Peninsula campaign and Lee's Moves North evened things, temporarily. The Peninsula is shaped like an arm giving thumb's-down, an omen for the British at Yorktown as for Union strategy.

"Navigable Waters", the underused "arms of the sea", ended at the fall line of water-powered cities. The Tidewater's easy access to the sea concentrated slaves and landholdings. In Virginia, slaves were voted by their owners, on the basis of taxation and federal apportionment, giving the Tidewater political dominance. Reconstruction gave the Whiter and more Unionist Southern uplands stronger apportionments, reflecting their later votes with Blacks excluded. Just before the Voting Rights Act, such apportionments were voided by the Supreme Court in *Baker v. Carr*.

with cashiering before his belated victory at Vicksburg. Grant's Virginia campaign suffered massive casualties by fighting around a series of rebel field fortifications. Starting near Fredericksburg (the Wilderness and Spotsylvania), Grant's continually bled and transfused army reached the old positions Mac had reached by the Union naval taxi, inflicting, with naval support, thrifty attrition upon desperate Confederate counter-attacks, **and** causing the scuttling of the *Merrimack*. The prior capture of most Confederate ports meant that not only had two years of bloody war already been wasted, but that the South could concentrate its engineers and artillery at Richmond, with no other remaining target of the Union worth as much. Grant's siege would take nine more bloody months, as he no longer had the massive local advantage in siege troops that McClellan had enjoyed by his timelier onslaught.

The Union war-effort took on more than just Lincoln's strategy, it took on much of his character. Generals were put on notice that casualties were expected, and were more of a proof of effort than were victories. Fearing relief, men in field commands would order fruitless attacks to give an appearance of activity. Sherman ordered one such effort early in the Vicksburg campaign, and Grant one at the end, when the Rebels were only days away from being starved into surrender. Grant not only repeated the pattern later in Virginia, he also continued his refinement of waiting several days for a truce after such fiascos. Letting his wounded die in screaming agony after several days in no-man's land left fewer live men to complain, and reminded the Union troops in nearby trenches just who was still in charge. And being put in charge was largely determined by politics, as the President accepted professional determinations that supported his ignorant prejudices and partisan biases, and rejected those that did not. The improbable Pope and Grant were rewarded with commands of Lincoln's inept Virginia thrusts, while the much abler McClernand, also a western victor, was doomed to relief by his Democratic affiliation (a friend of Stephen Douglas and a former congressman); the army he had raised was decimated under Republican mismanagement. Lincoln's disfavoritism of McClernand nauseated even his Republican Postmaster-General, a partisan man filling a partisan office that throughout the 19th century was more concerned with party patronage than with merit.

The excuse of Civil War is given, as though the depredations of Sherman in Georgia were inevitable; years later, Americans in Vietnam were exorciated by Modern Liberals for burning huts from which they had been fired upon, with the propaganda gibe that they had to burn the villages to save them. But in historical memory, a 60-mile swath of Georgia, from which there was no discernible fire, was burned in Liberalism's First Crusade. Lincoln suspended *habeus corpus*, no problem, for there **was** a rebellion; being unfashionably White, no one was compensated for running afoul of Mr. Lincoln and his broad definition of Rebel (there **was** an invasion of various national territories when the *Nisei* were interned: they later got reparations -- from the taxpayers, not from the liberals who imprisoned them). By the same token, the deified Lincoln also offered to shoot Rebel prisoners out of hand, if Union Black troops were shot; such a policy of retaliation would be denounced in our liberal century as contributing to "an endless cycle of violence" (the media never hesitates at wild extrapolation, far more ideologically useful than recitation of refractory mundane facts), if undertaken on patriotic, rather than leftist, grounds. Even the famed Gettysburg Address has been sanitized by decontextualization, as Lincoln's brevity was more a matter of public hostility to his previous visit to Gettysburg (right after the battle, the drunken fool had shouted witticisms, about the mounds of amputated limbs, over the screams of the newly crippled in the field hospitals).

Occasionally, the historical treatment of these tragedies itself ascends to unintentional farce. Allan Nevins, journalist/historian/biographer, and twice Pulitizered in the third category, may have been all over the landscape in describing Kansas Governor Lane, but it took the Civil War for Nevins to hit his stride. General Wm. Farrar "Baldy" Smith, a McClellan and Rosecrans subordinate given credit for Mac's and Rosie's victories, so inconvenient for the Lincoln Cult, is described as "tall" and "impressive" beside his flawed commanders. Later, with Grant and Butler pursuing Lincoln's murderous Virginia strategy, "Baldy" Smith was relieved of his corps command because he had lost too few men. This time, Smith is "short" and "portly", as though putting his physique into such desperate play would add luster to the idol Lincoln and his altar boy Grant. To point up these revealing contradictions to a cultist is of course to engage the irrational in argument. Cultists who acknowledge the contradiction will praise Nevins for his resourcefulness. And by their lights, those phantom lights resolutely from within, Smith did indeed shrink in his duties, for what is a human sacrifice but the sincere form of the humanistic religion, and who but a churl would stint in the effort? And who but the frequent advocates of "peace" would so gorge themselves on binges of bloody war, temple feasts between fasts? When the throbbing consciences of those seeking to prove their superior morality are at work, real considerations -- blood or the blood-money called taxation -- are ignored, save as props in lunatic morality plays. No mere ritualistic consumption of a sacrificed human scapegoat, no transubstantiation, will do with the liberal cult; real cannibalism, the sincerest form of religious ritual, is required. Liberal culture, with its theatre of the absurd, actually lags behind mainstream liberalism; the pretentious *avant-garde* is only the rear guard of pretense.

Of all Americans, Lincoln is the one Communist true-believers love to compare to Lenin, Stalin and Mao; tragically, they are right. Compared to giants like Polk, McClellan, McClernand, Lee, Jackson,

Stephens and Benjamin, Lincoln was an appalling man, one to whom "the dawn is not an awakening, but mostly an opportunity to wait for the evils of the next night", as an admiring English leftist later privately wrote to a *sympatico* American Supreme Court Justice. There is a gap between the metaphors, excretory or otherwise, used to describe the vile, that simply fail to include either the moral dimension or the way a specimen like Lincoln leaves it befouled; the battlefield tourist who would refer to one of his appointees as a bluebottle (carrion) fly was himself little more than a culpable maggot.

Lincoln was the American Nero, and the effusiveness with which liberals puffed him into legend has its modern counterparts, the sanctimonious deification of the tin-god Kennedy brothers and Martin Luther King, or the tasteful funeral procession for Khomeini. Such investments in extravagant irrationality always have their little sideways denials; all four "great" Americans became the centers of conspiracy fetishists (unlike Garfield and McKinley, rational men attacked by obvious kooks), because it was entirely plausible for their countrymen to have wanted them dead. The first two, Lincoln and Kennedy, were slain by completely cognizable opponents, a Southern sympathizer and a Soviet-aided assassin, respectively, but others are designated villains, Stanton or the right, respectively, as ludicrous projections of bogeymen designed to discredit the "bad radicals" or the other side of the political spectrum. 1968 assassination charges were symptomatic of the split in liberal ranks, between the Cold War Liberals and the re-emerging Modern Liberals; the liberal establishment, or vague right-wing conspiracies, had to be conjured up as villains to define the Modern Liberal outlook, besieging the right while posing as its victim, by the usual aggressively spurious charges, looking to both widen the gap between left and right and to take undisputed command of the left by destroying the more centrist liberals.

Those who find Lincoln a political genius are usually those moaning about such foreign pestholes as Northern Ireland, Beirut and Bosnia and their endemic civil wars. In some situations, it does not take a genius to start a civil war; rather, political genius may be needed to stop one. Although American liberals babble about the "inevitability" of a war over slavery, many other nations ended slavery without resort to war. That is political genius, unrecognized by those who habitually attack the healthy aspects of American life while wishing to ape foreign pathologies. If civil war is political genius, give us political idiocy.

Obviously, Lincoln was a Republican, but as the exemplar of American liberal ideology in action -- the political alliance of sordid interest and high-pressure self-righteous moral superiority -- he was the prototype, and the assiduous maintenance of his culthood has kept the pattern in view, a minimal respect for fact usefully equipped to tap the irrational wellsprings of liberal conduct. Cult development was pendular, Northern fire-eaters first controlling the national government with the South absent. Union had been maintained, an armed government dragooning its erstwhile citizens, but partisanship and ideology suspended democracy in the South, for the putative extension of democratic rights. Radical advantage in Northern elections was fairly widespread, but re-union brought the spectre of a return to political gridlock. With war-time tensions cooling and the South returning to its normal hostility to the Northern radicals, the effective loss of radical power loomed.

Instead, the Army was sent in to seize the Southern state governments and the 1868 elections, for Grant and the Republican Congress, making the so-called 14th Amendment possible. The 14th ensured Black (Republican) political rights in the South, even as the White majority (in all southern states, except sometimes South Carolina and Mississippi) was disenfranchised by the same alleged amendment's unconstitutional retroactivity (an "*ex post facto*" law prohibited by the real Constitution). Liberal ideologues, demagogues with bad breath, love to woof at the Constitution as a "*coup d'etat*", although it was utterly legal and consensual (Rhode Island, the last holdout against ratification, would have had to pay tariffs, like any other foreign nation, if it did not rejoin the nation; how Draconian!). The 14th, besides serving the corporations as it was designed to do, also added sexual preference to the Constitution; instead of mere pronouns, the protected class was specifically "male", although neuter corporations would benefit after 1876. Even with the refusal of the radicals to countenance rescissions of ratifications before definitive enactment, the 14th was too much for radical Massachusetts, which only ratified the 14th in 1939, 63 years after it had become a dead-letter in racial politics, and 43 years after it had been held not only to not ban segregation, but to actually uphold it.

With the South occupied, and under the administration of the military and carpetbagger/scalawag "Reconstruction" regimes (so like the original "Construction", bleeding Rhode Island), the Republican alliance of fading ideologues and partisan hacks and profiteers stayed in power, but their hold on the North was threatened by their obvious viciousness. In 1876, the Republicans agreed to suspend Reconstruction, to keep another Presidential term and its patronage. After 1876, Southern Republicans, Black and White, continued to send sizable delegations to Republican national conventions; as their only support was federal patronage from the winner based upon delivery of their nominating votes, these delegations helped lock in the renomination of incumbents or the nomination of otherwise slender front-runners.

The broad mass of people in the North had seen enough. Having burned their passport to chaos and lacking another domestic firebrand, the forces of moralistic arson had to await a suitable international incident.

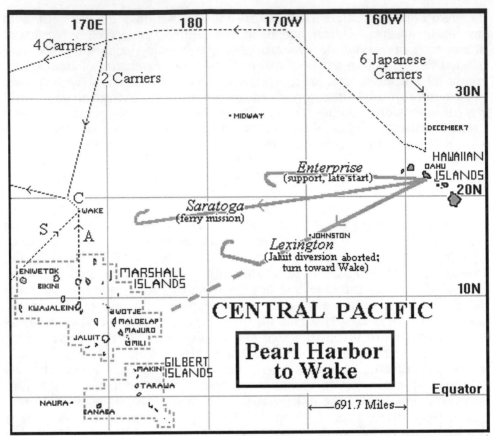

The first of four chronological Pacific War maps (others at 66, 98 and 110), showing the connection between the retreat of Japan's Pearl Harbor Strike Force and the attacks upon Wake Island. A = Amphibious force, attacks December 10 and 22, 1941; S = Gunfire support cruisers from Truk (later Savo Island core) for second attack; C = Seaplane cruisers *Tone* and *Chikuma*, with ability to accomodate passengers in their hangars. Their crews massacred Wake prisoners and later Indian Ocean missionaries. At Midway, their bungled scouting led to Japanese disaster.

Oahu to Wake and back was the unrefueled maximum range of American destroyers operating at 25 knots. The three American carriers had only two oilers between them, the *Neosho,* which the Japanese had passed upon at Pearl Harbor and which they sunk a month later to abort a raid on occupied Wake, and the *Neches,* which had fueled the first aircraft ferry mission to Wake and which was sunk 6 months later in the Coral Sea. Admiral Halsey's oilerless *Enterprise* force was accordingly given the shortest mission. Admiral Fletcher's ferry mission was also slowed by the aircraft depot ship *Tangier,* meant for Wake's aborted18 fighter-load.

Chapter 3 - **Intervention**

As with most items of liberalism, Progressivism was subject to subsequent caveats and denunciations, with most items anathema but the tradition, and its exemplars, given a nugatory embrace. The armed imperialism of Progressive nationalism has evaporated into a legacy that only patriots are proud of, and Theodore Roosevelt's championship of the "gun-nuts" of the National Rifle Association is as embarrassing to Modern Liberals as the later militaristic volunteerism of the Plattsburgh camps, where the liberals would play at sabre-rattling, to be ready for the opportunity offered by World War I's trench warfare. Today, of course, such activity would be investigated and harassed by modern left-liberals as right-wing insanity. Even in middle retrospect, the World War II liberal caricature of the "Japs" as buck-toothed thickly spectacled mustached sabre-waving lunatics upsets liberalism not because of racism, but because they resemble a race of Theodore Roosevelts.

One current way to be labeled as a right-wing nut is to point out the obvious leftist bias of the American media. Only in distant retrospect is the media's power admissible, and then in pursuit of goals now derided by the media and academics. Modern Liberal legend has it that the Spanish-American War was caused by the "yellow journalism" of Hearst and Pulitzer, but the critical events were hardly within their control. It was not newspapermen who blew up the American battleship in Havana harbor, nor was it the United States Congress that first declared war. It was Spain, and there were no Hearst or Pulitzer yellow presses there to pressure the *Cortes*.

Also carped at is the swift and efficient achievement of victory by the U.S., such as Dewey's rapid descent upon the Spanish flotilla at Manila Bay. First, the rapidity of the American attack prevented the Spanish from laying new minefields there. Second, Dewey's victory enabled the rapid detachment of the battleship *Oregon* for its long voyage to Cuba, where it joined the rest of the American battleships, already short the destroyed *Maine*, in time for the concluding naval battle off Santiago. Contemporary naval opinion over-valued the armored cruiser type possessed by the Spanish Atlantic force, but the Spanish tactic of high-speed flight sacrificed their armored cruisers' advantage in close-in fighting, putting their guns out of range while the American battleships' heavy guns and superb marksmanship ended the Spanish flight. Third, Dewey's action also ended the threat to American commerce posed by the Spanish Pacific flotilla. Although McKinley was not regarded as very progressive, he had quickly concluded an anti-privateering agreement with Spain, the typical Progressive/liberal fetish that agreements with foreigners -- the U.N. or disarmament treaties -- can over-ride the Constitution's grant of various war powers to the Congress. Dewey's public relations problem with modern neurotics is that his actions were effective and meritorious; he destroyed a legitimate military force aware of the state of war, with no loss to the men he was responsible for, his own. Unfortunately, that sort of Theodore Roosevelt-attitude was not to last.

The Democratic Progressive, Woodrow Wilson, got elected only because of a split in the Republican ranks between Roosevelt's Progressive come-back and Taft's regulars. Wilson's domestic effort was hardly encouraging for his future prospects: he found the economy sputtering, and stalled it completely with his policies. Fortunately for Wilson's re-election campaign, there was not only a running controversy with Mexico, but also a big war in Europe to provide a convenient distraction, a peace theme for electioneering and the opportunity for electoral leverage.

Crucial to that effort were the big electoral swing-states of Illinois and Pennsylvania, where large numbers of Poles, Serbs and Czechs resided in the key cities of Chicago and Pittsburgh. Even as he was campaigning as the peace candidate, Wilson was plotting the future dismemberment of Germany and Austria-Hungary, both countries having Poles under their rule, and Austria-Hungary also having the Czechs and some Serbs under its control. The opposing alliance had Russia, with many Poles, but that was the exception to Wilson's anger; the huge empires of France, Britain, Russia and even Italy were not targets, providing no electoral magic, although frequently occasioning European wars and American embroilment. Additionally, America's Germans were primarily Republicans and also opposed to the existing German Empire, so that, although very numerous, they had no political leverage, with Wilson or otherwise.

Wilson's tinkerings with the map of Europe began well before the U.S. declaration of war, which was done on the pretext of being against German submarine warfare and German intrigue with Mexico. Academics such as Germany's Professor Fritz Fischer, have argued that German maps, made **after** the outbreak of World War I, somehow showed that Germany had planned the war from the beginning; Wilson somehow escapes that standard, in spite of his maps pre-existing U.S. involvement, and foreshadowing his 14 Points, which happened to be handy when the successful peace candidate chose to become nettled to the point of war over German submarines and diplomacy. Wilson, as a historian, was disposed to an anti-German view dating from the end of the 19th century, when a German fleet had attempted to interpose itself between Dewey's force and the Spanish fleet in Manila Bay, and other incidents, before the division of Samoa, when American and British shells had landed on territory claimed by Germany. In all cases, British forces were present but escaped censure.

When early in World War I a German submarine sank the British passenger liner *Lusitania* "without warning" (the German government's ad in *THE NEWSPAPER OF RECORD*'s shipping news section evidently did not count as a warning), Wilson concealed his knowledge that the British "civilian" ship was carrying more than 20 rifles per passenger, enough to equip an entire infantry corps in the then-rapidly expanding British Army (growing from a miniscule 6 divisions in 1914 to 37 in early 1915). The information that the U.S. was aware of the *Lusitania*'s cargo became public only in the 1970s; in the 1980s, some rifles were raised. One copy of the deceptive munitions manifest had been kept by Assistant Secretary of the Navy Franklin Roosevelt, also in on the creation of that "German atrocity". The Wilson Administration tried to keep the rifles' existence a secret from the American public, if not from foreign governments -- London lied that the *Lusitania* had been carrying just ammunition, had blown up and had sunk immediately. The ship had actually been beached on its torpedoed starboard side in Irish shoals, and a hole was chopped in its top (port) side to remove the guns from its forward hold. This hole helped start a legend that the British had blown up the alleged ammunition "magazine" to provide a propaganda sinking, but conspiracy theorists had the wrong conspiracy.

The only stocks of sufficient rifles in American hands in early 1915 were those of the U.S. Army, and there was no congressional authorization for their sale, lease or other transfer (such as later replacing them in U.S. inventory with new production); the rifles were supplied to the British with Wilson's connivance. The possibility of impeachment was one decreased by the right kind of secrecy, and the political backlash against Wilson's re-election bid, due the next year, would have transferred much of the blame for the hundred-plus dead Americans from Germany to Wilson's own shoulders. As with American involvement in World War II, the initiative was mainly American, liberal intrigue leading to a series of incidents, and finally to war with the exasperated designated enemy. The war message was one of the first acts of the re-elected Wilson's second term; the renewal of German unrestricted submarine warfare and anti-American diplomacy proceeded not just from German hubris or some purely anti-American bias, but from a country which Wilson had sought to damage and which Wilson had slandered in trying to cover up, successfully for a long time, his own misdeeds.

Winston Churchill, First Lord of the British Admiralty at the beginnings of both wars, was also involved in similarly discreditable incidents in World War II. In 1939, for example, with Poland falling and the possibility of peace returning, Churchill took to the floor of the House of Commons with a dramatic story about an atrocity at sea, the torpedoing without warning of a British ship, sixty dead, and the story confirmed by the captured captain of the German submarine. The sixty "dead" were in fact picked up by a British transport -- summoned in the initial instance by the submarine's radio call -- and held incommunicado by the British while being transported to safety on land -- distant Brazil, an illogical military destination for a military transport in wartime, but a logical propaganda destination for the critical mission of whooping up support for the war. If you don't have a *Lusitania*, make one up. The submarine's captain ruined the story, however, when he was interviewed by CBS Radio in Berlin (P.G. Wodehouse, interviewed by CBS from Berlin, faced post-war censure for broadcasting for the enemy; the newscasters, and CBS itself, somehow escaped such censure, although they were there voluntarily, while Wodehouse had been interned in fallen France). Churchill's policy during the rest of World War II was that fast liners were not to sail in convoys, which would have slowed them down; instead, they were to sail alone, and any sinkings used for *Lusitania*-type propaganda. That was the policy less explicitly employed in World War I, when Churchill argued that the Royal Navy could not spare warships to escort large fast ships, only the slow small ones, more time at sea!

After World War I, with the economy still in a shambles, and a wave of leftist terrorism sweeping the country (aided by the new American Civil Liberties Union, ever anxious to help the exercise of such "civil liberties" as arson, bombings and riots, or resisting a legal declaration of war), Wilson tried to get the U.S. into his hare-brainchild "League of Nations", an early United Nations and just as successful. Although other countries had joined with stated reservations of their sovereignty, Wilson refused to ratify the Versailles Treaty after the U.S. Senate's constitutionally necessary "advice and consent" specified similar reservations. The Senate, actually a recalcitrant lawful minority, merely recognized that a treaty made under the Constitution cannot transcend the Constitution. Liberals always want to believe that some treaty, court decision or other legal gimmickry can, by virtue of origin from a constitutional organ, supersede the Constitution itself, that a legislative veto, or a judicial usurpation, such as the "legalization" of abortion, or a Federal Reserve Board, or a joining of some international organization, can transcend the Constitution. Such practices are known by lawyers as bootstrapping, or by the rest of us as power-grabs. The problem is that there are simply too many liberal gimmicks without the necessary widespread public support for a constitutional amendment to give them a sound legal basis, and liberals must improvise and re-interpret away constitutional bars, building their expensive and inane programs upon the foundations of shifty pretenses.

Liberal historians and other propagandists love to blame the U.S.'s absence from the League of Nations (the U.S. is always at fault, and always critical to anything happening in the world, fulfilling essentially a theological role for liberals) for its failure to uphold the other provisions of the Versailles Treaty. The U.S. was far more distant than the European powers from the areas where the terms were to have been enforced, and not in the habit of intervening in Europe. The structure of peace was doomed from the start, with the failure to prevent the rise of the criminal Soviet regime in Russia, or to enforce treaty compliance by newly re-risen Poland or even defeated Turkey. All of these were fact by 1922 (and American involvement, hampered by the new franchise for women and the resulting outburst of pacifism, would not have changed things a whit), so that the young League proved its fatuity long before the appeasement of the 1930s. What did change, too late, was that German national desires began to be treated as legitimately as those of its neighbors, a parlous situation. Before that occurred, however, the German leadership which had treated with the victorious Allies was fatally sullied by its acceptance of a continuation of the war-time blockade, forced demilitarization, the loss of German territories, blame for the war (Serbia, which of course had actually started the war by sponsoring the assassination of the heir to the Austro-Hungarian throne, doubled in size) and some occupation.

In the U.S., the fall of Wilson and the League led to domestic peace and prosperity, the return of normalcy which made the left so angry they had to deny the validity of the very word, chalking up the Victorianism to Warren Harding, the former newspaperman whose various speeches were drafted by a Johns Hopkins professor or by a future *Baltimore Sun* editor; when academics and journalists chortled over Harding's usages, they were merely indicting their own. Economic chaos, sabre-rattling, internationalism and the Wilson naval build-up were stopped; the reformers' enactment of Prohibition, uniting left and right as would the equally fatuous "War on Drugs", proved a poor substitute, but did provide a measure of chaos and corruption. Although the opposition to Harding, both within and without the Republican Party, soon resorted to scandal-mongering in lieu of issues, the accession of Coolidge kept liberalism out of the driver's seat. But with Coolidge's reluctance to stand for re-election in 1928, only slippery cabineteer Herbert Hoover was quick enough to pounce on the Republican nomination, the only such elected nominee without previous electoral or military experience.

Although enshrined by inept history and partisan twaddle as a conservative, Hoover was a pacifist, an internationalist and an economic interventionalist, things that had served him well while making a name for himself for international relief efforts. But his dogged energy in following a plan led to disaster when the stock markets panicked in 1929. Convinced that the key to restoring the situation was to keep up prices, Hoover embarked upon heavy federal regulation of agriculture (the AMA, overshadowed by Roosevelt's follow-on AAA, M for Marketing followed by A for Adjustment) and the heavy subsidy of business credit (the RFC). But keeping up prices merely prevented a quick recovery, because, lacking bargains to overawe their fear for the future, people stopped spending. Keeping up prices while employment, wages, profits and values were falling just tightened the screws upon the mass of people; prosperity is not being squeezed. Money spent on programs was just wasted because the programs were ill-conceived.

The accession of Franklin Roosevelt was far less a matter of policies than of party and personality. Hoover's chilly detachment had played well against the chaos of World War I and its aftermath, a determined American trying to forge some order, but it struck Depression Americans as callous. Roosevelt had a jaunty smile, a staggeringly favorable press and lots of hoopla -- Blue Eagle Parades, as the country tried to hootenanny its way out of a fix which Roosevelt's policies, most importantly Hoover's failed fix of keeping up prices, would prolong and prolong. But as long as there was political mileage to be made out it, there really was no Democratic need to change -- the Democrats, and their leftist hangers-on, had jobs. Contrast how quickly Vietnam became "Nixon's War" (before he even took office) with how long the Depression stayed Hoover's Depression; the very idea of Roosevelt's Depression (and it was for seven years, more than twice as long as Hoover's watch) is blasphemy to our civic religion of liberalism.

Although Roosevelt's announced program had been a modification of Prohibition and balancing the federal budget, the huge number of new programs -- some long over-due and beneficial (power dams and flood control on the Tennessee and Columbia Rivers, a federal highway system, new schools and post offices and a follow-on naval building program to the Coolidge cruisers and carrier) and therefore controversial to future leftists -- soon made a legitimately balanced budget impossible. What Roosevelt did was to take most of the new debt off the books, so that a semblance of a balanced budget was always within sight. While criticized by some economists as not running a high-enough deficit to cause recovery, the New Deal indeed really ran up Keynesian debts, although off the books, but there was no recovery from that panacea. And lest it be said that the cooking of the books prevented people from realizing the boost in "aggregate demand" that occurred; such should have produced its effects without publicity and psychology. It didn't, because the theory was wrong, looking for relief from psychological misconceptions in abstractions and graphs.

Roosevelt's interventionism, on hold while mileage was made out of "Mr. Hoover's Depression", had flowered first under Wilson and soon after as the 1920 Democratic Vice Presidential nominee. Orwellian Newspeak came to America first when Franklin Roosevelt actually coined the "Big Brother" phrase, in a speech in Butte, Montana, describing the attitude the U.S. should take toward Latin America. Roosevelt also claimed authorship of a Haitian constitution, leaving him gun-shy on Latin American politics; his New Deal "Good Neighbor Policy" would let Latins steal American property. Sympathy for Roosevelt's illness and the early "Memory-hole" of a captive press also left him off the hook of a juicy Navy Department homosexual preference scandal; Roosevelt's claims of a war-record (a brief European tour) were also taken at face value. Although such a sympathetic support system had been invaluable in shielding Roosevelt from his own short-comings, it was insufficient to justify a third term.

Only the coming of war -- military production for re-armament and export and the draft -- brought the nation out of its self-imposed funk, curing domestic failure with international catastrophe, and leading to a prolonged binge of global interventionism. The end of the "merchants of death" congressional inquisitions into World War I (wherein the U.S. government escaped obloquy for its role in the *Lusitania* affair) had produced a spate of neutrality legislation. This tapered off only in 1939, as Roosevelt found neutrality in war-time more difficult than in peace-time, when neutrality was effectively a dead letter anyway. Aside from rushing the build-up of the American armed forces via a draft and new ships and planes, old ships were due for rebuilding. The first of four groups of American battleships, the three *Idaho* class, had already undergone a recent rebuild, with the lapse of disarmament treaty tonnage limitations permitting such weighty and long-desired items as anti-torpedo bulges and thicker deck armor against plunging shells and aircraft bombs; later, the new American "pom-pom" gun gave these ships the best close-in anti-aircraft protection in the American fleet.

The tragedy of treaty tonnage-limitations was that other existing warships were limited in their ability to survive bombs and torpedoes; such ships were death-traps, and to no good end. The weight penalty of additional deck armor and anti-aircraft guns and radar could have easily been paid from a **design** (engineering plus economics) standpoint by adding needed anti-torpedo bulges to raise buoyancy by increasing displacement, but such synergies were anathema from the **ideological** standpoint of disarmament diplomacy. One ideological wrong prevented the adoption of several engineering rights, and thousands of Americans (on eight battleships and on a series of treaty cruisers too busy with war work for lengthy modification) died because of it.

But further improvements, although congressionally mandated, were stymied by Franklin Roosevelt's vacillating policy of shifting the fleet hither and yon against phantom threats and as a supra-diplomatic "signalling" device. Although Congress in April of 1939 ordered the rebuilding of a second echelon of American battleships, the "Big Five" of the fleet's total of 15, in 1939 and early 1940, the U.S. fleet was concentrated in the Atlantic Ocean lest the Nazis suddenly leap across the Atlantic and invade Iowa. As the rapid fall of Poland was followed by the "phony war" (or "*Sitzkrieg*"), Japan's war with China became a more pressing distraction, although there had been no material change. The Navy's 12 strongest battleships and the five strongest of its seven aircraft carriers were sent to Pearl Harbor to threaten Japan. This was a silly move on several accounts: First, the fleet was vulnerable there to a surprise attack from aircraft carriers, as had previously been pointed out in several books in the 1920s, by a fleet exercise in the 1930s, as well as repeatedly by Admiral J.O. Richardson, commander of the fleet in a pre-war situation, and with 80% of that fleet under his personal command. Early in 1941, the outspoken and insubordinate Richardson, rocking the boat to save a chunk of that fleet, was replaced by the compliant, and complacent, Husband E. Kimmel. Second, Congress in May 1940 ordered the rebuilding of the third echelon of American battleships, the three older vessels left in the Atlantic, but that would have meant stripping the American battleships from an area of actual, and increasing, naval belligerence, so it was never really accomplished. Third, nothing was really happening in the Pacific at the time, except progressively harsher American sanctions against Japan, so that ships were eventually detached from the Pacific fleet for Atlantic duty (the only American carrier with radar, the *Yorktown*, and the only three large American ships with pom-pom guns and modernized protection, the three *Idaho*s), as well as for tardy modernization (carrier *Hornet*, leaving it in the U.S. to prepare for the later famous "Doolittle Raid" on Tokyo, and even the "Big Five" battleship *Colorado*, which, being sped back to the war along with its damaged sister *Maryland*, ended up less modernized than two of the "Big Five" sunk at Pearl Harbor and raised).

With none of the eight previously ordered battleship rebuilds underway in early 1941, Congress had not ordered the rebuilding of the fourth, and last, echelon, leaving eight unmodernized battleships at Pearl Harbor unprotected by cheap-but-effective sheet-metal bulges. (Anti-torpedo nets were ineffective, because they "gave" with a torpedo's momentum, still allowing the warhead to contact the ship's side and explode. Bulges had enough rigidity to detonate torpedo warheads, were far less draggier and cumbersome than nets, giving protection at sea, and gave buoyancy for more deck armor.) Four of those unmodernized, and unbulged, battleships would succumb to torpedoes; a fifth, the *Arizona*, to an aircraft bomb (a converted battleship shell dropped by an airplane, which would penetrate its unmodernized deck armor, unaugmented by an additional 3-5 inches to keep such would-be penetrators from reaching its powder magazine and killing the ship and its crew); and three others would be damaged by bombs.

Had Congress forced Roosevelt to obey the law, all American battleships could have been modernized by December 1941 (as *Newsday* implied they had: "even before Pearl Harbor[,] the Navy ... had added more armor and more anti-aircraft guns"; such improvements to the non-*Idaho*s had been extremely minor, cramped by disarmament treaty tonnage limits). Even a real modernization was only a 6- to 8-month process. Instead, in December 1941, 20 of the fleet's 22 capital ships were being used for political charades, such as the backfiring gesture at

Japan or such Grenadaesque episodes as the occupations of Iceland, Greenland and Dutch Guiana, all to forestall a Nazi war-machine unable to leapfrog the English Channel, let alone the wide Atlantic. American Atlantic warships, operating out of the range of any German aircraft except passenger-carrying flying boats, boasted most of the Navy's pom-pom guns and most of its naval radar (the only radar aircraft carrier, the *Yorktown*, two of the three radar-operating battleships and two of three radar cruisers). The Pacific fleet, still half of the U.S. Navy and in real danger as American sanctions against Japan intensified, had no modernized ships (most important against a surprise attack was their armor lack -- both radar and guns were more active measures, requiring time to be brought into action, unlike armor and torpedo bulges, which did not have to be manned, loaded or switched on), few pom-pom guns and only two operative radar ships, one soon sunk at Pearl Harbor (battleship *West Virginia*'s radar was newly installed, but not yet activated, when it, too, was sunk).

Theodore Roosevelt had advised walking softly and carrying a big stick; cousin Franklin had clumped around, dividing his stick and letting it waste. Roosevelt's shift of the U.S. Navy's main base to Pearl Harbor was meant to have been provocative, but the gesture was so successful in that regard that it failed. There was also a close tie between American fears of an Asian rapprochement and the Japanese troop movements preparing for the possibility of a Pacific War. Most such Japanese troops were being withdrawn from China, something Washington was demanding. Had Roosevelt questioned Japanese troop movements instead of drawing aggressive conclusions from them, he might have continued to soften his stance. War might have been averted, or at least delayed until started at American behest and advantage. The U.S. ended up with a two-front war, with a string of defeats in the Pacific and with American merchant ships soon lustily burning all along the East Coast. And with war, in late 1941 and early 1942, the ships earlier withdrawn from the Pacific were shuttled back there (the three *Idaho*s and the carrier *Yorktown*) to make weight for the five battleships sunk at Pearl Harbor. Constant shifts had left the U.S. Navy vulnerable and off-balance, plunged into foreign wars with a string of defeats.

The measure of tactical surprise at Pearl Harbor is also ever "controversial", somewhat to conservative gadflys, but mainly to doctrinaire anti-militarists. The U.S. had neglected its Pacific bases, by disarmament treaty, for fifteen years, so it was playing catch-up ball in that regard. It had essentially two long-range planes available in 1941 for reconnaissance, the PBY Catalina flying boat and the new Boeing B-17 bomber. But the Catalinas were not yet available in sufficient numbers for a total long-range patrol of the Hawaiian approaches, and available B-17s were being concentrated in the West Pacific, a bomber "deterrence" that failed with their destruction mainly on the ground, lacking air-warning radar (the Japanese had tactical surprise on **both** large raids on the B-17s' Clark Field base), or with their expenditure against Japanese landings (B-17 crews were not trained for such anti-ship operations except sporadically later in the war). In the days after Pearl Harbor, before the propaganda campaign against MacArthur was underway -- or before his own publicity machine had begun to hum -- his B-17s reported bombing the Japanese battleship *Haruna*. That ship was nowhere nearby, but the B-17s had indeed sunk a tiny minesweeper, less valuable but harder to hit.

Similarly, the three U.S. Pacific carriers were all pre-occupied on Pearl Harbor day, with the *Saratoga* detached for voyage home for a tardy rebuild (a Japanese submarine torpedoed it on the way) and the other two ferrying short-range fighter planes to Wake (that Japanese target receiving its first fighters four days before attacked) and Midway Islands, respectively. Even the only Pacific radar cruiser was busy guiding a convoy of troop transports to the Philippines (diverted to Australia). There was no cheap observation available pending the build-up of PBYs at Pearl Harbor (in 1941, most PBYs produced and all other twin-engine reconnaissance planes, such as the Lockheed Hudson, were going to Britain and Russia); B-17s and carriers were busy helping other bases. The Navy scorned small patrol boats, and the Neutrality Patrol was an Atlantic gimmick Cruiser patrols would have been vulnerable to a real enemy and, even had carriers been available, the State Department had vetoed carrier patrols to the northwest of Hawaii as "provocative"; the provocative combination of baiting Japan and hanging out the fleet at Pearl Harbor might have been made less costly by such patrols.

Strangely enough, what liberals find most galling about Pearl Harbor is the allegation that Franklin Roosevelt planned the whole thing. Allowing for Japanese actions being beyond him, there was the tawdry pattern of U.S. intervention already underway, as well as the liberal policy of also denying the truth. Samuel Eliot Morison's inept way of denying a conspiracy by the icon Roosevelt was to link him with the then-current icon, JFK. "But let us not forget that we were surprised ... in 1961 by discovery of the attempt to overthrow Castro in Cuba", when in fact we had organized, supported and ordered that effort. The denial at Pearl Harbor started with the throw-away allegation that the fault was the division of command in Hawaii in 1941. The initial political impulse was obfuscation, blaming local commanders for the effects of Washington's policies, both diplomatic and bureaucratic. And if two military chains had each failed, a single one would have had even less chance of success.

One disturbance in the inter-service relationship at the command in Hawaii was that the Army was due to take over defense of the outlying islands. This was opposed by the Navy, and was hardly the type of disruptive thing Washington would have ordered had its appreciation been that an enemy onslaught was imminent. No such re-assignment of responsibilities occurred, and in fact two American carrier groups were at sea at the time of the attack, ferrying Marine, not Army, fighters to Wake and Midway. If this was rivalry, it was exceedingly beneficial rivalry -- the carriers were out of Pearl during the raid, and Wake had fighters to beat off the first Japanese landing, two things which might not have happened had there been inter-service co-ordination, with the outer islands left to await Army relief. Here, Kimmel's obtuseness saved most of the day, although the Japanese dive-bombers that would have attacked the carriers in port were freed up mainly to attack Army airfields.

Short-wave radio atmospherics played a paradoxical role. Some duplicative intelligence was available in Hawaii, but orders based on more complete such information were delayed in their transmission from Washington. Had short-wave radio been working, that confirmatory information and the orders for vigilance could have been received sooner. But, had the atmospherics been better, Japanese radio deceptions would have been more effective, and American intelligence would not have considered that it had lost touch with the Japanese carrier force. That force would have been located in Japan, falsely, from the dummy radio traffic being generated there, and the alerts would have been cancelled. Although the Japanese had changed their high-level code, as they had done periodically before, deceptive lower-level messages were being sent in clear, and by the big carriers' regular radiomen with their distinctive "fists". The traffic just wasn't bouncing off the solar-occluded ionosphere well enough to hit most American listening posts.

But suppose the main U.S. fleet had been based safely in San Diego, further away from surprise and too far away for a Japanese raid (the Japanese launched the war almost totally because of the American-sponsored oil embargo, and their Navy did not have the extra range to reach California in strength at the time). Japanese carriers would have been freed up for supporting the attack on Wake (the Japanese force actually sent there was too weak) or even for occupying Midway, and might have then encountered either American carrier or cruiser *Pensacola*'s troop convoy, three lucrative targets for a carrier fleet. There is a school of hindsight that the main Japanese Pearl Harbor target was aircraft carriers.

Aside from air-launched torpedoes that would not lodge in shallow harbor mud, the main innovation for the Japanese attack was their development of fin-modified battleship shells for bombing (by nominal "torpedo" planes, as the shell-bombs were too heavy for Japanese dive-bombers). Such bombs would have been almost totally ineffective against any of the smaller American carriers, because they would have plunged through without exploding inside the ship (on two later occasions American cruisers and carriers facing Japanese battleships were mistaken for bigger ships and attacked with armoring-piercing shells instead of "general-purpose" shells, more easily detonated and with far greater explosive power, not needing a heavy jacket of steel to pierce armor, appropriate to such unarmored targets). Would-be armor-piercing shells had to strike thick armor to cause their fuses to detonate, after a pause to allow the shell to penetrate, which they sometimes did; thin armor, or none at all, caused such shells to just pass through, although the scores of such hits suffered by the later American targets did cause some to sink from the sheer multitude of holes, even without explosions. Even the two somewhat armored American carriers, the *Saratoga* and sister *Lexington*, had three separate armored decks -- to save top-weight -- possibly none of which would have detonated such "bombshells" as were dropped by the Japanese at Pearl Harbor. Of course, had Japanese intelligence revealed carriers in the harbor, the Japanese would have assigned dive-bombers to them, to rip up their flight and hangar decks, elevators and aircraft with lighter, general-purpose bombs dropped from those more accurate, and more available, types. Carriers, although not possessed of battleship protection, had some defensive advantages of their own. They were lighter and therefore more buoyant, and they were roomier, giving more scope for protection through light subdivisions, compartmentalization, than through thick armor. But they did not require special-purpose weapons to seriously damage, unlike armored ships.

Although it is fairly obvious that the Pacific War was primarily an aircraft carrier war, its American leaders have gotten the official treatment. The official heroes, Admirals Halsey, Spruance, Kincaid and Turner, are dutifully praised for their beauty marks, and the two official villains, Fletcher and Theobald, damned for their smaller warts. Turner had been a Washington War Planner, forecasting a 1941 Japanese attack on Russia, instead of upon the U.S. Later, Turner was an amphibious force commander whose cruiser force was annihilated at Savo Island, with some ships' captains court-martialed for a lackadaisical attitude from higher-up. Subsequently, however, as the overall U.S. position improved, Turner's shortcomings were made up or less important. A cruiser squadron commander at Pearl Harbor, Theobald's later war action was restricted to the early Aleutian campaign, where his mediocre performance in that side show was treated leniently in early retrospect; but after Theobald attacked Roosevelt, his own record was savaged. His Aleutian successor, Kincaid, was in charge during two fiascos, the "Battle of the Echoes", where big ships dueled for hours with radar mirages, and the Kiska landing, where the Japanese evacuated under his nose, leaving three dogs to face the enormous bombing, shelling and landing. Before and after, Kincaid was a carrier admiral, first a subordinate and later a commander of huge forces. In neither capacity was he distinguished.

There were in the Pacific War six carrier battles between the U.S. and Japan. The first two came in mid-1942, when the Japanese had a clear advantage and the military initiative, which they lost at the two battles, Coral Sea in the South Pacific and Midway in the Central Pacific. These were followed by two later 1942 carrier battles in the South Pacific, those of the Eastern Solomons and the Santa Cruz Islands, where the sides were fairly evenly matched. Later, with its industrial supremacy, the U.S. had the advantage, leading to two big West Pacific carrier battles in 1944, while the Japanese still had a navy with which to resist. To examine the results, in carriers (CVs) sunk, achieved by the various American commanders, a chart:

Date	Battle	Pac.	U.S. Admirals	CVs Lost, U.S.	/Japan
05/42	Coral Sea	SW	Fletcher/Fitch	1 Large	/1 Small
06/42	Midway	Cen.	Fletcher/Spruance	1 Large	/4 Large
09/42	E. Solomons	SW	Fletcher/Kincaid/Noyes	---------	/1 Small
10/42	Santa Cruz	SW	Halsey/Kincaid/Murray	1 Large	/--------
06/44	Phil. Sea	W	Spruance	---------	/2L, 1 Md
10/44	Leyte Gulf	W	Halsey/Kincaid	3 Small	/1L, 3 Sm

Admiral Fletcher commanded the first three American carrier battles, turning back the Japanese conquest of New Guinea in the first at a cost of a large carrier, and achieving victory in the others. Fletcher was not a carrier admiral, and so deferred to more experienced subordinates in his first two battles. In Fletcher's last battle, he achieved victory despite the absence of one carrier refueling. His own sank a Japanese carrier, and also damaged a seaplane carrier, while Kincaid's carrier was ineffective and took three bombs. Yet it was Kincaid who was kept on and Fletcher beached.

Official historian Morison held that "[d]efeat at Pearl Harbor brought no immediate consequences except the capture of Wake Island", yet he also managed to chalk up that "fiasco" as "more the fault of Admiral Fletcher, who wasted time on unnecessary fueling, when he should have pressed on to relieve Wake." (Combining those inconsistent conclusions would make Fletcher responsible for Pearl Harbor.) The situation at Wake was that its planes had been expended, and Fletcher was trying to bring in more, with his lone carrier, in an area patrolled by land-based Japanese bombers and with two Japanese carriers about. Two other American carriers at sea had at first kept their distance. The senior officer of the three was Admiral Halsey, who escaped blame for the incident. The delay was primarily a product of the initial decision to split up the carriers, with a tardy order for concentration rapidly followed by orders for Fletcher to withdraw. Fletcher's refueling, then and subsequently, was mere prudence, a habit copied by Halsey, Kincaid and Spruance, who eventually were rotating out groups of four or five carriers at a time (each had a group refueling at the time of their 1944 battles).

Halsey and Kincaid commanded at the only American defeat of the six battles, losing one carrier while Kincaid's took its usual three bombs. The two Japanese carriers primarily responsible had first been encountered at the Coral Sea battle, which Halsey's two carriers sat out for no good reason (only after the Japanese withdrawal were they sent south). The two American carriers at Coral Sea, beside sinking the small Japanese carrier and saving New Guinea -- and possibly Australia -- from invasion, did damage the two big Japanese carriers present. This kept them out of the attack on Midway, when the American Coral Sea survivor teamed up with the Pearl Harbor pair to inflict a big defeat. But had all four American carriers been available at the Coral Sea, perhaps the American carrier would have been not lost, and the two big Japanese carriers sunk, instead of being repaired and popping up again and again, most effectively at Santa Cruz.

Halsey and Kincaid also commanded at the complex battle around Leyte Gulf. The main Japanese break there was when each American assumed the other's force was guarding San Bernadino Strait. Neither was, and the main Japanese surface fleet broke through to oppress one group of Kincaid's "jeep" carriers, also disorganizing another jeep group at the beginning of the very first "*kamikaze*" attack. Halsey, decoyed north by planeless Japanese carriers even as Kincaid's surface force had been decoyed south by a small Japanese surface force, failed to detach a force to pursue the Japanese carriers' escorting pair of battleships, and also failed to get south fast enough to prevent the escape of the main Japanese surface remnants through still-unguarded San Bernadino Strait. Although Halsey's raids -- Wake and Marcus, Doolittle, Formosa and China Sea -- were considered successes -- and the Formosa raid indeed ranked with Spruance's Truk raids -- his two fleet battles were respectively a failure and a flawed victory. How Halsey, Turner and Kincaid could be rated over Frank Jack Fletcher, the giant of the war's first year, is as big a mystery as why the U.S. entered the war at all.

The best American admirals -- Spruance, Fletcher and Kincaid -- were not specialists. They were not exemplars of the battleline, like Kidd, Pye, Lee and Oldendorf, nor carrier mechanics like Halsey and Mitscher, nor submarine mavens like King, Nimitz and Lockwood, nor feuding Washington honchos turned feuding amphibians like Turner and Wilkinson. They were admirals of cruisers, whose old tasks of independent operations and scouting had been largely absorbed by the task force concept, with the cruiser's search role taken over by carrier aircraft. In contrast to the specialists, cruiser admirals had a better handle on operating a fleet against an enemy fleet, where the search role and the waiting game were vital. Carrier airmen considered search a demeaning role, a bad attitude dating from the carrier's subordination to the battleline (when carriers had also gotten a cruiser's "C"); consequently, cruiser admirals were better air admirals than were carrier admirals. Cruiser admirals were less threatened by thinking of the fleet as a functional whole, rather than thinking of battleships, or carriers, or submarines, as the fleet and all else superfluous.

America had already entered the war prior to Pearl Harbor, with the lead taken by experienced interventionist Franklin Roosevelt. Roosevelt's first act was an executive order forming a secret department within the White House. This came in the first week of World War II (September 1939), and showed the real trend of Roosevelt's policies, although his hypocritical rhetoric would continue its syrupy homilies to peace for years to come. Secrecy and concentrated power is not needed for neutrality, or even open partiality. But it was necessary for a Roosevelt too cautious to chance his popularity, or his shot at a third term (already facing intra-party challenges from Vice President Garner and Postmaster-General Farley on purely domestic political grounds; for far less, Republican presidencies have been trumpeted by the media as "Administration in Disarray!"), with policies liable to plunge the nation into full-scale wars. The Japanese onslaught upon China was well underway, with the U.S. supporting China with credit for arms exports, but that conflict in and of itself had not brought Roosevelt to the measures he advocated for Europe, even when Americans had been attacked by the Japanese in the *Panay* incident (Japanese planes sank an American gunboat in China, in area where Chinese boats had taken to flying neutral flags; allegations of Japanese governmental responsibility remain mere charges). Although there were European distractions -- the possibility of Italian neutrality, and the Russian attack on Finland -- Roosevelt's clear thrust was anti-German (not anti-Nazi, merely a refinement of Wilson's policy). Aside from the seeds of secret intervention in September 1939, the U.S. Navy immediately began following unarmed German merchant ships at sea, broadcasting their positions every hour until they were intercepted by British warships, the goal of that particular "neutrality" farrago.

The *Lusitania* affair had affected both the nation's perceptions and Roosevelt's policies. Neutrality legislation had been passed and signed by Roosevelt when war seemed unlikely, and the legislation therefore pointless. With the outbreak of European war, Roosevelt moved to a cash-and-carry policy for munitions sales. As Germany was blockaded, specific sanctions were needed only against the Japanese, whose trade was unimpaired other than by governmental policies, its own or those of other nations. But Britain, and later Russia, soon lacked cash, so Roosevelt called for an official policy of giving away American weapons (as part of a policy of re-armament). Lend-Lease legalized a *Lusitania* policy under the fiction that the weapons would be returned when no longer needed. Lend-Lease trucks sustained the Soviet economy throughout the Cold War, and Lend-Lease weapons helped Mao conquer China; Roosevelt's "garden hose" was used against its American lender, including to undermine that very Chinese government we had vexed the Japanese into war in order to save. But then, war for Poland and China had always been lies of the Western statesmen; paradoxically, only the Germans and Japanese were sincere in their goals.

As German appetites turned back from the stubborn distraction of Britain to subjugating the Slavic Aryans, the apparent danger to the U.S. decreased, necessitating more provocative actions by Roosevelt to keep up the heat. Lend-Lease was followed by American convoys, the three Atlantic occupations and a shoot-on-sight policy against German submarines. As an uninvited side show to the German attack on Russia in 1941, Roosevelt's secret government of intervention, under later OSS/CIA head "Wild Bill" Donovan, took its first giant steps in covert activities. To lure German arms into the Balkans, and delay the onslaught upon Russia, the governments of Bulgaria and Yugoslavia were subverted, the first with lies about American aid against the Soviets if Bulgaria delayed helping the Germans, and the Yugoslavs with an American-engineered coup by Yugoslav Army officers against that country's neutralist government. This at a time when the Soviets and their foreign clients were still clinging to the Russian alliance with Germany! The Germans quickly conquered newly hostile Yugoslavia, with the bonus of having a clearer path to Greece, whose "fascistic" government had successfully resisted both Mussolini and Communist subversion. The German assault against Yugoslavia was aided by such Communist treachery as "non-violent" obstruction of Yugoslav troop-trains by Moscow loyalists. Such actions sped the shift of the German Army back into position for a good-weather assault against the Soviets themselves.

The fuller war soon expanded into a desire at high levels to sustain the Soviets as a German distraction, and a loyalty to the Soviets helping to push that policy forward in some operational echelons, where American spies, in Europe frequently with British accompaniment, helped push forward the local Communist agenda, ostensibly in the guise of war against Hitler or the Japanese. Suddenly patriotic Communists were helped in France, Italy, Yugoslavia, Greece, Bulgaria, China and Vietnam, with virtually all such efforts resulting in anti-American efforts by the Communists, beginning as soon as Soviet survival was assured, mid-1943. Tragically, most victims were civilian, or even non-Communist military partisans, and none of these activities had an iota of difference upon the prosecution of the war. In France and Italy, the seeds of Euro-Communism were fertilized with Allied arms and other aid, such as the smuggling of Italian Communist leader Palmiro Togliatti back into Italy (Mussolini had imprisoned titular Italian Communist head Antonio Gramschi). In Yugoslavia, Donovan's Yugoslavia Army junta was gunned down by minions of its backer seeking to massage Communist sensibilities; at least there the Moscovite peaceniks of 1941 eventually fell under the control of a more nationalistic Communist, Tito, who resented foreign interference with his incipient dictatorship. Bulgaria, the victim of American promises, saw its government subverted by Communists, including those aided by the British in the witting or unwitting expectation that doing so was aiding the war-effort against Germany. Churchill fell in with Communist ambitions because he hoped to convince Roosevelt to invade the Balkans, partly to forestall post-war problems there by over-awing local Communists and the Russians; instead, British and American covert aid increased Communist strength to the point of making the British occupation of Greece, the truncated flower of Churchill's Balkan ambitions, yield bitter seeds. Aid to Greek Communists resulted in an early anti-Allied mutiny by leftist "Free" Greeks in 1943 followed later by a lengthy civil war.

In Vietnam, part of French Indochina whose occupation by the Japanese had nettled Roosevelt more than it had Petain, the Free French were denied the facilities of the U.S. and Britain for operations north of latitude 16 (one degree south of the later so-called DeMilitarized Zone). Instead, Vietnamese nationalists, including those duped into Ho Chi Minh's Viet Minh movement -- nationalism in the service of Communist internationalism -- were given aid for anti-Japanese activities which never happened. The main Allied targets, Saigon airfield (from which two huge British ships had been attacked and sunk several days after Pearl Harbor) and Cam Ranh Bay, were in the area of Vietnam where covert aid was funneled through French or French-loyal activists, but the only Allied attacks in the entire Indochinese backwater during the war were a pair of American B-29 bomber raids from their early Chinese base on the Saigon area, and a Halsey carrier romp through the South China Sea in January 1945, which briefly savaged Japanese facilities at Cam Ranh Bay. Although it was in China that the most disastrous fruits of covert intervention ripened, sowing the seeds of further wars, and becoming a political football within the U.S., the mutation of the Yellow Peril from Japan to North Korea, China and North Vietnam was caused by an American publicity stunt. Read on.

Trenton and Princeton

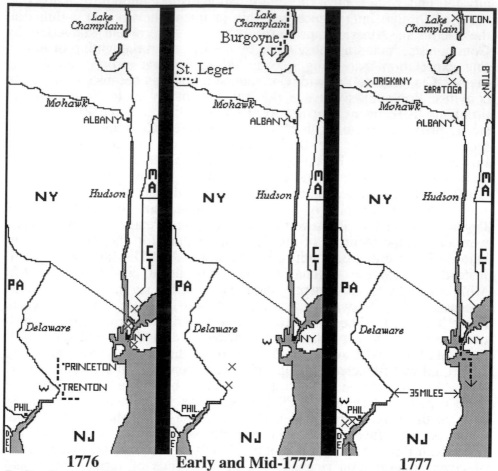

1776   **Early and Mid-1777**   **1777**

Left: Large British force descends upon New York area in fall 1776, defeating Washington's army at Brooklyn Heights, Harlem Heights and White Plains and driving it across New Jersey. The British leave small garrisons at Trenton and Princeton for next year's planned descent on Philadelphia.

Center: At year-end 1776, Washington's remnants surprise Hessians at Trenton and British regulars at Princeton. Washington's re-energized army bottles British up in New York, unable to advance back across New Jersey or to support British advance from Canada under Burgoyne and St. Leger.

Right: Garrisoning New York and planning to capture Philadelphia by sea, Britain's New York force can't advance up the Hudson to meet the British from Canada. Philadelphia is captured with two minor defeats of Washington, but northern American victories at Oriskany, Bennington and Saratoga bring France into the war as an American ally. And Washington had only crossed the Delaware, not the wide Pacific.

Chapter 4 - **The Doolittle Raid**
(Thirty Seconds of Public Relations Over Tokyo)

<u>Diplomacy and Pearl Harbor</u>. What slavery was to Lincoln, international chaos was to Franklin Roosevelt. World War I had made his Navy Department a source of publicity, the worldwide Great Depression had made him President (although "Hoover's Depression" had struck hard in Soviet Russia, Weimar Germany and Imperial Japan, various locals were scapegoated), and the rise of the Axis gave his flagging presidency new hope for a third term and beyond. Clearly, Roosevelt did not want to enter the war via Pearl Harbor, in the sense that someone crossing a river's thin ice doesn't want to fall in, but he did plan to achieve belligerence at American initiative. Roosevelt's main interest was Europe and the Nazi menace, even if his sympathy was often ostentatiously with the China his ancestors had traded with.

While a large segment of the American Navy was baiting Hitler in such safe locales as Iceland, Greenland and Dutch Guiana, the bulk was busy at Pearl Harbor as a gesture against Japan to match diplomacy and trade sanctions (Mr. Hoover had tried the same Pearl Harbor strategy at the Manchurian introduction to the Chinese War; the signalling gambit had been unsuccessful, although not as deadly due to the lack of sanctions, the smaller Japanese aircraft carrier force at the time and its lack of air-launchable torpedoes suitable for the shallow water at Pearl). Despite the later havoc wrought in China by Japanese troops, acceleration of American moves did not occur until the event which tied the European and Pacific wars into one. The Japanese began occupying French Indochina, leading to American protests at its initiation and an "American" oil boycott of Japan at its consummation (Roosevelt had indeed written his wife that an oil boycott would make an "actual necessity" for Japan to attack the U.S., but he was a habitual dissembler then putting off his wife's advocacy of an oil boycott). That was the beginning of American embroilment in "Vietnam", the drift to more immediate war obscuring the drift to later wars.

It is notable that Britain, already hard-pressed in Europe and North Africa, and the Free Dutch, with their main outpost in the East Indies vulnerable to Japan, were indispensable to the anti-Japanese oil boycott, because they could have supplied Japan's oil needs from the Sumatra and Borneo oil fields controlled by British Petroleum and Royal Dutch Shell. For those governments, antagonizing Japan would've been inexplicable, even suicidal, without American co-involvement in the boycott and in the war that would follow. Mexico, also indispensable, agreed to the boycott in return for Roosevelt's letting it keep its stolen oil fields. That was the how the U.S., with Roosevelt's connivance, was dragged into war with Germany -- the main concern of the British and Dutch -- via the "Back Door to War" in the Pacific. No archival revelations are needed to understand this.

Various diplomatic notes were exchanged between Japan and the U.S., while the U.S. military was told to expect a Pacific war in 1942 and Japan was seeing that a different Pacific war happened. Although the U.S. was drifting along with secret agreements with the British to enter the European war and defeat Germany First, the mechanics of procuring a war in the Pacific were more advanced. In addition to early sanctions, part of the initial American reaction to the Japanese in Indochina was to consider how American military aid to China could be used to get the U.S. into war with Japan, "a nation with which we were at peace", as it were. The plan was to equip China with American pilots and planes (all bought with American money), the so-called Flying Tigers. Eventually, these mercenaries were to have been given 100 Lockheed Hudson bombers, with range enough for a direct surprise raid upon Japan itself. Flying Tigers, initially with fighter planes, were indeed set up after the full occupation of Indochina. But the bomber project was to have been delayed until 1942 for want of the long-range Hudsons, also in demand for British anti-submarine patrol against German U-boats (reconnaissance for Pearl Harbor and Army East Coast maritime patrol being even lower priorities for FDR). "I hate warrrrrrrrh!" Roosevelt had proclaimed, falsely, given his childhood attempt to enlist in the Spanish-American War, his enthusiastic junket to Europe during World War I, and his eager planning for war east and west. Note that the collection of target information in Japan had been underway in 1937, the year of the *Panay* affair, when a group of American All-Star baseball players had included utility catcher Moe Berg, asked to photograph strategic targets.

In late November 1941, Roosevelt did consider moderating U.S. economic sanctions against Japan, but, after receiving reports of Japanese military movements, he abruptly cancelled conciliation and sent an angry ultimatum stressing the American commitment to the Chinese government. Those Japanese maneuvers were preparation for an attack which might not have occurred had Roosevelt followed through with his concessions, but which was definitely given impetus by Roosevelt's ultimatum. Lost by this early onset of war and Japanese momentum was the chance for the quick implementation of the American Pacific war plan, which envisioned war beginning in early 1942, followed by the united U.S. fleet protecting a series of amphibious operations across the Central Pacific to win bases successively nearer Japan.

How Roosevelt intended to have first gotten a declaration of war by Germany, as part of the agreed-upon Germany First policy with Britain, is unknown, but the parade of U-boat brushes could have been fortuitously capped by, say, the loss of the old *Arkansas* to a presumed German attack. Why else was that ship, by far the most vulnerable American battleship to torpedoes, being paraded about in submarine-infested waters?

But the Pacific War came first, at Japan's reluctant beck. Again, not only was there the irony of the liberal drift toward immediate war, but the scent of war to come. The Chinese government so stoutly championed in Roosevelt's ultimatum was to be systematically undermined by Roosevelt nominees, from Wallace and Truman and a series of emissaries on down to the Foreign Service, leaving the successor Chinese Communists to kill Americans in the Korean War. Finally, at Yalta, a moribund Roosevelt would sow the seeds of the Cold War by agreeing to the Soviets' predominance in an Eastern Europe whose last indigenous governments had shunned them, and of the Korean War by inviting the Soviets into Manchuria and North Korea. The wars for Poland and China had been thereby fully stitched together, by the betrayal of both. But the prerequisite for these future American disasters was a failure to prosecute the war.

Fifty Years of Doolittle Hype. After Pearl Harbor, carrier-borne aircraft were obviously going to be critical in the Pacific. There was both the Japanese example of what could be done and the American lack of other resources -- the battleline had been crippled but the carriers had not. The initial American response was confusion -- protecting Hawaii after the threat had passed and failing to help Wake when the opportunity was present. While the Japanese spread out over the West and Southwest Pacific, and their carrier fleet raided Darwin, Australia, Java and the Bay of Bengal, the U.S. Navy launched a series of carrier raids on outlying Japanese possessions in the Central Pacific. In Washington, there was another plan afoot: Roosevelt was to get his Tokyo Raid, after the reason for it had passed. Former racer Jimmy Doolittle's squadron of twin-engined B-25 Mitchell Army bombers was training for carrier take-off.

Roosevelt's palace guard of historians long sought to portray the Doolittle Raid as a product of his military advisors, the venerable theory of the evil counselors. Supposedly. "[o]nly seven" men knew of the plan, with Admiral King of the Navy, either directly or through two aides, hatching the plan. The notion is precious that Roosevelt, a naval buff and a geography buff visiting his White House map-room twice a day, was unaware of what two of the four functioning American carriers in the Pacific were up to for weeks. Then there was the genesis of Roosevelt's famous quip about Doolittle's planes having taken off from the fictional Shangri-La; **before** the raid, Roosevelt was asking an aide whether he had read the book referred to.

In fact, there is ample evidence that to Admiral King the main priority of the time was to protect Australia and New Zealand, what he referred to as "white man's country", from the Yellow Peril then overrunning the East Indies and New Guinea. King's take, three weeks before the Doolittle Raid, was that the main American priority, after holding Hawaii, should be to support "Australasia" by driving northwestward from the New Hebrides, into the area which subsequently became known as the Southwest Pacific area of operations. It is impossible to square these priorities with a raid in the North Pacific, and there is been ample evidence that the North Pacific raid was Roosevelt's baby, not King's.

From Theodore Roosevelt on, American planners had been dismayed by the vulnerability of the American-occupied Philippines to attack, particularly from Japan, the closest well armed power. At the beginning of his third term, Franklin Roosevelt was still pessimistic about holding the Philippines, although he was glad to see his bugbear MacArthur, "the second most dangerous man in the country" while Huey Long had still been alive, in command there. The Doolittle Raid was actively contemplated before the formation of the Flying Tigers, an alternative in case the U.S. failed to initiate war first. In January 1941, General Marshall noted the decision that "there should be no naval reinforcement of the Philippines; that the Navy should have under consideration the possibility of bombing attacks against Japanese cities."

The Doolittle Raid as it actually happened was superbly successful in its main mission, distracting American public attention away from major military disasters with an artfully publicized attack that was an unpublicized minor disaster in itself and a major strategic disaster. Decades later, that raid is still falsely credited with diverting Japanese resources away from battlefronts where those resources had ceased to have use because of the Allied surrenders being minimized. British Malaya and Dutch Java had fallen and the Philippines were falling, with Bataan followed by Corregidor. American dead in the Philippines numbered nearly 10,000, and 80,000 more Americans were being hung out to die. 57% of those Americans did not survive captivity, bringing America's death toll from the Philippines disaster to more than 55,000. The total was comparable to that from the entire Korean or Vietnam War, and it was from five months of combat, not from three years' or ten years' worth. And the relation to Korea and Vietnam was not just quantity.

And what did the raid accomplish? The plan had been for just a raid on industrial targets, followed by flight of the planes on to China. Russia was closer and had better airfields, but, being our ally when getting aid for its war against Germany, was not willing to aid America in its war with Japan; China was the closest landing area. Although it was possible for some landplanes to take off from a carrier when weather permitted, and that was the basis of using carriers as aircraft ferrys for such operations as the frequent flyings-off for Malta, they lacked the strength, tailhooks or pilot training to land on one. Doolittle's Mitchells were also too large to use the carrier elevators of that era, and used up flight deck space. Indeed, their clogged-up carrier was as vulnerable to enemy action as had been the over-loaded and ill-fated

Glorious off Norway.   For that reason, another carrier escorted the Doolittle carrier, half of the American Pacific carrier strength.

Discovered by Japan's picket line of civilian fishing boats while still a good distance from Japan, the carriers were reported to Japan. Knowing that carriers were involved, the Japanese authorities figured that a raid with typically short-ranged American carrier aircraft could not take place until at least another day; consequently, they were unprepared when Admiral Halsey and Colonel Doolittle launched the longer-ranged Mitchells that day.   But at the longer distance, Mitchells lacked the ability to bomb Japan and still reach unoccupied China.   Instead, 15 crashed in China after releasing their bombs over the designated industrial targets in Japan.   Some aircrew were killed or injured; the crews of two planes were captured and killed.   One pilot disobeyed orders and saved his plane and crew by going to Russia; the penalty was internment there. The raid did little beyond causing a few civilian deaths to go with the slaughter of the five fishing boat crews, who had been killed to prevent the loss of the carrier "secret"; no effort had been made to capture them. In the U.S., President Roosevelt announced the raid with great hoopla, echoed by the propaganda apparatus of the Office of War Information; the meager results and high losses were not disclosed, and the origin of the raid was smarmily laid up to the fictional Shangri-La.   Jimmy Doolittle got the Congressional Medal of Honor for this fiasco, a bungled low-risk pinprick which initiated American strategic bombing.   Although Mitchell had called for the abolition of the Navy and denounced carriers as futile, and the Air Force and its partisans would later rage at the idea of a special carrier for strategic attack, bureaucracy is momentum, not logic.   From that time on, April 18th would no longer be the day that Americans remembered Paul Revere's Ride, when that Boston celebrity had been captured while humble Billy Dawes warned the countryside; it would be the day of Doolittle's great victory.   Such hoopla helped the Democrats retain a narrow control of Congress later in the year.

Liberal partisans, the kind who sententiously recall that truth is the first casualty of war (if not that "force and fraud are the cardinal virtues in war"), 'fessed up later to the plane losses and the lack of damage inflicted.   But they called the Doolittle Raid a great victory on four accounts.   First, the nation was cheered up after a long string of defeats.   Second, the Japanese diverted aircraft from other areas to home defense.   Third, Japanese pursuit of the American carriers after the battle helped American intelligence pinpoint deployments because of the radio traffic generated, intercepted and decoded -- according to Lundstrom, "The greatest benefit of the Tokyo Raid would appear to be the wealth of radio intelligence garnered from the many orders sent by Tokyo to mass the pursuit forces.... [M]any facts regarding Japanese order of battle began falling into place, particularly submarine deployment".   And fourth, the raid caused the Japanese to attack Midway, and be decisively defeated, on the belief that the Doolittle planes had taken off from there; in Morison's words, the Japanese "higher command, disconcerted, expedited plans for an overextension which led directly to the Battle of Midway. That alone was worth the effort."

The propaganda triumph is the easiest to refute: Self-deception does not win wars. Moreover, there is ample documentary evidence after the Doolittle Raid that American propagandists thought apathy and complacency were the big problems, not glumness. Ironically, the victorious Japanese were happy to have seen the Doolittle Raid. With their victories, complacency was a real problem, and they joyfully used the quintessential media event to battle apathy and promote hatred of America. A well publicized trial of captured Doolittle Raiders was part of their campaign.

In the case of Japanese aircraft redeployment, the main cause of that was that the Japanese had won and largely occupied the developed areas of South Asia. What was left were the frontier regions of Burma, New Guinea and south of New Britain. The problem in those areas was a lack of airfields; Japanese aircraft were in surplus. Many Japanese air units accordingly returned home. The relationship of the Doolittle Raid was not directly causal. Rather, Japanese victories caused both the Doolittle Raid and the Japanese redeployments. More complex is the timing of Japanese offensives.

The intelligence value rationale for the Doolittle Raid of course contradicts the Shangri-La and Midway hypotheses, and the excuse for bumping off the Japanese fishermen. Why were the Japanese chasing carriers if they didn't know about them? The intelligence rationale ignores the fact that American carriers had been attempting and conducting raids on Japan's Central Pacific bases since the week after Pearl Harbor. Admiral Brown, in carrier *Lexington*, had been slated to attack Jaluit in December 1941 to divert the Japanese from Fletcher's attempt to fly off planes to besieged Wake Island; as their superiors Pye and Halsey dithered, neither attempt came off. The next month, Brown's planned raid on occupied Wake was cancelled. It was at that point, when no raids had happened, that Morison had King panting for "a really spectacular diversionary raid on Japan. Marcus, Kwajelein and the like were all very well, but something better was wanted -- a proper retaliation for Pearl Harbor." That was an early view, possibly ignorant of Roosevelt's past plans, but it ignored the chronology of events. No American carrier raids had taken place at that time, and although Kwajelein and Marcus were indeed raided, in between an attempt upon the new Japanese base at Rabaul was detected, attacked and aborted (as was Admiral Brown, after his third abortion in three months). Even twenty years later, Morison thought Rabaul had been attacked.

What Brown did achieve before his relief, in company with Admiral Fletcher and another carrier, was to raid the new Japanese holdings on eastern New Guinea, but Fletcher was a target of the late-arriving Morison, who sneered at a praiseworthy effort at the battlefront as "paled in comparison" to the Doolittle Raid. Fletcher was to have attacked Eniwetok while Halsey attacked Marcus, but had been ordered off to escort a convoy in the South Pacific, soon putting him near Brown and New Guinea. The previous month, Halsey and Fletcher had indeed attacked Kwajelein and nearby islands. The advantages of such raids were that they could inflict some military damage while being low in risk, because the fast American carriers could withdraw rapidly, as they could not when supporting amphibious invasions, for example, and that the Japanese reacted with pursuit and radio traffic, generating the same type of intelligence uniquely chalked up to the Doolittle Raid. Most importantly, such military raids left the American carriers in a strategically sensible position of being easily concentrated for any important task between Hawaii and Australia, the area the Japanese high command was considering for offensive operations.

There was before the Doolittle Raid already pressure in the Japanese Navy for an attack upon Midway, one that would lure the American carriers into decisive defeat. There were a number of alternatives, such as continuing Japan's own raids, which had been fourfold -- Pearl Harbor, Darwin, Java and the Bay of Bengal -- and profitable without more loss than a few aircraft. Waiting on the defensive for an American amphibious invasion, and a tied-down carrier force, or seeking a series of smaller engagements, a defeat-in-detail of the American fleet, were also obvious alternatives. But the operational plan favored by the high command ashore was to isolate Australia by first taking the rest of New Guinea and the Solomon Islands, and to follow that quickly with the capture of New Caledonia, Fiji and Samoa. Isolated Australia and New Zealand were then to be conquered. The first step was the conquest of Port Moresby, the Australian toe-hold on New Guinea, and the establishment of a seaplane base at Tulagi in the Solomon Islands. The latter was to provide some security for an airfield to be built on the nearby island of Guadalcanal, which was to be protected in the meantime by air cover from the new Japanese airfields around Rabaul. Cover for these expeditions was to be by a Japanese carrier force in the Coral Sea.

As noted, the U.S. was to get two carriers in position, and to prevent the loss of Port Moresby, at the cost of a large American carrier, the establishment of the Japanese in the Solomons and a long war of attrition that postponed the beginning of the definitive American counterthrust in the Central Pacific until November 1943. The Doolittle Raid diverted half of the American aircraft carrier strength away from what is generally recognized as the first carrier battle (which was actually the Bay of Bengal Raid, where the British carrier *Hermes* had been too slow to flee and where the opposing warships had not sighted each other). Used in the North Pacific raid, 45 degrees of latitude and dozens of Japanese air bases and submarines away from the Coral Sea, the two Doolittle carriers had been forced to return to Pearl Harbor and to refuel before taking a further roundabout to the Southwest Pacific. They arrived days after the battle, while Japan's fastest big carriers had been able to move south in time. As a result of the U.S. Coral Sea force's weakness, it lost a chance at a crushing victory against a major Japanese detachment, the chance to finish off the two large Japanese carriers involved and to forestall a Solomons campaign which would lose two more American carriers and eight cruisers. Additionally, the narrowly lost *Lexington* and its planes were absent from Midway, where American torpedo planes, with no fighter escort, were butchered, and the outnumbered American carriers lost the *Yorktown*, again by a narrow margin (an American submarine reported torpedoing an aircraft carrier under air attack, but the only carrier torpedoed at Midway was the *Yorktown*).

The Doolittle Raid prolonged the war. All four American carrier losses, in 1942, were directly due to the failure to win decisively at the Coral Sea, and that failure was due to the diversion of American carriers in the Doolittle Raid. Instead, the Pacific war dragged on, making future wars. Why has this simple process been so neglected? Obviously, propaganda past and present has crowded out rather elementary fact. There were plenty of disasters which had actually occurred -- Pearl Harbor with its premature build-up and defiance of congressional appropriations for fleet maintenance, the fall of the Philippines and the instigation of the Solomons campaign -- or would occur -- the late war diplomatic fiascos that set up the loss of China and the Korean and Vietnam Wars -- unpleasant enough without dwelling upon the responsibility for them. Then, too, the Battle of Midway was an important tactical victory, although the absence of a fourth U.S. carrier there helped caused the loss of another. And, had the American carriers been free to concentrate in the Coral Sea, the commander would have been the frequent bungler Admiral Halsey, although maybe even Halsey could have managed a crushing victory against a smaller carrier force tied down by two invasion fleets. Under favorable tactical conditions, even such comparable Civil War bunglers as Pope and Grant had pulled off victories. On the higher command level, FDR the commander-in-chief had equaled FDR the diplomat or FDR the defender of the Constitution.

FDR had been a great Assistant Secretary of the Navy, as his cousin Theodore had been. Unfortunately, the parallel did not end there. As President, TR and a compliant Congress had loaded down the Navy with pre-modern battleships and armored cruisers, ships whose time was passing or, in respect of their vulnerability to torpedoes, had already passed. Fortunately for the U.S. of TR's day, his Navy had faced no more challenging task than the grand gesture of the Great White Fleet's world cruise. Gestures in a more dangerous age would prove deadly, however. FDR's gesture of basing the fleet at Pearl Harbor to overawe Japan backfired, with five unmodernized battleships sunk. The Doolittle gesture backfired, causing four carriers to be lost and stalemate to occur. With that stalemate came attrition, cruiser/destroyer battles in the Southwest Pacific. There FDR's first gesture, removing torpedoes from American Treaty cruisers (removed from the Coolidge cruisers, omitted from New Deal Treaty cruisers), backfired. American cruisers were unequipped for the night battles of the Solomons, and the resultant U.S. tactical thinking left America's torpedo-equipped destroyers too closely shackled to the cruisers and their guns.

It can also be argued that the Japanese, without the distraction of the Doolittle Raid, would have marshaled their full carrier force in the South Pacific. But that too is speculative. There is no proof of it, and the planning for the Coral Sea foray had preceded the Doolittle Raid. The modern Japanese Navy was very much in the habit of making such detachments, in the service of audacity and confusing an enemy. In the first week of the war, they had detached another carrier pair to aid the renewed second attack on Wake, an audacity which succeeded because the U.S. was not reacting decisively during that crisis. And the Japanese were frequently successful in night battles by hurling in available detachments instead of gathering their forces. When the U.S. took back Tulagi and Guadalcanal from the Japanese, Admiral Mikawa's detachment of mostly older ships, five cruisers with heavy torpedoes and reloads and three smaller ships with light torpedoes and no spares, smashed two Allied cruiser detachments guarding the invasion ships. With only one shell hit, full magazines and dozens of heavy torpedoes left, Mikawa withdrew, losing a chance to destroy an entire invasion fleet and to strand an entire Marine division. For that, he was exposed to submarine attack during his withdrawal, losing a cruiser to the only significant American submarine accomplishment in the first half of the war, and being relieved of command. But unlike Doolittle's Raid, Mikawa's had inflicted significant and important military damage, and without disrupting the deployment of the main Japanese fleet.

The flip side of detachments is that they can be defeated in detail, swept up by a larger enemy force. The sterling American example of a weaker army inflicting such defeats is not the overly written-up Confederacy's, but rather Washington's. Unable to defeat the British in their assault upon New York City (or a year later against Philadelphia), Washington was able to maintain his army intact, avoiding decisive defeats by falling back against a superior but bloodied opponent. In early 1777, by surprise attacks on the forward British details at Princeton and Trenton, Washington drove the British substantially out of New Jersey. In the summer campaigns that followed, this was crucial to frustrate the British plan to capture the Hudson Valley. From central New Jersey, Washington was able to delay the British taking of Philadelphia as well as to detach enough troops to stymie a British attack north from New York City and even some to help trap a small British army that had moved down from Canada to Saratoga. That victory brought the French into the war, and eventually, in 1781, Washington and the French were able to trap another detached British army at Yorktown, capturing it and effectively winning American independence. That is how we came to be, and why criticisms of Washington's leadership are so silly. He confronted the main mass of the enemy when victory was possible or battle unavoidable, and kept his forces intact, ready and positioned for when smaller victories were available; this won. Compare that with a Doolittle Raid squandering victory in the South Pacific, modern America's misdirected riches proving the worst sort of poverty.

What made the Japanese attack Midway was not the Doolittle Raid; rather, it was the defeat in the Coral Sea which the Doolittle Raid had prevented from being decisive in itself. The planned series of Japanese expansion following the Coral Sea campaign had been put on hold because the main goal of taking Port Moresby on New Guinea had not been achieved; the New Caledonia-Fiji-Samoa campaign would have started with an exposed flank. Instead, while the Japanese Army plotted overland attack on Port Moresby, Japan's naval shore planners abandoned their opposition to the Midway campaign previously plumped by the planners at sea. Without the Coral Sea stalemate, Midway would have remained a low priority. That Midway was a priority at all was due not to the Doolittle Raid, but to the earlier American carrier raids in the Central and South Pacific.

The effect of the Japanese defeat at Midway was exacerbated by the meat-grinder campaign that developed in the Solomons. With the Japanese having lost the strategic initiative and the U.S., ultimately because of the Doolittle Raid, too off-balance to have seized that initiative, the Solomons campaign no longer had much strategic sense for either side. Shorn of their main carrier strength, the Japanese were too weak to seriously threaten Australia and New Zealand. Stalemate favored the U.S. operationally in the long run, because the U.S. could eventually replace its losses better than the Japanese could theirs, but strategically the decisive American cross-Pacific march was delayed, opening the way for diplomatic disaster in East Asia.

After the late 1942 carrier battles, Yamamoto's commitment of his new carrier planes and pilots to a long land-based campaign prevented the Japanese from ever effectively rebuilding their carrier strength. This last policy slackened off after Yamamoto's death, but his successor soon died also, leaving an 18-month hiatus in carrier battles because of the lack of pilots, planes and leadership. The availability of oil and bases in the East Indies left the Japanese some training capacity, but their thirst for the big battle caused the premature commitment, and effective annihilation, of their new carrier strength in the Battle of the Philippine Sea in June 1944, and all for Saipan (a situation somewhat like that at Midway, but the Japanese, lacking good intelligence, could not arrive until their very substantial land-based aircraft had been completely defeated, and their carrier pilots were very green). The Japanese had two obvious alternatives to that. They could have raided the new British build-up in the Indian Ocean, getting another big raid to get their pilots experience, confidence and accomplishment, or they could have committed their full Navy, or even large surface forces, to discombobulate MacArthur's advance along New Guinea's lengthy north shore. Late in May 1944, the Japanese did have on tap a strong night raid, built around their biggest battleships, against MacArthur's Biak invasion and its cruiser and jeep carrier support, but the lure of the big battle proved decisive; those Japanese ships were committed to the Philippine Sea carrier battle, with no effect other than an opportunity forgone. Fortunately for the U.S., the Japanese did make mistakes; that is why they lost. The reason they fought so well is that they didn't make mistakes as stupid as the Doolittle Raid.

Winston Churchill, warlord and navalist, was fond of an old saw about a battle being lost for want of a nail for a horseshoe. Consider that the Doolittle Raid was not "For want of a shoe", but for want of horse-sense. Instead of concentrating for victory, "the firstest with the mostest", half of the American Pacific carrier force had been diverted for a minor raid, and that a disaster except to cheerleading controlled news and historiography. With 5/6 of the Japanese fleet carriers and the fast Japanese battleships away in the Indian Ocean and their sixth fleet carrier being overhauled in Japan, the way was fairly open toward the besieged Philippines, but those and the American and Filipino troops there, if not Roosevelt's bugbear MacArthur, had already been written off. The Doolittle Raid was and is instructive liberalism, victory forgone for chaff, chaff doted upon by the type of people who nowadays treat victory as a disaster. Failure to divert Doolittle's planes to Russia when the carrier force was repeatedly sighted merely added a tactical defeat to the strategic disaster in the making, as 15 of 16 machines were lost instead of being interned by a country then dependent upon American largesse.

The Seeds of Future Distractions. Hundreds of the same type of bombers used and lost by Doolittle were soon being delivered to Russia through occupied Iran, the U.S. thereby picking up its first installment of enmity there by co-operating with the joint Russian and British occupation and its sponsor, the young last Shah, promoted by the removal of his obdurate father. In microcosm, the American imbroglio with Iran was a typical bitter fruit of Roosevelt's intervention. The birth of Lend-Lease had been initially a gift to Britain, with the largesse making possible British aid to Greece, and British defeat there, and then to the

Soviets when the Germans turned on them. But how to get the aid to Russia? The Turks controlled access to the Black Sea, and were hardly going to allow help to their glowering neighbor. The Germans were in possession of Norway, able to advantageously attack the sea route which had been the principal source of foreign supply for the Russians in World War I. The way to Vladivostock was open, with the Pacific War not affecting Russian neutrality in that conflict, including the shipping across the Pacific war-zones, but the excess capacity of Russia's Trans-Siberian Railroad was insufficient for the mass of war materiel being shipped.

The best remaining way was overland in Asia, with by far the shortest and best trail being through Iran to European Russia. But the Iranians did not like the Russians, who still possessed various hinterlands long claimed by Iran. The initial fact of American aid, and the circumstances of how to deliver it, soon led to the British-Soviet occupation of Iran, with the stubborn old Shah replaced by his pliable young son (assorted leftists were ever after blabbing about this mousy last Shah's autocracy and nationalism, the hallucinations of disordered minds). British troops were nearby in 1941, because they had just conquered Iraq, which had been showing signs of the independence it had nominally received in 1932, and re-installed a local puppet later overthrow by a clique including young Saddam Hussein. Iraqi hostility to the West was guaranteed and Iranian hostility was soon added; the three prerequisites of Non-Shah Iranian hostility -- American aid to Russia, American acquiescence in the occupation and a commitment to the new Shah -- being products of intervention. And the success of that intervention, the survival of a Soviet Union no longer contained by the Axis, led to the Cold War, with Iran and its Shah American, and British, clients until overthrown in 1979, as had been the Iraqis until their earlier overthrow. In the new interest of stymying the Soviets, things just rolled down the ruts that had been made helping them.

Liberal historians brashly affect to discern the exact cause of World War II as the failure of the League of Nations, and that failure stemming solely from American non-membership, failures to follow their ideology, but their appreciation of the bitter fruit of liberal intervention is far more bashful. For the last two generations, America has been pre-occupied with the Cold War, involving massive military expenditures on arms, on reconstructing Western Europe and on the reactive buying of political influence throughout the world. Long small wars were fought on distant and disadvantageous battlefields in Korea and Vietnam, and other distractions have impended, such as long spats with Castro's Cuba and post-Shah Iran. And the origins of most of these fiascos go no deeper than Franklin Roosevelt's policies of intervention and their continuation under Harry Truman.

The decision to oppose the Axis was at least defensible, and the diplomatic effort was also a full commitment to achieve that end, and to spite other considerations in the process (including, oddly enough, efforts to ameliorate the damage being done by Axis evil). But the nature of the conflict, with Soviet Russia split off from its previous deal with the Germans, but always capable of approving a new deal with them, left the U.S. with little leeway in implementing the particular policy it chose; with American independence and options foreclosed by liberal priorities and the decisions made to implement them, catering to the Soviets became a bad habit. By going too far in that direction, the U.S. ensured both the economic devastation of Central Europe and Soviet dominance of Eastern Europe, a far more immediately ominous situation than that produced by Russian collapse in the First World War. And aiding Communist Russia had been accompanied by aiding Communists in Europe, China and Vietnam, who would turn on their U.S. benefactor when doing so became even marginally more advantageous to them.

For there to have been the Korean War, and 50,000 dead Americans, there first needed to have occurred several prerequisites. First, the Soviets had to have survived, flourishing enough to be a viable entrant in the war against Japan; American aid was indispensable in achieving that. Second, the Soviets needed to have set up a Communist Korean government, and one American concession at Yalta ensured that. Third, for the late, and longer, phase of the Korean War, Chinese Communist surrogate troops would be needed. There again, the indispensables were American aid, military supply and diplomacy. Soviet aid in setting up Communist China was largely passed-along American aid and the Soviet occupation zone in China, as conceded at Yalta and as enlarged by Chinese Communist and Soviet truculence, was used for the consolidation of Communist control of the former Japanese-run Chinese constabularies and of the former Japanese arms stocks. Later, Truman's aid to the Communist effort consisted in sabotaging their Chinese opponents through an ammunition embargo, at a time when Soviet aid (no longer Lend-Lease arms, however) was flooding the Chinese Communists.

For Vietnam, the Pentagon Paperboys have long since assured us that the American presence there was to spite their good buddies the Russians. But of course that sort of omits the beginning of the story. There was in fact a major American interest in Vietnam during World War II, one that in some respects exceeded the American interest in China, including the Japanese attack on a Navy vessel there in 1937. For it was not until the Japanese began infiltrating Northern Vietnam, part of a colony of Vichy France, that Roosevelt first directly reacted to Japan, rather than as previously via protests and aid to duressed China. And when in mid-1941 the Japanese fully occupied Indochina, Roosevelt implemented an oil embargo of Japan, which he had previously characterized as a measure which would force the Japanese into war with the

U.S. During the early part of the war, with U.S. power at a low ebb, Indochina was divided up into spheres for covert activities, with Vietnam north of 16 degrees allocated to the Communist-dominated Viet Minh and American operatives (such operatives worldwide were volunteers, leading to a plethora of sympathetic American leftists helping foreign leftists, frequently at odds with prosecution of the war, distractions that more sanguine agents would have avoided). The first American bombings of Vietnam were by B-29s, from a Chinese base constructed by hundreds of thousands of Chiang's volunteers, against Japanese bases near Saigon (Japanese seizure of the Chinese base ended the early B-29 attacks, including marginal attacks on southwestern Japan). The burgeoning American carrier forces, aside from seizing island bases for more advantageous B-29 attacks upon Japan proper, also raided South Vietnam in early 1945, probably with the first American use of napalm there. Against the Japanese, and therefore praiseworthy.

American aid to Russia, although saving the Soviets and later helping the Chinese Communists by being passed along, was not relayed to the North Koreans, the Chinese Communists in Korea or the North Vietnamese or their Viet Cong surrogates. Soviet-pattern weapons were the key, despite leftist dysentery about captured American supplies. North Korea's assault was spear-headed by late model Soviet T-34 tanks, just as North Vietnamese victory over the French at Dien Ben Phu was achieved with heavy Soviet machine guns and masses of Soviet 122mm field guns, hardly a guerrilla weapon. While the early MiGs in Chinese service over Korea had fizzled, those in North Vietnamese service were more effective in air-to-air combat. The Viet Cong fought with Soviet AK-47 assault rifles and artillery rockets, and the final North Vietnamese push was columns of Russian-made tanks covered by clouds of Russian-made helicopter gunships. Those weapons were not American-made, but in the long run it was Franklin Roosevelt's garden hose which primed the Russian pump to supply a gush of malevolence. Liberals in pacifistic moods love to bloviate about the long-term cost of wars, but they have been rather reticent about the extended cost of Lend-Lease, including in American blood. And that cost, especially in East Asia, was driven up and up by the prolongation of the war caused by the Doolittle Raid. Instead of seizing the strategic initiative in 1942, the U.S. had split its important forces for a propaganda coup, the liberal imperative, war for public relations. The loss of 55,000 American boys in the Philippines disaster was sanitized with press release perfume and FDR's jocularity. Shangri-La was on the road to Yalta and Potsdam, to the loss of China (up to and including T'ien An Men Square), the division of Korea and the setting-up of Communist North Korea, with Red China ensuring a second phase of the Korean War and the fall to Communism of North Vietnam first and three other countries later; all from that same *Lost Horizon*. And with the fall of Communism west, the Doolittle legacy in the East is all that keeps us from a new age.

And was it surprising? What sort of American strategy would take half of the most critical items in a war -- two carriers and their escorts, two mobile airfields with 10,000 men and 180 aircraft operating with clear decks -- and send them on a month-long publicity stunt, one which featured the loss of a squadron of medium bombers? No sort of strategy at all. The strategy which the Navy had planned for early 1942 had been set aside, although the loss of battleships at Pearl Harbor was not decisive; seven were available. What was decisive was the loss of four big American carriers in 1942, a worst catastrophe than Pearl Harbor. Even with the loss of five battleships at Pearl Harbor, the Navy had the chance, with its pre-war carrier force intact, of winning strategic control and implementing its Central Pacific plan. Without those four carriers, and even with Japan's carrier losses (four big ones and two smaller), the American Navy did not have sufficient carrier airpower left to loiter in support of amphibious invasions near enemy islands outside of American land-based airpower but within the network of Japanese air bases. The Central Pacific plan had to wait upon new carriers, purpose-built or converted. The war dragged on. The first Central Pacific target, Tarawa, had an extra year to have emplacements for big guns captured at Singapore and other fortifications built by a Korean labor battalion, for example. And by the time carrier battles began again, the Japanese could field their own new carriers, purpose-built or converted.

In economics, Herbert Hoover had taken a financial disaster early in his term and frantically frozen it, with subsidized off-the-books federal credit and efforts to keep prices up, into a long-term depression. In the naval area, Hoover had quashed the Navy's Coolidge renaissance by stopping construction in favor of new negotiated limits; soon, however, he was sending that Navy out to exposed Pearl Harbor, as a gesture. And, of course, Hoover the pacifist and internationalist was also putting his faith in "cheaper" bombers; liberals love that bombing. FDR was a Machiavelli on wheels when it came to electioneering, but he was Hoover with tail fins when it came to policy. Even as he continued Hoover's economic policies with the inane fanny-wiggle of NRA (National Recovery Act) "Blue Eagle" parades, he was soon bizarrely echoing Hoover's military policies, but with a little difference. For example, instead of blocking new construction, FDR blocked the rebuilding of U.S. battleships, and that at a time when the expiration of treaty tonnage limits had made such renovations faster, cheaper and more effective. The Pearl Harbor gesture was institutionalized, making Japan's long-term planning easier, and the battleship renovations impossible. And then there was the Doolittle Raid, the Blue Eagle parade of war-making, signaling and prolonging war (the contemporary as well as those of the future) as surely as FDR's policies, like Hoover's, had prolonged the Depression. It will always be "Hoover's Depression" to some, but it will never be "Democrat Wars" to that same group.

Look at the traditional claims about the Doolittle Raid – that it was Admiral King's idea, that it raised morale, that it confused Japan, causing its leaders to panic, pulling back air units from the fronts and causing a gamble on Midway which lost Japan the war. There is not a weak link in that chain, because there isn't even a single link, let alone a chain. The Doolittle Raid was Roosevelt's pet scheme as adapted to circumstances; it camouflaged defeat with a spectacular nothing; it didn't cause Japanese withdrawal from combat zones, their victories had; it weakened the U.S. at the Coral Sea and then at Midway, causing the loss of all four big American carriers sunk in the war; and, by making American victory dependent upon future production, it made that war longer and bloodier while opening the way for foolish liberal diplomacy to manufacture future wars and American corpses, unpopular wars without pre-fabbed villains.

Chapter 5 - **German-Bashing**
(Lafayette, don't tell Steuben we are here)

For a variety of reasons, the German people have come to serve as stand-ins for America and the White race in general for the purpose of being a negative model, albeit for subtly shifting traits. The large wave of immigrants to America from Germany in the mid-19th century included a large politicized contingent, many Jews, embittered by the defeat of their revolutionary aspirations by traditionalism and monarchism, especially that of Prussia. While these emigrés remained proponents of German culture (including German Jews against more easterly Jews), they were also opponents of German politics, as exemplified by Prussia and its supposedly militaristic tradition.

A later cause, soon glossed over, was the collision of German and American interests in the Pacific. The newly united German government had claimed Northeast New Guinea and several nearby island groups, and later on China's Shantung Peninsula. Germany was also supporting Spain, a counter-weight to French bellicosity in Europe, in the retention of its colonial empire. With the Spanish-American War, the German Pacific squadron attempted to deflect Dewey's American Pacific squadron from engaging the Spanish Pacific squadron in Manila Bay, the sort of high-handed interference that in more degenerate days would come to be referred to as a "peace-keeping" exercise and, like virtually all of them, a failure. This incident was sandwiched by a more prolonged German-American-British spat over Samoa, which was settled with a German foothold there, after a cannonball had landed on soil claimed by Americans (although not American soil, of course). German support of Spain paid off momentarily for German imperialism when Spain, bereft of the Philippines, sold the friendly Germans three groups of smaller Pacific islands and their inhabitants. But in World War I this German Pacific patchwork was liquidated by the British Commonwealth and Japan. As an otherwise aggressive regional non-White power, Japan soon received renewed American opprobrium, but to contemporary American imperialists, Progressive militarists soon to become militant internationalists and crusaders for peace, the old German actions and their former presence still rankled. In Japan-bashing retrospect, these episodes and their impact upon American leadership go unacknowledged, but they were important at the time for mediating later American actions.

Yet a third source was British propaganda, starting long before World War I. It can be found heavily in the influential Victorian Whig Macauley, incensed that British Tories had aided Prussia almost as much as Prussia had aided Britain. Macauley's scruples about force did not extend greatly to Britain's own Empire, a fit object for his reforms. More conservative Britons were incensed that the arrival of the Prussians at Waterloo had co-incided with, and possibly caused, the French rout there, casting a shadow upon the achievement of a "British" army (large-ly Dutch and German). With the planned improvement of the German Navy from 1900 interpreted as a threat by influential Britons, British semi-official anti-German propaganda, in English and therefore acces-sible to Americans, increased, with fictional speculations of surprise German invasions by sea. This was conceivably bad conscience, co-in-ciding with British planning for a surprise invasion of Germany's Baltic coast, but the required new ships were not built until war had actually started, however.

British hypocrisy about public opinion was particularly obnoxious in view of its obvious instigation by the British Government and Crown. German official initiatives had been closely preceded by the formation of various Leagues -- Colonial, Naval and Pan-German -- but German statesmen did not try to hide behind such organizations, nor were such enthusiasts honors-listed, as were Lord Northcliffe, Lord Baden-Powell or Sir Jim Jameson, Baronet, leader of that "unofficial" Jameson Raid aided by three British Army Colonels. And there were others. House of Commons employee and British Intelligence agent Erskine Childers wrote a big anti-German novel, heavily promoted. Childers is often cited as an anomaly in that he was a supporter of Irish nationalism, but the pre-World War I Irish nationalists in the House of Commons were all in favor of war against Germany, seeking to use the tense situation to wring concessions such as the weakening of the Unionist House of Lords. While Germany did later sell arms to the "Irish", they were the otherwise pro-British Northern Irish, and Childers was one of the agents trying to intercept that traffic. Nor was it just civilian or on-leave propaganda. Major DuMaurier's anti-German play was written and pro-duced while he was on active service, with the British Army recruiting in the theatre's lobby. In the Royal Navy, serving officers used official journals to press, as it were, for a surprise "Copenhagening" of the German Navy. Consider what has happened to prominent American of-ficers who did not toe the line: McClellan, Mitchell, Richardson, Mac-Arthur, Walker (an enthusiastic Cold Warrior turned out by the bungling Cold War Liberals of the Kennedy regime, Walker's Southern lectures were a target of "civil rights" Communists as much as he himself was the first target of one Lee Harvey Oswald), Singlaub and Clinton's re-cent Air Force critic; it is permissible for generals to be politicized to the left -- praising Clinton is favorably publicized, not fined $7,000.

Aside from economic and naval rivalry, the possibility of a peaceful German unification of continental Europe, not German milita-rism, was the British nightmare. With the coming of war, ostensibly because of Germany's invasion of Belgium, British propaganda began in-flating, or creating, atrocities, some that are still with us. One accusa-tion of German "germ" warfare had, and still has, German agents in the

United States afflicting horses to be sent to Britain and France with anthrax. But the outbreak was all in Europe, and although earlier attributed by the British to shaving brushes made with pig bristles from China, had finally been traced to the sale of infected horses by dishonest Scottish horse-traders (and what other kind of Scottish horse-traders are there?). Another World War I canard had Germans killing people to make soap. Such morbid phantasies tell more about the people who make them up and keep passing them along; the soap was passed along again for World War II. There is in fact little evidence that many Germans use soap at all. They are more likely to cover an odor with *Kolnwasser* (cologne, perfume) than to wash it off.

Britain of that era was a nation on top but losing its lead in industry, finance and trade. The new movers were the U.S. and Germany. The classic response would have been to foment war between the two, making British actions at Samoa and Manila explicable. Failing that, Britain decided to make war itself, and Germany happened to be the easier target. The reason the British moved against Germany was the mirror of the reasons that they did not move against the U.S. The U.S. was a distant target, the British would not have been able to enlist any serious allies, except maybe Japan and Mexico, British trade would have been imperiled, American trade was not critical to American survival, Canada would have been directly at threat -- a target instead of the source of cannon fodder it was in the two wars against Germany -- and Britain's European neighbors might have taken advantage of its preoccupation in North America. These lessons had largely been learned during Britain's two previous wars with America. By contrast, Germany was a close target, nations which might take advantage of Britain if it were occupied in North America could be enlisted against Germany, Germany's trade and naval capabilities were thought more easily blockaded and its foreign trade was more easily disrupted and more critical to the survival of Germany, which could not feed itself. Germany was targeted not because it was a threat, but mostly because it was much more vulnerable than the U.S.

Modern self-defense by the German nation is roundly damned as aggressive militarism. Germans are always a bashable commodity, as in an April 1990 Mary McGrory column, wherein the vicious hag put her spin on a century of propaganda, blaming Germans for plunging Europe into war and ravaging it in 1870, 1914 and 1939, "three times in a row". German resentment about such outrageous lies is then chalked up, by the liberal masters of denouncing ethnic stereotyping while simultaneously practicing it to the maximum, as a national trait of self-pity. As Al Smith used to say, let's look at the record.

In 1870, Napoleon III's France successively blackmailed, threatened, declared war on and invaded Germany. That invasion was quickly repulsed, and France in turn invaded by the Germans and defeated.

After Napoleon III's overthrow, France's succeeding Third Republic put up further token resistance before lapsing into civil war with rival leftist "Communes" in Paris and Lyons. Germany was responsible for nothing save a vigorous defense against a demented and frequent peace-breaker, Napoleon III, at once far more aggressive than the original Napoleon, but far less successful. Germany's three short "Bismarckian" wars were instigated successively by Denmark (trying to grab two predominantly German duchies, the act of a small nation, newly and nationalistically democratized, unsuccessfully trying to get bigger -- big nations having already done so), Austria (also trying to get the duchies) and France. Germany and Bismarck got blamed because they were left-wing bug-bears already (because of their opposition to left revolution in 1848, the one which in France had empowered Napoleon III), successful largely because their self-appointed enemies were both aggressive and incompetent. Napoleon III, the active fomenter of five long, expensive and generally profitless wars (the Crimean; the Mexican invasion -- prompted by the usual Latino prideful failure to keep their word and honor their debts; the fraught-with-later-misery-for-the-Fourth-Republic-and-others conquest of Indochina; the Austrian; and the 1870), gets short shrift by Francophiles as well as by the left. After all, both the modern left and the Napoleons were legacies of the sacred French Revolution, of which Bismarck and his tradition were and remained stalwart opponents. Napoleon III, a target of other leftists while he lived, departed from historical memory, and substantial left-wing sectarian attack, with the overthrow which quickly followed upon his last defeat. Liberal opinion is only raised against successes, like Bismarck. For those non-reasons, history must be bent, and "Europe", instead of a small chunk of Germany and a larger chunk of France, deemed ravaged, and by Germany, in 1870.

Between 1870 and 1914, there were four Balkan Wars, in three of which far more of Europe was ravaged than in 1870, but with no German involvement, except, ironically, mediating peace. All four interrupt the "row" of 1870 to 1914, but remain missing from the kens of McGrory and other smear artists. Militaristic Germany went on to two generations of peace, the first two decades under presumed war-monger Bismarck. But, of course, Germany was undoubtedly saving up its energy to plunge Europe into war in 1914. That Serbia would conspire to assassinate the heir to the Austrian throne was Germany's responsibility in no manner whatsoever. World War I was caused not only by Serbia, but by its aggressive ally Russia, as well as by France, Russia's ally. Serbia, possessed of the Austrian contingency plans for an attack upon Serbia, needed to provoke that attack to profit militarily, and did so; Russia's war plan was immediate attack on two fronts, against Austria, via the Galician frontier, and its ally, Germany, via East Prussia; and France, with no Austrian border, plunged into Germany. Austria, the original victim with a clear legitimate *casus belli*, did plan a punitive expedition against Serbia, but its main armies were defensively oriented. Its ally, Germany, planned to attack France by violating Belgian neutrality, but its dispositions in the east were purely defensive, against the expected Russian attack.

The usual liberal explanation for World War I is a naval arms race between Germany and Britain, caused by those usual suspects the Germans. The British, as islanders, and major imperialists, are conceded the right to have a navy bigger than any two other nations, a right which in the nature of things cannot mathematically be extended to others, and which Britain's apologists, past and present, have shown no sign of doing anyway. Of course, the war which happened included far more than just those two nations, and was primarily a land war expending military structures built up through years of peace and prosperity. Apologists obsess upon the naval threat to Britain, which at unmet worst would have been a three-to-two British **advantage**, but, on land, the situation facing Germany was far more perilous. That is why it lost.

The main strength of 1914 armies was infantry divisions, then more comparable than units of the past or future. Most had eight infantry battalions with bolt-action rifles, grenades and a few machine guns, with a few batteries of light artillery, or field guns, and maybe a battery of medium guns; much more typical than the wrinkles introduced by motorization, armored divisions, and later reductions in infantry strength even in nominally infantry divisions to only two or three battalions, etc. Away from convenient railroads, men marched, while the guns and supply wagons were pulled by horses. By the start of the war, Germany had 87 divisions, a lead over its primary opponent France, with 62 from its smaller population. But Germany had only one major ally, Austria-Hungary with 49 divisions, while France had Russia with 114 and Britain with 6 (but with an untapped population at home and in its Empire). Although Italy, incensed with France's seizure of the Tunisia it was coveting itself, had for twenty years been a German and Austrian ally, in 1902 the French had mesmerized Italy with promises of future Austro-Hungarian, Turkish and Albanian territory, diplomatic generosity.

While Germany tried to win Spain's and Turkey's friendship as respective distractions to its main adversaries, the French and Russians, those two nations, incapable of credible threats to either power, were at best mainly targets themselves. Germany's dilemma was that it could count on 136 divisions, while its three main adversaries could field 182, a 3-to-2 disadvantage. The presence of Serbia added another 6 divisions, and of Italy 36, for a possible anti-German-Austrian coalition of 228 divisions, nearly a 2-to-1 German disadvantage, and with the coalition possessing even greater manpower resources for a longer war. Germany needed to whittle down those odds, which actually **did** occur, and were then exceeded, far more than Britain needed to fret about its naval supremacy, only threatened in remote theory by counting Britain's future "associate" the U.S. as an opponent for the Royal Navy. Initially, with Russia and France moving close together, Germany planned to meet war by those two powers with the von Waldersee plan, defensive operations against the inevitable French attack and offensive operations with the Austrians against the Russians in the more open east. But Russia was a big country, and the von Waldersee plan, militarily meritorious, would have left Germany heavily engaged on two fronts.

French diplomatic success in wooing Britain and Italy had made a prolonged two-front war unacceptable to German planners, so the more famous von Schlieffen plan was adopted for a Franco-Russian war. France, the smaller country, was deemed easier to conquer quickly, knocking out 62 divisions and possibly preventing Italian entry, and thereby making German victory possible. But although a gamble, and involving an invasion of Belgium and thereby risking opposition by its 6 divisions, the likely alternative was German defeat in a long war against a more powerful coalition. As it turned out, the German swing through Belgium left its most powerful armies somewhat disorganized -- like the Union armies on one of Lincoln's cross-country brainstorms -- and vulnerable to French and British counter-attacks, a major stand, but not a Miracle, on the Marne. In addition to the greater ability of the French on the defensive to use railroads, they also used taxis near Paris, the first important motorized troops. France's own attack had earlier sputtered so ingloriously that stalemate appeared a product of heroically resisted German aggression.

The comparative success of German efforts, and massive doses of propaganda, still being pumped out by professional liars, helped cement the legend of Germany starting the war; its policies were in fact designed to prevent, rather than to fight, a war. Fearing that a vengeful France would turn any war into a general war, Germany sought peace in Europe for generations. Nor was German policy one of attacking France, as German inaction during and after the Russo-Japanese War proved. Germany chose not to attack a temporarily isolated France while its Russian ally was first embroiled in war and then prostrated by internal collapse. Conservative, rather than militaristic, German leaders were far more concerned about the spread of leftist rot, and rightly so, as it turned out, than in attacking other countries, even those that meant to attack Germany at the first advantageous opportunity. But their moralistic policy of forbearing to attack a momentarily isolated France and cripple its military capacity left the French capable of striking when Russia had revived and the favorable opportunity of 1914 arrived. German militarism was in fact victimized by the scruples of its political leaders, rather than a victimizer by reason of its bloodthirst.

In the diplomatic sense, Germany was only a minor accessory to the start of World War I, through two actions more praiseworthy by liberal standards than censurable. First, in defending itself so intrepidly against France in 1870, Germany had sapped France's strength in its traditional role of supporting Turkey against collapse from attack through Europe, first by Austria and later Russia. Russia's repulse from expansion into the Balkans by its Crimean War defeat, when Britain had joined France in aiding Turkey, was undone. Checkmated in Central Asia and the Far East by the Anglo-Japanese Alliance, Russia returned to its former effort to undermine Turkey (denouncing Crimean War restrictions upon itself with the outbreak of war in 1870), this time with France as an ally, helping to undermine Turkey rather than supporting it. With Russia less active in their respective primary areas of concern, the Anglo-Japanese Allies became viable partners, rather than opponents, for the vengeful French and the still ambitious Russians.

Second, Germany, anxious to disentangle with those same ever-more-nettlesome Russians, with their successive sabre-rattling against the British, Turks, Japanese and Austrians, had dropped the restraining Bismarckian "Reinsurance" Treaty with Russia in favor of unrestricted military alliance with more pacific Austria-Hungary. German diplomats further hoped to prevent Russian expansion by supporting Turkey, whose support from Britain eroded (the last gasp was in 1908) as that nation moved into the Franco-Russian orbit. Their goal was peace in Europe, trying to head off any serious German Eastern or Balkan embroilment that would nerve up the French to attack Germany from the West (the French were up to Plan 17 in their schemes for this). They failed, from Serbian intrigue, Russian expansionism, French malice and the Anglo-Japanese Alliance's success in deflecting Russian energies from Asia back into Europe; German militarism, intrigue or expansionism, the usual demonic scapegoats, were virtually non-existent, and, where present, irrelevant to the course of events which occurred. Mainly, Germany failed to launch the requisite preventative war, a political decision, the consequence of not being militaristic enough for its own needs.

Germany's conduct regarding Belgium, submarines, poison gas and the aerial bombardment of London have helped make more plausible the legend that Germany started the war, and certainly all helped to extend the ravages of the war. But other nations were guilty of similar offenses. That Belgium suffered heavily was due not simply to the German invasion, but in large part to the Belgian decision to resist. Greece, similarly invaded (by France and Britain, seeking an easy path into Turkey and Bulgaria as Germany had into France, as morally guilty and for the same reason as the Germans), chose not to resist and did not suffer. That of course is a choice a country should not have to make, and the Greeks lucked out, compared to the later bloodbaths in Austria and Czechoslovakia, which failed to contest Nazi occupation, or the Baltic countries and Bessarabia, unresisting hosts to Soviet massacre. Germany was to acquire a massive load of opprobrium for its cavalier denunciation of its guarantee of Belgian neutrality and sovereignty, yet Belgium had already abandoned that neutrality by fortifying its border with Germany, although not its long borders with France and the Netherlands. Furthermore, Belgium sovereignty itself had been in violation of a solemn diplomatic covenant, the Congress of Vienna settlement of 1815, which re-established the unity of the old Spanish Netherlands under Dutch hegemony, making a large unit hopefully powerful enough to withstand the threat of any renewal of the French attacks last defeated at Waterloo. Under the impetus of yet another French Revolution, that of 1830 which established the Orleanist Monarchy, the Belgians had revolted against Dutch rule and the diplomatic status quo, with French aid such as an extended blockade of the Dutch in co-operation with Britain. Neither nation wanted a powerful United Netherlands, and the Belgian revolt gave them an opportunity to split it. The subsequent two guarantees of Belgium subscribed to by Germany were not guarantees against German attack; rather they were guarantees of Belgium against the possibility of renewed attempts at reconquest by the French or Dutch. The Dutch soon gave up the idea, while the largely French-speaking and Catholic Belgians soon found themselves more flirting with the French than neutral, even as Prussian Protestants engaged German Catholics in an extended spat, the *Kulturkampf* (part of purported German "cultural despair", nemesis projected upon confident Germany by cultural milieuritists who quiver with indignation at the suggestion that such leftist rot as Weimar decadence or French existentialism, the glorification of perverts and criminals, is more the sign of cultural despair accompanying national defeat).

Belgium was hardly neutral internationally. It had joined in with other nations, most notably France, Austria and Britain, in sending troops to Mexico to force that basket case to pay its debts; Germany had remained aloof except for Prussian mediation. Belgium had grabbed the most lucrative rail concession in China, the only land link between its two giant river valleys and the capital at Peking, and had also grabbed a giant empire in central Africa. This last, disputed with France, had also been mediated by Germany, with the Belgian King getting a personal empire, the Congo (now Zaire). French objections to Belgian rule there were withdrawn as Belgium moved closer to military cooperation with the French, and the Belgian Congo moniker resulted.

By the twentieth century, Belgium had determined to resist any German attempts at what international law had called transit (movement through neutral territories to attack a rival belligerent); French attempts at transit against Germany were not to have been resisted, but none were made early in the war that actually ensued, before the German invasion had tipped the Belgians into becoming official allies of the French. A French invasion of Belgium was eschewed by French military doctrine; the French were content to launch more direct aggression against "Alsace-Lorraine" and the German Rhineland, in accord with contemporary French theories about the direct attack and its "natural superiority". Neither the French attack nor the German attack through Belgium (nor the Austrian invasion of Serbia, nor the Russian invasion of Prussia) proved successful, however, so that the war became a long one.

German foreign policy, painted as provocative, had three general features. The first was compulsive mediation, in such basket cases as Mexico, Turkey and the Congo. The second was military aid, but, as with German foreign investment, not really closely linked to any aims of German political expansionism. The Kaiser was lambasted in the British press for sympathizing with the Boers dying in British concentration camps; the British press lords evidently did not feel any pressure from their government to play up similar French statements, as the two countries were moving toward a common anti-German policy. The most famous example of German meddling came in Ireland, but that was after Britain had begun planning to invade Germany. Mostly Germany sought to mollify potential foes and to cultivate potential allies with military missions. Starting a battleship for Greece ended with Greece at war with Germany; helping train the Japanese Army left it in shape to over-run Germany's Pacific possessions; and later training Chiang Kai-shek's Army left China at war with Germany. But all of those things were products of geo-politics rather than of German stridencies. Only in Turkey did Germany have much diplomatic success with a military mission, as Turkey which in 1908 had needed British and French diplomatic pressure against Russia, and had then lost two wars to the Balkan states and to Italy, was a surprisingly strong ally in 1914, cutting Allied supplies to Russian Black Sea ports and tying down Russian and British troops. The third German characteristic was steadfastness toward Austria, criticized by historians as vociferously as Frederick the Great's descent upon Silesia or Bismarck's (and Napoleon III's) far more justified war with Austria. Evidently, liberal historians think in retrospect Germany should have taken part in an Austrian partition (such a partition was part of Woodrow Wilson's 14 Points), should have been aggressive, although when it belatedly did so in 1937-39, it was immediately damned as aggressive even though its actions were overwhelmingly popular among the Germans of Austria and the Sudentenland, the first "victims".

The aerial bombardment of civilians was a rare genuine Russian first, but an obscure one, considering the famous man involved. The Russians, having ordered an Igor Sikorsky design as a strategic bomber even before the war started (one of that era's host of innovations by militaries ludicrously stereotyped as hidebound), organized a bombing force, which began the first of hundreds of raids, attacking undefended civilian German targets only, early in 1915, a generation before the practice's supposed start (by the Germans of course!) at Guernica. The 1914 Russian invasion of East Prussia had however been repulsed, so the Russian bombers were never within range of big German cities. In retaliation for the bombing of the small eastern towns, the Germans began using poison gas, first against Russian troops (obscure but true), and later against the French (first against French Senegalese Black troops, a German peeve, who used their own Blacks in Africa) and the British, who retaliated in kind. The Germans also began air raids on London, at least achieving two more legitimate purposes than did the Russians' slaughter of East Prussian villagers, the serious disruption of British munitions manufacture and the diversion of British air strength from the front in Flanders and France to defend London. It was to be the Americans, under General "Billy" Mitchell, who were to try combining city-bombing and poison gas, along with a dash of other new technology; for a 1918 spectacular raid on Berlin, cancelled by the Armistice, Mitchell was going to use radio-controlled poison gas-laden bombers, the first cruise missiles, to crash on Berlin. Sort of makes one glad to be an American, sort of. Mitchell, of course, by his later defiance of purported civilian and Army mossbacks (including innovators Spaatz, Arnold and MacArthur -- himself a liberal bugbear for later obeying orders to disperse a "Bonus Army", a bogeyman to Roosevelt and pilloried by liberals for defying Truman), remains the pre-eminent American liberal military hero, along with Private Eddie Slovik.

Conceding McGrory's 1939 point (if Poland be Europe), she was wrong on two out of three assertions, and omitted eight serious wars altogether (five Balkan, the Italian-Turkish, the Russian Civil and the Russo-Polish). That is a score of 1 out of 11, 9% accuracy, standard for a Pulitzer Prize yellow journalist of the leftist media establishment. But more than just basic malicious inaccuracy, the ritualistic pontificating smear of entire foreign nations, is involved. For instance, the condemnation of Germans for attempting to justify their own misdeeds by referring to previous maltreatment at the hands of others is typical liberal hypocrisy. Criminality is routinely excused by the same German- (and America-) bashers for the very same non-reason.

And praising the Germans, by way of the late new East German Parliament, for apologizing for World War II was no great shakes, for that was something the left, and everyone else, knew all along and about which there was no public demurral. On the other hand, the left had for two generations generally attributed the charge that Russians massacred Poles in the Katyn Forest as a product of Nazi propaganda or right-wing paranoia; the liberal exceptions have been politicians courting the Polish vote and gentlemen of the press sniggeringly patronizing the same ethnic bloc. But, of course, Senator McCarthy and friends were right all along; Gorby spilled the beans. Does McGrory apologize on behalf of fellow leftist smearers? Hardly. Worming her way into a pose of having professed it all along, an obviously upset McGrory nervily attacked Gorby for the quality of his admission, before ending her column with the usual unquestionably patriotic liberal sign-off, a couple of paragraphs of America-bashing.

William Buckley's specious observation that anti-Catholicism is the anti-Semitism of the left leaves the reality obscured. In leftist anti-Americanism (weirdly combined with the left's massive but subconscious ethnocentric grandiosity -- America is responsible for all of the world's ills, and throwing its money at them is supposed to miraculously effect a cure), Germany is the great stand-in for America ("Amerika"), left-liberalism's bayonet dummy. It is most hilarious when America becomes belligerent and expansionist in the service of liberal ideology. In 1936, American liberals were aghast at Germany occupying its own Rhineland; three years later, Franklin Roosevelt was proclaiming that America's frontier was on the Rhine, to no one's surprise. German-bashing, the left's mania, also quickly causes the mask to fall away from liberal pieties other than the pathetic pretense of patriotism, as making fun of cripples side-steps into anti-Semitism.

Bismarck was denounced as a crocodile-teared hypocrite for his purported lack-remorse weeping, but he had no tear ducts (to drain excess eye moisture into the nostrils). The second, and last, Kaiser was vilified for his withered arm, with personality deficiencies projected onto him by hostile amateurs (American political life has two famous sweetheart personalities with crippled arms, Senators Dole and Inouye). In fact, most of the Kaiser's public relations problems stemmed from his accessibility to the press, which his contemporaries, including foreigners, thought undignified for a monarch. But it is Nazis who get the full treatment (as though their extravagant sins were insufficient for condemnation); childish name-calling, including for traits routinely defended in others by liberals (homosexuality and drug use, for example), must be undertaken. *Wockenfuss*ed Goebbels gets the Kaiser treatment (Hun gout too dry?), while Goering gets lambasted as a drug addict (a teen-age victim of spinal arthritis, first volunteered for the cavalry and then served as a fighter pilot, rubbernecking his way in agony into succeeding the Red Baron between landings on grass fields in an unsprung aircraft; try that with spinal arthritis, and you too may wind up a morphine addict). Goering's other claim to fame is that, as Himmler's rival, his portly pumpkin-headed physique apparently provoked the SS counter-model of tall, thin and narrow-headed. Of course, both Goering and Hitler, distinguished war heroes, must be denounced as cowardly. Hitler is even denounced for not having had blond hair, a scorching indictment his childhood photos refute (blond hair darkens when too much time is spent out of the sun, in beer-halls, bunkers and opera houses, for example).

Herr Hitler is also castigated as anti-tobacco (trade "protectionism", not health, was early charged); possibly, having been gassed twice had given him lung problems. When Hitler's behavior is not being chalked up to some probably also mythic scrotal inventory deficiency (you can see it in many locker-rooms, a common minor defect), it is whispered that he, or Heydrich, or Quisling (real middle name: Abraham!), may have "really" been Jewish, as fatuous a speculation as it is troubling in its implications. Who is "really" Jewish is a hot potato even in Israel. And are the posers of these rumors anti-Semites, even though some are Jewish?

By the usual standards of leftist ideology, in those odd troughs between militant crusades, anyway, the problems of security and an economy are inextricably intertwined. The problem, so they would tell us, is that military spending is bad for an economy, which is why Israel, Russia and the United States were in such bad economic shape while Japan and Germany were prospering. Of course, the three countries cited as bad examples are also those with the world's largest Jewish populations and political influence (Israel from majority rule, Russia with its legacy of Jewish Bolshevism, and the U.S. from the disproportionate Jewish control of the media and political finance). The relative absence of Jews from Germany and East Asia compared to the countries with purported war-economy problems is as plain as the nose on Seymour Melman's face, as is the ample evidence of countries prospering, or restoring their prosperity, while heavily arming themselves (Germany, Britain and the U.S. of the 1930s and 1940s, for example, or present-day Taiwan and South Korea). And, of course, while Japanese and German prosperity might be laid up to their **lack** of a military by foreign leftists for foreign consumption, their own leftists were **finding** militarism, adamantly opposing re-armament, which proceeded with and accompanied their economic "miracles". It was no co-incidence, although prosperity did not flow primarily from re-armament; rather, both re-armament and prosperity flowed from the two nations' disregard of leftist cant. Other nations with large, or medium, or very small, militaries have stagnated economically; the main common denominator has been the attempt to apply left-wing ideology to those societies' problems, multiplying them rather than solving them.

The roots of many twentieth century events go back to the tenth century, leaving propagandists a rich area from which to select. German history is particularly complex, which not only makes honest generalizations more difficult, but makes selective distortions by the mendacious easier. The later core of Kaiseric Germany was little Brandenburg, a small garrison state known as a *Mark*, or March (roughly the area that could be covered by a central garrison with a single forced march). This process had been started by the Franks with their empire, which had been split among Charlemagne's descendants. While the part which became France was beset by British Celts, Arabs and then Vikings, the eastern third, the "East German" Kingdom, was enabled to expand in two areas.   To its west, the middle kingdom of Lothair, later called Lorraine, and including the modern Low Countries and a strip inland to modern Switzerland, was absorbed, giving the eastern kingdom the undisputed title of the "German" Empire.   In its east, the German Empire continued the Frankish attempt to halt Slavic and other incursions (partly possible through the migration of Germans from the east into the old Roman Empire) through Marks, such as Brandenburg, or the core of Austria.

The old Frankish area safest from the Vikings had been Swabia (both sides of the modern Swiss northern border), whose nobles (those who had gotten their locals to grant hereditary privileges in return for effective leadership in chaotic times) were therefore respected and called upon by other localities to restore order.   Branches of the Swabian Hapsburgs soon established a stronger base in what became Austria, expanding their territories and titles through military success and dynastic marriages.   Next in importance were the Hohenzollerns, who branched out first to the *Burgravate* (from *Burg*, city, and *Graf*, a Frankish-German name for royal, later frequently hereditary, officials, such as English Shire-reeves, or sheriffs, or French, Luxembourg and Channel Islands *Greiffers*, variously spelled) of Nuremberg, and later to the vacant *Margravate* of Brandenburg.   German notables, by virtue of having been less affected by the Arab and Viking onslaughts than were France or Britain (to say nothing of doubly vexed Spain and Italy), had maintained their ancient liberty of selecting their own overlord.   Unlike the hereditary, and more absolute, monarchies that arose from the throwing-off of foreign yokes, the Imperial German dignity of the Middle Ages was electoral.   While the Hapsburgs were most successful in getting elected Emperor, others got powerful by becoming electors, institutionalized Warwicks.

In 1356, Brandenburg was made one of the seven electors, and in 1415, the Hohenzollerns were rewarded for past and future service with the Brandenburg vacancy and its electoral power.   Both such promotions were by Luxemburg Emperors, dynasts of the Czech dominion, yet another Swabian noble family flowering, albeit briefly, to unite various past and future cockpits -- parts of old Lorraine, Bohemia and Silesia -- with the Imperial dignity.   Obscure crusades to the East had been followed by the deflection of the military order of the Teutonic Knights from Palestine to the Baltic, and a Hohenzollern fortuitously (talent plus opportunity anyway) became Grand Master as the religious impulse totally faded away.   In 1525, this Hohenzollern Teutonic Knight made Prussia a secular duchy, with himself as hereditary Duke, of course. Poland, another elective monarchy and occasionally a nominal dependent of the German Empire or sharing rulers with parts of it, made the area briefly a fief (as Poland had previously been a Frankish Imperial duchy), but in 1618 it passed to the Hohenzollern Elector of Brandenburg as an inheritance. Thus was born "Prussia", first usually known as Brandenburg-Prussia, with the Prussian aspect more laterly notorious for its militarism than for its religious origin or its German colonization. In many eastern areas, Slavic and other rulers sought to people empty domains with revenue-generating productive settlers; the Poles did so in Prussia and Silesia, the Czechs in Bohemia, the Hungarians in Transylvania, the Czar in Russia and the Lithuanians with German-Jewish refugees from Crusader pogroms in South Germany. All such areas would see the interests of the colonists' and their hosts' inheritors diverge, and all would see persecution.

Tired of his domain being over-run and impoverished by wars, Brandenburg's Great Elector built a powerful military machine, through training, long service time, reserves and depots, to defend his domains. Some success was had against Poland and Sweden, leading to a Kingdom of Prussia (unlike Brandenburg itself outside of the increasingly irrelevant Empire), even as such duchies as Poland, Muscovy and Austria had already become kingdoms or even empires. The strong army also let his successors conquer some areas of prosperity -- Silesia and West Prussia by Frederick the Great; the Rhineland and the Ruhr by that army rebuilt to Napoleonic-era standards by Scharnhorst, Clausewitz and Gneisnau; the other German states by consent and the old Empire provinces of Alsace-Lorraine through conquest by Bismarck and his King. This last Hohenzollern promotion, from *König* to *Kaiser*, caught up with the Romanovs and Hapsburgs in the race to political dinosaur status. Contrary to the ideo-swill dished out by Yale's Paul Kennedy, the path to national greatness was not economic rather than military; instead, it was the economically efficient use of Brandenburg-Prussia's slender means for military purposes, by the Great Elector and by the organizers of the rebellion against Napoleon, which brought expansion into more prosperous areas. A politically important economic backwater (the electoral dignity) became a military power through economic efficiency, and only then could it become economically prosperous. It was in fact this last which proved its undoing, along with British jealousy.

As to the Frenchness of Alsace-Lorraine, that was a product of the late 17th century, the successful expansion of Louis XIV's absolute state, shorn of foreign domination and seeking to dominate weaker foreigners, with their more archaic governments, in turn. The acquiescence of threadbare Prussia was purchased by French bribery (although Lorraine was definitely not Prussia's to bargain away), but less headway was made toward the traditional goal of controlling the Spanish/Austrian Netherlands. The Dutch were prosperous enough to be set upon by the English in various wars, but the English were also big and rich enough to help Austria fend off the French from Belgium; unlike Alsace-

Lorraine, the old Lower Lorraine lands were close to the coast and close to British concerns. Years later, the French returned the Prussian favor, supporting Frederick's seizure of Silesia from Austrian dominions weakened by an anomalous female monarch. Undermining Austria, usually the dominant German and anti-French power, was the French motive, however, not a love of Prussia.

Britain, with a stake in Germany due to its Hanoverian monarch, did oppose the Prussians initially, fighting the French in so doing, but, in spite of Macauley's later moralizing, the British soon supported Prussia when French-backed Austria tried to regain Silesia. The British motive was quite clear, colonial rivalry with France; although Pitt's observation that "Canada will be won in Silesia" proved optimistic, the French were distracted enough for British victories in Quebec. There is no specifically German, or Prussian, immorality in these transactions (merely the ordinary lack of morality, of private standards, which is sovereignty, whether French, British or Prussian). In the case of Silesia, German-settled and usually German-ruled through legal succession to the Bohemian monarchy by German families, there was only a sliver of Polish claim to the area (the usual invasion, and the later immigration of Poles once their unstable state had been completely absorbed by its stronger and more predatory neighbors). Yet Silesia was partly occupied by the Poles in 1918, who defied a League of Nations plebiscite by its inhabitants for German rule. The result was sympathy for strutting Poland when it was invaded and despoiled of its ill-gotten gains. Silesia became completely Polish, for the first time really, only after 1945, when German settlements six centuries old were ended. Of what relevance is this sad record of duplicity to America? None, save that the censored official version exculpating France and Britain helped get more American boys killed in France in 1918 than died in Korea from 1950-53 and in Vietnam from 1964-75. Counting the interim World War II, the cost in dead American boys exceeded 500,000.

There is also a studied demonstration of any case for French control of Alsace-Lorraine, other than their having grabbed it for a few months in the 12th century and for nearly two centuries later on, and to have repeatedly overthrown the family that did the trick, the Bourbons. The Cross of Lorraine was so French the French began killing those flaunting it. The true inheritor of the later Bourbons and their policy of "natural frontiers" -- French expansion to the Rhine -- was Franklin Roosevelt, with America's frontier on the Rhine. Had a German said that Germany's frontier was on the Mississippi, it would have been treated as an aggressive statement; Roosevelt knew of course that the Rhine also cuts through Germany, not just touching on its occasional frontier. After 1918, as after 1945, French aggression and war-mongering were rewarded, with Alsace-Lorraine restored to France at the minor inconvenience of a few hundred thousand dead American boys.

France proved its mettle in both cases by launching new occupations and wars (the Ruhr and 1939; Vietnam, Algeria, Suez and the Gulf); without Alsace-Lorraine, France had been less militaristic than with it.

The extent of German or other militarism can be gauged by examining foreign military terms entering English. There are of course a number of old Latin and Greek words, such as legion and phalanx, but those were already widespread before the birth of English. Since then, we have added arsenal, magazine and admiral from the medieval Arabs' conquestatorial spree; musket, bomb, attack, parry, scimitar, cannon, private, corporal, infantry, cavalry (instead of foot and horse), canteen, squadron, frigate, torpedo, battalion and regiment, 16 from medieval Italy's warring patchwork, mercenaries and Hapsburg levies; the Catalan barracks and the Spanish guerrilla; the medieval Czech pistol and howitzer; the Bangalore torpedo and the dum-dum bullet (the first "shaped charge" and the first soft-nosed bullet or "squash-head" round), and that Gulf War terror weapon, the pundit, from India; and only four from German, and two of those medieval, sabre, haversack, strafe and blitzkrieg. By far the largest group comes to English from the French: enfilade, ambush, ruse, rifle, feint, reveille, echelon, artillery, caisson, troop, materiel, sabot, platoon, company, soldier, ambulance, aide, lieutenant, general, major, marshal, corps, chevron, division, camouflage, bayonet, sergeant, triage, guard, siege, trench, embrasure, court-martial, epaulette, barrage, avant-garde, reconnaissance, march, combat, parachute, carbine, sabotage, espionage, fusillade, garrison, treachery, skirmish (sounds German, isn't), grenade (literally pomegranate, preceding the modern pineapple and potato-masher types), assault and maneuver (the last two chalked up by dictionaries to Latin but obviously French spellings), 50 words, enough for *War and Peace*, and the bulk of the words modern. (Not included are French engineering terms used for other people's discoveries -- the parts of an airplane, for example -- except for the term sabot. A sabot is a ring of matter at the base of an artillery shell delaying its departure until extra pressure has built up to rapidly squirt the shell through the gun barrel by forcibly shedding the extra matter; developed by the Germans with soft lead, the French gave it a name by moving to plastic rings.) While some may quibble and say that there are more French words in English because England was last conquered by the Norman French and centuries of war followed, that is hardly a refutation of French militarism. What European nation sings about drinking blood, anyway?

Look at the semantics of Alsace-Lorraine: Europeans call a **German** sheperd, not a **French** poodle, an Alsatian. Alsace and Lorraine were so quintessentially French that the French Revolution abolished them for bureaucratic purposes, making the assertion of their identities, *even as a part of France*, punishable by death. That's rather straightforward compared to the confusion generated in the Cold War.

Chapter 6 - **Past Tense: The Cold War**

While superficially the atomic era, the post-war (World War II) era, the "modern" era and the Cold War might be deemed to start at about the same time, the birth of the Cold War came first, even before the end of World War II. As Soviet survival against the Nazis was ensured by Russian military power, as rebuilt with American and British aid, by mid-1943, the task Roosevelt and Churchill set for themselves was dangling incentives in front of Stalin to keep him from concluding a separate peace with Hitler, and later to enlist Russia in the war against Japan. But although this was successful partly because the Soviets looked forward to controlling East and Central Europe through victory over the Germans, it did not mean that Russian malice would be deployed only against Germany. Before the German defeat, Soviet truculence against the West took various forms, mostly through the worldwide network of Communists and Communist agents. Dock strikes were encouraged in Australia and the U.S., and U.S. plans were leaked to Japan, in order to slow down America's Pacific progress. In the Mediterranean, Jewish and Greek Communists and fellow travelers were encouraged to revolt against British command. In Europe itself, the process of undermining local nationalists that had started under the Nazi-Soviet pact from 1939-1941 was again taken up, this time directly killing Communist opponents instead of turning them in to local Gestapo units. In British domestic politics, Churchill's National Unity government gave place to both Labour leftists and to "Tory" closet-Communists, so that Communist agitation there was somewhat stilled; but that tactic helped legitimize Atlee and the Labourites, including Moscow's fan club, all of whom had initially opposed British armament and entry into the war. In American Communist politics, the Soviet line hardened, Stalinist figurehead Gus Hall bowdlerizing the eclectic Earl Browder, Red out of the Party, as it were.

In less straightforward U.S. politics, the left outside of visible Communist organizations, *e.g.*, socialists, underground Communists and fellow travelers, was quiescent as long as Henry Wallace was Vice President and heir-apparent to the increasingly feeble Roosevelt. A believer in things occult as well as things leftist, agriculturalist Wallace, a sort of Shirley Maclaine in bib overalls, worshipped Russia's collective farms. Wallace and such mooncalf followers as young George McGovern, the future agricultural expert of the Senate, evidently thought Russian breadlines were ghosts from Czarist times. But for the 1944 ticket, the dying Roosevelt dumped Wallace and installed Harry Truman, and Truman soon became President. The problem for Truman, aside from being President, was that he needed to steal domestic issues from the Democratic left and to avoid a break with Roosevelt's old leftist cronies without giving away so much to the Soviets abroad that the Republicans would take advantage.

The atomic era, by contrast, can be fairly accurately dated, from 1945. The spectre of atomic war, aside from Hiroshima and Nagasaki, was for several years a product of troubled leftist minds, projecting their own hatefulness onto the U.S. Only with Russian possession of The Bomb, in 1949, was there ground to fear an atomic exchange. While Truman had been quite willing to use the Bomb to end an on-going war, he refrained from using it to enforce an American monopoly. As a result, the U.S. was to be threatened for the next four decades, and may be again. The Russian test did occur only after Truman had been re-elected, but it also co-incided with the fall of China to Communism. Those two events, with their manifest connection to New Deal perso-nalities, made the Cold War a political football in spite of Truman's domestic and foreign policy peregrinations. For although the left was to be cast out of control of the Democratic Party, it was not cast out of the party, but merely bided its time. Both Truman's Cold War Liberals and the left wanted their falling-out forgotten. Having failed outside of the Democratic Party, the left thought it key to a national power-grab, and wanted its *mala fides* obscured. Cold War Liberals were willing to for-get the left's treason in return for temporary loyalty to a putatively united Democratic Party, governing and then in opposition. The liberals knew about the Commies under the bed; like that fairy tale princess, they were aware of the peeve under the mattresses.

On the domestic front, aside from an economy cooling from war-fever, Truman's problem was the restiveness of the left. Those who had accepted Roosevelt's nominal leadership, even while working for the international Communist movement, soon challenged the weaker Truman and his supporters in various components of the Democratic coalition. By dint of massive infusions of patronage, Truman was generally able to save large parts of such organizations as the New York Labor Party, the Minnesota Democratic-Farmer-Labor Party and the CIO. The situation was similar to the American Civil War, when sectional splits had divided first national religious bodies, then the Democratic Party, and finally the nation itself. The rump of abolitionism, civil rights, was soon seized by Truman, however. Lacking a focus for its efforts, the ideological splits of 1948 saw the left too weak on its own to flourish under Henry Wallace or under a more official leftist banner.

The New York Labor Party saw the defection of non-Commu-nists to form the Liberal Party, which survived in spite of Wallace's drawing a half-million Labor votes in 1948 to throw the state to the Republican Dewey (Dewey's own state, but one he had lost to the Roosevelt/left coalition in 1944). In Minnesota, the hard-core leftists of the old Farmer-Labor Party, whom Roosevelt had coddled, backing their Governor and Senator in return for their electoral support for himself, were booted out after trying to domineer. Young Minneapolis Mayor Hubert Humphrey carried the day by emphasizing civil rights, drawing in wavering liberals with a statement of principle very seductive in lily-White Minnesota. In other states, there were acrimonious caucuses and primaries, such as in Texas, where New Deal lickspittle Lyndon Johnson ran against the Red Menace which Roosevelt and Truman had cozened, in the person of former Texas Governor Coke Stevenson, who had actually opposed the New Deal's leftism and its leftists. Because only one-third of the Senate is up for election at a time, this process of Neo-New Deal Red-baiting continued into 1950. California's 1950 Senate primary saw leftist Rep. Helen Gahagan Douglas, denounced by the retiring Democratic Senator and called the "Pink Lady" by her opponent, a Trumanite Representative, seek to offload this reputation onto her Republican opponent, Richard Nixon, whom Douglas called soft on Communism. In the swift bastardization of history undertaken by left-Democratic loyalists -- which is to say by media and academia -- Nixon was blamed for the Pink Lady tag, intramural Democratic wounds laid up to the opposition party. Later, Red-baiter Lyndon Johnson and Pink Lady Douglas were to become bed-mates, anticipating the rebirth of Modern Liberalism, letting the Reds back in bed with the liberals -- no longer **under** the bed. The CIO unions were kept in line with the usual union thuggery (countering in part the usual leftist thuggery), with Truman pledging to turn a blind eye to it and to work for the repeal of Taft-Hartley. "Repeal 14B!" became a union grail, as the possibility of open shops struck at the heart of union bosses' ability to cartelize labor to a particular employer, and hence to extort favors from the captive. Fellow travelers in the federal bureaucracy, and there were plenty, were intimidated with loyalty oaths. The **House** began re-investigating Hollywood, with so-called innocent victims of politically incorrect publicity blamed on the later-arriving **Senator** McCarthy.

Northern liberals in general were courted with Truman's Humphreyesque emphasis on civil rights, which proved successful in limiting both Henry Wallace and in cutting into New Yorker Dewey's independent support. Truman lost scattered votes to Wallace and gave up the Deep South to Dixiecrat splinter Strom Thurmond, but carried enough states to win the election against the complacent Dewey. The northern Democratic strategy in 1948 was almost the mirror image of Nixon's Republican southern strategy of 1968, done with the aid of Strom Thurmond and against Hubert Humphrey; the difference was that Nixon did not have Truman's control of the federal patronage spigot, and had the luxury of the moral high ground in opposing the Brobinagian excesses that had accumulated in the name of civil rights. In marked contrast, the Democrats had repeatedly had the opportunity to embrace civil rights from positions of power -- Cleveland's, Wilson's and Roosevelt's -- and had not only chosen not to, but had usually embraced and extended segregation.

The left was eclipsed for many years in controlling the Democratic Party itself, although certainly not threatened in its control of press and academia. McGovern made his peace with the Kennedy Administration, but never really had to explain his support for Wallace. In 1988, seeking the Democratic Presidential nomination, Illinois Senator Paul Simon was unable to explain why it had been "politically correct" for him to have supported the Republican Dewey in 1948. The answer is that some leftists thought a Truman defeat would have enabled them to gain control of the Democratic Party; the Vietnam War eventually achieved that end. Of course, the poser of the question to Simon was Michael Dukakis, who had made a speech in 1948 backing Mao Tse-tung. But that was the type of thing that Democrats no longer bothered trying to justify in 1988.

On the foreign policy front, Truman had tardily hardened American positions in Europe after the Russians had begun to increase their demands. The result was the Marshall Plan and aid to Greece and Turkey, being somewhat later enlarged and then militarized as NATO. Initially, the Marshall Plan was also meant as a sop to the Soviets, but Marshal Stalin was having none of it. The American military and intelligence community was re-organized, the Air Force becoming independent and the War and Navy Departments being joined with it in a new Defense Department. But the first initiative took place in the intelligence community. Early in 1946, before the congressional elections which returned a Republican Congress for the first time since Hoover, Truman attempted to lock in his partisans with re-organization through executive order, a parallel to Roosevelt's similar electoral/foreign motive in unilaterally establishing the executive intelligence (or covert intervention) apparatus, except that, in late 1939, Roosevelt had successfully been planning to save his own electoral neck, while in early 1946 Truman was ineffectually trying not to lose Democratic control of Congress. Only when a deal had been struck with the new Republican Congress, courtesy of the abandonment of isolationism by some, was the National Security Act passed, legally ratifying the OSS/CIA and National Security Agency, and enabling their growth as governmental agencies with a newly constitutional basis. The Republican Congress which accomplished all of this, along with the Taft-Hartley Labor Law and appropriations for a jet fighter Truman didn't want, was what Truman ran against in 1948, as the "Do-Nothing Congress".

Aside from that lying rubbish, Truman also tried to blame the Republican Congress for the state of the economy. Leaving aside the anomaly of decades of Democrats running against President Hoover, not against Congress, it was an accurate enough charge, at least compared to later Democratic charges of an "Eisenhower" recession (Democratic Congressmen running for re-election were prone to describe it as prosperity) or the post-1986 Democratic Congress trying to offload responsibility for its tax raises' stifling the economy. The emerging Hiss scandal also enabled Truman to deny any Democratic cozening of such treasonous wrong-doing in the past, to stonewall a congressional committee with "executive privilege" and to use the opportunity to denounce the Hiss investigation as a "Red herring" by Republicans trying to distract attention from their handling of the economy, for which he, Truman, seizer of railroads and later steel mills, was not responsible. Truman's famous plaque, "The buck stops here", was ludicrous coming from that source; the only time the buck stopped in Truman's office was when his herculean efforts to pass it had failed. Of course, the politician who will not answer embarrassing direct questions is typical, but the jump from Communist subversion in the Democratic executive branch to the economy and the Republican Congress was a nifty move. Traveling light is good advice; unburdened by the truth, Truman was quite nimble. But the attempt by Truman and other Democratic partisans to disguise their problem fooled people only in the short and long runs. A new nominee in 1948, Truman wanted a scandal-free election campaign, so the long-over-due White House-cleaning was postponed; mountains of subversion and corruption would fester. But in Modern Liberal legend, and at the polls in 1948, Truman's cover-up worked its sinister magic, and with coattails. There was therefore a Democratic Congress dragged in with the Democratic President, so that the disasters of the next several years -- loss of China, loss of the atomic monopoly, war in Korea, hundreds of security risks (under beds and in closets) and thousands of convicted Democratic office-holders -- discredited Democratic incumbents, demagoguery justly rewarded, with no Republican Congress to blame.

The end of the U.S. atomic monopoly, along with its roots in security lapses stemming from the New Deal, greatly affected American nerves and defense expenditures. But because there was no atomic war, and there were other wars, the fall of China was more important. While the Democrats spent decades denying that China had been theirs to lose, they have of late taken up the refrain that the recent Communist suppression of dissidents in T'ien An Men Square is an American responsibility, and a Republican one. But at least it is now permissible to admit that there were indeed Chinese Communists, a view condemned in years past from a curious blend of subversive coyness and Russian discipline. As with Castro and assorted other leftists who eventually accepted mainstream Communist discipline or extemporized their own, foreign Communists were often sanitized by such euphemisms as "agrarian reformers", making them into local Henry Wallaces. Other Americans had an interest in seeing China keep fighting Japan, so that China's on-going Communist movement was wishfully denied.

One mini-controversy in the Chinese epic was the role of a half-dozen U.S. Foreign Service Officers in the calamity. Americans who had seen Franklin Roosevelt provoke a war with Japan, on behalf of

Chiang Kai-shek's government, according to the last U.S. diplomatic note which preceded Japan's final decision for war with the U.S., were more or less dismayed to see that same government progressively undermined, and even embargoed by Harry Truman, in its civil war with the Communists. Among those who had wasted a few years on once obscure Pacific isles were Kennedy, Nixon and Joseph McCarthy. Unconstrained by loyalty to the Democratic Party, the latter duo, especially McCarthy (sometimes assisted by Robert Kennedy), charged that American policy had been badly affected by the Foreign Service Officers' treason or incompetence. And what were the areas of disagreement?

The view of the Foreign Service Officers was, and of their defenders still purports to be, that Chiang's government was run by venal fascists, united behind the sinister *min tzu* slogan, who were totally uninterested in fighting the Japanese, only in crushing the real resistors of the Japanese, the Communists (who, of course, were "democratic" "reformers" before they were contaminated by Nixon, Kissinger and Bush). The problem for the opponents of Senator McCarthy is that the Foreign Service Officers were always grotesquely inaccurate in their calls, and the pattern was in complete accord with the Communist program of the moment. Mere stupidity should be random, not follow a pattern, and the possibility of stupidity on the part of the Foreign Service Officers is belied by lengthy testimonials from themselves and their defenders (considering the source, such testimonials are important only for the rallying of the liberals to the left cause after the Republican accession; the word of liberals is empty of content). Chiang's government was the rump of the Sun Yat-sen movement in which the Communists had treacherously participated; although the expelled Communists too retained Sun's *min tzu* slogan, the fascistic charge was obviously not going to be chalked up against them by their sympathizers. Indeed, such nationalistic posturing by Communists would be used by sympathetic propagandists to downplay their Communism in China, in Vietnam, in Cuba, in Angola, in Mozambique, in Ethiopia, in Afghanistan, etc. Nationalism is apparently a wart when sincere, but a beauty mark when some Communist movement is being tarted up.

Chiang had been at civil war with the Communists long prior to Japanese encroachment into Manchuria and further south. In fact, the previous encroachment along those lines had been the Soviet occupation of Manchuria in 1928, abandoned after Soviet power over Mongolia was recognized and the Russians had made other deals with Chiang. Within China, the Soviets simultaneously engaged in a massive portfolio of subversion and influence-peddling, aiding a half-dozen different competing Chinese factions in hopes of increasing their odds of picking the eventual winner; inevitably, they also backed all of the losers, too. That the

Russians were also backing several different factions *within* the Chinese Communist Party is cited by defenders of the Foreign Service Officers as justifying their refusal to characterize the Chinese Communists as real Communists, when the question is even tepidly brought up at all. Who after all would be so crude as to expect that Foreign Service Officers, then America's most carefully selected bureaucratic mandarins (And won't they let you know it!), could make the difficult determinations involved in cutting through the haze of "Marxist", "scientific socialism", "progressive thinkers", "strugglers for social justice" and the other semantic fans that Communists play peek-a-boo behind. Highly qualified bureaucrats would been wasting themselves on mundane tasks such as understanding the country where they were deployed, and preferred to pine after wider and deeper powers such as Chinese mandarins enjoyed while plunging that country into the extended dark age that the American Foreign Service Officers seemed so bent on widening and deepening.

Mao Tse-tung's main base in southern China had eventually been destroyed by Chiang's repeated offensives, and the survivors mainly wiped out during the Long March retreat. Their final annihilation at their last refuge in remote Yenan was Chiang's highest priority, but of course preserving the Communists, via a "Popular Front" between remote Yenan's small band and the gigantic mass of Chinese under Chiang's rule, was the improbable program of the Communist sympathizers. By taking Chiang hostage, that program was indeed effected, just in time to let Chiang's forces take the brunt of the Japanese offensive against China. Chiang's forces inflicted approximately a million casualties, by Japanese Army record, before American entrance into the war, but in turn took far more casualties from the better equipped and trained Japanese. Meanwhile, the Chinese Communists, with their little Yenan Army, had been doing little fighting and less damage.

With formal U.S. involvement, both sides in the suspended Chinese Civil War realized that the war against Japan would be decided by the actions of other nations, and their main priorities shifted to maintaining and increasing their strength for the aftermath of an eventual Japanese defeat. While Chiang exasperated American advisors by doing little beyond tying down the bulk of the Japanese Army and its air strength, and sending troops into northern Burma to allow the British to set up a defense of India, the Communists were doing nothing for the war-effort, and much more of covert collaboration with Japan. With American help, a second Chinese Communist Army was set up in the south, nominally to work with Chiang's troops, who were at least somewhat active against the Japanese. But when ordered into action against the Japanese, the new Chinese Communist Army rebelled, and was annihilated by Chiang's troops, who, to hear Roosevelt's advisors, Foreign Service Officers and media and historical apologists tell it, were unable and unwilling to fight at all. In fact, it had been the Communists who were first unwilling and then unable to fight. As during the crushed outbreak of Communist rebellion against Chiang as Sun's successor, as during the destruction of Mao's southern base, as during the Long March and as during the period of Communist whining for the Popular "Front" they were so quick to betray, the Communists had proven unequal on the battlefield to Chiang. But two things were going to change all that: Mao's collaboration with the Japanese, and Franklin Roosevelt's dealings with the Russians.

In Yenan, Mao was probably not greatly concerned with the fate of his second army, because his Yenan Army had maintained its strength, while collaboration with the Japanese was producing renewed Communist strength in large areas of Japanese-occupied China. Pro-Chiang organizers were betrayed to the Japanese by Communist organizers, who bought further gifts of goodwill by turning in downed American flyers for imprisonment, torture and execution. Arrangements were made with Chinese in Japanese pay, enabling the Chinese Communists to form a secret alliance with two new large armies, the constabularies of the Japanese puppet governments in Manchuria and East China. Aside from organizing cadres for future use against Chiang, Mao's main "guerrilla" warfare in China was killing Chiang's agents or eliminating dissident collaborationists who might have been leaning toward aiding Chiang or eventually asserting their own independence; belligerent exile Kim Il-sung was re-exiled to Russia. Japan bought peace in its rear areas, as the Japanese Army's high command, like Mao and Chiang, realized that American involvement had reduced the Chinese theatre to secondary status. Until Japan's defeat, anyway.

Behind Chiang's lines, the main vehicles for Communist propaganda were three small "democratic" parties, which Chiang's people claimed were Communist fronts, something indignantly denied by the god-like American Foreign Service Officers. As usual, freedom meant the right of the Communists to be heard where they were not in power, and their right to crush all discussion where they held power; there was no need for a pretense of "democratic" parties in Yenan, only Mao's long forbearance in bumping off the local Communist leader whom he had supplanted by virtue of arriving with the Long Retreat. After the Communists took over all of China, officials in controlling numbers of all three small "non-Communist" parties were part of the ruling Communist apparatus, and all of them at levels of seniority indicating Communist Party membership from the late twenties or early thirties, making them veteran Communists by the time they were pronounced non-Communists by the Foreign Service Officers. Yet another absolutely wrong call, that just happened to help the Communists, had been made by what the media likes to call "an authentic corps of American heroes". It is in fact easy to have one's mistakes recognized and to be damned as a bungler, however: just be out of ideological step for a moment.

By late 1944, the Japanese had been reduced to suicidal desperation in the war against the U.S. Their fragile cities were being heavily bombed and their merchant shipping was sunk, their Navy largely destroyed and the bulk of their Army's heavy equipment trapped in Manchuria. The bulk of Japanese troops was also unavailable for defense of the home islands, trapped in China or on strings of unsupplied Pacific and Indian Ocean islands. Even with the atomic bomb nearly complete, Franklin Roosevelt had his dying carcass hauled off to Yalta to invite the Russians to violate their non-aggression treaty with the Japanese; the same Roosevelt had previously accused Mussolini of stabbing France in the back for attacking while France was already at war with Italy's German ally. How does one top the twisted morality of luring another nation to do the same, without even the justification of an alliance and in spite of the additional legal obligation of a written undertaking not to do it? With Nuremberg and its "conspiracy to wage aggressive war" bunco just around the corner, if you are Franklin Roosevelt, you offer to sign over part of the country you have nominally gotten into war over in the first place. To save China, we had to give it away. And the fallback position, to be defended to the last charge of witch-hunt, was that although it was ours to fight for or give away, "China was not ours to lose". Good enough to die for, maybe, but only if it was deliberately arranged that the deaths were in vain. And what of Joseph Stalin, whose morals were being traduced by the U.S. offer of a corrupt bargain? That worthy's appetite had by now been whetted by the Japanese investment in Manchurian mines and industry, which had more than a decade to grow since the Soviets had made their third solemn renunciation of the area and its industry, as well as its railroads (cutting the travel time from the bulk of Russia to Vladivostok, much as annexing southern Ontario would cut the travel time from Buffalo to Detroit) and harbors. Besides, Stalin had just been on the receiving end of a non-aggression pact violation, courtesy of his buddy Hitler, and wanted to resume the pattern of his own violations. But this time, he gave notice, the extent of his reformation.

The upshot was that, in return for a few hours of fighting, Russia got, in addition to an occupation of North Korea pregnant with the possibility of more dead American boys, control of Manchuria and the Japanese arms there, preventing the U.S. or Chiang from punishing those who had collaborated with the Japanese, and enabling Mao and his newly enlisted collaborationist armies to be lavishly equipped with formerly Japanese weapons, exported Russian arms, and even American equipment Lend-Leased to Russia for the war against Germany. More important, Mao's troops were lavished with ammunition, even for the U.S.-made weapons (the U.S. had graciously supplied the Russians with modern manufacturing equipment for the calibers involved). After sea-lifting Chiang's best troops to exposed positions in Manchuria (Mao's troops had first blocked the agreed-upon U.S. Marine landings, the sort of defiance usually rewarded by further liberal concessions), the better to make him amenable to extortion dressed up as negotiation, Truman embargoed Chiang from American ammunition, something he was uniquely able to enforce easily, with the rest of the world economically prostrate and a hostile Stalin for once dealing only with one party in China, Mao's. Truman's goal for China was a coalition government with the Communists, like those taking shape in Eastern Europe, which of course soon proved paths to Communist take-overs. Although Chiang saw through the coalition scheme as did most Eastern European nationalists, military force was decisive. The part played by Soviet forces in Europe was done in China by Mao's triple threat of his Yenan force and the two collaborationist constabularies. For Chiang's troops, the supply situation -- no fuel, no ammunition, no spare parts for their modern weapons -- was decisive. As their munitionless opposition crumbled (semi-official American liberal apologists blamed inflation!), China's Reds grew more openly hostile toward the U.S., in an incredible display of ingratitude toward Roosevelt, Truman and maybe even those Foreign Service Officers who did so much to make it all possible.

But, aside from murders of individual Americans, the initial act of hostility between the U.S. and the new Communist regime was an attack upon an American consulate. At the time, of course, the Consular Service was still largely independent of the Foreign Service, so that the sneers of the latter were at bureaucratic rivals who had refused to embrace the Reds. Guilty of loyalty, the Consular Service was eventually completely absorbed by the Foreign Service, survival of the snittiest.

The American nation was not noticeably grateful. So lame had been the performance of the Foreign Service Officers in China that a series of in-house investigations was held, culminating in the usual bureaucratic cover-up. When the military has an accident and investigates itself, the liberal press is indignantly sceptical, and ravenously bellows for a fulminating congressional lynch mob. What was the situation when the State Department, after nearly two decades of liberal Democratic rule, investigated itself? Only the American military is suspect bureaucracy, while that smug bunch of would-be aristocrats at "Foggy Bottom" is of the liberal establishment, and gets whitewashed, while the American people get eyewashed. State Department conclusions were respected by Democratic lackeys, and the Foreign Service Officers duly considered "cleared", while the congressional committee plowing the same ground was and continues to be roundly damned for all time. For the young and middle-aged who have only seen **Democratic** Congressional committees in fervid action, the absence of a media claque, let alone opposition, is incredible, but it **did** happen. The Foreign Service Officers involved departed to a typically bitter McCarthy-era exile; with China already lost, there was much less demand for their peculiar services, anyway. They were put out upon the path of tears, ground under the iron heel of McCarthy, with easy jobs in prestigious universities, cushy book deals and media lionization, as much victims as the millions falling before Mao's firing squads and forced labor "re-education" efforts.

One emerging book was by the Foreign Service Officer identified, from a photo, by Whittaker Chambers, the main witness against Alger Hiss, as having visited a Communist newspaper office in New York nearly twenty years before. The officer had done so, and Chambers had identified him accurately without a stitch of embroidery to the incident. Why the Foreign Service Officer was seeking information from a Communist newspaper was never really probed; maybe the New York library was too small. The so-called mainstream media's long-term conclusion? Chambers was unreliable, and Hiss was proclaimed the first innocent victim, albeit convicted, and of perjury. The statute of limitations had run out on that part of the Hiss treason to which Chambers could attest in the legally necessary role of eyewitness, so Hiss put himself in prison through his lies under oath, which were never dignified by such media yahooey as "cover-up" or "stone-walling". Instead, Hiss received a constant stream of sympathetic coverage, and the solicitude of such unquestionably patriotic Americans as Massachusetts Governor Dukakis, who also toasted Helen Gahagan Douglas in the same year as Hiss was re-admitted to the bar. Consider that Hiss got himself in jail through his attempt to censor Chambers through a nuisance law-suit, and the lengths to which Joe McCarthy's enemies went to censor him, including a recall attempt of dubious constitutionality (Senators have six-year terms) and Senatorial censure. Who was doing the persecuting, anyway?

Modern historians of the left fare little better with regard to their credibility about the actions of whole nations, rather than the mere skulking treasons of various slimy individuals. The Soviet practice of picking governments for countries which then invited the Soviets to invade was long-standing, with the results still rumbling in Afghanistan and still reflected in some European borders. During the first quarter century of Soviet rule, the Comintern existed, so that the Soviet government would smugly assure the world that its own actions were not its own actions, but the product of the only supposedly autonomous organization allowed in the largest country on earth. With the capture of the Chinese Communist Party Chairman in the wreckage of the Soviets' Peking Embassy during the twenties, that cover was blown, but the Comintern maintained a perfunctory separate existence as a cover for

Soviet subversion until its ostentatious abolition in 1943 smoke screened renewed Communist sabotage of Russia's war-time allies.

But even in late 1939 the Soviet government was rather openly sponsoring clumsy forgeries of governments for its neighbors. A week before the invasion of Finland, a new Finnish government was proclaimed on Russian soil, with a couple of unemployed Reds, some of them maybe even Finnish. During the period of the "phony war" of Germany against France and Britain, such doings were big news on the international front, as war-fever had not yet gripped the world's left-wingers, except for a few obligatory sheepish demonstrations against those about-to-be-attacked war-mongering Finns. When the Germans and Russians did fall out, the Russians were able to cobble up their own Polish government in exile, Communists and opportunists not at all bitter that the Russians had only recently invaded their country in co-operation with the Nazis, but rather grateful at having escaped the full play of Stalin's hospitality, his firing squads. With diplomatic chessmen like those, military force, victories and occupations were indispensable; the Soviets were able to grab Eastern Europe with their inimitable lack of finesse.

But it was in Asia that New Deal diplomacy spilled more blood, some of it American. The sign-over of North Korea meant that the Soviets were able to form an armed proxy (under a "nationalist" who had served the Chinese Communists in Manchuria, light duty) for a more direct test than was prudent in Europe, where the U.S. might have used nuclear weapons for a violation greater than the Berlin blockade. And although the Korean War was never popular in the U.S., the U.S., through the Soviet-boycotted U.N., was able to defeat the purely North Korean effort in 1950, with the possibility of liquidating that stupid division. But the loss of China meant that more Soviet proxies were available, as supposedly war-weary China proved capable, via massive Russian support, of re-inventing North Korea. Truman's belated refusal in 1949 to face fighting a land war in Asia, for China itself, had the next year seen that policy bring war in Asia, the two phases of the Korean War. Loss of China, the high ground in Asia, also saw the Chinese Communists able to serve as a funnel for Soviet aid to the Vietnamese Communists, with the North Vietnamese establishing themselves against the French, and then later out-lasting the U.S. to defeat South Vietnam and its neighboring dominoes. Chalk up another land war in Asia to the Roosevelt-Truman legacy, a legacy which has still not run its course, as China continues lost, North Korea remains a potential attacker, and Indochina a source of multiple disorders.

The pattern persisted through Czechoslovakia in 1968, when Russian troops arrived to install the government which invited them in, what lawyers call a bootstrapping operation. As with the Finnish, Polish and other escapades of a generation earlier, such peradventures put only a minor snag in the American left's love affair with those big Soviet lugs. The Mongolian and Manchurian operations of the late twenties had put no brake on Franklin Roosevelt's lust for a Soviet Embassy in Washington, just as the Russians' ham-handed interventions in Spain and a half-dozen Eastern European countries during the alliance with Hitler put no shame on good old Uncle Joe Stalin that the American left could discern. Nor did the dropping of the Iron Curtain put a kibbosh on the one-world nonsense or the insane schemes to send American tax receipts to rebuild Russia (it was faint-hoped the money would not have been misused). The liberal blind spot persisted into the fifties, when the re-crushing of Hungary brought only a temporary pause in the tendency to nibble at the proffer of "peaceful co-existence". The sixties were the decade of the "spirit of Glassboro", which did not prevent the re-invasion of Czechoslovakia any more than it brought an end to Soviet aid to North Vietnam. Instead of seeing people crushed by Russian tanks, the American left preferred to dwell upon the altercations in Chicago between police and rioting "demonstrators". In the seventies, the Russians began installing new regimes in Africa, in such garden spots as Angola (still fighting in the nineties), Mozambique (still fighting in the nineties), Somalia (deserted by the Russians in favor of its enemy, larger Ethiopia, but still fighting in the nineties) and, of course, Ethiopia (still fighting in the nineties). The Soviets sanitized this activity, at least to the satisfaction of the ever unfinicky American left, by the public relations gesture called détente, a few smiles in between sabre-rattles. Came the eighties, and the era of *glasnost* and *perestroika* and the war in Afghanistan dragged on into the nineties, with the Czechoslovak Embassy of Afghanistan providing the post for a Moscow-appointed Afghan President, whose incumbency was proclaimed by the invading Russian troops before he was flown to Kabul to retroactively roll out the Red carpet, as a good nationalist puppet will. The question for the nineties was not whether Gorbachev would survive, as American experts proclaimed, but what new slogan will arise to enable American liberals to again shut their eyes to Communist chicanery's production of the next new trouble-spot, or which reliable old cauldron will be selected for some new stirring and bubbling. Whatever happens, excuses will issue from the usual suspects. The source of Soviet conduct was a topic of respectable speculation only briefly; the continuity of Communist actions and the American left's response to them can seldom be a fit subject of study in the land of the unfree, liberalland.

The fall of Russian Communism might have been predicted by a Soviet dissident in "Will the Soviet Union Survive Until 1984?" That was a fairly accurate call, considering that it was the year the dim-witted Gorbachev became the Soviet heir-apparent. Considering Soviet leftism as the European culmination of the French Revolution and its invention of the modern "left", the honors for prophecy should go to Thomas Carlyle, who, on the 50th anniversary of the French Revolution, said that it would take a total of 200 years (until 1989) to burn itself out. Given the guttering of that candle at the time of Carlyle's statement, he was thought a fool by many contemporaries (and missed Asia).

But what of the fate of American leftism cast adrift? The left has always been a patchwork of squabbling knaves, from the French Revolution through the various Internationals through the infighting within the Russian Party through the Sino-Soviet split and prospectively onward. Indeed, the Chinese Reds had long been a magnet for American Communists, from the orientiphile Browder to those "innocent" victims of McCarthy (guilty victims of Truman) to the slavish devotees of "*Pinyin*" (Chinese written in a Latin alphabet with a German accent). Lineal descendents of the Peking-Beiping-Beijing flapadoodlers, Pinyinheads are careless that the English spelling for many foreign locales is different from native tongues, or from the French spelling. Would it be politically incorrect to write Cologne, Vienna or Rome for *Koln*, *Wien* or *Roma*, or to use the clumsy "official" Japanese transliterations instead of more familiar words? Not as long as those places are not the New Jerusalem of some leftist splinter. The decline of Moscow is merely the passing of one center of attraction for leftist evil. Members of the sinister congregation may find some new minister from abroad, they may elect one of their own, or they may split off and join the other tabernacles always looking for new supporters.

The fruits of interventionistic diplomacy and disarmament had been the lost of China, quickly followed by the Korean War. The landing at Inchon, site of the Japanese landing of 1904 and the American occupation landing of 1945, rescued South Korea and its hard-pressed American defenders, but Red Chinese intervention, a shock to the U.S., produced a stalemate with American failure to press for a victory. The first American landings at Inchon had been necessitated by the refusal of Chinese Communists (including the two ex-Japanese constabularies) to allow the peaceful landing of American Marines, as had been agreed upon be all parties, including the Chinese Communists and Russia. Delaying the U.S. Marines helped the Chinese Communists consolidate their position in Manchuria, leading with further American help to their control over all of China, and therefore to the Korean War's launch by North Korea as well as its maintenance by Chinese Communist troops.

That war may not have elected MacArthur, but it certainly did not hurt Eisenhower, whose election still rankles liberals. Sneering at that demonic "I like Ike!" slogan is the usual unconscious liberal hypocrisy, however, for its true counterpart was not saintly Adlai Stevenson and his ponderous banalities (or even his career, from serving as Alger Hiss' press secretary to wrecking pinball machines), but rather the counterslogan, "Win With Adlai!", as profound as it was prophetic. With Eisenhower, the U.S. got a Cold War Liberal (where MacArthur was simply an old Progressive), breaking with old corruption and maintaining defense efficiency, but continuing unfortunate ideology in civil rights, judicial activism, anti-militarism and internationalism.

The advent of Kennedy, and his Missile Gap hysteria, was literally a short-term problem. But Lyndon Johnson's five years as President saw the American tragedy re-assert itself, as a corrupt opportunist (Quincy Adams, Van Buren and Fillmore in their would-be come-backs were the first three to clutch at a single issue) seized on the civil rights issue to gain office, and then plunged the U.S. into war made bloody by his mismanagement (as Lincoln and Truman had before). But the fall of Cold War Liberalism came in Vietnam, slightly preceding the Chinese atom-bomb and the fall of Khrushchev as the Korean War had been preceded by the Russian Bomb and the rise of Mao. Stalemate this time meant division in the Democratic Party, leading to defeat in 1968. As the Republican Nixon continued the war, opposition to the war became partisan. Eugene McCarthy and Robert Kennedy, generally dutiful supporters of the war under Johnson, soon transformed themselves into peaceniks. Others also tried to advance their careers; George McGovern was an unlikely vice-presidential nominee on a ticket headed by fellow Midwesterner McCarthy, or by still hawkish Hubert Humphrey, but a natural match for a Robert Kennedy nomination. But it was Humphrey who won the 1968 nomination, though foundering against Nixon's Strom Thurmond-assisted southern strategy and the George Wallace third-party bid.

From 1968, the Democratic Party moved leftward, the McGovern debacle confirming that drift as surely as the Goldwater debacle had confirmed a rightward drift in the Republicans after 1964. Even Humphrey, the typical Cold War Liberal of 1948 to 1968, began aping McGovern and company as he had once endorsed Roosevelt and Henry Wallace. The incompetence of this synthetic leftism, along with some media scandal-mongering, gave us four years of Jimmy Carter, a man convinced that the Shah of Iran was a ruthless dictator and the Khmer Rouge were harmless nationalistic peasants. We moved from Gerald Ford's bloody heroism in rescuing the kidnapped *Mayaguez* sailors, savagely denounced by candidate Carter, to the bloody fiasco of Carter's failed Iranian hostage rescue, followed by Carter's Secretary of State resigning because attempting to rescue kidnapped Americans was "bad faith", as cogent an exposition of Modern Liberalism as has ever been made. The doings of the Carter Administration in defense were of similar quality, but mostly it is congressional Liberal Democrats who have opposed executive efficiency in defense while promoting waste in foreign aid and other purported do-gooding.

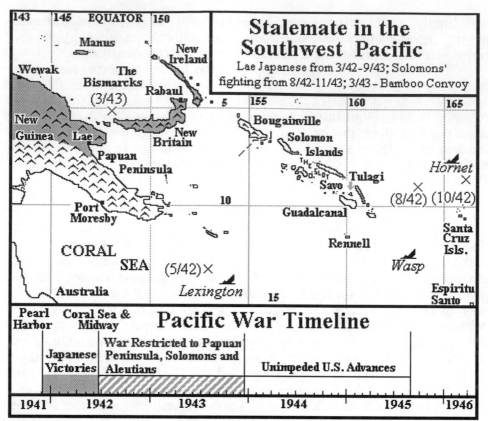

Stalemate in the Southwest Pacific

Lae Japanese from 3/42–9/43; Solomons' fighting from 8/42-11/43; 3/43 – Bamboo Convoy

Pacific War Timeline

Doolittlism weakened America at the Coral Sea, but Japan's South Sea Plan of using Port Moresby, Tulagi and Guadalcanal to move on New Caledonia, Samoa and Fiji (see map, page 62) faltered. After Midway, Pacific fighting was restricted for a year and a half to the Aleutians (see 62) and the Southwest Pacific, with Japanese surface ships formidable in the Solomons. Seeking to bolster Rabual's land-based aircraft, Admirals Yamamoto and Koga threw in their new carrier crews, which wasted away. Fighting on the Papuan Peninsula was capped by the aerial destruction of the Bamboo Convoy, causing the Japanese to stop reinforcing that end of New Guinea. The same month, outnumbered American surface ships ended Japanese reinforcements of the Aleutians in the day-battle of the Komandorskis. Carrier raids on Rabaul caused withdrawal of the Japanese fleet, with cut-off Japanese armies withering at Rabaul and Wewak. Next map, page 106. (In September 1994, Rabaul, Papua New Guinea's largest city after Port Moresby and Lae, was evacuated because of volcanic eruptions; Klara Hitler had married into the namesake Rabaul family, and her half-brother Adolf had romanced her daughter, who committed suicide.)

Chapter 7 - **Semantics and Secrecy**
(Ingresses of Water Sink Ships)

The decline of outright leftist omission (such as the fellow travelers tactfully not publicizing their observation of evidence of Soviet massacres) and the substitution of semantic distortion were products of the "Popular Front" era, when worldwide Communist movements affected reforming themselves to seek political alliance with other leftist movements against the Nazi/Fascist menace. There are several meanings to the word front, including the military sense of a battlefront, but the main meaning is of a surface different from that behind it -- in the same word, a front, especially a false front. The Popular Front era internationally co-incided with the Show Trial era within the Soviet Union, at least the Show Trials of big-wigs, not just the workers and farmers previously crushed. Military or political, the Show Trials were an opportunity for worldwide leftists to display their priorities, or even to change them. The spectacle was accepted at face-value by some, the hard-core and the credulous, and disputed by others, convinced that revolutionaries could never plot and scheme as they had previously against fellow leftists when out of power (the Mensheviks and Kerensky) or in power (Anarchists, the "Right" Social Revolutionaries and the former "Left" Social Revolutionary Trotsky, followed by NEPmen, "wreckers" and the "Right Opposition", the last anticipating the 1990s' liberal oxymoron of "conservative" or "right-wing" Communists). Such an orgy of drill ground lock step hardly advertised a tolerant coalition, but most leftists lurched along with the parade.

On the international front, as it were, Popular Front movements took political power in France and Spain, and were of some importance in China, the U.S. and in various colonies, such as French Indochina. The French Popular Front, although nominally committed to an anti-Nazi/Fascist policy, was dominated by pacifism and trade union goals, so that the modernization of French armaments was actually retarded, meaning that French strength had not recovered by 1940. Another distraction was the Spanish Civil War, where the military and assorted Spanish rightists had revolted against the Spanish Popular Front government following upon scores of incidents, including the official murder of the head of a rightist political party, selected reporters invited. For the French left, this was a trial of sorts, with the only effective French aid coming via the most reluctant Popular Fronters, the Radical Socialists. Typically, secrecy and the collapse of the French Popular Front kept this French intervention out of notice -- aside from disregarded Nazi, Fascist and Franco statements -- until the post-World War II French treason trials, when a Radical Socialist Popular Front cabinet minister admitted diverting French munitions stocks to the Spanish Popular Front.

Within Spain, the capture of the current short-lived Spanish Republic by a coalition of its leftist enemies was fig-leafed by the actual presence of a few Republicans amongst the motley collection of Basque and Catalonian Separatists, Anarchists, Communists, Trotskyites and, for bulk, two large Socialist parties. When the Right won Spanish Republican elections (there was no center in Spain), various factions of the left -- most prominently the Basques, Communists and Anarchists -- had engaged in their own bloody revolts, albeit unsuccessfully. As usual, the left, having failed at insurrection, played the victim, and through its transient unity captured the guise of legality, before embarking on an orgy of murder, of course. Aside from killing priests, nuns (pre-Liberation Theology), rightists, Trotskyites and suspected Trotskyites (pre-Death Squads), the Popular Front's various armed forces put up an extended opposition to the right-wing insurrection, for which they were rewarded with the names "Loyalists" and "Republicans". The right-wing catch-all of Reds ("*Rojos*") was far less sentimental, and, apart from the Separatists, 98% accurate. The main aid from abroad came from Communist agencies -- the French Communist-supported Popular Front, arms from Russia, and the International Brigades, a motley collection of Communists and fellow travelers frequently culled by Stalinist firing squads, something glossed over by Stalinist survivors. One of many enduring hypocrisies of American leftists, those who maintain that "China wasn't ours to lose" in spite of our deep involvement there, is to chastise the U.S. for "abandoning" the Spanish Republic, when the only U.S. involvement was by those charitably described as Un-American (few Flying Tigers died, none by Chinese firing squad). The finish of the Spanish Republic, after Italian and some German aid against it, was the withdrawal of Soviet support. Stalin, looking for a German deal, was no "Loyalist".

The Spanish Republic, a monument to chicanery, toppled, leaving no more than a nostalgic attitude-check for leftists and an obligatory resumé item for Warner Brothers characters. Although contemporaneously billed by the left as the opening act of World War II, the Spanish Civil War had about the same importance in international affairs as the "Hokey-Pokey" was to have for culture ("You put your left foot in, you pull your left foot out, you shake it all around. You do the Hokey-Pokey, that's what it's all about!"). Rightist Spain proved neutral; war started with the Nazis, Fascists and Soviets on the same side, not opposed. The password for the rightist coup, *sine novedad* ("without novelty" or as usual), had proved correct insofar as it applied to yet another Spanish *coup* and civil war, but this one did provide some stability for Spain; most ideologies withered to the profit of a society which matured under Franco as it had not under chaos -- Franco was the father of Spanish stability, modernity, democracy and prosperity. Although the Popular Front era served the Communist purpose of fomenting World War, it was soon disadvantageous to many Communists, although they were rescued by the usual dupes. (FDR's Administration, if not FDR himself, was the American Popular Front, from Henry Wallace on down.)

In China, the Popular Front was a microcosm of the worldwide effort, consisting in getting non-Communists to fight with Russia's powerful neighbors and to neglect Communist subversion in the process. In China, Russia itself provided more aid to the national war-effort than did the Chinese Communists, as the Russians had provided some tanks and planes to Chiang Kai-shek while there was some fear that he would ally himself with the Japanese, while American aid provided to the Chinese Communists was first a diversion from aid to Chiang, and second was used against Chiang, not against the Japanese. The Chinese Popular Front was utterly cosmetic, concocted to fool Washington and gullible Chinese, but hardly fooling Chiang, Japan or Russia. In today's America, the term "gung-ho", Chinese for "work together", has idiotically come to mean enthusiasm, although in the American lexicon it was merely one of the whoppers from FDR's Office of War "Information" puffing the Chinese Communist effort against Japan. That effort was non-existent, as the highly disciplined Communist military cadre had been restricted to the Yenan backwater, never a Japanese target; there were no Communist forces in the south, where the heavy fighting was. After U.S. entry into the war, Communist gung-ho was with the Japanese.

The official entrances of Russia and the U.S. into World War II, June 22 and December 7, 1941, are somewhat inadequate in describing the unfolding of policies. The U.S. had done its occupations and made its other minor interventions, attacks on U-boats and the shadowing of the German battleship Bismarck by a Coast Guard cutter operating from occupied Iceland and by Navy PBY flying boats (the kind Pearl Harbor was starved of) operating from Northern Ireland, while the Soviets had joined in the invasion of Poland, attacked Finland, invaded Roumania and occupied the Baltic countries before the "official" historical Russian involvement in World War II, Germany's invasion (initially of course only of areas recently occupied by the Russians, what Lillian Hellman was pleased to describe as peaceful frontiers). Finland was again drawn in by Russia's first "defensive" measure, the reflexive terror-bombing of neutral Helsinki. Although Washington's early response had been moral support for Finland and the Baltics (Soviet incorporation was not recognized and they were commemorated on American stamps' "Occupied Nations" series), the Soviet Union in difficulty was another kettle of borscht. Americans were soon engaged in the running of supplies through newly occupied Iran, around perilously German-occupied Norway, and past "neutral" Japan, a favorite milk-run for left-wing American Merchant Mariners too valuable to be risked on the dangerous Atlantic or Murmansk run.

For the strident left, echoing and amplifying Soviet demands for a "Second Front" against Germany was the main job for much of the war. The Nazi-Soviet Pact rogues had fallen out, and rescuing the Red rogue would spill American blood. Second Front implicitly meant that the attack on Mother Soviet Russia was the First Front, a classification which ignored a rather blatant historical precedent. World War I Germany had lost despite triumphing on its Eastern Front; Russia had been irrelevant to that war's outcome, even without massive Western bombing similar to that of World War II. The first Second Front in World War II had been the Russian attack on Poland, which Franklin Roosevelt tactfully refrained from describing as a hand plunging a dagger into its neighbor's back, as he fatuously described Italy's token declaration and feeble attack on France and Britain (overran British Somalia and western Egypt) in the following year. There was one standard for tiny Russia and another for giant Italy, allowing for clumsy metaphors (a hand's neighbor is its own wrist, an inadvertently accurate description of Italian policy). But the U.S. attempted both to warn the complacent Soviets and to delay the German attack, through diverting German strength into the Balkans in early 1941. Momentarily, American deception shifted, from the semantic to covert operations and military secrecy.

Military secrets are the answers to idealized journalistic questions -- who, what, where, how and why. Unfortunately, truth is not the first casualty of war, credibility is. Nations have frequently been warned of impending attack, but the motives of the provider of such information are susceptible of distrust. After Finland, put on notice by Soviet propaganda, Norway was the first victim of a surprise attack, following months of fencing by British and German violations of its neutrality. Norway's heavy water production, its use as a conduit of shipping -- especially Swedish iron ore to Germany -- and its desirability for Allied aid to Finland or for German commerce-raiding in the Atlantic made it a target. The German prison ship *Altmark*, perfunctorily searched by Norwegians, was boarded in Norwegian waters by a British warship, and hundreds of sailors freed, the British mined Norwegian waters (Operation Winifred) and planned an invasion (Operation R4), but the German invasion arrived hours earlier. One German transport bound for Norway, the auxiliary cruiser *Schiff 9 (Koblenz)*, was torpedoed by a British submarine in Norwegian waters, and the German troops on board admitted their destination, telling the Norwegians that they were on their way to rescue Norway, true enough given the late cancellation of the British invasion. Yet many Norwegians were caught napping, much as the Low Countries would be a month later, despite the 1939 crash in the Netherlands of an off-course German plane carrying invasion plans (for that winter; redrawn after their loss for spring 1940). The Soviets, repeatedly warned of their invasion, chose to believe Hitler over Roosevelt (always a close call), even as there was ample evidence of an impending attack upon the U.S., with Pearl Harbor sleepy even after a Japanese midget submarine had been sunk entering the harbor. As with Orson Welles' famous hoax, many people suspended their disbelief only at the prompting of the radio. Most people prefer to have someone else make up their minds for them; self-direction takes more mental energy that most people budget themselves.

Once all main parties were mainly in the main war, the main Allied problem became mollifying the Soviets, who were anomalously not in the Pacific War. Prior to its very late entry against Japan, Russia passed through two distinct phases, exemplified by two Halsey raids. The Doolittle Raid showed to what extent the Americans were willing to lose planes and men to the icon of Soviet neutrality -- only one plane proceeded to Vladivostock. Later, the Russians returned the favor of American warnings, American supplies and American forbearance by leaking American secrets to Japan. The Japanese acted in direct opposition to the leaks, putting their trust, as it were, in Russian duplicity. One big episode was Halsey's raid on Taiwan (Formosa), which the Japanese were informed was coming, and that it was just a raid, not an invasion. The Japanese fleet was too far south, and temporarily too weak to intervene, so the Japanese put all of their land-based airpower into action. With no surface threat in sight, and not tied down with an amphibious fleet to guard, the raiding Halsey was able to move fast and hit hard; the Japanese lost many hundreds of aircraft, without sinking a single American ship, and left themselves greatly weakened for the coming Philippine battle (the *kamikaze* expedient was one result), for which their closer and rested fleet would lack air support. But why should the Japanese have accepted the word of a Russia betraying its ally, anymore than we should accept the stream of apologia and abuse from the American left, the scum who fed the Russians with their information in the first place? There was no media outcry, as both Truman and Eisenhower mainly covered up, the first out of habitual guilt and the second because he was in power and did not care to have someone else's scandals pollute his watch.

The leaker of war-time secrets from the Navy had been penalized, if not reformed, by being transferred to the low-priority Yacht Division. Papers from there were part of the non-Alger Hiss-supplied balance of the infamous "Pumpkin Papers". Unlike the perjurer/traitor Hiss, who received his academic honors much later, after an endorsement by Michael Dukakis, the head of the early discovered spy-ring was soon honored by the memorial of the Philip K. Jessup International Law Moot Court Competition, boasted by those fine law schools with the petitioning deans. What we really needed was a Julius Rosenberg Chair in Unquestionably Patriotic Studies -- send your extension cords to Bard College! After Soviet archives had revealed the Rosenbergs as decorated spies, they were cleared anyway by the ABA (talk about a moot court!), as American lawyers attempted to upgrade their own image by hiding behind enemy agents.

The German onslaught on Russia was stalled in 1941 partly by American supplies, but its renewal the next year soon led to the chant for a "Second Front". The Soviets had of course shown no interest in opening up their own Second Front against the Germans during the 1939 Battle of Poland, the 1940 Battle of France, the later 1940 Battle of Britain, the 1941 Battle of the Balkans, the Battle of the Atlantic or the Air War over Germany. Indeed, their loyalists abroad had sabotaged early anti-German efforts, as they would later Western initiatives, when it was safely possible for them to do so. The effect of agitation for an invasion of occupied Europe was the premature build-up of Allied troops in England when the Mediterranean, Indian and Pacific Theatres needed them, and a premature emphasis on landing craft construction. The German U-boat campaign was aided by the resulting short-sighted de-emphasis on anti-submarine ships.

Activities short of a direct invasion by the Western Allies were successful. The invasion of Vichy North Africa (partly trans-Atlantic) trapped the reinforced *Afrika Corps* (*Panzer Armee Afrika*) in a haul of prisoners more than twice as big as Stalingrad's, a far more salutary effort than the disastrous Dieppe Raid of 1942, a fair indication of how deadly "Operation Sledgehammer", the 1942 Second Front plan, would have been. 1943's invasions of Sicily and southern Italy, although botched by allowing German island garrisons to escape, did destroy Italian resistance and led to the call-back of a score of heavy German divisions from the Eastern Front (about the size of the German mobile force for the onslaughts on Poland and France, although fleshed out with recruits), leaving no German reserve there to defeat successive Russian advances. The Germans had to continue garrisoning France from cross-Channel invasion, and they also had to replace the Italian units which had garrisoned the Balkans (more peacefully than the unpopular Germans were to do). These last two commitments took a half-million German troops and made German manpower, rather than its deployment, a serious problem for the first time.

Had the Allies invaded France in 1943, Italy would have been able to stay in the war, keeping the Balkans and Italy garrisoned and its three corps in Russia. Failure of "Operation Round-Up", the Second Front plan for 1943, might have meant a massive German shift of troops and aircraft to the East, instead of the other way. Strategic bombing of Germany prevented the *Luftwaffe* from rebuilding its offensive capacity. The Germans still had attack bombers, but both the fighters which would have protected them in assaults against enemy airfields and many attack bombers themselves -- fitted as night fighters and interceptors -- were needed in Germany, as were a large percentage of *Luftwaffe* troops; anti-aircraft fire was a very manpower-intensive operation with the large guns needed to reach even the middle altitudes used by British bombers. With its tactical air operations superseded, the *Luftwaffe*'s forward air-field manpower, a quarter-million strong, was formed into more than a dozen *Luftwaffe* infantry divisions. Lacking the superb training of *Luftwaffe* parachute units, these formations melted away in ground combat. Had the Western Allies not conducted the strategic bombing campaign, all three assets -- planes, *flak* and airfield crews -- would have been available to support efficient German counter-offensives as they had supported decisive German offensives earlier in the war.

By 1944, the Western Allies had troops, landing craft, air super-iority and a more worn-down foe for cross-Channel invasion, but even then tactical surprise was crucial. In one April 1944 incident, German small craft interrupted an Allied landing exercise off England's Dorset coast, torpedoing three large landing ships and killing hundreds of U.S. troops. On the 40th anniversary of that feat, during the Reagan Admini-stration, that incident was brought up in the press; the source was the same as for virtually all alleged news, the leak, and in its ghastliest form, the dreaded press release. Among those with breathless now-it-can-be-told stories about the Lyme Bay attack were *THE NEWSPAPER OF RECORD*, CBS and right-wing media critic Dorothy Rabinowitz (who seemed uniquely certain that submarines were involved; they were not). The up-shot of their stories was that there was a time when mili-tary secrecy was desirable: for Rabinowitz, all of the time, and for mainstream media leftists, whenever there was some sort of leftist cause they could identify with, as with Lyme Bay's then-upcoming D-Day invasion of Normandy. D-Day was the 1944 version of a Second Front, still in demand by Soviet sympathizers. Allied troops dying in Italy, Allied airmen dying over Europe, or Allied sailors dying at sea did not count. What did count were the Soviets and their priorities and de-mands; frontal attack by the U.S. and Britain to rescue the Soviets from the consequences of their misplaced trust of Hitler. A sound enough rea-son, to leftists anyway, for getting Americans killed. By 1944, howev-er, the Soviets were confident of their survival, and would probably have betrayed the D-Day landings had they been trusted with the information, as they attempted to betray other Western Allied operations in the Medi-terranean and Pacific.

What the mainstream media had in mind running the story was that there was a time -- then, during a war sanctioned by the left -- for keeping the lid on secrets for our boys. They are our boys when dying for the left; when dying for their country, they are the enemy and the "socialist", "progressive" or "nationalistic" regimes that kill them are the media's heroes. In that latter circumstance, the mainstream media em-phasis was clear, blabbing out the secrets of Reaganesque war-monger-ing was their unquestionably patriotic and professional duty. But what a scoop, to have such a secret revealed after all those years.

Scoop of dung is more like it. The Lyme Bay exercise was **NOT** a secret in 1944 or subsequently. German air reconnaissance had recognized it as a landing exercise and informed the German Navy. With the weather improving and an Allied invasion of the Atlantic Coast expected, such landing craft were a high German priority, and two flotillas of torpedo boats were sent to intercept them. Not only were the Germans fully aware of the types of landing craft involved even before they set out, what an exasperated Churchill referred to as "some God-damned things called LSTs", they had encountered them before. Off Tunisia, the Germans had in late 1942 even captured an early model (the British "Maracaibo" type, based on small oil tankers); specifications of this had been provided to the Japanese, whose own versions were produced quickly enough to be used for troop and supply movements between occupied Philippine islands under successive siege by the Americans in late 1944-45. After North Africa, the Germans had also encountered LSTs off southern Sicily, then off Calabria and Salerno, and finally, for long months that were just winding down a bit in the month of Lyme Bay, off Anzio, whose LSTs were then being withdrawn to the Atlantic for D-Day. Their disappearance from Anzio cannot be said to have been unnoticed by observers from the dozen German divisions there, situated on high ground with splendid views of the Anzio beaches and the two tiny harbors. In addition to the historical background, the assumption that the nature of three burning and exploding ships attacked at close range would be a secret to naval officers on eight enemy vessels is imbecilic. Even U-boats identified their victims.

Nor were Allied landing exercises in England some kind of secret, as the media implied. Although specifics were not released for planned or on-going exercises, the ones that had occurred were amply newsreeled, for morale purpose and to convince itchy Second Fronters that something would be done. Some deception of the Germans was also attempted by these means. The location of the planned invasion was not known to anyone at Lyme Bay, and could hardly have been deduced from exercises there. The Normandy-like beaches of England, East Anglia's hundreds of miles up the coast, were far more circumspectly used, mostly for surveys that could be extrapolated to the practice beaches, deliberately as unNormandy-like as possible. Also kept very secret was the timing of the invasion, then and until just a few days before it happened unknown, because of the critical weather factor.

Weather was extremely important to unsheltered across-the-beach invasions. German fortification of harbors and the fiasco at Dieppe had convinced the Allies that attacking another port from the sea would have been suicidal. But a plan or intent doesn't necessarily become a fact; Churchill's feet were always chilly about the direct invasion route, and some rougher weather might have inclined him to withdraw his vital consent. About the only people benefitted by keeping the Lyme Bay fiasco a secret were the Allied naval and air commanders charged with stopping German small craft, who did such a miserable job during the war, until saturation bombing of ports accomplished the task.

The futility of trying to stop small supply efforts, especially when large ones are easily stoppable, was illustrated by World War II, when the Germans, totally outmanned at sea in large craft, were able to use their small craft for supply, transport and interdiction of similar Allied efforts, right up to the end of 1944. German achievements included the evacuation of more than 100,000 men (with their equipment), more than were captured at Stalingrad, from Sicily, Sardinia and Corsica; the re-taking of the eastern Mediterranean's Dodecanese Islands; the evacuation of a German corps by barge through the English Channel after Patton's breakout from the Normandy beachhead; and the harassment of English convoys throughout the war. But even tarnished brass-hats were not to benefit by the secrecy, because there was none, then or later. They had even been taken to historical task before the Lyme Bay anniversary flash, as for example by General Gavin in his memoirs, particularly annoyed that the later barge convoy was not intercepted, to make good the sacrifices of his troops in Normandy by capturing the enemy, instead of letting them escape, re-organize and fight again, some undoubtedly against Gavin's own unit. Rifling old newspapers and books is a cottage industry for the U.S. press, which issues unattributed rewrites and collects Pulitzers for doing so with monotonous regularity, any time it wishes to stop running press releases for a brief moment and do some "research", instead of just waiting for some publicist to hand in the story. The research for the Lyme Bay press release was a bit shoddy, not only giving the misleading impression that the whole thing had long been secret, and hoaxing the press, who gladly fell for it, but also getting the casualty figure off by a hundred, a dead give-away. The facts of Lyme Bay had been long in print. There was no scoop.

The lengths the media will go to bias a story are incredible. The F-14 fighter plane was the most opulent project in the history of Grumman, usually Long Island's biggest private employer. So how did local rag *Newsday* describe the plane, about as heavy as a World War II B-17 bomber, although in the same size range as other high-performing fighter-bomber/interceptors? In enemy hands, only Iran fortunately, the plane was described as "tiny". Against Libya, with the Reagan Admini-stration being savaged, the "tiny" F-14 was described as "Godzilla", with *Newsday* going to the Washington office of a British organization to solicit that misleading comparison regarding a plane made in *Newsday*'s own Monster Island backyard (Godzilla is a 900-foot high fire-breathing Japanese movie star). The F-14 was journalism's equivalent of General "Baldy" Smith, who was short and portly when he wasn't tall and impressive. But none of it flys.

As fervent internationalists, except when pretending to be nationalists, leftists make a to-do about the "One World" fetish, especially when criticizing European colonists as interlopers (from another world, as it were). Multiple Asian invaders of Europe are taken as givens, in that strange ethnocentric complex that holds non-Europeans out as morally idiotic paragons. The odd number is apparently important, as "One Worldism" soon simpers about the "Third World", a variegated group of basket cases, Latin, Black and various Asian cultures also euphemized as "developing"; the reflexive leftism of the bunch has pretty much prevented development, however. With the Soviet Empire officially dismantled, does the Third World move up to the Second World? Note that the continued predominance of Communist dictatorships in East Asia does not affect the official announcement of the "fall of Communism"; evidently, Asians don't count except for scoring bogus domestic American points about the Khmer Rouge or the T'ien An Men Square Massacre. Look in any self-righteous newsroom, and you'll see yellow "Mongol" pencils.

In the Latin department, opponents of Nicaragua's Communist dictatorship were stigmatized as the "*Contras*", as the American media lurched along the ruts of Communist logic, although never described as such. In Communist terms, a movement that puts them in power is "revolutionary", and one that tries to block them from power or to remove them from it is "counter-revolutionary", Spanish *contra*. The media down-played a Communist presence in the Nicaraguan government while simultaneously using a Communist code-word for its opponents. Meanwhile, in nearby El Salvador, those fighting Communist terrorism with their own were described as "Death Squads", while Communist terrorists were sanitized as "Guerrillas" or "Liberation Forces". What the media hated about right-wing violence in El Salvador was that it was effective in targeting the media's fellow leftists. Certainly, the American mainstream media has been notoriously reticent about describing anyone as a Communist before the Communist involved finds it advantageous to drop the masquerade, even as Communist atrocities were usually denied or down-played. There are never admissible Communist Death Squads until the left desires to parade its own horrors, for whatever reason. Bolsheviks and Spanish "Loyalists" got a free pass from their friends, as Guernica became the atrocity of choice, so much so that even some Germans were hoaxed into thinking they had bombed the place (the German *Kondor* Legion had a scant three squadrons of bombers, and the Russian-supplied "Loyalist" Air Force had air superiority at the time and place of the alleged massacre, with its instant and "exact" casualty roll invented by journalists in France). The deaths of approximately 70,000 Spaniards at the hands of their "Republican" government and its supporters is remarkable. How the "Fascists" were able to command the loyalty of so many is inexplicable, except that many were evidently prepared to pay with their lives to end the leftist dictatorship. The roseate leftist view is of Ernie Hemingway resolutely stumbling past mounds of victims to drink himself further into a celebration of his murderous leftist buddies. The left even resurrected the old French canard about a German "Fifth Column" to describe Franco supporters behind their lines. Although attributed to the "Fascists", that particular charge of German subsidization dated back to Bismarck, when French leftists denounced each other as the Prussian Fifth Column, in an era when the Prussian Army was usually organized into four groups. Later, when Mussolini distinguished himself from the emerging Bolshevik classification, he was stigmatized as a British "Fifth Columnist", largely by socialists in German pay, aping the Bolsheviks again.

As long as it isn't McCarthy "looking for Reds under the bed", that is as long as it is Communists killing and torturing, it is generically OK with the American left. Only Communists can be innocent victims: in leftist calculus, guilt is innocence, and lying about it is commendable. But then, sometimes a measure of honesty is politic. More recently, Russian horrors have been acknowledged, at the behest of the head of the Russian Communist Party, and not before, and Communist horrors in Cambodia and China have been trumpeted, for domestic American political reasons, to embarrass Republicans in office. Of course, it was liberal Democrats who lost China, just as it was leftist Democrats who disarmed the opposition to Communism in Southeast Asia.

Neither academia nor media was purged by McCarthy, although the bashfulness of America's "Marxists" -- those tedious little games of semantic hide-and-seek -- was somewhat exacerbated by the trauma of that era, personified as Wisconsin's Republican Junior Senator. Steely revolutionaries are so easily bruised! Just how many victims of McCarthy there really were, and the extent of their innocence, has not yet been explicated; opportunism, not accuracy, is ever the leftist goal. By its strong and unstinting barrage at the strawman of "McCarthyism" (a *Daily Worker* coinage hawked by the dutiful "mainstream" claque), the left has attempted to shift the onus from itself to its real critics. Criticizing the 1988 Democratic nominee for his support of Mao, Arbenz, the ACLU, Alger Hiss, Sacco & Venzetti (before Willie Horton's passes, those killers were pardoned) and Helen Gahagan Douglas was politically incorrect. But Dukakis got no loyalty from the disloyal -- enroled Communists at his convention were Jackson delegates.

Such fragmentation and duplicity is ubiquitous among the left. When Rosenberg accomplice Morton Sobell was released from prison, for example, some of the "faithful" were shocked when he divorced his wife, who stood by as a Party member while he was in prison; they were shocked at the traitor's **disloyalty**. The left's shameless contempt for truth helps it promise anything, including to itself. Effective governance is hampered both by the sham as well as by the people who put it on. It is the inept and deceitful left that wants government to do more, while ensuring that nothing is done well, from fighting wars to providing "social programs".

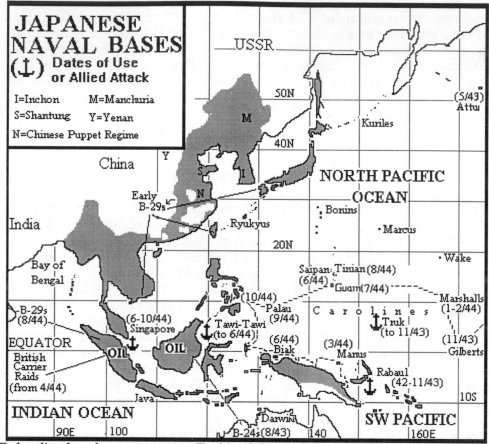

JAPANESE NAVAL BASES
(⚓) Dates of Use or Allied Attack

I=Inchon M=Manchuria
S=Shantung Y=Yenan
N=Chinese Puppet Regime

Rabaul's abandonment meant Truk's also, leaving the US free for amphibious hopping and carrier raids. Japan's Navy withdrew to Tawi-Tawi lagoon, near Borneo; harassed by American subs, it eschewed the Indian Ocean and Biak to battle for the Marianas and lose its newest aircrews. More retreat, to Singapore, defeat at Leyte and the final retreat to Japan followed.

The Marianas were easier to supply and closer to Japan than the old B-29 base in China. Real strategic bombing in the Pacific had started from Australia, attacking South Borneo oil in the same month as Ploesti, but with more than twice as many B-24s. Re-basing the Chinese B-29s in Australia, instead of Ceylon, would have covered all of Borneo's oilfields.

Chapter 8 - **Liberal Distractions**

During World War II's New Guinea campaign, airdrops of supplies went astray and were recovered by the natives. These unexpected riches from the sky were greatly appreciated by gullible locals, who organized themselves into the Cargo Cult, building straw simulacra of aircraft, in hopes that the sky might again rain goodies from this exercise. Those natives were sniggered at by initiates of the Eastern Pacific Pork Barrel Cult, whose planes had misdirected the goods in the first place. When not at war in distant hellholes, the natives of the Eastern Pacific Pork Barrel Cult build straw simulacra of statesmen, in hopes that the sky might someday rain goodies from this exercise. The only rain is the sweat from fevered brows, disappointed hopes and people working harder at swindling themselves.

The federal government's main employees from its constitutional responsibilities are postal, treasury and military, with those line employees spread throughout the nation and world, and with their functions despised and neglected by liberals looking for newer and sexier fields for governmental expansion. As ideological anti-militarists, except when their penchant for interfering in the affairs of other nations turns to intervention, liberals tend to focus on cutting military capabilities more than budgets. The huge Washington civilian Pentagon staff and the plush upper military officers of that same building are immune from cuts; they are necessary to Washington's real estate boom (the Oil Patch may have its ups and downs, the Snake Oil Patch, never) as well as drags upon American defense, huge wastes of money being something liberals are for rather than against.

The military has, however, served liberalism better in modern times than it has served itself, its men or the nation. It served as a laboratory for integration, with lost lives and battles not dissuading liberals from trying the same hare-brained stunts with other American institutions. The veterans' affairs bureaucracies, another wolfish liberal shenanigan tricked up in patriotic wool, were strengthened by the larger number of both veterans and wounded produced by the longer wars. Veterans' affairs served as yet another laboratory, and a crack in the door, for federal governmental expansion into medical care, housing (VA loans) and the education business, even beyond the older military experiments in those areas. The veterans' medical care experience was partially cloned as Medicare and Medicaid, with different bureaucracies and slightly different procedures for each, expansion letting the incumbent administration plant a new culture of party patronage. Sponsoring legislators flexed their political muscles to impress the public and themselves, as if a hodge-podge of ramshackle agencies pursuing non-public ends is positive rather than grotesquely wasteful.

The federal educational bureaucracy began via the military track, the service academies and freedmen's schools forming the first two early, and anomalous, waves. In between were the land-grant colleges, Civil War Republicans using federal patronage to establish beachheads in various state schools. Of much more modern cachet was the GI Bill, providing the thin edge of the wedge for federal funding of various groups into state and "private" colleges. The GI Bill definitively departed from aiding schools, to nominally aiding students to attend school. Subsidized demand merely guarantees artificially higher prices, so money is usually wasted as far as actually helping individuals, who are transitory in their roles; it is the institutions, and those who run them, who profit. What was first an "entitlement" for veterans soon degenerated, by way of the "National Defense" misnomer, into a madcap scheme for draft-dodging, on the strange theory that backing junior off to college on the tax-tab would improve national defense. Later encrustations led to the plethora of student loan and grant programs, with similar rules enforced differently via bureaucratic quirks.

By contrast, solid procedure uses an organization's strengths. As the military in its designed role, if not its liberal laboratory roles, from giveaways to racial and sexual integration through women in combat units and homosexuals, has come under attack, so have the roles most collateral to the military's nature and tradition. These are engineering and exploration, where military skills and command structure and operational self-sufficiency have been efficaciously employed for national goals. Military engineering officers have designed cities (some of Brooklyn by archeuntypical temporary Brooklynite Robert E. Lee), built dockyards and fleets (Oliver Hazard Perry), bridges (Eads, across the Mississippi), many forts and the occasional canal (Panama). One indication of the emergence of modern liberalism was its rejection of the actual accomplishments of liberalism, including the employment of the Army Corps of Engineers; it was more politically useful to attack the useful than to be of use.

American military exploration has extended from before Lewis and Clark and Pike (Pike's Minnesota expedition largely repeated a British Army captain's four decades before) through the coastal surveys of Maury, the polar expeditions of Greeley, Peary and Byrd to a majority of the pre-Shuttle astronauts. But even there, early Modern Liberalism had intruded its ideology into the Eisenhower Administration, causing the early rejection of American military rockets for space exploration. The real instigator of the "Sputnik Gap" was liberalism, also, with massive infusions of government aid into "education", its primary profiteer. As usual, the "new approach" was more of the same. The quack diagnosis fits the "cure".

A.   **Democracy and Meritocracy**
        (Majority Rule and Minority Privilege)

Before there was an American nation with political and military needs, there were separate colonies with the same problems. Defense against Indians was largely a matter of local militias. These furnished the bulk of many "British" operations against French Canada, with the snide attitude of British officers and regulars grating on colonial susceptibilities. The post-war occupation of Boston and other plans to station British regulars in an otherwise secure set of colonies put regular troops in a bad odor. From the Revolution onward, political currents ran against a large professional military establishment, while those within the American military establishment, tiny as it frequently was, wanted professionalization as an alternative to dependence upon war-time levies of the state militias, with their usually elected officers. It was an incipient national military bureaucracy against local democracy.

But there was a constitutional crack in the doorway, the power of Congress to commission officers. At the lower officer ranks, that soon became the congressional power to name appointees to the new service academies, at West Point and later at Annapolis. Even as many states had only just founded public universities, so was the federal government setting up its colleges, albeit as military engineering schools. The national mania against "standing armies" might scoff at the Prussians' describing their army as the university of the nation, but America's national colleges were themselves nominally military. But these schools remained primarily engineering schools, with very little advanced military theory. Lacking nearby large-scale military threats, there simply was not a large enough American military establishment for such a thing, and the country's rough-and-unready frontiers required more mundane skills.

While such emergencies as the War of 1812, the Mexican War, the Civil War and the Spanish-American War did strain the system of volunteers and the militia, the system did work well enough for victory. Although the combination of a rebellious Philippines and a massive war in Europe soon persuaded the more politically susceptible that a larger military was needed, in the name of "preparedness" (for jumping into foreign wars), World War I saw another combination of the federalized militias (the so-called National Guard), volunteers and a draft accomplish the job. Like the Civil War, an unpopular war and a draft were soon followed by agitation for a veterans' "bonus". Both wars spawned veterans' organizations, a ready-made lobby for pork barreling politicians.

With the growth of veterans as a political lobby, the opposition of Cold War Liberals to a professional military as regards the lower ranks was ensured. Long-term service would have meant fewer veterans, and therefore fewer "clients" for the burgeoning "veterans" bureaucracies. But while liberals had been glad to use veterans as a thin wedge to pry apart constitutional government, once the precedents had been set for expansive federal government, the narrowness of the veteran class was a barrier. The veterans' chisel had done its work, and was tossed aside in favor of minorities, the poor, women -- progressively larger groups with more useful nebulosity regarding the delivery of programs. It took more leftist agitation against the Vietnam War, and the accession of Richard Nixon, to end the draft. Nixon got an end to anti-draft agitation, and an effective damper upon so-called anti-war agitation by extension. In the long run, however, the left put a crimp upon a liberal fiefdom, veterans affairs, which the left was long impatient to transcend on the two-fold ground that governmental largess was limited by the veteran categorization, and that the military was an area which should be abandoned on general principles -- it was just too constitutional.

No matter how agitated the rhetoric about their programs, liberals despise the people who are taken in, especially partisan opponents. In the 19th century, when Republicans were the liberals, they financed their assault upon the South and the Constitution with various measures, including a provision whereby men could buy themselves out of the draft at $300 a head. Given the bloody fiascos when Lincoln attempted to procure quick victories to aid bond sales, this was not a bad bargain for the nation. But after future President Grover Cleveland obeyed the law and provided the needful funds, he was ever afterward denounced by the Republicans as a draft-dodger, when all Cleveland had done was to follow the procedures set up by a Republican President and an overwhelmingly Republican Congress. In modern times, the draft-dodging escapades of Bill Clinton -- aid from a Senator and various perjuries -- brought a desperate counter-attack upon conservative Republicans. Perhaps the most ludicrous was that upon Pat Buchanan, dropped from an ROTC scholarship and expelled from college after a brawl with police, for which he was fined $25; liberals described this as Buchanan dodging the Vietnam War, when in fact the incident occurred in 1959, five years before official American combat involvement there. Of more immediate moment were the actions of younger men. At a time when liberals were booming education as the keystone of national defense, Dick Cheney was in school, and at a time -- the McNamara era -- when the Cold War Liberals had earmarked the National Guard for a possible war in Europe or intervention in the Caribbean -- the 2½-war plan -- Dan Quayle was inviting future censure for joining up. All four programs -- the bounty, education deferments, ROTC (non-career military officers) and the 1960s' war plans -- were liberal programs with liberal goals; in that respect, at least, anyone participating should have known that those programs were in bad faith.

But before there were attempts to bring fully fledged "social programs" out of "veterans' affairs", there were other rumblings from within the military. Integration of the military became a presidential mania only with Truman, a weak successor seeking a constituency, even as later the weak successor Lyndon Johnson would bid for the same constituency by extending integration from the purview of the commander-in-chief to everything in the nation, including Lester Maddox's Pick-Rick beanery, a focal point of interstate commerce or the general welfare at no time whatsoever. Both accidental presidents were merely emulating their low-life predecessors, Van Buren's unsuccessful Free Soil comeback and Lincoln's unquestionably patriotic accession. Truman and Johnson each succeeded in his immediate task, winning the next election, but their control of the Democratic Party, or of themselves or the government, was transitory. The Democratic Party styles itself the party of civil rights by virtue of embracing the concept only after it had become an excuse for yet another gush of corrupt patronage (much as the rival party of Lincoln had come to see its ghostly Southern federal patronage wing -- Black and White -- go to the highest bidder at Republican conventions). But standing for nothing at all except demagoguery, the Democratic Party has also been the party of racism; once they reached rocky spots, Truman's and Johnson's desperation tactics left them outcasts within their party, dumped largely by mealy-mouthed lip-servicers of their policies, but not of their leadership. Generally, someone who can develop a constituency for the presidency is not going to settle for the vice-presidency; barring future presidents-by-succession from their own elective terms might limit such coalition-building hi-jinks, the attempt to substitute corruption and minority-coddling for the majority rule of law. Better a lame-duck than a frantic weasel.

Civil rights is yet one more demonstration of the lack of a real political opposition to liberalism. Between Truman and Johnson, there were Eisenhower and Kennedy. Eisenhower's commitment to civil rights was unenthusiastic, but when federal law was flouted by Arkansas he sent in the troops far quicker than did the Kennedys to Alabama and Mississippi in the next decade. As demonstrated by his horrific Supreme Court appointments, even worse than Nixon's, Ike did not have any appreciation for liberalism as a philosophy with pernicious consequences. After Johnson, the next four Republican Presidents lurched along in his wake, tossing out patronage to the Democrats in a continuing slap-in-the-face to American taxpayers, more and more addictive civil rights medicine for conditions which disappeared long ago. Most damage to minorities in this country is self-inflicted, and includes the politics they endorse.

Integration is merely the flip-side of segregation; in the latter, laws separate races, in the former, laws mix them. Both are coercive and have no contact with freedom except to suppress it. In the military sphere, there was an incentive to use Colored troops, to lower more politically damaging White casualties, but the way of doing so was the main problem. Since the Civil War -- and on a smaller scale before that -- Blacks had been used at sea on a non-segregated basis and on land in segregated units with White officers, such "Black Jacks" as Logan and Pershing.   But there were a number of incidents with that system: Pershing's troopers in Mexico failed to catch Pancho Villa (a killer of Americans, and therefore an obligatory hero for American liberals), held against them but not against Pershing.   Later, there was a race riot by Black troops in Houston, leaving few Black American units to fight in World War I.   When U.S. Marines occupied Iceland in 1941, Black Marines embarked on an orgy of murder, robbery and rape of the "German" "racists" there; Admirals King and Nimitz, with responsibility for the Central Pacific Theatre of Operations, refused to have Blacks or Black units in their area, except for Black replacements for the cut-off supply of Filipino mess-boys.   The Civil War *Monitor* had been more integrated than the King-Nimitz theatre, but the duo did have a better combat record.   One famous "ex-Marine" of that era was New York City Mayor David Dinkins, who, faced with the possibility of seeing combat in the Army, Navy (accepting many Blacks for service on Atlantic-based "jeep" carriers), Coast Guard, Merchant Marine, or Army Air, chose to keep agitating for a position in the Marines, then operating primarily in the segregated Central Pacific and therefore with a very small Black quota.   Dinkins got his wish, and although he has waved his service affiliation proudly, he has not chosen to emphasize that he spent the war integrating Marine training facilities in the U.S., stuffing straw back into bayonet dummies, for example.   "Violence is never ever the solution for problems", huffed the pacifistic "ex-Marine", although we have a Marine Corps on exactly the contrary assumption.

In Europe, two mostly Black divisions had bad records, one having both Black regiments completely desert in Italy, the other sustaining thousands of casualties in the Battle of the Bulge, to no good effect. While smaller units of Blacks had better records, most notably amphibious vehicle drivers in dangerous landings, the most well known Black units were the Red Ball Express long-distance behind-the-lines trucking unit, and Black airmen, such as the Tuskegee Airmen.   The claim that the Tuskegee Airmen never lost a single bomber they escorted may indeed be true, but that was largely because they were escorting very long-range bombers, B-24 Liberators, and could not fly their shorter-range Mediterranean-based Thunderbolt fighters all of the way to the bombers' targets.   German, and Roumanian, fighters engaged the bombers over their targets, and shot down dozens -- 61 Liberators were lost on the first Ploesti raid, for example (and dozens more crash-landed). Black Thunderbolt pilots in England lost more bombers in more hectic skys, but also shot down more German fighters.

It was not that spotty record, but rather his political needs, that prompted Truman to order the integration of the armed forces, whose manpower he was also cutting down by more than 90% at the time. If a shortage of men had really been the cause, integration would have been done during the war. And post-war reliance on the atomic bomb caused neglect of conventional forces, so when the Korean War started, four short months after a Truman spokesman defined Korea as outside of the U.S. security perimeter, it was Truman's politically integrated Army which responded. In Korea, as later in Vietnam, Blacks were far over-represented in disciplinary cases, and far under-represented in officers. Although each was a product of the inferior Black talent pool, each was to be charged by liberals to racism. As usual, the back-firing of a liberal quick-fix was disguised by the usual bureaucratic shower of medals (as in the Civil War, Korea, Vietnam and Grenada), and there were de-mands for more liberal quick-fixes, more Black officers to somehow obviate Black indiscipline (vintage liberalism, rewarding malefactors). Thus far, the American military officer corps, and other supporters of an effective American military, have succeeded in warding off quotas or set-asides for ineffectual officers in the American military (the bureaucratized American military already generates enough, and "merit-based" services see most of that carefully selected merit trapped in place anyway, bugs in bureaucratic amber).

Unfortunately, the civilian side of America has been less suc-cessful in dodging integration and other reforms. Those other reforms have included quickie divorces, welfare dependencies, the early release of criminals and the abdication of social responsibility for imprisoning many types of criminals and psychopaths (the insane are allowed to roam on the ground that they are responsible for their own actions, and simul-taneously to escape jail on the ground that they are not responsible for their own actions), and the free trade policy which has gutted American manufacturing. So at the same time as liberals have slyly promoted in-tegration (and the liberals' gravy is really in the promotion, not the achievement, of their stated aims) of schools and housing, black families have disintegrated, crime has skyrocketed and manual labor jobs have dried up. (Even though liberals also promote feeble efforts at "job"-training, they don't care to prevent the jobs from leaving for areas where unskilled people will work for less money; in a free trade environment, job-training is the willingness to be exploited, foreigners for their labor and America for its market.) Not surprisingly, Whites have responded by leaving integrated schools and neighborhoods when possible, result-ing in the premature expenditure of housing stock for "social" reasons, slumification to the point of depopulation, followed by gentrification of the remaining housing stock and homelessness for the last displaced. Whites in general realize that at best the Blackening of a neighborhood makes it more dangerous and less desirable. Even if the new entrants are "middle-class" Blacks, an ephemerality for most "tipping" neighbor-hoods, the presence of Blacks makes infiltration by the numerous Black street-criminal population easier. Crime skyrockets, Whites flee, middle-class Blacks also flee and open the way to a new neighborhood, and liberals win Black support for affecting to espouse their cause.

Before the wave of integration broke upon the military meritocracy, that meritocracy had first to solidify, and it did so in general isolation from racial considerations. Civil service reforms were the first wave of the Progressive Niagara, and the strident nationalism of that stage of liberalism made a military meritocracy a goal. Occasionally, of course, meritocracy meant merely renaming old systems. Some of the militias became the National Guard, and others the Reserves; Texas A&M University had provided the Texas Rangers and the Texas Militia with their officers, and was soon doing the same for the Texas National Guard and Texas-based Reserve units. The inexhaustible need of a bureaucracy for officers led to the extension of that old militia approach, the ROTC program for young college gentlemen of the time, as well as an up-from-the-ranks democratization of meritocracy, OCS, or the Fort Jackson Vacation. Early in World War II, a military lacking confidence in America's allies had established another officer program, ASTP, for those Depression-era youths who had been unable to afford college and therefore a shot at ROTC. This program ended by the middle of the war, with these potential leaders drafted into the infantry; the war was suddenly winnable, and they became expendable.

B.   Post-Constitutionality

But the urge for improvement had entered the liberal program, and needed extension. First, there was the post-World War II GI Bill, yet another veterans' boondoggle, putting many affluent vets through college and/or graduate school at taxpayer expense, supposedly in retroactive pursuit of the constitutional power (duty) to raise armies. The older veterans' medical care programs were also in fuller swing, with more veterans, many of them initially serious war-related injuries. But each of these essays in socialism was limited to veterans, a serious handicap for the enlistment of other social groups into liberal patronage clienteles. The liberals' first big break was in the American satellite boondoggle, wherein the delay engendered by forgoing military expertise in rocket development led to a useful panic when the Soviet satellite orbited first. Liberals who had protested against the military rockets, or against the idea of space exploration at all, were quick to hitch the hysteria to their wagon-load of pork. National Defense became the moniker for a reform of the nation's then-efficient school system, in the rather careless assumption that educational mediocrity, not a failure of political will, was to blame for America's tardy leap into space. National Defense was just an excuse for putting young people into college and graduate school, and keeping them out of the draft and out of National

Defense. In reality, the program was just the last attempt of mutating liberalism at maintaining a constitutional blush.

The epic electoral victory of Lyndon Johnson against alleged war-monger Goldwater provided the opportunity to totally cut the constitutional apron-strings of liberal patronage. In the first instance, Johnson's coattails pulled in enough Democratic Congressmen to allow the steamrolling of a New and Improved Deal, the "Great Society", most importantly Medicare and Medicaid. In the second instance, Johnson's immediate plunge into war in Vietnam led to an upsurge in anti-military activity. McCarthy's innocent victims had recovered their revolutionary nerve, and the figleaf of National Defense educational aid was re-embroidered to National Direct educational aid. This aid was of course not direct to students, being aid to universities which individual students became responsible for paying back. After all, if educated students were so important to the national security, or social well-being in the new calculus, then keeping the schools' balance sheets in working order must therefore have been even more important. The educational bureaucracy was what was being coddled, after all, because students' identities as such were transient, while educators remained a potent lobby. For primary and secondary schools, a flood of money from the more affluent states stifled those states' previously well functioning public schools. With the upsurges in both medical and educational spending, the American military actually shrank as a proportion of GNP, even as the nation desultorily waged a war in Vietnam and its environs.

That trend of a shrinking defense co-incided with the full flowering of the free trade philosophy. Protectionism by any means was anathema to liberals, superficially determined, like Blanche DuBois, to depend upon the kindness of strangers. But there was a bit of strategy amongst the blowsiness. For all of the talk about international competitiveness, there are really only two areas where a nation competes internationally -- militarily and economically; and those are two areas, patriotic courage and real productivity, where liberal shenanigans are unfortunately not taken as seriously as they should be. Economically, competition across national borders is in goods, not in services. Smarmy liberals characterize an America being gutted of its productive capacity by the export of jobs as an emerging service economy with the same frantic verve as chilly Herbert Hoover cackling over apple-sellers. But the service economy is not only the parasitic portion of a functioning economy, it is also the stronghold of liberalism. What liberals despise is the military (a.k.a. the services) and people who work with their hands. Such people just do not have an interest in higher leftist catechisms, especially when they are employed, prosperous and self-confident, so they are thrown to the wolves of peace phantasies or the international market by the liberals, who shed some perfunctory tears along with other peoples' jobs. After all, if those jobs go to Mexico, it must be because

Mexicans are so well educated and productive, not because they will work for $1.64 an hour in unsafe and polluting factories. Keeping those jobs in America, through trade barriers favored by such American giants as Hamilton and Franklin (fearful of European industry and Oriental frugality, respectively), will even be opposed by some alleged conservatives, who evidently think that "family" values would somehow be enhanced by $1.64 an hour. The free trade oxymoron that motivates both liberal and "conservative" anti-protectionists is fundamentally the assumption that forgoing the revenue generated by efficient tariffs (those that maximize revenue through the highest rate with the least effect on trade volume) will produce a greater good -- **somewhere** -- that is worth the cost of raising the same revenue through other taxes -- those that disrupt only domestic activity -- as well as the costs of forgoing the measure of protection afforded by tariffs. The free trade position is that giving up a public advantage will give someone somewhere a **private** advantage that is or will be greater than the **public** disadvantage. That is typical liberal nebulosity, the elastic public concept filling some private pockets.

Of course, to real liberals, not just pseudo-conservative dupes, there's also the frantic pursuit of the social program treadmill. Not only is the Constitution itself speciously misread and misinterpreted as mandating active unlimited government, the Bill of Rights is also pilfered, and plundered of its meaning; and the Constitution was actually designed to set up a government, while the Bill of Rights wasn't. The Bill of Rights was and is designed to protect individuals against government. Modern liberals have turned the Bill on its head, affecting to have it mean that a big government is needed to give us those rights, which are nothing if not restrictions upon big government (liberals frequently denounce the 9th and 10th amendments as "meaningless" because they attempt to restrict government in general as the other eight do specifically). Instead, liberals look to the restrictions as permissions, willfully confusing liberty from government with license for big government. Privacy becomes subsidized abortions (with the 9th and 10th amendments pressed into service). The right to keep and bear arms becomes gun-control (by tax, and in denigration of the government's constitutional power to regulate militias -- repeated in the first part of the Second Amendment -- so that a raid in Waco is by Treasury agents instead of by the military). The right to counsel begets a liberal bureaucracy (Legal Services, once headed by Hillary Antoinette herself) and "civil rights" others (for the civil rights of minorities -- liberals believe the Bill of Rights doesn't apply to everyone). Free expression means tax-subsidies for such politically correct governmental agencies as PBS, National Public Radio, the National Endowments for the Arts and Humanities and others that we can be imprisoned for not supporting.

The extension of rights is also used to taint original constitutional organs. But of course the military was perverted when it was used to impose Reconstruction upon the South, thereby imposing it upon the nation. The so-called 14th Amendment was rejected by Georgia and the Carolinas, and its ratification was rescinded by Ohio and New Jersey; with the U.S. Army used to impose new Southern governments, the opposition to enactment nationwide was nullified by that *coup d'etat*. And consider the spectacle of a liberal Supreme Court nominee babbling about the "equal rights" provision of the 14th as helping feminine rights, when that sacred cow in fact introduced sexism to the Constitution, protecting only "male" inhabitants, as befit one of those innumerable causes espoused, so to speak, by the early insufferablettes (the Constitution proper used male pronouns, which were and are substantively meaningless). And, of course, it is liberal dogma that the Bill of Rights applies only to minorities, so equal protection should mean no protection; given the history of the 14th, it often does. Consider the mindset of the "Radical" liberals who gave us the 14th, wherein the main drafter, the massively corrupt Roscoe Conkling, could point to the amendment's genesis as ensuring corporate rights, so that "born or naturalized" came to subsume "incorporated" in Supreme Court interpretation (at the foot of Madison Avenue stands a statue of Conkling, facing toward Wall Street). What good was "equal protection" of the laws when this so-called amendment set up an *ex post facto* bill of attainder against old Confederates? One stop on the road to Modern Liberalism is the sociological school of jurisprudence, where the law means "the prophecies of what the courts will do in fact, and nothing more"; obviously, law as a guide to conduct is pretty useless when conduct becomes criminalized after it occurs or when existing statutes are negated by future interpretations. Another aspect of Modern Liberalism is its coddling of minorities, at least as long as they play their designated roles.

Liberals smirk agreement when Blacks moan about the Constitution calling them 3/5 human, although they will not point out the obvious truths that that classification cut the congressional delegations of the heavy slave-holding states along with their presidential electors, and that the 2/5 was subtracted at the insistence of the Northern states. The 14th provided a penalty for states which discriminated in voting rights -- the loss of a proportion of seats and their electoral votes; in effect, 0/5. Why no outcry from "civil rights" advocates at "0% human"? -- the 14th was a liberal enactment, not a product of those evil old Founding Fathers. From the end of Reconstruction through the Voting Rights Act, this provision went unenforced, letting the Democratic Party control the House of Representatives for six sessions it was unentitled to, re-electing Grover Cleveland and Woodrow Wilson and electing Kennedy-Johnson (along with massive fraud in Texas, Illinois, Missouri, Michigan, New

Jersey and maybe even Pennsylvania). Why didn't the "Civil Rights" auxiliary of the Democratic Party protest? The answer is that they were partisans first; when it came to rights, the rights of the Democratic Party to power and patronage were what they stood for. Civil Rights was a mollifier for the national Democratic Party, and an electioneering option when the party got into trouble. For its part in helping put the 14th into whatever place it has, the military has lately been perverted in a more literal sense, and it has also seen "equal protection" applied to women seeking to fly carrier jets -- there is a quota, in the name of equal protection, of course! And why are women, proclaimed the Majority when being courted by liberals, given the protection supposedly reserved for minorities?

C.   The Peace Dividend: More Inputs to Failure

The concept of diminishing returns is difficult for some in the abstract, but in concrete terms is more accessible. Any good used as an input, such as water or oxygen for our bodies, is needed in certain minimal amounts. A severe shortage below some threshold leads to quick death of thirst or anoxia. Somewhat above that level, a chronic shortage of water damages kidneys, and of oxygen damages heart and brain. There is a middle range within which life flourishes, but above that there are ranges within which or beyond which more water or oxygen is harmful. Too much water intake damages kidneys, or even destroys cells throughout the body, such as water on the brain (no connection with a crick in the neck); too much oxygen leads to a loss of consciousness, the body protecting itself from slow combustion of its tissues. The same principle applies to bureaucracies and their principal intake, money.

Several decades ago, the principal foci of state and local governments were road-building and law-and-order, including asylums for the unwell. Education and other so-called welfare functions were lesser priorities. Came the baby-boom and Sputnik, and there was suddenly a greater mass of gullible parents willing to spend more on local schools, and a patina of un-Americanism for those questioning large new spending on education. In the affluent states, such as Connecticut and New York, spending on education moved to the highest political priority, as the states which were first and second in state SAT scores moved to do something about that parlous situation. And they did, with Connecticut falling from first to thirty-third in the nation, and New York from second to forty-fourth. And that was after television viewing had peaked, and well after those states' Black and Hispanic populations had peaked, including the percentage of those groups attending college.

While the SATs are hardly perfect, they are essentially the only national measurement available over a period of years. Although it is true that more young people started college over time, the decline in scores has been more than a result of the recruitment of the "less aca-demically skilled"; there has been an absolute decline in the number of those scoring in the highest categories, which would not have occurred if the problem had been mainly one of new types of entrants. The decline was across-the-Boards, but not necessarily across the nation. For 1991, the state-by-state correlation of SAT scores with average state spending for five years previously (because skills are cumulative, only spending in the students' senior years would hardly be relevant) was not only not positive, it was actually **negative**, -.368. Which is to say that virtually all Americans states (and even localities), having at best reached and at worst long passed the optimum level of educational expenditures, that boost their per pupil expenditures by another thousand dollars per year will not only not see an SAT improvement, they will see an average **decline** of another 22 points per pupil.

The problem is mainly a flood of money, mostly in the Northeast U.S. Two rural states, Alaska and Wyoming, generating their revenue from mining taxes, are also very inefficient with educational funding, Alaska with the worst results. Another state, Iowa, spends more than its neighbors, but, as the home of the Iowa Test of Basic Skills, stays more focused than do more faddish states. Many Southern states, still with large Black populations and scorned for not spending money, get among the best results in the nation. Their reward is to be scorned as educa-tional backwaters, because they get value for their money, instead of spending themselves below mediocrity. Of course, even local liberal demagogues in Arkansas and Louisiana will damn their states as being at the bottom of the states in **spending**, but both are in the top fifteen (along with Alabama, Mississippi, Utah, etc.) in **results**. They are in fact presently spending at levels which generated good results for Con-necticut and New York before the flood of money swept in cathedrals of learning, teaching fads and liberal indoctrination and pushed education, the inculcation of facts and skills between a child's ears, out the door. Of course, liberals who vehemently deny that spending money on educa-tion can ever be bad usually bray about "overkill" and "Pentagon gold-plating". "Think of the children" is the bleat of every politician or other scoundrel that ever lived, but what good does a Massachusetts child get from the extra $70,000 (present value of excess spending above the efficient level of many Southern states) that the Commonwealth spends to put her through the 12th grade? The money, enough to put the child through college, goes to adults, and she gets an inferior education in return for serving as a poster child for higher taxes.

The flowering of the "military-industrial complex" under the Kennedy-Johnson Administrations also co-incided with a number of oth-er phenomena. Johnson, the successful peace candidate with a war to sell, had embraced civil rights as a means of popularity with the left, but this also lost him his old oil money backing. Johnson went further left, advocating a measure of socialized medicine to raise political capital. Whereas other countries had controlled doctors' wages, the U.S. did not, making that largely Jewish group move from the comfortable to the rich; the house call died, in the cause of national health, of course. The old economic saw was "Guns and Butter", but there was no butter, just political grease. Along with the coddling of doctors, Johnson also made tax-break gifts to Jewish media lords, along with, as 1968 neared and his search for contributors grew more frantic, an embrace of Israel with tax-payers' money. Of course, not every thing Johnson did was for his political ends. The Highway Beautification Act, after all, was only incidentally political; mostly, it was just to put the screws to those highway signs cutting into the ad revenue of the Johnsons' CBS TV and radio stations, and casting the Johnsons as public benefactors in the process, with a generous assist from their national media lackeys.

The advent of Medicare and Medicaid in 1965 came upon a nation which had achieved extended private insurance coverage to the bulk of its population and had among the world's best indices in such things as infant mortality rate (13.3 per 1,000 births as early as 1951). And this had been achieved at 5-6% of GNP, as compared to the 8-9% level typical of nations with socialized medicine, with its usual flight of doctors to the U.S. and its rationing of health services to make money available for the scads of bureaucrats deemed necessary to do the rationing which their presence on the public payroll necessitated. American spending on health has zoomed to 14% of GNP in a generation ("inflated American health costs are chiefly a consequence of medical insurance policies adopted to evade the government's World War II wage and price controls" gibbers conservative columnist R. Emmett Tyrrell, Jr., who evidently blacked out during the reign of LBJ), and health indices which had been improving leveled off or even decreased. And the spending increase was not merely the 4% of GNP gobbled up directly by the two new programs; by the mechanism of third-party reimbursement, wherein governments enforce equal protection of the laws by mandating different rates for different types of payers for health services, private patients were soon subsidizing Medicare and Medicaid patients, as doctors and hospitals gouged their quickest-paying and most reliable debtors with ever higher rates, in order to ratchet up the "Blue", private insurance and government-reimbursed rates.

2% of the nation's entire GNP was soon involved in this particular cost-shift of money from people actually needing health services to the extent of being willing to spend their own money to other people using ambulances as taxis and expensive emergency room visits for routine medical treatments. After all, it was cheaper than spending pocket money for a taxi, or cheaper than spending their own money on a visit to a doctor's office. The healthy poor soon became the nation's most frequent seekers of medical treatment, a government-subsidized way to get out of the house that those in poor health were less able to enjoy. And that was perfectly foreseeable at the advent of Medicare and Medicaid, that stripping responsibility from consumption would lead to irresponsible consumption (including of course fraudulent billing, which is almost impossible with cash customers aware of the treatment they received, but ever more likely the more separate the payer is from the putative recipient). The old and the poor, those previously with the greatest incentive to economize and avoid unnecessary care, had been stripped away from the medical market, if not from medical care. Those left over were usually more affluent on the average (some of the old are very rich, and hardly needed Medicare), and had both fewer chronic conditions as well as jobs and families to look after; they were less price-sensitive to the gouges that would soon occur. Medicare and Medicaid performed the work of marketing segmentation, wherein an industry with nothing new in the way of production looks to subsidize its inefficiency by differentiating its customers beyond the mere matter of their needs for particular services. It is like the airlines trying to sell the same seat for more money to those whom they can gouge; strangely enough, while scrambling for such a cheesy advantage, they lose sight of their business, and even go out of business.

And, of course, Medicare and Medicaid, having done miniscule good for massive expenditures, are now sacred cows. The so-called "debate" on national health care lurches forward on the ground that the previous fiascos are not fiascos, and that despite all of that money spent on these liberal programs, more such reforms are needed, more expensive pillaging in the name of the public health. The threat of too expensive health care for the non-insured is naturally enough precisely the product of Medicare and Medicaid, the unshackling of financial control for need, and the posited cure is the usual, more of the same snake oil. Note that Bill Clinton, bragging in the 1992 primaries that he "had" a plan for national health care, went through a song-and-dance about waiting on the Hillary Commission's revue before taking any action as President. Taking no action including proposing and signing a 1994 tax increase on all American payrolls to continue funding Medicare's hit on the economy. Paying more for the same system is insane -- we need an end to price-fixing by organized medicine and government, including an end to artificial barriers to medical education. More doctors, from less expensive programs, would bring down medical prices if price-fixing were banished.

The tragedy of money wasted on bootless health programs, bootless gold-plated edudoctrination, bootless job-training, etc. is that money is not being spent on things more needed, on defense, on prisons, on asylums, on housing, on roads and other transportation needs, on less polluting energy sources, on American manufacturing capacity. One effect of spending an extra 6% of GNP on wasteful health programs has been that the drag upon the air conditioning industry of America alone has produced more offsetting ill effects than all of the good produced by Medicare and Medicaid. Air conditioning in hot months has three positive effects on health. First, cutting temperature and humidity cuts down on household molds that cause future asthma and allergies in susceptible children exposed to them. Second, cutting temperature somewhat for sleep aids in cardiac maintenance; air conditioned people have less heart disease than do the over-heated. Third, domestic and other violence skyrockets in hot months among the non-air conditioned, enough to make a measurable demographic impact (guns, there all year, and also there all year where gun deaths are insignificant, get blamed, such as that HBO "special" about a "typical" American day, which just happened to be in July, when violence peaks). Air conditioning is just another of those non-interventionistic health advances such as clean water, cheap washable clothing, adequate food and sanitation.

To liberals, however, something useful that works is wasteful, conspicuous consumption; send in Wee Jimmy Jerkie to monitor the nation's thermostats (if there is a crisis of political leadership, some nit panicking over high oil prices, well, depriving people of efficacious shelter will take their minds off politics). But there is no need for a federal Department of Air Conditioning, because people can still spend their own money for it, just as they used to for efficient medical care. The real need in that direction is less government, and less waste in government, so that people will have more money to spend on their doctor bills, or on air conditioning, or even to save. The liberal need is the exact opposite of that, keeping their political pump primed with all sorts of rubbish, the more useless the better. After all, when something actually useful isn't working, people notice. But Modern Liberalism, having long since moved away from anything useful (the Tennessee Valley Authority, dams and Army Corps of Engineers projects became anathema during the Kennedy Administration, with the Peace Corps, do-gooders donating their precious selves, most auspiciously making up the slack), has nothing to worry about on that score. None of their projects is useful, so the fact that none of them works is not noticed; it is sufficient for the purposes of liberalism that enough people assume that they do. The military, and its various weapons, cannot, liberal legend aside, operate on that basis because they face reality-testing.

Chapter 9 - **Radiation** (More InfraRed than Light)

There are two main types of radiation, ionizing radiation caused primarily by radioactive decay particles, and electromagnetic radiation, such as that emitted variously by the sun, the earth, atomic or hydrogen bomb blasts, or radio and television stations. The damage produced by nuclear weapons is primarily from their blast effects -- hard, light and heat radiation and shock waves destroying and burning areas proportional to their proximity to the blasts, as well as the "fallout" of radioactive atoms contaminating a somewhat wider area. Aside from death, quick or lingering, fallout offers the possibility of mutagenic damage, cancer and birth defects. It also offers the opportunity to parade naturally occurring genetic anomalies as the product of fallout, from nuclear testing or nuclear power. The birth of radiation propaganda meant the death most quickly of that old garden curiosity the "sport", since chalked up, near Three Mile Island or most distantly from Chernobyl, to radiation damage. Anti-nuclear propagandists are not the types to overlook a four-leaf clover, but the mushroom cloud is more dangerous.

The area of a single blast's damage is limited by several factors: the curvature of the earth, the blast's tendency to radiate in all directions (up into the air and down into the ground, wasting most energy instead of effectively targeting it) and the centrality of damage (the blast center, or "Ground Zero", is massively "overkilled"). Doubling an individual bomb blast only increases the area of destruction by about 41% (not 30%, as reported by the "reputable" media), with the proportion declining as the horizon dips away. Any increase in the power of a radiating blast increases the area affected only by the square root of the increase -- that of 2 being 1.414. A 1-megaton bomb 500 times more powerful than the 20-kiloton Hiroshima bomb would destroy an area only 22.3 times as large, for example. The principle is the area of a sphere, the same that Newton explicated as his Inverse Square Law for solar radiation, the main source of his day, as it were. Most nuclear nations make many bombs, so the possible areas devastated are greatly increased by increasing the number of possible blast centers. Two blast centers of a given power devastate twice the area as one, as opposed to only a 41% increase obtained by doubling the blast size of the one. It may be cheaper to make existing bombs more powerful than to build more, but only for awhile.

But such considerations as the death of millions or hundreds of millions have not proven lurid enough for left-wing propaganda. With the incredible all-too-possible, leftist rant has to stretch farther than ever in its attempts to transcend truth in the name of its self-proclaimed monopoly on higher morality and sensitivity. The initial effort in this direction was the propaganda concept of overkill, the proclamation that nuclear arsenals contain the energy-equivalent of a thousand pounds of TNT, or some greater amount, for "every person on earth!" and consequently that America should disarm while trusting other nations to do likewise.

But, of course, most such overkill takes place in the center of atomic explosions, and most of the hundreds that have taken place so far killed no one. Many combat uses would be against individual aircraft or ships or submarines, or against individual strategic missile silos in rural areas, with fairly light casualties in spite of expenditures of TNT-equivalents of thousands of tons per person. There is ample precedent for wastage incumbent upon the use of much more frugal and directed weapons. Most artillery shells, bombs and bullets miss, as witnessed by leftist propaganda during the Vietnam War, when opponents of America professed anguish that it was costing so much per enemy killed, so many bombs and shell and bullets wasted at such a cost. For their money, the hypocritical advocates of so-called "peace" (American defeat) suddenly wanted more killed.

Under this sort of macabre accountancy, all the nation needs is a single bayonet, and enemies stupid enough to successively impale themselves upon it. In the real world, of course, the situation resembles the parable of the mustard seed; just as well over 99% of an atomic blast is wasted energy, so do well over 99% of all bullets miss. If they didn't, wars would be much shorter and deadlier. The dull calculus of overkill lives on, over 99% missing, but still striking some luckless dullards as meritorious. For most people, however, such quantification, even if spurious, was too rational in appearance to tap their emotions to the extent requisite for leftist propaganda. Something scarier was needed, first the vividness of Ground Zero, then the intellectual squalor of Nuclear Winter.

The jab by the irrational at the subrational vulnerabilities of others took a morbidly comic turn with the Nuclear Winter hoax, a left-wing project that was meant to derail Reagan's not terribly efficient effort to rebuild America's military defense by moating the Pentagon with money. The old scares about Ground Zero were funny enough in their way -- Ground Zero being a bad place to be when any weapon is being tested, a switchblade for instance, but the Nuclear Winter folks tried to reach mental places where old fears about firestorms and radiation sickness had not penetrated. There are other fears, with their own subrational neural circuits, and Nuclear Winter tapped into fears of cold and dark, leaving only a few primals, such as falling and being bored to death, incapable of being worked into the scenario. But they are working on it.

The working of perpetual winter into the threat of nuclear war was, except for the hard-core cheerleaders of every leftist bowel movement, more than just a bit strained. There was an old George Carlin routine about Al Sleet, the Hippy-Dippy Weatherman, who tells viewers not to worry about thunderstorms on the radar, because he has picked up some Russian missiles. While the character might not have had the local appeal to most as did Carlin's spoof of a sportscaster to those of us who grew up near Kingston, Ontario, it had a wider appeal to the atomic-aged, those who had grown up in the shadow of the mushroom, if not of Biff Burns, the cliché-barking chihuahua. But even the mushroom had lost the immediacy of its threat, by virtue of just not happening, so it was jazzed up. Add a video game ("computer model" to the impressionable) or three to Al Sleet's radar, program it with alarmist foolery, and out comes "Don't sweat the missiles, though, because it's gonna snow later!" And, of course, the left finally provided an opportunity to actually do something about the weather, Disarm America.

Naturally, this hokum grew out of the Greenhouse Effect in one of its troughs, when people looking for alarmist rubbish about normal conduct decided that war, as normal human conduct, could be mined also. Although the point of the Greenhouse Effect was the supposition that dirty air makes the planet warmer by sopping up solar radiation (like it gets hotter in the shade, hey!), that leftist franchise had been taken. But, if stuff added to the air by man in peacetime makes the earth warmer, than stuff added to the air by man in wartime must, therefore, by indisputable computerized New Age logic, make the earth cold, and, *voilà*, Nuclear Winter! After all, the prospect of a billion or more people dying suddenly and many others slowly is just not terrifying enough, so someone has to go the extra mile and tack on cold, dark and, yes, what's that, suffocation, and the fear of suffocation.

Developed from the defective Greenhouse Effect, with its underestimate of the earth's oxygen supply and its refusal to admit that the earth too radiates (why it gets cooler at night usually), the Nuclear Winter scenario just did not make sense. It ignored both global amounts and their accounting rules. To illustrate that in miniature, in the early 1970s, it was put forth that the ship *Glomar Challenger* had been built, at a cost of hundreds of millions of dollars, to mine metal nodules found scattered under the oceans. A geologist's calculations showed the ship costing almost as much as the value of the minerals, and with expenses and the vast territory needed to be covered by the scooping, the purpose was denounced as folly or fraudulent. It was fraudulent, as the ship was CIA-funded, meant for salvaging Russian submarines.

Nuclear Winter/Greenhouse Effect calculations ignore the effect of superfluous terrestrial oxygen, and both also ignore the core statement of the Black-body Rule: a perfect emitter is a perfect absorber. What goes up into the atmosphere may either hinder or aid incoming energy in reaching the earth's surface, but to that same extent it will do the same to re-radiating heat trying to entrop (the venerable Second Law of Thermodynamics) off into space. Clouds may block the heat of the sun from reaching the surface, but if they are around at night they prevent the earth's heat from radiating back into cold space the same way. Thin atmospheres like the earth's just do not have that big an effect on global energy balances, and what effects there are largely offset. The problem with nuclear explosions is damage and fallout, not fallup.

Venus was once thought to have the potential to support life, in spite of receiving almost twice the solar radiation of the earth by the handicap of its closeness to the sun. The source of these delusions was two-fold, the thick cloud-cover of Venus and its high albedo, or apparent reflectivity, of solar radiation. But upon closer examination, it turned out that Venus's atmosphere is not reflecting, it is just radiating the heat that has built up from solar proximity. Venus, with nearly twice the solar radiation that the earth gets, does have more than twice the temperature differential with space normal than the earth has. Although Venusian heat is attempted to be turned to support the Global Warming mania, as though Venus' atmosphere is at fault and not its lack of distance from the sun, the planet apparently just does not have the hydrogen that the earth does, so that the compositions were never the same. Venus may have more than twice the temperature, but it is only twice as hot; the reason is that Venus has no water, or steam, so that it's a *dry* heat -- there's no humidity, as a Venusian Chamber of Commerce might point out. The same amount of heat raises the temperature of Venus more than it would if the planet had more water or other hydrogen compounds and their capacity to absorb heat; it has only a trace of hydrogen-containing sulfuric acid in its atmosphere, opaque but not important as a global heat repository.

But the water would still be very hot steam, and the type of atmosphere is otherwise irrelevant to a comparison with earth. Venus' thick blanket developed because of proximity to the sun and its heat; the heat did not develop as a result of the thick atmosphere catching and retaining heat, as in the Greenhouse Effect, or in blocking it while still somehow managing to lose it, according to the Nuclear Winter theory, which the surface heat of Venus rather bluntly refutes. Venus' heat is due to the sun's heat; its gravity traps the air that such heat thickens. And that thick opaque atmosphere is trillions of times denser than any increase in the earth's atmosphere possible from an all-out nuclear war using current weapons. But there is always progress. (Contrary to Greenhouse Effect hysteria, a greenhouse in fact traps heat by stopping convection -- the rising of heated air -- with glass ceilings, not by carbon dioxide, which is piped in and consumed by plants without playing a heating role. Liberals **do** know about glass ceilings -- they even use them as a paranoid metaphor for discrimination.)

Nuclear Winter, or the Disarm America crowd's new spin on the New Ice Age (also a practical certainty on a longer-term basis than Global Warming, but no betting pay-off) otherwise deep-freezed by the Greenhouse Effect, assumes that the atmosphere is a major determinant of global climate, instead of just the messenger, with ocean currents, of solar radiation. And what is the record of global weather change from the climatic carnage predicted even from a few hundred warheads? The assumption is that nuclear war, or burning oil fields, or any other liberal anxiety of-the-moment, would ape the cold snaps after the explosions of huge Indonesian volcanoes, Tambora in 1815 and Krakatoa in 1883. There **was** a tremendously harsh summer in 1816, when the Northern Hemisphere missed its annual warming and snow fell during crop seasons. New England rivers were frozen over even in July, and the Paris Conservatory burned the wooden frames of its harpsichords because of a summer shortage of firewood. Unlike some situations when a cold polar air mass tilts toward one hemisphere while the other is warmed by air draw up from the Equator, both hemispheres were chilled. Krakatoa certainly did not tardily cause the American East Coast's Blizzard of 1888, the product, as with so much weather in so-called "temperate" zones -- tempered like metal heated and suddenly chilled -- of a strong direct wind from an area of extreme weather, in that case the North Pole in winter.

In this century, Mt. St. Helens blew off a few cubic miles of dust that girdled the Northern Hemisphere, but to no discernible weather effect. By the same token, before World War II and its bombings were well underway, the European winters of the war's first three years were all extremely cold, while the large-scale burning of cities (Hamburg, Dresden, Leningrad, Stalingrad, Tokyo, Hiroshima and Nagasaki and dozens of other major cities with less spectacular, if serious damage), and the destruction of oil fields at Ploesti, Borneo and Sumatra, with the burning of German synthetic oil factories, should have, according to Nuclear Winter, brought even colder winters. Instead, they got somewhat warmer, until peace broke out; only then did inordinately foul weather re-occur, with bergs in the English Channel. If something large is supposed to produce a catastrophe, a smaller version should be expected to produce measurable results. World War II did not, being not a climatic event but a massive human tragedy, as nuclear war would be, also without being a climatic event.

Such a predictive scenario was rushed out by the Cringing America Society in time for the great debate about whether or not to throw Iraq out of Kuwait. While the computer-generated cartoon, Conventional Winter instead of Nuclear Winter, did not have quite the academic panache of a hundred law school deans' synchronized dysentery about a Supreme Court nominee who is not a loony leftist, there was the indubitable air of high-tech to fool someone, somewhere, maybe. As with the Nuclear Winter scenario itself, however, the same basic program was part of the Greenhouse Effect's computerized grab-bag, wherein stuff added to the atmosphere is supposed to either make the planet hotter or colder, instead of just dirtying its air. The oil fields did have some slight resemblance to volcanoes, but volcanoes are just too big to be really photogenic for more than a few seconds of a real big eruption. Tambora and Krakatoa exploded from beneath, and near the Equator, massively injecting dust into the high atmosphere by the tropic-generated world-girdling jetstream. The hundreds of Kuwaiti oil fires, by contrast, were simply fires producing more soot than usual, as if the oil had all been burned by the diesel bus engines of Holy Mass Transit. There was no explosive propulsion to altitude, and even Kuwait is much farther from the equatorial up-drafts than were the burning oil fields of Sumatra and Borneo in World War II. Such things are supposed, on alternate weeks, to produce the Greenhouse Effect, but Nuclear Winter was the key for warfare. The monsoons were supposed to be prevented, Asia to starve and the U.S. to see summer snow. Instead, Bangladesh got its usual flood and New York City was hot and humid. The author, listening to the Conventional Winter-in-Summer blather and considering the reliability of such sources as filibustering academic wacko Carl Sagan, got an air conditioner.

What is the public to think when no less than Carl Sagan -- and you really can't get less than Carl Sagan -- pronounces? After all, he is, besides being a chronic leftist agitator, an ex-Ivy League astronomer and a television scientist, a certifiable authority. Should he be taken as seriously as he takes himself? Let's look at his record in astronomy. Sagan has pronounced that for its climate the proximity of Venus to the sun is not "significant", when at .72 of an astronomic unit it receives 96% more solar radiation on an area than does the earth. Nearly twice as much of the only significant source of planetary heat isn't "significant"? The difference between liquid water and liquid lead isn't "significant"? This from a Greenhouse Effect raver. And look at Sagan's record on the "gas giant" planets, whose distance, size and gravitational effects on other bodies have long since shown them to have densities approximating that of water. Sagan, here joined by many other deep thinkers who should have known better, thought these planets would have atmospheres loaded with methane and ammonia. Those compounds are built around carbon and nitrogen, fairly heavy atoms for gases. Why would planets of light density have fairly heavy atoms in their atmospheres, their least dense areas? Quite obviously, they wouldn't, their atmospheres would have to made up of the only very light gases available, universally abundant hydrogen and helium, to give them any chance of attaining their accurately calculated densities. The observations? Why, hydrogen and helium, of course. Sagan was wrong again, and on his professional turf. Not surprisingly, he is even more unreliable when skylarking about his morbid political beliefs. Note that Sagan is an exponent of both Nuclear and Conventional Winters and the Greenhouse Effect, and note that Newton's Inverse Square Law, which astronomer Sagan ignored for Venus, is the same formula used to boost Ground Zero, another cause endorsed by Sagan. Sagan's is the authority which Lord Acton called Accredited Mendacity, crankery with a variety of cushy soapboxes. Solar activity, beyond our control, and other natural factors, such as earth's orbital wobbles (during a long-term solar cool-down, a major wobble puts an ice sheet on North America, and an additional minor wobble puts one on Scandinavia, but the cycle continues, and the cold-spots formed by sun, orbit, continents and currents disappear when the sum total of effects dips the other way), are the major determinants of earthly climatic conditions, including weather spells that only seem unearthly and unprecedented, bombarded as we now are by instant satellite reports on them. To say otherwise is hysteria, and when too many people believe such rot and try to "govern themselves", the predictable result is confusion and waste from panic-driven actions fed by misinformation and personal interests. The more technical matters of nuclear radiation are fields for similar activity.

Aside from the attempt of leftist environmentalism to generate manipulable fear from the general spectre and effects of nuclear war, there are collateral campaigns of misinformation about more specific items. One set of fears is subsumed under the category of ionizing radiation, mainly that produced by radioactive elements. To explain the realities that these fears build upon, a quick review of the atom is desirable.

All matter directly apprehendible by humans is composed of atoms, and those atoms are composed essentially of three particles: electrons, protons and neutrons. The proton is a fairly large particle, with a "positive" charge; in a stable atom, it is orbited by an equal number of small electrons, each with a "negative" charge. The number of protons determines the atomic number, or type of atom. Hydrogen's atomic number is one, helium's is two, carbon's is six, uranium's is 92, etc. A single proton forms the nucleus of an ordinary hydrogen atom, with a single electron orbiting. But atoms more complex than hydrogen require a third particle in the nucleus, the neutron, usually a combined electron and proton, which enables protons to remain in close proximity without flying apart from the repulsion of their identical positive charges. Neutrons are electrically neutral outside of the nucleus, but they are as heavy as protons, and make up half of the weight of most of the lighter atoms and even more of the heavy atoms.

While neutrons are necessary for complex atoms, two items about them are destructive. First, the neutron itself needs, under earth-normal conditions, the presence of a nucleus, preferably a stable one. A neutron by itself will soon decay into a proton and an electron (ejected too quickly to form a stable hydrogen atom from the two pieces) or an equivalent, and in many unstable, or radioactive, atoms a neutron will also decay, usually expelling a fast electron, or beta particle, and thereby becoming a proton. That changes the element involved. For example, carbon-14, a 6-proton atom with eight neutrons, two more than normal carbon atoms, will usually see one neutron expel its electron and become a proton, changing the mix of the nucleus to seven protons and seven neutrons, a normal nitrogen atom.

If there would not be enough remaining neutrons to form a stable nucleus, the neutron might leave, or the proton left by its decay will be expelled. A nucleus of deuterium, an unstable isotope, or nuclear variety, of hydrogen with the definitive single proton accompanied by a single neutron, cannot turn into a two-proton helium nucleus because there is not present additional neutrons for a stable two-proton nucleus. Instead, one neutron leaves to decay and become another hydrogen nucleus. For the light nuclei larger than hydrogen, there is generally a near equality of protons and neutrons. Small atoms with extra neutrons are unstable, or radioactive, and will eventually decay; but, for such light atoms, the decay is simple and usually produces a stable nucleus fairly quickly. The typical decays tend toward the beta variety, the transmutation of an excess neutron into a proton, with the expulsion of a high-speed electron-equivalent from the nucleus.

But larger atoms require disproportionately more neutrons to keep their higher concentrations of positively charged nuclei together. Radioactive decay of the largest atoms tends to produce other radioactive elements, until the final products of the many possible chains reach the lighter element range. The decay is also more complex at many stages, with heavier atoms tending toward decay by emission of an "alpha" particle, or a helium nucleus, two protons and two neutrons. While beta decay cause an atom to move up one in atomic number, alpha decay causes it to move down two. Alpha decay is more energetic than beta decay, but among heavier elements it usually produces a more stable atom than existed prior to its occurrence, because the left-over nucleus has that higher proportion of neutrons to protons desired by heavy nuclei. By contrast, beta decay in heavier atoms tends to make them more unstable, because one neutron is subtracted to add one proton, a double whammy against the stabilizing proportion of neutrons.

It was this process which was taken advantage of to form plutonium-239, the equivalent of fissionable uranium-235 with an added alpha particle, and hence also fissionable. The actual process first bombards non-fissionable uranium-238 with neutrons, preferably and economically in the company of uranium-235 being used for power generation, with uranium-239 resulting in some cases. By two quick beta decays, a uranium-239 atom becomes first neptunium-239 and then plutonium-239. 99% of natural uranium is uranium-238, only mildly radioactive as a "heavy" element, with enough neutrons (146) to stabilize its 92-proton nucleus. The same heavy element with slightly fewer neutrons, the isotope uranium-235, is more unstable, and therefore a good natural source for a chain reaction of fission, the splitting of a uranium-235 nucleus producing smaller nuclei, which, needing fewer neutrons per proton for their smaller nuclei, eject left-over neutrons to split other uranium nuclei. This is the paradigm of a fission chain-reaction, atomic, or nuclear, energy, including atomic, or nuclear, bombs, plutonium acting like U-235.

The atomic bomb requires heavy nuclei, for their instability and consequent fissionability. The resulting outburst of energy makes possible the opposite process, fusion, at the opposite end of the atomic scale. For if very large atoms make energetic splitting possible and easy for those with a shortage of neutrons, it is more profitable as an energy-releasing mechanism to fuse small atoms, because more can be fitted closer together, and because more energy is released by the fusion of smaller atoms. But fusion requires a greater investment in starting energy, because it takes more energy to weld nuclei together than it does to simply aid unstable ones to break apart.

Simple hydrogen is inadequate for fusion, however, because larger atoms, even those of helium, require neutrons which ordinary hydrogen atoms do not have to supply. The best compromise is to use the radioactive isotopes of hydrogen, one-neutron deuterium (hydrogen-2) or the rarer and more useful tritium (hydrogen-3). A further compromise is to combine deuterium and tritium, stabilizing them chemically by compounding with another light element, lithium.

The H-Bomb is an impressive combination of an atomic bomb, based on plutonium or uranium-235, whose fission triggers a fusion explosion, based on the tritium variety of hydrogen, in the bomb's jacket. Yet the various parts are themselves comparatively harmless, and it is only in the expensive and laboriously assembled bomb that the purified uranium-235 (or the mostly man-made plutonium) and tritium are seriously harmful. However, left-wing propaganda, as unstintingly promoted by the American media and its *laissez-faire* attitude toward its fellow leftist liars, has managed to demonize both ingredients, quite apart from their dangerous high-tech applications. Aside from media promotion of left-wing ideology, fear sells newspapers and boosts television ratings, although not as much as media presenters want -- when some sensationalized batch of misleading trash fails to click, the public is faulted for not paying attention. The failure of leftist marketing can never admissibly be attributed to the shoddy product, leftism itself.

In the 1988 presidential election, for example, the media's generation-long campaign to portray plutonium as "the most toxic substance in the universe" had been part of the build-up to elect Dukakis, or someone like him, President. It was with anger sullen or hot that the media, Dukakis partisans all, reacted when the Reagan EPA announced new research showing radioactive radon contamination of American housing to be a bigger and more ubiquitous health problem than previously thought. Radon, after all, is natural, and of little use in attacking the American military, or atomic power, or anything else that liberals despise. Dukakis supporters were upset that their panic-mongering had been nullified by the Republican exposure of a genuine health threat; the Republicans had hopped the Democrats' ideological freight-train and were free-riding on left-wing fear of radioactivity and other enviro-babble. Leftists threw a snit when they did not go into complete denial; the facts were politically inexpedient, and the radon story had, for ideological reasons, to be denigrated as a political ploy.

Of course, there are natural substances that are radioactive. Among the lighter elements germane to living tissue, radioactive isotopes of three elements are likely to be absorbed. Carbon-14, formed by solar radiation, is taken up by plants and thereafter may be absorbed by animals eating the plants. Water, fresh or salt, may be formed in small amounts from the radioactive isotopes of hydrogen. Because living tissues contain a great deal of water, and because of the faster decay of the heavy hydrogens than of carbon-14, more radiation is absorbed from water than from carbon-14 (although it is one effect of carbon dioxide in the air, a "Greenhouse Effect" villain and indispensable to terrestrial life, that more carbon-14 is formed). A trace mineral important to life, plant or animal, is potassium, which frequently consists of a radioactive isotope, but although it is fairly "hot" as a beta/gamma emitter, it is not taken in in great quantity.

But all of these items are useful and nutritive, something radon, or plutonium and uranium, are never (radon is in fact completely chemically inert, a noble gas, while uranium and plutonium form simple compounds). In fact, uranium compounds are so non-toxic, they were once used to color china a bright orange, and plutonium is chemically similar to uranium. And, of course, plutonium is similar in radioactivity to uranium-235, the percent of naturally occurring uranium which was present in that uranium dinnerware. Today, even using uranium depleted of plutonium or uranium-235, the 1 percent of natural uranium that gives it 99.8% of its radioactivity, is unthinkable for dinnerware. Plutonium, that most toxic substance in the universe, at least for attacking the military and atomic power, was the real target for liberals, so it needed to be constantly portrayed as a villain in and of itself. Except, of course, that plutonium is not only non-toxic, but its radioactivity has been grossly exaggerated -- it is important in bombs and power plants not because of its radioactivity *per se,* but because it can emit energy and neutrons in a chain reaction with other plutonium or uranium-235 atoms, explosively as atomic bombs (including as triggers for hydrogen bombs), or gradually to provide heat for electrical power generation.

Radon is not toxic either, but it is **TWO MILLION TIMES** more radioactive than plutonium, and, because it is chemically inert and naturally a gas, it gets into people's lungs, where the damage of its radioactivity can be maximized (the isotope of radon called thoron is even more virulently radioactive, about six billion times as radioactive as typical plutonium, but it is so rare and short-lived it seldom reaches anyone's lungs). A typical radon atom's beta/gamma decay is only about 5/6 as radioactive as a typical plutonium atom's alpha decay, but the unstable radon atom is about 2.4 million times as likely to break down at any given moment. The gas radon is also eminently inhalable and in people's houses, not just in small lumps in distant bombs and in fuel rods. The comparative danger of radon and plutonium might best be summed up as two packages of dynamite. One package of six sticks, the plutonium, can be expected to go off, in some distant location, sometime in the next 25,000 years. The radon package of dynamite is smaller, only five sticks, but it will go off sometime in the next week, possibly in your cellar or even in your lungs. Which is more dangerous?

The other H-Bomb ingredient, tritium, an isotope of hydrogen with two neutrons, also has had to be demonized, although it is naturally occurring, from solar radiation acting upon water vapor in the atmosphere, and ubiquitous, in every glass of water and in New York harbor, for example (where there is enough tritium to make many H-Bombs). So what was the ploy of opponents of a New York naval base? That a nuclear weapon might fall into the harbor and, for a few hours, raise the level of tritium even higher than it already naturally is, before the tides and the Hudson quickly equalize the radioactivity to its natural background level.

The reason that there is a background **level** is that tritium breaks down quickly (or, in the periodic table sense, breaks up, into helium), so that there is a natural equilibrium between that produced by solar radiation and that lost through the substance's intrinsic instability and radioactive decay. For that same reason, tritium in H-Bombs has to be periodically recharged, because it naturally vanishes, lowering the potency of the bomb as it sits, and eventually, if unrecharged, just leaving it as a plutonium or uranium-235 trigger bomb with not enough tritium for fusion chain-reaction. To maintain an H-Bomb arsenal, then, a nation must continually refine and concentrate natural tritium from water (old ground water has the least, because its solar-exposed tritium has broken down and not been replaced, and deep quiet lake bottoms have the most, because water molecules with tritium are heavy and concentrate at the bottom), or manufacture it by artificial radiation.

American tritium manufacture is done in South Carolina, with the American nuclear arsenal again under leftist attack because of tritium leaks. Hysterical and ill-considered multi-billion dollar schemes were afoot to close the plants and "clean up" the tritium in lengthy projects. Yet there is no need to clean up tritium, other than when it is convenient and economically practical to recover it instead of producing it, because it is an ephemeral substance. Leave it alone and it disappears anyway, half of an amount in 12½ years, with no cost other than shutting a few wells in a South Carolina neighborhood that is practically unpopulated anyway. Some tritium absorption is natural anyway -- even dysentery is natural -- but as a particle emitter it has to be absorbed to do damage. Usually, this is through water, but bodies use water and most other hydrogen compounds quickly, so that most is quickly replaced by other intake (quarts of water per day, lesser amounts of starches and fats, a percentage of body weight per day, as against an atom that typically does no damage in an average decade). Although far more tritium atoms can be concentrated in a small space, in reality such things are rapidly diluted, such as by leaching into a river. (Radon in your cellar is a similar quantity, and the effective way to handle it is to dilute it, by releasing it to the atmosphere, where its decay would be completely unlikely to affect anyone.) But when tax revenues, or federal borrowings, are available, and political capital can be made by expensive "solutions" (including the generous awarding of contracts to apolitical contractors) to military-related non-problems, efficiently addressing a condition for a few hundred thousand dollars must be foregone, and the Treasury pillaged. After all, it is an archetypical "national problem", a temporary situation in a small patch of South Carolina; therefore let money be authorized and contracts let.

The greatest unappreciated hazard of nuclear war comes from the left-over uranium-238 that does not turn into plutonium. In a reactor accident, uranium-238 obviates the so-called "China Syndrome" by preventing the fissile uranium-235 and plutonium already formed from a totally "run-away" reaction (as was belatedly shown at Chernobyl -- after the panic and attention had passed -- and at less publicized incidents, where melted uranium clung to cooling pipes rather than burrowing into the earth). In nature, uranium-238 probably had a similar effect, preventing the dispersion of natural deposits of uranium in the manner of those of thorium, also potentially fissionable, but evidently lacking a similar non-fissile brake like uranium-238 in early terrestrial history, when there were greater concentrations of radioactive materials because they had not yet undergone eons of slow decay. Extensive, if not intensive, thorium deposits occur in India and Brazil, two nations on the fringe of nuclear weaponry.

But for atomic bombs and most reactor fueling requirements, there is far more left-over uranium-238 than is needed for atomic purposes. This uranium-238 waste-product, purified by removal of its more economically valuable isotopes, is however somewhat valuable because of its weight. Lead has a specific gravity of 11.34, but depleted uranium is nearly 68% heavier by volume mostly because of its greater load of neutrons. Among the uses of such depleted uranium, two are on account of this weight. Depleted uranium is used as a counterweight in thousands of large jet aircraft, with many jumbo jets utilizing a thousand pounds of it, because it can fit the necessary weight into small and aerodynamic fairings. High-velocity shells of tanks, armored personnel carriers, light anti-aircraft guns and aircraft machine guns are mostly made out of depleted uranium. Some late-model American tanks even have depleted uranium armor. The reason is that a shell of a given size has more armor-penetrating power, or other damaging ability, proportionate to its weight, and depleted uranium is simply very heavy. For the modest cost in velocity for the much heavier shell, the greater weight gives a much higher payoff in momentum and kinetic energy. Consequently, thousands of aircraft, thousands of anti-aircraft guns, thousands of tanks and tens of thousands of armored personnel carriers carry hundreds or even thousands of pounds of depleted uranium apiece. There is a lot of it out there.

Another use of depleted uranium is for jacketing atomic or hydrogen bombs, with the blast producing far more fallout than a normal atomic or hydrogen blast. For example, Hiroshima and Nagasaki were fairly radioactive for only a few weeks after their 1945 bombings, because the bulk of their ten thousand-pound atomic bombs were of iron and aluminum, which do not form long-chained radioactive isotopes. Depleted uranium does, however, as proved by the use of less than two hundred pounds of it in a 1953 hydrogen bomb test. Fishermen a hundred miles away were killed, and forty-one years later the island used is still not safely habitable.

The use of tactical nuclear weapons against airports or concentrations of armored vehicles, with their supplies of depleted uranium, would repeat that test experience on a massive scale. It is that possibility, not phantoms like "Nuclear Winter", or plutonium or tritium scares, or China Syndromes, that is the principal danger of nuclear war apart from the immediate blast casualties. Here again, however, the initiative of President Bush in ending the deployment of American tactical nuclear weapons, a move made possible by America's previous resolve in outwaiting the Soviets and in refurbishing its conventional arms capabilities, stole what should have been a legitimate peace issue. The danger of depleted uranium in tactical nuclear war just never hit home to the left, because it was an actual danger, something those who aim at the irrational, in politics and policy, just cannot grasp.

And also in reality, the ubiquity of depleted uranium means that a nation assembling a nuclear weapon can easily make it into a more terroristic weapon with a depleted uranium jacket. But since leftist rant requires all fallout to be equal, the short-lived light isotopes from the relatively clean bombs of the super-powers to equal the potential long-lived and heavier radiation from a deliberately dirty bomb, the left will have trouble grasping that real calculus also. The abstruseness of the subject has been relatively unimportant to the propagandists, however, for most of the perceived complexity is their own obfuscation. But fear of nuclear war certainly affected policy-makers, exacerbating their inability to deal with conventional war, such as the Vietnam War, the conventionaliity of which was reflexively denied by liberal policy-makers. The refusion of left and liberal took place in the crucible of the Vietnam War, and their calculus there was also defective.

The next chapter compares the Vietnam and Gulf Wars, with more accuracy than that of old opponents of winning the former trying to prevent the latter from being fought at all. They were happy to denounce the Gulf War before the war, obsessing about the presumed toll of American boys; they were happy to continue to denounce the Gulf War during its short waging, finding ecological damage and potential catastrophe from a vengeful Iraq's destruction of the Kuwaiti oil fields. But Arabian oil is sweet, with less sulfur than American crude, and also light in weight, tending to float more in water. The water being polluted was the sunny Persian Gulf, where sunlight and oxygen quickly combusted the volatile light oil as the dour Alaskan sun failed to do with the heavier and sourer oil dumped by Exxon's tanker. The Persian Gulf's ecosystem proved durable, having been tested by the hundreds of tankers attacked during the Iran-Iraq War. And, of course, the earth's weather failed to yield up the prophecised New Ice Age of Conventional Winter. But even after victory, the nay-sayers were still probing for a hot-button, more angrily than ever, having been proved wrong by the facts and politically impotent by the adoption of policies they had railed against. They now sought to repeat their post-Vietnam War propaganda victory over the defoliant "Agent Orange", to which various maladies had been attributed despite the lack of those problems among eaters of American rice, long weeded with Agent Orange, or among those living along power-line rights-of-way kept clear by the demonized defoliant. Their target was depleted uranium, with the initial salvo fired from London, co-incidentally the export center of weapons and armor using competing technologies (laminated, rather than spaced depleted uranium, armor and hot-or-hard, rather than heavy, projectiles). The logical problem of this alleged syndrome is that uranium and its compounds -- including the ceramic with that magic orange color -- depleted or otherwise, have long been used industrially without producing the complained-of symptoms. In short, it was the usual agitation with no more foundation than the usual electronic and chronic soapboxes, another media event, the same old hoopla with no point sharper than its shabby falsity.

New media plutonium hoopla in September 1994 was to protect the budgets of liberal intelligence agencies, domestic and international. As their Cold War rationale faded, plutonium terrorism was trotted out, with "only one millionth of a gram!" the supposed lethal dose. At that rate, the Nagasaki A-Bomb would have killed 25 billion people. Fissionable uranium-235, the chemical and radioactive analog of plutonium, is naturally present at one millionth of a gram per **ounce** of typical rock or soil. Bureaucracies preserve only themselves, and at our expense.

Chapter 10 - **Vietnam and Iraq**
(A Tale of Two Wars)

The first large issue in Vietnam was the political context of the war. America's goal was fairly simple, preventing the conquest of South Vietnam by Communist North Vietnam. Opponents of U.S. involvement, whether isolationists, pacifists or more or less coy supporters of the Communists, proclaimed the on-going war a civil one, describing the North Vietnamese not as expansionary Communists, but as mainly nationalists. Why there had to be only one group of "nationalists", the side supported by international Communism, in what was supposedly a civil war, has never been explained. Such half-truths are like a coat of paint, strictly two-dimensional, only meant to be seen from one side and designed to cover something, in this case a ramshackle of lies, from the corrosion attendant upon exposure to fresh air. The most typical expression of the media and the other Communist supporters was the proclamation of Ho Chi Minh as the North Vietnamese George Washington, seeking to expel the U.S. from its (non)colony of South Vietnam, and seeking to re-unite "their country", which had in fact been three countries, before being united, with Cambodia and the two Laotian states, into a French colony.

Southern Vietnam, or Cochin China, had been the alien Champa Empire, whose Vietnamese settlers broke away from Annam, or Central Vietnam, which still controlled one of the Laotian states. Prior to the permissible onset of "colonization", by Napoleon III's France, the entire area was a hodge-podge of contention, with China usually occupying, attacking or otherwise exerting influence in Tonkin (Northern Vietnam) and Cochin China vying for control of Cambodia with Thailand, which also controlled a Laotian state rivalling Annam's. As against the others, the Cambodians were the senior surviving settlers, while the French were only more recent invaders than the Vietnamese, Thais, Laotians and Chinese, all from the north, or the destroyed Chams from the East Indies. What the French did was two-fold: restricting Chinese influence, with much of nearby southern China instead falling under French influence, and unifying the area under one government. The "colony" thus produced was not a true colony, however, in that there was little French settlement; rather, it was a protectorate. By contrast, the rebellious American colonies were European settlements more than they were dominions over natives.

Even more fanciful flights of the George Washington allegory had North Vietnam in the role of colonial America, but what the scenario writers left out was something to play the role of South Vietnam. The obvious choice would have been Canada, but that haven for American draft-dodgers had been far better treated by the U.S. than South Vietnam was by the North. The first U.S. attempts to recruit Canada had been an invitation that it send delegates to a meeting; Ho's group had dealt in murder and betrayal. Like the U.S.'s early efforts, albeit with a frequent disregard for the rules of war, North Vietnamese victory had resulted in partial independence. Flights of refugees to the still "colonial" area occurred in both cases, with the less scrupulous North Vietnamese using such movement between the Vietnams to infiltrate a cadre of terrorists, something the evil U.S. somehow failed to think of when the Empire Loyalists decamped to Canada. The North Vietnamese attempt to conquer the South, by then independent of France, was supported by the left, who oppose colonialism except when it is being done by Communists; by contrast, the American repeat effort to incorporate Canada, a minor cause of the War of 1812, is still condemned by liberals, because it was an action of their favorite villain, the U.S., even though Canada was at the time and subsequently still a colony, part of that Empire cottoned to by those Loyalists.

And what of the vexed question of Vietnamese elections, supposedly sabotaged by the U.S. in the 1950s? That Red herring still smells, as the North Vietnamese have had nearly four decades of control in the North, without bothering to hold elections, and nearly two decades of control of all of Vietnam, again without an election in sight. Plainly, the U.S. is not at fault, stifling the democratic inclinations of a bloodthirsty Communist dictatorship. But it was always North Vietnam that tried to disrupt elections, the ones that were held in the South before its conquest quashed them, and any other manifestations of freedom. But all of that could have been easily extrapolated from the early career of North Vietnam's "George Washington".

Ho had (A) first left his purported country for France, the colonial power, and joined the French Communist Party (although the organization was of course unquestionably patriotic to some, its small quotient of loyalty was to the enemies of France, so Ho was not necessarily being an unpatriotic Vietnamese by joining it, just a master of ambition and intrigue); (B) then moved to Moscow and worked for the Communist government there (invaluable for freeing distant Vietnam from the distant French, possibly); (C) then moved to China and Hong Kong as a Communist activist (freeing China from itself, and Hong Kong from the iron heel of Britain, are the sort of activities all patriots put high up on their lists of priorities; besides, Hong Kong is indubitably closer to Vietnam than is Russia); (D) become a "political prisoner" in Hong Kong (invaluable to the resumé of an authentic revolutionary: getting caught proves your commitment, if not your competence, and the fact that you were let go proves that you are probably willing to betray your leftist comrades, something respected by those inveterate intriguers, if by no one else); and (E) as the Japanese occupied French Indochina, returned there to collaborate with them, trying to exterminate legitimate Vietnamese nationalists before the expected return of the French, in the hope that killing off the real leaders would make Ho himself the top dog among the natives. Just like a George Washington to murder his opponents! Such a man was emphatically not patriotic, the view peddled by American journalists and academics, people whose own patriotism is beyond question. Just ask them, they'll tell, as honestly as they would if they were Ho Chi Minh, their George Washington.

In Vietnam, as in China, there was a chummy relationship between the local Communist Party and a right-wing foreign power not at war with Mother Soviet Russia. The Vietnamese difference was that there was no local government, no Chiang Kai-shek, to do some fighting against the same Japanese invaders. There was in Vietnam therefore no need for a "*gung-ho*" propaganda effort, to silk-screen collaboration with the Japanese, including the murder of Americans who fell into Communist hands. Ho's career recalls George Washington's in only one respect, the latter's principal historical vice of having been a slave-holder, albeit by inheritance, and of people who were a distinct minority, not the mass of inhabitants of the U.S. Ho, by contrast, helped extend the internal passports and labor camps of Communist Eurasia.

The Communist explanation of the America goal in Vietnam? Those massive deposits of offshore oil that we used to read so much about, and so often, back while the war was going on, courtesy of those unquestionably patriotic journalists, still working on or so nauseatingly eulogized. Since there was no on-shore oil in Vietnam, that angle was what Al Haig used to call a non-starter. We hear much less about that offshore oil with the North Vietnamese victorious, even less than about World War II atrocity comics; the question which liberals prefer to bring up is how much money we should be giving to the Communists, for their violation of the "peace treaty". Of course, duly ratified treaties do have the force of law in this country, so we would therefore have to even disobey our laws, but as long as the purpose is to help our enemies, the liberal Democrats will favor it. Why the inhabitants of an oil patch, long allied to Soviet Russia, the world's largest oil producer, need money is left unexplained. The oil has not flowed, and we know it is there, because the same people who called Senator McCarthy a witchhunter said that it was. But the U.S. cannot sue for slander, and treason statutes have fallen out of favor, unlike treason, the only economic activity which flourishes courtesy of the American left. The nearest oil is closer to Borneo than to Vietnam, out under international waters. The same distance would put Memphis, Tennessee in the Louisiana oil patch and Hartford, Connecticut in the Pennsylvania crude class, oil for the lamps of Vietnam, shedding a lurid light upon the generosity of journalistic/academic cant in this country; drilling rights in Vietnam, Memphis and Hartford can safely be said to be dirt-cheap. If there were oil in Vietnam, undermining America's war effort would have been even more paramount in the aims of this country's leftist liars: perhaps they would then have tried to circulate innuendo that there was no such oil.

For years, Vietnam has indeed been offering oil exploration rights, but the bidding has been tepid in the extreme, with the absence of gushers in the Philippines having put a damper on already dim prospects. Ironically, the Vietnamese Ministry of Oil, usually the official importer for whatever oil a straitened socialist economy can afford, is located in the old American embassy building in "Ho Chi Minh City", a building that Ho's troops repeatedly attacked. Supporters of the Vietnamese Communists have been trying to get permission for U.S. oil companies to explore offshore Vietnam, the right to have the Communist government collect American fees for mere exploration, and then to "nationalize" any deposits discovered. One cause of South Vietnam's collapse was the cut-off of American aid, including the money to buy oil, at the urging of these vermin. As with their support of the Communists during the war, *cui bono*?

The context of American aid to South Vietnam was two-fold. First, it was an adjunct to U.S. treaty obligations under the SEATO rubric, a duly ratified instrument to which the U.S. was a party, and which specifically contemplated South Vietnam as an object of aid. Second, American involvement was a response to North Vietnamese retaliation for the aid, attacks on Americans in the South and in the Gulf of Tonkin. The increase in U.S. efforts was authorized by a 98-2 Senate vote. Why Lyndon Johnson did not ask for a declaration of war is not, like many policy decisions of that era, fully known, in large part because the documentary record was rifled by leftist moles Daniel Ellsberg and company, seeking to demonize the war as it shifted to the ever-eager shoulders of Richard Nixon. The Pentagon Paperboys advanced their own careers as rapidly as that copy they sent to the Russian Embassy with the alacrity and homing instincts of an Alger Hiss, a Julius Rosenberg, a Lee Harvey Oswald or a Jim Jones. Liberalism, always quick to find honor among thieves, bestowed such as its meager stores permitted. Morton Halperin, for example, an Ellsberg supporter within the Nixon White House and the outraged target of wiretaps, was with the ACLU and the "Center for National Security Studies" (no kidding, espionage and wreckage of archives constitute "studies"!) before being invited aboard the Clinton Administration as Assistant Secretary of Defense for Democracy and Peace-Keeping, so we know that both he and it have continued to find their own level. Supporting a Communist dictatorship, Communist spies and Communist terrorism are undoubtedly the sort of things Bill Clinton considers relevant; the failure of the tri-national U.N. observer teams in Southeast Asia is of course ignored -- split three ways, they didn't report any violence.

In the Gulf of Tonkin episodes, the second incident is the one most often disputed by North Vietnamese supporters, on the claim that it did not occur. As usual with the pleading of the low-lifes that defend criminals, there is a contradictory alibi for the North Vietnamese: the attack (which did not occur) happened by mistake (the North Vietnamese thought the American ships were South Vietnamese ships attacking the North's coast) or in self-defense (the American ships were helping the South Vietnamese ships attack the coast of North Vietnam, something that neither nation did by surface ship at any point in the entire war, even when an American battleship was brought out of retirement). How the state of mind of those on the North Vietnamese ships, which were sunk, was known has never been explained. The evidence that the attack did not occur is that some American crew members and flyers did not see it, at night and in bad weather. A ship under attack does not have its crew lounging at the rails, but rather at action stations. Sonar operators did not hear the high-pitched whine of noisy old torpedoes because the sonar of both American ships was low frequency, geared to screening out extraneous noise, not for hearing it or amplifying it; at high speed, as with ships maneuvering to escape torpedoes, the sonar sets did not work at all. Few people saw wakes of the torpedoes (as with the whine, the wake was a feature primarily of older torpedoes; those put into service for the twenty years prior to the 1964 incidents were extremely quiet and almost wakeless, especially in the real world). And the radar of F-8 Crusader day-fighters would not have been able to pick up wooden torpedo boats, and didn't. Obviously, anything which does not resemble the clarity of movies -- where the "realism" is fakery, underwater shots in the clear water of studio tanks, clear wakes and the soundman's added whine -- must needs be faked.

Of course, when the U.S. is attacked, but not damaged, the result is a fabrication, unless there is an anomalous situation where the left wants war. The left-wing's "good guys", America's enemies, never attack and never miss when they do attack. "Right-wing" bad guys, German U-boats, used to indeed miss, and sometimes even hit, after themselves being the target of unprovoked American attack, but reports of even the misses were soaked up by left-wingers eager for war, and for U.S. rescue of Mother Soviet Russia. Pete Seeger would start pencilling down lyrics in short-hand, without waiting for confirmation or controversy. If attacked and damaged, the U.S. has either been caught flatfooted or, more often, properly punished for provocative actions. The only innocent Americans are executed left-wingers; that is why they are executed by America the Bad, our country, always wrong. By deliberately prissy standards, it can be easily argued that there were no "real" naval battles in World War II, because there is only one (1) photograph, from hundreds of sea battles involving thousands of ships, showing two opposing ships on the same plate, and even that is far from clear, particularly to the willful with partisan reasons for denial. Maybe there were no battles, and the accounts were all concocted. Right-wing conspiracy buffs thought it peculiar that all three American carriers were out of Pearl Harbor -- hey, maybe **THEY** did the bombing!

Paranoia aside, America's Vietnam War split-imperative of both defending the South while punishing the North, as well as other morbid fears, led to Johnson's restricting the war's conduct, making the North free from U.S. invasion and leaving the most concentrated and important targets free even of U.S. aerial bombardment. As in Korea, victory became off-limits, but even earlier. Leadership, the social phlgistron most noticeable by its absence, is finding a strategy for achievement with available means. The U.S. has usually had superfluous means in this century, but, to repeat it yet again, misdirected riches are the worst sort of poverty. The absence of leadership in Vietnam came when Johnson gave a vote of confidence to American military power; a vote of confidence is usually taken when confidence is waning, and Johnson showed no confidence in victory, but an overweening faith in the power of micro-management. America was trying not to lose, instead of working to win. The selected strategy, or lack thereof, left the enemy's core strength intact, and not even seriously threatened. Ho and his fellow murderers would not flinch from a war of attrition in which their subjects' lives, but not the leaders' own lives or their power, would be sacrificed. After all, Johnson **needed** the enemy leaders to negotiate with. Johnson's overall misjudgment, the political context, largely determined the four military contexts, the mismanagement of the war.

First, the war became a matter of tactical collisions -- local defenses, search-and-destroy missions and bombings -- without a coherent strategic objective. The costs of a breakthrough were assumed over and over, but with the exploitation to make the cost worthwhile either prohibited or not sought (unused to winning, the U.S. military had some weaklings "sickened" by the Gulf slaughter of enemy troops who ran rather than surrendering). Enemy strategy more often sought large battles, which miscarried, but the long-term effect was to their sanguine advantage, as their side had eliminated dissent while the U.S. was being stabbed in the back by Communists tolerated by the society they were trying to undermine. Johnson's chosen path was harassment of the enemy, trying to drive them to the peace talks by gradual pressure and the proffer of the reward of lessening it, like trying to grease a bill through Congress. Battle and tactics (instead of the military itself) became political tools, rather than a means to the political goal of military victory by destruction of the enemy's war-making power or will to continue fighting -- "... nor will we bluster, bully or flaunt our power", was Johnson's pledge. But winning a war requires blustering, bullying and flaunting your power, to convince the enemy to give up. Shorn of the goal of victory, strategically pointless tactical fire-fights led to more tactical fire-fights, while bombings led to bombing pauses.

Johnson's quandary was partly a misapprehension of physical realities. Destruction is accomplished by the sudden and explosive release of energy, not by prolonged and episodic releases of far greater energies.

Push a door and it will open, if unlatched; the same amount of energy released quickly enough will destroy the door. An hour of a small thunderstorm releases more energy than an atomic bomb, but slowly and therefore not destructively, except in a child's imagination. The Ho Chi Minhs of the world are not frightened by thunderstorms or by ultimate weapons left unused. What defeats them militarily is the use of force in massive and devastating quantities against their power structures, the societies they control through violence and the monopoly of opinion it ensures. A society maintained by force, such as North Vietnam's, is impervious to gradual pressure, but even as it is hard it is also very brittle, and fairly easy to shatter with force applied to its center. Gradual escalation and warfare by gesture merely prolonged war's death and destruction, something of more concern to the open society which allows its enemies to undermine it. Broadcasting, itself a relatively new endeavor, used to be punishable when done for an enemy, by death (as of the British "Lord Haw-Haw" (William Joyce) for his work for the Germans) or imprisonment (as of the "Tokyo Roses"); but that war, at least the part when Mother Soviet Russia was at risk, was popular with the left, so the "right to dissent" did not exist.

The second military effect of Johnson's constraints was naval. There was no blockade. Command of the sea, never absolute, although always most effective against large vessels, was instead utilized in the Vietnam War solely as an adjunct to aerial bombardment. Large un-armed freighters were allowed to proceed peacefully with their massive cargos of war materiel and to unload in ports politically sheltered from U.S. action. Supplies were fair game for U.S. interdiction only after being loaded onto individual trucks or bicycles, as the Americans tried finesse, affecting a sporting touch, which just kept the killing going on. Enemy units in South Vietnam continued to be supplied by sea to "neutral" Cambodia (by allowing itself to be used as a supply conduit to invade a neighbor, Cambodia was no more neutral than Thailand, with its U.S. air bases, whose planes rather regularly overflew both Cambodia and similarly "neutral" Laos), and thence by regular truck convoys (uninterrupted for years by the U.S.) to the South Vietnamese border, where the supply line fragmented. There it became subject to U.S. attack, causing attrition but not a decisive break in Communist supply. American foolishness politically protected North Vietnam's Cambodian supply line at its three choke-points, vulnerable freighters en route to Sihanoukville, their unloading, and the long overland haul in Cambodia. Until 1970, only the last of these was ever really attacked by the U.S., and that sparingly, allowing years of steady use and cumulative effect upon South Vietnam and upon American nerves. The vaunted Ho Chi Minh Trail was important mostly as a source of fresh troops, at least until the freighters to Cambodia were cut off by the overthrow of its collaborationist government. Blockade would have been less destructive.

The re-activated battleship *New Jersey* was destructive only for a year. Vietnam was a long, largely coastal, country, maximizing the area reachable by the *New Jersey*'s guns. Furthermore, the coastal areas of South Vietnam were farthest away from the North Vietnamese supply lines from Cambodia and Laos, so Communist coastal supply centered on smuggling sampans convoying supplies past the "DeMilitarized Zone" or down the Mekong River from Cambodia, or indeed transferring seized food supplies within coastal South Vietnam.

Critical to this effort was the network of Communist tunnel-complex strongholds along the coast. These depots proved vulnerable to the *New Jersey*'s guns, much more penetrating and disruptive to tunnels than was napalm or the usual 750-lb American bombs used in Vietnam -- battleship shells need to survive the trauma of being fired, and so have more penetrating power against soil than do conventional bombs, high explosive wrapped in sheet metal. (The U.S. did use much heavier bombs to clear helicopter landing strips in the jungle, but tunnels, in areas away from annoying tree roots, were unaffected.) The major North Vietnamese objection to the full-scale start of the prolonged "peace talks", along with a strange emphasis on the independent repre-sentation of their puppets the Viet Cong (the North was apparently proud of presenting itself as intervening in a civil war, something its partisans accused the U.S. of doing), was the withdrawal of the *New Jersey* from the war. The U.S. capitulated on both issues, showing its essential loss of nerve and failure to grasp the nature of the war, or its conduct, and consequently to prosecute either or, in the court of public opinion, to defend either.

The North objected to the battleship because it had been effec-tive; the Pentagon, under Nixon and Laird, spinelessly remothballed it as if it were obsolete. The media, which had long since denounced the battleship as obsolete, continued to do so, despite the enemy's (the nation's enemy, not the media's!) position that a battleship was of more concern than were clouds of U.S. bombers. Not realizing the import-ance of the enemy's tunnels, neither the U.S. Air Force or Navy took the obvious step of converting available battleship shells to bombs, as the Japanese had so profitably done with the armor-piercing variety in 1941.

North Vietnam itself, in addition to its rail links with China, also largely immune from American attack, received the bulk of its war materiel by sea, including most of its 100,000+ Soviet surface-to-air missiles, more a threat to the North than to American aircraft. 99%+ missed their American targets, and just blew random holes in the North, including Hanoi, often off-limits to American bombs but not to "un-friendly fire"; the North's massive anti-aircraft gun batteries, also supplied by sea, achieved the same effect. Gunfire did shoot down far more American planes than did the missiles, however, due to their flying at fashionable, and dangerous, low altitudes.

The third military ramification of Lyndon Johnson's political confusion was the shackling of American airpower. Airpower is most effective against large ships (off-limits), rail traffic (concentrated along the Chinese border and in the Hanoi-Haiphong area, and usually off-limits), large population concentrations (Hanoi and Haiphong, usually off-limits) and airfields. The enemy air force was concentrated on off-limits fields, allowing the North to initiate air-to-air combat when the odds were most favorable to it; the U.S. attacked airfields empty of planes but with heavy anti-aircraft defenses. The least effectual targets for aircraft, sparse road traffic, bridges and dispersed enemy units, were chosen the most often, because efficient airpower was politically eschewed.

The misspent American air efforts were exacerbated by the prolongation of the war, which made North Vietnam's ground fire, on the tactical level contemptibly ineffective compared to American anti-aircraft capabilities, cumulatively impressive over the span of years engendered. In the early part of the war, there were also unexpectedly high losses (compared to Korean War experience), easily foreseeable under the circumstances, to MiGs in dogfights. Those losses tapered off with the end of the first dogfight phase. When American fighters re-equipped with guns and better tactics became deadlier, the North Vietnamese switched to the unpublicized offensive, sacrificing most of their Air Force in suicidal attacks on U.S. air bases in Thailand. Both the North Vietnamese attacks on the Thai air bases and their crushing defeat, the loss of nearly two hundred aircraft to American Hawk anti-aircraft missiles, went unreported; the U.S. did not want to announce the victory, for fear that the war's critics, American Communist supporters, would call it a "widening" and an "escalation" of the war. The North Vietnamese were happy to keep a fiasco secret, while not offending diplomacy or "opinion", as if either were going to desert them. Some ever-loyal American "reporters", hearing of crashes in the Thai jungles, did accuse the Air Force of concealing losses -- of American planes (which, when damaged in missions and crashing in Thailand, were reported as losses). The explosions produced by some shoot-downs were also attributed by the media to new Communist guerrilla activity, the war being deemed to have widened into Thailand in a politically correct context.

The U.S. was also "secretly" bombing Cambodia in this period. Both Cambodia and North Vietnam obviously knew about it, but they also wanted the bombing kept secret from diplomacy and opinion, because the existence of legitimate targets rather obviously implicated both North Vietnam's use of Cambodia and Cambodian complicity. The bombing was somewhat belatedly revealed, as a "scandal", by the U.S. media, which offered no explanation for the extraordinarily heavy level of Cambodian imports in the preceding years, or Sihanoukville's becoming a boomtown by virtue of the munitions traffic through it. The provocation both for the bombing and the subsequent U.S. incursion was substantially ignored, and the Cambodian incursion was bloodiest in the U.S., due to the "anti-war" hysteria whipped up by such selectivity.

Cambodia's neutrality, like Thailand's, had already been violated by the other belligerent, leaving each particular opponent under no obligation whatsoever to respect what had ceased to exist. The moral ground for the position of not censuring the second, or responsive, violator is quite solid, hoping to enable neutrals who wish to preserve their status to do so, by making one-sided exploitation of a haven impossible. A country whose neutrality has been actually violated should not be a reward for the aggressor, even if the violator is as politically correct as our free press. Neither Thailand or Cambodia had been violated in the first instance, the U.S. and the North Vietnamese being there with the consent of the respective government; Cambodia obviously dealt with the wrong side, and has paid a justly high price. Use of Cambodia as a supply conduit, the bombing and the incursion could all have been easily obviated at the outset. Blockade, or a Q-as-in-Cuber Quarantine, should have been the first U.S. act in the war, at a time when the future rock-throwing pyromaniacal international law scholars of Kent State were still officially in junior high school, in an earlier phase of their liberal indoctrinations.

The fourth military effect of Johnson's misjudgment lay in the misuse of ground troops, their supply, organization and use. South Vietnamese troops were always inadequately equipped and supplied. Media legends about guerrillas being supplied by abandoned or captured arms were never less true than regarding the Viet Cong. Only when large units defect with their units, a happenstance of civil wars, of which the Vietnam War was emphatically not one, is such a source of arms important. The myth is largely a liberal projection: only such break-down products of civil society as liberals steal from the poor, usually by claiming to act on their behalf. The South Vietnamese Army was too poor to steal from, and the North Vietnamese and their Viet Cong surrogates were already lavishly equipped with Soviet-pattern arms and ammunition, including artillery rockets, which had no modern U.S. equivalent after World War II and Korea, as well as early furnished and superior assault rifles, years before the South Vietnamese tardily had their decades-old bolt-action rifles retired and replaced. Liberal opponents of the National Rifle Association love to moan about "assault rifles", in the hands of Americans, as a threat in the "war" against America's overmatched police (whom liberals despise anyway), but in an actual war, where the complained-of situation actually did occur for years, the liberals ignored it or lied about it.

George McGovern, damned with faint phrase as supposedly the most well informed liberal in the U.S. Senate, variously attributed Communist arms to "home-made" weapons (their home-made weapons were minor, booby traps such as the *pungi*-sticks smeared with dung to produce a septic wound, germ warfare applauded by the left for its ingenuity), and then "80%" to captured weapons, while occasionally conceding that the Soviets and Chinese were really supplying the arms. McGovern's domestic agenda on arms was similarly opportunistic: he supported the Second Amendment while protecting his South Dakota base, but turned into a "gun-control" freak as a national liberal candidate. Compared to Senator Joseph McCarthy, McGovern was a gibbering idiot; while McCarthy had merely quibbled over the number of Communists in government, McGovern was all over the landscape not just with numbers, but with basic facts. Although talking of peace, he also urged a South Vietnamese guerrilla invasion of the North at one point (another liberal strategem treating the enemy as vulnerable to pressure) and voted for the Gulf of Tonkin resolution and years of war appropriations out of loyalty to the party he hoped to control. The defeat of Johnson and then Humphrey in 1968 made McGovernism the future of the party, even as the Vietnam War suddenly became "Nixon's War". Toward that end, McGovern joined with the American Civil Liberties Union in trying to shield American war criminals from the light sentences dished out by a society rotted by leftist coddling of criminals. Nothing could be allowed to stand in the way of Nixon's "blood" responsibility; it was almost as if he had done McGovern's voting in the Senate, to hear McGovern tell it. Another typical piece of McGovern rubbish was his plan to end the war by inviting North Vietnam to join in development of the Mekong River. Did McGovern, with his fund of geographical info from his bomber pilot days, know that North Vietnam was the only country in the area with no connection to the Mekong? Maybe he did and maybe he didn't, being a man who mixed deep ignorance with deliberate dissembling, but it would have made more sense to invite the other three Indochinese countries, or Burma, China and Thailand, to join a Mekong River project, because those were the only six countries it and its tributaries flowed through. Throw in the spectacle of McGovern campaigning as the National Organization for Women's anti-abortion candidate in 1972, including the seconding of his nomination by a Right-to-Lifer, and his later efforts to make "Pro-Choice" a litmus of political correctness, and you have vintage McGovern, a man of ambition and enough terminal self-righteousness, for whatever deceit he is spouting at the moment, to convince the gullible of his sincerity.

U.S. troops were usually heavily armed, but in some cases Pentagon management, the Kennedy-McNamara Whiz Kids at work (a pack of credentialed jerks labeled "The Best and the Brightest" in fatuous liberal hindsight), led to pointless re-organization. U.S. infantry units were stripped of effective anti-tank weapons, because they were supposedly fighting a guerrilla war in country deemed unsuitable for tanks or other armored vehicles; running into Communist tanks was therefore a nastier experience than it need have been. The Communists had their own superb bazookas, of the modern Soviet type, but their troops, lionized as stalwarts in the always kow-towing American media, feared using them, as it meant giving their positions away, even against those South Vietnamese troops who supposedly wouldn't fight.

Pentagon micro-management of small-unit equippage had its blind spots, fortunately. American Hawk anti-aircraft batteries were separate units, which missed being weeded or even completely axed by Pentagon leaders convinced that the U.S. commanded the air. But the work of the Hawks was done anonymously, until the media found it politically correct to actually report one telling episode. A North Vietnamese helicopter attack across the "DeMilitarized Zone" was slaughtered by a Hawk barrage, dozens of helicopters shot down in minutes. That destruction made the papers, reportable by the military as it occurred in an acknowledgeable war zone, and played to the media's contemporary fascination with showing a burgeoning war, and the doom awaiting Americans near the DeMilitarized Zone. The later liberal phantasm of "Another Vietnam" had not yet been fully fleshed out, but its early incarnation as "Another Dien Ben Phu" was in fine fettle. The liberal media's masturbatory dreams of massacred Americans were repeated so relentlessly that the fatuity of the attempt at prophecy, in lieu of reportage, was overwhelmed by the cumulative effect of the doom-mongering. Khe Sanh was one frequent focus of defeatist obsessing, but neither it nor any other sizable group of Americans was defeated in battle. Defeat came later, in 1975, when accumulated errors, the doom-cult and Watergate had left the South Vietnamese isolated, disorganized and subject to defeat. Prior to that, of course, no sizable group of South Vietnamese was ever overrun after the fashion of Dien Ben Phu; although their panicky retreat from the Laos raid was well publicized, those troops lived to run away another day.

The arrival of Richard Nixon meant a relaxation of at least some of the Johnson-Whiz Kid stupidities. Although North Vietnam remained safe from invasion, and negotiations rather than victory remained the goal of the semi-liberal Nixon, two active measures against supply to Communist troops in South Vietnam were quickly undertaken. A U.S. division was soon posted astride the Ho Chi Minh Trail in Laos, something its accompanying reporters, no map-readers, seemed unaware of, and the Cambodian route was also sanctioned, even if blockade remained prohibited to the giant U.S. Navy. With huge Northern units in the South, piece-meal bombing of the North was largely abandoned for several years, in favor of bombing in the South, where Communist air defenses were weaker. U.S. troops were slowly withdrawn, and the North's acquiescence in a settlement was obtained, after Nixon's re-election, by mining Haiphong's harbor and bombing Hanoi. Treaty enforcement depended upon U.S. resolve, however, and the Watergate *coup* left American leadership weak. The North seized its chance, and the South, between dominoes Cambodia and Laos.

South Vietnam had been left almost totally without anti-aircraft weapons, without heavy anti-tank weapons, without fuel for its few squadrons of modern aircraft, substantially without vehicles and without ammunition. The North Vietnamese, after Haiphong was cleared, were lavishly resupplied with tanks, aircraft and helicopters, and their army swept down South Vietnam, encountering a South Vietnamese Army organized and scattered for garrison duty against low-level guerrilla activity, and lacking the mobility to unite for concentrated resistance or the weapons and ammunition to resist at all. Bits of the South Vietnamese Army were defeated by the massed power of the onslaught, concentrated and forceful attack blowing away each attempt at local resistance, each time a weak local unit against a strong and violently employed mass. Having no ammunition proved just as demoralizing to the South Vietnamese as it had in 1947-48 to the Anti-Communist Chinese, when Harry Truman embargoed them; Truman's advisors had duped him first into supporting a coalition government, and then into the blockade to force it upon Chiang. In China, as later in Vietnam, the Communists did not really need to negotiate because they were trying to win, not just deal, and their allies gave effective aid, instead of stupid liberal advice and obstruction. The Democratic betrayal of China had made both Korea and Vietnam war-zones, and disadvantageous war-zones. Meddling by Pro-Communists and liberal clowns was repeated in Vietnam, from Democratic ranks, but after the expulsion of Halperin at least not from within the Administration.

The South Vietnamese Army, prepared by liberal thinkers to fight with guerrillas, had been conquered by an armored and air-supported blitzkrieg that Patton would been proud of. The early "lesson" about fighting a guerrilla war had been learned by the liberals, who had re-organized the South Vietnamese Army out of its conventional posture after disposing of a succession of South Vietnamese political leaders who knew a bad idea when they heard it, and who were more aware of the conflict's nature than were Washington's Whiz Kids and their colleagues in Intelligence and the State Department. Leaving the initiative to the North Vietnamese, courtesy of first fighting a liberal war and then withdrawing entirely, merely exacerbated the error.

The political lesson of Vietnam for other countries reinforced previous experience, that the liberal U.S. was inconsistent and ineffectual, sometimes violent in action, but not steadfast in purpose, wise in policy or efficient in execution. Even the U.S. guaranty of Western Europe remained open to question, the French continuing to develop their own nuclear force, for example. Who is going to trust a country that has one major party being constantly taken over by leftist lunatics, and the other major party being constantly hobbled by harassment from the lunatics' control of the press and bureaucracy?

The military lessons of Vietnam have been generally left un-learned, as reportage, historiography and analyses have ascertained neither the nature of the war nor the patterns of conduct in it by all concerned. The military issues of the Vietnam War have been even more variously misinterpreted than more routine defense matters. But the nature of war itself means that military professionals can re-apply old verities, except when political parameters prevent it. In the Gulf War with Iraq, blockade was one of the first American actions, instead of being eschewed for seven years as in Vietnam. In the Gulf War, use of force was preceded by a build-up, and then the force was explosively released, unlike the sporadic and ineffectual escalation used against the Communists in Vietnam. In the Gulf War, airpower was used immedi-ately against the Iraqi Air Force, command structure and supply apparat-us, and later concentrated against visible battlefield targets, unlike the off-limits targets in Vietnam and the area bombing of jungles. In the Gulf War, Allied troops were equipped and used in decisive attack upon enemy formations, and those urging that Iraq itself be immunized from attack were properly ignored; there was no North Vietnam off-limits to Allied troops. The result in Iraq was military victory, and at relatively low Allied losses, but even enemy and civilian losses from the shortened war were far less than in the Vietnam War, dragged out as it was by politicized incompetence. Liberals were left to squawk that the Gulf War had been deceptively easy, although the deception had been their own, gleefully anticipating "tens of thousands" of dead American boys. They also squawked about Saddam Hussein being left in control of a de-feated Iraq only weeks after they had sought to undermine any effective resistance to him at all. But at least there was the comedy of liberals combing the Constitution (that "Compact with Hell") for loopholes and turning their back upon the sacred United Nations; the U.N. had set the political parameters of opposing Saddam while not solving the problem of his continued existence. Military virtuosity had been prevented from achieving full political victory because of political cowardice, but even that cowardice had been too bold for American liberals. There were calls for cease-fires and bombing halts, trying to get George Bush, and those American boys. bogged down in more futility.

The political leadership that lost both wars was remarkably simi-lar to that of Fascist Italy. Lyndon Johnson had set out to fight to nego-tiate, after the manner of Mussolini casually entering World War II in the expectation of losing a few men to secure himself a seat at the nego-tiating table (lacking a negotiating table, Mussolini had to settle for a lamp-post). The Kuwaiti takeover was very much in the pre-World War II dictators' manual for the *fait accompli*, the abrupt taking of an action leaving the onus for counter-action on divided and timid third-parties.

The modern paradigm here is the Indian descent upon the Maldives, supplying the guerrillas for a revolt and Indian occupation units in rapid synchronization; to cut the time for diplomatic quibbling, the Indian troops were dispatched *before* the revolt. Saddam's straw vote in the U.S. Congress was only a scant few votes from deadlock, so it was a close call for the prime-mover in the anti-Saddam coalition.

If the liberals had once again self-destructed in their fatuous fantasies of an American bloodbath, American conservatives were not without their own stupidities, although of minor details. Saddam Hussein, the former and prospective Kurd-killer, was denounced as the new Saladin by Evans & Novak and by Jeanne Kirkpatrick. Saladin had not been an Arab, of course, but rather a Kurd in the days when "Saracens" had been a force, in between the Arab outburst and the late-blooming Ottoman Turks.

But the main chant of the left, American and European, was a reprise of the moldy Vietnam "War for Oil" theme, only this time, there was indeed oil. Of course, once upon a time, the three major western powers had owned the oil of both Iraq and Kuwait, with two Standard Oil arms, the British-Dutch Shell and some French companies with the Iraqi concession, and Gulf Oil and British Petroleum sharing the Kuwaiti concession. If the Western countries had indeed been willing to fight a "War for Oil", the times of the various seizures would have been ideal. The U.S. under Franklin Roosevelt, zealous guardian of Poland ("War for Polish Sausage"?) and China, let Mexico steal a multi-billion dollar investment in oil by Americans for about one-tenth of a cent on the dollar, an abrupt and meritorious occasion for patriotic war, but not for liberals. National sovereignty, even that of oil thieves or authoritarian governments, was a more cognizable goal for liberals, killing for principle, not for something real and useful like oil. Note that liberals did not even call for sanctions following the contemporary Maldives seizure by India, an aggressive basket case they dote upon.

And while Kuwait was a rich prize in itself, wiping out many of Iraq's external debts while grabbing one of the sources of subsidy for several otherwise bankrupt Arab causes, the real prize was Saudi Arabia. That was the meaning of the support for Saddam from Jordan and Yemen, poor Saudi neighbors both envious of Saudi wealth and with their separate axes to grind. Jordan's royal family had once held the prize cities of Mecca and Medina, but had been expelled from them by the Saudis; the Jordanians had been fobbed off with the third prize for Islam, Jerusalem, whose Grand Mufti had been too pro-German in World War II. And then Jordan had lost Jerusalem to Israel, blaming the Saudis and others for not supporting it. Yemen, in the most naturally bountiful part of the Arabian peninsula, had seen the desert Saudis flourish, taking central Arabia with Kuwaiti help, taking the holy cities with British backing, getting rich from oil and impinging upon Yemeni claims on some weak and potentially oil-rich sheikdoms when Yemen was politically divided and poor.

From the political standpoint of threatening a wider war but settling at the moment for Kuwait, Saddam's strategy of hunkering down in Kuwait was very appropriate. It bluffed massive casualties against military counteraction, and it left the Iraqi army concentrated on the Saudi border. But once the political decision had been made by other countries to reinforce the Saudis, the military calculus swung against the Iraqis. They had lost the opportunity to invade Saudi Arabia and to destroy its military infrastructure or to convert it to their own use. Instead, Allied troops were able to use the huge Saudi air bases and to run short supply lines from the Gulf. Desert War **is** logistics -- deserts being short of all things necessary to sustain large numbers of people, military or civilian -- and a war against Iraqi-occupied Saudi Arabia would have been a nightmare, with Allied troops lacking ground-based air support and ports to sustain a decisive onslaught against Iraq itself, and their supply train lacking Gulf oil. Because Turkey near Iraq is a wilderness and Iran was as hostile to the anti-Iraq coalition as it was to Iraq itself, the feasible alternative would have been a dragooning of Syria and Jordan, forcing them to yield the right of transit to Allied troops or to fight on Saddam's side. As Israel would have inevitably been involved, probably both of those Arab nations would have fought against the Allies. But Saddam chose the arena of aggressive-passive politics, and lost. For awhile, anyway, thanks to the decision not to root him out.

On a more generic plane, it is also clear that the political nexus, although most critical, is not the whole picture. There are more purely military, technological and engineering problems, although these can be obscured by assuming more politicization than actually exists. The question of military bases is the easiest starting point, one with a ready relationship to both the Vietnam and Gulf Wars.

Chapter 11 - **Touching the Bases**

Although not quite as importantly as leadership, political or military, the effectiveness of a modern military hinges upon its economic basis, including the simple question of where the military is kept when it is not being used. Basing affects the training and employability (such as to Southeast Asia or the Persian Gulf) of a military, and the expense of its maintenance. Basing is also usually conceptually simpler than more esoteric matters of technology, equipment and organization, so examining it can illuminate politicization that might be less blatant in subtler areas.

Although the question of basing is mostly a peace-time consideration, and therefore remote from the hurly-burly of wartime, pertinent historical perspective is frequently therefore obscure compared to the lore of wars and battles. Liberal demonology fixates upon base location, calling it a matter of political pull (or clout, etc. as local usage varies). Grotesque exaggerations of political influence assume the quality of folklore, and Congressmen up for re-election every two years use what they can. The camera's invention was but the prelude to the photo opportunity, the chance for politicians to pose in front of some local military manifestation -- a new base, an enlargement, a business that just got a contract -- seeking to associate themselves with some newsy local activity, where the military is popular, anyway, to take credit by the association. Such a low-cost tactic has its flip side: turn over the associate-with-the-positive theme, and the other key is simply to avoid being seen with the negative; Representatives from liberal districts do far less ribbon-cutting at local bases, although they might do some more discrete politicking among people who work at such places, and before veterans groups. The same office-holders are also wont to be seen with the famous, the colorful and the successful, but only to the extent popular with the folks back home, their bosses. That is why Presidents invite celebrities, newsmakers and the talented to the White House, or call the winners of sporting events; the calls are televised, for it is "news", a politician mugging for the camera, trying to identify himself with a happy occasion, a positive image.

If the politician is lucky, things that positively affect his district are chalked up to him. South Carolina was a hotbed of military bases long before the arrival of the seemingly eternal Representative L. Mendell Rivers, who, with his "Rivers Delivers" slogan, took credit for old patterns much as a naughty child might carve his initials in a very old tree. Charleston was the best port on a long stretch of coast, from New York to the Rio Grande and beyond, making it a military target and the focus of defensive measures, such as the installation of both forts and harbor facilities, both British/federal and colony/state. Fought over in the Revolutionary War and even more so in the Civil War, Charleston is well into its third century as a naval bastion.

There are three constitutional branches of government, and the legislative branch has two Houses, the lower House with 435 members; each Representative has 1/3 of ½ of 1/435th of the federal power, about 1/26th of 1%, and delivers accordingly. Himself, every two years, back to Washington and the 434 others who share his secret. The only thing Mendell Rivers ever delivered was Mendell Rivers. Had he been a Representative from landlocked Wyoming, and all of those naval installations been put there, that would have been a story. But congressmen from such landlocked states are prone to denounce naval bases, such as Coloradoan Pat Schroder's denunciation of naval sloth in economizing while her state was faced with cut-backs of its bases, Army and Air Force. She did, however, neglect to praise Colorado for not having demanded its own naval base, its fair share.

And why does the press play along with the press agentry and electioneering hogwash? The press is lazy and stupid, but it is more. Newshawk acceptance of the braggadocio of politicians, at face value, is not merely the foolery of cynical sophisticates gulled like greenhorns, but an ideologically opportune stigmatization of the military as pawns of political power-brokers. By creating these devils, or at least winking at their posturing self-creation, anti-defense liberals with their own padded credentials, and spouting any sort of insane rubbish, can be paraded as reformers, and the press can rewrite their speeches as potboiler exposés. With the cardboard villains created, there is a demand for plaster saints to fight off their shadows. The co-operation of the press in congressional legend-making is just liberal marketing in action, which is liberalism.

Some pre-eminent Representative or Senator, a Carl Vinson or a Richard Russell, may indeed lead Congress in making necessary commitments to the nation's defense. But both Georgians were proponents of a powerful American Navy, and not from a state then or since any sort of hotbed of naval bases or production activity. Although their land requirements are smaller than those of the other services' bases, naval bases, in the traditional sense of being for the use of ships, must be located in ports, of which there are a finite variety of relatively fixed quality, also tending to be centers of commerce. Even naval air stations for the training and operation of land-based aircraft tend to be put near coastal areas, in large part because the air missions or training involved are nautically oriented, such as maritime surveillance, anti-submarine patrol and carrier-related training. South Carolina on one side of Georgia has Charleston and Florida on the other has Pensacola, each with a harbor superior to Savannah's, and each with naval bases that Savannah just did not merit, in spite of having such powerful and pronaval Congressmen. Such men may be temporary favorites of liberalism when intervention is momentarily in fashion, but usually get downgraded and despised by liberals. But it is the nature of fashions to change, just as it is the nature of verities to remain, fops notwithstanding.

Georgia has long had two Army bases and an Air Force base with a nearby Naval Air Station. Both air facilities are located near a huge government-owned factory which produces Air Force cargo planes and all of the nation's maritime patrol planes. Planes from the Naval Air Station can patrol both the Atlantic and the Gulf of Mexico, something ships based in Georgia couldn't do without steaming around Florida. Georgia did eventually get a naval base, at Kings Bay, during the Carter Administration, one president, even Carter, having the same constitutional weight as many senators and more representatives. Carter accomplished this pork barrel fiasco by cutting back the production of new submarines to carry the new Trident missiles, charging mismanagement at the Connecticut submarine-builder. The new missiles supposedly in such dire need were put into older submarines, which thereby somehow needed a new base, co-incidentally in the President's home state. Later, Trident submarines themselves were based there, on the excuse that the missile facilities were already there. Another rationale was that the Kings Bay facility was more suitable for the larger Trident subs, although they drew only four feet more water than did the older missile-carrying subs which had long been based at Charleston. Carter delivered for his home state, a waste of tax money, but fortunately he could not deliver himself back to the White House.

Another thing the South suffers from less than do other sections of the country is a concentration of whiny liberals. When the Navy was recently establishing a small naval base on New York Harbor's Staten Island, liberals began fretting about it making the city a target. "Ground Zero" stencils were blazed on sidewalks all over Manhattan (as if there weren't already enough dead-body stencils in Manhattan anyway), giving the distance to Staten Island and the presumably inevitable hydrogen bomb blast at this "target". Of course, the Ground Zero nonsense had been going on for years before the Staten Island base, and the main result of the "contriversy" was that Ground Zero was shifted from the old bulls-eye of Wall Street or the Empire State Building to Staten Island. Focusing on the base was just routine hypocrisy.

Large military bases tend to be located in sandy wastes -- desert, swamp or pine barren -- cheap land with no intrinsic use. The direct cost of obtaining the land (frequently land the government had been unable to sell) and the indirect cost of relocating other activities are minimized. The South has tended to be the land of military bases for a number of reasons. First, it has the largest stretches of sandy waste with sufficient water to support habitation; the low regional land values drive the cost of the land even lower, unlike the sandy wastes of Long Island and Los Angeles, where urbanization has driven the cost up enormously. Lower Southern land values were ultimately a product of its warm climate. The really Old South was unglacierated, so that the soil built up, instead of being scrapped off, like the Northeast's soil, which mostly became Long Island. Rich soil and warm weather made the South good for America's early export sources of hard cash, the plantation crops tobacco and cotton. The plantation's ability to absorb extremely unskilled labor nearly all year made slavery economically attractive. But with slavery came economic maturity and social stagnation; more productive Whites and their industry favored the North, where the land was less tied up and where social mobility was unhampered by a planter class. The North's Civil War victory meant occupation of the South and further stagnation, keeping land low and political values even lower, with a Post-Reconstruction one-party reality of Democratic congressmen perpetually re-elected into seniority.

Second, the South was part of the old U.S., and many sites are traditional military locations. Third, military occupation permanently federalized many former state or Confederate sites, reinforcing the traditional element. Fourth, the South's warmer weather cuts construction and heating costs, and troop cold weather miseries, the Reverse Valley Forge Factor. More modern considerations include minimizing the loss of aircraft from bad weather, the Kitty Hawk Factor. Weather was also a big factor in both the aircraft industry's and the movie industry's centers-of-gravity shift from the sandy wastes of Long Island to the sandy wastes of Southern California, and its then-cheap land; companies made money off the rising Long Island market, and then got in on the ground-floor of California's real estate boom. There was less reason to close or abandon old military installations in the South than in other parts of the country, less favored by weather and less watered. Many in the West were often small in scale originally, due to their Indian War nature, and thus were prime candidates for memorialization or less dignified closure.

The American North has many disadvantages, compared to the South, for the location of military bases. Yet, because of population presence, some training activities have long been conducted in the Northeast, many at sites originally pioneered by those unofficial Progressive volunteers, back when Progressives were hawks, before U.S. entry into Liberalism's Second Crusade, the edification of the trenches. More notorious, but briefly so in a nation's memory (usually jogged during anti-military jags), was the encampment at Yaphank, Long Island, where Americans returning from the Spanish-American War were slowly demobilized, by mustering out or dying out. The mortalities were products of inadequate clothing, as troops who had sweated in winter clothing in Cuba, before discarding it, were finally issued tropical uniforms just in time for a very cold winter in a poorly heated encampment with bad water and bad sanitation. Yaphank today has been absorbed by suburban sprawl, and is a Suffolk County administrative center; local liberals, such as academics -- professors of history and political science, for example -- consider it a deliberately "obscure" location chosen by Machiavellian local Republican politicians. Long Island liberals tend to be both paranoically ungenerous and ignorant (like all liberals), having heard of neither the Yaphank encampment nor the nearby Brookhaven National Laboratory (except during anti-military spasms or anti-nuclear spasms, that is). The reason Yaphank was chosen for its three government tasks was that it was a sandy waste, cheap and available for an encampment, for a sprawling laboratory and for a governmental center for suburban spill-over from expensive New York City onto transiently cheaper real estate.

During the heady days of Continental Air Defense, when the U.S. briefly tried to have a serious defense against Soviet aircraft, the Northern U.S. was alive with related activity, such as scattered anti-aircraft missile batteries (Nike and Bomarc) and interceptor airfields. The main radar installations, located farther north, in Canada and Greenland, have been more well kept up, because they fit more into the strategy which succeeded Continental Air Defense. They became warning devices for massive retaliation, the Cold War Liberal innovation of McNamara and his Whiz Kids, and completed in scope by Nixon and Laird, of gutting defense in the name of attack. With a U.S. defense against aircraft in place, the Soviets had changed their emphasis to rockets, more difficult to defense. Steps to indeed defense those rockets were planned by Nixon and Laird, as later by Reagan and Weinberger. The initial defeat and later obstruction of those efforts, the prospect of more Northern bases -- such as for the aborted Safeguard/Sentinel antimissile system -- was done not by the posited "Iron Triangle" of contractors, congressmen and the Pentagon, but by a recoalescence of liberals. The Modern Liberals of Northeast peace-disarmament-and-we-don't-want-to-be-a-target persuasion (if a base's mere presence would invite attack, a country would seem to have malevolent foes, and really need more military bases, not fewer) had joined with the fading Cold War Liberals, proponents of the offense as cheaper than real defense.

By themselves, the disarmament crowd could not affect national policy, only its nuances. Mobilization against local bases was simple opportunism; such bases were not really targets: agitation against national policy was the goal. Cold War Liberals were simply wrong about the costs of defensing aircraft and missiles. Missiles used for defense are in fact cheaper than their larger foes, which have to go farther. In the Iraq War, Patriot defense missiles were cheaper than the Scuds they shot down, or twice as cheap as Tomahawk cruise missiles, the U.S.'s own cheapest strategic missile. An interceptor and its missiles are usually similarly cheaper than the bomber they defense; the bomber, traveling further while carrying a heavier load, has two reasons to be heavier and therefore costlier. Another item of interest and usually down-played by the Whiz Kids was the cost of the destruction averted by successful defense.

Of course, the liberal coalition's victory could then be ascribed to the demons of the "Iron Triangle", a splendid enough quasi-Masonic bogeyman propaganda term and concept (one man's paranoia being another's persecution mania), who would be held responsible for the continued build-up of offensive weapons. The bases for these -- bombers, missiles and missile-battery submarines -- were also, as the Continental Air Defense system had been, located mostly in the Northern United States, with a few in other northern hemisphere locations -- bomber bases in Spain and Guam, submarine bases in Scotland and Spain. (Tactical bases -- Army, Navy, Marine, Air Transport and training -- were concentrated in the South; the Whiz Kid advents, not congressional influence, re-energized this concentration.) Defensively, offensively or observationally, the nearness to the potential Soviet foe of the strategic missions to be undertaken was far more important than the presumable influence of "Iron Triangle" log-rolling. Just when those Southern Congressmen had as a group reached their peak in seniority and control of committee chairs, their ability to hog the pork barrel was strangely most questionable, but left unquestioned. Would-be liberal interrogators had other priorities, propagating useful legends. Personal political considerations and vanity led some Congressmen to play along, but their motives and actions were ultimately patriotic, enough reason for liberals to hate them.

The end of the Cold War, with its emphasis on strategic targeting of the Soviet Union, has seen the disproportionately strategic North air bases hit again. New York's Griffis (Rome) and Plattsburgh (the prototype Progressive volunteer camp, lately a SAC base) are to be shut down, while the tactical light infantry base at Fort Drum (once the Pine Camp "Plattsburgh" camp) is unaffected. Troops from Fort Drum were about half of the American contingent sent to Somalia, an assignment where traditional ground troops were more germane than were bombers or missiles. The "Iron Triangle" proved ephemeral -- it had no more existence than as a propaganda term of art.

The peaceniks were also helpful to Whiz Kid "efficiency experts" in getting shut-downs or cut-downs at many shipyards, including some government installations. The first generation of the "no nukes" crowd was not disappointed at the stunting of the nuclear generator capacity at Bethlehem's Massachusetts shipyard (later taken over by conglomerate General Dynamics), nor was it teary-eyed to see the cessation of nuclear-powered submarine construction, and hence of submarine construction for the modern U.S. Navy, at New Hampshire's Portsmouth Naval Shipyard or at other locations around the Northern U.S. Nuclear construction was thereby concentrated at two locations, submarines only at Connecticut's Electric Boat (now part of General Dynamics), and both submarines and the few nuclear-powered surface warships and aircraft carriers vouchsafed to our Navy at Virginia's Newport News.

Evidently, the mojo of the "Iron Triangle" does not extend to nuclear power on the ocean's surface, nor does the medusa stare of the pacifists penetrate the ocean's surface. The majority of America's nuclear reactors are naval, and the great bulk of those are in submarines. Two American nuclear submarines have been lost at sea, as have several Soviets, and with no discernible ecological catastrophe, except to the crews and those who mourn them. The type of ship propulsion has a massive effect on the type and quantity of naval bases needed, however, and also on their locations.

Possibly OPEC, oil companies and the tanker industry also have an opinion on nuclear power, or, even better than a mere opinion, an economic interest in not wanting it, for warships or other uses. But the cost of new nuclear-powered construction, in the small-scale, one-at-a-time way it has been used for surface warships, is too much to make up for the oil not used, or the tankers not used, or the escorts not needed for the tankers not used, or the space not taken up on board ship by the fuel tanks (which average about 45% empty, anyway), or the weight not taken up on board ship by the fuel and its tanks (about 1/5 of the tonnage when the tanks are full), or the fire hazards decreased by nuclear power (as in the *Belknap*'s post-collision oil fire, amidships, not near its nuclear weapons), or the explosion hazard reduced by getting away from gas-fired turbines (very chic for new destroyers), or the time and fuel not used at sea for steaming to and from refueling points every ten to twenty days, or the decreased vulnerability of ships made less predictable and more long-legged in their movements by virtue of not being convention-ally fueled, or the cost of the extra naval-basing capacity needed for more numerous and less capable ships, or the enormous cost of the manpower for the preceding massive inefficiencies.

Or so the experts tell us. They can also tell us that serial or mass production of nuclear-powered surface ships, as with any similar item, would enormously bring down their main cost, that of construction; that occurred with nuclear-powered submarines, the main reason for concen-trating their production. Meanwhile, there is no realizable efficiency of scale to be gained in the higher maintenance costs of a conventionally powered fleet, whose bills keep running up after its ships have left the shipyards. We can be absolutely sure that when oil prices go up again, and gutting nuclear power ensures that they will, and sooner, and higher, the Navy's already unnecessarily large oil and gas bill could easily shoot up by another ten or twenty billion dollars. Per year.

The leftist animus against nuclear power (except for submarines) was given snide vent during the Gulf War. Because the Gulf oil supply from the Saudis and the non-occupied sheikdoms was provided free, the U.S. commitment of a half-dozen aircraft carriers was made predominantly of oil-fired ships. The Pentagon thriftily took advantage of temporarily cheap oil, at a rate of more than ten million dollars a week, and used its nuclear-powered carriers to patrol other areas, where the oil subsidy was not available. Keeping the oil-fired carriers on their normal non-subsidized training and patrol missions would have cost nearly a half billion dollars compared to the tactic of sending ships which could take advantage of the subsidized oil. Liberals sneered at Pentagon thrift, using the occasion to attack nuclear-powered carriers. Of course, had the Gulf situation been more serious, with world oil supplies threatened, the nuclear-powered ships would have been even more of an asset than they already are, and the oil-fired carriers a burden instead of presenting a unique opportunity for economy.

Aircraft carriers, particularly nuclear-powered ones, are indeed themselves a type of floating air base, one whose main competitor is airfields, land bases for aircraft. Both carriers and airfields are the large Chinese puzzle boxes of a technological military, containing quantities of aircraft, medium-sized boxes, that shoot missiles or drop bombs, small boxes filled with explosives. Most of the earth's surface is ocean-covered, and most of the rest is accessible to carrier aircraft, as carried around by their larger boxes.

Airfields, in marked contrast, are fixed in their locations, and the aircraft at any single one are restricted in the terrain they can cover or reach. Besides their handicap of being immobile, airfields are subject not only to the type of obsolescence produced by the flow of military events to another area, but are also hostages to politics to a much greater extent than are carriers. The U.S. poured billions into a huge Libyan air base, only to be forced out when Libyan policy changed, and to see the airfield fall into hostile hands when Colonel Khadafy took over Libya. The Da Nang complex and five of the six large Thai airfields were victims of national wimpery and peace, the first being taken over by the North Vietnamese and then leased to the Soviets, and the Siamese bases being taken over by the jungle (or, to be politically correct, the doomed tropical rain forest's local comeback). The U.S. was long shackled by restrictions on the use of the now-abandoned Clark field near Manila in the Philippines (political and then volcanic) and Torrejon field near Madrid, Spain. Clark was off-limits for U.S. raids during the Vietnam War, as were Torrejon and all American air bases on continental Europe during the Libyan retaliation. With aircraft carriers, there are no host country foreign politics to contend with, because there is no host country but the U.S. The total cost of the construction of the seven lost bases? About the cost of the half-dozen all nuclear-powered carrier task forces not built, none of which would have had to pay rent to foreigners, a year-in-and-year-out budget and balance of payments negative; nor would any have been captured or otherwise used by America's enemies, as the Da Nang and Libyan complexes were.

And what do left-wing critics say about an America that used carrier-based aircraft in Vietnam, instead of just flying them in from distant Guam (three times as far from Vietnam as Clark, although the flights of B-52s from Guam overflew both the Philippine Sea as well as the Philippines itself), or waiting for the building of the new-but-soon-to-be-outdated airfields in Thailand and Vietnam? Two of the usual suspects, Admirals Carroll and LaRocque of the liberal-letterhead complex's think-tank and "public" television department, have the answers, they profess to think. The Navy was horning in on the Vietnam War, to find a use for its billions of dollars worth of carriers and aircraft and to protect its slice of the future budgetary pie. The Admirals do not explain why the Navy did not also find a use for its dozens of atomic submarines, with their relatively large slice of the Navy budget, and still considerable portion of the whole Pentagon pie. The Admirals' view omits such data and other considerations, including the Navy's role in having been attacked in the first place, or Johnson's decision to retaliate before the Air Force could begin its gigantic Southeast Asian construction job. Carriers, available and mobile, were on the job first because of their intrinsic utility. It was the Air Force that not only protected its slice of the budget for the near trillion dollars worth of aircraft and airfields it already possessed (at a cost nearly that of the entire Navy), but even cut itself a bigger piece by the cost of its new airfields' construction. The Navy, by contrast, did not build any more carriers because of the Vietnam War. It did not need to, because it could simply move some of those it had to positions off the coast of Vietnam. Indeed, some carriers were taken **out** of service during the Vietnam War; such false economies were used to save money for the unnecessary expenses of the prolonged war, and its vast construction budget, as well as the even more costly War on Poverty, still going on and multiply more costly than the Vietnam War.

What carriers cannot do is carry wisdom about the use of naval power, either its ability to blockade, or the use of its airpower to support strategically decisive offensives, rather than to chauffeur reluctant diplomats to interminable negotiations. The French had only a few carriers, one relic and two smaller donations, to support their troops against the Viet Minh, but even their few aircraft were less prone than many of America's to political interference, or even worse, such as the dozens lost to enemy sabotage while vulnerable on the ground. There are fewer saboteurs on U.S. aircraft carriers; although one would-be leftist hero did jam bolts in one carrier engine, he was just being unquestionably patriotic, with little bits of metal instead of little bits of nonsense.

But the issues of service roles and mastery of responsibilities transcend such minutiae as why a carrier should be made to sound huge at a length of "more than three football fields" when its closest comparison is criss-crossing strips of concrete each more than twenty-five football fields long (that's eight aircraft carriers to us regular folks being talked down to with football field yardsticks). And the airfields require thousands of men for construction, maintenance and operation of the roads, hangars, repair shops, power generators, radar, command and communication systems, messhalls, hospital, barracks, water supply, fire department and field security systems, including an anti-aircraft missile battery, not to mention the aircraft, the sort of things that make aircraft carriers so apparently costly because they are all lumped in with "just the ship", or "the ship and its escorts", or "not even including the airplanes". The Air Force budget is much more amenable to being spread over a number of cost centers, but all are part of the cost of each airfield. The Navy, by contrast, has a much lower bill for land-based facilities, including ports for the carriers. Should the daffy Admirals succeed in abolishing the aircraft carrier for their left-wing paymasters, the expenses of the airfield would suddenly loom up as the next liberal bugbear, the expensive shoe on the warrior's next leg to be amputated. But there is other quackery than surgery, the copper bracelet of service reorganization, for example.

Chapter 12 - **Foreign Organization: Things Up in the Air**

The founding of America was undertaken in a military era when ships, having become large enough and sturdy enough for the North Atlantic, required a different type of military organization that did land forces. In smaller and less stormy waters, or in such barbarous times as the Viking epoch, smaller boats could utilize military skills more readily. But that had its last triumph with the galley battle of Lepanto in 1571, and its last gasp with the poor performance of the oared Spanish ships in 1588's defeat of the Armada. For the bulk of American history, then, there were large ships at sea -- naval, privateers or pirates -- using a few "marines" as specialists for more military sharpshooting, boarding and shore parties, but mostly using nautical skills needing a specialized service.

With American independence, there was not really a national army because of the end of the war, the weak national government and the unpopularity of standing armies; the early attempt at an American Navy had been pretty much sacrificed in hopeless battles against the British. When the Constitution was enacted, for the common defense and other reasons, the greater initial investment needed for a Navy kept it part of the same department as the Army, under the Secretary of War. With the Federalists, proponents of the Constitution and therefore of a national military, in control of the government, the construction of six excellent frigates was the first order of business. The nation was too small and poor to construct a battlefleet of ships-of-the-line, or sailing battleships, so it made ships that were faster than those but good individual matches for any other ships afloat. As "Anti-Federalist" agitation grew, leadership provided by renegade Federalists Jefferson and Madison (moving to the dominant mood of their home state of Virginia, antifederal parochialism of the "Old Dominion" and jealousy of New England influence), the Federalists moved to establish a separate Navy, recognizing the new importance of the planned six big frigates while ensuring their patronage in its establishment in the event of a Democratic presidential accession in 1800. Thus did we have an Army and a Navy, and two departments, for much of the nation's history. This completely common-sense division between areas of operation, competence and technology was controversial -- done, and opposed by the Anti-Federalists, on partisan grounds -- but the independent Navy co-incided with the entry of its first real warships into service.

It was a much later development, heavier-than-air flight and its quick use by the military, that began the modern debate about organization. Some argued that the new field needed a separate service, three balls instead of two. Others argued that there would be intractable problems of squabbling and budgetary jealousy, and that one super-service should be formed. Partisans of individual services argued for the shrinkage or abolition of the others as outmoded or no longer necessary. Although all approaches were broached in America, their actual implementation, for better or worse, occurred mostly in other countries.

A.   The Third Ball: The Royal Air Force Takes Off

Existing armies and navies took quick notice of the emerging aircraft well within its first decade. As with balloons (hot-air types in service with the Union Army in the Civil War) and airships (powered and more aerodynamic balloons), the main military and naval use for winged craft was scouting enemy dispositions, finding belligerents ashore or afloat. Britain's small Army formed the Royal Flying Corps, and the much larger Royal Navy formed Coastal Command for patrolling the coast and other operations by flying boats and other seaplanes, types quickly spun off by the rapidly developing aircraft. As early as 1912, the wheels of bureaucracy were in their usual pointless motion, and Coastal Command was absorbed by the Royal Flying Corps. Phantasies of German invasion were partly responsible, but giving control and the earliest notice to the Army made no sense, as a putative seaborne invasion should have been opposed first by the Royal Navy. Part of the fear was bad conscience, as the Royal Navy had for several years been planning a sudden descent upon the German coast.

But the actual outbreak of war two years later led to the growth of specifically naval needs for aircraft that were being neglected by the Army's Royal Flying Corps and its Coastal Command, in part because of the RFC's massive expansion for its Army-oriented missions in the war in France and the Near East. Among the tasks neglected by Coastal Command were scouting for the Navy and patrolling against the new peril of the submarine, which in those years as for long afterward operated at night and during much of the day on the surface, where it could move under full power and have more opportunity to scan the horizon for targets. The Royal Navy's new Air Service did a much better job in those areas, as origin and goal-oriented use proved more important than experience and bureaucratic categorization.

But the growth of all British airpower provided a seductive new opportunity for bureaucracy. Instead of again concentrating all airpower in just one of the two existing services, as previously in the Army, the push now was to combine all air into a separate service. That way, instead of depriving one senior service of its air, both could be shorted. This was done on the auspicious occasion of April Fools' Day of 1918. It had no great effect on the war, because the planes, crews and operations then underway were largely continued, including Coastal Command's lackadaisical effort against submarines. The third service approach had several appeals. There was that of specialization, the new thing of airpower supposedly mandating its own service. There was the huge size of the Royal Navy and the enormous growth of the British

Army; but, of course, merely cutting away the air units did not create new managers, it just moved the old ones away. There was the possibility of preventing jealousy between the Army and the Navy over the air, but the creation of a third service, while scotching the second gasp of purely naval airpower, created a third center of jealousy, the air itself. There was also the possibility of co-ordinating production of aircraft, but the different types were even then not really comparable except in terms of engine need, and that was a long-term problem.

April 1, 1918 had not seen a true birth; it had been more like cutting the tails off two animals and stitching them together to make a new animal, with each tail not only fighting the other, but also dividing and fighting against itself. Taking the air away from the established services caused the neglect of their needs, in a world in which the seas were the keys to trade and control of the ground key to success in battle. Aside from the neglect of maritime patrol from shore, a naval responsibility in virtually every other country, RAF absorption of the Royal Naval Air Service caused the neglect of the aircraft involved when the Royal Navy changed its priority from catapult launch of ship-board seaplanes to the installation of flight decks on specialized ships for wheeled aircraft. The biplanes of the time were more adaptable to these aircraft carriers than were later monoplanes, with their need of longer runways, but they were also rather fragile, wire and fabric structures, for the beating that carriers would give even biplanes. The 1924 change of name to the Fleet Air Arm for this low priority of the RAF did not change things; British carrier aircraft development continued to stagnate for the next 15 years.

But grand strategists of politics, press and the RAF's new Bomber Command were proclaiming the superiority of the attack as French ideologues had before World War I and as the Kennedy-McNamara "Whiz Kids" were to do in the middle Cold War. British Prime Minister Baldwin's dictum that "the bomber will always get through" is usually mistaken as his defeatism in the face of ballyhooed German airpower, but it was in fact a trenchant epigram from an unwarlike man who commanded quite a few bombers. That lead shrank under Chamberlain, but the basic organization, pilot pool and British engine and airframe design and production saw Bomber Command re-assert its supremacy during and after the Battle of Britain. At that crisis, Bomber Command was already so big and obstreperous that it could not be bothered to attack the airfields where German aircraft were massed between onslaughts on England. Although bombing some German invasion barges in French harbors, Bomber Command's main contribution was carrying out its old ideas under the new master Churchill: bombing German cities to draw the Germans into a retaliation for which the *Luftwaffe* was unequipped. German aircraft were designed for shorter range, smaller bomb loads and more accuracy, for day use in military assignments, not, legend aside, for terror bombings; it was a rerun of the old German High Seas Fleet, built for short range and then pressed into service for pinprick attacks dwarfed by paranoid British anticipation. Bomber Command had gotten its way before the advent of Churchill, and the aircraft on the way for it were bomb buses for indiscriminate night bombing of large urban areas.

The RAF's second priority was Fighter Command, which somewhat blossomed with the emergence of new fighters and radar, a chance to redress the bomber's offensive advantage pushed by the out-of-office Churchill. Fighter Command prevailed in the Battle of Britain, but not by dint of help from the other RAF commands. The just-independent-of-the-RAF Fleet Air Arm had suffered under its long tutelage as the RAF's fourth banana. The RAF, though allowing a separate series of biplane torpedo planes to be obtained in niggardly numbers, had attempted to unify the observation, fighter and light bombing roles for carrier aircraft, resulting in one type of plane, misusing the new Merlin engine but too slow and unmaneuverable for shore-based service in the Battle of Britain. There were too few and inappropriate Fleet Air Arm aircraft, and too few pilots, particularly for the hasty war-time need to flesh out existing carriers and to replace combat losses and to equip new ships. The old Royal Naval Air Service had done better against World War I's airship menace, launching the first-ever carrier raid against a zeppelin hangar.

In fact, the Royal Navy's carrier contribution to the Battle of Britain was strictly negative: only weeks before it began, Norway was being evacuated by its British Expeditionary Force, and the aircraft carrier *Glorious* took on board a mass of old Gladiator land-based biplane fighters, so many it was unable to operate its own few planes. Intercepted by two German battleships, the carrier and its escorts were destroyed, with less than fifty survivors, none aircraft. The Germans, typically, wanted more, and their Admiral for the week-long battleship spree was beached, for lack of aggression. In the real world, if not in Billy Mitchell's gee-whiz exercise, the battleship won the first round, more than a thousand hands down, and more than a hundred aircraft down, including several fighter squadrons and their pilots weeks before the Battle of Britain. The incident recalled the first mortal conflict between the modern battleship and the submarine, a generation earlier, when the archetype *Dreadnought* had rammed and sunk a German U-boat (Falls, in *The Great War*, had a French battleship sunk by a submarine, but, being modern, it was only damaged, was repaired and saw further action, even in two more wars).

With its planes under RAF control, development of British carrier doctrine and practice lagged far behind the standards achieved by its appropriate comparisons, the U.S. and Japan. All three countries had been permitted by the Washington Treaty to convert or to build from scratch significant strength in aircraft carriers, and the Royal Navy had indeed taken the first step before that treaty, with several big conversions underway. But the other two countries had their carrier aircraft under naval control, so that not only did they develop the ships, they also developed their air strength, in quality, in quantity and in concepts tested by exercises. The Royal Navy had the ships, but got only a few and inferior RAF aircraft, and so could not really develop its expertise. Because of the lack of experience and of planes, British carriers were only expected to carry about 40% of the aircraft load of similar-sized American or Japanese carriers. RAF control until 1939, and then war, prevented the Royal Navy from getting a high priority for new planes; numbers were only half met, and the planes that did show up were only half as capable as those of the other two big naval powers. If Japan's and America's carriers were rated each at 100, the Royal Navy/RAF melange was worth about a 15, hardly a ringing endorsement for the unified air approach.

Three European countries which aped the nearby British example had similarly dismal results. The French aircraft carrier did not have adequate planes in its decades of service until it was interned into American custody. Newly Fascistic Italy passed on its option of converting a battleship which had to be disposed of under the Washington Treaty. Later German and Italian carriers were kept unfinished because their air forces, in control of the planes, considered them a low priority; the navies involved gave the carriers an accordingly low priority, because without planes, they would have been useless. Modern Italy has had a replication, with its *Garibaldi* equipped only with helicopters for eight years, because Italy's Air Force was apathetic about Navy carrier jump-jets and the Italian left considered them "aggressive". There was no "Iron Triangle" to push for a few imported jets, just a Navy which needed years of bureaucratic struggle to push for the concept of naval control of naval aircraft, a necessary adjunct to mustering force for the political struggle to get the aircraft themselves. Trainers were soon in service, and jump-jets were due in 1993, **16 years** after the carrier was authorized. Note that the *Garibaldi* was equipped with a large ramp for jump-jet take-offs, making that part of the flight deck useless for the embarked helicopters, which require extensive flat deck space.

The combat experience of British carriers bore out their inferiority. The carriers were unable to be risked against land targets, at best attacking ships near enemy coasts. With the Germans and Italians having only land-based aircraft, the British carriers were able to accomplish some things by staying mostly out of range, except for surprise attacks. A small plane attack on Taranto torpedoed three Italian battleships in shallow water. Off Greece, another attack damaged an Italian battleship at sea, and the Italians lost three modern heavy cruisers and nearly two thousand dead in protecting its retreat. Heavy damage was inflicted by torpedo plane attacks on two modern Vichy French battleships in African harbors. And the German battleship *Bismarck* was crippled by one of three torpedoes to strike it from two attacks launched by two British carriers, enabling a mass of British ships to catch it and sink it. All of those accomplishments were by the famed Swordfish biplane torpedo bomber, capable only of operating in the absence of opposing air cover, because its contemporary British carrier company -- fighter-bomber/observation compromise models -- was incapable of escorting it against enemy air cover. In Europe, those handicaps had, with prudent usage against opponents without tactical air cover, been worked around.

But war with Japan impended, and in the Bay of Bengal, the British would pay the price of the disorganization wrought by the political meddling of the 1918-1939 "reform". The British had amassed a force of four carriers there, with a battle force of other warships and a strong force of land-based aircraft, in all three of those respects more than the Americans had at or available for Midway weeks later. But the carrier air groups were still weak, with old planes and some newly navalized land-based models with bad teething troubles. When the Japanese carrier fleet arrived, all that the British could do was have their local merchant shipping annihilated, the same thing happen to their unsupported land-based air (prior to the special case of the Gulf War, carrier and land-based aircraft had never co-operated successfully anywhere; the methods of operation are too different, ability to concentrate being an intrinsic part of the carrier's superiority, and second nature to a navy skilled in its usage), as to a small British carrier which did not get away in time, and lastly to two fleeing British cruisers. The big British carriers and battleships could only flee and live to fight another day. Their Admiral was **not** relieved, and justifiably so; the inter-war bureaucratic mess had not been his responsibility.

Before streams of American purpose-built carrier planes became available, the expedient had been to navalize land-based designs, because it was thought quicker than awaiting new designs. The choice was not really the Royal Navy's, with war-time calls for other uses of aircraft-builders' resources and with aircraft production concentrated under a separate wartime ministry run by British press Lord Beaverbrook. (Unlike the classical models, the modern pillar is hollow: Beaverbrook, formerly Max Aitkin, was an old Lloyd George hanger-on pressed into service as part of the "National" government, Churchill's device to enlist Liberal and Labour support for continuing the war and his government against the mass of Conservative M.P.s who detested him; "Rex Mottram" in Evelyn Waugh's *Brideshead Revisited* was Max Aitkin.)

But land-based designs are built for taking off from and landing on very long runways, building up speed slowly, and landing the same way. They are simply not capable of sustainedly taking catapult take-offs and the rough abrupt landing by arrester cables on pitching decks.

The requisite strength cannot be just slapped on like a coat of salt-resistant paint. The British aircraft involved took years to semi-navalize, the early ones quickly destroyed by routine use, not combat. By the time the designs were durable enough for extended use, the war was over and they were outmoded anyway. Britain made up ground by importing thousands of American purpose-built carrier planes, high-performing enough to compete with the most advanced land-based planes, and with the built-in airframe and landing gear ruggedness to keep working. (Most of these Lend-Lease loaners were simply pushed overboard in 1945, with the British keeping on their own navalized mediocrities.)

Such ruggedness makes carrier planes easily capable of the reverse transition, operation from airfields. Corsairs, Skyhawks and Phantoms were the carrier planes to go into the most extensive land-based use, each for decades, and each in the thousands. No land-based monoplane has ever really been able to meet the challenge of transition to carrier use; they simply are not built for it, and rebuilding takes more time and expense than developing a new purpose-built model. A carrier plane can come from a land-based project, *provided* that it is done early enough in the design process: the McDonnell Douglas F-18 Hornet in current carrier use -- and in future foreign land-based use -- was developed from the land-based Northrop F-17 proposal, but the changes were massive, fundamental and lengthy during the redesign. It is far easier to simultaneously develop an aircraft for land or carrier use, as the French have done with their new Rafele; additional toughness never hurt a land-based plane.

The RAF experience shows the pitfalls of re-organizing a particular activity into one organization, when the definition of the activity is intrinsically flawed, and therefore essentially arbitrary, because it neglects fundamental differences in an activity as it takes place under varying conditions and with varying goals. In that respect it is socialism in place, lumping disparate things into one inefficient mass, to give a roseate glow of rationality and consistency to the resolutely simple-minded. But such plausibility has a certain Darwinian value in democratic politics, a camouflage similar to the flu virus' varying coats, and enabling the same essentially bad idea, the "essence of reform", or of socialism, or of bureaucratization, to slip into an activity like the genetic material of a flu virus into a cell. Such bureaucratic imperatives are a parasitic infestation of real needs, the virus replicating itself to the detriment of the infected body politic.

There is no real air activity *per se* to be lumped into one air force, with its own parochial outlook and its own set of priorities. There are naval air activities, most notably carrier operation and maritime patrol, best kept exclusively under the operating service, with its already integrated priorities, that will try to find the optimum combination of aircraft (or other new technology) and more traditional tools to accomplish those priorities. That process is best left undisturbed by not artificially dividing away air functions. In the naval arena at least, the U.S., since the maritime patrol crisis of 1942 (when the coastal German submarine threat and the low priority afforded by the Army Air Corps/Force to land-based maritime patrol led to months of slaughtered merchant ships off America's Atlantic coast), has prospered by keeping everything naval under the senior naval service, maximizing capability and minimizing waste compared to the planeless carriers and extemporized aircraft of other countries that tried the unified air approach for naval purposes.

B.   The Canadian Snowball: Three into One Won't Go Far

One pole of reform for handling presumably pernicious service rivalries is the Canadian method of unification. The unsentimentalized result of the Canadian experience argues strongly against unification. An industrialized country with a fairly small population for its size, Canada gets, in return for its medium-sized defense budget, three small roles filled: a small NATO contingent for Europe, a small anti-submarine force mostly for the North Atlantic and a small Continental Air Defense force in co-operation with the U.S., which de-prioritized Air Defense from 1961 through 1981. All three roles were expected to be filled, should the balloon go up, by the use of tactical nuclear warheads; there was therefore a sense that sharpened skills and abilities were beside of the point. The three roles left to the unified Canadian military are roughly those of an army, a navy and an air force; Canadian unification was largely a political cosmetic for lassitudinous pallor, a failure to achieve real economies commensurate with the substantial lack of capacity realized. Compared to a politically similar Netherlands with about 10 million fewer people, Canada has less air and ground capability and a dramatically smaller and less able sea force.

Compared to even smaller countries with lesser industrial bases, such as Norway, Sweden and Israel, Canada's unified system is inefficient and backward. Norway has designed and built its own anti-submarine weapon and anti-ship cruise missile. Larger Sweden designs and builds its own supersonic fighters, tanks, self-propelled artillery more advanced than the U.S.'s and cruise missiles. Israel produces its own cruise missiles, Merkava tanks, Kfir jet fighters (a combination of a Mirage body, B-70/late Mirage/Concorde/Swedish airfoils and a GE engine) and is working on more advanced aircraft and ballistic missiles. Meanwhile, Canada's most notable military innovation has been a device for grabbing hold of helicopters trying to land on board ship in rough waters, the "Bear-trap".

Since American liberals generally wish to cut defense capabilities without cutting governmental expenditures, the Canadian experience has been a satisfactory one; unification of the services remains a liberal holy grail. Compounding this is the separation mentioned in the Constitution liberals despise (an army and a navy, joined at the President, as commander-in-chief), although, for public relations purposes, the sham of strengthening U.S. defense is proffered. The Canadian example is not the only one, however, in spite of the selective interest of liberals shopping for support for military reductions or for socialized medicine. Aside from the more obviously negative British experiences in both areas, or even the domestic experience with both leftist manias, the Soviet Union provided instruction in both areas.

C.   The Russian Bear Juggles More Balls

Fortunately for the U.S., its main foreign adversary, Soviet Russia, had the same multiple priority problem as that muffed in the house of the inter-war RAF. Structural dissimilarities with American and British society disprove, yet again, the "Iron Triangle" rubbish; two apexes of such a triangle (contractors and vote-grubbing politicians) were absent for Soviet Russia's three generations. Real Soviet politicians did not need votes, except a half-dozen in the Central Committee, and there were no contracts, just do-or-die directives from the top. The third apex, a military and its bureaucracy, was present, but was for nearly seven decades made up of men who advanced in rank due to their predecessors' execution by the political leadership, not a prospect to cheer boat-rockers and swivel-chair empire-builders. Communist leadership **was** Russian politics, long supreme and in command through terror or its memory; patronage consisted of better food, clothing and housing, not contracts. And the result was a far more massive Soviet military, consistently taking up more resources, and from a much smaller economy, than America's. The cause was a force-oriented political prime-mover, both paranoically defensive and opportunistically expansive; the bureaucracy affected only details, as is bureaucracy's nature (power either establishes priorities, or it dithers and delegates them to organizational tables and red-tape artists, who simply fight over them eternally). Liberal confusion and drift promote U.S. mismanagement, part of the confusion being devil theory smoke screens spewed out, and lead to more confusion and drift. But Soviet patterns have been both newsworthy and instructive.

The original Czarist forté, heavy bombing, had gone with Igor Sikorsky, who changed first countries and then fields to invent the helicopter. The Soviet Air Force developed as part of a huge build-up made after defeat by the glowering colossus of Pilsudski's Poland (both Polish victory and Soviet build-up being aided by Germany), although the Russian Army received the bulk of the pie. Much like the Italian build-up of the thirties, the premature Soviet build-up saw an exhausted economy entering a new era of accelerated technical growth unable to provide its forces with the new weapons to replace huge masses of suddenly outmoded equipment. Much old stuff was lost early in World War II, along with the troops it equipped; but Russia, unlike Italy, had the resources, land, numbers and foreign aid to survive. Both the Soviet Army and Air Force entered the post-war era with massive numbers of a few well designed weapons; foreign-pattern equipment was left available for export to cause new trouble. America did not get its Lend-Lease garden hose back from the Soviets either, as Dodge and Studebaker trucks kept the Soviet economy sputtering along longer than Studebaker, and American equipment helped Mao win China.

Unlike ground equipment, aircraft were still evolving rapidly, so Soviet Air, previously restricted to ground support and interceptors by the nature of its war and equipment, was unhandicapped by possession of large categories soon to be outmoded anyway. The limiting factor would have been jet engines, but foreign aid made up the ground, both captured German engineers and engines and, more infamously, the British Labour Government's gift of Rolls-Royce jet engines and specs -- rather than exporting, post-war Britain, prostrate and getting heavy American aid, was giving away its valuables, and to the common enemy.

Political appreciations, the lack of modern bombers and the capture of German rocket scientists led to the swift development of Soviet rocketry, its strategic role institutionalized by the status of two separate services. The first of these, a product of the American possession of heavy bombers and atomic bombs, was the Soviet Air Defense Force, the Soviet Air Force's interceptor branch, which then rapidly developed surface-to-air missiles and deployed them in staggering numbers. There was also soon a plethora of strategic bombardment rocket models, with the older ones kept in service. The new Soviet Rocketry Service knew that the most truly obsolete weapon is the one scrapped, and the Rocketry Service grew by adding new units to operate new models, instead of stagnating in size by retiring the old models and re-equipping their troops. The captured German engineers had specialized in liquid-fueled designs, something the Russians long persisted in, but mainly for strategic rockets. The Russians had a clear understanding of solid fuels dating from the early thirties (the Soviets had co-operated with the Nazis in developing solid-fuel tactical army bombardment rockets, which both nations soon used on each other), and probably understood how to scale up that knowledge to strategic rockets, had they wished.

Cumbersome liquid fuel, in the age of first-strike fear, was not a great way of getting a rocket off the ground to escape an enemy first strike; that was however a consideration irrelevant to the nation seeking only a first-strike capability, a nation that long had no real fear of being attacked itself, even after the U.S. had added fast missiles to its slow bombers. The rocket is a faster weapon because it does not need the atmosphere to breath and fly, and can rise above its friction to move fast. Bombers, to accompany a first strike, would have to start hours in advance, and would forfeit surprise due to their longer approach. Soviet emphasis on rocketry was an emphasis on a maximum first-strike capability, to catch American bombers on the ground. But then, any pursuit of military virtue is an opportunity for attack, as opponents of the U.S. Strategic Defense Initiative maintain; not only will it **not** work, they say, but when it **does**, the U.S. could use its security to attack other nations, surely an excuse for them to mind their manners.

The Soviet Air Force maintained its old priorities of ground support, by political edict, as well as its interception role, an air defense made more critical by American possession of both bombers and Bomb. The fighter branch was joined by a profusion of Soviet anti-aircraft missiles, more successful in peace-time than in service with the North Vietnamese (well over 99% ineffective, with B-52s bombing Hanoi with about 1/5 of the loss rate of World War II raids on heavily defended area targets such as Schweinfurt and Ploesti, and far less than in many contested raids on small difficult targets, such as ships or the Sedan bridges) or Arabs. Missile lapses led to a loss of Soviet confidence in them, with the Kremlin commanding more effort than performance. Long after the U.S. bomber force had ceased to be a main threat, Soviet factories continued churning out small fighters for its clients and customers. Bombers for its own use were a distant aerospace priority, behind Air Defense and Strategic Rocketry. But had the large American bomber fleet not forced the Soviets into Air Defense, they would probably have added their own Bomber Command, rather than eventually making their Navy a priority again.

The principal beneficiaries of the Russian strategic bomber de-emphasis were the U.S., which followed its Air Defense buildup by overtaking Russian rocket progress, as well as the Soviet Navy. The Soviet Navy got bombers of its own as well as cast-offs from the Air Force, using them for long-range patrol and as bomb buses to offset its long-time lack of aircraft carriers. The Soviet Navy also early developed the cruise missile to arm its ships, using intermediate guidance from other ships or patrol aircraft to make up the early shortcomings of "smart" guidance. Air-launched cruise missiles for the patrol planes themselves followed. With the competing priorities of a huge Army, a burgeoning Rocket Service, a growing Navy and an Air Force with the third role of strategic transport added, Soviet industry could not keep pace with its aircraft and engine designers. Large body production was stuck on subsonic production of transports, airliners and naval patrol bombers, while fighter aircraft was geared to small designs.

Large new high-performance fighter aircraft were desired despite the economic performance of Soviet-made fighters against the U.S. after the MiG-15 debacle in Korea. But the MiG-15s had fallen mainly to the light F-86 Sabre, hardly an endorsement of the large fighter concept. This had seduced the U.S. first, but aside from the able operation of such large fighters by the Israelis after 1967, it was other American innovations, and Soviet megalomania, which made large fighters attractive. The spectre of low-altitude bombers and cruise missiles placed an apparent premium upon fighter size, the extra weight needed for look-down radar and a crewman to operate it, as well as the greater range applicable to a fighter no longer tied to local radar vectoring. These large high-tech new fighters strained Soviet production facilities, both as to capacity and as to quality, and the whole armaments program strained the economy in a fashion that did not happen in the modern U.S., despite liberal prattle. In the Soviet case, armaments were the economy to a great extent, while in the U.S. the greater economy was more under a long drumbeat of liberal attack, on behalf of more patronage ("social programs"), the chimera of free trade and higher taxes, than under strain from a war economy. While liberals opportunely obfuscated various procurement issues, American military organization was more quickly and fundamentally put into play.

Chapter 13 - U.S. Organization, Re-organization, Disorganization

A. A New Ball and a New Juggler:
American Air and the Defense Department

Despite liberal hype about inter-service rivalries, the effect on American defense of the traditional rivalry and its animosities between the Army and the Navy has been negligible, each having its own sphere, and the Navy's possession of the Marine Corps making the problem of co-operation with land forces one usually harmoniously resolved within the Navy Department, or operationally with the Army in larger campaigns, each service understanding its job and co-operating without a new layer of deadweight bureaucracy. The main problem in actual operation was who was to unload and care for supplies on the beach, important but properly addressed by local improvisation and new equipment. It was the twentieth century and the advent of the aerial dimension to war that complicated matters, making the RAF a seductive bureaucratic solution as well as making for some more American pitfalls: the ideological problem of aerial supremacy, the tactical problem of battlefield air support, the emergence of guided missiles with their utility for atomic warheads, the problem of intra-service rivalry and the "roles and missions" fetish.

The cult of re-organization is a favorite of the liberal-letterhead complex, and when its dynamic co-incided with events and the need for patronage, a re-organization of defense and airpower was undertaken. Unlike previous executive branch re-orderings (1939 -- Franklin Roosevelt; 1946 -- Harry Truman) of the non-military national security state, making possible secret intervention, the post-war military re-organizations co-incided with a massive build-down from war-time mobilization. Two big services, the Army and Navy, with their respective Army Air Force and Marine branches, had managed 11 million men to victory. But that managerial apparatus was deemed insufficient after a massive 90% cut-down of the services. A third service was somehow needed, an independent Air Force, and the three somehow needed a new civilian Defense Secretary, inserted between them and their constitutional commander-in-chief, the President. While superficially eliminating one cabinet post (through the combination of the old Navy and War Departments), each service still had its own secretary, answering to a new level of bureaucracy, the Defense Secretary, so that the 90% reduction in military manpower was administered by a 100% **increase** in civilian brass (a 20-fold increase in the secretary/field force ratio), doubling the old number of secretaries, from two to four (Air Force and Defense the additions, with War changed in title to Army). The new secretaryships included associated staffs, military and, especially, civilian. The Democrats' long hold on national power was slipping away in congressional elections, and the unpopular Truman was thought headed for defeat. It was time to lock the gang into their jobs, to withstand the expected Republican renaissance. The Republicans, confidently looking forward to a 1948 sweep of the White House and an increase in their control of Capitol Hill, saw themselves soon filling the additional posts. Otherwise, the birth of the Defense Department was the last gasp of the New Deal tactic of swelling existing agencies with new offices and responsibility. Henceforth, the number of cabinet posts was to swell also, one under the reluctant liberal Eisenhower, and more under Lyndon Johnson and Jimmy Carter.

For the first two decades of the independent Air Force, the main determinants of political policy, and of the shape of its forces, were Cold War Liberalism, the later Truman, Eisenhower, Kennedy and Johnson. One typical bureaucratic response of the Air Force was the perceived need for a service academy of its own, as though the traditional academies had been turning out dolts. The Air Force leadership, widely painted as thick because its brilliance detracted from that of the Billy Mitchell anti-military icon or was of the dour LeMay type, had seen its galaxy of leaders perform well in World War II, after having emerged from the engineering background of West Point in the initial instance, even as Annapolis had poured out the leadership for the Navy's enormous modern and high-technology aircraft operations, as well as of the Marine Corps' air wings. But bureaucratic imperatives prevailed, and a new Air Force Academy was decreed for the nation's governmental western hip-brain, out in Colorado among the fossil beds of its non-functional predecessors. At a time of general military shrinkage, and larger planes with fewer officer pilots, the supply of officers strangely had to be increased, as though the older academies, Reserve supplements and promotions from the ranks were or would be insufficient.

Technomania had arrived, and one bureaucratic academy started a whole series of liberal military dominoes falling. With ROTC downgraded in importance by the arrival of another service academy, the way was further opened for other government aid to higher education's gold-plated treadmills under the excuse of "National Defense", until it became habitual and the defense moniker mutated to "National Direct". The money was a deadweight loss, puffing up the nation's collegiate liberal patronage mills with students to rake instead of leaves, and generally supporting the indoctrination of those students in leftist ideology, with its unpatriotic and anti-military stridencies. The bill was a measly few hundred billion dollars and hundreds of millions of student-years wasted chasing, and catching, sheepskins.

The atomic era meant more than just adjustments to the American psyche and balance sheet. For the Air Force, that mushroom cloud had a silver lining, the possibility of achieving full actualization of the bombardment weapon which, even the misnamed and overrated *Strategic Bombing Survey* realized, had not been achieved in World War II with conventional explosives; Billy Mitchell's theories had proved to be over-blown. Strategic airpower had been the key to expanding the Army Air Force and making it independent; with the Bomb, the new service's su-premacy seemed assured. Because nuclear weapons had a large umbrella effect for a brief historical moment, and still do in some vital areas, the concept was somewhat valid. The U.S. could threaten other countries with the Bomb, but they could not threaten us. America the Bad used that transient superiority to otherwise disarm itself, rather than to have its way with the world. The world repaid by developing its own atomic bombs, threatening America the Stupid with annihilation on one hand and brushfire wars on the other.

Deterrence became mutual, although other U.S. inhibitions also helped keep it from victory in Korea, so there were other effects on that conflict than the non-use of atomic weapons. The uses at Hiroshima and Nagasaki were not followed up, as the U.S. did not seem to want to pick on an alliance that could fight back in that same way. The blizzard of leftist "peace" propaganda did not help American resolve. (An irony of the Iran-Contra "scandal" was Ronald Reagan rhetorically asking report-ers if they remembered where they were on August 8, 1985. During the Cold War, the defeatist media was busy that week with dewy-eyed fast-breaking "news" about little Japanese girls who died of leukemia decades ago, or about the latest "Ground Zero" terror-mongering; with the end of the Cold War that sort of "news" has tapered off, giving way to the "need" for a "national health care system", for example.) For American defense, as the atomic umbrella effect diminished with mutual deter-rence, the cost of necessary tactical expedients increased; but the atomic spear-chucking role still remained a plum, for the Air Force as well as for the other big two services trying to horn in.

B.   The Navy Wants its Bomb

The Navy, which had launched Doolittle's Raid in 1942, had started for it a purpose-built islandless aircraft carrier strategic bomber base during the Truman Administration, the *United States* project, but Congress balked at its completion. The Navy did proceed with designs for nuclear bombers designed for smaller carriers, as well as with rock-ets for naval launch of nuclear weapons, but another big project still had some appeal. The Navy tried to break the Air Force's atom-bomb stra-tegic monopoly with an atomic-powered aircraft, apparently thinking such a beast would qualify as a ship. The Air Force responded with its own such project. Steam-powered aircraft (oil-fired or otherwise), with the weight of boilers, feedwater, and step-up gears (or generator, wiring and electric motors) to spin the propellors at the requisite speed, were not common, to say the least; the weight of the lead and/or concrete shielding for the reactor would have been tremendous. Even diesel engines, only slightly heavier than gasoline engines, were never really practicable for aircraft use because of their weight (a heavy engine block is needed for strength to contain high-pressure compression for fuel ignition; gasoline engines have spark plugs to do the igniting without pressure's bulk requirement), although for less weight-sensitive applications -- ships, tanks, locomotives and trucks -- their fuel efficiency and other economies are valuable. But some thought atomic-powered turbines practical for a very large plane. The cost would have been astronomical, and even if someone could've built it, they couldn't have afforded to risk losing it in a war. And no one wants nuclear reactors flying around, and possibly crashing -- although that fact was probably the Navy's trump card in the mad race: use them over water only. According to the budgets (not always reliable), each competing service spent more than a billion dollars on its separate lunatic project, mostly during the 1950s, and therefore hard and valuable pre-inflation dollars.

The Air Force did fly a nuclear reactor in a B-36, but the plane was too heavily loaded for even electric motors, let alone nuclear turbines or a bomb-load. The B-36 was the Air Force's post-war big gun, although it had been a pre-war project meant to bomb Germany from across the Atlantic. With the Democrat Truman in office and the left-media still biding its time, the B-36's shift in "role and mission" went uncommented on, as did its Old Western nickname of the "Peacemaker". Much later, Reagan's designation of the MX missile in old Minuteman holsters as the "Peacekeeper" was harped with the usual witless overkill, but at least Reagan had the excuse of having been host of a syndicated Old Western television show -- "Death Valley Days".

The wits had missed not only the New Deal's nostalgic evocation of civilizing the old frontier, they had also missed the earlier irony of the pacifist Herbert Hoover's hot new bomber, Boeing's "B-9". They had also dutifully refrained from remarking upon the High Noonish implications of Kennedy's New Frontier, or of their hero being shot in the back after the face-offs at the Havana Corral, even as their predecessors or younger selves had dutifully parroted Franklin Roosevelt's whooper about thinking of Lend-Lease as a garden hose. A multi-billion dollar garden hose that kills millions of people is quite remarkable, but at least it wasn't some ghastly assault rifle.

The idea of the atomic-powered plane limped on into the 1980s. The July 1, 1982 issue of *The Lockheed Star* ("Official Publication of the Lockheed California Co.") reported that that company's "Advanced Concepts Design Division [was studying].... a proposed nuclear-powered flying aircraft carrier. Designed to carry fighters, support aircraft and missiles under its wings, and supplies, troops and crew members in a five-story fuselage, it appears to be Lockheed's answer to Battlestar Galactica. Weighing in at a hefty 11 million pounds, from wing tip to wing tip it's longer than four football fields [there they are again!

-- and they might even be the longer Canadian football fields of Bill Loughhead's youth] and has an overall surface area of nearly three acres. Using 54 auxiliary engines on takeoff, it would have a nuclear reactor to take over at 17,000 feet to power four large cruise engines on missions of up to a month in duration before having to land."

Battlestar Lunacy was more like it. "Battlestar Galactica", a syndicated television show about a race threatened with extinction by machines, had already been shot down by the deadly combination of low ratings and high production costs, after a flight even longer than a month in duration. Another and more advanced 1950s' project, the Flying Wing, had been featured as a nuclear weapons carrier in the 1953 movie "War of the Worlds" (the Martians were unaffected by the Bomb). A syndicated television series loosely based on the movie appeared in the late 1980s, just as the Flying Wing, like the Martians, was, "from a state of deep hibernation,... resurrected, more terrifying than ever before", as the half-billion-dollar-apiece Stealth Bomber. Made of exotic radar-absorbing materials, the plane's huge cost showed the perils of going to Wells once too often, even as the movie proved that a movie studio could get a jet for a prop.

But for the atomic-powered plane project, wasn't it refreshing to have an aircraft company refer to one of its projects, even one on the very rearmost burner, as hefty? In this public relations-conscious age, an airplane about 50 times as heavy as any previous plane would usually be described as "a slim and nimble 55 hundred tons". But rockets more than half that weight *have* worked, the Saturn V Apollo moon rockets. Nor was the flying aircraft carrier without precedent, and not just from stillborn designs and development. In the 1930s, the Navy had two dirigibles carrying modified Curtiss Sparrowhawk fighters (hook on upper wing instead of under tail; because the airships could match "landing" speed with the aircraft, no real structural modification was necessary); both airships crashed. Blimps, however, have been used into the atomic age for observation tasks, atomic attack and drug-smuggling sentinels equipped with large radar antennas in their gas-bags.

Even as Lockheed had kept open its appeal to the Navy by characterizing its phantasy as a flying aircraft carrier, so had the Air Force hoped for its own aircraft carrier. Contracts were let for McDonnell to develop a small parasite fighter, the Goblin, to be carried by long-range bombers on their assigned missions, presumably outside of other fighter-escort range. But research ended after the Goblins had trouble reconnecting to the B-36s used as test carriers. And so ended the arthritic Truman-era controversy of press and Congress about "the B-36 versus the aircraft carrier", one of the frequent rewrites of the Billy Mitchell mess, and just as stupid as the rest.

During the 1950s, the Navy, in addition to its atomic-powered plane project and much more successful carrier-launched atomic bombers, also dithered with cruise missiles for warship and submarine launch of atomic warheads. Cruise missiles, a Nazi invention as the famed "buzzbombs", were tiny unmanned jet aircraft packed with explosives. Early solid-state electronics gave the Navy unsatisfactory results hitting small targets like ships with conventional explosives, so it abandoned cruise missiles for a long spell, using its carrier aircraft for long reach, nuclear or otherwise, and working on ballistic missiles for longer range from smaller ships. Other nations, including the long carrier-less Soviets, continued work on cruise missiles with various guidance systems. The lack of modern naval battles blinded the U.S. Navy to cruise missile progress until minor conflicts, beginning with the 1967 Arab-Israeli War and including the India-Pakistan Wars, showed Russian and other cruise missiles to be a potent weapon even in relatively backward hands. U.S. Navy cruise missile development and defense became a sudden priority, with light anti-aircraft machine guns suddenly making a comeback. The big nuclear-powered cruiser *Long Beach*, originally a strategic, cruise and anti-aircraft missile ship, had lost its early cruise missiles, its anti-aircraft guns were removed as obsolete and its strategic role was kidnapped by submarines. After a lapse of years, a new generation of each was installed -- the old gun positions went unreplaced, as the new designated anti-cruise missile guns instead replaced the radars for the ship's stripped-out Talos anti-aircraft missile system, a marvelous success from the ship's original equipment. The more things changed, the more they cost.

C.   Submariners Grab the Navy's Atomic Role

The Navy's ultimate success in the battle with the Air Force was the marriage of the new nuclear-powered submarine, with its independence of the ocean's surface and hence largely of detection, to the Polaris missile originally developed for launch from surface ships, including from the *Long Beach*. The first shotgun wedding in the series saw the Navy cut some of its first large batch of standard nuclear-powered submarines in half, adding a section with sixteen missile tubes for the Polaris modified for underwater launch; it was a success, and the Navy had its main strategic role. *Sic transit gloria mundi*, however, for success in the strategic rivalry with the Air Force simply made for a greater rivalry within the Navy, as the submariners, the garrulous "silent service", became a law unto themselves, and began to fight for control of the Navy's command and budget against the carrier-dominated surface fleet.

Imitating the carrier groups with their high percentage of officer-pilots, the submariners fought back by over-organizing. Unlike surface ships, which, not being invisible, can routinely communicate with each other without giving away an advantage, submarines cannot communicate with each other and co-ordinate their activities well. Should they do so, they simply effectively become visible surface ships with a massive deficit of weapons and detection devices. Submarines that stay hidden just do not need floating admirals as carrier and battle task forces do. The submariners established massive training and engineering departments, very over-officered, as well as instituted a policy of double crews for many nuclear submarines, with a double dose of officers. The specious rationale for double crews was that modern nuclear-powered submarines, with their clean air, bright lights, fresh water and spacious pastel decor, were too stressful for a single crew, although the old submarines, the "pig-boats" with their buried-alive-in-mechanical-Hell ambiance, diesel and chlorine fumes choking a cramped and greasy labyrinth of low-hanging pipes, had somehow managed with one crew each; at least the popping ears and the powdered eggs were the same, anyway. The submariners, with more officers and dozens more submarines from the new strategic role (and a new training establishment for "ballastic" missilemen), were able to out-breed the surface Navy, eventually flooding the admiralty with their candidates.

The result of the flood of submariners was to put too high a priority on the submarine. Although able to play hide well, the submarine is not particularly good at seek: when it fires in combat, it generally gives up its main strength. It is also not capable of the military virtue of concentration and co-ordination for tactical decisiveness, something surface ships, including sub-hunting groups, can do well. Submarines are snipers, and snipers do not win wars. They may pick off merchant ships or the occasional warship, but that is not a great bag when the submarines themselves are extremely expensive items. Despite the plethora of small wars since World War II, many quite bloody and extended, submarines just have not done much. They have sunk an Argentine cruiser and an Indian frigate, but they have had little effect on the outcomes of their wars. Mostly, submarines have been irrelevant to events ashore, unlike carriers with their versatile aircraft or surface ships with their guns. They do have a strategic missile carriage role, but that involves either blowing up the world or, and more frequently, not.

In the two Cold War Liberal Crusades, Korea and Vietnam, submarines were of no use whatsoever, and even though we have spent more than a trillion dollars on them, they still have little utility for war on land. Now, with a cruise missile-launch role, submarines can send the same explosive charge with a million-dollar missile as the surface Navy can with a $600 bomb or battleship shell; and, of course, the bomber or battleship is much more evasive or well armored than the submarine which has given its position away. In the Gulf War, U.S. submarines finally did break their decades-old drought. Adding a late wave of Tomahawk cruise missiles from a safe distance, where their underwater ability was bootless, the subs supplemented the bombardment by carrier aircraft with guided missiles and bombs and by surface ships with shells and far more cruise missiles.

The surface Navy's problem is more than just its having been out-maneuvered on officers and that it does not have a big-time strategic missile role. As the generalist portion of the Navy, in contrast to the submarine Navy's specialization, surface ships use more unskilled labor. The Navy, in the age of a volunteer American military, is no longer an out for the brighter enlistees seeking to escape draft into the Army by opting for the Navy, with its better food, less marching and no foxhole-digging. Newer and more labor-efficient ships, cutting up to 60% off the manning requirements for former standard types (except carriers), and higher wages have failed to close the gap completely. The useful surface fleet has become handicapped by its large numbers of social misfits, borderline cases for the jobs that the more technical, and lily-White, submarine service does not have. The force with race riots tends to be at a public relations disadvantage when pressing its case for appropriations. By contrast, less versatile submarines, capable mainly of an aquatic mole routine, can tunnel in to grub for budget requests, coming off as the more disciplined, more tightly run, more military, more ship-shape part of the Navy. To quote Karl Marx, "Well-grubbed, old mole!" It is really the only time the submariners have to get their hands dirty.

D. The Army Gets Atomic Missiles, for Awhile

The Navy's bifurcation resultant from its appropriation of a ballistic missile role was not repeated in the other two services involved. The Air Force, partly in response to other circumstances -- the vulnerability of its airfields to Soviet missiles, most notably -- was to develop land-based missiles, also underway by the Army, which was stretching the possibility of missiles for tactical battlefield bombardment into a longer-ranged strategic role. The Army, deprived of aircraft by the cleaving-away of the Air Force (which had of course been the **Army** Air Force) as well as by Eisenhower's later orders (1956 dealing with strategic missiles and a later extension to combat aircraft, but not helicopters), wanted a bigger atomic role than gun-fired bombs, an entrée to aerospace. Missiles were the vehicle, for the battlefield and beyond.

Early missiles were comparatively short-ranged for the strategic role, and had to be placed in bases abroad to be within reach of Soviet targets. The Army was later fended off, helped by the emergence of longer-ranged missiles, which could be based in the U.S. and hit all of Soviet Russia, instead of just the large areas, primarily of European Russia, reachable by the older generation (more like older siblings, really) of foreign-based models. The new missiles were intercontinental, and therefore had less of a blush of an Army tactical weapon. Eventually, Army tactical nukes were victims of a diplomatic thaw, the Reagan build-up followed by the Bush tear-down. But both were justifiable, the Reagan build-up on diplomatic grounds, and the Bush cut-back on the grounds of radiation.

Although the Air Force, like the Navy, was now split between a ballistic missile portion and an aircraft-dominated portion, its split was far less organizationally profound. The main goal of the flying Air Force was still the strategic atomic delivery role, so that the Strategic Air Command, after early failures of the air-launched cruise missile to extend its bombers' capabilities, could easily absorb ballistic missiles as complementary means within its mandate, unlike the Navy, which had only a small aircraft-based strategic role. On an entire-service basis, however, both services were neglecting other roles for their respective top two.

The Navy, with its carrier and submarine rivalries battling for the top-dog spot, and its amphibious role getting the next priority due to its Marine branch, was neglecting both minesweeping (being left to presumed allies, including by giving them most of America's minesweepers, as well as giving them money to build newer ones) and the cruise missile aspect of surface warfare. Like the old RAF, the Air Force's top units were the Strategic Air Command, literally Bomber Command all over again, also later with missiles, and Continental Air Defense, literally Fighter Command all over again, with its interceptors and radars supplemented by anti-aircraft missiles. Although the U.S. Air Force had no carrier-based or coastal patrol role to neglect, it did have several other roles to battle for the third spot, and, with the later denigration of Continental Air Defense by Cold War Liberalism, even for the second spot. The other three roles were tactical airpower, which the Air Force considered mainly a job of commanding the air against an enemy, transport and battlefield support of American troops.

The eventual outcome can best be looked at via the Reagan Administration's later priorities in filling the Air Force shopping bag. The Strategic Air Command finally got its new supersonic bomb-bus, the B-1B, as well as extensive development of the Stealth Bomber and two land-based missiles, the MX and the Midgetman. Continental Air Defense's rationale got massive sums spent on research and development of the Strategic Defense Initiative, looking at various exotic ways of shooting down missiles, and incidentally putting the planets within reach as the German V-2 rockets had put space into reach. The transport role of the Air Force's third independent command, the Military Airlift Command, was expanded with a new batch of dozens of huge C-5B Galaxy transports. Tactical Air received a wing of the new Stealth Fighters for command of the air through intruder raids, but it failed to completely shake off the ground support role by dumping its purpose-built planes for that role in favor of more aerially oriented tactical fighters for the squadrons and their pilots devoted to ground support. (Larger and less numerous fighters also meant that Tactical Air's flood of candidates for generalship had lessened, crimping its hole-card.) By 1980s' standards, the Air Force's priorities had shifted, with Strategic still on top as always, Tactical Air up to second and Airlift a strong third. Air Defense was a distant fourth, and ground support in the cellar, below ground.

E.   The Army Gets Helicopters, the Hind-Tit of Aerospace

The Air Force, with the supersession of both its and the Army's medium-ranged missiles, had retained the land-based strategic missile role, restricting the Army to much shorter-ranged missiles for tactical nuclear weapons. At the same time, it had repelled an Army attempt to restart an Army Air Force of its own for ground support and battlefield command of the air, which the Air Force's Big Three commands, Strategic, Air Defense and Airlift, were uninterested in. Pursuant to Defense Department directive, the Army was prohibited from having fixed-wing planes, being restricted to helicopters. The Army, the least successful of the three services in moving outside of its primary mission of the battlefield, at least had a definite mandate for helicopters for battlefield support, but that was more a triumph for bureaucracy than for the efficient achievement of military capability.

The Army, and its role for the nation's defense, had really been bureaucratically defeated; the Navy had its own fixed-wing aircraft and helicopters, as did its sub-branch the Marines, with Marine ground troops very well integrated with the Marine Corps' own air wings as well as with the Navy's carrier forces, from which the Marines derived most of their aircraft and from which they often flew and otherwise co-operated operationally. The Marine Corps has consistently been the service branch most exemplifying the qualities praised by liberal reformers in the abstract, such as versatility, mobility, economy and integration of its operations, and it has also consistently been the target of those same liberal reformers, seeking its abolition. Obviously, when liberals do make pertinent criticisms, such are not well meaning. Occasional liberal truthfulness is only incidental; there is always a sinister purpose.

The Army, on the other hand, had its primary air support in separate hands, and was left with the third-best alternative of over-developing the helicopter, an intrinsically limited technology that was also more suited to Navy and Marine needs. The helicopter's key ability is that it can take off from and land just about anywhere. That ability for heavier-than-air flight was pioneered by the autogyro, which had a propellor for forward speed and a free-spinning rotor for lift; but autogyros had less utility for specialized missions where freer lift was required. Before military use was really contemplated, the helicopter was made by removing the autogyro's prop, powering its rotor, and adding a small spin-countering prop to the tails of the single-rotor models. Helicopters act, as we all know, by spinning large rotors, causing huge rushes of air downward, to lift the helicopters, with slight tilts of the rotors making forward airspeed and changes of direction possible. As the helicopter flies through the air, the downward flow is almost perpendicular to its progress, so that the craft is constantly battling the inertia of its own downdraft, as well as other drags. The huge cross-section of body, rotor and downdraft makes the 'copter an inefficient flier, with an exceedingly restricted airspeed, restricted payload, altitude restrictions, high fuel consumption and limited range in return for its verticality.

In Marine and Navy operations, conducted near sea-level, the 'copter's need for thick air is not important. But at the high altitudes of mountain warfare, as in the Soviet Afghanistan campaign or the Nicaraguan Communists' anti-Contra campaign, crashes from loss of control in narrow valleys, from mountain winds and from loggy controls were added to enemy fire and the helicopter's usual miseries, the weather and mechanical mishaps attributable to what is "basically a toy". Even the debits that go with the helicopter's useful attributes do not exhaust the list of negatives. Because the rotors must be on top of the copters for gross balance reasons (copters hang from their rotors, and having them underneath would be extremely unstable, as well as restricting the craft from landing anywhere to just clumsy hanging devices) and the engines and their gearing must be close to the rotors to avoid lengthy and even more fragile connecting shafts, helicopters are top-heavy. Einstein told us that inertia and weight are the same, so in helicopters with moving rotors and turbines, as in taking-off, flying, hovering and landing, the inertia of the heavy parts' movement adds to top-heaviness. Copters thus tend to flip over on the ground, smashing their rotors and shredding themselves and anything else around, and do not float well. The tipping-over problem is compounded by the use of narrow skids or by the adoption of retractable landing gear, more expensive, complicated and fragile, for the purpose of an insignificant reduction in the copter's massive drag, and an invisible return in speed and range in return for greater danger. The ability to land anywhere is also the key to landing on soft soil, where tipping-over is even easier. The helicopter's military potential lies in its ability to avoid the loss of life expended in the tactical breaking-through of an opponent's front lines. Instead, it can fly over the battle and deliver troops on an enemy's rear areas. In actual operations, however, it has been used as an expensive taxi to, not away from, the mortality of tactical fire-fights.

In the contrasting case of the Marine Corps, with its main mission of hitting the beach, the helicopter makes possible far more effective amphibious landings than the old-style craft. The sea-land interface of operations is no longer restricted to harbors or narrow strips of beach with deep water close in-shore, all readily ascertainable in advance by an enemy. Instead, **any** coast can be attacked, not just **at** the coast but well inland. Although the Marines would eventually need a beachhead or port for the landing of heavy equipment and supplies for extended operations, the hardest part, hitting the beach under fire, can be worked around or over by using helicopters. Sure, there was no amphibious operation in the Gulf War, but had Saddam Hussein continued into Saudi Arabia -- if the situation had been worse -- an amphibious invasion would have been far likelier.

For the Navy, the helicopter is a primary anti-submarine weapon because it can operate from shipboard and, equipped with its own dipping sonar, is faster than subs and able to change locations faster than a ship. Formerly, but before airborne sonar, such anti-submarine patrol was performed by floatplanes, flying boats and blimps. Such alternatives, although not landplanes, were retired in favor of helicopters, including those called DASH, drone anti-submarine helicopters, which were to have been carried on nearly a hundred American ships. In preparation, dozens of ships had some of their light anti-aircraft guns replaced by small hangars during the Whiz Kid era. DASH proved a DUD, however, as remote control of a temperamental helicopter proved very difficult, especially whenever the helicopter was out of sight -- just the sort of absolutely foreseeable problem that bypassed the liberal experts, until Laird pulled the plug in 1969. The hangars proved too small for other military use, and ships entered the cruise missile era with their last line of defense against them eliminated. Most of the ships were eventually given away or sold to foreign navies, however, so it ceased to be an American problem; the other navies were left to rebuild the ships' light anti-aircraft batteries against modern electronic *kamikazes*.

Small old seaplanes had operated from catapults on regular big warships, and via water take-offs from ships too small to carry catapults; flying boats were too big to be catapulted. Many of each were handled by seaplane tenders, which came in two sizes. Small tenders were converted destroyers or other destroyer-sized ships of from one to two thousand tons each, too small to do a good job with the large flying boats that were far more capable than the small floatplanes carried by the warships. Large tenders were a separate item, and expense, from the general run of warships, and they were retired or converted when flying boats went out of fashion. The Navy's last such vessel was the *Norton Sound*, later converted to a test ship for the Aegis radar system, and also the scene of another modern Navy episode, a lesbian and sexual blackmail scandal. The advantage of the helicopter over floatplanes and flying boats was that the carrying ship did not have to stop dead in the water to hoist the helicopter aboard with a crane; instead, the helicopter could just land directly on board, and the ship could avoid the danger of stopping and making itself temporarily vulnerable.

Today, of course, stopping dead in the water in pursuit of submarines is considered a bragging right of warship design and operation, the stop-and-listen strategy, helped by gas turbine-power that in some navies comes from derated aircraft engines; the only advantage of naval helicopters has thus been flagrantly waived, so the objections to flying boats fail. Helicopter-carrying anti-submarine ships, the frigates, destroyers and even cruisers which would once have been called hybrid helicopter-tenders, are now much larger, ranging from three to ten thousand tons, capable of carrying seaplanes at the lower weights and fully fledged flying boats in the middle and upper weights. Why are flying boats, with the same ability to dump sonar buoys as helicopters, and to land in the water and listen like a modern ship (instead of having to hover to listen while using up fuel at a horrendous rate), as well as tremendous advantages in range, flying time, payload (both detectors and weapons) and reliability in cost, maintenance and operation over helicopters, not utilized in the anti-submarine role (or in the role of replacing light cruise missile boats)? As old technology, they are "obsolete", and not as chi-chi as "modern" helicopters.

Also not chi-chi is the ground support role, particularly that falling under the Air Force's fixed-wing monopoly. Specific planes for that role were rare indeed, until in the late Nixon years a strange alliance of New York liberals, seeking job training and business for the state, and the salvation of the fading Republic aircraft company, joined with actual patriots to support a new ground-attack aircraft. Designed by Long Island's Republic around a small-caliber high-velocity anti-tank gun made by New York's General Electric and capable of penetrating armored personnel carriers and the upper armor of many tanks, the A-10 was also powered by two GE engines.

Not sought by the Air Force because it would distract from meatier and more glamorous roles, the A-10 was forced upon the Air Force by a momentarily awake Defense Department and sold to liberals as a job-training scheme. Republic, already having trouble holding onto its trained and experienced staff due to its lack of work, would train a large number of unemployables to assemble the plane. Liberals who were prone to complain about the bloated payrolls of defense contractors eagerly joined in the effort, confident in the belief that they would not have to fly in a plane assembled by misfits -- "Nothing is too unlikely for our boys!" The phenomenon is the same for liberals' support of affirmative-action surgeons, confidently believing that they will get someone else to operate on themselves -- "Thanks anyway, Doctor Washington, but I have another surgeon in mind. But how about a shot of novacaine for my painful earnestness?" Produced by the hundreds, the A-10 arrived in service under the command of Jimmy Carter, lending a spurious semblance of effort to a regime not only bereft of defense accomplishments but incompetent and sometimes actively destructive of the arsenal already assembled.

And what are the long-term prospects of the A-10 in Air Force service? Another aircraft New York-built around an anti-tank gun in its nose, the Cobra/Kingcobra by Bell (of Buffalo; the anti-tank gun was originally incorporated for shooting down enemy bombers), was produced during World War II to the tune of nearly 13,000. The P-39's abilities as a fighter plane were reduced by an unsupercharged engine ineffective at high altitude, the same Allison used for the largely ineffective P-40 and the failed early P-51 (the high-altitude interceptor role was filled by Lockheed's P-38, with its twin Allisons finally supercharged as was the later P-51's British Merlin engine to complete a fine fighter). But the P-39, available for low-altitude missions and like the later A-10 conveniently armored for ground attack, was generally high-hatted by the war-time Army Air Force, not yet even fully independent of the Army. Instead, it was given away to other countries starting before Pearl Harbor, principally Soviet Russia, with more than 7,000, and Britain; the remainder in U.S. service ended the war, not as interceptors or attacking still relatively numerous German tanks, but rather towing practice targets at U.S. training bases.

Unless the Air Force is kept in line, prospects for the A-10 are similar, with allies, the National Guard and the Reserves the likeliest beneficiaries of bureaucratic Air Force munificence. This was completely obvious before the Gulf War, and even more so from the results of A-10 use, as well as from its relative absence from the self-accolades of the Air Force. The A-10s, fairly few in number and often diverted to hunting distant Scud missile-launchers, still managed to destroy about half of the Iraqi armor that succumbed to air attack. By contrast, higher-tech Air Force fighters got far more publicity, as did Army helicopters. The Air Force has the A-10s but doesn't want them, or battlefield support other than with its glamor fighters. The Army is stuck with the helicopters, and has to protect that expensive and ineffective franchise. The A-10s had the range to concentrate anywhere on the battlefield, including the wherewithal to undertake the Scud-hunting tasks outside of helicopter range. Army helicopters, by contrast, were able to operate freely only in the absence of enemy airpower, but with their own expensive mobile air bases needing yet more and bigger helicopters, as well as winged transports, to keep the short-legged combat helicopters close to the front. By 1993, the Air Force was again trying to rid itself of the effective A-10s, trying to export them.

Transferring the A-10 to Army control would make more sense, however, and might tone down the Army's love affair with the helicopter as a ground-attack tank-buster. But the proper step is more radical surgery, cutting the Air Force down to its core big three beloved independent commands, Strategic, Air Defense and Airlift, giving the

Air Force three priorities it has already adopted as its own, and putting its foundlings up for adoption. All tactical airpower of the Air Force, including the A-10 and the "fighter-bomber" squadrons, should be placed under the Army, as Army Air, to fulfill the battlefield role effic- iently, under one command for both organization and operations, giving Army managers an alternative to helicopters and an incentive to restrict their use in favor of more capable and economic fixed-wing craft. The Marines already have an opportunity for the fixed/rotary mix appropriate to their operations, including opposing enemy interception, with their beach needs causing more of a bias toward rotary than Army Air should show. In the chess-game of battle, the Army's infantry pawns deserve more support than they get from their knight-ranged 'copters, like the more powerful pieces the Marines already deploy. And don't dog-faces deserve as much as jar-heads?

There are purely strategic goals to be achieved by an independent Air Force, not directly related to the needs and goals of the Army or Navy, and those should be united in the same umbrella organization for land-based strategic roles without interference from the needs and ambi- tions of rival services and their separate priorities. The Army, despite the misleading commonality of also being land-based, has its own needs for the mortal demands of the battlefield: observation, bombardment, supply and operational transport, as well as preventing an enemy from having the same. Tactical airpower for the achievement of such ends should be under that service's control, to ensure proper preparation, ope- rational integration, and bureaucratic support for the mix of air and other Army effort proper to the needs of the battlefield. It was by the colli- sion of the emerging goals of land-based strategic airpower with the needs of traditional Army battlefield support that America's airpower has been most distorted. The Air Force, even while still nominally part of the Army, had its own chief sitting in with the other service chiefs.

The Air Force, which has for decades preened itself as the stra- tegic service, could get used to the idea of losing its mundane tactical battlefield role, but the big helicopter-makers (Bell, United Tech- nologies' Sikorsky, Boeing and McDonnell Douglas' Hughes) would not like it. But the helicopter-makers have already profited overmuch from an institutional anomaly, and that public institutional problem deserves the proper institutional solution. The same cannot profitably be done with the Navy, where the proper solution for submarine mania is fewer of them, rather than an adjustment of service structure. But the Navy's experience provides a perfect analogy for the transfer of the Tactical Air Force to Army control to accomplish an Army mission. For, before the split-off of the Air Force away from the Army, there had been the early split-off of mid-1942. The maritime patrol function of the Army Air Force had been taken away and given to the Navy, putting the means for a naval mission within the full control of the naval service. The same should be done for the full panoply of land-based aircraft appropriate for battlefield service, for the Army's purpose. A background map of the Helicopter War:

One, Two, Many Vietnams

Southeast Asia's major rivers start near the upper Yangtze River, and most of its peoples came down those rivers, starting about 3000 BC, apparently because of a cooler and drier climate. As ethnic Chinese moved up the Yangtze, other groups followed, the last – Laos, Meos and Kachins – staying in the cooler highlands. Also around 3000 BC, the East Indian Chams invaded the area of South and Central "Vietnam", with the Viets originally restricted to the Red River area. After 4500 years, the area's first extended Malays, the Chams were conquered by the Viets' Annamese Empire, which soon split. Ho Chi Minh was trying to revive this archaic dominion, under other principles: not another George Washington of a new American republic, but rather a Hitler or Mussolini with a reborn *Reich* or *Impero*.

Chapter 14 - **Types of Warships**

The arms race myths -- beginning with the premise that if we do it, someone else will, and if we don't, no one else will -- are liberal narcissism at its most typical. Those peculiar assumptions are buttressed by misreadings of the past to disarm the America of the present. Looking at historical cases, where most facts are in and the distortions and their patterns are clearest (except of course in selective dredgings-up for liberal propaganda), we see the concept of obsolescence not only clanging merrily about, but even allowed to hamper scapegoating of the more usual suspects. If a weapon is effective, it creates an arms race, so get rid of it; if a weapon is old but still has some effectiveness, get rid of it, because it's obsolete.

The naval sphere provides an instructive look at evolved technology, one now mature and fairly easy to understand in its early stages. As with the newer air warfare, sea warfare is on a medium foreign to land animals; consequently, transportation is definitive. Armies can fight with stones, but air forces need airplanes and navies need ships. The seas are a path for transport and trade, as well as a source of food. Particularly in barbarous areas, with no real roads, hostile patchworks of small societies and no law, ships were essential to trade. But most land societies needed some sort of rudimentary security, such as a walled town or geographical isolation -- an island, or an uninhabited hinterland -- to develop sea-borne trade enough to require a specialized navy. And even that impetus could be lost through defeat on land (for navies cannot remain forever at sea) or through social disintegration. When that happened, naval technology backslid, and even barbarians could build simple ships. It took the triumph of German barbarians to destroy Rome, and the corruption and decay of Byzantines and Arabs left Vikings, with their puny single-oarbank long-boats, masters of the Atlantic Ocean and the North, Mediterranean and Black Seas, in addition to their own Baltic. One resistor was Alfred, who built a navy for Wessex, before his kingdom was conquered -- from the land.

Before that, the Mediterranean and even the Atlantic had seen contending fleets, Greek, Egyptian, Phoenician, Carthaginian and Roman, all putting out big ships in big numbers at various times. Although the technology was simple in concept, it was occasionally difficult in execution. The existence of five-oarbank galleys was long thought a myth by later writers, because they could not figure out the internal arrangement of such a ship. Even the Romans had to find a washed-up Carthaginian specimen they could copy, and their own navy had fought side-by-side with the Carthaginians against the Greeks.

While the Mediterranean world did recover some of its equilibrium, and again build galley navies, the primacy of that type and the area did not last. The galley's last big triumph was the Battle of Lepanto in 1571, and its last important gasp, other than occasional captures of becalmed full sailing ships, was the unsatisfactory performance of Spanish galleys, full or hybrid, in the Armada of 1588. What doomed them was not just the introduction of cannon, giving a surer method of destruction than ramming and boarding, but the growth of trade beyond the Mediterranean.

While the winds of the Atlantic are frequently credited with calling forth full sailing vessels, that is less a simplification than simpleminded. Galleys had always been mainly sailors, not rowers, because manpower for more than auxiliary purposes was not practical even in the Mediterranean. The crew would have required too much food and fresh water if worked so hard. Instead, rowing was mostly for getting on and off the beach, where fresh water was obtained and the ship frequently spent the night, and for maneuver in battle, including ramming, or its avoidance, and boarding, or its avoidance, depending upon the abilities of particular ships and crews and the circumstances of meetings. But in the Atlantic, bordering on areas nearing civilization but without the richness of the Mediterranean, trade was done in bulky goods and in bigger ships. At first, piracy and the lack of regular ports still made large crews economical: besides rowing, they could fight and handle cargo. But as trade and civilization grew together, traders and governments could not afford galley-sized crews, and the new larger full sailing ships could not beach easily, but required more regular ports, with more reliable sources of cargo-handling labor and more reliable middlemen, even if there were fewer ports than beaches. Smaller crews relative to ship size made longer cruises possible, however, so that distant trade and exploration became profitable or apparently profitable. Trading posts paved the way for colonies, whether settlements or protectorates.

The countries which traded in the Atlantic tended to become both the big naval countries and colonizers, as long as their prosperity, diplomacy and luck held out, anyway. Frequently, the three arenas met with evil result, such as Britain's loss of its American colonies (enforcing trade laws upon colonies while letting fleet decay) and in the Opium War (forcing China to buy opium so that Britain had silver to pay for tea, taxation of which supported the Royal Navy and its Opium War). Before the growth of Turkish power throttled trade through Asia, Denmark and the German League of trading cities had feuded, but neither were important in later years. Instead, Atlantic Portugal led the way, and Spain with its possessions (most notably Italian and the Low Countries) soon became important. After that, the Dutch breaking away from the "Spanish" Netherlands, the French and the English became the top-ranked contenders. America of the sailing age never really competed on the high seas with such fleets.

Sailing ships had their sides available for the mass-produced cannon of their era, and the larger ships would have banks of cannons where old galleys used to have banks of oars. Ships with three or more rows of guns per side were ships-of-the-line, or battleships, and fleets of them would fight by trying to bring their sides to advantageously bear upon ships of the opponent's fleet. The Spanish had been the last to rely primarily upon soldiers fighting and boarding, but that was most difficult between the largest ships, and ceased to be a critical factor between battle fleets, as did ramming. Getting the wind advantage for maneuver, to bring the broadsides of guns to bear, was more important. Destroying masts or rigging was one frequent goal, so as to render enemy vessels incapable of maneuver (in galley days, masts and rigging had usually been taken down before battle as vulnerable, too valuable to lose and redundant when maneuvering under oar).

Next below these sailing battleships were the sailing frigates, not as powerful in guns but usually faster and long-ranging (detachable without weakening a nation's battle line), followed by brigs and lesser types of ship. Federalist America produced numbers of frigates, excellent ships that, with two ill-fated exceptions, were long useful against pirates -- Barbary, Atlantic, West Indian and East Indian -- and against individual frigates of Revolutionary France and officious Britain. The U.S. did not finish any real battleships for the high seas, but during the War of 1812 it was attempting to control Lake Ontario, against such British ships as were small enough to pass up the St. Lawrence River or had been built on the lake, by building the world's biggest ship-of-the-line at fortified Sacketts Harbor. This battleline-in-itself was mooted by peace, succumbing over the course of seven decades to the effects of fire, storm and scavenging upon its uncompleted hull.

The Federalist frigates were not opposites from Jefferson's spavined gunboats save in being efficient. The true opposite there was the American disease, the extravaganza, in a naval form. The first of these was the Revolutionary War project, the *America*, unfinished when given to France in 1781. In the War of 1812, the Ontario battleship also proved useful, as a bugbear to the enemy rather than as a gift to an ally, although it, too, was never finished. Later extravaganzas included the pre-Civil War ironclad, the *Stevens Iron Battery*, and the islandless Cold War supercarrier; both expensive projects only provided employment and scrap metal.

But before that pair became possible, something had to have happened. What happened was that Mr. Fulton built a steamboat. This technology quickly meant that, although coal or wood and available engines and boilers could not supersede sails and their rigging for long-distance cruising, steamships could out-maneuver sailing ships in battle. In turn, because paddlewheels took up space and were vulnerable, the cannons of steamships and of their opponents became feverish objects of improvement, from Baconian to Draconian. Steamships wanted to be able to destroy the old types of ships with their dozens or hundred of stubby cannons from a safe distance, while ships opposing steamers wanted to be able to damage their paddlewheels or to penetrate their hulls further than old cannonballs had been able, to destroy boilers and engines, or even magazines. By the advance in gunpower, wooden walls which had been adequate before were wanting, and the rebirth of armor was underway, at first as rudimentary as the old hanging of shields at a galley's sides.

The process came to a premature fruition in the American ironclad *Monitor*. Vulnerable paddlewheels were replaced by a screw propeller, and sails were done away with altogether. This was possible because the ship, and its scores of sisters and cousins, was built for domestic blockade duty, not the high seas. The entire topside was armored and, aside from a small pilothouse, featureless except for a rotating turret, with its two large guns as the ship's armament. Although not as versatile as later refinements, this turret centered the armament, delivering the ship's "broadside" over a much wider area. At Hampton Roads, the largest and most significant of the Civil War's many "sunken roads", the *Monitor* famously fended off the second sortie of the Confederate ironclad, the *Virginia* (a.k.a. the *Merrimack*, its old name as a Union sail/steam cruiser), a larger and more primitive type, even after having been rebuilt as an ironclad battery-ram.

But although both ships were advances over most warships in service, their famous dueling contemporaries, the Confederate raider *Alabama* and its nemesis, the Union *Kearsarge*, were more like the transitional ships which constituted oceanic navies for the next several decades. These were large steamships with large guns, but for ocean sailing they still needed sails, and masts, and rigging, and for turbulent deep water such ships also needed freeboard, something heavy armor and high turrets would have discommoded. Some protection was afforded at the most vulnerable points by chains and other extemporizations. Turrets would have been disadvantaged by the sailing apparatus, so the few large guns were placed along ships' sides, in casements or other positions (the same thing occurred in early tanks, until the maturing of the type resulted in the use of the turret, or in accepting a limited gun traverse in return for a lower silhouette).

But ocean-going ships already had several disincentives for hugging coasts. There were shallow waters, and the fewer and fewer ports open to deeper- and deeper-draft ships were easily fortified. Moored mines, called torpedoes after a bottom-feeding ray, were already a potent threat, and loading a ship up with heavy armor and riding it further down into such hazards was not attractive. Moreover, protection upon the seas may have been new, but upon land fortifications it was still quite viable, especially against ships. Forts, not having to float, could always pile up more protection, and their guns fired from stable land. Ships were larger targets, and ship guns were more inaccurate while firing at smaller targets, a fort's individual guns instead of an entire ship as a target.   That is why the blockhouse and emplacements were able to fend off the British Ontario flotilla from Sacketts Harbor and why Fort McHenry was able to save Baltimore from an ocean-going British fleet. It is also why Jefferson's gunboats were so negligible in their effect, far less important than forts and not a supplement to their strength, and why Lincoln's and Jeff Davis' ironclads were more important in American coastal waters than as immediate models for the high seas.   The ironclad had superior protection, but in the state of ship-building and engineering of the time, it was more a matter for limited use "coast defense" ships than for regular naval vessels.

But as the 19th century came to an end, navies came to be more dependent upon steampower.   One reason was that the larger ships, because of larger guns and more armor, required more power than wind could provide for such heavy and deep-draft objects.   Another reason was that the competitive navies were owned by colonial powers, which could maintain the requisite coaling stations throughout the world, generally in areas where their trade was concentrated and their colonies were also already located.   The main technical development, apart from incremental improvements in armor (steel, carbonization, heat treatment, other alloys, sandwichs, plating, decremental or angled mounting), engines and guns, was Commander Whitehead's wonder weapon, the mobile torpedo.   This was dolphin-shaped (quite unlike its namesake the bottom-dwelling ray, or like the immobile torpedoes at Mobile Bay), streamlined and self-propelled.   Although its explosive was a mortal threat to any contemporary warship (because of their weight and their large internal subdivisions, a single hit could sink the largest), the early torpedo's range was not great.   But all sorts of ships soon carried them, from battleships within their hulls to small craft from their decks. Unlike large guns, torpedoes had relatively little recoil at their firing, similar to the later cruise missiles, and so did not require ship size proportionate to their size.

Most such ships could be kept out of range, by gunfire in daylight and by prudent withdrawal from proximity to enemy fleets at night. Surprise attack was one answer to that, vital to the destruction of Russia's Pacific Fleet by Japan.   When the Russian Baltic Fleet set out for the Pacific during the Russo-Japanese War, it opened fire on a fleet of fishing boats, mistaking them for British torpedo boats out to help Britain's ally, Japan.   Russian diplomacy and British propaganda legended that the Russians thought the British boats were Japanese torpedo boats a long way from home.

Another new item, proceeding mainly by a long genealogy of American experimenters, was the submarine.   Soon equipped with torpedoes, submarines were quickly thought by the more fashionable to have rendered the battleship obsolete before it had even become a really standard type.   The Russian battleship *Petropavlovsk* was sunk by a mine in the Russo-Japanese War, and the evolving terminology of the time confused some into thinking a submarine had done it. As the torpedo had become the accepted name of Whitehead's mobile kind, mines were being called submarine mines by contemporary precisionists, a name shortened by others to submarines even as the title of submarine torpedo boats was being more successfully shortened to submarines. The Russian battleship had been sunk by a drifting mine, not by a submarine or a Whitehead torpedo but, long after the incident itself had been forgotten, the impression remained.

Mines and torpedoes delivered by surface ships were important from the beginning of the Russo-Japanese War, however. Two Russian battleships were crippled in Port Arthur by torpedoes on the day the war started, and others fell victim to mines -- two of each country's battleships mined, one of each sinking. Such vulnerability had been shown by a previous very public incident, the demonstration of a new French anti-torpedo armor, during which the target sunk "at once" (strangely enough, the French later named a cruiser after the faulty designer). Soon after, Germany, covertly and much more successfully, began using its own mock-up for nine years of tests; the construction and materials were superior, like those of the ships Germany was building.

At this point, the types of ship were as follows: First, there were battleships, with a few large guns in big turrets and more rapid-firing "semi-heavy" and medium guns in smaller turrets; battleships, slower than cruisers, were the most heavily armored ocean-going ships. Next, the various types of cruisers were faster, smaller in armor if not size than battleships (the weight of battleships' armor lowered their profiles), and also fairly long-ranged. The cruisers themselves were of various types, armored being the biggest and most formidable, with armor, many rapid-firing "semi-heavy" and medium guns, range and speed, and accordingly expensive. Such armored cruisers, with battleship tonnage and more ship showing above the waterline, were expected to be able to help out in battleship battles, with their guns, as heavy as all but the few heavies carried by contemporary battleships, doing major damage at the close ranges thought likely. Protected cruisers were less well equipped in everything except speed and range, and smallest were the light cruisers, with virtually no armor and smaller guns. Those were the ships depending primarily upon gunpower (although they had torpedoes also) and possessing long range at sea; smaller ships were torpedo boats.

Torpedo boats were small unarmored ships, usually used in flotillas to threaten bigger ships, or to shield bigger ships from an opponent's torpedo boat flotillas. The smallest were frequently made of wood, similar to types later called motor torpedo, patrol-torpedo (PT) or Schnell-boats, fast but also depending upon stealth for a chance to deliver their torpedoes, which seldom happened. Also depending upon stealth, although not upon flotilla tactics, were the submarine torpedo boats, more with an ability to wait than to move underwater, to surface at night and move to unexpected locations.

The first question asked by every reporter covering the *Iowa* turret explosion was -- "Is the battleship obsolete?" -- thus showing that their military thinking was advanced to the level of the 1922 popular press. The contemporary sinking of a titanium-hulled Soviet nuclear-powered submarine, a ship that would have cost billions if the U.S. knew how to build one, was greeted as blasély as a rash of similar Soviet incidents, or the loss of the two American nuclear submarines, the *Thresher* and the *Scorpion*. The *Thresher*'s loss was news when it happened, for it was new and nuclear-powered, but there was no suggestion that it was obsolete. Despite those incidents and the submarine's expensive lack of utility in modern conflicts that do occur, a trillion dollars for irrelevance, there is no question as to whether the submarine is obsolete, or at least cost-obsolete.

Submarine technology failed as early as the American Revolution; succeeded marginally in the Civil War (sinking a Union ship but destroying the Confederate submarine involved, the third crew to die on the *Huntley*); received a spurious commendation in the Russo-Japanese War; failed to win World War I or II for Germany or to do more than ice the cake against Japan in World War II; and has done little since. The submarine is a conspicuous underachiever for the funds and attention lavished upon it. Submarines moved to the front of public consciousness for three reasons. First, other competitors, surface and carriers, had been declared obsolete. Second, merchandising by submariners has exceeded the sub's merits. Third, the submarine's microcosmic appeal for the movies has helped -- its lone wolf battles are more suited to the dramatization of men at war than are the fact of massive interactions of surface fleets and aircraft carriers, too broad in scope for actual portrayal even on the big screen, and usually cut down to small-scale plots for dramatization anyway. When the submarine does prove useful for some purpose other than killing its crew or the economic destruction of merchant shipping or of the treasuries financing the submarines, as in the sinking of the *General Belgrano* or the *Lusitania*, then it becomes an instrument of atrocity, a terror weapon.

Much has been made of submarines as atrocity weapons, as terrorists in their attacks upon merchant ships, violating the laws of war. There was some early international agreement on such laws, some directly indicting the submarine. But in general those agreements dealt with cruiser warfare, and submarines were **not** considered cruisers. Usually, they were considered a coastal defensive weapon, on a par with shore guns and monitors. Submarine cruisers were eventually built by a few nations -- Britain, France and Japan -- but proved impractical, expensive and more dangerous to themselves than to merchant ships (the French *Surcouf* sinking after colliding with a merchantman, for example). In actual operations against merchant shipping, submarine warfare was largely conducted under the legal rubric of necessity, the imperative that a submarine commander do as much legitimate damage to enemy shipping at as little risk to his command as possible. Slow submarines could not order fast passenger ships to stop at sea, for example, because even slowing as rapidly as possible brought a typical liner (a fast ship without brakes) out of range quickly, and hence out of danger and compulsion to obey the submarine's orders. The charge that merchant and passenger cargo was not a military target was usually proffered by Britain's supporters, who of course also argued that when intercepted by the Royal Navy such ships and their cargo were subject to seizure or sinking in the event of resistance. Britain also ordered its civilian ships to resist, legitimating their sinking by Germany.

Particularly during the submarine's early days, professional navalists considered the main threat to large warships the next higher level, the torpedo boats proper, warships smaller than light cruisers but not really boats. To deal with this type (never really important in American service), the largest type of torpedo boat was evolved, one designed to fight torpedo boats, the torpedo boat-destroyer. This type, name shortened to destroyer, only tardily broke into large American service, to become the main opponent of the submarine, screening warships and merchant ships. The American Navy prior to World War I featured ocean-going battleships and armored cruisers, but the German submarine menace called forth masses of destroyers, even as World War II produced a smaller and more specialized type, the destroyer escort, which began to be called a frigate for no good reason (the *American Heritage Dictionary* incorrectly says that frigates are "intermediate in size between a cruiser and destroyer"; while there are a few modern frigates larger than a few older destroyers, destroyers are virtually always larger than their contemporary frigates).

In the case of the technical merits of large ships, the development of oil-fired steam turbines and long hulls, with their high fineness ratios, led to a peak in the essentials of ship design fairly early in the century. Water resistance made ship speeds above thirty knots possible only with extreme hull types and/or massive expenditures of power and fuel for slight gains in speed. The main box for all naval functions has therefore been fairly fixed, meaning that hulls and their engines, as with some weapons, are valuable according to their replacement cost and remaining life, rather than necessarily devalued by the obsolescence consequent upon age in less mature, and more rapidly improving, technologies.

Although copied by other nations, streamlined hulls were pioneered experimentally and actually by the British. But some of their ships were overly tapered. A more squared stern than that used by the British enabled many American ships to have much greater tactical maneuverability -- a much smaller turning radius -- than the overly tapered ships, at an exceedingly modest cost in speed. Off Malaya on December 10, 1942, two overly tapered British ships, albeit fairly fast, were repeatedly torpedoed and sunk by twin-engined Japanese aircraft, Churchill's bad day. Although a catastrophe, it was far from the shape of things to come. More nimble fast warships repeatedly evaded torpedoes launched from such comparatively clumsy torpedo planes. The Japanese plane types involved never enjoyed another such triumph, and masses of German and Italian large torpedo planes, twin- or triple-engined, seldom if ever sank a big warship by themselves.

U.S. battleships had been less extremely tapered to begin with, but the desire for more efficient scoutplane operation led the U.S. to adopt squared sterns for its post-treaty cruisers and battleships, even as the desire for more efficient handling of depth charges led to squared sterns on its anti-aircraft cruisers and destroyers. In the case of the Royal Navy's bigger ships, seaplane development had been hampered by RAF control, so that only biplane seaplanes were available until the RN gave up on them entirely. Biplanes and their air resistance had meant not only short range, but also the need for large solitary steam catapults located amidships, over a ship's boilers. With monoplane seaplanes, the U.S. could put two smaller catapults and more seaplanes on a square-sterned ship's fantail, removing a battle fire hazard from amidships while enabling a ship to be more maneuverable against enemy fire. This was critical against air-dropped torpedoes, because a shorter and more maneuverable ship could make a far sharper turn against such a visually obvious threat, presenting less area for contact by a torpedo dropped even within a mile or two. Navy control of Navy air led to a defensive advantage against enemy air. But all Allied and many American cruisers exposed were those with the old tapered "cruiser" hulls. Only *Helena* of the large new ones was lost to torpedoes, at night.

During the inter-war naval treaty period, re-engining big warships was done mainly to save tonnage for other uses; most such expense would have been forgone had the ships involved been less restricted in having new equipment added without taking out old weight. Since then, there have occurred only a few detail improvements in the ship box, such as the development of nuclear energy as a steaming agent. A large and durable nuclear-powered hull of the late 1950s, the *Long Beach*, was built. Although its roles and missions have altered with time -- planned Polaris missiles never added; cruise missiles and light anti-aircraft guns installed, deleted and then re-inserted after new American appreciation of cruise missiles and their defense; Talos missiles deleted -- the usefulness of the hull and its engines remained as capabilities and virtues independent of the weapons suit of the moment. Similarly, aircraft carriers grew more powerful over their lengthy careers by having the aircraft types used change as technology improved and new models became available, their capability growing in common with the rest of the world's aircraft. Carriers' capability grew as their planes grew stronger, and the planes had escaped treaty armaments limits if not those imposed by technology and procurement.

Two post-World War II innovations have been important mostly for smaller warships. Gas-powered turbines give acceleration possibilities for stopping and starting in the water for anti-submarine warfare. Small stabilizing fins add immensely to the underway comfort of ships equipped with them, usually the narrow fast ships most prone to rolling in heavy seas. There was some hysterical media and congressional claptrap about Aegis cruisers being top-heavy and liable to capsize, but as wide ships their ability to make sharp turns at high speed even without such fins was assured, although not of course preventing them from shooting down airliners. The stability ruckus arose in part because the ships were more heavily loaded than the *Spruance* class destroyers from which their hulls and engines were copied; but the *Spruance* class had been originally designed to be as heavily loaded as the Aegis ships, until their weapons were decreased in number and capability to save money, for fiscal, rather than physical, stability. Not only were the Aegis ships not overloaded, the Reagan Administration put more weapons on the *Spruance*s, bringing their capabilities up nearer the capacities and costs of their hulls and operating expenses.

In fact, the American Navy has been among the least capsize-prone of the world's navies. Recovering their old capsized vessels seemed to be a Swedish activity ranking with chasing Russian submarines out of their harbors. In the 1930s, the Japanese rebuilt dozens of ships because of instability caused by too many weapons on treaty-restricted tonnage, hardly a factor in cheese-paring modern American armaments. In World War II, virtually all German destroyers had stability problems, something experienced by only about 2% of their American contemporaries. The main post-war American problem was the addition of enlarged radar masts at the end of the design process, a typical Pentagon specialty, as was the solution to the small *Mahan* class most affected. They were scrapped, destroying fairly modern and usable hulls, rather than just removing the problem masts.

The Aegis radars, by contrast, even if unfortunately not installed in the slightly larger nuclear-powered hulls first planned, were put in ships well capable of handling them, and not in high masts directly above a ship's center of gravity only in calm water, but fixed lower in its superstructures and balanced between sides of the ship. Pictures of the Aegis ships on trials merely alarmed the gullible; such awakened credulity, "being informed" (of what and by whom?), is catnip to media and electoral demagogue alike. The Aegis ships, along with their near-sisters, incorporated another modern characteristic.

The fourth major modern detail change in ship design was flat or transom sterns extending below the waterlines. These gave ships a more efficient box-like carrying and working shape (mines, depth charges, so-nar arrays, decoys, landing craft, etc.) and maneuverability and, above 27 knots, an effectively longer shape and fineness ratio, as the water be-hind a ship so built forms a facsimile add-on cruiser stern, making the ship a more efficient mover at high speeds where conventional hulls be-gin to maximize the drag of water resistance. Transom sterns are prac-tical for ships usually operating at high speeds, as at lower speeds the stern's suction makes it much less efficient than a regular tapered stern; only at high speeds does the suction pull the water into a hydrodynamic mass to aid movement rather than to retard it.

Wisconsin Senator William Proxmire was under a delusion, one of many, that the Pentagon was trying to fool people about the construc-tion of transom-sterned Soviet aircraft carriers. On national television, Proxmire called the Pentagon analysts budget-padding liars, saying the ships being built were bulk-grain freighters (nautical Molotov Bread-baskets, as it were), not usually a high-speed trade. All four ships are now, like ex-Senator Proxmire, at sea, festooned with guns, five types of rockets and missiles, and planes and helicopters. Proxmire and his scummy accomplices at CBS have yet to retract or apologize for their slander. The bestower of the "Golden Fleece" award had pulled the wool over the eyes of the gullible, perhaps even himself.

Could anyone believe that a Wisconsin Senator would engage in deliberate or careless fibbing just to rake in publicity? Not a liberal Democrat, shades of Joe McCarthy, no! Proxmire's charges tended to reinforce his thoroughly undeserved reputation as a waste-detector, be-cause they were usually aired as gospel by the fawning media, and the truth limped far behind, coughing from the dust and smoke screens, its quiet voice drowned out by the cacophony of the propaganda machine, the syncopated humdrone of "The Selling of Liberalism". Dare we call it Proxmirism? That would give the man far too much credit, for he was merely the loudest of the claque, a convenient patrician thug screaming the right lies for the media megaphone, the Senator with lying eyes be-ing lionized by the press. There are accessories before the fact, there are accessories after the fact, and there is CBS, accessories to spite the facts.

Around the turn of the century, three naval wars affected future naval designs and strategies. The naval battle of the 1894-95 Sino-Japanese War was seized upon as showing the effectiveness of "quick-firing" guns of middle calibers. That German-built Chinese Krupp ironclads had not suffered a single penetration of their armor was as overlooked by naval strategists as by governments placing orders abroad. The Spanish-American War of 1898 had not showed the armored cruiser in a favorable light, because the Spanish armored cruiser fleet, in fleeing five American battleships and an American armored cruiser, had for-feited the presumed close-range and broadside advantage of their quick-firing medium guns. The battleships' forward-mounted heavy guns had been able to destroy the armored cruisers before their speed could put them out of the battleships' range. But armored cruisers lived on, particularly in French service (where the possibility of war with cruiser-rich England required armored cruisers as powerful commerce raiders), and also with the British and Germans (watching the French and each other). The U.S. had earlier built only a pair, concentrating on battleships and monitors, until Theodore Roosevelt splurged on them.

If there was an unappreciated side to the Spanish-American War, it is the fear of mines. It is entirely possible that the explosion of the *Maine* in Havana Harbor, an important precipitate of the war, was from a mine left over from the previous Cuban rebellion, with its Spanish fears of official American aid. The dash of Dewey to Manila was also explicable as an attempt to strike before new defensive minefields could be laid there. But the Russo-Japanese War-loss of battleships to mines showed the inadequacy of contemporary underwater protection, a vulnerability demonstrated ten years later. In World War I, older battleships were frequently exposed to mines while bombarding coasts; of 21 old battleships lost in World War I action, only one was sunk by gunfire alone, the other 20 mainly from inadequate underwater protection against torpedoes or mines.

The destruction of Russia's Pacific Fleet in fallen 1905 Port Arthur (unlike the Spaniards who fled falling Santiago and died fighting ships at sea, the Russians, with three of five battleships previously crippled by the surprise Japanese torpedo attack or by a mine, died hopelessly at anchor fighting shore batteries) had shown the helplessness of even the most heavily armored ships against heavy land guns, and the importance of secure bases. The Japanese would repeat their Port Arthur triumphs in World War II, the surprise attack that time against Pearl Harbor, and a different naval base taken from the land, Singapore.

But the biggest and most influential naval battle between the *Monitor* and the *Merrimack* and the World War was the Japanese victory at Tsushima Strait, the annihilation of the late-arriving Russian Baltic Fleet (with British diplomatic support, Turkey had kept the small Russian Black Sea Fleet from joining it). The battle was fought at long range, medium guns (those of armored cruisers and of the side turrets of the day's battleships) had little effect on battleships, and the bulk of damage was done by the heaviest guns of the battleships (then usually only four, two in a front turret and two in a back turret). This time, there was no Santiago-excuse of a running battle for the medium guns' failure. After Tsushima, the lessons of Santiago could no longer be ignored; new battleships would soon feature all heavy-gun batteries, with elevation of guns and sighting equipment developed for greater range than previously thought needful (without medium guns, however, such ships would need more smaller close escorts). The British built theirs first.

Jackie Fisher, the man behind that first, and the man behind the Baltic Plan for invading Germany, was also behind another innovation, the battle cruiser. Battle cruisers were in virtually every way a big step up from armored cruisers. They were bigger; they had numerous heavy guns, like modern battleships, instead of the more numerous medium guns of older battleships and armored cruisers; they were more heavily armored than armored cruisers; and they were faster than armored cruisers. They were exactly what one would want for hunting armored cruisers, but the size, expense and utility of the battle cruisers caused them to be used in collisions with enemy battleships and battle cruisers, where the battle tag showed its limitations. The problem in battle turned out to be less the type than a specific flaw -- British battle cruisers had inadequately armored connections between turrets and magazines.

Although battle cruisers were about 20% faster than contemporary battleships, and had armor about 20% thinner, those two factors did not quite cancel out. Battle cruisers were also big targets, needing some width to accommodate their massive engines, numerous boilers, bulky fuel stowage and heavy turrets and armor, and needing disproportionate length to give that width a speedy hull-shape. This size characteristic caused the Germans to label them large cruisers, as in large targets. The combination of thin armor and large size meant that, although high speed would cause some shells to miss, some heavy shells would still hit and would do greater damage than against battleships.

But the battle cruiser's speed and range meant that it could be used aggressively, and would see more action than the tougher, but tardy, new battleships of the main battle fleets. The four biggest naval battles of World War I were all primarily or initially battle cruiser actions and, in the Mediterranean, the refugee German battle cruiser *Goeben* helped bring Turkey into the war, concerning and embarrassing the British and French ships there and their governments, while frequently bringing chaos to the Russian Black Sea Fleet, two countries trying to trap the *Goeben* and a third fending off its raids.

Note that Britain built only one modern battleship at first but three battle cruisers at once. Had Germany indeed been the main target of the battle cruiser, as legend has it, these anti-armored cruisers would have made no sense. In 1906, Germany was already five armored cruisers below authorized strength when its parliament increased that authorization by a further 43%; none were built. France had been the main armored cruiser rival to Britain; Theodore Roosevelt was building 13 (including three "second-class cruisers" larger than the two armored cruisers left over from the Spanish-American War); and Japan was in fourth place, by virtue of its eliminating Russia, including the capture of some reparable armored cruisers. Bringing up the rear was Germany, and the battle cruisers were not built on its account. Teddy Roosevelt's burgeoning Navy was the target.

The military is ever blamable as mossbacks when they stagnate and as aggressive when they don't. The new trends, co-inciding with European political tensions and Germany's 1900 decision to build a real fleet (by slowly replacing old coastal defense ships and transitional ships with so-called first-class battleships), soon resulted in bigger and innovative new ships. As always, however, such things were more a matter of national assertion and prosperity than of incipient bankruptcy. Nations are ruined by arms races less frequently than women are ruined by books; books read, or arms races engaged in, are more matters of opportunity to demonstrate existing tastes. The same growth of modern technology fueled economic growth, trade and other national rivalries as it did the state of specialized naval technology. Nations can always refuse to participate in arms races, but if they are imperiled by demurring, that is reality intruding.

Britain, an island nation with its empire, felt it needed a navy as big as the next two naval nations combined. Events and trends caused those nations to change. Previously, Russia and France, soon to be Britain's allies, had the largest foreign navies and were therefore the subject of British naval obsessions. But the destruction of the two biggest Russian fleets (the loss of six of its seven Pacific Fleet battleships and all eight of its Baltic Fleet's), and the continuing American build-up, soon paired the combination of the U.S. and France as Britain's projective nemesis. But France's land arms race with Germany pre-occupied it, causing neglect of the French Navy. The German build-up was underway, so rather than Britain's debt-slowed ally Japan being lumped with the U.S. as a threat, Germany and the United States combined were the British standard.

This standard was barely met by old numbers, leaving a two-power battleship balance at the end of the T. Roosevelt build-up (Britain with 32, Germany with 13, and the U.S. with 19, combined 32). The spectre of the German build-up and other current trends brought forth new technology, but which, compared to the Whitehead torpedo, the submarine and the new aircraft, was really just a fuller extension of the old technology. Such a complex episode as the naval race between Germany and Britain at the century's start assumes a lurid light only courtesy of liberalism's special effects department. Britain is condemned for building the first "modern" battleship, the *Dreadnought*, with all sizable guns of one large caliber instead of some heavy and some medium. The charge is that the new ship made the rest of Britain's fleet "obsolete", as if it were going to attack the others, instead of being on the same side and helping. Walter Millis' statement, in his *Arms and Men*, that the new battleship and new battle cruisers "would at a stroke render obsolete not only every battleship and armoured cruiser in other navies but every one in Britain's own huge fleet as well", even implied that the new ships themselves were victims of this conceptual nightmare;

after all, they were part of that huge fleet. And if Britain hadn't got there first, someone else, foreign and possibly hostile, would have. Given British assertiveness, such might have meant immediate war against the offender. In the specific case, the U.S. was ahead on designs for such a ship, Germany had a parliament mandate to build to that standard, recently defeated Russia had two fleets to rebuild and would seek a qualitative advantage to cut the numbers otherwise needed, and Japan, although financially strapped, was innovative. The lessons of the recent Russo-Japanese War were generally available to all navies, although in greater detail to the British; what they did do was build in a hurry, setting a record for battleship construction that was never broken. As the Royal Navy was then the world's most powerful, the *Dreadnought* simply increased its lead, helping to keep the Royal Navy ahead of the combined power of the world's second and third most powerful navies of the moment. A similar weapon in the hands of one of them would have decreased Britain's lead and caused, if not war, at least the construction of two dreadnoughts to match a single foreign one.

And the British effort was successful. The Royal Navy of 1908 barely met the Two-Power Standard, yet by the end of 1914 it exceeded a Three-Power Standard based on the new all-big-gun battleships and battle cruisers. Britain had 34, while second-place Germany had 21, the third-place U.S. 8 and France, Russia and Japan tied for fourth with 4 each, giving a maximum of 33 for any three non-British navies. Moreover, the building programs underway for Britain in 1914 were sufficient to keep a Two-Power Standard against the U.S. and Germany even had both nations completed their own building programs (Germany did not, giving up on two of six ships). Furthermore, Britain seized three battleships under construction for foreign order, completed its own program of ten large ships, and even added two battle cruisers to its war program and completed them. And, of course, due partly to the large modern orders produced by the arms race, British shipyards could cope with not only the old program of ten large ships and the two new battle cruisers, but also with building nearly a hundred coastal defense ships, then merchant ships, and finally anti-submarine craft. By the time the war started, Britain had "won" the so-called arms race, which the Germans had already conceded through their more leisurely program.

As the British build-up continued far beyond the Two-Power Standard, a London fog of alibis moved in. Threats other than the battlefleets of major powers were advanced, with British battle cruisers fobbed off as a reply to German passenger liners and the possibility of their being armed. In fact, of course, it was Britain which armed merchant ships, most auspiciously as the hundreds of "Q-ships" of World War I and armed merchant cruisers of World War II, as well as using other merchant ships camouflaged as capital ships. In neither war were German liners armed; they were too valuable to Germany and ended up in both wars as part of the Allied booty. Germany's best World War I raider was a sailing ship, and its dozen or so World War II merchant raiders were fairly small motorships, albeit very well armed. Britain's next artful panic was over Austria's and Italy's battleship programs, two rival countries with little naval tradition -- what they built stayed in port in World War I, two being lost there. Britain's Mediterranean squadron of six old battleships was hastily recalled by panicky Winston Churchill on the putative assumption that they were safer nearer the presumed German threat than from the ineffectual Austrians or the Machiavellian Italians -- until his Gallipoli brainstorm caused the re-introduction of such ships to the Mediterranean, with the co-incidental loss of six. Finally, even as proponents of an ever larger Royal Navy moaned about the "world" build-up of battleships, Britain built them for Chile, Brazil, Turkey and Japan, most ending up seized for that Royal Navy.

But these phantoms were plainly fiddlesticks, so the Two-Power Standard was altered to justify the British build-up. First, Prime Minister Asquith declared that the Two-Power Standard meant not as many ships as the next two naval powers combined, but 10% more -- If A had 20 and B had 12, Britain would have to have 36, instead of just 32. Next, British apologists began complaining about Britain's "need" for 60% more than the next largest navy. If A had 30 and B had 6, Britain needed 48, instead of 36 or 40. And when the Kaiser signified his acceptance of that 60% ratio, an acceptance which British diplomats had solicited, Churchill brusquely announced, with Cabinet support, that Britain needed 100% more, two ships for every one of Germany's, then the second naval power -- the kind of Munich pressure and blackmail that Churchill later railed against. If A had 30 and B had 6, Britain now "needed" 60, instead of 48, 40 or 36.

Since Germany's battleships were already inferior in gun size, with each new British battleship already having 60% more gunpower, so the emerging "threat" of the U.S. was seized upon for another British escalation, the move to a 15-inch gun. This gun's shell was nearly "40% heavier than" that of the U.S. 14-inch gun which had just been introduced for the first American super-dreadnoughts, the *New York* and the *Texas*; America proved as important -- although not publicly for smarmy Anglophilia -- for Britain's 15-inch-gunned ships as it had for the *Dreadnought* itself and the first battle cruisers. Nine U.S. battleships, four with 14-inch guns, ended up deployed against the already outnumbered and vastly outgunned Germans, with four British monitors already long-equipped with the American 14-inch bogeyguns. America had provided a reason for Britain to feverishly arm, and an aid in using those arms, but its role as a dupe would mutate into that of providing an atmosphere of disarmament convenient to a financially pressed Britain.

In the German-British naval race, the goals of the Germans were strictly defensive: the fleet, by its existence, was to prevent an invasion of its coasts or a blockade, then thought possible only close by the coast. The German battleship fleet being born was not designed for operations even as close as Britain; instead, the short range thought necessary for the main mission led German designers to omit coal bunkerage in favor of ships' armor. German battleships had no possible utility for an attack upon the British Isles except small raids on the closest parts; more extended operations were impossible because of coal limits (and unlike the German oceanic cruisers, their battleships had no provision for coaling at sea). Only later German battle cruisers had range, and they were few; the title of the German High Seas Fleet was a bluff (Germany initially diverted a gun*boat*, not a war*ship*, to 1911 Morocco, followed by a light cruiser, with both vessels in an obscure southern port away from confrontations). But facts do not gibe with liberal historiography, where more democratic Britain has to be retrospectively shielded from the bellicose "militarists" of the Kaiser's Germany; rather blatant British sabre-rattling has to be ignored or, liberalism squared equals Marxism, chalked up to economic interests.

Edwardian Britain (1901-1910) had quickly adopted a policy of peace-time allies to militarily isolate its chosen economic and naval rival Germany. Japan was first, solidifying Britain's Asian flank. In 1904, Britain allied with France, and in 1907, Russia, defeated by Japan and less of a rival in Asia, was directly added (Russia had long been allied with France). With Britain's motive clear and the military and diplomatic means secured, partly by Russia's eventual recovery, all that was needed was opportunity and execution. That came in 1914, after an assassination and the German invasion of Belgium. British consciences which had proved insensitive to their own slaughter of tens of thousands of Dutch farmers and their families in South Africa soon found a peculiar outlet in convenient concern over Belgian farmers. Atrocities were not waited upon, but were instead invented after-the-fiction. Warship design was intimately linked to this larger design.

British Army planning with France for war against Germany -- featuring an invasion of Belgium -- had contrasted with the Royal Navy's own 1909 Baltic Plan. The latter was nominally cancelled by a political shake-up, but its influence continued. Early in each World War, with Winston Churchill running the British Admiralty, the Baltic Plan was revived. The second time, in 1939, involved the conversions of existing ships, but these were not undertaken because of the possibility of an extended war with hostile neutrals Italy and Japan; even old battleships otherwise in need of rebuilding could not be spared, and one was soon sunk by a submarine (finally, the first "modern" battleship lost to a submarine, and that by a surprise attack in port), making the shortage of these valuable obsolete items even greater. Instead, Churchill prepared a plan for invading another Scandinavian neutral, Norway, for three purposes: blocking German iron ore imports from Sweden via Norway and its coastal waters, getting Norwegian heavy water production for Britain instead of for Germany, and helping to get aid to Finland, then being invaded by Nazi Germany's Soviet ally. The British force for the invasion of Norway was at sea when the Germans struck first; Churchill's less-than-doughty Brits turned back to port and re-organized their force for intervention against a prepared and aggressive foe, a different proposition than the surprise invasion of a lightly armed neutral.

In Operations R4 and Winifred, the British were merely extending -- by mining or occupation -- their blockade of Norway, otherwise similar to that inflicted on Scandinavia, the Netherlands, the United States and other neutrals during World War I. Blockade was, of course, an act of war, one which neutrals put up with to avoid worse -- mining or occupation, for example. Why hadn't Woodrow Wilson, instead of getting us into full-scale war, tried convoying American merchant ships to British-blockaded countries? Because although Americans were told they were fighting for "freedom of the seas", Americans weren't to be protected in that exercise as long as Britain objected, or even as long as Anglophiles thought that America's protecting its commerce would be "unfair" to Britain (being "unfair" to Germany was OK). Norway, having been previously blockaded, was between the wars a prospective future war-zone, along with the Low Countries. German naval theorists posited Norway's capture as desirable for less easily blockaded raider, naval, submarine and merchant ship bases than Germany's own.

The first Baltic Plan had indeed seen the requisite fleet constructed, after the outbreak of World War I and the jamming-up of the Western Front; Fisher the innovator was brought back by Churchill after having fallen out of favor before the war. But, before the Baltic Fleet could be finished for its appointed task, a similar attack on Europe's other flank, from the deep waters off Turkey's Gallipoli peninsula, had failed, and the sponsoring team of Churchill and Fisher was out. Another Churchill-backed project, destined to see service on the Western Front itself, was the tank.

Churchill himself went to the Western Front as a junior Army officer, and the Baltic Fleet mostly spent the war in use on that front's flank, Belgium's shallows. The three largest ships of the hundred-plus built had been large cruisers, fast and extremely heavily gunned, but so unarmored and lightly built, to save weight and draft for the Baltic shallows, that just firing their own guns caused damage. Refused by the de-Fishered Royal Navy and attacked in the British press, a sure sign of official sanction during wartime censorship, the trio was later converted to aircraft carriers, by a strange alliance between a forward-looking naval leadership and a disarmament treaty. One of the three was the *Glorious*, later sunk during the winding-down of the Norwegian improvization for the substitute of the revival of the cancelled plan for which it had originally been built twenty-five years before. A victim of mischance rather than bad redesign, the ship could have proven immensely valuable, in spite of having its role and mission so frequently altered in violation of the canons of liberal defense jargon.

Unlike the orphaned trio, the other ships of the Baltic Fleet were not built for speed, but rather toughness, sacrificing their speed for armor in reverse from the trio's design. Off the coast of a Belgium violated by the Kaiser's Germany instead of off the coast of a Denmark violated by King George V's Britain, the British ships soon encountered a German innovation then new to warfare, but since periodically hailed, in other manifestations, as a new "breakthrough". The German invention, dating from the same year as the first Baltic Plan, 1909, was wire-control (as many "breakthrough" modern anti-tank weapons making tanks "obsolete" still are), of speedboats filled with explosives, with a 30-mile range and even capable of receiving over-the-horizon guidance from an aircraft, still a common Russian method.

Off Belgium, the German boats struck and exploded against their targets with full force, but no practical effect, because the targets were equipped with another Churchill device. Not hailed as a breakthrough for some reason, these were bulges, also called blisters, buffers and even crinolines (hoop-skirts), of sheet metal-clad air-pockets, designed to protect against mines or torpedoes; these caused an explosive boat to explode at a safe distance from the ship's main hull, preserving flotation and other functions. The same method, spaced armor, defeats the bazooka-style war-heads of modern anti-tank weapons, both guided and unguided. The Baltic ships themselves were coastal dead-ends, however (many were actually called monitors after their American coastal namesake, also a dead-end for fleet operations), because slowness kept them from main fleet use, and their cautious deployment kept them from decisive coastal use, for victory or defeat.

World War I's end brought the speedy release of most specialized coastal warships, as well as the scuttling of the German High Seas (Baltic & North) Fleet, but the Royal Navy's supremacy on the high seas was threatened immediately by the U.S. The Japanese, though still allied to Britain, were outbuilding it with money they had saved by not getting heavily involved in the fight (although they had grabbed German colonies, threatened China and escorted Allied ships against German raiders and submarines from the Pacific into the Mediterranean). Britain wanted to keep as much as possible of its vastly extended lead in modern battleships and battle cruisers against the world. After the release of a confiscated battleship to Chile, the Royal Navy had 42, one more than the next four naval powers combined -- the U.S. with 19 (2 of those not yet complete), Japan with 10 (2 of those not yet complete), France with 7, and Italy with 5, making 41 for a contemporary Four-Power Standard). Britain's dilemma was that it had only one foreseeable addition, the battle cruiser *Hood* delayed by its incorporation of some lessons from

Jutland, while the U.S. soon had twelve more huge ships under construction (6 of the *South Dakota* class, and 6 of the first American battle cruisers, the *Lexington* class) and Japan six underway (2 *Tosa* class and 4 *Amagi* class battle cruisers). Although the full achievement of these programs would have only slightly exceeded the Two-Power Standard by the numbers (and the British really had a bonus due to their early carrier program), the bulk of the British ships were smaller and weaker than the new construction, as the United States and Japan sought qualitative improvements.

The United States built its turn-of-the-century navy because it had been humiliated by a series of international incidents where its lack of a modern deep-water navy lost it leverage. The *Virginius* affair with Spain in Cuba, the dispute with Britain over the border between British Guiana and Venezuela and the first Samoan incident with Germany and Britain indicated the perils of American naval weakness even in a fairly settled world. The Monroe Doctrine had proven enforceable against Napoleon III with the U.S. heavily armed immediately after the Civil War, but now needed new backing. Diplomatic reverses made for a political consensus -- President Cleveland and Congress -- to procure new warships. Only then were industrialists consulted; Andrew Carnegie, making armor and engines, was himself processed into a leftist bugbear.

The American build-up made the U.S. a factor in British naval calculations; T.R.'s Navy actually became Britain's main fetish. To the extent that innovations devalued old construction (and liberal ideologues certainly profess that they did and still do), this American battlefleet of transitional-era warships, as well as France's collection of armored cruisers, made the British transition to the battle cruiser and the "modern" battleship worthwhile. There was indeed a German political pledge to construct a larger fleet, but their existing navy was small, and their new construction could be quickly changed to the new standard (only later were German canal, shipyard and port facilities challenged by the further British innovation of the super-dreadnoughts). When the U.S., under stand-patter William Howard Taft, failed to keep pace, the Royal Navy had moved beyond a Two-Power Standard to exceed a Four-Power Standard. After the Woodrow Wilson interlude of a Big Navy and interventionalism, the return of Republican stand-pattism under Harding made negotiated naval limits, Washington-style, possible.

Chapter 15 - **Warships Limited**

Even without an assurance of that future American role as its "Associate", the temporary removal of America as a serious naval rival, by British innovation, had made British offensive operations against Germany safer. War became safer, and happened. But after completion of the extensive operations, laterly with American assistance, the U.S. was too big and distant to be bullied, and Britain too broke; the British resorted to diplomacy. Newly Japanese-held islands astride American communications to the Philippines had re-awakened American fear of Japan, the only other Pacific naval power since the T. Roosevelt era. Japan on its part was both expansionary and pensive, fearing a deal between the new Bolshevik Russians and the U.S., expressed as "the Bering Straits Tunnel".

Britain's Lloyd George government, that gaudy collection of hard-faced men, was interested in saving money on naval construction to enable it to continue its active diplomacy and intervention in post-war hot-spots -- Greece and Turkey, Russia, Palestine and the Arab protectorates. Although Lloyd George was habitually hostile to his cabinet, calling young Neville Chamberlain a pinhead and throwing ash-trays, for example, the only person he regarded himself as mistreating was the eccentric Foreign Minister, Lord Curzon (Curzon, visiting the front in the war, had remarked upon some British soldiers bathing that he had never realized how White the lower classes were). The Tory Curzon had been a key figure in forming the political alliance which carried Britain into World War I. When Chancellor Lloyd George had swung from pacifism to naval armament -- and high taxes, the coddling of Irish Nationalists and the curbing of the House of Lords -- Curzon had brought in dozens of his fellow Conservative Lords for the crucial vote when their House voted itself into impotence. But Lloyd George as Prime Minister had footpads of his own for the conduct of foreign policy from Number 10 Downing Street. While Admiral General Sir Eric Geddes was wielding his famed ax upon London armaments, his brother Sir Auckland was Ambassador to Warren Harding's Washington.

Because Auckland Geddes was a Lloyd George intimate (unlike his nominal boss Curzon), habitually devious and an actual occultist, the proposal for a Washington Conference on the linked matters of naval building programs and Pacific affairs cannot be unambiguously credited to him, but he is by far the best suspect. (Those who paraded themselves after the conference was considered successful are merely suspect.) At any rate, Secretary of State Charles Evans Hughes was amenable to Geddes' suggestion, as were other men and governments. In broad scope, Britain would end its Japanese alliance in return for the U.S.'s abandoning its naval building program, and the isolated Japanese would be forced to forgo their building program and to accept a permanent third-place naval status. The U.S. would apparently actuate its

1916 law calling for a Navy second to none, a program impossible to achieve had Britain possessed the will and the wherewithal to meet a Two-Power Standard. Although this represented a step back from British ideals, there was more continuity than change through the treaty regime.

The ideology of the arms race, even after the German-bashing had temporarily subsided, left naval arms limits a plausible phantasy, and hence politically possible. But technology had moved forward. Moving from sailing ships to "modern" naval technology, Britain was the leader and only the U.S. was otherwise important. American accomplishments were the fitting of steam engines to ships, various naval artillery innovations, the *Monitor*, with its turret, armor and screw propeller, and the submarine, from Bushnell and (attempted) Fulton, through the Confederate *Huntley*, through practicality at the beginning of the 20th century, and nuclear power and ballistic missiles after mid-century. But the British were more important, with the automobile torpedo, although not itself a type of ship, mandating the noncapital torpedo boats -- large, small and submarine -- and the torpedo boat destroyer, as well as with such modern capital types as battle cruisers, battleships and aircraft carriers. Another aspect of modernity was public opinion, the massaged demand for such international nostrums as disarmament.

1922's Washington Naval Treaty provided for scrapping some old battleships and new ones being built, and for limiting new construction. Limited conversion to, or new building of, aircraft carriers was permitted, however, and undertaken by the big three of the U.S., Britain and Japan, as well by France (Italy passed on rebuilding its allocated carrier, until the treaties had long expired and there was no time to build one). Treaty tonnage restrictions were 8,000 tons greater on aircraft carriers than on battleships and battle cruisers, and other cruisers, initially limited to 10,000 tons to prevent them from becoming euphemisms for battleships or battle cruisers, also came to be further restricted by later treaty. These limitations effectively prohibited some design features which had been both cheap and efficacious. Bulges had to be both air-filled (liquid would have transmitted shock too well and coal, an acceptable shock-absorber, had fallen out of use as a warship fuel, too bulky and heavy for the power yielded) and below the waterline to be effective, cutting speed somewhat but more importantly raising tonnage, suddenly treaty-limited. Ships such as aircraft carriers and cruisers were therefore built without such cheap and effective underwater protection, making them and their crews (*e.g.*, cruisers *Indianapolis* and *General Belgrano*) unnecessarily vulnerable to mines and torpedoes. Cruiser restrictions were the main topics of subsequent discussion and treaty, and those built by signatories as late as the late 1930s still had both gun and weight limits.

The Washington Treaty had been preceded by the Versailles Treaty, which was designed to keep Germany, with its fleet scuttled, disarmed at sea as well as in the air and on land. It was therefore left to the Germans to pioneer evasion; for example, tanks were kept contrary to the treaty by keeping the turret and its weapons separate, but easily joined in the event of war, a system that lasted until complete denunciation of the restrictions uniquely forced upon that country. On the water, the Japanese were somewhat subtler, but more thorough, in evading naval treaties they had undertaken voluntarily. Turrets containing guns too heavy for treaty cruisers were kept in readiness on shore, along with extra armor and even extra bulges. The U.S. and Britain, seeking to speed cruiser production and acting in somewhat better faith for once, built mostly within the old limits even a bit after the old treaties had expired, hoping for their extension or replacement.

From Armored Cruisers to Treaty Cruisers

Combining great range with high speed for shorter distances, armored cruisers had mounted numerous "semi-heavy" and/or medium guns (10- to 6-inch) and armor heavy by the standards of smaller "protected" cruisers or even smaller unarmored "light" cruisers. Often with the tonnage of contemporary battleships but with far more ship showing above the waterline, armored cruisers were meant to raid or to protect commerce and to battle enemy cruisers, as well as to scout for battle fleets, joining in heavy battles at close range when advantageous. The main armored cruiser builders had been Britain and France, with large empires, foreign trade and habitual rivalry. Other operators had included Russia, Japan, Germany and the U.S.

With the Russian Navy gone in 1905, several nations had joined France as threats to Britain's Two-Power Standard insofar as it pertained to armored cruisers. Japan, facing the end of its British alliance in 1911, had built large new armored cruisers (possibly seeking diplomatic leverage with an anti-British commerce potential), but the main threats were American actuality and German potentiality. But in two wars before World War I, armored cruisers had proved vulnerable to heavy shells at long ranges and to mines and torpedoes, with their own semi-heavy and medium guns ineffective against heavy armor. Something better was wanted, something less vulnerable while able to take advantage of the armored cruiser's weaknesses.

Britain's technologically innovative 1908 battle cruisers effectively negated all opposing armored cruisers, causing France, Russia, Japan, Germany and the U.S. to drop their construction. Only Germany took up battle cruiser construction immediately, however, followed slowly by Japan, with British help once Anglo-Japanese Alliance renewal was assured (Japanese battle cruisers escorted British troop convoys during World War I). By its early start on battle cruisers (three times as many as with the single *Dreadnought*), Britain assured itself a sufficient lead in the most versatile of big ships. And despite British battle cruiser vulnerability to heavy shells at Jutland, they were far less vulnerable to mines and torpedoes (always surviving two hits) than the armored cruisers they supplanted (usually sunk with first underwater hit, never surviving two). In addition to fighting at Jutland, Britain's hyperactive battle cruisers accounted for three German armored cruisers and five German light cruisers in three battles.

Lumped in with capital ships by the Washington Treaty's terms, the less valuable armored cruisers were scrapped or ignored along with many pre-modern battleships. A 10,000-ton limit left new cruisers lighter than the old armored cruisers, but, with prudent naval architecture, better against underwater hits; no new 10,000-tonners were sunk with only one such hit, but only one survived two. Higher tonnage would have saved many such ships and their crews. Once the limits were exceeded, no cruiser succumbed to only two underwater hits -- the German *Blucher* sank from two torpedoes **and** several ll-inch shells, while the American *Houston*(II) survived two torpedoes (the American ship was still officially described as a 10,000-tonner, but such American cruisers had hulls similar to, but with about 15% more draft than, legitimately 10,000-ton Italian Treaty cruisers). Treaty cruisers were also limited to 8-inch guns (2 such wrecked the old Japanese battle cruiser *Hiei* in a close-range World War II night battle), and later to 6-inch guns, but non-signatory Germany built 3 ships with ll-inch guns (so-called pocket battleships, used as commerce raiders, but with little effect on the outcome of World War II).

The German trio was a product of the Washington Treaty's more spectacularly failed predecessor, the Versailles Treaty. Disarmed Germany had been unilaterally restricted in capital ships by the *Diktat* to old battleship tonnage and gun-size, leaving Germany with the future choice of coastal defense ships or anomalously powerful cruisers as replacements. The Germans chose cruisers larger than the Washington limits with ll-inch guns multiply more powerful, and, with eight small diesels instead of one big one, with the long range previously sought in vain for German battleships at last achieved. Locked outside of the Washington and London arrangements, Germany's trio was, as part of a small navy, interesting for the anomaly it left in classification.

But, as part of appeasement, in 1935 the British government unilaterally made Nazi Germany a party to the Washington-London protocols, with the Anglo-German Naval Agreement providing for a German Navy 1/3 the size of the Royal Navy, the Washington Treaty allotment for France and Italy. The terms of the Anglo-German Naval Agreement therefore allotted five new battleships to Germany, with the Germans actually building four (two of a small class, and later two *Bismarck*s).

Along with legitimizing new German submarines, the German trio's classification as cruisers, rather than *ersatz* battleships, helped doom new naval treaty limitations. It was their finest accomplishment.

The highly regarded German trio had many parallels to the infamous trio of British Fisher cruisers. Both were products of World War I, the British trio as part of a stillborn plan to launch the war and the German trio as a response to the fact of defeat in the war as it had already occurred. The British trio was converted to aircraft carriers, the first under naval air but the others after the Washington Treaty and RAF control. The two survivors of the more compact German trio were contemplated for carrier conversion, but the same organizational flaw, *Luftwaffe* control of putative aircraft, had already doomed Germany's two more advanced carrier projects, one purpose-built and the other a conversion of a more conventional cruiser. But, in most other respects, the British and German trios were remarkably parallel:

Category	Br. Trio	Ger. Trio	Comments
Displacement (Standard Tons)	19,000	12,000	Armored cruiser tonnage.
Main Gun Size (")	15" or 18" (double or single turrets)	11" (triple turrets)	Battleship-sized guns, each ship with single fore-and-aft turrets like old battleships. Br. double 15" turrets re-used on late World War II battleship *Vanguard*. Similar 11" turrets also used on German battleships, the Germans planning to replace them with double 15" turrets.
Armor (mm):			
Side	76	60-80	Protected cruiser hull armor.
Deck	25+19=44	40-45	Discrepancies mainly from lar-
Bulkhead	38	40-45	ger English units.

Intent:

Malevolence: With world's strongest Navy by far, Br. design for surprise attack on German Baltic coast.

Impotence: With old Navy destroyed by defeat, Germans maximize fighting power on Treaty-restricted tonnage.

U.S. Equivalents:

Monitors: Shallow-draft coastal vessels for big Navy's offensives.

Frigates: Deep-water ships to run from big foes and to fight smaller ones, including merchantmen.

Total: Each class is a variety, deep-water or shallow-draft, of the same triple hybrid type.

By losing its war, Germany had temporarily lost whatever naval influence it had possessed, primarily that of a British target. The main course of naval disarmament proceeded, as had the course of naval armament, under British auspices.

Battleships and Battle Cruisers

British Battleships and Battle Cruisers Through the Treaties:

					Number Disposed Of:				*
		Main Guns		WWI	Pre-Wash.	Quick Wash.	Slow Wash.	By Lond.	Left For
Class	Year	#/"	#	Loss	Conf.	Conf.	Conf.	Conf.	WWII
a) Simple dreadnought and CB Types (10 and 8 12" guns, respectively):									
Dreadnought	1908	10/12"	1	-	1	-	-	-	-
Invincible(CBs)	1908	8/12"	3	1	2	-	-	-	-
Bellerophon	1909	10/12"	3	-	3	-	-	-	-
St. Vincent	1909	10/12"	3	1	2	-	-	-	-
Neptune/	1911	10/12"	1	-	1	-	-	-	-
Colossus	1911	10/12"	2	-	2	-	-	-	-
Indefatigible(CBs)	1911	8/12"	3	1	-	2**	-	-	-
b) "Super-dreadnoughts" (upon premature rumors that Germany was adopting 12" guns, Britain adopted 13½" guns, BBs with 10 and CBs with 8, increasing class size from 3 ships to 4):									
Orion	1912	10/13½"	4	-	-	4	-	-	-
Lion(CBs)/	1912	8/13½"	3	1	-	2	-	-	-
Tiger(CB)	1914	8/13½"	1	-	-	-	-	1	-
King George V	1912	10/13½"	4	1	-	-	3***	-	-
Iron Duke	1914	10/13½"	4	-	-	-	-	4	-
c) 1914 British seizures (for sale prior to Washington Conference, 2 unsold):									
Agincourt	1914	14/12"	1	-	-	1	-	-	-
Erin	1914	10/13½"	1	-	-	1	-	-	-
Canada	1915	10/14"	1	-	1(Chile)	-	-	-	-
d) British follow less frequent German increments of 4 BBs by increasing planned class size to 6 and 8 and respond to U.S. 14" and rumored German 12" guns with move to 15" guns (British complete 12 such ships for WWI, most seeing combat, Germans only 2, with no combat):									
Queen Elizabeth	1915	8/15"	5	-	-	-	-	-	5
Revenge	1916	8/15"	5	-	-	-	-	-	5
Renown(CBs)	1916	6/15"	2****	-	-	-	-	-	2
Hood(CB)	1920	8/15"	1	-	-	-	-	-	1
Nelson	1927	9/16"	(2)	-	-	-	+2*****	-	2

Key: BB = Battleship; CB = Battle Cruiser; Year = First ship commissioned. * Disposed of means sold, hulked, scrapped or used as target.
** Paid for by and named after Dominions Australia and New Zealand,

these sole politicized 12"-gunned survivors of post-war weeding-out were willingly sacrificed in the Washington Treaty. *** Replaced by *Nelsons*. **** Extemporized war CB substitutes for 2 cancelled *Revenge* class BBs. ***** The new Nelsons balanced some unscrapped Japanese and U.S. new construction.

The *Dreadnought* and *Invincible* concepts, speed of construction, introduction of new classes, swift growth of gun and ship size and progressively larger numbers for the frequent classes were unilaterally British vis-à-vis the Germans and, usually, vis-à-vis the world. However, the description in chart item d) above of British battleship classes of 6 and 8 is based upon the largest appropriation; actually, each class was initially planned as 5 ships and ended up that way. The description of Britain as initiating the trend to larger battleship classes omits the anomalous German 5-ship *König* class. This originally included 4 ships, with another being built to a similar plan but with a large diesel engine. The large diesel flopped, and the ship became the fifth *König*. In two successor classes of four, the Germans planned large diesels for two ships of each, but they flopped again, with the early pair built as turbine ships and the later pair never completed. The Germans were belatedly trying to remedy the short range of their battlefleet with these diesel projects; the only two "High Seas" battleships to reach the high seas under German control were two of the *König*s on a peace-time cruise just before World War I, frequently refueling in ports that would be hostile or only briefly available in war-time.

Designed by Rudolf Diesel as a "rational engine" using internal combustion but fewer parts than gasoline engines, the diesel is "rational" only where the cylinders are small enough for efficient internal combustion; with larger cylinders, diesels do not run well (they are balky and leave unburned carbon even in their "efficient" range). The usual way around the diesel's inefficiency of scale is to multiply the number of cylinders per engine and/or the number of engines in lieu of enlarging individual cylinders and their engine blocks. Instead of a single large diesel with few parts, there would be many with more parts, making very large applications -- high-speed ship propulsion, for example -- more efficient for easily scaled-up turbine technology (inertial Newtonian rationality) than for diesels (Charlesian principle).

British Washington Treaty scrappings, given by Morison as 20 (14 battleships and six battle cruisers), were exaggerated. Because of prior British economizing on money and inefficiency, the Washington Treaty produced only 13 British disposals (9 battleships and four battle cruisers), four of which (the two unsold seized battleships and the 12"-gunned Dominion battle cruisers) Britain didn't want anyway. Morison's figures were simply wrong; the British were hardly sacrificial. Although Morison found such details important enough to include, he just didn't get them right. Even after 15 volumes, he still hadn't mastered U.S. battleship guns. He screwed up on the *Arkansas*, the London orphan, describing it on D-Day as firing 14-inch shells nearly **twice** as heavy as its guns could fire, and on the *West Virginia*, the near-victim of the Washington Treaty saved by Japanese insistence on less scrapping, describing it at Leyte Gulf as firing 14-inch shells only about **half** the size its guns could handle. Both ships had been key items in hard diplomatic haggling -- four months' worth after the British agreed "in principle" to the American plan for the destruction of the *West Virginia* and more before and during the London Conference which doomed the other three U.S. battleships of the *Arkansas*' vintage -- and the battles involved were the biggest of their type, in World War II or ever. If you do not know the details of such dealings as diplomatic treaties, you really have no basis for evaluating them; the way is left open for careless assumptions, wishful thinking and reworked propaganda, for the sloppy bowl of mush that is official history. It merely extends the effect of censored war-time press releases and willful media inaccuracy, substituting faulty detail for suppression, aiming not for accuracy but rather for keeping the misleading mood previously generated intact.

The Washington Treaty left the U.S. with a battle fleet slower than every British and Japanese capital ship, and also with the four weakest and only 12"-gunned capital ships possessed by the five Naval Treaty signatories (also weaker than the big ships of Russia, Spain, Argentina, Brazil and Chile). This was largely redressed in 1930's London Treaty, when the five remaining British 13½"-gunned ships were scrapped in return for only 3 U.S. 12"-gunned scrappings, but the smaller Japanese fleet lost only the demilitarized *Hiei*, and that temporarily, because it was the only such ship later re-activated. With eight opposing capital ships gone, Japan grabbed Manchuria, a *démarche* similar to Germany's later march into the Rhineland following Britain's attempt to shoehorn it into the Washington/London naval system.

Not only did the British have the strongest fleet from the Washington Treaty, they also sacrificed the least in giving up new projects. They gave up nothing, only the pretense that they had laid down four new battle cruisers commencing on the eve of the Conference, all claimed started on the same day. That was rubbish, a transparent negotiating ploy. Both the Japanese and Americans were more advanced upon their programs, each with one new battleship completed and with three others launched. The divergence came with more advanced programs, as the Japanese had really laid down only two further capital ships, although they followed the British lead by claiming two more paper lay-downs, while the U.S. had an enormous 12 further capital ships actually laid down.

Even given the two expensive conversions to carriers, the Washington Treaty forced the U.S. to scrap the work-equivalent of three more new capital ships (the 75% completed *Washington* and 10 other unconverted lay-downs averaging more than 20% complete). Furthermore, the original U.S. proposal had contemplated scrapping two recently launched American battleships and one such Japanese battleship, so that American had proposed sacrificing the equivalent of four of its new capital ships. Absent complete stupidity on the part of the Americans, that premium was the price that the U.S. was willing to pay for the abrogation of the Anglo-Japanese Alliance and for greater leeway for China. Damage done to the U.S. by the Washington Treaty was followed by that to Britain by the London Treaty; the home-team losses of such double disarmament made Japanese militarism feasible.

Battleship Rebuilding Limited

Modifications of 18 U.S. Battleships under the Washington Treaty:

Ship	Fate	Years	Treaty Modifications	Scheduled/Actual Later Modifications
London Treaty Discards:				
Florida	E	24-26	PO, Large TBs	None/Discarded
Utah	E	26-28	PO, Large TBs	None/Target, Sunk PH 2Ts
Wyoming	E	26-27	PO, 6'TBs, 1"DA	None/Mostly Disarmed-Training
Oldest London Retainees:				
Arkansas	A	25-26	PO, 6'TBs, 1"DA	5/40 Approp./Not Done, only AA
Texas	M	25-27	PO, 5+'TBs, .75"DA	5/40 Approp./Not Done, only AA
New York	A	26-27	PO, 5+'TBs, .75"DA	5/40 Approp./Not Done, only AA
Second Group:				
Oklahoma	S	27-29	P, 6'TBs	41 Prog./Sunk PH 4Ts, No Repair
Nevada	A	27-29	P, 6'TBs	41 Prog./Beached PH 5Bs&T, AA
Arizona	S	29-31	P, Medium TBs	41 Prog./Sunk PH 5-8Bs, None
Pennsylvania	A	29-31	P, Medium TBs	41 Prog./Damaged PH B, AA
Idaho Class: (modified under London Treaty, very heavy new DA)				
Mississippi	W	31-32	P, 4.5'TBs, 3-5"DA	42 Prog./pre- and post-PH AA
New Mexico	D	31-33	P, 4.5'TBs, 3-5"DA	42 Prog./pre- and post-PH AA
Idaho	D	33-34	P, 4.5'TBs, 3-5"DA	42 Prog./pre- and post-PH AA
"The Big Five":			All Big Five:	4/39 Approp./Little pre-PH;
Tennessee	L	None		PH B, Later 8.3'TBs,4-4.5"DA, AA
California	L	None		Sunk PH Bs&Ts, raised, Tenn. mods.
W. Virginia	L	None		Sunk PH 6Ts, raised, Tenn. mods.
Maryland	L	None		5'TBs 1941/PH Bs, AA
Colorado	L	None		Getting 5'TBs during PH/AA

Key: P = New Engines & Boilers, generally larger and fewer; PO = New Engines & Boilers, all oil-fired; B/Bs = Bomb hit/hits; T/Ts = Torpedo hit/hits; TBs = Anti-Torpedo Bulges; DA = Deck Armor **added**; AA = Large Anti-Aircraft Augmentation; PH = Pearl Harbor. Fates: E = Early Discard (London Treaty). A = Post-World War II Atomic Target. M = Monument. S = Sunk and Not Repaired (PH). W

= Test-bed (Missile Launch). D = Delayed Post-World War II Scrapping. L = Late Scrapping, after 1959 Decommissionings.

The London Naval Treaty, although depriving Britain of battle strength greater than the entire Italian battle threat in the Mediterranean, and the U.S. of three recently rebuilt smaller battleships, permitted the rebuilding of the *Idaho*s with very heavy new deck armor. This was planned and begun under the pacifist Hoover, but was the last program of American battleship rebuilds until 1939. Hoover's gesture at Japanese aggression in Manchuria -- massing the available American fleet at Pearl Harbor -- did not interfere with rebuilding battleships as FDR's more sustained, and more disastrous, similar gesture did; FDR's interruption of rebuilding greatly exacerbated the disaster.

With the lapse of all treaty restrictions, the old weight-saving expedient of expensively replacing boilers and engines was unnecessary. Heavy deck armor could be added and buoyancy and stability restored by larger anti-torpedo bulges. But by the time these cheap and effective measures were truly needed, fear of war made them appear too time-consuming, even though they were far faster than the old replacing of boilers and engines, which had meant ripping up a ship's decks and taking out the innards, instead of merely adding outside protective gear.

All boiler and engine replacements were unmerited by the minor improvements in efficiency. They were solely to save minor amounts of weight made critical by treaties. The result was that the nation paid to scrap relatively new propulsion systems. The last group of ships, the "Big Five", despite having boilers and engines virtually identical to the discarded originals of their predecessors, were kept in commission until 1959 (nearly forty years) and not scrapped until the early 1960s; they may have later spent time mothballed, but their middle-aged engines had seen grueling war usage. Two *Idaho*s, more thoroughly modernized, were decommissioned in 1946, and the third made a test-bed. Their second set of boilers and engines got only slightly more use than their originals had.

FDR's perception of the war threat and/or the need to bluff and bait Germany and Japan led to the 1939 and 1940 appropriations going mainly unspent. All money was supposed to have been used by June 30 of the respective following year, 1940 and 1941, and a 1941 follow-on could have had work begun on July 1, 1941 and, if expedited, completed by December 1941. With the backlog, however, other due rebuildings (the 1941 and 1942 "Programs") were not even funded. After World War I, the concentration of the U.S. fleet in the Pacific was so routine that Puget Sound naval shipyard was assigned all modernizations actually done.

What was different about the Japanese threats was that the U.S. fleet was concentrated at Pearl Harbor, first by Hoover for the Manchurian Crisis response, and later by FDR, instead of at its normal San

Diego base, with detachments to Puget Sound for work. In June 1941, with the Nazi threat to Britain at a low (the German invasion of Russia was imminent and the Italian and Vichy fleets at low ebb), the U.S. began an Atlantic build-up unprecedented since World War I, with the normal three battleships there doubled with the three *Idaho*s and the carrier *Yorktown* added to the *Wasp* and *Ranger*. But by that time, the executive decision to substantially pass on the battleship modernization program had already been made. Of the ships ordered rebuilt by Congress, only *Maryland* had received anti-torpedo bulges by the time of Pearl Harbor, but not new deck armor. It was of course bombed.

Also at Pearl Harbor were three of the other "Big Five", along with the four battleships that would have part of the next allotment of rebuilds (the stillborn 1941 Program). Without bulges, *Oklahoma*, *California* and *West Virginia* were sunk with hundreds dead and salvage difficult (the *Oklahoma* actually capsized, while the other two settled, with fewer deaths and salvage easier, though still lengthy, pursued partly because they were better ships). The only bulged ship at Pearl Harbor, and that with bulges only half as big as those later given to *Tennessee*-type rebuilds, was the *Maryland*, shielded from torpedoes by the unfortunate, and unbulged, *Oklahoma*. Without heavy new deck armor like that added to the *Idaho*s nearly a decade before, the *Arizona*'s inadequate deck armor was penetrated and its forward magazine detonated, killing more than a thousand of its crew. Lacking bulges and deck armor, the *Nevada* took enough water from five bomb hits, along with a single torpedo hit, to merit the ship's deliberate beaching.

Because of FDR's policy of delaying battleship rebuilding, five of the eight battleships at Pearl Harbor ended up on the bottom, with many dead. Had FDR timely obeyed the congressional appropriations, he could still have had eight or more far more battleworthy battleships at Pearl Harbor for his gesture, but with none permanently sunk, or even long-disabled, and far fewer dead Americans.

Failure to modernize the battleships led to the majority of the American dead at Pearl Harbor. Aside from the 188 American planes destroyed, largely on the ground and therefore without their pilots and other crew, the major damage was the five battleships sunk:

Battleship	Cause	Out of Action	Dead	% of US PH Dead	% From Non-Modernization*
Arizona	Exploded	Perm.	1,103	45.9%	42.6%
Oklahoma	Capsized	Perm.	415	17.3	13.1
W. Virginia	Settled	2.5 yrs.	105	4.4	
California	Settled	2.5 yrs.	98	4.1	
Nevada	Beached	1.3 yrs.	50	2.1	00.0%
5 BBs Sunk	-	-	1,771	73.7%	55.7%

* Non-modernization dead are total dead on the disaster ships minus the death level occurring on the non-disaster ships -- about 100 for the torpedoed ships which did not get underway, and about 10 men killed per bomb on the ships which received bombs (includes the other 3 American battleships at PH). *Arizona* dead do not include those on the repair ship *Vestal*, moored alongside, from the approximately 2-kiloton blast; the assumption is that the *Arizona* was hit by 8 bombs; and the figures for an expected non-disastrous torpedoing of the *Oklahoma* are extrapolated from luckier, but still unbulged, ships; the figures are therefore conservative. 70 civilian and 64 Japanese dead not included. The majority of American dead at Pearl Harbor stem from the explosion of the *Arizona* and the capsizing of the *Oklahoma*. Both disasters -- the permanent loss of the ships with large parts of their crews -- would most likely not have occurred had the *Arizona* possessed a modernized armor deck and the *Oklahoma* anti-torpedo bulges. The latter might still have sunk and the former been heavily damaged, but the death tolls would have been far smaller and the ships respectively reparable and salvage-able. The U.S. was indeed rather fortunate that only one of the three heavily torpedoed ships capsized, because such an event made evacuation of the hull by survivors difficult and salvage extremely difficult.

With the arrival of war, the battleship shortage from sinkings, damages and commitments meant that only two raised battleships, *West Virginia* and *California*, and the formerly damaged *Tennessee* were fully rebuilt (the repaired but unmodernized *Tennessee* had been needed during the period of U.S. weakness, but it received its full post-treaty battle modernization in only eight months after the Battle of Midway). Circumstance and luck meant that the main damage to them would be *kamikazes*, against which new deck armor and bulges were irrelevant. Instead, the new anti-aircraft defenses helped shoot down many attackers, although anti-aircraft crews were the main casualties of those that did get through.

Carriers

Even as Britain had innovated the battle cruiser and the modern battleship, it had also invented the aircraft carrier, and under war conditions. The *Furious* was the test-bed, fitted first with a flight deck in place of its forward turret. Planes could take off easily, but landing was totally impractical (attempts at landing planes by swerving around the stacks and bridge ended in tragedy). Even with that handicap, the partially converted *Furious* was a success, but for safe landings a bigger deck was added on the fantail, replacing the rear turret. Planes were hauled between the two decks on elevated runways on both sides of the stacks. This was the rig of the ship for its first carrier raid in July 1918, and was the rig adopted for a smaller cruiser conversion, the *Vindictive*.

In addition to the transient organizational matrix aiding the Royal Navy in converting the first of its orphaned trio into an aircraft carrier, the more narrow "role and mission" for which those ships had been built proved a boon rather than a handicap for their utility as aircraft carriers. By virtue of their shallow draft, their area for supporting a flight deck was larger than that for less extreme designs of the same tonnage. The comparable later German trio of "pocket battleships", by virtue of their broader "role and mission", proved less likely candidates for conversions from a design as well as from an organizational standpoint. As more compact ships (more than 100 feet shorter than more conventional cruisers of the same tonnage), their tonnage, such as it was, could not support a flight deck as long or as broad as that which their same tonnage could have done with a shallow draft.

The general principle is that, in a changing world, the most useful items are frequently those which, having been given specific capabilities for a demanding specific role, may be more adaptable to other, unthought-of, future roles than are designs purposefully left vague and generic. Examples include the numerous types of artillery adapted to different shells and targets; purpose-built Roebling swamp amphibians working on coral reefs and snow; and purpose-built interceptor aircraft, with their engine power harnessed to tactical bombing, frequently proving better fighter-bombers than those designed as such.

Hybrid, or hybridized, naval designs -- the early *Furious* and *Vindictive*, Japanese World War II battleships/carriers (the 2 *Ises*), Soviet helicopter (the 2 *Moscows*) and jump-jet (the 4 *Kievs*) carriers and NATO jump-jet carriers (Britain's three, Italy's *Garibaldi* and Spain's project) -- have not proved effective compared to more specialized aviation designs. Indeed, fully fledged carriers can operate jump-jets and helicopters (if not the seaplanes that the Japanese hybrids were meant to carry, but never did) with no problem, better even than the hybrids designed for them; but hybrids cannot operate fully fledged aircraft and are limited even in their helicopter capacity (because of ramps, other armaments and too large islands taking up deck space begrudged to the air mission by hybridization).

Before the *Furious* was fully converted to a through-deck carrier, Britain had completed another conversion to that standard, a confiscated Italian liner project becoming the *Argus*, the first true flat-top carrier (completed 9/1918). By that time, the first keel-up carrier project was well underway, the *Hermes* having been begun in January 1918, the same month the *Vindictive* was launched. As the U.S. and Japan began their first projects, the conversion of the collier *Jupiter* into the carrier *Langley*, and the keel-up construction of the tiny *Hosho*, Britain was already undertaking its fifth, the conversion of a seized Chilean battleship into the carrier *Eagle*.

That British lead was cemented by the Washington Conference and its aftermath, with Britain able to dispense with the *Vindictive* as well as to spare the *Furious* for true flat-top reconstruction, applied *de novo* to its near-sisters the *Glorious* and *Courageous*. The Washington Conference permitted other nations to convert or build, but newly flat-topped *Furious* was the first such built. Instead of the parity with the U.S. affected by the Washington Treaty's terms, and demanded by the 1916 American Naval Act, the British kept an All-Powers Standard in carriers, fell to a Two-Power Standard in 1927, were still superior to any single nation in 1928, were back to a Two-Power Standard in 1931, and were still the carrier-richest nation until 1939.

The two Japanese conversions as well as their first keel-up fleet carrier were ineffective as first built, too complex with three take-off decks placed on top of each other. As the Washington Conference had extinguished the Anglo-Japanese Alliance, the Japanese were deprived of inside information from Britain, the type of advantage which had previously let the Japanese get their first battle cruiser, an improved super-dreadnought, directly from a British shipyard, incorporating the lessons learned on previous British projects, and therefore superior to them. The Italians passed on their Washington Treaty carrier opportunity, while the French carrier completed in 1925 was negated by the same Air Force disinterest which nobbled Britain's much larger carrier force. In the end, however, Britain's organizational funk negated the advantage won by its effective diplomacy.

Between the wars, not only possession but carriers themselves were restricted by the Washington Treaty; the size of conversions and new construction were restricted, as was a nation's total carrier tonnage. Britain gained by this, as its conversions were largely (4 of 5) from unarmored ships, while Japan and the U.S. converted two new capital ships each and France one. From aviation and battle damage points-of-view, this left the more conservative non-British designers tempted to build ships to withstand shell damage, rather than to use their tonnage for efficient air operations or to protect against the bomb and torpedo damage that would become by far the more common peril for such ships. The British squandered both advantages, from the organizational view-point of the Royal Navy having lost control of its aircraft and from the design standpoint of having ship subdivisions below the hangar decks too big and too weakly buttressed to contain torpedo damage. Bulges, except to a limited extent, were difficult under the Treaty, raising both individual ship and a nation's total carrier tonnage.

Faced with two large aircraft carrier conversions and wanting big protective bulges for them, Assistant Naval Secretary Theodore Roosevelt Jr.'s response was to cheat -- "there was another 3,000 tons somewhere else" in the Washington Treaty. His father's Progressive latitude in constitutional interpretation -- "what is not specifically prohibited is legal" -- had been passed on to the son and extended to the interpretation of the "Treaties made" thereunder. Thus illegally equipped, the two U.S. carriers proved robust, the *Saratoga* surviving two torpedoings and other damage and the *Lexington*'s crew being saved after heavy damage had doomed the ship to be sunk by a further salvo of American torpedoes. Less well bulged conversions, Britain's *Glorious* and *Courageous*, and Japan's *Akagi*, took their crews down. The *Akagi* was sunk by bombs, but the loss of buoyancy from smaller bulges was probably a factor; they would not have hampered it in most operations, since it was always paired with the slower *Kaga* when the latter was available.

Large conversions meant a few large carriers, while global limits for a nation meant that no country built up to 27,000 tons, the Treaty standard for new carriers. Consequently, there were carriers weaker than they need otherwise have been from a damage control standpoint -- the British and the Japanese *Ryujo*, *Soryu* and *Hiryu* -- or from a speed standpoint as well -- the American *Ranger* and *Wasp*. The best of the Treaty lot were the three American *Yorktown* class, but these were soon surpassed by the end of the Treaty restrictions (the third *Yorktown*, the *Hornet*, was actually built after the end of Treaty restrictions). Britain quickly built the *Ark Royal* and more slowly the *Illustrious* class, while the U.S. greatly improved upon the *Yorktown* design as the *Essex* class. But the best carriers were Japan's quickly built *Zuikaku* and *Shokaku*, fast, long-ranged, large and well designed to absorb bomb and torpedo damage.

Such considerations had a clear effect on the potentials of opposing fleets in specific instances. The American opportunity to defeat the second Japanese invasion of Wake in 1941 had been heightened by the fact that it had potentially three larger carriers to oppose two weak Japanese treaty carriers, the *Hiryu* and the *Soryu*, numbers and quality. By the same token, the Japanese Coral Sea force was stronger than the American force sent to oppose it. The U.S. fielded two treaty carriers in that battle, a conversion and the *Yorktown* (with the Doolittle Raid occupying the other two *Yorktowns*), while the three Japanese carriers, in addition to a small carrier, included the strong *Zuikaku* and *Shokaku*, whose loss would have disproportionately curtailed Japan's naval effort.

The U.S., to keep within its nominal carrier tonnage cap (as exceeded in reality by the extra 3,000 tons each used for its battle cruiser conversions), had to eventually demilitarize the *Langley* by removing its arrester gear. It kept its flight deck, however, being allowably listed as an aircraft ferry. Morison was unaware that the ship could still fly off wheeled landplanes, losing the sense of besiegement of 1942 Java, where ships had troubling getting within hundreds of miles of its or its neighboring islands' staging airstrips. In the Mediterranean, conditions at Malta were frequently as bad, with some carrier-loads of reinforcements launched at such extreme range that a majority of some flights were lost at sea from running out of fuel. Loss of the *Langley* led to even more desperation at Java, the risk, and loss, of ships attempting to carry in crated fighters. The policy of liberal disarmament (by "conservative" Republicans in the American case at a time when militarism was still tainted as "Progressive") followed by liberal coalition war made for military disaster, the attempt to hastily build up and defend bases -- Manila, Hawaii, Singapore and Java -- weakened by decades of neglect, disarmament and spurious economizing.

After World War II, the British were again carrier-innovative, pioneering the mirror landing assistance system to guide down aircraft and the angled deck to mitigate the hazard of landing aircraft being headed directly toward the forward take-off area. This became of major importance when the entry of jet aircraft into carrier service overwhelmed the capacity of raisable deck barriers against landing overruns; these had previously sufficed for smaller prop aircraft with lower landing speeds. The angled deck was also important in increasing the size of the flight deck in relation to the tonnage of a carrier, because this original extension was carried beyond the main hull by a sponson well above the waterline.

A sponson is a sort of naval balcony; smaller ones had been used just before and during World War II to carry anti-aircraft guns. Hitherto, full flat-tops had deck sizes and construction costs directly proportional to their hull sizes. With sponsons, new aircraft carriers, mostly American but some British, French and Soviet, had flight decks increase in size by sponsons without a proportionate increase in ship size. In American use, large sponsons on both sides accommodated all four elevators, angled decks beyond the British standard, two of four catapults for take-offs, a carrier's larger island and some deck parking space. Putting the elevators outboard -- on the sponsons -- rationalized hangar deck operations compared to previous conditions, when at least two elevators had gone to the middle of the hangar deck. The precursor was the U.S. *Essex* class's third elevators, foldable for docking in those days of small aircraft and operated over the deck edge.

For all large warships -- battleships, cruisers and carriers -- naval restrictions were not the path to a safer world, but rather the path to frailer ships. Ships with less tonnage for protection, or even for raw buoyancy, sank faster and took their crews in doing so. The nebulous ideological goal of arms limits ran into the very real consequences of following-through; in the real world, do-gooding killed thousands. The shortest distance between two contradictions is always a rationalization: do-gooders claimed they were making the world a better place, but it was as dangerous as ever, with some less protected than they would have otherwise been. The pursuit of military advantage, within the constraints imposed by limitations, was made wasteful precisely by those limits. Ships underway were scrapped, losing the value of the money spent on them (the cost of their resources wasted), and other ships were wastefully rebuilt, taking years of expense in failing to achieve within tonnage limits results that could have been far more economically met by exceeding those limits, limits set not by means or by knowledge, but on account of ideology.

Destroyers

Even as the Washington Treaty, to restrict capital ships -- battleships, battle cruisers and aircraft carriers -- had of necessity restricted tonnage and gun size for cruisers (so that capital ships couldn't be built in the guise of cruisers to evade the restrictions), so the London Treaty, to restrict cruisers, also had to restrict the next lower class, destroyers, to prevent evasions. Future Axis powers Italy and Japan had been first in building enlarged destroyers, Italy with the *Leone* and *Navigatori* classes, and Japan with the three "Special Types". New destroyers of such strength were banned by the London Treaty, although Italy and France did not sign. Italy, typically, neglected the type, while France built superb specimens which had little effect by virtue of their incorporation into France's ill-fated Navy.

During the course of the London Treaty, its signatories built smaller destroyers, and the Japanese smaller torpedo boats. Designers still aimed at putting pre-treaty armament levels onto smaller ships, prejudicing stability. Japan's Special Types 2 and 3 had pioneered the twin dual-purpose 5"-gun turret (the first such ship was the *Amagiri*, the ship which rammed *PT-109*), but using such turrets in smaller ships made them unstable, necessitating a regime of rebuilding by the Japanese, and helping end the London Treaty system. With that treaty out of the way, Japan resumed building only large destroyers; the Germans, by the peculiar virtue of re-armament in the context of their bilateral deal with Britain, sought to evade their numerical disadvantage with quality, building only large destroyers; and both the U.S. and Britain took flyers in large destroyers.

The British supplemented their alphabetical series of small destroyers with the large Tribal class (also the name of an earlier World War I destroyer class and a later class of missile destroyers). This Tribal class carried twin gun turrets, but British dual-purpose main battery destroyer guns were not introduced until very late in World War II, after dozens of British destroyers had been lost to air attack. German and French destroyers were similarly flawed, with larger single guns for surface fire, but the French ships were better "sea boats" than the unstable Germans. The U.S., while building mostly smaller destroyers, albeit with single dual-purpose guns, until World War II, produced two classes of large destroyers, five *Somers* class and eight *Porter* class, with twin guns, originally single-purpose, causing instability; that hurt when Admiral Halsey began sailing into typhoons. The toll of destroyer victims of earlier treaty limits and their fallout was in the hundreds, a small increment to the 10,000 odd victims in bigger ships.

Then and Now

The initiation of the Washington Conference and its Treaty co-incided with a post-war mentality in international relations, a placebo that lasted for somewhat less than a decade. Even as the Conference was going on, however, the Soviets were invading Poland, and being held off with the unofficial help of "disarmed" Germany's *Freikorps*, and the Turks were successfully defying the Greeks and the Western European Big Three of Britain, France and Italy. Peace was obviously a pipe-dream, a wish rather than a fact. That situation didn't improve in the mid-1920s as Hirohito took the Japanese throne under the expansionistic mantle of Baron Tanaka's "Memorial"; the Soviets turned toward massive domestic savagery, rebuilding their army and air force for foreign expansion in the East that preceded Japan's; and Italy saw a consolidation by Mussolini, with his more dilatory plans for a military machine and expansion. The problem for naval planners, and for sailors, was that warships are durable goods, and those forgone or crippled by the transient illusion of international harmony were left that way after the passing of the mood. The U.S. was in better financial shape than Britain and had better naval architectural concepts than France or Italy; consequently, it was most disaffected by artificial treaty restrictions. Only Japan was more active in rebuilding. And that showed.

In modern times, military power has also been forgone for ideological diplomacy. Trust in transient moods and paper guarantees has scrapped billion-dollar missile loads from billion-dollar missile submarines, filling their silos with concrete. There are some who believe that this makes the world more secure and that the world will also be more prosperous, but underwater cement haulers are irrational. One-shot missiles -- usually not shot at all -- at least have no crews to be lost; this is technology, however, not because any disarmer has ever admitted the carnage wrought by earlier naval disarmament. Whatever the moral quibbles about military means (loving your enemies is at least admitting that status), paper provides no security; some may fervently wish it did, and others may temporarily prosper by pandering to that wish, but it doesn't. And, of course, the moralizers and disarmers are the first to find new enemies, generally people they have extolled in the past. Those who praised Tito's Yugoslavia and drooled over Mao's China turned into today's interveners and boycotters. Tragically, such ideologues cannot even handle basic facts about what does in warships, what limits warships in battle rather than in treaties.

Chapter 16 - **Troubled Minds and Troubled Waters**

Although the U.S. had sent a battle squadron to Britain in World War I, the main American naval effort was against German U-boats, with the focus on escorts, seaplanes and merchant ships. Widespread American experience with the mainstream "modern" types had to await another war. World War II led some to conclude that the surface warship was obsolete, that the present and future belonged almost exclusively to the submarine and the aircraft. But such blanket statements about technology should have been applicable across national lines; they weren't. Looking at the patterns of major surface ship losses, there are massive discrepancies between Pacific combatants, and also over time. Major Allied surface sinkings at the hands of Japan:

Ship Type:	Cause:	Air	Surface	Comb. Surf./Sub.	Submarine
Battleships		7	0	0	0
Treaty Cruisers		3	7	0	1
Small Cruisers		0	5	1	0
Totals:		10	12	1	1

All battleship losses came in the first four days of the war, and the air loss of two treaty cruisers came soon after from the Bay of Bengal Raid. Only the *Chicago* (1943) was lost to air attack after the early months of the war; the ballyhooed *kamikazes* were ineffective against major warships: many hits, no sinkings. Japanese submarines were also ineffective against major American surface warships (although they did affect the carrier balance on several occasions), finishing off the *Juneau* in late 1942 and much later sinking the *Indianapolis* a week before the atombomb was dropped.

By contrast, Japanese surface tactics -- emphasizing night battle with advanced optics and big torpedoes from cruisers and destroyers -- were early successful even in daylight battles in the East Indies (1 treaty and 4 small cruisers) and later at night in the Solomons (6 treaty and 2 American anti-aircraft cruisers, 1 finished off by a submarine). But after the achievement of American naval superiority -- air, surface and submarine -- all Japanese arms were ineffective. The Japanese pattern had been a successful air phase, followed by an effective surface phase, followed by defeat.

There were few surface battles in the beginning of the war and especially in 1944 and 1945, because commanders could husband their ships from close-range surface battles easier than they could evade wider-ranging aircraft and submarines. The Japanese had opportunities for surface action, but the Indian Ocean had been eschewed (where gradually renewed British naval strength cost the Japanese 3 heavy cruisers in 1945) and the Biak operation cancelled for carrier battle in the Philippine Sea, while in the major Leyte Gulf surface battles the Japanese Southern

Force had been overmatched and the Central Force twice hammered by air attack without reaching major surface targets.

Admiral Halsey's Balaam's Ass strategy of dithering between the Japanese Northern and Central Forces at Leyte Gulf also caused two possible surface battles to be avoided. Japan's two slow hybrid battleships and two cruisers escaped to the north as Halsey failed to pursue a beaten foe, and the main Japanese surface force, with the anti-aircraft guns and gun-directors of its four battleships and five cruisers heavily damaged by previous bombing, substantially escaped Halsey's carriers and battleships by retreat through the same San Bernadino Strait that Halsey had earlier left uncovered; the chance to annihilate Japan's Navy, and to force peace in 1944, was lost. Finally, the "Last Sortie" of 1945, with only the *Yamato* and a light cruiser, was destroyed by American airpower, the ten other major surface ships in Japan lacking fuel to take part.

Looking at the accomplishments of Japan's Navy in isolation could lead to the following misleading conclusions: First, airpower was a surprise weapon which soon lost its effectiveness, and Japanese Army airpower was completely ineffective against ships (no heavy ships sunk, compared to 7 for the carrier airmen and 3 for land-based naval air, or compared with the slaughter wreaked by MacArthur's Army Air against the Bamboo Convoy, for example). Second, the submarine wasn't very important. Third, the way to defeat surface ships was with other surface ships. And fourth, co-ordination between arms wasn't important, accounting for only a small cruiser and the finishing-off of two carriers. The *kamikazes* had come into play at Leyte Gulf only just after the Japanese Central Force broke off its attack on the American jeep carriers; had the attacks been simultaneous or in the opposite order, the bag of American ships would have been much greater.

Co-operation between U.S. branches -- after the two naval battles of Guadalcanal, at Truk, at Surigao Strait (including Army aircraft), off Samar and in the Manila Raid after Leyte Gulf -- was simply better. Just look at Japan's major surface ship losses in combat, the debit side:

Ship Type: Cause:	Air	Comb. Surf./Air	Surface	Submarine
Battleships	5	2	2	1
Treaty Cruisers	7	3	2	5
Small Cruisers	9	1	3	10
Total:	21	6	7	16
By Year:				
1942	3	2	1	2
1943	0	0	2	0
1944	9	4	3	10
1945	9	0	1	4

In the early years of the war, there was a balance in the causes of losses. By 1944, however, Japan had lost so many destroyers that its light cruisers were pressed into service as escorts. American strategists, taking note, then made destroyers a priority target for submarines, which also bagged a number of light cruisers that year. But American submarines had not been a serious cause of Japan's destroyer shortage, sinking only six of the 43 Japanese fleet destroyers lost from 1941 through 1943. Air attack and surface battles made the shortage, and incidentally made the job of American submarines somewhat easier (for Japanese destroyers, anti-submarine work was a low priority, after surface combat, anti-aircraft and, for most of the war, mine warfare, both sweeping and laying). Even with that advantage, however, submarines accounted for only 26% of the Japanese fleet destroyer force. Furthermore, although U.S. subs sank 27.7% of the 88 Japanese destroyers with little anti-submarine equipment (17% and 35.5% of such lost in 1941-43 and 1944-45, respectively), they sank only 17% of an anti-aircraft class which packed some anti-submarine equipment, and a miniscule 3% of the Japanese destroyer-escort class, both classes entering service as the U.S. submarine effort reached its tardy crescendo. And Japan's destroyer-escorts were still far more oriented to surface warfare than were America's more varied destroyer-escorts, with 50% more gunpower and 50% more torpedo-power than their strongest U.S. counterparts.

The meditation on Pacific (and Indian) Ocean major surface warship losses omits the fate of carriers. The facts in a table:

Carrier Lost	Type	Date	Cause	Activity When Lost
Allied:				
HMS *Hermes*	CVL	04/42	Air	Raided (Ind. Ocean)
Lexington	CV	05/42	Air (Scuttled)	Amphibious Defense
Yorktown	CV	06/42	Air/Submarine	Amphibious Defense
Wasp	CV	09/42	Submarine (Scuttled)	Amphibious Defense
Hornet	CV	10/42	Air/Surface	Amphibious Defense
Liscombe Bay	CVE	11/43	Submarine	Amphibious Invasion
Princeton	CVL	10/44	Air (Land-based)	Amphibious Invasion
Gambier Bay	CVE	10/44	Surface	Amphibious Invasion
St. Lo	CVE	10/44	Surface/*Kamikaze*	Amphibious Invasion
Ommaney Bay	CVE	01/45	*Kamikaze* (Scuttled)	Amphibious Invasion
Bismarck Sea	CVE	02/45	*Kamikaze*	Amphibious Invasion
Japanese:				
Shoho	CVL	05/42	Air	Amphibious Invasion
Akagi	CV	06/42	Air	Amphibious Invasion
Kaga	CV	06/42	Air	Amphibious Invasion
Soryu	CV	06/42	Air	Amphibious Invasion
Hiryu	CV	06/42	Air	Amphibious Invasion

Carrier Lost	Type	Date	Cause	Activity When Lost
Japanese (continued):				
Ryujo	CVL	08/42	Air	Amphibious Invasion
Shokaku	CV	06/44	Submarine	Amphibious Defense
Taiho	CV	06/44	Submarine	Amphibious Defense
Hiyo	CV	06/44	Air	Amphibious Defense
Zuikaku	CV	10/44	Air	Amphibious Defense
Zuiho	CVL	10/44	Air	Amphibious Defense
Chitose	CVL	10/44	Air	Amphibious Defense
Chiyoda	CVL	10/44	Air	Amphibious Defense
Shinano	CV	11/44	Submarine	Shake-down Cruise
Unryu	CV	12/44	Submarine	At Sea*
Amagi	CV	07/45	Air	Raided
Aso	CV	07/45	Air	Raided (under cons.)
Ikoma	CV	07/45	Air	Raided (under cons.)
Kaiyo	CVL	08/45	Air	Raided

Key: CV = Regular Carrier. CVL = Light Carrier. CVE = Jeep, or Escort, Carrier, generally slightly heavier than a "light carrier", but with fewer planes and slower. * = May have been heading for an attack on the Mindoro amphibious invasion (Morison, *The Two-Ocean War*, page 479). Omitted are five aircraft ferry sinkings, the American *Langley* by air in 1942 and four Japanese converted liners sunk by American submarines in late 1943 and 1944.

All "Air" is carrier-based aircraft. Aside from the light carrier *Princeton*, the only land-based air to sink carriers, and those escort carriers, were *kamikazes*. All successful *kamikazes* here are believed to have been land-based Japanese naval air. Note that, as with surface warship sinkings, submarines were effective for the side with the initiative, which could pick the venue and mass its submarines there, the situation with six of the seven carriers sunk by submarines. Exception *Liscombe Bay* was sunk off Makin, part of the attack on Tarawa, an amphibious target that had been hardened during the Doolittle Raid-induced delay in America's Central Pacific offensive; while the hardened nut of Tarawa was being slowly and bloodily cracked, a Japanese submarine had a chance to reach the area and get into a firing position.

Note the carnage caused in carriers on both sides by amphibious operations. These were prime and slow targets, and required protection. Consequently, both sides' carrier forces were uniquely drawn together by these events. With hundreds of miles of air radius, the carriers involved still had operational mobility, and they could still maneuver while under close attack, their tactical mobility, but they had lost their **strategic** mobility. Land-based air had neither advantage, and was comparatively negligible in effect for the tremendous masses of land-based aircraft employed and lost in amphibious defense (the only victory there was the first defense of Wake, when the amphibious invaders had no fighter support).   Carriers in a **raiding** mode retained their strategic mobility; note the complete absence of carriers lost while raiding, and remember the frequently immense damage inflicted.   Note that under satellite surveillance such strategic mobility would be effectively forfeited *ab initio*, but that carriers continue to retain operational and tactical mobility vis-à-vis land-based air.

And note that Japan's surface ships had some effect against American carriers, nearly as much as its submarines.   By contrast, American surface ships had no effect on Japanese carriers, even as they were less effective than Japan's surface ships against opposing surface ships.   Plainly, usage, not obsolete technology, was a large part of the American surface warfare problem.   And last, note that Japanese combined arms did a much better job against carriers than they did against surface ships.   The misleading lesson from Allied surface ship sinkings is refuted not only by the sinkings of Japanese surface ships, but also of three American carriers.

There were some other carrier sinkings, in areas where American, and American-built, carriers also fought.   In the Atlantic Ocean and Mediterranean Sea, British carriers were lost:

Carrier Lost	Type	Date	Cause	Activity When Lost
Courageous	CV	09/39	Submarine	Anti-Sub Patrol
Glorious	CV	06/40	Surface	Amphibious Evac.
Ark Royal	CV	11/41	Submarine	Malta Ferry
Audacity	CVE	12/41	Submarine	Convoy Escort
Eagle	CV	08/42	Submarine	Malta Ferry
Avenger	CVE	11/42	Submarine	Amphibious Invasion

Once again, no raiding carriers were lost despite important raids on the Italian fleet at Taranto and the German battleship *Tirpitz* in Norway; indeed, no carriers were lost during purely naval encounters such as Cape Matapan and other Mediterranean battles and the pursuit of the *Bismarck*.   Note that all carrier combat losses were during World War II.   The *Furious* in World War I, Allied carriers off Korea, French and then American carriers off Vietnam, British carriers off Suez, British jump-jet carriers off the Falklands and American carriers off Kuwait all operated without loss.   And yet they are supposedly vulnerable.

Considered in isolation, the British experience, which is to say the European experience, would show a misleading pattern of submarine losses, no vulnerability to air attack and no losses in ports.   Although anti-submarine patrol was important in destroying German submarines, especially after the provision of American escort carriers, two early carriers were lost, the first with little experience in the role and the second after its planes had shot down five German bombers attacking or shadowing its convoy. In the Pacific, American anti-submarine sweeps using carriers sank more dozens of Japanese submarines. There were well over a thousand submarines lost in World War II, too many to profitably list

While American analysts fault Japan's World War II tactics of tying its submarines to fleet operations and of targeting warships, the best successes of American submarines occurred precisely when those tactics were used by the U.S. Before and at the Philippine Sea battle, Japanese tankers, destroyers and carriers were targeted, and American submarines were employed at the approaches to the Leyte Gulf operation, sinking two heavy cruisers, knocking out a third at the beginning of the battle and sinking two smaller warships at the end. These submarine uses succeeded late in the war because the U.S. had regained the strategic initiative which it had surrendered by the Doolittle Raid and its fall-out, and could post its submarines where action was likely to occur; Japan's submarines had been most successful early in the war, when it had held the strategic initiative. The Philippine Sea experience hardly validates the submarine as a technology, however, as the Japanese lost a large number.

These facts indicate that submarines were supplemental rather than decisive, their use reflecting results more than effecting them. In modern times, of course, American submariners boosted the combat capabilities of submarines against combat ships, from escorting carriers to sinking enemy submarines. The usual alibi for the American submarine failure in the first 70% of the Pacific War is bad torpedoes, which the submariners supposedly finally tested after 22 months of warfare. But the torpedo was developed before the submarine was perfected, with surface ships being the primary means of delivery up to World War I and the torpedo plane developed between the World Wars. And America's PT-boats, destroyers and torpedo planes, although getting few shots early in the war, had no noticeable torpedo defects -- and their torpedoes were produced by the same Navy Bureau of Ordnance which produced the submariners' excuse. The problem had been that the submariners, with their influential promoters such as King, Nimitz and Lockwood, had been able to force the introduction of some overly complicated wrinkles in the torpedoes issued to them. It was hubris, and neither the new gimmicks nor their problems were shared by humbler users.

The other torpedo carriers had their excuses The slow Devastators which had swarmed the *Shoho* at the Coral Sea with exploding torpedoes were shot down wholesale, nearly a third of total production, by Japanese fighters at Midway. The even slower Catalinas, which had proved torpedo-capable at Midway, were only slowly used for that role in quantity. American destroyers, which used their exploding torpedoes mostly to scuttle several American carriers and against the odd Japanese ship, were only later released to maneuver for night torpedo attacks. And America's British model PT-boats were largely ineffective, except in the movies, although they did sink three submarines and a big destroyer by themselves. But it wasn't their torpedoes that made American PTs a substantial failure, it was the Navy's failure to adopt the more efficient Franco-German boat design.

The choice of ship types has been influenced by more than the direct Anglophilia which gave us mediocre PT boats. There was also the legacy, official or unacknowledged, which gave us the naval disarmament treaties, Britain's road victory at Washington or its home loss at London. Even after those treaties had lapsed, the U.S. built some cruisers close to the old limits, diplomatic considerations and wishful thinking overriding defense value. One such cruiser type was the American *Brooklyn*s, lacking the underwater protection of bulges, as available treatyesque tonnage went for mounting larger numbers of treatyesque guns. Gun size, not number, had been restricted, first at Washington and then further at London, with some hoping to see the London regime in effect again; other nations, particularly the Japanese, concentrated on better torpedoes for their cruisers. Often mauled in World War II, which followed hard upon their building, those *Brooklyn*s which were damaged, but not mortally so (one was struck by a radio-controlled German glide-bomb, the wonder weapon of the moment), were rebuilt with bulges while being repaired.

In the early 1950s, a half-dozen war-surplus *Brooklyn*s were sold by the U.S. in pairs to each of the three major South American powers, keeping a pattern of balanced sales to A.B.C. (Argentina, Brazil and Chile) navies that the U.S. and Britain had begun early in the battleship era. The battleships were just going out of service in the 1950s, after four decades of service, although not of use. Argentina and Brazil, former possessors of two battleships each, also got a modern light British aircraft carrier apiece; Chile got no carrier to replace its battleship, but all three got numbers of American destroyers over succeeding years. One Argentine cruiser, previously lucky and undamaged, and therefore unbulged and vulnerable, was the *General Belgrano*, once the American *Phoenix* and a veteran of Pearl Harbor.

Torpedoed by a British submarine during the Falklands conflict, the *General Belgrano* sank more rapidly than otherwise necessary with a large portion of its crew, late victims of the decades of liberal disarmament madness. Also getting short press notice, although for more ideologically opportune reasons than the disarmament angle, were the previous naval actions involving the Falklands. In World War I, Graf Spee's German Pacific Squadron of two "obsolete" armored cruisers and three smaller cruisers, having previously sunk two British armored cruisers off Chile (they had left behind their consort, a slow old battleship), had mistimed a bombardment of the Falklands' Port Stanley. The old British battleship and two British battle cruisers were in port to load coal; the British battle cruisers emerged and shelled von Spee's squadron to pieces.

In World War II, the German armored cruiser *Graf Spee* was trapped in Uruguay after battle with three smaller British cruisers (all **late** treaty cruisers, and therefore very small, with the "heavy" cruiser short a turret to save weight even further below the old 10,000 ton limit, and the two light cruisers with two-gun turrets instead of the three-gun types later put into service by Britain, Japan and the U.S. when the particular temporary tonnage restriction had expired) north of the Falklands, and then scuttled by its captain following reports of British reinforcements. The only real British reinforcement to stop this *ersatz* battleship (the *Graf Spee*, although not a battleship, replaced one in Versailles parlance) was a heavy cruiser (early treaty cruiser, therefore larger than the other three, more modern and therefore more treaty-plagued) that had come up from Port Stanley, and which would have been the *Graf Spee*'s main opponent had the Germans not been hood-winked into scuttling their ship.

If an area needs to be a backwater for liberal propaganda purp-oses, why it must then be a backwater; if it has plenty of sheep that provide people with wool and mutton from an otherwise barren stretch of land, its usefulness, not its remoteness from the centers of liberal chi-chi, is irrelevant. Its previous experience as a naval lightning rod must be ignored. After all, democratic Britain, writhing under the electoral iron heel of Conservative Margaret Thatcher, had to be the villain, and the Argentine *Junta*, previously and subsequently denounced as blood-thirsty barbarians for their suppression of the country's left-wing mad-bombers, had to be the hero -- "Third World" will out. Making the Falklands obscure merely served to scapegoat the British war effort (although not the Argentine invasion; being liberal means applying no standards to non-Europeans entitled to their own immorality). Should oil be found in the Falklands, or off their extensive continental shelf, they will no longer be obscure (indeed, they will probably be found to be indispensable to some imaginary eco-system), and Britain will be condemned for new reasons.

The Royal Navy's dismantling was an indispensable prerequisite to the Argentine invasion, one Thatcher Government achievement vig-orously applauded by the British left (except the ship-building unions). Britain scrapped its last real aircraft carrier in 1978, beaching its Phantom fighter-bombers and its Buccaneer bombers (which saw service in the Gulf War to make up for British losses from excessive low-level operations), and scrapping its Gannet early-warning radar planes. With the Gannets gone, the Falklands fleet had to fall back upon the American anti-*kamikaze* device of radar-picket destroyers, and with the same mel-ancholy results. Two British destroyers were sunk by Exocet electronic *kamikazes*, because they lacked fighter cover from the beaching of the Phantoms, even as they were unnecessarily exposed while doing the work that Gannets could have done from farther away with an aerial height advantage. Instead of real aircraft carriers, substitute put-up jobs, built for some minor North Atlantic role, with a few slow and short-ranged Harrier jump-jets, returned the British to their inter-war standards for aircraft carriers.

This time, the problem was not the disorganization of one service running the ships while another ran their planes, but funding only for tasks too narrowly defined. Real need couldn't read a "Defence White-Paper"; some men died, while others alibied. Whatever the impression given by diplomats and politicians, the Falklands' seizure was made more feasible and less dangerous by substantial unilateral British disarmament, which mitigated against both the possibility of opposition and its success if attempted. What more encouragement does a *junta* need, except the predictable "dripping wet" carping about British resistance and operations, such as the torpedoing of the *General Belgrano*?

Just what the Argentine ship and its escorts were doing at sea that day, moving primarily toward the Falklands where the British counter-invasion was in progress, has not been explained. Perhaps they was on a mission of destruction, or on a mission to appear destructive, but it was definitely not a normal peace-time maneuver; the Argentine invasion had obviated such concepts as normal and peace-time. The *General Belgrano* possessed more gunpower, with fifteen guns firing shells twice as powerful as those of British pop-guns and 50% farther, and, made of armored steel rather than flammable aluminum, more resistance to opposing gunfire and cruise missiles than the entire British invasion flotilla. It was also equipped with anti-aircraft missiles, which the British, with their scant two dozen Harriers, were not really able to face.

What is the submarine commander sighting such a force supposed to do? Follow it, and risk detection by the two sonar-equipped escorts armed with homing torpedoes (although not with the additional large Swedish rockets on their French sisters), and more capable of detecting and destroying a submarine noisier in fast pursuit? Or does he attack, and risk offending the world's neurotics with a victory which might also preserve some of the lives of his countrymen, including his crew? As with Dewey at Manila Bay, or the U-boat that sank the *Lusitania*, the British submarine was a victim of its own success, at least in liberalism's shadow world, where virtue is shameful and the pathological worshipped. The fact of opposition to an invasion was more incredible to liberals than the invasion itself. The victory over the *General Belgrano* was even more hideous than the patently obvious fact that the submarine would have neither been there, nor sighted it, nor torpedoed it, nor sunk it, but for the fact of the invasion, so coyly excused with the plea that the Argentines did not think the British would mind.

To liberals, victory is a disaster, and the *General Belgrano*'s sinking was interpreted with the usual metaphysical omniscience as contributing to another endless cycle of violence (which ended a few weeks later with final British victory). The later sinking of British ships was credited to projected nemesis, the liberal god's vengeance, or to Argentine resolve increased by the torpedoing, instead of as a normal incident of war. Could the Argentines have been somewhat discouraged, and less effective in their subsequent actions, by the loss of their most powerful ship? Or, with twenty thousand Argentine troops on the island near Port Stanley, would not that country's Air Force have been attacking British ships anyway? Those questions are not even admissible in liberal court, let alone answered. Instead, the losses of the British ships were pure doom, if not caused by the shortcomings of their own weapons, although not by the previous years' fashionable disarmament. Passing up a submarine's shot at Argentina's lone functional cruiser would not have provided air cover for the British ships; the proposition is utterly irrational, which is to say trendy leftism.

Victories win wars, and giving up chances at them helps prolong or lose wars. No purpose is served by fighting and not trying to win, and triumphs are the medicine of choice for the occasional set-back. A nation as besot with liberal vices as modern Britain, with its scum rooting for the enemy, its compulsive diplomacy and its military disoriented by economies destructive of any capabilities other than those foreseeable by the latest bureaucratic position paper on roles and missions, is a nation needing the tonic of victory in a just and moral cause, which it got in the Falklands. But it is a nation with a severe problem -- its left and the rot it seeps into press and government -- and that is the enemy it has yet to defeat. Ultimately, that enemy is strengthened by Anglophilia and its sentimentalization of past British policies.

The left-liberal interpretation of the so-called naval arms race between Germany and Britain at the beginning of the century finds arms themselves the problems, and technological dynamics and procurement the prime movers. An official biographer praises British bureaucracy for its miraculous improvisation at the start of World War I of massive and complex regulations and forms for maritime insurance, for example. So assiduously is the myth of British amity maintained that the pre-planning of such measures, an obvious safeguard even for a pacific island heavily dependent upon sea-trade, must be denied. From such a willful dose of unreality past comes the unreality of the nearer past, where faith is put in the official version, the latest White Paper. The maintenance of a spurious pacifistic past is the prelude to the sentimentalization of disarmament -- ignoring its very real disaffects -- and denying a choice of responses to exigent circumstance. Give peace a chance? -- Tell the invader. Such alleged thoughts spill over into American politics, academia and publishing. One of the symptoms of the left disease, in Britain and elsewhere, is wallowing in morbid irrationality, leading to willful ignorance of not only military uses, but of any sort of technical, scientific or factual material, apart from its leftist distortions and their disabling of any analytic capacity.

Domestically, the Reagan Administration's refurbishment of the four *Iowa* class battleships was done against similarly sage advice; battleships are, after all, obsolete. And what does that mean, exactly? The bicycle as a military weapon has never shone enough to be rewarded with the epithet of obsolete, yet it continues to kill pedestrians in Manhattan, but then so do a lot of things. In Asian dry seasons, it proved an excellent, cheap and fuel-efficient source of operational (the area between tactical and strategic) mobility, most notably for the Japanese drive, or rather pedal, south through Malaya to capture Britain's Singapore bastion from behind (a hundred thousand British troops captured by men on bicycles), for the British advance inland from their D-Day beaches, and later for North Vietnamese movements through Laos and South Vietnam's back country. Obsolete is always with reference to an alternative, and when the alternative is walking, the bicycle is not obsolete, even on jungle dirt trails. Some people confuse obsolescence, real or imagined, with vulnerability. Battleships do have some vulnerabilities, but that is partly because they were long valuable targets, which truly obsolete things are not -- they are no longer valuable. On that raid's 50th anniversary, *Newsday* favored us with the sage observation that Pearl Harbor ended the battleship's "myths of invincibility".

Of course, the press had in fact been hysterically proclaiming vulnerability, not invincibility, from the beginning of the century through the *Iowa* explosion, first because of torpedoes and submarines, later because of bombers. To present a certain shading to a particular story, the press will deny its own sordid record, an option not open to the rest of us without press censure. The press had embraced charlatan bomber-prophet Billy Mitchell with as much gusto as it had earlier savaged the Wright brothers as hoaxers for several years. Aircraft, and submarines, were long unrealized threats to modern battleships, however, more threatened by groundings and internal explosions.

Only four modern battleships were lost to hostile action prior to World War II, three from comic opera navies. Two, a British in World War I and an old Spaniard in their latest Civil War, were mined at sea. An Austro-Hungarian battleship being taken over by the new Yugoslavia was mined by Italian frogmen in a port claimed by Italy. The one modern battleship lost in a sea battle until 1941 was another Austro-Hungarian sunk by an Italian torpedo boat. World War II saw a flood of battleship sinkings, but very few by aircraft at sea. Most sunk were in port -- fuel-burning steamships remain there far more than did old sailing ships -- but not necessarily by aircraft, as were the Pearl Harbor battleships. In 1939, the British *Royal Oak* was sunk in Scapa Flow when surprised by a German submarine's torpedoes. In 1940, with France attempting to withdraw from the war (by act of its legal government, the one that had declared war), a British fleet made a surprise attack on Oran, French Algeria's harbor, sinking one old battleship and damaging two others with gunfire; days later, a British aircraft torpedo detonated an auxiliary ship's depth charges, redamaging one hard-luck newer French battleship for its second triple-figure death toll of the week.

Japan's seizure of French Indochina, done with dragooned French consent, followed this British outrage, with the U.S. choosing to oppose only the later bloodless Japanese *coup* while lauding the earlier bloody British treachery. (Franklin Roosevelt would emulate both, with his own three dragooning seizures of 1941 and his full-scale invasion of French North Africa, sinking dozens more French ships.) November 1940 saw British carrier aircraft torpedo three Italian battleships in Taranto harbor, sinking one and beaching another; this raid was launched by a single carrier, and with only eleven slow biplanes. Italian battleships in battle at sea, with their tactical speed advantage and fine daytime gunnery, had already been frustrated by British tactics, carrier attacks at long range or smoke screens and the threat of destroyer torpedo attacks by day, and close-range night battles. Although U.S. ships would later similarly face Japanese carrier attacks at sea and night battles with Japanese torpedo launches, first came Pearl Harbor, as foreshadowed by Taranto.

Purely air attack upon battleships in harbor had thus been added to submarine attack and primarily gunfire attack with some air support upon battleships in harbor, and these incidents even made the papers. To 1941 observers, fleets in port had been targets of hostile action three times in the previous calendar year, and those who were ignorant of contemporary events might recall such incidents as Drake at Cadiz, Howard's fireships striking the Armada in port, Nelson's repeated "Copenhagening" of the Danes (without a declaration of war), "Dewey at Manila", a long-time toast of pre-neurotic America, or even the Japanese Togo at Port Arthur. And modern ships, fuel-burning and large, had larger and more complex bases than in sail days; encounters with ships more tightly tied to fewer ports were likelier than ever.

Only in 1941 did more battleships begin to be lost at sea. The British *Hood*, frequently classed as a battle cruiser, was sunk by the German battleship *Bismarck*'s gunfire, and then the *Bismarck* was successively damaged by gunfire from a pair of British battleships, three torpedoes from the aircraft of two British carriers, a destroyer torpedo, decisively ruinous gunfire from a second pair of British battleships, and then finally sunk by a British cruiser's torpedoes. In the fortnight before Pearl Harbor, the British battleship *Barham* was sunk at sea by a German submarine; the film of it turning over and exploding its boilers -- on full steam in a vain attempt to power pumps -- is standard footage for television sclockumentaries. In the fortnight after Pearl Harbor, two British capital ships were sunk at sea by Japanese aircraft from Saigon, an at-sea first for aircraft, and two more British battleships, mined by Italian frogmen, beached in Egyptian harbor. Battleships at sea had proven somewhat vulnerable, but the fewer carriers at war had proven more vulnerable -- three large British ones sunk -- and masses of submarines and aircraft had also been lost. But, as the beneficiaries of enthusiasm, they were not thereby obsolete, the flip side of invincibility.

If vulnerability to atomic bombs is the criterion, then just about everything is obsolete, but the battleship among the least so. Designedly strong and mobile, they are not easy targets, except in port -- Pearl Harbor most familiarly to Americans, but Port Arthur, Scapa Flow, Taranto, Alexandria, Kiel, Norwegian fiords and Kure also. After World War II, many battleships, along with other types, were atom-bombed in Bikini Atoll. Only at very close ranges were they destroyed, being heavily damaged at slightly greater ranges and barely affected at a few hundred yards (the blasts are common file footage, and most of the ships, about six hundred feet long, are visibly being overtaken by the main blasts). Even unmanned, with no pumps or damage control, and the latest battleship being more than twenty years, or four generations of designs, older than the *Iowa*s, many survived both atom blasts and remained afloat during subsequent years of bomb, missile, gun and demolition charge target practice.

Atomic blasts in water transmit energy efficiently, but only over short distances; a near miss is necessary to inflict serious damage. Atomic explosion in the air at slightly longer distances dismantled the superstructures on some older battleships. But even a hydrogen bomb would be less effective against an *Iowa* than against a steel-reinforced concrete bunker, because the bunker's rigidity causes it to absorb shock much more thoroughly and disastrously. The hydrogen bomb's circle of destruction is greater than an atomic bomb's, but not its efficiency -- most of the explosion destroys the center with massive overkill, and the edges are fairly well defined, so that, only a few miles beyond bunkers destroyed in tests, windows in wooden houses were left unbroken.

A battleship is designed to absorb shocks, in part to enable it to fire its guns; a salvo can skid a battleship 60 feet sideways in the water, roughly equaling the energy of a nearby atomic bomb-blast absorbed as a shock wave on the exposed portion of a ship beyond destruction range. And part of that energy travels at one speed through the air and another part through the water, and so do not strike simultaneously and more destructively. The battleship, man's strongest mobile structure, is least affected by unconcentrated force because it rolls with the punch and is blasé about heat blast and radiation. What sinks such a leviathan are direct, pinpoint attacks by traditional means, where the force is localized and far more concentrated than the energy from an atomic blast, which is 99 + % wasted overkill even when directly on such a hard target. But traditional means are what a battleship is armored and subdivided against, to minimize and contain such damage; therefore, it usually takes a number of hits to disable one.

Countries with atomic bombs have not yet used them on each other, just as they stopped using poison gas on each other, for fear of retaliation. Such weapons are not therefore commonly encountered, and most nations neglect their defenses against them, just as most people put away their gas masks early in World War II (but put themselves away in gas masks under Iraqi bombardment years later). Before that, it was feared that poison gas would be dropped on cities, although it had not in World War I; left-wing propaganda, the kind that shows up in "history" books, about Italian use of poison gas in Ethiopia (if at all, after victory) fed upon pacifistic terrorism about the doom of war, helping to feed impulses toward both appeasement and ineffectual resistance -- sanctions, diplomatic resolutions and petitions. The weapons that are actually used today are bombs, missiles and mines, things the *Iowa*s are unmatched in resisting, approached only by the four monumentalized battleships moored off America's East and Gulf Coasts in their namesake states.

Modern ships are thin-skinned, and often made of aluminum, so flammable at high temperatures it is an actually ingredient in many modern incendiaries. Such explosives are no threat whatsoever against a battleship's thickly armored vitals, even in such large warheads as are found on large cruise missiles such as America's Tomahawk or the Soviet Styx (or its Chinese Silkworm offshoot), or in the small gravity bombs in modern use, or in the smaller cruise missiles, from the Exocet on down. Soviet Russia, a useful example for liberals when it was not operating aircraft carriers and American carriers could be called obsolete by that peculiar standard, had no battleships, its old ones too moribund and its modern construction destroyed by German troops in World War II. But it had the world's largest fleet of gunned ships, about a dozen comparable to the old American *Brooklyn*s still in Russian service, but firing shells about one-tenth as powerful as the *Iowa*s', and less than all but the smallest cruise missiles. But cruise missiles are not designed to penetrate armor, unlike some battleship shells possessing the same amount of explosive, so that the *Iowa*s are little threatened themselves, but possess both armor-piercing shells for use against hard emplacements as well as high explosive shells, with less metal shell and more explosive powder, for use against area targets. Cruise missiles, accelerating more gradually than shells, do not need structural strength, and are thus poor kinetic penetrators against hard targets.

Bombs, with normally even thinner shells, were a major threat to older battleships with decks mostly unarmored against plunging shells or bombs. But as battle ranges, gun elevation and the threat of plunging shells all increased, as the airplane and the bomb threatened, battleships of the modern era were built with thick armored decks to stop all but the most massive bombs. Battleships were large targets, but mainly for disarmament treaties keeping them vulnerable. The real standard of what is obsolete is always relative; all other ships and structures are more vulnerable, and therefore more obsolete (although not literally, because of age), than the battleship. High explosive shells, whether artillery, bombs or missiles, striking thick armor are ineffective, and some armor-piercing shells just ricochet off, leaving dents for a crew often otherwise unaware their ship had been hit.

During World War II, two American battleships were struck by shells as powerful as Styx warheads. The *Massachusetts* was dented by a half-dozen large Vichy French battleship shells during the American invasion of Vichy North Africa, controlled by a regime with which the U.S. had diplomatic relations and which received no warning about the attack except the usual Roosevelt intrigues with dissident military officers conspiring against their civilian superiors. And unlike the several dozen unarmored French ships sunk that day by the British and the Americans, the firing French battleship lived on to fight another day. It drew American ire as part of the French-British-Israeli attack on Egyptian possession of the Suez Canal, offending Eisenhower's liberal foreign policy advisors as a breach of international good conduct, although the previous North African invasion had delighted the liberal Roosevelt and his advisors. (The Egyptian canal seizure substantially escaped the censure of American liberals; non-Europeans cannot be expected to meet European standards, according to the evangelicals of equality.) It was Belgium, 1914, all over again, but, being nominally directed against the Germans (although there were none in the sunken French ships), there was no breast-beating, just a celebration of treachery in a Good Cause.

Across the world, a week later and against a country which had attacked the U.S. as treacherously as the U.S. had attacked the Vichy French (in what would be described in trials of the defeated as "conspiracy to wage aggressive war"; it was the Vichy French who were put on trial for having the temerity to think that the government which could declare war was the one which could accept peace terms, not some rebellious general in foreign service), the battleship *South Dakota* was struck by dozens of heavy and medium Japanese shells, after its power had blacked out and left it unable to reply. Well armored, although not as thoroughly as the *Iowa* class, the ship suffered minor damage to its superstructure but no loss of vital function -- hull, big guns, magazines, engines and controls -- just damage to its anti-aircraft guns and unarmored gun-directors. The *South Dakota* was damaged in a battle to keep Japanese ships from bombarding an American airfield, as two Japanese battleships had previously done to the same field, leaving only a single aircraft operable out of 110 when the bombardment started, a better score than Japanese aircraft achieved at Pearl Harbor with the dual advantage of surprise and not being obsolete. Aircraft, far less effective than those of World War II, had been deemed to make battleships obsolete, something of little consolation to the dozens of planes shot down by the *South Dakota* three weeks before its scourging at the hands of a thirty-year-old Japanese battleship, or to the dozens more shot down by the *North Carolina* seven weeks before that.

Unlike Billy Mitchell's patsy, these were shooting back with scads of modern anti-aircraft guns, moving targets steaming about with active pumps and crews for damage control. Mitchell's target could have been sunk with a rowboat and dynamite, just as, under the same constraints as his target ship, Mitchell's planes could have been wrecked by a five-year-old with a hammer. The Navy itself had long been convinced of an air menace, and had installed 3-inch caliber anti-aircraft guns in its battleships four years **before** Mitchell's stunt. Mitchell's fragile bombers flew at 2,000 feet, chugging along at 80 miles per hour. The gun type already on American battleships could reach 20,000 feet and would shoot down far faster, far more agile and far less fragile attackers even after being supplanted on most battleships.

What had gone right? Far too sweeping conclusions had been drawn by the morbidly impressionable from an unrepresentative test (of the sort criticized by liberals when used to sell weapons, as Mitchell was trying to do), and continue to be made. The battleship did not become obsolete; rather it was gradually superseded by the aircraft carrier as the appropriate yardstick by which naval power would be measured; Mitchell, of course, had pronounced the carrier obsolete even in the early 1920s. The battleship had never ceased to be a warship of effective fighting strength in a tough shell, but its gun technology was rather mature. Although the battleship was capable of having its deficiencies further marginally reduced, by dint of not being capable of much further positive development, it slowly yielded priority to the aircraft, a younger technology capable of greater growth. But the aircraft grew at the expense of research, development and constant procurement, as well as greater operating costs (including bases, land or carrier, losses from peace-time accidents and weather) and shorter strategic radius.

The battleship's two drawbacks were its vulnerability to aircraft and its short-range weapons, compared to airplanes' operating radius. Vulnerability to aircraft was redressed initially by both greater deck armor and the addition of masses of anti-aircraft guns, 100 or more, with their crews soon the ship's feature most endangered by bombing. Later, surface ships became equipped with anti-aircraft missiles, and improved their striking power against more stationary targets with cruise missiles, not as flexible or effective as aircraft for all applications, but less expensive in peace-time and with smaller acquisition and operating costs.

The light and medium anti-aircraft guns and their numerous crews were deleted from the refurbished *Iowa*s, their role done by the anti-aircraft missiles of escorting ships as well as by both those dual-purpose guns retained and automated gatling guns added with their slaved radars.

Submarines are the doyen of the modern Billy Mitchells, and the *Iowa*s have been improved on that score, moving from floatplanes relying only on sight to the Navy's most modern anti-submarine helicopters, equipped with sonar buoys, radar, magnetic anomaly detectors and homing torpedoes, at four per battleship twice the number carried by the Navy's best purpose-built anti-submarine surface warships.

But there is more to winning battles than just surviving threats: dealing them out in turn and making good upon them. The main battery guns of the *Iowa*s are a type originally planned to equip two more ships of the same class, as well as a further class of ships with three more guns per ship. There is accordingly a huge supply of spare parts, including barrels (which wear out after hundreds of rounds), and with a further six battleships that used the same ammunition retired (three as memorials), there is also a massive supply of paid-for shells saved, with the ships, from the trendies and the scrap-heap. For a paid-for shell, a detonator and some silk bags of powder, an *Iowa* shot can deliver as big an explosive charge as a big Tomahawk cruise missile costing hundreds of times as much -- cost-effective, in Whiz Kid jargon, although that mindset usually finds value to be obsolete. The guns, as with any unguided weapon fired from a ship on the restless sea (and the *Iowa*s roll a goodly amount for large ships), are not terribly accurate, but with the ability to fire repeated salvos of nine large shells, they do not have to be. The targets which they are capable of dealing with, ships, concrete emplacements, other bunkers, airfields and troop concentrations, are still to be encountered in the real world, wishful thinking notwithstanding.

And the choice for dealing with them, when the decision has been made to deal with them, when they are within gun range of the sea, is usually between bombing, also not extremely accurate and involving the possibility of losing expensive planes and their pilots, or a battleship bombardment by a bombload-equivalent salvo every minute or so. Each battleship has the ability to deliver the equivalent of several tactical nuclear warheads in conventional explosives with a few hours' heavy bombardment, spreading the devastation like a cluster bomb, but not breaking the anti-nuclear protocols doted upon by the handwringers.

Cluster bombs are big bombs designed to burst so that their cargo of many little bombs can be scattered before exploding, spreading destruction over a larger area instead of over-killing one point and its immediate environs. Cluster bombs are the American term for the weapon and, as with all things American, are objects of liberal hatred. Of course, the type was originally developed by the Soviets, as the "Molotov Breadbasket" of left-wing propaganda fame, but that was

Mother Soviet Russia, about which the patriotism of the left was never in doubt. The equation of a death-dealing device with bread is not without its own implicit comment on macabre leftist humanism. That the weapon's Soviet origins are so dutifully obscured, after being so dutifully hosannaed, is typical. But, after all, the Molotov Breadbaskets were dropped on the Nazi Germans, so they must have been a good thing, and fully meriting that doubtlessly necessary warm-up against Poles and Finns.

In view of the expense of new American warship hulls and engines, with small cruiser-sized flimsy fire-trap hulls and their explosive propulsion systems running at nearly half a billion dollars apiece, before running another similar amount for a weapons outfit, spending less for a bigger and far better hull with fine engines and many weapons already on board was a bargain. The similar and following plan to partially reactivate the two remaining *Des Moines* class large heavy cruisers was also a relative bargain compared to new construction, but less so than the *Iowa*s. They were simply not as effective as the battleships, with smaller guns, much less armor and somewhat greater hull and engine wear, although hull and armor were much better than contemporary production, while the 8-inch guns are rapid-fire, with good range and four times the punch per shell of the Navy's standard 5-inch shells, and all cheaper than new construction.

The Navy had been experimenting with a single 8-inch gun turret for smaller ships, but for the expense it was not a better anti-aircraft gun -- part of its "dual-purpose" -- because its added range was irrelevant against fast targets at long range, and its larger but fewer shell-bursts effectively covered only the same area as the 5-inch guns already in service. That particular Carter-Brown decision, albeit criticized by frequently accurate voices, was correct. A third *Des Moines* class ship, the *Newport News*, had been deleted during the Carter Administration as non-standard; it had in 1972 suffered a turret explosion, and the 8-inch gun turret affected had been replaced with a 6-inch gun turret from a scrapped class of automatic-fire light cruisers (an offense against the old disarmament legacy of classifying cruisers by gun-size).

All such ships had been late World War II products, introducing cased shells (propellant and shell in same package, like a modern bullet or smaller caliber artillery shells) to be rapidly loaded by specialized machinery. Previous turret machinery had been unable to handle the awkward old shell and powder-bag combination used with large naval guns (like an automatic copying machine when the office fussbudget tries to economize with wrinkled paper and jams up the machine). With cased ammunition automatically loaded, ships could fire four times faster than conventional cruisers, but the cost was cased shells containing their own detonators, making the whole heavy package, not just a small temperamental separate detonator, explosive if dropped. Scrapping the *New-*

port News did increase the number of spares and relative ammunition supplies for the two surviving ships, but there had originally been five of the class ordered so that that situation was not really critical in spite of the relatively prolonged use of the completed three compared to the more often mothballed battleships. Numbers of older cruisers had been retired earlier or fully or partially converted to missile ships.

The liberal approach was the "effective-cost" Whiz Kid sale of two even larger cruisers, about midway between the *Iowa* and *Des Moines* classes in virtually all details, from size, armor and usage to main gun battery (12-inch caliber halfway between the 16- and 8-inches of the unscrapped classes). *Alaska*s worth a billion dollars apiece in today's dollars, and nearly a quarter of a billion dollars apiece in currency just about to slide in value from liberal mismanagement, were sold for scrap, at a few million dollars apiece. It was the sort of criminal waste practiced by junkies upon others -- kicking in a car window ($150) and ripping up a dashboard and ventilation control ($350) to get a stereo ($200) to be sold for the price of a fix ($10 or $15). Two armored hulls ($$$$), their engines ($$$$) and their weapons ($$$$) went for peanuts ($), the sort of bargain resuméd lunatics in power and other junkies understand perfectly.

The 12-inch gun was also in Cold War land use as the Army's "atomic cannon", until some wacky artillery men used a conventional shell to shake up cottagers at a resort lake near their artillery range. Rather than admit that an "atomic" delivery system had been so perverted, the Army preferred to profess that the incident had been an accident by an "inaccurate" weapon (about eight miles from its supposed artillery range target, but exactly in the middle of the lake actually aimed at). The dozens of "atomic cannons" were scrapped, and their tactical atomic shell role was split between rockets, which malfunction more often than guns, and smaller guns with less range, just the type of things atomic warheads should not be fired by. One positive was that both missiles, with no recoil, and smaller guns, with less recoil, were more mobile than were the railway-sized trailered 12-inch guns on land; at sea, with guns already mounted in a large ship, that doesn't hold up.

Compared to a modern aircraft carrier, a refurbished *Iowa* has a 70% smaller crew; uses less fuel for steaming than an oil-burning carrier (which has to keep up speed for flight operations, going into the wind and then back onto its base course, over and over, tacking like a sailboat but burning fuel to do so), and even less than a nuclear-powered carrier, whose planes are not nuclear-powered; has less costly cruise missiles instead of airplanes for long reach (liberal savants had been calling the carrier obsolete because it was vulnerable to cruise missiles, but with battleships equipped with them, carriers suddenly became the temporary cynosure of all virtue); and is far less vulnerable to modern tactical weapons. Carriers, because of their sheer size, buoyancy (little heavy armor), compartmentalization (copied by modern liberalism) and modern fire-fighting equipment, are themselves surprisingly tough.

Compared to modern submarines, an *Iowa* has more uses, against tactical targets (big and medium guns, 32 Tomahawk and 16 Harpoon cruise missiles instead of 12 or 15 Tomahawks and fewer Harpoons per gunless submarine, for example), greater detection and engagement possibilities against surface ships, and, in return for its own visibility and consequent targetability, the capacity to work in close co-operation with other ships without sacrificing a long suit of transient underwater invisibility. The submarine has hydrophones, as do the battleship's helicopters; sonars, which the helicopters can use without giving away the battleship's position, while the submarine's sonar use always gives its position, its best secret, away; a periscope, for the possibility of detection revealing a small patch of horizon; and radar, which involves surfacing, emitting an active signal and being detected, while its own antennas, smaller and fewer, are lower in the water than the great heights of a battleship's superstructure, and thus not capable of commanding as wide a horizon. Naturally, first into mothballs with budget cuts were surface bombardment ships, the battleships and cruisers (they **do** have much bigger crews than submarines), and even more naturally, they were quickly hauled out again when the Gulf War impended, need calling forth the useful.

Air crashes kill more and more frequently than explosions on battleships, but their particulars are less well aired than was the *Iowa* tragedy. Although if there is that ghastliest indication of plutocracy, the, ugh, **private** aircraft involved, then thinly disguised editorializations (from the salaried minions of corporate-plane operators) calling for their ban will echo through the nation's media like a splash in a cesspool. The private aircraft is a symbol of wealth and power, as great a distraction from liberal goals as the fact of national wealth and power of a battleship or an aircraft carrier; private, or public and patriotic, each must be brought low that liberal ideology might rise. Other air crashes are merely a chance to savage a corporation, airline or aircraft builder, or the civilian FAA, and thus intimate that Reagan caused the tragedy by firing those air traffic controllers, and that it's time for an amnesty and their rehire (as the Clinton regime is now doing).

The battleship explosion was a chance to attack America's military, an even more desirable target, more directly connected to patriotism and the proper function of the public sector. When American military people are killed, the result is a feeding frenzy by the ghouls of the national press, eager to consume dead American boys for ideological nourishment. They would steal a dead sailor out from under the pennies on his eyes. The peculiarities of the case, the relationship between two sailors, one of whom died and the other of whom stood to collect $100,000 in insurance on his life, and the discovery of detonators in the dead man's living quarters, proof that he had an outside interest in such things or that someone wished to make it appear he did, were swept away in attacks on the Navy for its presumed negligence in various ways. Attacking the military obscured the factor that $100,000 is the modern point at which life insurance companies start charging a murder premium, and at the same time below the cut-off for automatic investigation.

Buildings get burned down and people get killed for insurance every day in the U.S. (something the selling insurance agents are not going to point out in sales to the insured). Unlike some forms of industrial insurance, where companies change practices for lower premiums, life insurance is not a cause of safety but of danger. Occasionally a lot of people get killed at once to disguise the crime's nature, even as disgruntled ex-employees or jilted lovers have been known to cast their nets wide. When 87 innocents were torched in a recent New York case, what were the media's priorities? Whether the woman involved was being blamed by the neighbors and what feminists thought of that, and whether there were building code violations at the torched club, whose owner was a Hollywood actress's husband. Not the evil that made the tragedy, but the utterly trivial -- celebrity-gawking and scapegoating -- the reactions of a local press. Although the culprit had motive, means and opportunity (jealousy, gasoline and purchase near the place and time of the torching), he was beside of the point, which in a liberal press is always far from the facts.

But the national press has more focused ideological concerns, so the *Iowa* onus was immediately upon the Navy. After all, the ship was obsolete. Why smirking media know-it-alls even bother asking their leading questions is a puzzlement. But even more disgusting are the brain-dead stuffed-shirts they dredge up to sit still for their abusive yammering, followed by the liberal politicians who gather to feast on the corpses of dead American servicemen. When there isn't enough unquestionably "patriotic gore" to satisfy their bestial appetites, either they phantasize about disasters (Khe Sanh, Another Dien Ben Phu, Another Vietnam) or the cry goes up of a light body-count, a cover-up (during and after Vietnam, including Thailand, and during and after the Gulf War). Someone will occasionally sneak through to shed a little public light, but the bureaucratization of American society, besides spawning the liberal media, helps screen out anyone except accredited quacks or those with ideological or political agendas. The *Iowa* explosion initially caused amazement that the ship had not blown up, with the ignition of the magazines. Yet the turret was designed to withstand not just the explosion of a single gun charge, but the explosion of a combination of three gun charges, three shells and the incoming enemy shell which would have somehow defeated the armor and caused the big bang. The magazines, and therefore the rest of the ship, were in no danger.

The only American battleship to be blown up by a magazine explosion, including the *Maine* (not enough damage), was the *Arizona*, struck at Pearl Harbor by up to eight of those armor-piercing battleship shells which the Japanese had given tailfins and dropped as bombs. One penetrated the inadequate deck armor into a magazine and detonated it, destroying the ship. According to published legend in some history books, one bomb went down its stack and blew the ship apart; but the boilers, under the stack, were not under pressure and not therefore explosive -- a stack bomb would have simply filled a largely unmanned boiler room with lukewarm water (divers have lately located the armored grate incorporated in the stack; it was not penetrated -- there was no stack-bomb). The *Arizona* did show how far liberals would go -- for two generations -- in distorting responsibility for a disaster. FDR had blocked battleship modernization and hung the Pacific Fleet out to die, two indispensables for that particular disaster. And when liberals can savage the opposition, the distortion is also troweled on. In the *Iowa* case, this became a welter of contradictory theories to detract from the obvious. One such theory was unstable powder.

A generally unstable state was a feature of nineteenth century explosives, including those used for British charges in World War I, and of some twentieth century nitrogenous fertilizers (which must be absorbed by plants unequipped with detonators). Modern military charges have safety built in until someone negates it, whether for a military purpose, such as cased ammunition for rapid fire, or for other destructive purposes. After the disaster of the three British battle cruisers at Jutland, when turrets flared and burned down through their barbettes into magazine explosions that left the ships and their thousand-man crews as undone as Admiral Beatty's lowliest coat-button, large ships around the world had been rebuilt or redesigned in hopes of preventing future such occurrences. The men in the *Iowa*'s magazine, insurance beneficiaries or otherwise, were perfectly safe, and some of them even knew it.

German ships at Jutland were already so equipped with magazine protection, and, unlike their British rivals, also had modern powder charges of the American type, flammable at low temperatures, but only explosive at much higher temperatures. Such "powder", seldom really powder, burns slower than wood kindling when lit with a match. Even with less precipitously explosive modern charges, slow burning in a confined space makes temperature build-up to an explosion level possible, but there is time to flood the magazines before that happens. Outside of prospective immediate military use, such powder is kept stored in ventilated areas, such as on barges, to prevent runaway temperature build-up and explosion. Such powder requires deliberate detonation or a colossally bad accident to explode.

The media-inevitable Massachusetts congressional Democrat/ beneficiary theory was that the powder had become unstable by being stored at too high a temperature. That Markey malarkey ignored the nature of the powder, mostly nitrogen tied up in solids with an oxidant and a combustible element. Such a powder does not become more unstable, it combusts (or oxidizes) slowly, losing the bulk of its weight to the air as free nitrogen and various oxides are created or otherwise released from chemical bondage by the oxidation (or combustion) of other elements of its former molecular chains. Powder which has undergone this process is not more unstable, it simply decreases in weight as it is used up by oxidation; weighing the bags shows whether the process has occurred. The powder was supposed to have been kept stored at lower temperatures to prevent it from wasting away, making its charges less effective and standard for their job (and eventually needing repacking into properly filled new bags), not because temperature would have made them more unstable. For a training of turret personnel, such short-weighting would be incidental, and using short-weighted bags instead of those at the proper specs would just have saved on repacking.

At the report of the *Challenger* explosion, that time more accurately chalked up to inappropriate temperature use (the material used had been developed for missiles kept in air-conditioned silos, underground or underwater, not left out at night in freezing weather), the change in the particular material's strength was physically demonstrated by dunking it into ice water and crumbling it. No such demonstration was possible with the barge-stored powder charges exposed to heat, because they would've just burned at low temperatures as they are supposed to, and exploded -- burned rapidly -- at their much higher detonation temperature. If the powder had been unstable, why did one of the bags not explode on the barges, or during loading to transportation to the ship, or while being stowed on board, or while being loaded onto the hoist -- during heavy handling -- rather than just before it was to have been detonated anyway?

The Navy's subsequent experiments did show that such powder **could** be detonated by some bizarre misworking of the turret machinery, but the Navy could hardly show that this scenario had occurred. For some reason, the tests took place out in the open, where there was too much room for such an event; the experiment was not repeated *in situ*, although turret mock-ups are usually far easily more available to the Navy than are remote facilities in New Mexico with only limited simulations. When the Navy has a real reason to suspect a flaw or to look for one, it uses mock-ups, starting in the ship design process. Although for the usual public relations rationales the fantasy of an accident was indulged by the Navy (directly opposing a lie is contrary to professional canons -- acceptability, rather than truth, is prescribed), there were at least 100,000 reasons for there not to have been an accident.

So why was instability of the powder advanced as a hypothesis, when so much work was expended indicting the turret mechanics? Well, the beneficiary, in addition to getting the heat off himself and onto someone else, perhaps had a psychological predisposition (guilt, deserved or not) in favor of thinking that something was wrong with the charges sent up from his magazine, rather than there having occurred some accident in the turret. The media did rather idiotically emphasize the lack of the crew's training, in view of the fact that the ship was on a training cruise when the explosion happened. Because they were being trained, a lack of training was at fault -- had they already been well trained, too much training and its waste of money would've been charged. Also remarked was the presence of contraband in the turret, cigarette lighters, etc.; presumably, such items could never have been present at earlier stages of the charges' storage and transportation. Why it was assumed someone would have been smoking or flicking his lighter during a firing drill was unexplained; between drills would have seemed a much more likely time, but that was **not** when the explosion occurred. In a similar vein was the media's charge of an inadequate investigation and a cover-up by the Navy. The media, itself suffused with irrationality -- prophecising, pontificating and expostulating without evidence, seeking the fastest, most sensational and most ideologically opportune out -- is hardly an expert on the empirical. How many reporters investigating radiation stories bother to get a Geiger counter to tote around, except for their own photo opportunity?

Since the Middle Ages, progress in understanding has come partly through the rejection of magical multiplicative theorizing. The media has provided four contradictory theories -- bad powder, contraband, poor training and old or inadequate machinery -- as the "cause" of the *Iowa* turret explosion. The possibility of malice has been studiously, indeed maliciously, denigrated. Yet the powder happened to blow up in one particular time and place; it had shown no generic propensity for unscheduled explosion. As for contraband, that it was found also did not show that it was a cause; if there had been a dog in the exploded turret, it needn't have been chewing on the powder bags. Poor training has not been shown to have been a cause of the explosion as it happened. And the antithesis of the men's inexperience was the tried-and-true machinery, which had worked in World War II, Korea and Vietnam, and went on to work in the Gulf War. It took contrived efforts to get an explosion from special mock-ups set up to produce an explosion -- note that a *deliberately staged explosion* was taken to negate the possibility of a *deliberately staged explosion*! This last the media accepted unquestioningly, so that it at least "covered" the bureaucracy, even as it answered no questions about what happened. Occasionally, however, bureaucracies do come up with something.

Chapter 17 - **Landships, Their Breaking and Their Making**

The descent of World War I into the trenches, even bloodier and more stalemated than those of Lee and Grant or of the Russo-Japanese War of a decade earlier, led to a search for expedients. Aside from its interest in amphibious warfare, pushed before the war for the Baltic Plan and during the war against Turkey's Gallipoli Peninsula, the Royal Navy under Churchill began looking at "landships", or armored vehicles, to break the stalemate on the Western Front. Perhaps because Churchill was still officially a Liberal (he had abandoned Conservative Unionism when the Liberals had achieved a pro-war alliance with the anti-Union Irish Nationalists), this innovation, soon known by its code "tanks", was called a breakthrough rather bureaucratic empire-building. Of course, in Britain of that time, Empire-building was a prideful thing.

Tracked and armored vehicles were a step forward, but were not really decisive in World War I, or, by themselves, anywhere else. Early tanks, although used in an era before specialized anti-tank weapons, were unreliable and seldom available in great numbers for very long. The presence of landmines, other obstacles and mass artillery meant that the immediate task was difficult in comparison to the available engineering. Trenches were taken into account for the main lot of British tanks, whose overlarge tracks aped the trench-crossing arc of an imaginary wheel big enough to roll across. The French, originally hoping to advance soldiers behind armored wheelbarrows, were soon building tanks, and the Germans, aside from capturing tanks in counter-attacks, built their own, few, inferior, huge and unwieldy. But the wonder weapon called forth specialized opponents.

The first "breakthrough" "wonder weapon" to make the tank "obsolete" was the anti-tank rifle of circa 1918, a long hand-gun, heavy, slow-firing and only occasionally effective. The Soviets had a long affinity for the weapon, because it co-incided with their assumption of power, and because it promised a way to defeat the masses of tanks possessed by victorious capitalism from World War I. The Red Army's revolutionary ardor was expected to win with the anti-tank rifle, an ideology which affected the Russian infantry even after Russia began habitually possessing most of the entire world tank supply. The anti-tank rifle may not have won the Spanish Civil War for the "Loyalists", although it did not lose the later wars of their Soviet patrons, who were mounting the montebank Mauser in armored cars as late as 1943.

Most long hand-guns are rifles, possessing grooved inner barrels to spin their "shells", usually just solid bullets; the spin's gyroscopic stability prevents random air effects from accumulating and moving the projectile further off course. (Neither rifled nor fin-stabilized projectiles would be more accurate than musketballs in a vacuum, however, because all would be equally moved by gravity, unaffected by spinning or fins; and, yes, contrary to published pig-ignorance, a gun can fire in a vacuum, because gunpowder contains its own oxygen.) The rifle was a late 18th century innovation, gradually supplanting the musket and larger smoothbore cannons, except in such short-ranged weapons as shotguns and, much later, those for firing fin-stabilized projectiles.

Modern guided and homing anti-tank weapons strike and penetrate conventional armor with heat-jet warheads of the type pioneered by the bazooka. Such a warhead has a hollow space, exploding forward as a jet of heat rather than in all directions as a normal explosion. Although chalked up to one Monroe, the effect was that obtained by breaking open firecrackers and igniting the ends; without containment, the gunpowder flames in the open direction. Heat-jet (also called hollow-point or melt-through) weapons are the equivalent of the anti-tank rifle, which had been defeated by slightly stronger armor even on light tanks. To defeat heat-jets, an extra layer of light armor can be spaced in front of the main armor. Such spaced armor is effective in securing the premature detonation of fairly slow-moving objects such as the heat-jet warheads; anti-torpedo bulges were a nautical example. Spaced armor includes skirting (shields held out at a short distance from the vehicle) and even extemporized objects like sandbags (scorned in peace, rediscovered in war).

Two more modern defenses do away with spaced armor altogether, but are expensive and have appeared only on new weapons. A new British laminated armor, Chobham, has a heat-resistant sheet in addition to the usual hard surface. The Russians have put a reactive outer layer on some of their new armor, which explodes outward when heated, to disperse an igniting heat-jet. Iraqi vehicles in the Gulf War were not equipped with such modern, or simple old, protection. At best, they were buried "hull-down", but with their tops vulnerable to air attack from kinetic or heat-jet weapons. Fortunately for those behind the older light outer extemporizations, intrinsic limitations make all types of melt-through or other wonder weapons relatively slow and easily detonated. Water resistance makes Commander Whitehead's torpedoes too slow to penetrate the outer hull or bulge of a vessel, so the explosion is spent at a distance from the anti-torpedo bulkhead or the main hull of the ships so equipped. Merchant ships, small vessels and many thin-skinned modern warships are not so lucky, however.

Like many other military endeavors, the torpedo has itself periodically been accused of obsolescence. FDR's Navy of the 1930s stripped torpedoes from bigger cruisers, and left them off new cruisers. Not being defended (by virtue of being declared obsolete), any weapon ceases to be obsolete; not being restricted by disarmament, as gun size and armor were, made the torpedo, along with the aircraft and the number of guns, a priority for development for the ideologically unimpaired. The Germans had less luck with torpedoes from surface ships, planning to use them to sink vulnerable merchant ships, but were putting them even on battleships after the loss of the *Bismarck*. The Japanese improved their torpedoes, later using them to sink many inadequately protected American ships. Modern American torpedoes, approaching the performance of 1930s' Japanese torpedoes, albeit with modern guidance systems, have been the target of liberal cheese-paring, even though they are modest additional expenditures to make America's ultra-expensive submarines more effective. Liberals spend huge amounts only when it is ineffectual; spending enough to get results they call waste.

The air medium is less effective in slowing anti-tank projectiles of the melt-through type, whether guided or short-range bazooka shots. Such objects, lacking rifling-imparted spin, are unstable in flight, effective only at short range or by virtue of guidance to their targets. But three factors put a speed limit on heat-jet warheads and their shooters, and thus make cheap counter-measures, such as skirting or sandbags, effective against them. The melt-through warhead's nature limits its own effective speed, as striking too fast causes the carrying rocket to crash into its own heat-jet, dispersing it before it has melted through conventional armor and crisped the crew of the target. For the same reason, heat-jet warheads cannot be used on normal rifled shells, because the spinning would send the heat jet outward instead of keeping the heat going forward at one point of the target. The French did develop a rifled shell that spun, with a heat-jet warhead mounted on ball bearings on the shell's inside and not spinning from inertia, although the warhead was small and its shell not very accurate; useful in French, Saudi and Qatari service against Iraqi armor, its rifled cannon still required a medium tank carriage, so it was not really cheap and light.

Guidance systems also limit speed, because the wire has to unreel, or the human operator has to see the target or the rocket and have time to react, or the warhead's sensor has to be able to "see" a laser-generated hot-spot on the target for weapons so equipped, all actions degraded by too fast flight. The third factor to put a speed limit on heat-jet weapons is economic: they are made to be both cheap and easily mobile. Putting in extra propellants for the limited gain in speed possible near ground level (where the air is thickest and where targeted armored vehicles are found) would make them more expensive and less easily mobile, less of a cheap substitute for more costly and effective weapons, and less useful for equipping the mass of an army's infantry, light vehicles or helicopters, all weight- and/or space-sensitive carriages. Potential slow weapon-users know that, in most tactical situations, using slow weapons will make them targets for enemy counter-measures; consequently, they require opportunity or high morale.

Among anti-tank weapons, the indispensable tank-killer, and therefore the primary tank-mounted weapon, remains the high-velocity high-impact gun, which easily defeats spaced and reactive armor, seeking to penetrate the target's main armor, or at least to smash it enough to kill the people behind it with fragments. The high-velocity shell has the advantage over contemporary armor used against it of being capable of being made of the same material as the armor, and of being more easily updated: the shell only needs one point to get through, while replacing extensive armor is more expensive and time-consuming. Mobility and suspension capacity also limit the amount of scale-up for a terrestrial vehicle, but not for a ship; bigger ships can mount enough armor against smaller guns carried by smaller ships easier than tanks can against smaller tanks, because a smaller size range is possible for tanks. For lighter targets, high-velocity guns can usually take lighter shells, which explode more easily and more powerfully, extra explosive in place of metal no longer needed for strength of penetration. These less compact shells take up more breech space, meaning less propellant and less velocity, which improves their power more than it degrades their accuracy.

Tanks and military aircraft meant that artillery and its shells had to become more differentiated and complex. No longer was it a case of solid shot, high explosive and/or shrapnel shredding men, vehicles and wooden ships. Instead, there was a matrix of different targets with different optimum counters. Certain targets needed to be hit with pinpoint or otherwise specialized weapons (all-around rapid traverse for anti-aircraft guns, for example) that were costlier than old guns and therefore less numerous, but also less effective -- with less explosive, shells too fast for "effect", etc. -- against infantry, light vehicles and light ships, optimum targets for the old guns and the new rocket mortars. This matriculation **was** somewhat limited, however, because anti-tank and anti-aircraft guns shared many characteristics, but both were still expensive, manpower-inefficient and of less use against unspecialized targets.

There are two types of high-velocity guns, rifled and smoothbore. The rifle's spinning shell makes for greater accuracy, while the high-velocity smoothbore fires a fin-stabilized projectile (shell or rocket), not as accurately but even faster -- all energy goes to forward motion. A rocketed non-spinning projectile can use more propellant without making the gun barrel or breech too massive for a mobile vehicle, as would be necessary for a conventional rifled gun, where the propellant explodes inside the gun, rather than burning more slowly. Shellfire by explosion mandates a more massive breech and a more robust carriage for absorbing the recoil than does the smooth launch of a rocket. Such weapons are more modern, and can mount the same caliber of gun on a slightly smaller chassis than with a rifled gun, but were not as accurate nor as successful in use, possibly owing to their Soviet-client users, and the tendency of their frequently rifle-gunned opponents to seek longer battle ranges, where the fin-stabilized projectiles are least accurate.

On the latest American tanks, the Defense Department, as always with the consent of Congress, ordered laser/computer range-finders for each tank, adding hundreds of thousands of dollars to each tank's cost and more than a billion to the total procurement cost. And what did the military get? For a rifled gun that essentially shoots in a very straight line, nearly a mile a second, with minimal gravity drop and only small air effects (which the computer gizmo measures only at the tank), a gunner can point the gun at the target, with a slight adjustment for gravity drop on the cross-hairs at longer ranges. What the tank can see, it can hit, and quicker without the gizmo. The gizmo just takes time, which can cost lives with an enemy shooting back. And the expense of the gizmos cut into other needed procurement. The $econd $tep in this farce was to junk the rifled guns with their long-range accuracy and to replace them with smoothbores; the tanks went from guns not needing the computerized range-finder to guns less accurate at long range.

Less heavily armored than tanks, armored personnel carriers convey troops to and across modern battlefields. Occupants are protected against small arms and machine guns, grenades and the bursting effects of mortar and artillery shells and bombs, the main killers of soldiers on twentieth century battlefields. Modern vehicles usually also have NBC protection, sealing and filtration of their air supply, something men on foot, in the army or on the street, do not have. The major variant of the armored personnel carrier is the mechanized infantry combat vehicle, allowing its infantry to fire their weapons from an otherwise sealed vehicle, something from the Chicago gangster era. While liberals love to sneer at military nomenclature, and at presumed euphemisms other than their own, mechanized means fully tracked, as opposed to simply motorized or all-wheel driven (a half-track is a vehicle half on powered tracks), power for a vehicle carrying infantry who can fire while still mounted. The infantry's firepower can suppress enemy infantry, especially those with anti-tank weapons, while keeping the embarked squad still mobile. Convoyed infantry can easily remain with tanks, keeping a force united and fast-moving, to cut off an enemy rather than to waste time and lives in tactical firefights.

Such vehicles have been converted from armored personnel carriers or purpose-built and long since deployed by Japan, Russia, West Germany and France. Even the frugal Dutch bought hundreds, from an American manufacturer, of a design rejected by the Nixon/Ford Defense Department as not being ritzy enough for the military. The design the Defense Department wanted turned out to be the Bradley. Controversial only partly because of its cost, much greater than the Dutch vehicles, the Bradley was attacked by liberals because of its vulnerability. They were incensed that a vehicle lighter, with less armor and costing much less than a tank was, duh, more vulnerable to anti-tank weapons. If the Bradleys had the same capabilities as much heavier and more expensive tanks, even the Pentagon would have snapped them up as the cheaper substitute, unless blocked by congressional liberals. The Defense Department spends more for tanks, with the money appropriated by Congress, because they are less vulnerable and more effective against critical targets, such as an enemy's tanks and other armored vehicles. Armored personnel carriers and the more specialized Bradleys are more vulnerable and less apt at the critical anti-armor function; they must depend on tanks to protect them from enemy tanks while they perform subsidiary roles -- conveying troops to the next attack, defense or rest area, or providing suppressing fire.

Some tank roles can, should be and are performed by armored personnel carriers, because they are cheaper, easier to maintain and more plentiful. Their use saves wear on the tanks, leaving the tanks unoccupied and able to concentrate on the critical tasks which tanks can best perform, breaking tactical stalemates and busting enemy tanks, to prevent an enemy from concentrating his armor for victory. The absence of tanks leads to such tactical slaughter as the later American Civil War, the Russo-Japanese War, World War I, the U.S. involvement in the Vietnam War or the Iran-Iraq War. Absence is of course relative; tanks were present in some conflicts but mechanically broken down or not used in decisive masses.

Particularly when spaced armor or other cheap counter-measures have reduced the over-stated effectiveness of cheap anti-tank weapons, the gun tank remains indispensable. No matter what the bombastic technological breakthrough -- whether the anti-tank rifle, the bazooka, the wire-guided or heat-seeking missile, the cannon-toting aircraft or helicopter or, the latest, the mine/grenade-sowing artillery shell (cluster bombshell of track-breakers) -- no weapon or combination of weapons has achieved nearly the type of technological breakthrough which doomed the wooden fighting ship as a mainstay of the world's fleets (although some missile and torpedo boats continue to be made of wood). The tank's combination of cross-country mobility, armor and firepower remains pre-eminent (but still needing support from infantry and artillery, preferably mechanized, as recognized even in 1918, when the first such vehicles were built), concentrating force to get and keep the initiative to win in any situation short of nuclear annihilation. Controlling contested tactical ground for strategic purposes is the only alternative to defeat or bloody stalemate in war, and the tank is the means to achieve that end in most situations. In modern America, of course, liberals dote on defeat and stalemate, and victory is more off-limits to American troops than gay bars, as military virtuosity is circumscribed by confused policy both political and military. The Gulf War was anomalous.

Such demoralization is nothing new. After World War I, military-bashing by congressional committees accompanied pacifistic tracts and "neutrality" legislation. As a result, the cavalry was legally barred from having tanks, a typically political backwardness blamed on the military. The problem was only partially the pacifists who were afraid that a modern Army would fight in Europe as had the unprepared Army of

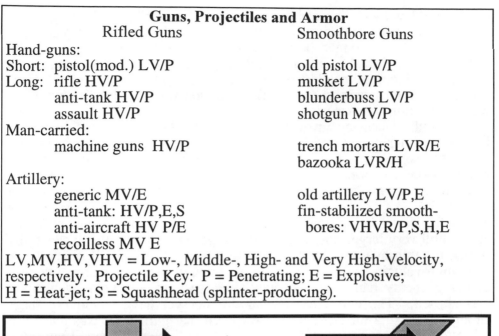

Guns, Projectiles and Armor

Rifled Guns	Smoothbore Guns
Hand-guns:	
Short: pistol(mod.) LV/P	old pistol LV/P
Long: rifle HV/P	musket LV/P
anti-tank HV/P	blunderbuss LV/P
assault HV/P	shotgun MV/P
Man-carried:	
machine guns HV/P	trench mortars LVR/E
	bazooka LVR/H
Artillery:	
generic MV/E	old artillery LV/P,E
anti-tank: HV/P,E,S	fin-stabilized smooth-
anti-aircraft HV P/E	bores: VHVR/P,S,H,E
recoilless MV E	

LV,MV,HV,VHV = Low-, Middle-, High- and Very High-Velocity, respectively. Projectile Key: P = Penetrating; E = Explosive; H = Heat-jet; S = Squashhead (splinter-producing).

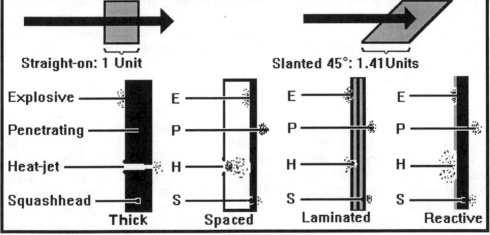

"Preparedness" when John Bull made Uncle Sam parrot "I Want You!" Pacifists were more favorably inclined toward the Navy, regarding it rather optimistically as a defender of the Atlantic moat rather than as the tool of Roosevelt's interventionism it became. Hostility to tanks was also evinced by the tobacco belt, which joined with the pacifistic/isolationistic Midwest in opposing them. The key was not tobacco, however, a favorite habit of servicemen and others prone to adding nicotine stains to the time on their hands, but the tobacco-growing region's other big product, horseflesh. The equine lobby, whose horses were no hobby, wanted to keep the cavalry horsed and themselves in the saddle, rather than seeing it militaristically mechanized and liable to stir up war instead of the horse trade. The Army evaded the law by calling cavalry tanks "combat cars", a subterfuge even thinner than the contemporary German one of dismounted turrets; such evasions were no longer being decried by the left-wing scum in the *Reichstag*, which had been completely replaced by right-wing scum. As part of the international left-wing reaction to those supposed reactionaries, Communist support for pacifist agitation was slowly withdrawn, as were restrictions on American tanks.

With "Germany invading Europe" and Japan presumably invading Asia, America invaded both; they did not get here, so we had to go there, for some reason. The European situation in particular led to a more serious re-appraisal of American armor, and an arsenal to make tanks was built in Detroit. The first jerry-rigged product was powered by a lash-up of five gasoline-burning automobile engines, a safer and less bulky diesel being unavailable. The engine arrangement made the tank's hull very large, not only a large target but causing the armor to be spread too thin over too great an area to cover a gasoline-filled target. A new high-velocity anti-tank gun large enough for use against rapidly evolving enemy tanks was not available, so a middle-velocity weapon was chosen. The new tank arsenal did not yet have machinery large enough to make a turret mounting for even that gun, so it was placed in a limited position in the side of the tank's hull, while a small anti-tank gun, just becoming ineffective against the larger German tanks entering service, was placed in a small turret on top. Besides the two guns, the tank was festooned with machine guns, some fixed in place like those on a fighter plane. Multi-engines, multi-cannons and multi-machine guns meant a large crew in the fairly roomy, if vulnerable and flammable, vehicle, which was called a Grant or Lee depending on which Civil War General one admired, sympathized with or wished to slander.

With all of its faults, the Grant/Lee had a reliable suspension and good cross-country mobility, imparted from predecessor models, and its automobile engines had the reliability of first-class industrial products, far superior to the engines of British tanks of that era, many unfit for active service. The Grant/Lee was able to provide a stop-gap for the British in North Africa and for the Soviets, who had lost their main tank forces in the mid-1941 German onslaught. Although Rommel destroyed hundreds by his tactics and their vulnerability, the Grant/Lee was the tank which stopped him, and it was the weapon the Russians used to stop the German First Panzer Army at Rostov in the autumn of 1941, the first, and most decisive, Russian defeat of the Germans, and the salvation of the Russian oilfields.

And what happened to the Grant/Lee, unsatisfactory when built and soon replaced in the armored divisions by the improved and evolving Sherman, the tank that the Detroit arsenal had been built to produce? The "obsolete" cast-offs were taken by the infantry, and used until the end of the war, because an obsolete put-up job, with armor, mobility and weapons, is better than no tank at all. Some Grant/Lee chasses are still in use as artillery platforms in various armies. Even the Sherman, soon recognized in the hothouse development of World War II as meriting a successor, was the mainstay of the Israeli Army in the 1956 War and is still in third-line service for Israel and several other countries.

Starting with a Sherman, in two years American designers had successively re-armored, re-engined and regunned the prototypes, before moving on to change the hull, turret and suspension. The new vehicle was the Pershing, in time for the invasion of Germany, mounting as its main armament a former anti-aircraft gun in violation of that gun's role and mission. With serial detail improvements, the Pershing was in production into the 1980s, later under the Patton and M-60 monikers. The model was in production from Franklin Roosevelt to Ronald Reagan, and possibly beyond, for the Israeli Merkava tank could be called the latest model of the Pershing series.

The Merkava uses the Patton's diesel engine and wheels, with a Grant/Lee/Sherman-type suspension, and the same British-designed gun utilized in the M-60 and later retrofitted in many Pattons. What is different, and better, about the Merkava is that turret and engine have been changed in their normal facing and the weight of the armor has switched ends, so that the lay-out is more like a tank chassis as heavily modified to carry a large artillery piece in back, firing over the vehicle. In a normal tank, the driver, the heaviest armor and the turret are toward the front, while the engine, drive sprockets and weakest armor are at the back. In the Merkava, like its namesake the chariot, the horsepower and pulling power are up front, with the driver behind them, making the reins, or controls, shorter. The bulky engine helps keep the crew protected from hits at the tank's front, whose armor, not handicapped by having to protect a crew member sitting at the extreme front, has been made to fit snugly around the engine and transmission, and made more ballistically efficient. More shells are deflected by offering the least perpendicular surface and a slanted, and therefore thicker, cross-section of armor to a non-deflected shell. Having the sprocket in front helps to maintain track tension with smaller return rollers than usual, so that a short skirt on each side, combined with the coverage afforded by large road wheels, suspension, sprockets and rear idlers, protects the tank's sides against melt-through weapons while minimizing the interference with the running gear that a larger skirt can cause.

Unlike the Israelis, the U.S., with an infinitely greater industrial base, chose the new suspension, gas turbine engine and spaced armor of the Abrams tank, a Chrysler project. The other major war-time tank-building nations have tended to follow the American pattern. Russia's main line of tanks have been incremental improvements of its war-time T-34, still utilizing the suspension American inventor J. Walter Christie developed in the late 1920s, but being upgunned with several different rifled guns before moving to fin-stabilized smoothbores, so that larger calibers could be accommodated on the same basic chassis. Russia also incrementally improved its heavy tanks, starting with the KV (Klementi Voroshilov) of 1939 through the IS (Iosef Stalin) tanks of late World War II, through the later T-10 and T-10M; Russian heavy tanks were up-gunned with larger rifled weapons. West Germany's only major project was the Leopard, with the same hull and armor contour (later improved with spaced armor) as the war-time Panther. The Panther had proved extremely efficient after its early troubles, which Hitler never forgave, comparing it to a failed bomber -- "The Panther is a crawling Heinkel, and the Heinkel is a flying Panther!" -- Marx's phrasing and humor.

Less successful previous tank-builders Britain, France, Japan and Sweden have tended to adopt new designs, abandoning even successful designs for fresh starts. After a run of limited successes and outright failures, the British ended World War II with a success, the Comet, but abandoned it for three generations of different designs, all successes (although the second, the Chieftain, had seen a return to engine troubles, more serious for its Iranian export-operators than for the habitually tinkering British themselves). The other three countries, with mainly failures to start from, went through two completely new designs apiece.

Converting the U.S. civilian economy to a war economy, both for World War II and Korea, was accomplished with an extremely logical grasp of realities, and some adjustments have carried over into the structure of the modern American economy. Tanks were built by the new tank factories, or "arsenals" (actually armories) -- Detroit run by Chrysler, Cleveland run by General Motors, and lesser locations -- or by locomotive factory conversions with the necessary founding capacity and overhead equipment for moving very heavy materials. American car-making capacity was switched over to aircraft production, with the assembly lines abandoned and the roomy floor space used to assemble the large pieces light-weight enough to be lifted by an automobile factory's overhead equipment as by airflows. New aircraft production facilities were also set up in areas with people untapped for war work, Oklahoma, Wichita-K.C.-Omaha, St. Louis, Dallas-Ft. Worth and, especially during the Korean War, Atlanta. Armored cars, although built by Ford and Chrysler on truck assembly lines, were not really militarily important enough to take up the huge American automotive production capacity, the truck portion of which was still concerned with trucks, a vehicle needed in huge quantities to carry the supplies needed for modern armies, as well as with half-tracks, the first purpose-built armored personnel carriers. Such vehicles were built also by railroad car-makers and manufacturers of equipment of similar size and complexity.

One such miscellaneous industrial firm was California's Food Machinery Corporation (later FMC: as the bulk of its business shifted to munitions, the old name became an embarrassment), a builder of salmon cannery assemblies and similar automated equipment. With the division of the world into service responsibilities for American conduct of World War II, the Navy and Marines, with their history of joint maritime operations, shared command and similar air fleets, drew primary responsibility for the Central Pacific, while the Army and Army Air Force were allocated the priority for the more land-oriented European and Australian/New Guinean theatres (compare Grenada, with four services vying for small roles in a very minor event).

For invasions of the atolled islands which studded the Navy/Marine area, Marines planned to use a version, later armored, of the Roebling Amphibian, a tracked vehicle first developed for the "role and mission" of live-saving during Florida floods. Coral reefs, which made the atolls possible, could rip the bottoms of conventional beachcraft or restrict their use to easily defended breaks in the reefs. The tracked vehicles could not only climb over the reefs, but could take their cargos of men and supplies across bullet-swept beaches (the whole sweep of an atoll's beaches, not just the ones near breaks in its reef), and inland to unload -- outmaneuvering the enemy, cutting the main early loss of life in amphibious assault, and not piling up supplies on the beach. Florida-based Roebling was a small firm, with inadequate production facilities and, although close to the regular Marine amphibious training area in North Carolina, far from the Pacific. FMC had its much larger, available and appropriate (the vehicle being about the size, weight and complexity of a cannery sub-assembly) facilities right on the Pacific Coast, the center of the salmon industry as well as the gateway to atoll islands. FMC built the bulk of the Roebling Amphibians, called AmphTracs or LVTs (Landing Vehicle Tracked) by the Marines, with modern variants still in service.

As President-elect Jimmy Carter's advent was being foreshadowed by the blizzard of '77, a large Marine unit was undergoing winter training at an Army base in Northern New York's snowbelt, preparing for possible deployment to NATO's northern flank. Using both its own equipment and that of Army, Reserve and National Guard units usually trained at the base, the Marines decided to embark upon a publicity stunt of "rescuing" the nearby city, whose locals were inured to snowfall averaging more than thirty feet per year. Marine-manned Army tanks sent out first got bogged down in the snow, and the Marines were rescued by locals on snowmobiles. The second Marine rescue effort, with Army armored personnel carriers, was a similar fiasco. Finally, the Marines used their own LVTs, the Everglades creature later used for coral-reefed Pacific islands; it proved light enough, with enough traction, to operate well on snow. The town was "rescued" by the Marines (as it was later by a special civilian dispensation of food stamps and their own scandal), and the late-model streamlined LVT proved to have an excellent winter capacity compared to heavier armored personnel carriers, another heretical departure from the roles and missions fetish. The training succeeded, unexpectedly showing that the Marines had a capability for winter combat that the Army did not. President Carter of course cut back training, relying on the Rapid Deployment of publicity to simulate a prepared military.

In spring, the snow melted, and the Army's vehicles, or most of them, were located in various dales and hollows. Getting lost under the snow had been as confusing as navigating on top of it can be, with limited visibility and maps distorted by varying snow coverage of land-marks. During the following year, a base Army Sergeant responsible for buying scrap metal (the military was into recycling before it became chi-chi) realized that the scrap metal he was being sold were pieces of an armored personnel carrier, a $100,000 vehicle, a local man getting a few hundred dollars for destroying a lost vehicle and selling it as scrap. There is no right of salvage on American military equipment, so the authorities were alerted, and the man arrested and jailed. Not a national news story, just a local incident where an alert sergeant spotted a prob-lem and acted. Of course, it was an isolated incident, in an obscure locality, and there was a liberal Democrat in the White House.

With a conservative Republican in power, the story was suddenly different. Procurement over-charges already detected by the sergeants were paraded as proofs of the administration's incompetence. The press and Congress posed as heroes "uncovering" "scandals" already found, as such things sometimes are, by the proper legal and bureaucratic authori-ties. The real detectors were brought forth briefly, but were mostly lost as usual behind grandstanding liberals, jut-jawing their indignation at waste that had already been detected and even largely reimbursed, just the sort of waste liberals abhor. The Democrats were not only flogging a dead horse, but one the federal government had already gotten a refund on. There is no refund on social programs, however, just the annual drain on the productive economy to keep liberalism's big guns on the firing line, instead of being spiked.

Military artillery developed faster in war. *Kamikazes* put a prem-ium on developing the automatic aspect of dual-purpose anti-aircraft guns, already improved by tiny detectors in the shells to enable them to burst close to enemy aircraft. Putting up more of those effective shells was a priority, as was cutting down the large and vulnerable crews of the smaller hand-loaded guns. FMC became the American leader in the ar-ea, as it did in replacing the half-track with the fully tracked armored personnel carrier, a more compact LVT with thicker armor but a much lesser amphibious (and snow) capability. As during World War I, in World War II, deturreted tanks were first utilized for a better cross-country troop-carrying role, but they were too heavy and cramped. FMC's M-113 series has long been the world's leading armored pers-onnel carrier, and favored by troops over purpose-built vehicles for such roles as reconnaissance. The U.S. Army's purpose-built recon vehicle, the Sheridan light tank, a GM-Cleveland project OKed by Ford alumnus and chief Whiz Kid McNamara, has been as unsuccessful an export (no sales) as the M-113 has been prolific (tens of thousands sold abroad). The Sheridan, like so many products of the Whiz Kid era, the Whiz Kids themselves for example, remains in service mainly because it received so much public attention and funding that some functionality was assumed. FMC also designed and built the Dutch Army's mechanized infantry combat vehicle, and developed another cheap version that Washington passed up; in addition to Pentagon gold-platers, liberals were also glad to see the more expensive Bradley, costlier and easier to delay.

And what is FMC's reward for a flawless record of achievement, employment, export and public service? Flinty investors shun its shares because FMC deals with a monopsony, a sole buyer. The federal government, a perpetual hostage to the whim of mental eunuchs, can both refuse to buy from FMC as well as refuse it permission to export, putting more than half of its business at perpetual risk. Does a prudent man invest in an enterprise at the mercy of rancorous ideological publicity hounds in Congress, the media and the academic/public interest/do-gooder liberal-letterhead complex? Not generally, but then the entire American economy and society is hostage to the busy-bodied loonies. Even speaking-out is called lobbying or violating so-called campaign laws, attacking the First Amendment in its most politically relevant forms, the petitional and the electoral. But when it comes to the propagation of liberal wars, or even liberal defense policy, the waste of public money becomes a sign of high virtues, even when it has to make up the yo-yo changes of direction of liberal defense policy. For example, a small military has to be periodically rapidly expanded, and with investors loathe to put their money into a long-term investment in liberal enthusiasm, which always lags, the government ends up going into the factory business. But liberals do not really understand that either, as their economic and business views are products of an irrational, enthusiastic mindset. Rather than embracing constancy or efficiency, liberals go for fads, which perforce don't get called fads.

The metric system, a product of the French Revolution and its manic search for the novel, merely relabeled measurements already in use, appealing to the weak-minded (most notably those who have trouble with decimals) as some worthy innovation. Compared to Henry VIII's standardization of measures, the foundation of all rationalized industry (his own or such extensions as Eli Whitney's standardization of manufacture, instead of just products), the metric system was theological in its triviality, and of course highly politicized and religiously motivated in its establishment. The metric system is scientific in that it allows easier use of the same set of units, to compare one's body size to the distance to the sun, or to atomic particles, and other invaluable applications. Itself constantly in flux, and having its parameters periodically redefined, the metric system is a source of pride to busybodies and those with something to sell, such as plastic bottles, too large for standard refrigerators, which leak when set on their sides. Liberals caused the federal government to spend billion of dollars "converting" the American economy to the metric system, in the fatuous belief that American products were not selling abroad because they were using the wrong measurements. Such money could have been spent -- cloying pregnant silence -- **HELPING THE HOMELESS**. Americans were buying foreign cars, and metric wrench sets, not because the metric system was more "scientific", or because it was different from the English system they were and are more used to dealing with, but because the foreign cars were better designed and made, and were cheaper, and the extra set of wrenches was a minor expense in comparison. What the American economy needs is better products and protection from dumping, not being saddled with a government obsessed with enthusiastic buffoonery like metrification, more expensive and wasteful than the atomic-powered airplane.

The metric system gives a common language to scientists, but they had one in the English system beforehand, even as the world had a screwdriver before someone invented the Philips variant and a new market for screws and tools. The metric system has been overtaken by events, and was never completed anyway. The French decimal calendar was one early casualty, as the world kept using Mesopotamian time. Other concepts were estimates, as one ten-millionth of the distance from equator to pole varied with "sea level" in a world of fluctuating glaciers. More arbitrary human-scale measurements do not have those problems, and they could be later precisionized as metric definitions had to be. The French, so insistent on common items, refuse to abandon their language and speak English. The metric system is like a common language: it is Esperanto on a stick, the sort of semi-theological non-accomplishment liberal weenies dote upon while denigrating real achievement.

Empirical observation was the scientific breakthrough, and it was possible, organized and achieved largely by traditional measurements, invented for the rational fact of economic convenience, rather than for semi-theological reasons like the metric system. At the same time, advocates of the politicized occult take the inside-out position that accomplishments themselves are theological, as Senator Proxmire's calling the moon project and the whole space program a religious exercise. Liberals heartily favor education, when they have made it into indoctrination, anyway, but usually oppose the search for knowledge. The extension of knowledge and technology is inherently anti-religious, and guarding it from the mummery of its opponents is as important as protecting it from the deification of the nugatory, such as measuring systems, by its sometimes rather titular supporters. There are things that work well and produce results, and there are other things that are merely beside the point;

the ability to distinguish them is the ability to move forward, and to avoid sliding back.

Liberals are vexed at the mere existence of defense. Those who wish to stretch the concept of public ever further are ashamed of defense, the original public good (or public service), because its existence belies the claims of modern political impositions to be truly public. The dole may be open to the public, and so passed off as public, but it is a private benefit at public expense. Defense, by contrast, is a public benefit because it benefits the entire public, not just the recipients or the organizers of doles in their seeking of popularity and the image of benefactors. With productive jobs exported, services are ballyhooed as vital, but not the military services. Liberal economists agonize about including defense in GNP at all. Everything else is accepted at its cost-price, including other governmental things without competing buyers, but not defense. But there is a split within economists, the liberals looking nostalgically upon public works such as roads and dams as public goods, and the more fanatical denouncing usefulness as distracting from ideology, with ideological objections (roads and dams are bad for the environment, bad for railroads and post-flood scavengers, etc.).

But any good will be used, altering the later socio-economic calculus. Successful rationalization of industry undermines itself, because it cuts its inputs. Those inputs, of people and resources, flow to less efficient areas of society, to government and education, to hair-dressing and other services, things where cost-control and efficiency are non-existent (it is the social Peter Principle). And that is where there are no imports, so that protectionism is implicit in a liberal society, where protection itself -- against criminals, foreign enemies, or the destruction of living standards -- is eschewed for fatuous ideology (society is guilty, and unleashing criminals is the proper way to punish it; peace is the best policy for everyone, one the evil will follow; and the world market needs us to fleece). Ideology denies that government, particularly defense, is one of the few potentially stable markets for research as well as for the products of rationalized production. Not that the budgetary wrangle is any guarantee, but procurement is more stable than the private marketplace in that individual orders are large and timely, making for such pioneers as Henry VIII and Whitney. Private trade takes time to create and maintain a market large enough ("world") to justify research and development and efficient production.

Some, opposing military spending, therefore call it unproductive. Professor Seymour Melman, favoring nuclear disarmament, demonstrates to the gullible that all military spending is unproductive. Being overrun by one's enemies is also unproductive, but that can never happen to a nation that boasts a Seymour Melman to defend it. The military is accused by the left (the American left, that is) of sopping up resources which would go to research more productive to economic progress (which the left is frequently against, of course). But defense tends to be less wasteful than merely political boondoggles (Jimmy Carter's "Synfuels" program, for a ludicrous example of utterly unproductive research built upon an economic dream-castle of high-cost production for a non-captive market). Much modern high-tech engineering has a military background, if only because the battlefield is an arena where capability counts. That is why an RAF cadet thought up the jet engine, why military transport demands first increased ten-fold or more the orders for, and the capacity to build, such civilian craft as the Junkers Ju-52 and the Douglas DC-3, and why that military transport market helped make the Boeing 707 and 747 the giants of modern air transport and American exports. Those things, prosperity and success, happen in societies that are dynamic, expansive and positively assertive, not passive, neurotic and fearful. Liberals have managed to intrude even into the development of both ships and landships, the pace of whose technical advance has been slow, because of intrinsic technological and engineering limits, the operating parameters of water and land vehicles. What hope for the air, where development is very much faster and the potential for expensive disaster much greater and much more frequent?

Chapter 18 - **Gaining Attitude and Losing Altitude**

In the late 1950s, development of anti-aircraft missiles had proceeded rapidly, with alleged experts heading toward the view that high-altitude bombing was becoming untenable, especially by subsonic craft such as the late model B-52s still entering service. And even the U.S. supersonic high-altitude bomber then being put into service, Convair's B-58, was held less able to reach its targets. In the view of these experts, the future of bombers was limited, and belonged to aircraft operating at low altitude, where ground echoes and the horizon would hamper an enemy's radar and therefore hinder radar-dependent interceptor aircraft and anti-aircraft missiles. The possibility of a defender using airborne radar to detect and oppose low-altitude attacks was grossly underappreciated, particularly in view of America's own continued efforts in that direction (blimp and prop AWACS).

The B-58's builder, the aircraft company which became the core of arms conglomerate General Dynamics, was a southern California maker best known for such large aircraft as the World War II B-24 Liberator, a fast, high-altitude, long-range bomber. Actually out-numbering the more famous Boeing B-17 Flying Fortress, and technically more advanced, the B-24 was more fragile, a condition important to its crews when damage from enemy fire was a problem. Much less advanced, and much stronger and successful, was the PBY Catalina, or Dumbo, a twin-engined flying boat that was by far the most numerous and widely used such craft in history. Earlier flying boats were the business which had brought the Consolidated Company west from Buffalo in the first place. After the war, the Consolidated firm again jousted with its fellow giant maker of large planes, Boeing, in bomber and other markets. Consolidated, renamed Convair, got the bomber business back for awhile, from Boeing's B-29, with its huge B-36 propelled by six pusher props, later supplemented by twin-jet pods under each wing for more speed. But the jet was the wave of the future, and Boeing's all-jet B-47 and B-52 series put the B-36 into eclipse, before Convair's brief come-back with the supersonic B-58.

Even before World War II, Consolidated had started growing by absorption, first buying a design for a training plane from the Midwest's bankrupt Dayton-Wright operation. After developing the project, and selling it to both the Army and the Navy, Consolidated went on to its first big corporate acquisitions, buying first Stinson and then Vultee, to beef up its small aircraft line, while the main part of the renamed Consolidated Vultee Air (later truncated to Convair) concentrated on large airframes, the bomber/airliner/transport market, for the same reasons its Boeing rival had. Unlike Boeing, Convair anticipated and helped cause the decline of the bomber market, as its California division switched from mainly flying boats to the new field of missiles, both strategic bombardment vehicles to replace the bomber, and the anti-aircraft variety to make life for enemy bombers harder. The Ft. Worth unit, home of trainer production expanded by the mammoth war-time B-36 project, became its main airframe unit in part through the decline of Convair's airliner production, which had been centered in California. The Ft. Worth division prospered during the brief Continental Air Defense boom by building first transonic and then supersonic interceptors.

What killed Continental Air Defense in practice was its effectiveness in theory. Since the bomber was theoretically so well defended, it was therefore obsolete. And since the bomber was obsolete, and missiles were thought too difficult to ever defense, defense itself was pronounced obsolete, so little effort was soon being expended on it. Just before bombers were declared obsolete because of the mere concept of effective Air Defense, the Ft. Worth division produced the B-58, bought in lower numbers than the B-52, but keeping the Ft. Worth facility open and giving it more supersonic experience, and with a larger body. The B-58 also helped maintain advantageous contact with the bomber branch of the Strategic Air Command (SAC, previously solicited for strategic missile sales and, before that, for the B-36), in the offensive emphasis of the Whiz Kids more important than the temporarily eclipsed Air Defense crowd. While winning a controversial new contract for the Ft. Worth facility, a combined-service supersonic tactical fighter/strategic bomber called the TFX, Convair renamed itself again, to become General Dynamics. But the corporate culture was the same.

A builder of Navy flying boats for three decades had first added trainers and a separate division to make the trainers, then added bombers and then passenger planes to its large airframe business, later switched to missiles as it lost out on large airframes (and in the more highly competitive trainer market, which just about any aircraft company could enter at any time), and still later parleyed its high-performance business into a record contract, even as its four-jet passenger plane succumbed to American competitors, most conspicuously its long-time rival Boeing and also Douglas. With Boeing dominant in the large and slow market, General Dynamics had moved to smaller and faster: missiles, interceptors, the B-58 and the TFX, but with no civilian market.

General Dynamics temporarily solved its classic monopsony problem -- one buyer, the government, with control over exports -- by market segmentation, splitting the American military into segments, and treating each as a possible customer with its own needs. In the Whiz Kid era, that would've had its own hazards, as those misdirected liberal experts were determined to cram the same product into as many military niches as possible, so that there would be fewer corporate winners. Although as the main contractor for the TFX General Dynamics was the early winner from this silly government policy, future shortfalls in the aerospace weapons market were possible.

The company decided on the paradoxical program of diversifying within the Defense Department market even further. It bought Connecticut's Electric Boat, and became the nation's largest submarine builder, reaching the Navy's submarine service, which had been buying its missiles from Lockheed. It bought Bethlehem Steel's shipyards, and got into the business of building surface warships and their support craft for the surface Navy, to whom it had sold its effective series of anti-aircraft missiles. And it tapped into the Army proper, as it once had tapped into the Army Air Corps with a purchased midwestern trainer, by buying, from a nearly bankrupt Chrysler, its midwestern tank arsenal. This Detroit plant was then flush with the Abrams tank contract and bolstered by the collapse of its only American competitor, General Motors' Cadillac Cleveland tankery (which had specialized in lighter tanks until the near extinction of the breed caused it to compete for the M-1 Main Battle Tank project with a heavy prototype defeated by Chrysler's Abrams). Submarines, warships and tanks were businesses Boeing was not in, and ones much harder for a new entrant to horn in on, unlike the trainer business.

By its compartmentalization, General Dynamics was somewhat protected against the over-reactions of Whiz Kid aerospace strategists, if not against the renewal of left-pacifism in the name of reduced world tensions or other fads. The naval anti-aircraft business was affected by the Air Defense farrago. Convair had developed a set of three missiles, Tartar, Terrier and Talos in order of increasing range, for shipboard launch against aircraft. The Terrier had been launched from an old battleship test-bed in the early 1950s, but procurement of the last of the series, the Talos, had been curtailed by denigration of Air Defense and land use as well as by its size and expense. To save even more money, most of the Talos missiles bought and some of the other two were put into refurbished World War II ships. One Talos-equipped new cruiser, the giant nuclear-powered *Long Beach*, saw action in the Vietnam War. Three Talos missiles, with their quoted range of "25+ miles", shot down three supersonic MiG-21s at ranges over 75 miles. The Talos was 100% efficient, and at very long range.

The predictable response, when the liberals got back into power, with former Whiz Kids Cyrus Vance and Harold Brown occupying Jimmy Carter's top two cabinet posts, was that the Talos missiles, and most of their ships, were scrapped. Sandwiched between the Nixon and Reagan Administrations, with their Watergate and Iran-Contra "scandals" inflated into constitutional quarrels over the power of the executive branch to refrain from spending congressional appropriations, the Carter mob was soon randomly refusing to spend appropriations, with no threat of impeachment from the ever-Democratic House of Representatives, however. The Carterites got congressional permission to scrap some of the Talos ships, and orders to rebuild others. Defense Secretary Brown did scrap the permissible oldsters, but refused to rebuild the others.

With some Talos ships retired (including one as a floating museum in Consolidated's old hometown of Buffalo), Brown had the conceptual inspiration to declare the Talos itself "non-standard", and thereby deserving the scrap-heap. That it was paid-for, deployed, well stocked (many more spares with fewer ships carrying it) and superbly effective against planes still in widespread hostile service did not strike his expert academic mind as relevant. One ship supposed to have been rebuilt, the *Albany*, became 6th Fleet flagship, an 800-man admiral's taxi cruising the coasts of nutty Libya, peaceful Israel and calm Lebanon with a gutted air defense. Another, the *Long Beach*, did eventually have its Talos radars (not the missiles or their launchers, just the radars) replaced -- by machine guns with about 1% of the Talos' range. Stone knives were evidently too costly. But a semblance of activity was offered by the Carterites' plan to replace the Talos and its two smaller relatives with a new series of three similar missiles, the "Standard" trio. General Dynamics, hostage to the government, co-operated with this farce by bringing back the old trio with modest improvements, including the introduction of a fourth, and non-standard, variant. With our taxes as burnt offerings, the gods of bureaucratic busybodiedness were thereby appeased.

The temporary ceding of the upper atmosphere put the B-58 out of favor; it was scrapped at the end of the Whiz Kid era by the Nixon-Laird team. Crucial was the B-58's apparent lack of versatility compared to the B-52, which had both a capacious bomb bay and a wing structure capable of flexible carriage, as had been proved by using it as a launch-carrier of research vehicles, both manned aircraft and a succession of experimental air-launched cruise missiles. The latter had been designed to give the B-52 a stand-off capability, where it would not have to use its bulk and slow speed to itself penetrate an enemy's air defenses, such as Soviet Russia's or their later clones in Hanoi and the Suez.

Underwing carriage would have been too much for the B-58's wings, large in area but thin for lower air resistance at its supersonic speeds, and the drag of the additions would have cut speed and fuel economy more for the B-58 than for the B-52. Both factors were important in the decision to scrap the B-58, although the B-52's stand-off capacity went long unachieved, as drones were embarked before the delayed development of successful U.S. air-launched cruise missiles. The B-58, with a single large body-slung "weapons pod" (large hydrogen bomb, launchable decoys and a gatling gun), was as limited in its repertoire as the later Russian Backfire bomber, also with thin wings and a body for fuel-tanks. The Russians re-equipped their Backfires with large body-slung guided anti-ship rockets, the Kitchens, and used them for ocean patrol-bombers. The B-58, having been scrapped, could not be adapted to such a role. Once again, billions in national defense assets were destroyed for foolish reasons, confusion crowding out imagination and value, cant making can't. The B-58 was obsolete, you see, and although an admittedly fine and expensive plane, incapable of filling its sacred "role and mission". Once the B-58s had been irrevocably scrapped, the Russian example was lost, except for convincing the same numbskulls that the carrier was now "obsolete", because of those supersonic Russian air-launched rockets carried by the unscrapped Backfire and its Commpatriots.

The other major conceptual factor in the bomber lapse was the high-altitude fallacy. In this 1960s' view, while strategic missiles whizzed through space, anti-aircraft missiles would rule the high air, and remaining aircraft would be the infantry of the very low sky, grunts hugging the ground while quick death whizzed overhead. What had happened to cause such an outlook? The loss of U-2 camera planes, in a series of high-profile incidents dating from the late 1950s, was extrapolated far beyond what was justified. The U-2 had indeed been a high flyer and long ranged, but it was otherwise a severely limited aircraft, with bad visibility for the pilot, no radar, other air-warning system or electronic counter-measure capacity, a very slow speed for a jet, among the frailest and least maneuverable planes to ever fly, with pieces regularly falling off upon landings. It was a plodding duck flying a straight line for anything with sufficient range and altitude for a possibility of interception.

In much the same way, satellites in low orbit have no airfoils and otherwise limited maneuverability, not much tactical detection or reaction capability, and tremendous inertia, and are therefore meat whenever someone launches an ASAT (air-launched anti-satellite missile) or other measure against them. But the Bush-Cheney team, in response to a contemporary bubble of international goodwill, spiked the American ASAT. Armchair liberals will again be able to moan about America's "vulnerable" carriers and their visibility to low-flying satellites -- even while the carrier is being called obsolete by peace, it seems it is also in imminent danger of enemy attack. LTV's proven ASAT might've been operable by Grumann's proposed improved F-14(D) carrier aircraft, more slowly aborted, but the Bush-Cheney team preferred to think of lessening future dangers to American servicemen as "destabilizing" a Cold War which supposedly no longer existed.

Unlike the old U-2s and satellites, modern high-performance aircraft have built-in and continuously updated electronic warning devices and counter-measures, large airfoils (for maneuverability at high altitude), high speeds in thin air (making the possibility of interception lower by reducing the time window, and making electronic confusion even more viable) and the ability to shoot back; they are not predictable camera platforms, winged or orbital. In addition to the B-58 and the aborted B-70 prototype, two other contemporary high-performers deployed were stunted by the high-altitude fallacy.

North American's A-5 Vigilante was designed as a high-speed, high-altitude, strategic hydrogen bomber to operate from aircraft carriers. With B-58 speed, same type of engines and single bomb, the A-5 was its naval equivalent, meant to replace the naval homologue of the B-47 and B-52, the subsonic A-3 Skywarrior, a carrier-based strategic bomber. Deployed originally in that role, with its H-Bomb ejectible to the rear (that the plane would have a better chance of escaping the blast) from between its twin engines, the A-5 was otherwise the paradigmatic configuration of a contemporary high-performance aircraft. It looked like nothing before, but about a dozen models since, from Russia, Europe and the U.S., have had the same type of large airfoils for thin air maneuverability, broad swept wings high on the body and back of its midpoint, and two large jet intakes below the wings.

The A-5, ordered in small quantities so that each carrier would have a few, was not victimized by submarines assuming the Navy's strategic role with Polaris missiles originally meant for surface ships. The Polaris merely greatly expanded the Navy's nuclear role. Until the Bush-Cheney team put the Navy out of the non-missile nuclear delivery business, other aircraft, most notably the F-4 Phantom for a generation, assumed the job of aerial nuclear spear-chucker, from the fashionable low-altitude angle, where they would supposedly have less of a chance of being shot down. Early in its own generation of service, the A-5 was converted to the photo-recon role, then becoming a Pentagon fetish, because it could operate at high altitudes, where it would not be shot down. Why the A-5 would be shot down at high altitude in one role but not in another was, of course, never explained. But at least the F-4 was more suited to the low-altitude role than was the A-5, so the role-fillers, if not the logic, were right. The Navy did get long hard service from the A-5 -- decades of carrier take-offs and landings -- so there was the good excuse of fatigue for retiring it, unlike Talos missiles retired from the unfatiguing task of laying cradled in ship holds. Other high-performance aircraft were available and already in quantity use on carriers, so the spare part situation could be rationalized with fewer models.

The interceptor victim of the high-altitude fallacy was the new Lockheed super-interceptor, first called the F-lll (designation later given to General Dynamics' TFX project after TFX had become a code for boondoggle), then the YF-12A (12 as in F-112, the Air Force later dropping the third digit), and then finally, in use as a reconnaissance plane (and the reason the B-58 did not assume that role), the SR-71 Blackbird. A gigantic plane more than a thousand miles per hour faster than contemporary supersonic fighters, as it proved thirty years later when it crossed the U.S. in 68 minutes, a respectable time for such an aged craft, the Blackbird as an interceptor was to have been the platform for the very long-range Phoenix anti-aircraft missile, under development by Hughes since the late 1950s. Possessed also of great range, the Blackbird, numbering in the several dozens, became the U-2's unhitable replacement, filling the fashionable photo-recon role for Pentagon photoanalysts, a slightly different department than the branch which had called high-altitude aircraft obsolete. But the act of not putting the Blackbird into service as an interceptor left American and Allied forces open to similar reconnaissance by an enemy, because there was nothing to get up and catch their planes in time.

Even fixed-base long-range Nike missiles had been scrapped, leaving Northern liberals to grouse that their states were not getting their fair share of defense dollars because of sinister conspiracies (their own, as usual). Yet again, something was declared obsolete and therefore not defensed, and left wide open to a potential foe. There was nothing left on the ground, except some relics based in Canada, to make up American forfeiture of the high air, as crucial to command of the air as the high ground is to control of land. America's defense (except for picture-taking) had lost ground for an inexcusable reason -- confusion.

Unlike Soviet anti-aircraft missiles, those put into American service were overwhelmingly successful, so that American Air Defense was not porous as a result of flawed designs or failure in use: the problem was solely errors in doctrine. The Reagan build-up did provide the Patriot for high-altitude defense, filling the hole left by the scrapping of the old Nike batteries. One extended Nike mission at times was shooting down missiles, but liberals had denigrated that possibility in spite of its achievement in tests (weapons tests only mean anything to liberals when the weapon fails, except rigged tests for liberal boondoggles, of course). When Patriots did indeed shoot down missiles in the Gulf War, liberals were faced with their deepest nightmare, an American success. The Scuds were old missiles, liberals breathlessly half-truthed (when not in outright denial), but it was not their age that stopped them, but rather the end of an age, that of listening to liberal twaddle on the impossibility of defense. One close-up of the extended disinformation campaign was that television pictures did not show the Patriots actually intercepting their targets, whose destruction was presumably by the "long arm of co-inci-dence"; liberals who had spent the 1988 presidential campaign drivelling about the need for a federal subsidy to develop "high-definition television" apparently thought they were watching it.

General Dynamics' naval groups were very much in American and Allied service. The ground-launched low-altitude Hawk was a Vietnam War and Israeli success (the as-yet-unscrapped Nike was not used in Vietnam or Thailand, as Cold War Liberalism in its Second Crusade was opposed to both Air Defense and the use of high altitudes). The North Vietnamese, operators of huge batteries of high-altitude anti-aircraft missiles, had themselves bought into the high-altitude fallacy.

Their MiGs, Beagles and helicopters stayed low, within Hawk operating parameters, because they were low-altitude operators generally and because they were conducting the ill-fated Thailand attacks or support missions when clobbered. Unlike the Nikes, the Hawks were retained (as the Improved Hawk, partly to restock the mostly unacknowledged Vietnam War usage, otherwise an over-publicized minor updating comparable to the "Standard" program) and got foreign sales.

American air-launched Sidewinder and Sparrow missiles, denounced as expensive failures by the media from the late 1950s, are still in massive and effective service, at home and abroad. This pair, by Raytheon originally for the Navy, was not only blasted when first introduced, on the basis of low overall shoot-down rates, 16% for the Sidewinder and 8% for the Sparrow, but since. Such things are relative because competing air-launched missiles, perforce also small, were far less effective overall, and most American launches were outside of design optima. A major problem lay in their use according to prevailing dogma, as high-altitude weapons.

In fact, missiles, especially the small-finned, small cross-section type of the two American models and other typical tactical air-launched weapons, have their greatest advantage not at the thin air of high altitude, but at the thick air of low altitude. Thicker air gives small missiles three advantages: a greater speed superiority over their targets, bulkier and draggier manned aircraft; a maneuverability advantage, because their small fins have far more effective purchase in thick air than they would higher up; and greater heat-seeking tracking ability, because an aircraft battling thick air has to use more fuel, giving it a bigger heat signature, as its exhaust is not dispersed as quickly as it is at the much higher speeds possible through thinner air at high altitude. Parodoxically in view of their high-altitude usage, both American missiles have been adapted to surface launch, where their short range ensures that their targets will be predominantly at low altitude.

The larger Sparrow, with its greater range, serves on hundreds of American and Allied warships, but is a bit too large for short-ranged land-mobile applications. The smaller and shorter-ranged Sidewinder is of less use at sea, where the long horizon causes users to seek more range; Sidewinder naval use is mainly on re-equipped ships of the South Korean Navy. Lighter weight makes the Sidewinder more desirable for land-mobile use, however, as a supplement between less mobile area weapons, Hawks and Patriots, and mobile, but even shorter-ranged, vehicle-mounted gatling guns and Stinger missiles. Topography usually cuts the land's horizon more than the sea's, making the Sidewinder's lesser range a less important land consideration.

In heavy air, with its radar locked in prior to launch, the Sidewinder will destroy its target up to 90% of the time in actual combat. But ground-launched Sidewinders do not generally have much lock-in capacity, both because of weight (ancillary radar systems, necessary for most initial target acquisitions which are then picked up by the missile's own little radar set before its launch, are not used) and because ground-launched Sidewinders do not have mobile dogfighting launch platforms that can maneuver to get a good angle and a lock-in shot on a target. The ground-based Sidewinder is a fire-and-hope weapon to what targets present themselves. It is not a 90% killer, with nearer to a 10% shootdown rate, but that is better than the 0% that would be achieved by not using it at all in the ground role.

For the plane launching tactical anti-aircraft missiles, dogfighting of a sort is involved when the missile's percentage is to be maximized. Soviet fighters tended to be cheaper, short in range and, in heavy air, better dogfighters, because their usually smaller control surfaces have optimum bite and lack drag in thick air. Risking larger, more expensive and less numerous American or Allied aircraft to get optimum missile shots was therefore not a good idea. If your plane isn't a dog, it should not dogfight, and Flop Gun programs to make it do so simply encouraged inappropriate tactics. The problem was failure to follow through on the logic which dispensed with small American fighter aircraft after the Korean War (where they had been extremely successful); once small fighters were dropped, the tactics appropriate to them should have been also. Tactical considerations, often disregarded by defense critics, dictate that a now-typical American fighter should stay high in fuel-efficient air, using its range and flight time superiority to await an advantageous opportunity -- numerical, surprise, good shot or opponent low on fuel -- before diving to the attack. Such was successful strategy in the olden days of aerial combat, as in fights between different-sized birds of prey, but Department of Defense Whizzes often fail to approach even the bird-brain level. Birds, however, are not equipped with missiles, especially the longer-range kind. Before deigning to dogfight, a typical American plane should use its longer-ranged Sparrow or other missiles first, hoping for a low-percentage kill to obviate risk to itself. Such prudent use was the major factor in making the Sparrow a criticized low-percentage weapon, but the same fools would have been more exercised over greater American plane losses.

All of this confusion had occurred before, during the bomber hubris which had accompanied submarine hubris. American bombers had been thought not to need fighter escort, so short-range interceptors against enemy bombers had been sought, partly for procurement convenience. Lockheed's long-ranged Lightning was a low priority. At high altitudes (**above** U.S. bomber operations), it was superior to the new German FW-190, and could even out-turn the Messerschmitt-109 to the right. Three other things helped stay the P-38 from escort duty. There were long-distance demands by two theatres, the New Guinea/SW Pacific and the Mediterranean. In the Pacific, P-38s supplemented carrier

Hellcats, jeep carrier Wildcats and Marine Corsairs, while in the Mediterranean the Lightning was out-ranged by the B-24 bombers used there. By the time of the full bomber offensive, the Lightning's strategic range was being wasted in tactical ground attack missions, while the shorter-legged P-47s and later P-51s mainly escorted the bombers.

Another American air weapon, the 20mm Vulcan gatling gun, has been adapted to both naval and ground-mobile uses. At sea, with its slaved radar system, it is widely used as a defense against cruise missiles. But sea mountings of guns are virtually always too heavy for mobile land use, just as land aircraft are virtually always too fragile for carrier use. The old 20mm gun was not noted for shooting down targets until too late (after the bomb or torpedo had been dropped or the *kamikaze* was going to hit anyway), because of its short range and low stopping power; not greatly superior in those respects, the gatling at least requires less deckspace and manpower, and its chosen enemy the cruise missile is more fragile than old aircraft, more explosive and with fewer pieces than a *kamikaze*. The gatling's radar also gives it much greater all-weather and day/night viability, an improvement over the old visually guided anti-aircraft guns. Most foreign navies have chosen somewhat larger calibers for their weapons of such type, however, often with twice the range and therefore a greater chance of stopping a given cruise missile. Many nations also use such heavier weapons in their aircraft, but in the air a gatling-equipped fighter can maneuver and close with its target, negating its lack of range as well as extending its window of opportunity (much lower closing speeds in a chase situation) in a manner that land- or ship-mounted gatlings cannot match. On the ground, the gatling can be radar-controlled, but unlike a missile it does not have to be locked onto its target for effect; its stream of bullets can be aimed like a firehose. The value of the American gatling gun in actual sea or land service is unknown, but Soviet-pattern weapons in Arab and North Vietnamese use were fairly effective against low-flying Israeli and American planes.

The Soviets also used higher calibers for land-based anti-aircraft, the larger shells with proximity fuses for optimal bursting. Soviet-made guns shot down more than a thousand each of American aircraft and helicopters during the Vietnam War, largely because planes were flying low to escape the "skidding telephone poles" (anti-aircraft missiles) and to attack small inane targets. Much of the American problem was the high-altitude fallacy, however. The closer to the ground, the closer to a greater variety of weapons; aside from the radar and the large long-range missiles, there are usually more numerous and cheaper (the two go together) short-range/low-altitude missiles and frequently guns. A plane can simply fly above far more weapons than it can fly under. And flying under causes the plane to approach its oldest and most fundamental enemy, the ground. There is less warning time from missiles, less ability to evade with thick air cutting speed, much less area to maneuver (because of both low speed and the presence of the ground cutting away an entire hemisphere of maneuver available at higher altitudes), and less time to recover from damage or to bail out. The U.S. began heavily favoring twin-engine planes in Vietnam, but at low altitude the loss of either engine is usually fatal, because there is not sufficient air cushion for regaining control of a heavy twin-engine aircraft suddenly flying on one engine.

Larger caliber modern anti-aircraft guns are more suitable for naval use, however, where their heavy fully automatic mountings are as mobile as the ship carrying them, and where they can also fire less specialized shells against other targets, floating or ashore. On land, such heavier calibers are not part of fully mobile units, because they are too cumbersome and would slow them down. Guns somewhat heavier than the American gatling can be accommodated on tank chasses, however, as foreign mobile mountings in the 35mm to 57mm caliber range prove. The Soviet twin 57mm and quadruple 23mm tanks in Arab service have effectively shot down Israeli planes.

A 57mm gun is classified by its caliber, which is both the width of its shell and of the bore of its gun barrel. Artillery guns were originally standardized and classified by the weight of their projectiles, originally round stones, later lead balls. The key moment in the industrialization of arms was the transition from artillery firing stones to the use of lead cannonballs. Because the natural supply of stones is of different sizes, there was earlier an active disincentive against standardized guns; the same-sized guns would have sooner exhausted the natural supply of round stones of a given size. Guns, with their articulated bores, are less forgiving than the older catapults were, with piles of likely stones showing ancient forts, camps and siege positions. By contrast, cast lead balls could most easily be made of the same size -- with the same mold or molds, easily standardized -- which placed a premium on making cannons the same size (the guns themselves, however, continued for centuries to be hand-bored or -built up, as size, not manufacture, was standardized). The six-pounder, or saker, started in Henry VIII's establishment of standard weights, done to simplify artillery ammunition supply and production, as well as future production of the guns themselves at the Royal Arsenal. Mentioned by Shakespeare in his usual anachronistic playing to his audience by updating the historical, the saker was a larger caliber than are more modern six-pounders, which kept the weight classification when more aerodynamic oblong projectiles were introduced, making calibers smaller for the same weight. The six-pounder was standardized at a caliber which metric system users call 57 millimeters (but 2¼ inches is closer to 57.15mm). The name saker faded from use except the Czarist and other Slavic corruption "Sokol" (the leader of the 19th century Czech nationalistic gymnasium movement was named Sokol -- Bohemia had long been a munitions center).

One misconceived form of standardization is the roles and missions gibberish. There are in fact only capabilities and the ability to recognize them. Capabilities are largely a product of technology, the development of previous efforts. The six-pounder gun, for example, had been superseded in normal use by the development of armored ships, but remained in service on some small light vessels. When Whitehead's wonder weapon, the torpedo, was mounted in small light wooden ships called motor torpedo boats, and posed a direct threat to the unsubdivided and unbulkheaded big ships of the turn of the century, navies turned to light guns with enough power, range and rate of fire to deal with such light vessels. In the British Navy, the six-pounder was rescued from obscurity to plug the gap.

It was thus greatly back in fashion when World War I, and the development of the tank, occurred, and was large enough to be mounted as the main gun of the "males", or gun-armed tanks, of what was after all a British naval project. The anti-torpedo boat six-pounder, by virtue of its size, became the tank's first gun, extending its role and mission. And when enemy tanks became a threat and outgrew the anti-tank rifle and the anti-tank artillery of the 1930s (25mm, 37mm/1-pounder, 40mm/2-pounder or 47mm/3-pounder guns in various armies), the six-pounder was pressed into service as an anti-tank gun. It equipped Britain's post-Dunkirk emergency anti-tank force of half-tracks and later many "Churchill" tanks, became the main American anti-tank gun to replace the 37mm, and supplied the Soviets in massive numbers through Lend-Lease, which also provided new equipment to make ammunition for it. It was also in Japanese service, as a man-dragged "infantry gun", and as Japan had lagged in tank development, only in the late 1930s did these "infantry guns" become Japan's first main tank gun.

With the gun in Soviet service, but soon superseded in anti-tank use by the continuing growth of tanks and their armor, the caliber was available for other development. During the post-war period, both the Swedes and Soviets developed 57mm anti-aircraft guns, the Swedes for export (to the French Navy), and the Soviets for tanks, because 57mm was large enough for bursting shells, easy to adapt to rapid fire and of a range fit for engaging maneuvering aircraft. Larger guns have more range, but aircraft so far away are not easily predictable in their movements; the increased range is largely wasted, and the larger shell bursts do not make up for a slower rate of fire. From swivel gun, to light vessel main armament, to anti-torpedo boat gun, to tank gun, to infantry gun, to anti-tank gun and to anti-aircraft gun, the key was the decision to utilize the six-pounder's capabilities, transcending roles and missions categorization and picking the best available tool for the job.

And the job does not stay the same in times of fast-moving technology. The anti-aircraft guns of the late 1930s, the German 88mm (or 20-pounder), the American 90mm, the British 3-inch (76mm) and later the 17-pounder and the Soviet 85mm, all shared the virtues of high velocity (to reach high altitudes), exceptional accuracy, to hit ever-faster bombers, and hitting power, to deliver large powerful bursts of *flak*. But the aircraft in use, although discomfitted by the guns, were soon of less menace to field troops than was the evolving tank. Adding a hardened shell for armor penetration made a new weapon to deal with a new threat. The Germans were the first to use their "88s" against tanks, using an area weapon in the field against doctrine. Rommel eventually began putting all of his possible anti-tank weapons together, concentrated on British supply lines, to await British armored counter-attacks; he used the 88s' range to winnow his enemy at long range, before the concentrated fire of his tanks, purpose-built anti-tank guns and 88s finished the survivors at closer range. Just as the 57mm anti-tank gun was passing back into limbo before resurfacing as an anti-aircraft weapon, contemporary anti-aircraft weapons were being used as anti-tank guns and then mounted in tanks (in the case of the U.S. 90mm gun, first into "tank destroyer" tanks and then into the Pershing-Patton series). Needs and abilities superseded roles and missions when war blasted away the fog of bureaucratic categorization.

The discrepancy between the light 20-lb shell weight of the German 88mm anti-aircraft gun and that of the slightly smaller 86.4mm caliber British 25-pounder shows how the initial design for a gun affected its specifications and its future adaptability. The 88 had a fairly light shell so that the powerful and heavy gun could give it high velocity for quick reach to altitudes considered high at the time. High velocity made calculating fuse length easier than with a slower shell, and, by cutting "lead" length, gave more chance of putting shells near fast aircraft. By contrast, the 25-pounder was meant for lower-velocity, indirect fire of as many high-explosive shells as possible against ground targets, by a gun meant to be as easily mobile as possible. It did not have optics good enough, a breech strong enough, a carriage strong enough or a barrel long enough for high-velocity fire, and was chambered for a large, slow shell.

The 25-lber was an excellent weapon of its type, a pre-World War II improvement over the old French "75"(mm; in use for four generations), but was not greatly capable of other roles. The more expensive 88, with a huge crew of 25 to feed the all-round, all-azimuth, heavy-recoil gun versus 6 for the more placid 25-pounder, had the gunsight, muzzle velocity and robustness for other demanding tasks. Fitting a harder shell -- armored for penetrating armored targets -- made the 88 a superb anti-tank gun against heavy armor. The 25-lber could have been used, as some French 75s were in 1940, as a short-range anti-tank gun against contemporary German tanks, but heavier tanks soon made such uses unprofitable, as thicker armor defeated both high-explosive and slow hardened shells. Indeed, 25-pounders were not later equipped with hollow-point shells for effective low-velocity use against tanks, from lassitude or their lack of gunsights, or from the availability of purpose-built or adaptive anti-tank guns.

For America's ground troops, there remains a gap between the short-range anti-aircraft protection afforded by hand-held Stinger missiles and the mobile gatling gun on one hand and the not terribly mobile Hawks and Patriots on the other, a gap only partly filled by vehicularized Sidewinders with limited radar capability. The French, Germans and Russians have all filled the particular role (with the ability to also effectively hit ground targets, enemy troops or light armored vehicles) with mobile radar-guided guns (Russian 23mm guns had radar, unlike earlier 57mm-gunned tanks), with range and hitting power far superior to American gatlings, and the Russian models combat-proven. The U.S. radarized attempt was the Sergeant York tank, after the Duster, a customized Korean War-era Walker light tank mounting two 40mm guns but without radar-control, had been sold off, retired or put deep into the Reserves a long time ago, during the Whiz Kid era. The Sergeant York made and failed to live up to bombastic claims, and its proponents were caught cheating on its tests. Perhaps, instead of being named after the famous sharpshooter York, it should have been named after a famous test-cheater such as Ted Kennedy or Joe Biden, or even Billy Mitchell.

Also an American candidate was the West German Gepard, an anti-aircraft variant of their Leopard (and hence Panther) series of tanks, with Swiss guns. The West Germans claim that the Gepard's 35mm guns can hit the target 75% of the time. Given that the guns' range is 2½ miles, and their shells take several seconds to travel that far, a target would have to be large and slow to be hit at that range; most high-performance aircraft could move forward about a mile in that time, and be anywhere within a cubic mile of space by the time the stream of shells arrives. Needless to say, the Gepard did not pass its American tests, although with much less publicity than the Sergeant York, which was thought to be more effective, cheaper and American-made. Of course, nothing at all is cheapest, but it is 0% effective in shooting down aircraft. The York, with possibly correctible defects of the type found in all new weapons, may have been fatally compromised by such minutiae as not correcting for patterned misses and not taking account of wind drift. In the Gulf War, the only Iraqi air attacks were missiles against Patriot-defended fixed targets and Iraqi aircraft were unable to perform offensive missions; there was no problem. But if there is a more desperate war, Americans may die because of a spavined battlefield-mobile anti-aircraft capability, and if they do, liberals will be braying for victims, someone to blame, someone else.

Chapter 19 - **The TFX** (Re-inventing the Edsel)

In addition to the other bugbears -- political influence, obsolescence and service rivalry, the vendetta against Air Defense, the high-altitude fallacy, the hopeless love affair with the helicopter and the roles and missions farrago -- the Whiz Kids were edging into Modern Liberalism with their new obsession about purported over-capacity in the American aerospace industry. They sought a shake-out of aviation through the medium of a new combined-service aircraft. The minor devil being exorcised was subcontracting, the closest thing to an Eisenhower defense scandal.

Some older missile contracts had reimbursed the main contractor for subcontractors' profits, putting a profitability premium on the number of subcontracting levels achieved. The solution, eliminating that contract feature, had already been done, but subcontracting itself remained a liberal phantasm. By banning subcontracting, thought to be evil in itself, the Whiz Kids hoped to totally freeze out the airplane companies not getting the single big new contract, driving some out of business. Military procurement had taken a back-seat to regulating the economy through manipulating the destruction of some large employers, just as eliminating the presumed evil of different weapons for different services (the birth of the "non-standard" fetish) would also crowd out considerations of military utility. Washington-based consultants to the Defense Department, the most productive and useful members of society at no time whatsoever, were going both to prune a large industry (but without affecting that vital Washington real estate market where the experts had their money), as well as to reform the military. And automobile king McNamara was going to put the same car in every service garage, something Ford had been unable to accomplish with its big Edsel, a company product contemporary with McNamara. A certain rancor about the wishes of customers was bound to be the result of that experience, and running rough-shod over the tax-supported military services was easier than getting back at the diverse automobile-buying public more directly. People who had saved their money by not buying Edsels were going to see their taxes go up.

When competition is present, with the incentive to keep costs low and prices low, the aviation industry is characterized as being in a state of over-capacity; when the industry becomes shrunken and inefficient in meeting fair timetables and cost goals, when over-capacity has been shaken out, it becomes anti-competitive, or monopolistic. The same quacks provide a different set of spurious cures to provide a new set of diseases, keeping the merry-go-round spinning, the paycheck and consulting fees flowing and the illusion of progress just up ahead; the only disease is the trumpery of the diagnosticians, with the real need for a "magic bullet" to kill liberals. The decision to move toward an industry shake-out was partly a belief of Cold War Liberals that the left-liberals and the home-state representatives of the winning contractor would be likely to pass a program otherwise aimed at cutting America's future defense capacity, the left-liberals in the name of peace and prosperity, and in the actual aim of harming the country, and the home-staters for personal political glory. The project was called the Tactical Fighter X, or TFX.

The TFX was in fact a long-term NASA proposal which predated the Whiz Kids. The Air Force's Tactical Air Command joined in, seeking to freeze out the Navy from future aircraft procurement even before the Navy's Phantom had proved superior to and more versatile than the Air Force's Thunderchief. The Air Force subsidized the first swing-wing experiments, the two X-5s, but the program early swung toward obvious bi-service poaching and a bomber role by experiments with a wind-tunnel mock-up of the new Navy Vigilante strategic carrier bomber re-equipped with a swing-wing (congressional testimony about the A-3 Skywarrior had the wrong plane -- the Skywarrior had engines in wing-pods, not practical for a swing-wing). These tests were studied by the aerospace industry, with North American, General Dynamics and Boeing the most interested in early developing their own swing-wing projects.

The TFX was the definitive Whiz Kid project in terms of goals, costs and results. It promised economies of scale through the rationalized concentrated production of a single aircraft to fill three distinct roles. It promised an end to purported aerospace over-capacity, as well as an end to subcontracting, blown up into an evil in itself as a mis-applied generalization from those missile contract provisions no longer in force anyway. The losers of the main bid were not to get part of the contract by bidding on subcomponents, staying in business by making the buy price of a component less than the cost of the main contractor's in-house production price. That meant that virtually all subcomponents would not have an option of being achievable at a lower price, and that the higher price of the subcomponents would push up the TFX's cost. But the Whiz Kids were willing to spend more tax money in order to put some taxpayers out of work.

In the otherwise boom-or-bust world of aviation, with either very successful designs or failures, stabs at contracts for the government or chancy deals with airlines stagnated by fares kept out of the general public's reach, subcontracting kept a company's workforce, factory, balance sheet, existence and design staff intact in the long intervals between striking it big on its own. Subcontracting was also the most competitively demanding phase of aviation from the economic point-of-view, as the out-source had to be sure to cut its fabricating price to get the bid, and thereafter trim its costs to avoid excessive losses, while if it had a successful design of its own those questions of price and costs were secondary. To the moment's design-winner, savings guaranteed by a subcontractor were solid, as the competitor would have to eat its losses

if it had bid too low, while in-house cuts in cost were inherently speculative. A winning bidder was almost always too lean to do all work itself -- winners were generally cash-poor and also chary of over-expan-
sion from having to cut back in the past. Subcontracting was the natural
response of an industry with large fluctuations, and it maintained a large
measure of competitive equilibrium. Aerospace had spread its scattered
capacity around for design competition, and subcontracting matched
manufacturing capacity to the demands of massive discrete projects,
smoothing demand over jagged bumps and keeping the competition in
designs alive while cutting costs.

Liberals past and present would criticize sole-source contracts
like the TFX as political deals and freeze-outs, just as they would criticize the opposite approach, the subcontracting system, as log-rolling or
spreading the honey around, when it was just cost-cutting and sensible
business. Indeed, companies which deliberately and systematically made
things for themselves, which they could have had someone else make
cheaper, would have probably been violating the anti-trust laws if they
had been trying to freeze out their competition by doing everything
themselves. The ugliness which liberals see is usually a product of their
mindset, seeing the world through dung-colored glasses.

Of course, the capacity of the aerospace industry had been greatly
increased by two previous wars, Liberalism's Third Crusade of World
War II and Cold War Liberalism's First Crusade in Korea. Because
war-time investment from traditional investors had shied away from the
boom-or-bust aircraft companies' factories in favor of traditional industries converted to war-work but with more stable future prospects, the
government itself had been most involved in expanding aerospace capacity, through building the facilities for vastly enlarged war-programs and
leasing them to the aerospace companies on a long-term basis. Putting
its tenants out of business was the new program.

The three roles which the Whiz Kids hoped to fill with the TFX
from one firm were: First, the title role, a new tactical fighter for the
Air Force, with the paramount qualification being an ability to operate
from rough short runways, so as to make the craft less likely to be destroyed on the ground by an enemy surprise attack on the limited number
of airfields capable of handling conventional jet fighters. (Conventional
jet fighters had become streamlined with sweptback wings for lower drag
at speed, but those wings did not generate sufficient lift at lower speeds
for short take-offs or landings.) Second, a new medium strategic bomber for the Air Force, with long range, a respectable bombload and, most
important in the heyday of the high-altitude fallacy, the ability to make a
final low-level approach for hundreds of miles to avoid enemy ground-
based radar and that enemy's air defenses. The possibility of airborne
radar was evidently not considered, possibly due to the Soviet tradition
of smaller fighters with minimal built-in radar capacity directed from the

ground, but the Soviets were already working on specialized large radar-carrying planes for airborne direction. Third, a carrier fighter for the Navy which, in the cringing days of pandering to frets about the carrier's obsolescence, the Navy characterized as a defensive, long-endurance platform for that Phoenix anti-aircraft missile still under development by Hughes. Rather than emphasizing a complete fighter with the ability to attack and destroy a variety of targets, the Navy was seeking something to keep Russian cruise missiles and their launching aircraft away. The most relevant criteria for selecting a TFX-builder were experience in high-performance supersonic aircraft, and the ability to build a plane rugged enough to operate from a carrier, the highest structural test faced by any aircraft, and one bound to help meet the Air Force fighter version's rough take-off and landing criteria.

The American aerospace industry had already seen three companies shaken out of the main airframe business, victims of fashion and their own incompetence in the field. Bell had gone to helicopters, and Curtiss had gone over solely to engine production, after substantial failures with its bulky and inefficient World War II Warhawks and Helldivers, large but not necessarily very strong planes. The Warhawk had also been greatly hampered by bad engines from G.M.'s Allison division. Army Air had wanted a liquid-cooled engine, for a more aerodynamic nose, although Curtiss itself had built far better radial engines. These were air-cooled and lighter than heavier and bulky liquid-cooled engines, but the Army thought radials too draggy. The builders of the first aircraft engines through the Wright Brothers line, Curtiss-Wright had vied with Pratt & Whitney for world supremacy in radial engines. But the rise of jet engines was Curtiss-Wright's fall, the new entrance by General Electric and the better transition by Pratt & Whitney dropping the formerly pioneering concern to a distant third.

Another aviation pioneer, Martin, had seen its flying boat franchise (the China Clipper, etc.) erode first with the end of the passenger business victimized by war and longer-ranged land-based planes and then with the post-war phase-out of military flying boats. Its bomber business had limped along in the isolationist inter-war period with limited peace-time sales of such transitional-era aircraft as the art-deco B-10. World War II, including foreign orders, had seen Martin take advantage of new engines and speed requirements with a line of light and medium bombers featuring fairly high performance but unsafe wing-loading (with take-off, flying and landing problems). The most prolific of these was the Martin B-26 Marauder, with its various nicknames -- the most notorious "Widow-Maker", "Lead Sled" and "Flying Coffin"; "One-a-Day-in-Tampa-Bay" for its training base accidents; and, most cutting of all, the "Baltimore Whore", because with its defective landing gear and overloaded wings it had no visible means of support. The Marauder was one of four American bomber models with 10-13 machine guns heavily used in the European war, but its ratio of enemy planes claimed shot down to its own losses was only about ¼ of that of the other three planes. Either the Marauder's gunners were unusually reticent in their claims, for which there is utterly no evidence, or the plane was a dog. The Marauder's quick withdrawal from service was followed by the rare re-assigning of its B-26 designation to a far more effective, and far safer, plane originally meant for ground attack.

This ground attack role became a possibility for a new jet, and Martin sought to revive its business with the B-51 project, a ludicrous three-engined design with two innovations, swiveling wings, still too small in the Martin tradition, and an engine in the tail, similar to many modern airliners. But a successful English craft by English Electric, and designed as a nuclear bomber, was seen by Martin as a superior design for ground attack, a better possibility for its lagging Baltimore factory to pursue. Martin turned out bomber and ground attack versions as the U.S. Air Force's B-57 Canberra, before stretching the craft's wings into a high-altitude photo-recon craft that presaged Lockheed's U-2. Specially adapting this superior foreign design stretched Baltimore production into the early 1970s. But as the company's main aircraft project, it wound down the plane business; Martin switched over completely, and successfully, to the missile-building and subcontract field, back to small wings, and away from the successful original designs that an aspirant to aerospace leadership must occasionally produce.

By the time of the Whiz Kids, there were essentially nine large American aviation companies with the size and experience to compete for the TFX project, or not to get the contract and face massive shrinkage or extinction. Another huge aerospace operation, Boeing, not really a serious TFX contender, was failed last for Machiavellian reasons, but it was not endangered, being jammed with civilian and military orders for its airliner/transport category. Boeing's SAC/MAC (Military Airlift Command) KC-135 tanker/cargo plane had been adapted from what became the civilian 707 project, helping it win the long-range passenger race for Boeing before being further militarized as an airborne radar and command plane, from Air Force One to more technical applications. Later, the even more lucrative 747 emerged from Boeing's futile stab at the C-5A project, the Whiz Kid fetish of increasing strategic mobility, the better to more quickly shoehorn Americans into distant brushfire wars.

Liberal phantasies of political influence had achieved a peak with Washington Senator Henry "Scoop" Jackson, supposedly hell-bent on obtaining big government contracts for Boeing, his state's largest firm. Yet Boeing had been a major military contractor, first for seaplanes and early fighters, and then for the bombers with their structural similarity to the emerging passenger/transport market, for decades before Jackson had heeled his first ward. The military adopted the 707 while Jackson was a minority junior Senator, and the ever more senior majoritarian failed to get any new big government program for Boeing (B-58, B-70, C-5A, TFX and SST (supersonic transport)); Boeing got only a helicopter project and some hydrofoils in 30 years. Jackson's electioneering masquerade fit the media's need for a Senate military-industrial complex villain to complement that base ogre of the House, Mendell Rivers.

Of the other nine aerospace companies, three met both main criteria for the TFX program on their own, combining supersonic experience and design ruggedness. McDonnell had been the last of the big ten to emerge, a child of the jet age and a Navy brat. McDonnell's first project, other than subcontract work mainly for a Douglas war-time C-47 assembly factory in Oklahoma, was a design for a twin-engine night-fighter, the P-67 Bat. This extended development project eventually lost out to Northrop's P-61 Black Widow, but it left McDonnell with spare capacity and experience in developing an airframe of the type soon to be in demand for new jet fighters. These would need two engines because individual jet engines of that transitional era were not yet powerful enough to propel a plane on their own.

With its Army Air Black Widow success, Northrop also got the early Air Force franchise for an equivalent jet night-fighter. But separate procurement left the Navy with its own jet needs, a market McDonnell tapped with a series of subsonic Navy fighters. McDonnell then broke into the supersonic, Air Force and export markets (Canadian, anyway) with its Voodoo interceptor, a victim of long delays which hit the Air Defense market just as it slackened. But it was the supersonic Phantom jet fighter for the Navy which put the St. Louis firm into the really big time, with Air Force interest and a developing export market. McDonnell had shown its mettle, and although another Whiz Kid project, the Vietnam War, would soon pump up its Phantom business further, the TFX appeared at the time a crucial contract for it. But while the Phantom was both big for a carrier plane and about the weight of World War II's famed four-engine B-17 Flying Fortress, it was small compared to contemporary bombers, a hint that the TFX project was inherently too much of a stretch.

Vought was an old firm which for a generation was the "V" in conglomerate LTV, and usually its dominant factor, especially after "L", Jimmy Ling, was dealt out by the SEC -- to become a partner in a brokerage house -- but it had no large plane experience, not even of the Phantom's size. After a couple of small Navy floatplanes, Vought's main carrier-based efforts had been handicapped by engine problems. The World War II Corsair, a gull-winged plane built around a huge engine, had been rejected early by the Navy for carrier use because its pilot sat so far back of the huge engine that deck landings were thought unsafe. Used by the Marines as a land-based plane, the Corsair's fighting virtues eventually led the Navy to risk its use from carriers. Although replaced in most carrier use by later and more advanced planes, the Corsair was still in use after the TFX contract had been awarded, for Marine ground attack during the early Vietnam War. Vought's next brush with engine problems involved its Cutlass fighter jet, a hyper-modern design knee-capped by defective Westinghouse jets. The quality of the airframe led to further contracts for Vought, however; it went supersonic with the light carrier-based Crusader, tilt-winged and the first "area rule' plane, still in service with the French Navy more than thirty years later. The Crusader was eventually replaced in front-line American use after nearly two decades, but its general lay-out was adapted by Vought for the Navy A-7 light attack bomber, still in some carrier and Marine use, but not totally replacing the older Douglas A-4 in Marine use or seeing any foreign service.

North American was the third company to combine supersonic experience, rugged plane design and even a third qualification of large bomber experience. As a larger operation than McDonnell or Vought, North American was more capable of doing all TFX work itself, a cruc-ial consideration for the shake-out role. But all was not rosy at North American, as shown by the California company's later merger with Pittsburgh machine tool-maker Rockwell (initially called North Ameri-can-Rockwell and then later just Rockwell International, although the North American division was its enormous aerospace business). Besides its supersonic Navy Vigilante bomber slighted by the high-altitude falla-cy and diverted into reconnaissance, North American had transonic ex-perience, Navy experience and large bomber experience, but none had been positive; that kind of thing, along with the curtailment of its most meritorious plane, makes a company a merger target.

North American had grown large in World War II because of a triple threat line-up of Texan trainers (still in civilian use today, by virtue of reliability and war-surplusage, and as stand-ins for historical films), Mitchell medium bombers, of Doolittle Raid and Empire State Building collision fame but otherwise reliable and effective, and Mus-tang fighter planes, still in civilian use as racing planes. All three were bought by the military in massive quantities, more than 40,000 in all, making North American big by numbers, while other companies got big by larger airframe products.

The Mustang had been a plug in its original "mission" as an RAF interceptor (for shooting down bombers), because of its inadequately supercharged Allison engine. The available design was turned by America's Army Air into a dive-bomber, legendarily because the budget for fighters had already been allocated to other Allison-powered craft, but the Mustang did receive dive-brakes and bomb-release gear. Souped up with a high-performance British implant, the Mustang became enough of a thoroughbred to totally outgrow the dive-bomber role, and its combination of high performance and long range made an ideal bomber escort just when such a thing was needed for daylight raids over Germany. In this third role, the Mustang was fighting nimble enemy fighters over enemy territory, far more demanding than its interceptor origin. But that was before hardening of the arteries had affected the calculations of the "Iron Triangle", when actual capabilities were allowed to transcend the categories of roles and missions. After North American's prodigious war-time feats, the post-war experience was bound to be a let-down, however.

North American's vastly enhanced reputation had led the Navy to seek its design expertise late in World War II for what was to have been the Navy's first all-jet fighter. Although this single-engine project was long delayed by slow jet development, so that other jets, twin-engined, broke in carrier service, the Air Force showed an interest in the project, a more advanced swept-wing design than the more clearly transitional straight-wing jet fighters it was receiving in the post-war era. Built and in service in time for the unexpected Korean War, the Air Force F-86 Sabre won the Korean air war hands-down, so convincingly that it both captured the European export market and re-awakened Navy interest. With the basic structure sound enough for carrier operations because of its Navy genesis, modifying the Sabre into the Navy Fury was not difficult, but the war and later production for the Air Force had priority, so it was only three years after the Korean War that the Navy got its Furys. Just in time to be outmoded by advances in jet engines, the Fury's brief service was ended by the advent of the Crusader and the Phantom, both hundreds of miles per hour faster. But at least the Sabre-Fury had given North American experience in building carrier planes, which it soon utilized for the Vigilante, its second supersonic plane.

North American's first project beyond the sound barrier was an improvement of the F-86 Sabre called the F-100 Supersabre. Unlike many planes handicapped by their engines, the F-100's single engine worked well to get the plane slowly through the turbulent transonic speed, but the design was inadequate for its slightly supersonic speed. The Supersabre crashed frequently, although never really getting the public bad rap that the far worthier, and far safer, F-104 Starfighter (a so-called "Widow-maker") and F-105 Thunderchief ("Thud") received. Fixed up, the F-100 ceased to be actively dangerous, just mediocre, undistinguishing itself in the early Vietnam War as a fighter-bomber.

With a true instinct for the nugatory, congressional criticism focused not on the F-100, but rather on North American's hiring practices. Young Senator Proxmire, liberal Democratic appointive successor to the late Republican Joe McCarthy, and anxious to build a reputation and help keep his seat from a usually contested state, began harping on North American hirees. The reticence for being brow-beaten under television hot-lights of one former Colonel, working on a guidance subcontract for the successful Minuteman missile, made Senator Proxmire exceptionally angry, the anger of a politician denied publicity long burning against North American. Recently retired military officers mistakenly believed they were living in a free country and could work for whom they damn well pleased. The privilege of not testifying before congressional inquisitions is one that extends only to left-wing subversives and those who wish to shield them just as the liberal propaganda term of art "double-dipping" is used only for retired military officers keeping active in their specialties outside of the military (while legally collecting retirement pay as compensation for past service), but not for the specimens who take up military-bashing for liberal lucre. It really is disgusting that people would wish to keep working on an important national program with which they are familiar, rather than moving to a completely new endeavor (frequently the prospect for those who stay in the rotation-happy military). In civilian life, of course, executive recruitment of people with whom a company has worked is common, generally not controversial, because it is utterly reasonable to hire people of demonstrated expertise already familiar with an area or a project. Only in liberalism, whether openly political or the coy media variety, is there a public arena for a yammering opportunist to manufacture controversy, publicity and an undeserved reputation as an opponent of waste.

Proxmire's extended vendetta against North American encompassed its space work, which he was prone to characterize as a religion. As a left-liberal, Proxmire was exercised that some larger goal had obscured the heady business of colonizing American society with liberal ideology. No distractions from doctrine were to be allowed, and the Galileos of the modern era had to be harassed as threats to the secular religion liberalism, just as later minor remnants of Christianity and infiltrators of its various hierarchies would be recruited as political allies. Knowledge is an enemy of both religion and its prop of faith, best cultivated in the dark of ignorance. Liberalism has subverted education, as Christianity once sought to do, in the active belittling of knowledge. Denying the possibility of knowledge, or prattling about "mere facts" and "so-called knowledge", or denigrating any other sort of rigorous thinking outside of the liberal catechism of fatuous assumptions and flabby lies, are the levers to pry open the door for liberal indoctrination. Sugar-coated bromides about "teaching people how to think" always becomes telling them what to believe, after denying them the mind-building exercises that do help make people think (which is why they are dispensed with, as promoting intellectual barriers to liberal indoctrination with its flabby load of nonsense). Ignorance is not bliss, it is liberalism.

In Proxmire's case, his left-liberal hostility to any extension of knowledge, particularly the space program of Cold War Liberalism, and his old rage at North American fused into beetle-browed indignation at North American's space shuttle, that "glorified space truck", which the

Soviets and West Europeans chose to emulate, to maintain their lead over China and Japan in the religion race. Imitation is the sincerest form of flattery and, by that standard, Proxmire was refuted, not for the first time. Proxmire's gloating over the *Challenger* explosion was somewhat damped by the revelation that the fault had not been North American's part of the shuttle, but rather the subcontractor's boosters and the space agency's decision to launch in cold weather.

The upshot for North American was that its public and political relations were frayed, just as its relations with the Navy had suffered during the Fury's delay and the hobbling of the Vigilante. The final millstone was North American's bad experience with the post-war strategic bomber branch of the Air Force, the Strategic Air Command that was to be a TFX user. North American's large jet bomber project, the four-engine and deservedly forgotten B-45, had been fobbed off onto the oblivion of the recon beat long before that role had acquired its later clout, cachet and sex appeal, and become the graveyard of fine aircraft.

Of the other six aviation companies that were possible contenders for the TFX, two, Douglas and Grumman, had loads of naval experience but had not built supersonic production craft. Long Island-based Grumman was working on its largest airframes ever, both for the Navy, the subsonic A-6 medium bomber, also later produced as an electronic-warfare vehicle and as a refueling tanker, and the radome-mounting Hawkeye, even slower. Grumman was the firm most likely to seek a partner with Air Force, supersonic and large airframe experience.

Douglas had also built Navy planes, larger than Grumman's; its A-3, 12 tons heavier than the Phantom, had been the first carrier-based medium nuclear bomber, and had also been converted to Tactical Air Force use as the B-66. Older Douglas planes had served with Army Air and as exports, a series of light high-performance bombers of which the late World War II A-26/B-26 Invader had served well in Korea and was still in service after the TFX bid. Douglas' California operation built thousands of transport/airliners, the most successful having been the DC-3/C-47 series, now in their seventh calendar decade in use. But more modern Douglas airliners had been less successful, its DC-8 surpassed by the Boeing 707 as its later DC-10 would be beaten by the 747 (except as an Air Force tanker). Douglas was in long-term trouble, in spite of its successful Missouri-built naval attack planes, especially the A-4 Skyhawk, the first purpose-built naval tactical nuclear bomber, but much more useful as a conventional light bomber from the late 1950s -- the Vietnam, 1973 Arab-Israeli, Falklands (Argentine service) and Gulf Wars (Marine and Kuwaiti service).

Eventually, Douglas merged with Missouri neighbor McDonnell to form McDonnell Douglas. The merger kept the huge California Douglas factory in the airliner business while appealing to liberals as a prospective shut-down of an efficient production line and design center for military aircraft. Cutting defense muscle is usually a liberal goal in itself and good for decrying the decrease in competition for military contracts. But McDonnell's failure to reform the inefficient Douglas California operation and such episodes as the Israel Lobby's repeated blockades of big sales of advanced McDonnell aircraft to Saudi Arabia have of late put the giant into jeopardy. Late in 1993, in return for Israel's help in greasing the North American Free Trade Agreement, the Clinton Administration agreed to allow McDonnell Douglas to export a few more F-15s -- to Israel. So much for "free trade"!

Grumman too would become the target of a merger, a 1981 un-friendly take-over try by Vought (LTV), its fellow supplier of naval aircraft. LTV's law firm, more famous for defending liberal media libel, chose to ignore the implications of the McDonnell Douglas merger for Grumman's main anti-trust defense against the merger. McDonnell and Douglas with Grumman and Vought had been the four large suppli-ers of carrier aircraft, all constituting critical suppliers in anti-trust approval of a merger under the FTC "Rule of Four". Possibly, the law firm was unaware of the previous merger and no one at LTV thought to tell them. Grumman's law firm, another firm more famous for shielding liberal media libel, had less reason to bring up the McDonnell Douglas merger, as it was unfavorable, a permitted merger, for heading off a Grumman-LTV merger. Grumman was largely owned by workers and retirees, so LTV stepped softly around the question of which production line it would shut down if successful. LTV said that its Texas line was going to be converted to missiles, and that the Long Island factory would stay open, but refused to make binding pledges to that effect; LTV had made similar statements about keeping some steel mills open when it bought up Jones & Laughlin, but shut them down anyway.

Ultimately, the question came down to the credibility of LTV management. Had Jimmy Ling's misconduct occurred later, LTV would have probably tried to keep him as a figurehead for minority preference; his successor was Vought's Paul Thayer, whom no one believed, with solid reasons as it turned out. Thayer claimed that a competitor's plane he had been flying had nearly killed him, but was not borne out by the plane's "black box". Later a Reagan Defense official, he was sentenced to prison for insider trading, leaking corporate secrets to relatives. Thayer was indeed a scamp, but LTV **did** make good planes when it got contracts. It survived the TFX drought with the A-7 adaptation of the Crusader design, but suffered when Carter's Whiz Kids by-passed its lightweight métier for the over-blown F-18. In 1992, Martin bought a bankrupt LTV's aerospace operation, leaving nothing of LTV except its initials and the old Jones & Laughlin steel operation; Martin had pros-pered in its niche. Former target Grumman announced in late 1993 that it was going out of the airframe business, and in April 1994 Northrop outbid Martin for it, stopping another merger with Vought.

Four other builders had Mach, but no naval, experience. Two, Long Island's Republic and California's Northrop (once a Douglas subsidiary and the originator of the Dauntless dive-bomber which sank four Japanese carriers at the Battle of Midway), were small operations and would seem to have been candidates for extinction. Northrop had built several large-for-their-time projects, but always in limited numbers. Its night-fighters were fairly capable but war was still mainly a daylight operation. The Flying Wing had been a Northrop development obsession, but had not been ordered by the Air Force. Northrop's modern productions were like its old Dauntless design, small and cheap, but fairly capable and good values, American equivalents of the MiG-21. The first of these was a transonic trainer/export fighter project called the Tiger, which received government sanction as the Freedom Fighter, after beating several other companies' proposals. It was a Tiger in the domestic trainer and export fighter markets, selling thousands. Otherwise the future looked bleak for Northrop, but it was not shook out of the business by not getting the TFX bid -- its development of the Tiger II, significantly boosting the Tiger's capabilities, sold well abroad and kept it going.

Republic, the Long Island operation victimized by the Curtiss Warhawk contract before Pearl Harbor, had rebounded by designing fighters around the biggest new non-Curtiss engines. Its first big success was the P-47 Thunderbolt of World War II, hulking, rugged, medium-ranged and successful both as a fighter and for ground attack. Republic's first jet achievement was the F-84, second to North American's F-86 as the P-47 had been second to North American's P-51. Thousands of three principal variants of the F-84 were sold to the Air Force and abroad.

Republic's third big corporate achievement was a supersonic fighter-bomber for the Air Force, the Thunderchief, which got an undeserved bad rap and therefore no exports, but the Air Force bought hundreds. Besides its high speed, the Thunderchief had given Republic experience with a bomb-bay, unique among fighters. But the fighter-bomber classification, a product of its procurement for the Tactical Air Force with its additional mission of ground support added to the concept of a more pure air-to-air fighter, showed that modern developments were becoming more specialized than the TFX plan of one aircraft for a variety of roles. Not only were there fighters and bombers, but an increasingly distinct category of fighter-bombers. And for that ground attack role, the single-engined Thunderchief was soon displaced in Air Force favor by the twin-engined and somewhat more capable Phantom. The Phantom, designed as a missile-chucking interceptor when missiles were overrated, had the engine power for a greater bombload without a bomb-bay, but, built for speed rather than for maneuverability, it too was not really a dogfighter.

The Phantom's poaching of the Thunderchief's designed role left Republic with bleak prospects as it faced rejection in the TFX proposal. But Republic did survive by merging with other troubled Long Island aviation concerns in different categories: Fairchild, a maker of small airliners, and Hiller, a small helicopter company. Struggling on into the 1970s, Republic had one run of prosperity with the A-10 ground-support aircraft, building hundreds to stay in business, although not in the front rank.

The two remaining firms, possible seekers for a co-bidder with carrier-based experience, were the California/Confederacy giants Lockheed and General Dynamics. General Dynamics looked at the time to be more in need of the project, as its Ft. Worth division would probably have been shut down without a contract, although its California missile business would have survived. But General Dynamics had solid experience in supersonic planes, one an Air Force interceptor and the other the supersonic B-58 bomber, so relations with the Air Force, especially the Strategic Air Command, were good. General Dynamics' relations with the Navy were also good, for its anti-aircraft missiles had been very successful in maintaining the carrier fleet's viability, something the TFX's naval aspect was supposed to complement.

Lockheed appeared a more solid prospect at the time than General Dynamics, as its airliner business looked to be buoyed by the dropout of that competitor, and its missile division was flush with the Polaris and other successes and up-dates. Not being a candidate for extinction made Lockheed a likely candidate for the TFX. Lockheed's carrier-based experience was ahead of it (the low-key Viking anti-submarine patrol platform), but its relations with the Navy brass were as good as General Dynamics', because Lockheed supplied missiles to the submarine branch as well as the Navy's shore-based patrol planes (converted airliner bodies) from 1939 to the Whiz Kid era to today. Lockheed had plenty of both large body experience, relevant to the bomber role, and supersonic experience, relevant to the high-performance aspect, but at different ends of the country. Lockheed's large airframe efforts were concentrated at its Marietta, Georgia plant leased from the government in 1951. Set up for Lockheed to build B-47 bombers under license from Boeing (while the Korean War raged, so did the Cold War), the plant later turned out airliners and military transports. But while Boeing had prospered despite the rejection of its proposal for the C-5A bid by successfully building its 747 airliner adaptation, Lockheed's own civilian jumbo jet, a separate design from its winning C-5A bid, ran into problems. Lockheed's executives got Whiz Kid help for this problem, as both Harold Brown and Cyrus Vance helped drain money purportedly for the C-5A into Lockheed's Georgia coffers, although the troubled civilian project was in California. This left them in fine shape when a Georgian later became President.

Lockheed's old California operation had more success concentrating on missiles and small or high-performance aircraft, such as the U-2 or the supersonic F-104 Starfighter, a big export success, and a victim of ubiquity and iniquity. The latter in German service had been labeled the "Widow-maker" by German leftists (Germans usually like to see the whole family wiped out), but remained in German service for more than three decades, an indication of some reliability. The F-104's main problem was Germany's nearness to the Soviet bloc and the plane's poor performance at low speeds -- flying fast meant risking border violations and being shot down, while flying slow was indiscrete with the Starfighter's little wings. Lockheed's follow-up effort, the 80-ton Blackbird super-interceptor, showed those in on the secret that the company could build stupendously capable planes with bomber size and range and matchless fighter performance, but it also showed that the TFX project's parameters were too wide, that bomber size and that for the carrier role were too far apart. Ironically, the TFX was later given the Blackbird's original designation.

From the potentially crowded possible field, four main bidders emerged, single companies or duos. The four became two, Boeing and the team of General Dynamics and Grumman. These were winnowed further amidst controversy to the single winning team, the combo of Ft. Worth's General Dynamics, for the two Air Force versions, backed up by Long Island's Grumman, for the carrier role. The selected design featured a swing-wing option, not previously accomplished on a production aircraft, and the most controversial feature of the project itself, otherwise attacked by political representatives of the losing bidders' districts as well as by trouble-makers generally. Political influence-peddling was charged, and deep suspicions were raised that the main contractor was from the Vice President's home state; Lyndon Johnson, sunk in that job's obscurity, was undoubtedly flattered that someone at least remembered him. Any winning bid would have been so attacked, because such charges are part of the ritualistic babble that passes for political discourse in this country's liberal dotage. The selection of a naval contract participant had in fact at least negated the initial bureaucratic impetus of the project, the Air Force's attempt to freeze out the Navy's usual builders.

Instead of the more exact swing-wing, the more pompous term variable-geometry wing was vaguely rolled out, for whatever reason. But well prior to the TFX, variable-geometry wings had been planned or used. Martin's B-51 project had swivel wings for increasing their "angle of attack", and therefore lift, on heavily loaded take-offs, while permitting a decreased angle of attack, and decreased drag, once the plane was airborne. Vought's high-wing Crusader carrier fighter had an analogous feature, a tilting mechanism in the plane's body giving more lift at low speeds for carrier take-offs and landings, and even for aborted landings (Vought's similar attack plane, the subsonic A-7, had a modified low-speed higher lift-to-drag wing and didn't need the tilt feature). North American's B-70 prototype had wings that drooped at supersonic speeds to reduce drag. Even Lockheed's C-5A had variable-geometry wings, but those were inadvertent and were eventually negated in their excess flexion by computer-controlled counter-pulls. And, of course, autogyros and helicopters had not proven practical until their rotors had been allowed to be flexible. The exception that soon proved that already well known rule was the Whiz Kids' billion-dollar Lockheed Cheyenne helicopter development project; rigid rotors enabled a small increase in a helicopter's usual massive drag, although at the cost of causing crashes. The swing-wing, not variable geometry, was new.

The more specific objection was that the swing-wing mechanism was excess baggage ("three tons of weight") used only for a couple of seconds during each flight. Approximately the same objection could've been made to landing gear or to carrier equipment, but those were traditional, and therefore not abhorrent to alleged progressives who praise "high-tech" in the abstract. The swing-wing in fact made sense for all three projected TFX roles. The sweptback position gave it the low-drag wing shape of a high-performance aircraft, for high speeds at high altitudes for long distances, as well as more compact storage for carrier use. The forward wing position provided more lift at low speeds and altitudes, useful for carrier operation, for cruising ability for the naval version's patrol role and for the Air Force's tactical short-field applications, although not for the long-distance low-level strategic bomb-run (semi-swept position for some speed in thick air). A swing-wing gave the project a slim chance of success, adding low-altitude performance and cruising hang-time to Vigilante-type performance. But the plane's combined size and rough operations criteria prevented the simple expedient of a lengthened nosewheel strut to increase wing angle and slow-speed lift, as was done with the Skyhawk and the Concorde.

Political critics of the TFX were from the Democratic left or from the states of disappointed bidders. Although the losing bids had also been swing-wing, that concept itself, not the TFX's roles, was decried. The swing-wing they denounced has gone on to be adopted for: first, Grumman's F-14, a carrier fighter project spun off by the TFX project when the TFX grew 15 tons too big for carrier operations (the Navy's alternative would have been to rip up the flight decks of its carriers to install heavier catapults, stronger arresting gear and larger and heavier elevators to haul the naval TFX to and from the hangar deck, tying up the fleet's strongest ships for more than a year apiece and running billions of dollars, to accommodate an overgrown turkey); second, North American's B-1, moved forward when the TFX's inadequacies for the strategic bomber role became obvious; third, the Soviet

Tupolev design bureau's Tu-26 Backfire bomber; fourth, fifth and sixth, the Soviet Sukhoi design bureau's Su-17 bomber (an early modification to the old Su-7 fighter's airframe), Su-19 fighter and Su-24 bomber; seventh and eighth, the Soviet MiG design bureau's MiG-23 fighter and its variant MiG-27 bomber; and ninth, a West European consortium's Tornado fighter-bomber. The swing-wing, around longer than the space shuttle, had even more chance to be imitated.

And what of the alternatives boosted by critics, the Boeing version with its thrust-reversing engines or the earlier rejected designs which featured a belly or back scoop for the engines? Thrust-reversers were in extended development for various vertical or short take-off projects, most notably the West German Kestrel/British Harrier. Redirecting propulsive airflow had begun with variable pitch propellors, such as those of Hamilton Standard, a component of United Technologies alongside Pratt & Whitney engines, Sikorsky helicopters and Norden bombsights. Lockheed's later Constellation airliners had completely reversible prop-blades, able to swivel on landing to help brake the aircraft or to maneuver it on the ground. Those also began a confusion of ground personnel, by making prop backwash or jet exhaust less predictable. Engines powerful enough to lift huge loads can also, when misdirected near terminals, blow cartloads of luggage and workers all over.

But thrust-reversers for jets such as the TFX were simply not very useful. On rough runaways, such as those demanded for the tactical fighter role, slowing planes could be over-taken by the clouds of debris blown up by their own exhaust, and their engines could be damaged by sucking in such debris. For the carrier requirement, the large size and high landing speed of modern jets, including those much smaller than the TFX, had long over-matched the capacities of raisable crash barriers once installed forward of flight-deck landing areas. Since then, carrier doctrine required forward clearance for landing, a feature made more realizable with angled decks, and that planes keep up power for a possible touch-and-go landing abort. The thrust-reverser offered no usable advantage for carrier take-offs or landings, and would have made crewmen blown overboard from already hectic flight decks far more likely with the more unpredictable exhaust direction. Unlike the swing-wing, thrust-reversers had no use in flight, high-performance or otherwise, and no relevance to the TFX strategic bomber version's low-level role. The weakness of Boeing's case, and its survival to the last round, are the best indicia of politicization, probably bureaucratic. The Whiz Kids wanted the weakest opponent for the General Dynamics/Grumman team at crunch-time; two subsequent Senate investigations finding that Boeing had been euchred just happened to precede the re-election bids of ranking member Scoop Jackson in 1964 and 1970.

As to the previously rejected innovative proposals, the Air Force opposed a back scoop for fear of stalls, and one has not yet been built for a production high-performance aircraft. The Air Force had also opposed a belly scoop for the TFX for fear that it might suck up debris from rough runways to be used as part of its tactical fighter role, disabling the engines. Only one plane has since appeared with a belly scoop, the F-16 day-fighter, one project generated by the TFX's failure, and more capable than the heavily compromised TFX actually built. Although adopted early by many foreign countries, the F-16 has crashed from unexplained engine failures, possibly as a result of matter being sucked into its belly scoop (with the same engines, F-15s have not been crashing). For that reason, and the lack of belly-scoop imitators, the F-16 is hardly a ringing endorsement of the TFX's critics, and its crashes have not generally been remarked by those so sarcastically scornful of the design work and alleged political influence of the F-16's builder, General Dynamics. Had North American built the F-16, Senator Proxmire would have attacked it.

As a Democratic politician (yes, despite media canonization, he **was** a Democratic politician), Proxmire tended to blame the Pentagon, military and civilian, and the contractors, while playing down the role of the top political leaders of his party for their negligent stewardship of Congress and the executive branch. When all is said and done, or press-released instead of done, the Pentagon and contractors are incapable of approving contracts without high executive authorization ("The buck stops here!") and congressional appropriation (the buck starts there); during Proxmire's extravaganzas, the buck got passed, quietly and deliberately, while the Senator became a star.

The process was remarkably similar to that which promoted Proxmire's fellow Wisconsin Senator, Gaylord Nelson. Nelson too had gotten raves from the media claque for the "environmental" Clean Air Act, whose built-in loopholes permitted major polluters to shoot their dirt into the upper atmosphere, making more air dirtier for longer, and raining acid onto the unbuffered soils and waters of wooded mountains and mountain streams. Trees and fish died, while Nelson went on to "double-dip" (never called that when liberals do it) as an environmental letterhead frontman. Proxmire too went on to double-dip, supplementing his retirement pay with media bucks for the spewing of his acid pollution. Proxmire was the Gaylord Nelson of Defense, and Nelson was the William Proxmire of Clean Air, the gold-dust twins of Wisconsin's Liberal Democracy, half-bright and getting it half-right. Proxmire's tirades against fiscal waste never extended to the federal government's surplus cheese program of which his Wisconsin was always the prime beneficiary (in spite of its notorious Fond du Lac), any more than Gaylord Nelson's environmental concerns extended to whey-dumping from the cheese factories, a potent water pollutant. Proxmire took full advantage of being considered a voice in the wilderness, distant howling not admitting a close examination of the specifics. Despite a pathetic

record of slander, error and aggressive ignorance, his shoddy carelessness was labelled integrity, so that he did not have to appear to campaign
for re-election, as the media did it for him, almost as if they were paid
to do so. But at least his move to the press has technically ended one of
the most despicable careers in American politics, the man who was not
the Real McCoy but the Real McCarthy.

The General Dynamics TFX was an expensive failure because it
tried to do too much, the insistence of the Whiz Kids. The concept was
flawed from the start, because strategic bombers had passed out of the
size range of carrier planes and of tactical fighters. In the case of
contemporaries of the different categories, of course, strategic bombers
had always been much bigger since their 1913 invention by Igor Sikorsky -- the TFX was a fools' errand from the beginning. As fighters had
grown, so had demands upon and therefore the size of strategic bombers.
The Vigilante had a low bombload and fairly limited range, long for a
carrier plane but short for a land-based bomber not carried part-way by
ship. Loading down such a concept with a swing-wing and a huge
bomb-bay meant far more weight, and the landing gear had to play
catch-up just for a long runway role. Belated attempts to deal with the
mismatched roles by improvised fixes during a truncated prototype process simply beefed up the plane but not its performance. Intrinsically too
small for a real strategic medium bomber, it became progressively more
mediocre for tactical applications, even as it exceeded an ability to use
rough fields. Increased weight did not make a better bomber, but it did
cut the plane's maneuverability, making it a poorer fighter while stressing the landing gear and structure out of the carrier and rough field
applications.

The actual TFX inadequately filled only two of the three design
roles, a supersonic bomber kept over the superior B-58 because of the
high-altitude fallacy and limited Pentagon imaginations, and a long-range
tactical aircraft, inferior in everything except range and payload to ten
other U.S. aircraft, committed to a NATO role. Long after disastrous
testing late in the Vietnam War, the TFX's long range, along with
foreign politics and the Reagan mania for including as many services as
possible in minor operations let the F-111 (nee TFX), flying from
Britain, into the 1986 Libyan raid. It could fly around France and
Spain, while 72 more capable F-16s were grounded in Spain because of
political cold feet by their base's landlord. Also because of their range,
F-llls were used in the Gulf War against some Iraqi targets, although not
against the distant Mosul region, where the Iraqi Air Force was still
extant. Blackbird interceptors were not there to escort them.

The strategic bomber role was occupied only partially by the
TFX, but still primarily by the aged B-52, kept in service as a subsonic
conventional bomb-bus, an electronics-warfare vehicle, a strategic bomber and a cruise missile-toting stand-off bomber. The supersonic B-1 has

supplanted the TFX bomber even further, with an underacknowledged Gulf War presence (media commentators on the scene did not recognize the plane, with its distinctive rear body-slung twin-engine pods resembling only the rare Concorde, at least one calling it a B-52, whose twin-engine pods are wing-slung) and there is on order one squadron of B-2 Stealth Bombers. Instead of one plane for the strategic bomber role we have three, the scheduling of a fourth, and the accomplished destruction of yet another, the B-58. For Air Force tactical use, the TFX joined the mass of supersonic aircraft already in service, of which the Phantom remained the most important, with others relegated to Air Defense (as designed interceptors some had little potential as fighter-bombers anyway) or to the Reserves.

To get away from long vulnerable runways, the West Germans simply mounted their "Widow-makers" on mobile rocket-assist platforms, but the U.S. Air Force was more procurement-oriented. First, the F-15, a twin-engine, high-speed, high-altitude and highly maneuverable fighter-interceptor built by McDonnell Douglas, was obtained. Although less capable than Lockheed's super-interceptor, the F-15 was completely superior to the TFX except in range and bombload. Although costly, the F-15 was sought by foreign buyers, as the TFX had not been (crash-prone, expensive, mediocre and difficult to maintain, only 24 were bought by Australia before the disaster had made front-page news; the Australians use their surviving TFXs as ocean patrol platforms for the Harpoon anti-ship cruise missile). The F-15, although much cheaper than the less effective TFX, had budgetary problems, so the single-engine F-16 day-fighter was obtained for American use and export. Congress was less obstructive toward foreign sales of the less capable General Dynamics craft than it was toward the superior McDonnell Douglas model, so superior Congress didn't buy more. Eventually, the Stealth Fighter, more of the former (good for bombing) than the latter, was also obtained, leaving the TFX, Phantom, F-15, F-16 and F-117 (equals F-17) Stealth Fighter all filling the same role, five for one.

The first spin-off from the TFX was a Navy fighter built by General Dynamics' erstwhile partner, Grumman. The F-14 became an immediate congressional whipping-boy, a target of congenital publicity hounds moved into open opposition to the country by the convenient accession of Nixon. Democrats were at least clever enough to avoid the obvious and inconvenient question of why the F-14 was necessary in the first place. Funding delays caused by congressional charges of unnecessary delays led to actual delays, the self-fulfilling prophecy in action, by people who wanted another quick and expensive put-up job like the TFX, to saddle the Navy with hundreds of duds as the Air Force had been. F-14 cost and size (15 tons less than the TFX) drew the ire of congressional hypocrites, and its foreign sales were only slightly more than triple the TFX's, 80 to Iran (inoperable by the Iranian Air Force left after the Khomeini purges). The F-14 is a superlative plane, as capable as the F-15, and it arrived in service just in time to become the platform for the long-awaited long-range Phoenix air-launched anti-aircraft missile, under development by Hughes for more than a decade.

As with the superlative but expensive F-15, the government sought a lower-cost supplement for the F-14, a Navy day-fighter equivalent to the Air Force's F-16. As with the F-14 and the F-15, the F-16 had been shaped by the Nixon-Ford administration, which had the general virtue of knowing what it is was doing. The Navy day-fighter was the F-18, and its final shaping was done by the Carter/Brown minions, the Whiz Kid revival. Instead of up-powering an analogue of Vought's old Crusader, light and with one engine, they added an extra engine, electronics and bombload, at least making the F-18 Harpoon-capable, but also making it an expensive and less capable version of the F-14; Navy carriers were saddled with two sets of airframe and engine parts for two high-performing fighter-bomber/interceptors. The regime which had eliminated existing and effective anti-aircraft missiles because they were "non-standard" was adding a non-standard fighter plane, expensive and less capable than the Phantoms and F-14s already in service. The TFX, shut out of naval service, had gotten its revenge in the Carter Whiz Kid revival. Three aircraft, the Phantom, F-14 and F-18, filled the role the carrier TFX was to have taken, which (counting the TFX and Phantom only once each) left the total scorecard reading, instead of one TFX for three roles, ten aircraft doing the TFX's job.

The TFX, in addition to leaving dozens of Air Force squadrons equipped with a lemon, left the door open for unnecessary additions to the American strategic missile force. Planned American bomber strength had made the whittling-down of the Minuteman force appear plausible, and the failure to achieve that strength made the addition of Trident and its enormous submarines cognizable, as it did the multiplicity of proposed land-based missiles and their development costs. The price tag of the TFX was probably in excess of a hundred billion dollars, and that in pre-Jimmy Carter hard money, the stunting of military capability, and the cost of the quick-fixes.

American defense would have been better served by keeping the B-58 in service, later adding the B-1, a real swing-wing strategic bomber, not building a new Navy carrier plane until the late 1970s (the Phantom was adequate for all of the tasks assumed by the F-14), adding the Northrop Tiger II as the Air Force tactical fighter, and cutting back on strategic submarines and their missiles. But the quick-fix was too tempting. Fortunately, we have learned since the TFX. We learned that liberals attempting by one program to shake out an industry would undo the process by their other buffoonery. Not only did the two TFX contractors survive, but McDonnell prospered by the use of Phantoms in the Vietnam War, Lockheed got the C-5A contract as part of the Whiz Kid mobility fetish, North American got space work via the New Frontier's Cold War Liberal space program, and the others all survived, if only through mergers, before programs dictated by the TFX's failures started to kick in and boost the industry even more.

We have also learned that Republicans can be at least temporarily seduced by the same nonsense of adapting the same body for grossly dissimilar functions. But the growth of stealth technology at least cut out the naval attack role, so that even if the Navy's stealth plane has been aborted, its separate existence may have prevented worse. The Bush-Cheney team, aside from cutting back the Reagan build-up, announced a new program for the 1990s, a new plane to fill three roles for the 21st century. Whereas the TFX, with its combination of Texas, California and New York builders against Boeing of Washington and Kansas and other disappointed suitors, aroused considerable interest and charges of political influence, the new program was far less controversial (possibly because there was no goal of an industry shake-out or a rival service purge, or possibly because there were only two real entries, the F-22 by the giant team of Lockheed, Boeing and General Dynamics against the F-23 proposed by McDonnell Douglas and Northrop, joint developers of the F-18). Remarkably, the trio's main states of operation (GD-California, Texas, Missouri and Virginia; Boeing-Washington and Kansas; Lockheed-California and Georgia) left it with the duo's home states blanketed, and their representatives largely indifferent to the outcome. The trio was able to enjoy the unambiguous backing of Texas, Georgia, Washington, Kansas and Virginia, cumulatively powerful and each the home state of a major congressional leader (but then, major congressional leader is a triple oxymoron). Of course, with McDonnell Douglas in trouble and with the curtailment or cancellation of Northrop's big meal-ticket, the B-2 Stealth Bomber, the losers did face extinction. But that was generally their own fault, the failure to control costs.

Only on isolated continents can an inferior design fill grossly differing niches; the world today is too close for the arms mandate to tolerate such mediocrity. If the Pentagon had ordered dinosaurs, they would have tried to start with one big model, making it for the three-fold role of giant plant-eater, armored dinosaur and carnivore, attempting to imitate the evolution of the types within one design. All dinosaurs, like all planes, had a common small ancestor, but have long since evolved beyond that commonality; the existence of discrete types with such gross dissimilarities makes a common mold idiotic. What the Whiz Kids did do was to shoehorn the Navy and SAC into a TAC proposal, in the interests of saving an entire "one billion dollars", about one percent of what the boondoggle program, with its quick-fixes and more programs to make up their deficiencies, ended up costing. The land-based bomber role was the biggest stretch of all, as the Vigilante itself had fairly short range (carried part-way) and only a small 5,000-pound bombload. With take-off swollen by another 25,000 pounds of bombs and five times the Vigilante's fuel load, the TFX goals moved well beyond fighter, or even fighter-bomber, parameters. But even after the program had been approved, McNamara was still down-playing the bomber role, referring to the aircraft's "dual" role in 1963 congressional testimony, for example. Even years later, with the program far over-budget and failing, his minions were referring to the TFX actually being built as primarily a fighter (which it never was), or sometimes as a fighter-bomber like the "F-105" (which it really wasn't), but emphatically not as a bomber (which it was, albeit a mediocre one).

Not being able to tell a bomber from a fighter, the Whiz Kids were also not going to be able to recognize the unsubtle requirements for carrier aircraft, and that adaptability only went one way -- a carrier aircraft could always be used from the land, but, since the end of the biplane, not the other way. Although the swing-wing superficially attempted to regain the biplane's landing and take-off advantages, it was still functionally only a straight-wing monoplane, and such with a land-based genesis had never proven carrier-adaptable. The Whiz Kids' 1962 "common inter-service reform" of aircraft changed just numbers and letters, not fundamental capacities. The Marines had already pioneered multiple-use aircraft, using carrier training and tailhooks to operate several squadrons per special prefabricated short cable-equipped land-strip -- forward restricted terrain, in small clearings and without massive landscaping, drainage and huge concrete runways. Edsel-maker McNamara just never learned that, although you can always park a small car in a big garage, you can never park a big car in a small garage. The Edsel, coming at a time when America was a huge net exporter of cars, was not a big seller abroad, but other tail-finned items were.

Chapter 20 - **Merchants of Political Merchandise**

The international arms trade is ever contriversial to liberals. The problem is the complexity of international politics and economics, which liberals over-emphasize when it is convenient for them or deny when their appetites demand simplistic formulas. Complexity, and the intractable givens of particular situations, are just not going to meet liberal demands for some ideologically palatable panacea -- Sisyphus, you see, just needed a boulder policy. This neurotic need for rigidity is one of several fetishes causing liberals to behave irrationally toward military, and virtually all, matters. Policies, planning and rigidity are also frequently military characteristics and, like most people, liberals tend to see their own flaws most clearly in others. Both military and liberal scenarios tend to reflect the most extreme cases, with the military having the onus to determine maximum needs and possibilities, while liberals usually are keeningly pessimistic in opposing their phobias and just as pessimistic in finding conditions so dark as to require the panaceas generated by their obsessions. Consequently, worst-case military scenarios of huge battles and massive deaths are emotionally and politically attractive to liberals, even though both such scenarios and liberals have a poor track record of actually predicting military events, including their own liberal disasters. But there is a liberal problem with just weapons themselves, a paradigm for the liberal problem with reality in general. Liberals have a problem with guns.

Insisting on the Second Amendment's right of the people to keep and bear arms gets one labeled a "gun-nut" by the media -- "people" is supposed to suddenly mean the government, a construction that would make the 2nd Amendment, much of the rest of the Bill of Rights and the Constitution itself meaningless. As noted, the Bill of Rights as a series of prohibitions upon government is anathema to Modern Liberals, who find freedoms "meaningless" without government hand-outs. The plain meaning of the written statement of America's government, a limited government, is a barrier to the apostles of unlimited government; lacking support for a constitutional revision, they have to lie. Aside from its selfish pursuit of profits and power, liberalism's co-dominant symbolic and irrational side expresses itself in attacks on gun-owners. Liberals' sexual inadequacies are paranoiacally projected onto gun-owners and their guns.

But phallic symbols are just that, symbols, of interest in revealing the patterns of neurotic thought. Guns, like telephone poles and skyscrapers, or even tunnels, are functional, not symbolic. Guns efficiently project small missiles, telephone poles carry telephone, telegraph, power and cable lines cheaper than burial, skyscrapers maximize floor space on expensive real estate, and tunnels can save ferry costs or more travel time on round-about roads or trackage to justify their expensive construction. The sexual symbolism of these things is irrelevant to such practical things, and mostly misplaced.

After all, squirt-guns are better phallic symbols than real guns, but only left-loony Sweden is so addled as to ban them, and toy soldiers, too (Surgeon-General Elders, a Clinton appointee and Arkansas native, has urged the same for this country). Selling or giving toys can get you a longer sentence than homicide in "the world's freest country". Profit and self-seeking keep Sweden exporting real arms big-time. Rather than risking children being warped by toys (never a problem in the real world), Swedes prefer seeing them dead. Or maybe Swedish weapons never kill civilians. But then in Sweden, according to statistical stereotype, ovens and tall buildings are deadly weapons, suicide vehicles in an otherwise progressive society. Such media-appointed conservatives as Pat Buchanan (employed by Jane Fonda's boyfriend) and William F. Buckley, Jr. (public television's lawn jockey) are hard on the case, so to speak, finding the cause of Sweden's high suicide rate in pornography and sexual permissiveness. The assumption of these Catholic boys is that Sweden's suicide stats are comparable to those of other countries. But the Swedes puff up their suicide rate by attributing large proportions of varying deaths to possible unacknowledged suicides. By that tactic, Sweden gets its high suicide rap (actually about the same as most other predominantly Caucasian countries) and some fire from ax-grinding conservative ignoramuses, while whitewashing most of its other social indices. Sweden's construction, housing, fire protection, highways and automobiles, medicine and hospitals and domestic gun use all look safer than they really are, because many accidental deaths are attributed to suicide -- "There is no such thing as an accident" in Sweden. Sweden pretends to be a safer country than it is, helping to export its pointless ideology of taxation, socialism and symbolic legal harassment, as well as "safe" cars whose domestic victims are labelled suicides.

Modern liberalism has more or less consciously left utilitarianism (the philosophy of usefulness), emphasizing that ideological shift while obtaining the goal of every ideology but of no truth, real and practical political benefits for itself and its adherents. The consequence is neurotic politics, part of a neurotic society. With the transparent slyness characteristic of troubled minds, giddy liberals try appealing to the gullible vulgarians who accept at face-value the folk rumor that the 23½-inch weapon contained in an FBI glass case is John Dillinger's penis, not the tommy gun he used to rob banks. American Puritanism did not disappear; rather, it mutated into New England liberal busybodiedness, with crusades and other fetishes purporting to enlighten the world, but providing no insight within.

For example, it has been an American belief since Webster that the word penis originally derived from the Latin *paene*, meaning almost. That is so psychologically deficient a discounting of male pride as to constitute a certain fallacy, so to speak; a man would not refer to his most prized possession as an almost. The official alternative is that the original word meant tail, another deficit; tail means tail, everywhere. Moreover, the older spelling used not "ae", but "oe". The origin of the word penis, or poenis, is far more cognizable in the earlier Greek legend of the Phoenix, one long available to the Romans. The Phoenix was the bird which grew, consumed itself in fire and then rose again from its ashes; the myth comports with the usual phallic requirements of a bird-like entity hotly rising, reaching a crisis and subsiding to rise again in its realm of reproduction. Compared to that, the sexual symbolism of guns is as forlorn and strained as other liberal mentation.

The logic of modern American weapons systems is rather simple; liberals try to evade it, high-tech being something to tout abstractly or merely frivolously ("high-definition television", the Quemoy and Matsu of the 1988 Democratic primaries, and not needing government subsidies to develop any more than did records, radio, or the original idiot-box), but to denigrate when national defense is involved. But the box is the proper gross conceptual device, both in the compound sense and for each particular level of a system. Different boxes may fit inside one another, but each type -- gun, missile, mine, torpedo, tank, airplane, helicopter, flying boat, warship, carrier and submarine -- has intrinsic operating characteristics, delineating its lines of profitable further development.

Despite rubbish about the military being hidebound, the aircraft was in massive use a decade after its development, the submarine shortly after it became a practical, if limited, weapon, and the tank in less than three years had spun off the self-propelled gun, the armored personnel and ammo carrier, the bridging tank and the mine-clearing tank. Such extemporizations were swept away by civilian peace-time budget cutters (for Britain, first Liberal Eric Geddes, made a knight, a general and an admiral within one year, the perfect resumé for the job, and then newly re-Conservative Minister Winston Churchill, cutting defense in his least autobiographed period) until they had to be rediscovered for the next war, Mr. Churchill's.

But cheese-paring is incidental to fundamentals -- the tank will always be limited in size and weight by the need for cross-country mobility (roads are easily blocked or targeted), as tracks and suspensions can only take so much weight upon their multiple moving parts. Any design will be a compromise, but with the prospects of a technical breakthrough rather remote, tank design is easily and safely made cheap, incremental and conservative without forfeiting a technological edge. Water admits greater tonnage (except when restricted by disarmament treaties or canal size, as in the super-dreadnoughts too big for Germany's Kiel Canal, McClellan's aborted Northern Virginia campaign or the modern ships too big for canals), but also exacts a speed limit. Air has the least load-bearing potential, but its low drag makes power increases yield greater dividends there than anywhere else, as long as there is no disproportionate weight or size penalty from new engines.

Rather than the air medium being the limiting factor, engine technology was the bottleneck, developing high power-to-weight engines and the related airframes to accommodate and maximize their power and fuel and cooling requirements. Piston engines had the disadvantage of reciprocal, power-wasting motion, each piston changing direction thousands of times per minute, which caused their replacement by turbines first in large warships, where weight was not initially a problem. Turbines spin in one direction, and there is therefore less wasted energy.

The turbine concept came to aircraft as the supplemental turbo-supercharger for piston engines and then jet-turbine engines, the main line of air-breathing engine development for the past five decades. Power was the key, and the streamlining which followed, and which had not really been profitable on less powerful models, could be understood by the old-timers. Britain's Gloster works went directly from its last biplane fighter to that nation's first jet fighter, an all-metal monoplane, with less airframe problem than waiting for the Rolls-Royce engines; design teams around the world abandoned old strategies as new power rewrote possibilities and expectations. Similar German jet break-throughs were later exploited by the Russians and, if not by France itself, at least by designer Marcel Bloch (builder of some pre-war clinkers, only partly the victims of underpowered French engines, his unimpressive record was obscured by a name change to Dassault), who got financing to assemble a team of occupationally unemployed German jet-scientists from Junkers.

As the cutting edge of aerial high-tech was engine power, America's jet engine industry became concentrated in its Northeast, with N.Y.'s General Electric and Connecticut's Pratt & Whitney taking the lead. And that lead was not because of political or bureaucratic wire-pulling, but because the competition (Curtiss-Wright, Westinghouse and Allison) was building more expensive, delayed and less capable products. The two companies whose products could cut it grabbed the market and grew, employing more people more efficiently; if more former government people were employed, it was because the hiring shingle was out instead of the company hatchetman. GM's Allison did eventually bounce back by producing effective large turbo-prop engines for cargo and patrol planes, and it is tying in with Saab, which used to buy its jet engines from Volvo, now being absorbed by France's Renault. This is a rare time: Swedish cars have signalled a turn.

The priorities of military development were in the post-war American sphere determined largely by technology. Where not much rapid progress was possible, as with tanks and surface ships, not much effort was expended, and product venues shrank in number and size. Capabilities that could be extended, as of the submarine by nuclear power, were rigorously pursued, even if the technical limits were easier to surpass than were intrinsic operating limits on the military use of the weapon made more capable, but not more useful. But it was aircraft and missiles which promised the greatest improvement, as well as being the nuclear-warhead deliverers; aviation survived the uneasy peace-time, with the overall number of companies remaining constant, although a few shifted their priorities and some prospered more than others. The institutional utility of the air lay in its appeal to all four services (the Army first in missiles, then in helicopters, which the Air Force was never really interested in), whereas tanks were only for the Army and Marines (leaving out two big services, the Navy and Air Force), while ships were only a Navy and Marine concern (also leaving out two big services, the Army and Air Force). Modern American arms exports have reflected the pattern established domestically by the services and their technological priorities, although that pattern has not held true for the ever controversial international arms traffic.

Despite florid rhetoric about merchants of death and arms races, the origins of such are never simply in the marketing of technologies. Things were clearer in the old days, when much of the world was held in the grip of colonialism, and hence a larger measure of law and order than we experience in these heady days of national liberation. The market for arms exports, such as they were, the airplane and tank lying in the future, lay mainly in two fertile areas of political disagreement, between newly independent Greece, and later other Balkan countries, and the Turkish Empire in Europe and Asia Minor, quarrels now wound down to Cyprus and the Serbs and their neighbors; and between seven South American countries, with Argentina, Brazil and Chile as the big arms importers (Peru had border disputes with Ecuador, Bolivia and Chile, while Argentina had a territorial dispute with Chile and rivalry with Brazil over the buffer states of Paraguay and Uruguay). Without such quarrels and their occasional wars, there was no worthy arms market in those countries. With tension, there was an export market for munitions, even battleships (much more easily traced than cannons or smaller arms). All five nations (A., B., C., Greece and Turkey) ordered modern battleships in the years before World War I, with the suppliers being Great Britain, on top by a wide margin, followed by the United States and Germany.

Britain built six battleships for foreign order, three for Brazil (the first two delivered, and the third bought by Turkey but never delivered), one for Turkey and two for Chile (both delayed, only one ever delivered to Chile). None ever saw battle action under foreign flag, despite the Chilean ship and the two Brazilians each being in service for four decades apiece. When World War I broke out, the Brazilian ships had already been delivered, but Britain seized the undelivered four (the two Chilean and the two Turkish orders, the original and the Brazilian default, the last having gone under the successive sea-change of names of *Rio de Janeiro, Sultan Osman I* and *Agincourt*). The completed three seized battleships fought under the British flag at Jutland, with one sent on to Chile after the war, and the other two scrapped under the Washington Treaty. The other Chilean ship, construction less advanced, was later converted to a British aircraft carrier, and was in heavy British Mediterranean service until sunk in 1942. Britain was an unreliable supplier, and its buildings profited mostly its own power.

The United States, by contrast, only undertook two projects. First, it built and delivered two Argentine battleships. Next, it built guns and turrets for a Greek battleship ordered from Germany. With war on, and the ship itself cancelled, the United States took full advantage, selling the guns and their four turrets to Britain, which armed four large monitors with them, and selling the Greeks two old battleships from the U.S. inventory. The U.S. turned out to be a reliable and opportunistic supplier; if not quite the full Titan that Britain was, the U.S. at least attracted Promethean hostility for its reliable deliveries. U.S. Argentine orders reached their destination but never saw hostile action, while the war-time extemporizations were bloodily used, long service for the monitors, action in the early 1920s for the Greek battleships in the lost war against Turkey and, for the ship which survived being scrapped, a sinking by German dive-bombers while trying to flee fallen 1941 Greece. Just missing by a few months the dubious distinction of being the first battleship sunk by aircraft in battle, the former *Idaho* was the only American-built battleship sunk by hostile action between the *Maine* and Pearl Harbor, and maybe the first ever.

The Germans had only the Greek order for a single hull, but failed to exhibit Teutonic efficiency in its construction or use. "Militaristic" Germany refused to use the nearly completed hull, and it was eventually scrapped after the war, Greece, with its two former American ships and losing a land war in Asia Minor, no longer needing it. Although the Greeks had shown good sense in having the Germans, with their as-yet unappreciated armoring techniques, build the hulls, Greece's decision not to buy German guns strikes propagandized hindsight as strange. But the arms of Krupp were not yet a hissing and a by-word among the world's morbidly susceptible. Germany's last wars, two generations before, had been fought by mobile, not heavy, guns, except for the late siege of Metz, after seven large French field defeats. The U.S., in contrast, had fought two naval battles and a siege in its Spanish War, its artillery, especially naval, overwhelming the Spanish, German-supported and even somewhat German-supplied.

The good old days of far fewer national rivalries and old technologies have gone. There are not only more weapons, such as tanks, airplanes, submarines and missile boats, in international commerce, there are a dozen more fires produced by modern decolonization. India-

Pakistan, divided Korea, China-Taiwan, Iran-Iraq, Israel-Arabs, Malaysia-Indonesia, Indochina, Libya against the world, Algeria-Morocco, Ethiopia-Somalia, South Africa-other former British colonies and Cuba against the world, as well as miscellaneous OPEC arms bingers (Venezuela, Saudis, Kuwait and Nigeria) and the Western re-armament of former Axis powers, have been added to the old duo of Greece-Turkey and the South American rivalries. Decolonization was destabilization, and the main cause of modern wars, from Serbia to the Polish Corridor to independent Iraq, Iran and Kuwait throughout the "Third World". New technology just changed the means employed in new quarrels as well as in the old ones. The international trend of arms exports held from the end of World War II, mainly surplus weapons at the beginning, into the mid-1980s, when the market softened somewhat (an OPEC slow-down from lower oil prices; Israel building its own weapons; embargoed South African weapons drying up as a supply bargain; and Iran's incompetent fanatics and Iraq's politicized military ceasing to flail each other with customary gusto).

In this modern period, the United States exported more than 15,000 military jets, and the Soviet Union a similar quantity (although a higher percentage were bombers). Britain exported many military aircraft early in the period, until its aircraft industry collapsed under governmental control and domestic disarmament. British aviation companies were squeezed into one large combine, much like the non-Ford automobile companies had been; labor stoppages became more frequent and serious, so that paralysis became endemic. In spite of, or maybe because of, government backing, the British seemed unable to initiate new aviation projects themselves. Even the small Harrier required West German participation to start up. Later, various consortia were begun with European partners for bigger projects, civilian airliners and military aircraft, the Jaguar and the Tornado. Saudi Arabia bought Tornados when Israel vetoed U.S. sales (thirty years ago, the Saudis had re-exported old British armored cars to Iraq, which nearly used those marginal items against Israel). Usually, France's Dassault is in third place for military jet exports, having sold thousands to pass Britain after 1960. The goals of most nations, except influence-driven Russia, were jobs, export earnings and the amortization of development costs of new planes. Since most aircraft were ordered at a building government's development cost (often otherwise half of the order cost) absent exports, building governments were enthusiastic supporters of early exporting, to recoup some of their development costs. The technological effort for new engine and airframe development was far more involved than for more limited technologies, such as ships or tanks, so there was much more to amortize; the U.S. government therefore favored U.S. aerospace exports, while opposing those of other new weapons.

American missile exports have been large in numbers and dollars, although the Soviets have exported more in sheer numbers, due to the ineffectiveness of their anti-aircraft missiles, and their early possession and export of effective cruise missiles, especially the Styx. America did promise Britain exports of the Skybolt air-launched cruise missile (in return for a Scottish submarine base), both countries hoping to give their bombers, B-52s and Britain's "V" force, an early stand-off capability to increase their utility in the modern era. Skybolt was an early Whiz Kid cancellation, to British mortification, but the British received Polaris missiles for their submarines in lieu of the Skybolts, and in return for the Scottish base. Only in the 1980s did the U.S. begin exporting cruise missiles in quantity. Prior to that, the effective American anti-aircraft missiles, the air-launched Sidewinder and Sparrow, the ground-launched Hawk and the sea-launched General Dynamics "T" and Standard series, were the most numerous, financially remunerative and best values for foreign buyers. U.S. missiles were exported for the same reason as American aircraft, Soviet missiles as Soviet aircraft, etc. Britain, early fading as a missile-maker, did not really export that many, being easily surpassed by France, and later by Italy.

In comparison with aircraft exports, American tanks sold abroad have been primarily war-production surplus, from World War II and Korea (the Patton and Walker tanks), except for emergency exports to Israel. The first American-built sales to Israel had been Shermans in the early 1950s, a drug on the world market, and then resale of Pattons from West Germany (with American permission) in the early 1960s. Only after DeGaulle's break with Israel in 1967, and Lyndon Johnson's preparations for the 1968 elections, did the U.S. become Israel's virtually only foreign supplier, to be repaid by having its sales to other countries bloced by the Israel Lobby. Emergency exports for Israel were taken out of low American inventories, and at a time of high inflation were valued at their lower acquisition cost, rather than their cost to American taxpayers paying for expensive replacements to inventory. Unlike American exports, tanks from Russia, France, Britain and West Germany have tended to be current production for export earnings, political influence and, in the last three cases, jobs. Russian exports have been large even in comparison to its huge Army and swarms of armored vehicles in service. The three Western European nations, selling more tanks than they kept for their own uses, were in the market for export earnings and jobs. Development costs for tanks being low, they were not a factor in exports, except for some European models produced solely for export.

International ship exports, in all three major modern categories, bear a far greater resemblance to the pattern for tanks than to that for aircraft. The U.S. has exported surplus warships and submarines to its allies and to South America, as has Britain and, to a smaller degree, the Netherlands and Sweden. Other nations had lost their navies, and the

Soviets wanted to keep their old ships; indeed, aside from being rewarded for being Hitler's ally and betraying Japan with the three Baltic nations and parts of six other countries, the Soviets got German submarines, rocket and jet scientists, six modern Japanese destroyers, an Italian battleship (*Giulio Cesare*, a namesake like "Tsar"), a British battleship (*Royal Sovereign*, a fine name for socialist solidarity) and an American cruiser from future Red-baiter Truman's boss, FDR (*Milwaukee*, an old socialist town).

The pattern of large (frigate and above) modern surface warship exports is vastly different from the traffic in reconditioned surplusage. Unlike many countries, the U.S. had a huge inventory of old ships, with its new construction moving to nuclear submarines and very large aircraft carriers, neither as yet ever export items. Smaller post-war American constructs were failures: the *Mahan* class large destroyers scrapped because of instability, and flimsy hulls; the *Dealey* class of sub-chaser replacements, swollen beyond the required size but in extensive foreign service due to American generosity (dozens **given** away to Norway, Portugal, Italy and France; a baker's dozen remained in lethargic U.S. service, but only two of those were sold to Latin America while the rest were scrapped); and the *Claud Jones* class destroyer escorts, four ships built thirty years ago and **given** to Indonesia in the early 1970s. Of the last 208 modern warship exports, the U.S. has had only 16, Russia leading with 57, Britain close with 53, West Germany with 26, Italy ahead of the fifth-place U.S. with 17, France and Spain with 13 each, the Netherlands with 10 and China and Yugoslavia with the balance. The 16 U.S. exports were of two classes more than 80% of which remained in American service (*i.e.*, they were not designed for export), the six of one class were from the Whiz Kid era, and the bulk of both orders for the ten were from the Carter Whiz Kid reprise. The Carterites also approved the sale of a third, purpose-built class, the four *Kidd*s, to Iran. When refused by Khomeini, the ships entered American service, beside 31 near-sisters built to a less well armed standard, the *Spruance*s. American boys got second best, while liberal Dems played the merchant of death game, with a minimum of adverse publicity, of course, because liberalism always lives down to its principles. At least Lend-Lease or some other sleazy euphemism wasn't deployed.

Of 284 post-war submarines sold, or produced abroad in co-operation with the recipient, 188 were Russian, 54 West German, 20 French and 14 British. The Dutch and Italians are planning to enter the submarine export market, abandoned more than 30 years ago by the U.S., when the Eisenhower Administration pressured Electric Boat to shut down diesel submarine production after an order of four for Peru had been finished (to run the "modern" American total up to eight, good for fifth, and last, place). Other nations got the business, and the world improved not a whit, especially the bureaucrats at the State Department's

Latin American desk, who had a gesture harmful to American interests to flourish against Chilean and Ecuadorian complaints about sales to Peru. Peru took its business to West Germany, as did Ecuador; Chile's submarine business went to the British. The U.S., spat upon by Israel for considering sales of tanks and aircraft to the Arabs, did consider opening up a new production line for diesel submarines, including exports -- in Israel. And that when Detroit's tank factory was about to be shut down while France got Arab tank business; while McDonnell Douglas, since in financial jeopardy, lost a huge Saudi F-15 order to a European consortium; and while Connecticut and Virginia have experienced pools of sub-builders, and while a half-dozen other U.S. localities have proved capable of producing diesel submarines in the past from shipyards still in business.

The third category of modern warships is the new one of missile craft, up to 800 tons. The type started with the decades-old elongated Franco-German *Schnell*-boats, the French making a torpedo-less copy, mounting the new guided anti-tank missiles first, then later larger missiles, such as the new Exocet, as the anti-tank missiles were moved to helicopters for ship-attack. The carrier-poor Soviets developed the much larger Styx, and the ships to launch it. The U.S., with cancelled cruise missiles, naturally long had none, and consequently no cruise missile boats to sell. Missile craft, in addition to direct exports, have seen the most rapid rise of new production lines around the world, as the boats are more within the grasp of lesser industrial nations than the high-tech of aviation or submarines, or the heavy industry of tanks or large warships. The Soviets, usually operating about 100 missile boats, have exported, directly or through offshore production, nearly 600. China is the main secondary source of both Soviet missiles (their Styx anglicizes to Silkworm) and boats, and both countries have set up further production facilities abroad. France, with usually only a scant three missile boats in national service for the past two decades (it mounts its own Exocets primarily in larger warships and on carrier planes), has been responsible for about 200 in foreign service, through a multiplicity of new production lines, the main secondaries being in West Germany (near where the old *Schnell*-boats were built) and Israel. The West Germans have built French-pattern craft for their own use and for export, setting up new lines in Turkey, Spain and Singapore, with Singapore's tertiary works apparently setting up a quaternary operation in Taiwan. Israel, building for itself since the French began courting the Arabs and tried to embargo Israel's missile boats, has also exported and set up a tertiary line in South Africa. Two other West European nations, with only Italy having six hydrofoils in its own service, have dominated the larger end of the missile craft market, with 26 sales by Britain and 17 by Italy. Even Norway, with 39 missile boats in service, has exported 16, to Sweden.

The U.S. backed into the missile boat business in a minor way via the usual suspects, the Whiz Kids. Small gun-armed patrol boats, the *Asheville* class, were built at the insistence of experts who insisted that the U.S. was neglecting small craft (not minesweeping or cruise missiles, just small craft for the sake of their size). An additional fillip was that the *Ashevilles* had gas-turbine propulsion, the first U.S. ships to have it, but too small to really need it. Possibly if there had been plans to use the *Ashevilles* as sub-chasers, such propulsion would have made more sense, but the ships were given no sonar, not even the small sets usually mounted in helicopters, or anti-submarine weapons, nor even helicopter-portable small torpedoes. Scorned by the deep-water U.S. Navy as had torpedo boats generations earlier, the *Ashevilles* were early foundlings, given away to a Massachusetts vocational school, the Environmental Protection Agency and foreign nations.

One *Asheville* ended up in South Korea, becoming the basis of a joint Korea-Tacoma effort making 24 more as cruise missile carriers. A Carter-era order from Saudi Arabia added 4 more of a larger class from a Wisconsin builder. During the Carter era, the U.S. and Italy persuaded each other to spend a quarter billion dollars apiece on six hydrofoils each, the American production order courtesy of Congress. Unlike his refusal to implement other congressional appropriations, Harold Brown went through with this one. The high-tech ships were extravagantly expensive, of negligible utility, and less capable than missile-armed flying boats would have been at a fraction of the cost. Brown blamed Congress, but Congress knew it was dealing with a spine of jello -- you do not worm your way up to be Secretary of Defense in a liberal Democratic administration by virtue of brains, character or backbone. The contract was in a sense a back-payment, for the hydrofoil builder was Boeing, the victim of the Lockheed Galaxy/Tristar funding scam perpetrated by Brown and other Whiz Kids during the old days.

The missile craft, as with the exported large warships, were built in Democratic strongholds, so politics did not have to enter into any of the decisions, they already **were** the decisions. But, of course, liberal Democrats are nothing if not inconsistent, clumsy even in patronage. Warship production in Democratic areas such as the shipyards of Quincy, Massachusetts, Brooklyn, New York, New London, Connecticut, Bay City, Michigan, Puget Sound, Washington, Philadelphia, Pennsylvania/Camden, New Jersey and Oakland/Alameda/San Pedro, California, and tank-making in Detroit and Cleveland, continued to stagnate as the U.S. government opposed most arms exports, except in aerospace. Moreover, the U.S. was actually subsidizing production of such items abroad, by giving away so-called offshore funds. The U.S. was not a merchant of death, a military profiteer, but rather a philanthropist, with motives as tangled as those of any other donor. San Jose's FMC, builder of lighter armored vehicles and gun turrets, escaped actual ban on most of its exports, but received far less government help than did the aerospace people.

To sum up the pattern of American naval exports, the U.S. has been responsible for 8%, 3% and 4% of world exports in the three modern warship categories, surface, submarine and missile craft. The American proportion for tanks was similar. At the same time, the U.S. energetically worked the aviation export market, selling nearly 40% of world military jets, and having other sales fall victim to the Israel or China Lobby when they were considered to the Arabs or Taiwan. Despite left-liberal charges to the contrary, American arms are not in South African service. There was a smuggled shipment of artillery shells, and some South African warships have cruise missile defense chaff dispensers, which throw out streamers of ultra low-tech aluminum foil strips. South Africa operates British warships and aircraft, French submarines and Israeli missiles and missile boats. The World War II shipment of American aircraft (Curtiss P-40 Warhawks) to South African forces fighting in the Mediterranean probably did not last out the war, let alone survive until the institution of *apartheid* in 1948, due to the pace of aviation change and the inadequacy of the particular model. Aside from the few shells and the aluminum foil, the largest amount of American-designed equipment in *apartheid*-era service was World War II Canadian-built Grant/Sherman tank chasses equipped with British artillery pieces. Should a Black leftist dictatorship arise in South Africa, there will doubtless be calls for sale on taxpayer-guaranteed credit or outright gifts of munitions by the usual half-gullible/half-hypocritical liberals -- "merchants of death" and the "international arms traffic" will fade away as rapidly as the $450 million dollars Carter sent to the Nicaraguan Communists, before they, like the American people, decided they could do without his sanctimonious drooling.

Of a similar kidney was the media drooling about sales of American arms to Iraq. The Iraqis had thousands of Russian tanks and other armored vehicles, Russian, Austrian and South African artillery, French and Soviet aircraft and missiles, Russian ships and had on order Italian ships and missile boats. Equipped with Italian-made American-pattern torpedoes and Italian versions of the Sea Sparrow anti-aircraft missile, these were embargoed at American urging. The result? A "scandal" about the financing of weapons purchases where no delivery took place, because of that same U.S. Administration that was supposedly "behind" the arms sales. The misuse of agricultural export subsidies? Why not end such programs entirely? What did reach Iraq from the U.S.? Some plans for new types of large long-range cannon, never completed or used, with the parts for the few planned ordered in Europe (the man largely responsible, Canadian-American Gerard Bull, is believed to have been murdered by Israeli agents in Belgium). Maybe artillery shells from a shipment smuggled to South Africa from the U.S., but those were 155mm, a caliber not noticeably in Iraqi service because not in Russian service. That was piffle compared to the massive Iraqi arsenal imported from other countries, and even miniscule compared to the American arms Iraq captured by overrunning Kuwait, a small lightly armed country with mostly non-American weapons, thanks to Israel.

Lacking a real American weapons traffic with Iraq since the overthrow of the pro-American government there during Eisenhower's tenure, the media's other charges involved sales of industrial goods, machines, metals and chemicals, all with multiple civilian uses. *THE NEWSPAPER OF RECORD* published a massive list of materials supposedly critical to Iraq's atom-bomb project, virtually **none** of which were available to **any** of the countries which had previously produced nuclear weapons; why Iraq needs such high-tech input to what is a fairly low-tech industrial process is liberally inexplicable. Interestingly, when such supposedly military things were bombed in Iraq, their media description shifted to civilian, pronouncing the U.S. guilty on two directly contradictory counts. But the media and the Iraqis were consistent, the Iraqis more so. They always claimed the materials were civilian, even when put to military use in Iraq, and they joined the media in consistently abusing the U.S.

The extent of American government interest in foreign aviation sales was demonstrated by the "Freedom Fighter" competitions, both won by Northrop with its Tiger and Tiger II designs. The purpose of the Freedom Fighter was to provide a cheap and simple aircraft to low-tech and financially strapped allies. But the Northrop planes had been so capable that many more advanced countries had bought them, possibly undercutting sales of more high-tech, and more expensive, U.S. planes. It took the Reagan Administration to say no to a third round, refusing to help Northrop by subsidizing the latest update, the Tigershark (Reagan had spoken at the 1972 Tiger II roll-out). Caspar Weinberger's acuity was borne out by successive crashes of Tigershark prototypes, with only one left to man the ranks of television commercials and other ads starring the plane, by companies seeking images of high-tech glamor and even reliability. Congressional supporters of American Tigershark acquisition tended to be liberals trying to look patriotic and concerned about high-tech and jobs. Most of the jobs would have had to be undertakers for the Tigershark pilots; to non-liberals, high-tech is something that works, not something to waste lives and tax money on.

The government is concerned about selling old equipment and new aerospace materials because the government and its bureaucrats care mostly about themselves. Since a government creeps slowly forward on its wallet, its most direct concern is with where the money is coming from, its departmental budget and what it can do to justify the next appropriation. Jobs and exports are fine items, but they are outside of the government, and the prospect of indirect revenue from the economic activity generated, taxation of the wages and profits made possible by sales of tanks and ships abroad, although certain, is abstract and far from more purely governmental and departmental concerns, too subtle to be actionably grasped by bureaucracy without the specific mandate to help expedite American arms sales. Sales to some countries, on the other hand, get automatic opposition from the State Department or Congress, who prefer to see other countries get the business generated by Turkey, the Arab countries, Taiwan, South Africa and South America. On the other hand, getting back a portion of the cost of old war equipment is the type of thing that brings in money, and looks good to congressional oversight committees, and passing along the cost of reconditioning work done by government arsenal and shipyard workers helped keep them on the payroll, and Defense's bureaucratic empire unshrunk, until the supply of surplus equipment gave out, anyway. In the meantime, revenue from selling old equipment was less taxing, and looked like initiative; but, in a bureaucracy, anything which looks like initiative is usually a dressy sort of sloth. The business equivalent would have been letting the factory close while selling inventory, not a sustainable proposition.

The more sustainable export mechanism the government was interested in was sales of new aerospace production. Once again, the primary, in fact the sole, government concern was keeping government-owned factories busy, and cutting the research and development costs of the high-tech input to all four services. By exporting expensive aircraft, as many as possible, the burden of research and development, as well as tooling costs, could be shifted to the foreign buyers, cutting the unit costs to the American services and helping to stay near budgets. Cushy financial deals took away some of the real savings realized, but that was from another agency, and the books of the services were kept freer of red ink than was really the case. That the high-tech research staffs of this country were being maintained and replenished (the latter more difficult as liberal education took off, and indoctrination replaced capabilities as a teaching priority) was an utterly negligible factor in the government's calculations, as were the overall retention of jobs and export earnings from the production involved. Amortization and assumption made the weapons in American hands less expensive to the taxpayers, but they occurred because the structure of government made it also somewhat easier on bureaucrats. Despite comical liberal pretenses of governmental largess and compassion, government cares mostly about itself; that is why it has such an unctuous band of salesmen in the liberals. Anything that anyone else gets is incidental, a trickle-down from the big feed-bag, and liberals have shown themselves to be hypersensitive to the spectacle of anything trickling down. Knowing how little escapes their own grasping, they project it onto others. Accusations that Republican programs benefit the rich and that only a little trickles down are absurd.

There is only one really rich person in this country, and that is Uncle Sam. Trouble is, some of the shadier relatives seem to have too much influence over the old man.

The intellectual incapacity of liberals to maintain perspective and distance from any affairs more substantial than publicity and campaign fund-raising soirees is stunning. From the Whiz Kids to Jimmy Carter to Gary Hart's airport whistle stops to announce "new ideas" (drowned out by jet engine noise like Reagan's helicopter noise) to Michael Dukakis and beyond, liberals love to yap about high-tech, jobs, the economy and "industrial policy", but cannot discuss defense matters without getting Proxmired in opportunistic twaddle, any more than they can discuss industrial policy without jumping straight onto the next ban-the-carcinogen bandwagon. Any sort of constancy other than ideological twitches, spasms and tics and self-seeking eludes these people. The budget is supposedly so complex that "the urge to understand everything is the path to insanity"; but the urge to avoid understanding is the closest liberalism comes to sanity. The lunatics make some effort to cover their tracks, but the effort is handicapped by their lunacy. The willful ignorance and inattention of liberalism is the freeway to waste and national decline. And when the level of performance is so low on military matters of life and death, and within governmental agencies, what hope when the issues are esoteric, such as economics and social policies, and the consequences of actions felt only very indirectly by cloistered bureaucrats and politicians? Liberalism demands ever more intrusive and expensive government, gives us bureaucracy and proposes to top it off with the next Jimmy Carter, or the next George McGovern, or the next Lyndon Johnson (or someone on all three of those knave-lengths, the current Bill Clinton). The next chapter is an in-depth look at one two-dimensional icon.

America Fifth: Post-Korean War Arms Exports (to 1986)

Warships:					Tank Rank:	Type
Surface	#	Submarine	#	Missile #	1. Soviets	T-10;-72(H)
Soviets	57	Soviets	188	Soviets		-54/55;-62(M)
Britain	53	W. Ger.	54	& China 600		PT-76(L)
W. Ger.	26	France	20	France &	2. Britain	Centurion*(H)
Italy	17	Britain	14	W.Ger. 200		Chieftain(H)
U.S.	16	U.S.	8	U.S. &		Vickers(H)
France	13		284	S. Korea 28		Scorpion(L)
Spain	13	(Italy and		Britain 26	3. France	AMX-30(M)
Dutch	10	Dutch enter-		Italy 17		AMX-13(L)
China	2	ing export		Norway 16	4. W. Ger.	Leopard/II(H)
Yugo.	1	market)		900	5. U.S.	M-48*(H)
	208					M-60(H)

Tank Key: L = Light (series); M = Medium; H = Heavy; * = Late Models.

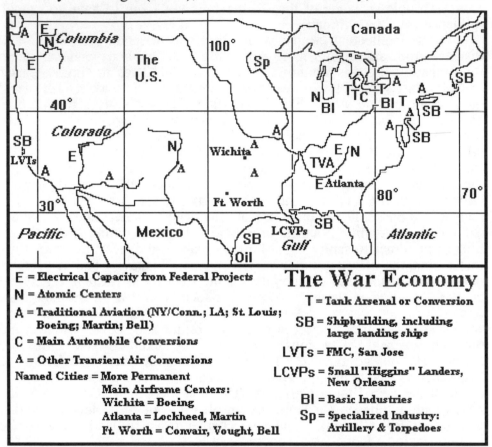

E = Electrical Capacity from Federal Projects

N = Atomic Centers

A = Traditional Aviation (NY/Conn.; LA; St. Louis; Boeing; Martin; Bell)

C = Main Automobile Conversions

A = Other Transient Air Conversions

Named Cities = More Permanent Main Airframe Centers:
Wichita = Boeing
Atlanta = Lockheed, Martin
Ft. Worth = Convair, Vought, Bell

The War Economy

T = Tank Arsenal or Conversion

SB = Shipbuilding, including large landing ships

LVTs = FMC, San Jose

LCVPs = Small "Higgins" Landers, New Orleans

BI = Basic Industries

Sp = Specialized Industry: Artillery & Torpedoes

Ft. Worth and Atlanta were also centers of corporate re-organization. Texas saw Bell's substantial relocation courtesy of war-surplus plant and manpower, mostly North American's, and the 1993 acquisition of Convair's local ops by Lockheed and of Vought by Martin. In 8/94, Lockheed and Martin agreed to merge, leaving high performance work spread over three states but subsonic work concentrated in Georgia.

The Hoover project on the Colorado, generating electricity useful for aluminum farbrication, helped aviation move to Los Angeles and later to the temporary hubs at Phoenix and Albuquerque, the latter cities' resulting growth enduring more than their aviation businesses. The New Deal Columbia and Tennessee projects were more useful for aluminum refining, which needed vast quantities of water in addition to the electricity, and to the heavy engineering of the atom-bomb project, concentrated at Hanford, Washington and Oak Ridge, Tennessee.

Chapter 21 - **Proxmire at Length**

For prototypical liberal drivelling, including drivelling out of both sides of the same mouth, look no further than Senator Proxmire's 1970 opus. Proxmire, or rather his congressional staff (royalties and salary source unspecified -- or maybe government employees dependent on a Senator's whims "volunteered"), set forth his rationales, conflicting or otherwise, for the beginning of his anti-military offensive. This co-incided with the birth of Modern Liberalism, with Cold War Liberal Democrats backsliding into pacifism and isolationism as the Vietnam War, and management of the Defense Department, shifted to the Repub-licans, courtesy of previous Democratic ineptitude. Proxmire denies the charge of isolationism, although his book front-loads reminders, from the introduction by then-Illinois Senator Paul Douglas to the mention of Montana's Mansfield. And what had been the big three states of isola-tionism? Proxmire's Wisconsin, from pacifism and German socialism and including favorite son Bob La Follette, Sr., fervent foe of the League of Nations, along with the Montana of Jeanette Rankin and the Illinois of Colonel McCormick's *Chicago Tribune*.

Remarkably, only about 1% of Proxmire's book dealt with the on-going Vietnam War, scapegoating it for having purportedly distracted the attention of Democratic icon Robert McNamara, when not using it to controvert a few of McNamara's pet weapons or to build up the resu-més of a few newly designated Modern Liberal heroes. Proxmire's own record of supporting war credits and the Gulf of Tonkin resolution is thereby obscured (in this period George Romney gauchely claimed that he had been brainwashed into Cold War Liberalism, Republican style). Proxmire's tacit silence during the horrific Whiz Kid abuses (not Kenne-dy's or Johnson's, or McNamara's, just the usual evil councilors) is ignored; Proxmire and the rest of his reborn yahoos had sat like stone images while their party was committing massive abuses, waiting until the opposition was in control of the executive branch before contesting them. Sympathizers may moan that Proxmire and company, including proxies Goodwin, Schultze, Stubbing, Fitzgerald, etc. had just been pro-tecting their careers, but people with careers can seldom afford the truth; when political conditions, not the merits, changed, so did their tunes.

While piggy-backing upon Eisenhower's "military-industrial complex" speech, Proxmire ignores its timing and import, that it had followed a campaign by Proxmire's party against a spurious "Missile Gap", coming just before the industrialist McNamara took office with his retinue of lawyers and academics (Ike's speech was written by an academic, of course), and also industrialists. Proxmire even blames the military for talk of "a missile gap where none existed" (page 72), when it was Democratic partisans such as himself.

Proxmire's method might charitably be described as McCarthy-ism turned against the nation. Consider how many howls of media anguish there would have been had Proxmire been searching for Communists or their sympathizers in the government. Consider also that the downfall of McCarthy came in his attacks upon the Army, under his own party. On the subject of the defense bureaucracy, just who did promote Peress? Or later, in the Kennedy Administration, who fired Otepka? Proxmire was sanitizing the left his party was moving toward, but the same disinfectant was hardly going to be applied to that party's new targets, the presidency and executive branch it had been voted out of. Nor were attacks upon military deficiencies going to be followed up by attacking the same deficiencies in Proxmire's proxies, and not just for resumé items. His weapons were association and innuendo.

Attacking a new Republican defense commission, for example, Proxmire called two insurance company executive members "defense contractors" because their very large insurance companies, complying with the investment diversification rules of the bulk of states, had slivers of their huge portfolios invested in stock and notes of defense contractors. Democrat McNamara, the prime mover for more than seven years, gets a specifically free pass from Proxmire: "The fact that Secretary McNamara was President of the Ford Motor Company, the fifth ranking military contractor when he took over at the Pentagon, implies neither an illegal nor unethical relationship." (page 140) Meaning, of course, that Proxmire, who prided himself on seldom missing a Senate vote, voted to confirm him, giving a different standard to a high appointee than to lesser blights. "In [McNamara's] case, he disposed of all of his Ford stock at a huge personal financial sacrifice." -- In other words, he sold his stock for money, and paid taxes on his profits. If Ford's common stock price was depressed, McNamara had been running the company!

Of course, Proxmire also attacks those with no defense connections at all as ignorant and likely to be misled, so that everyone, except himself and people who agree with him, are tarred as biased or ignorant. Proxmire himself, according to the book jacket, worked on Wall Street and at Harvard, a defense contractor, so his own bona fides are similar to those of the people he criticizes. Proxmire attacks movement between the military and the civilian defense sector, yet his two exemplars, McGee and Fitzgerald, respectively moved from two military services to a civil government job monitoring the military and from a defense contractor monitoring other defense contractors to monitoring the same contractor as an Air Force civilian employee. In McGee's case, Proxmire recites his resumé, including naval service (page 26), before puffing his record as a waste detector, and than reprisals against him for allegedly not having revealed his Air Force employment (pages 32-33), which Proxmire himself had earlier omitted (page 26), castigating the Defense Department for having deliberately faked surprise at McGee's earlier record. (Proxmire's citation of a Defense Department document is oracular, as it could have been referring to just McGee's previous Navy experience; McGee's reasons for having left Air Force employment, a usual resumé requirement, are not mentioned.)

Fitzgerald, "Deputy for Management Systems, Office of the Assistant Secretary of the Air Force" (page 35), is cited as a victim of bureaucratic machinations, although his type of position -- "the deputy assistant to the assistant secretary" (page 135) -- is otherwise described as for "those who combine lethargy with servility in a feudalistic system", a "Kafkaesque bureaucracy" (page xv) for "faceless" "time-servers" "who, long ago, made peace with their consciences and whose adaptability is their main virtue" in "stay[ing] on forever" (page 135). It seems to make a great deal of difference if one follows Proxmire's party line whether one is lionized or denigrated.

The subsequent refusal by "free spirit" "Ernie" Fitzgerald (page xv; CBS later portrayed the rogue bureaucrat as a cheapskate, the complete opposite of a free spirit) to take seriously his "meaningless job" (page 25) of examining "'the construction of a 20-lane bowling alley'" or "'[t]he other item ..., which [he] ha[d] not yet looked into at all, ... the problem of food service cost, that is, high cost in our mess halls.'" (page 35, Fitzgerald testimony before Proxmire's Subcommittee)? This bureaucratic spurning of an assigned task is vintage time-serving arrogance. Proxmire was willing to see "reviewed" "abuses" in "PX's and commissaries" (page 236), "the disproportionate amount of our resources the military services spend on marginal luxuries. This includes the maintenance of post exchanges, commissaries, ships' stores, officers' and noncommissioned officers' clubs, expensive jet planes assigned to generals who could travel by commercial airline on routine business, and similar items." (pages 1-2) There must be some metaphysical distinction in there somewhere, to leave out bowling alleys and messhalls, not to have someone whose praises he sings do the job of looking into their abuses. The difference is that between Fitzgerald's assignment and Proxmire's book there had been some scandals and publicity; the area that was suddenly "hot" had to be denigrated in specific retrospect to lend "Ernie" some lustre. (Several years later, working in an Army messhall near another being daily pilfered, the author notified the Army that the food storage area was infested with insects, of which he collected 35 different varieties (some may have been larvae), taping them to a piece of cardboard; for his efforts, he too was doused with insecticide.)

Proxmire's recap of history is similarly confused. He attributes World War II training in Southern states to the seniority of Representative Rivers, who took office only in 1941, after most of the bases had long since been established (the Civil War, Reconstruction and the Plattsburgh Camps of WWI "preparedness" hysteria). "When [American servicemen] were assigned to duty in Alaska or fought over Western Europe's snow-laden ground with Patton or Bradley in the winter of

1944-45, their curiosity about why they were trained in the South to fight wars in the cold must have been aroused. Climate had little to do with it. Seniority in Congress did." (page 109) Seniority in Congress didn't cause the fleet to be based at Pearl Harbor, because there were no congressmen from there until twenty years later, nor was California a political power when it became festooned with bases.

And the story of Southern training omits the glib confidence of FDR's Administration, convinced it could whip the U-boat menace in thirty days and that it would be in Berlin by Christmas of 1944. The first U.S. ground troops fought in the Philippines, New Guinea and Guadalcanal in the Pacific, and in North Africa (you know, the Sahara Desert) and Sicily in the "European" Theatre of Operations. Southern training was more helpful than harmful. Most American operations were predicated upon amphibious landings, and therefore good weather, making cold weather training a low priority. Most veteran units under "Patton or Bradley" in 1944-45 (all of Patton's troops, including Patton, were under Bradley) had been withdrawn from the Mediterranean in 1943, and received colder weather training (good weather was unavailable) in England up until the summer of D-Day. Why no training in Alaska? It was a war zone. Cold weather training for World War II did take place, in winter, at such locations as Forts Dix, Devers and Harrison and Camp Drum (formerly Pine Camp, becoming Camp Drum after the 1942 fall of Fort Drum, an island remodeled to resemble a concrete battleship in Manila Bay), in the American North. Only later, with semi-permanent commitments in Central Europe and Korea, did cold weather training become a higher priority.

The standard Proxmire advances for contemporary bases is similarly fanciful, if more Utopian: "Do we need [our military bases] for the purposes for which they were originally established?" (page 222) -- is the criterion, when the proper response is that they were established as military bases and still are, and we still need military bases (including for various types of weather). The proper economic measurement is the cost of alternatives, including for some foreign bases that are subsidized by foreign governments and for some domestic bases with little alternative economic utility. The bridge between the historical and the era of Proxmire's book was the McNamara (Kennedy-Johnson) regime. But charges from that era are similarly defective. "'In the war game rules and around the conference table,' [former Kennedy honcho Goodwin] said, 'we [Whiz Kid theorists, not White House aides] developed our options in the name of flexibility -- amphibious forces, airborne forces, helicopter forces, special forces -- seemingly unaware that when you have the ability to do something you will become powerfully tempted to do it.'" (page 128) What the New Frontier shriekers about the "Missile Gap" were doing was moving toward, not away from, the simplistic (Proxmire) view of the world as islands about to toss missiles at each other. But, of course, the amphibious forces, airborne forces and special forces (Rangers and other fatuous Commandos) were largely developments of World War II, Army helicopter mania was a product of technology and its incorporation into the American military organizational matrix after 1959, and the Eisenhower Administration had seen the first amphibious helicopter carriers. The McNamara regime merely gold-plated non-nuclear items eclipsed in public attention by Missile Gap hysteria. Nuclear delivery remained the priority, and even though its ability was constantly being raised by massive multiples beyond Hiroshima and Nagasaki, no one became "powerfully tempted to do it", possibly because they thought they might not be able to get away with it.

Virtually all of that capability, conventional or nuclear, was achieved through Eisenhower-era programs already in operation, especially "divisions, airlift capacity, fighter squadrons, ... the increase in numbers of both strategic and tactical nuclear warheads, the submarine program, and in almost every other way" (page 127); the exception was new follow-on conventional warships, instead of nuclear-powered, to escort the aircraft carriers Proxmire elsewhere condemns as useless (the 8 anti-submarine carriers, page 237, which Proxmire advocated spurning in favor of, among others, "land-based patrol planes") or vulnerable or costly (the bigger and more modern carriers, pages 85 and 193). McNamara did increase airlift capacity with jets (the Lockheed C-141) and then turbofans (the same company's C-5A, which became newly "controversial" under Nixon largely because of Proxmire and company), by replacing most old prop haulers and many turbo-props from the Eisenhower regime. But that program, although making twice as speedy planes with slightly more capacity, did so at high monetary and procurement costs, and at the cost of agitating anti-defense loonies, including Proxmire with his hypocritical praise of higher airlift capacity.

Although Proxmire extravagantly praises McNamara's purported establishment of a "combat-ready" military (page 127), after eight years of McNamara he found it "'unable' to respond to a major crisis" (page 6); combat yes, a major crisis no: "we are incapable of defeating small guerrilla forces in the jungles of Asia" (page 5) but we are "combat-ready" (page 127). But then, these may just be echoes of Proxmire's ineptitude -- we may give "a blank check to the military" (page 5 and the title to Chapter 5, pages 48-75), but the contractors and the Pentagon "deliberately lie about the cost" of weapons (page 7); why does someone with a blank check need to lie? "We have heard cliché after cliché" (from the Pentagon, namely such purported clichés as "'striving to do better" and "dedicated to cutting waste", but "[w]e need someone to lay down the law, pound the table, crack heads together" (page 227), etc.; it is *Proxmire* spinning out the clichés.

The confusion is partly one of quantity: Proxmire has two left feet, and types with them. There is the listing of American defense assets at the time, including "423 warships and 17 carriers,... 15,327 Air Force planes in 72 wings, of which 21 are strategic [and] 43 tactical..... Additionally, there are ... 41 Polaris submarines ..., 646 nuclear-armed strategic Air Force bombers, numerous medium-range missiles and bombers deployed on the periphery of the Soviet Union and China as deterrent forces" (page 11). Except that the 41 submarines were already counted in the 423 warships, the 646 nuclear bombers were already counted in the Air Force strategic wings, and the other "bombers" were already counted in the tactical wings. There were **no** medium-range American missiles at the time, just the submarine-launched and intercontinental missiles already mentioned. The 72 combat wings of the Air Force included far fewer than 15,000 aircraft, with the balance committed to transport and training, support roles, not combat roles.

The figure of 17 carriers is interesting, as Proxmire elsewhere asks "What cause is served by adding a fifteenth attack carrier" (on page 85, in the context of two other projects that had also been deferred), while "[w]e have fifteen attack carriers" (page 193); $15(14?) + 1 = 15 = 17(15?)$. Interesting, but then "[t]he eight ASW (anti-submarine warfare) carriers ... should be abandoned" (page 237); $15(14?) + 8 = 17$ (22?). Recall that Proxmire's predecessor Joe McCarthy was accused of a "numbers game" in describing Communists in the State Department. Communists, and they are not yet extinct, are quite fond of euphemisms, protectively colorizing themselves with the patina of the pinker hues they embrace or damn when convenient. Aircraft carriers, each about the size of the Empire State Building, are not as easily disguised. An accurate census is seldom a problem. And the carriers, although supposedly "sitting ducks for modern missiles" (page 85; more than 20 years later, in 1991, an elderly American helicopter carrier was indeed struck by a missile; some cans of paint were the only casualties), are part of America's "ability to strike back at an enemy so audacious as to strike first. With ... aircraft carriers from which planes can fly" (page 92; tautology amidst contradiction). When it comes to carriers themselves, cut them because they're allegedly vulnerable, but meanwhile use them to justify the throttling of other weapons.

Although affecting to be a partisan of missiles and the Cold War, Proxmire's heart just wasn't in it. He is surprised that, at North American's aircraft plant, "[i]nstead of an easy-going, fun-loving place...., [s]ecurity was tight." (page 171). How unpleasant for such "free spirits" as "Ernie" Fitzgerald! Proxmire himself would ostentatiously reject access to secret documents, so as not to be bound by pledges of secrecy. But it is hardly surprising that a factory doing defense work with 30,000+ employees would be highly organized and security-conscious; what uproar might have ensued from some publicity-hungry Senator had it not been! But then, Proxmire does affect anger at the less than

1/3 of 1% former high-ranking military officers employed there. Who could possibly want people with military experience, used to supervising from hundreds to tens of thousands of people, working at a huge defense factory?

And Proxmire affects some knowledge of more than just the micro-economics of huge factories and projects, the structure of whole economies and their capacities to support defense work. But it is the usual confusion. Obsessing upon Soviet Russia and Communist China, in the apparent belief that the U.S. possesses military forces only to deal with those transient menaces and with no others, Proxmire finds that "Russia under Stalin followed the course of building up investment at the price of consumption. The price paid in human terms was excessive. [But the price was being paid on Stalin's terms, not in human terms.] On the whole, the policy was self-defeating. And ..., China under Mao followed the same policy with the same disadvantages to efficiency and initiative." (page 188). Investment is bad when Proxmire wishes to belittle opponents who have invested heavily. But when the U.S. is being scoped, in the guise of a universal statement, the standards change: "In the long run, resources poured into the military tend to limit a nation's fundamental military capacity. Only those funds and investments that greatly broaden the base of an economy ultimately strengthen that economy." (page 185) In other words, investment is bad for the enemy, but not for us, especially when we define investment as liberal social programs, as an alternative to a strong military.

But if the Soviet and Chinese Communist economies were so weak, why shouldn't we have challenged them in a flat-out arms race which they couldn't have won, when "even their best efforts to build superior military power can be met and matched by this country with a smaller relative sacrifice", when, in the Soviet case, for example, "the end result would be a weaker economy, a Russian worker poorly motivated and, perhaps, dangerously alienated, an even greater lag behind the West in capital equipment, and an agriculture that continues to absorb nearly a quarter of productive Soviet manpower" (page 191)? One partial answer is that as command economies the Communist countries were in their element in a military race, their system not really allowing a civilian economy capable of functioning.

Another answer, from the American side, is that the Whiz Kid calculations didn't allow for these relative strengths and weaknesses. Instead, the calculations were narrowly military, save for some politicization by liberal ideology. This introduced a desire to pull American punches in the arms race, cutting Minuteman procurement from 3,000 to 1,000, for example. Their research and development was finished, a production line was expensively set up, and then actual procurement was cut, raising the relative costs of R&D and tooling by three times. With American strategic force thus weakened, other projects --- the B-70, the

B-1, Poseidon, Trident, MX and Midgetman -- were called forth, more or less slowly, to make up for the Minutemen forgone.

To Proxmire, the problem was also one of belittling the Communist military threat, after having focused on it to the exclusion of all else. Denial of Soviet carriers became paramount -- "The Soviet Union has ... not a carrier" (page 193) -- even though its first was being laid down as his book was published. The Soviets were building a supersonic bomber? Just deny or denigrate in the usual mish-mash of tautology and confusion. First, deny the existence of the threat: "one of the great Pentagon rationalizations brought out of reserve whenever military judgment is challenged", "the 'scare-the-hell-out-of-'em' syndrome", which "created a Russian long-range-supersonic-bomber threat where none existed" (page 72), the Backfire bomber. Except that it existed, and Proxmire had already admitted much of it! "[T]he Russians are testing a new F-111-like, swing-wing bomber.... The Russian plane is a medium bomber with a limited 2,500-mile range. It raises more questions about the efficiency of our intelligence than it threatens the security of the United States." (page 71) The Russian plane, freed of the Whiz Kid confusion foisted upon the American TFX with the demand for two tactical fighter roles, had been large enough for a strategic role from the beginning, with a range 50% greater than that admitted by Proxmire. It is notable that, even after the TFX fiasco, Proxmire did distinguish between the F-lll, repeatedly referred to as a fighter in the Whiz Kid tradition of dissembling, and its nearly identical bomber version, the FB-lll (pages 69 and 207), but disingenuously choose to refer to the Backfire as an F-lll, rather than as a designated FB-lll strategic bomber. Combining range, cruising ability, sprint speed and payload, the huge Backfire became a Russian naval patrol bomber, an expensive weapon diverted to meeting the threat of those sitting duck American carriers, while the Soviets were slowly building their own carriers, to go with the bomber which Proxmire denied or belittled, depending upon his mood.

Proxmire uses legal and governmental standards with the same selective hypocrisy he mines economic concepts. The military, and laws governing it, are treated with a specifically constitutional standard, even with the conservative standard of original intent (page 110) misapplied to statutes (Congress is simply too careless with its language and with the constitutionality of its enactions to be taken seriously by anyone except an ideological opportunist). The money that Proxmire saw wasted on defense he wanted spent on such items as the Job Corps, Head Start, etc. etc. One cannot look at the constitutional basis, the original intent, for such programs, simply because there is none; they are liberal patronage, pure and simple, and hence "uncontrollable" (page 78) spending, according to the then-Chairman of the Congressional Subcommittee for "Economy in Government".

And, of course, there are the usual semantic twists, "military budget requests" versus "domestic needs" (179), which even-handedly would be military needs versus domestic needs, or military budget requests versus domestic budget requests, or even constitutionally mandated military responsibilities versus corrupt patronage dressed up as compassion. Although the military budget is only part of the federal budget, the problem is supposedly not government spending as a whole but "the sheer size of the military budget.... almost impossible ... to comprehend" (page 91); to Proxmire, the politically expedient part is greater than the whole. If Fitzgerald called defenders of government waste who talked about jobs in defense the high priests of waste, Proxmire, just wanting "jobs" (page 87) without **any** input to defense, was the pope of liberal waste, speaking *trans mitre* as usual.

Proxmire's contractual standards of performance are similarly misplaced. Even carpenters, plumbers, mechanics and repairmen are not usually bound by their estimates, and they deal with the routine, simply because taking the time for an estimate would be a diagnosis that is part of the expertise they are selling. For large projects on the cutting edge of new technologies, the uncertainty is much greater. One hates to compare political and legal systems, but **even lawyers have better faith than does Proxmire**.

The double-talk continues with Proxmire repeatedly criticizing the "abandonment" by the military of various missile projects. But most he names failed during development, with the rest replaced by better models (early Sparrows, Polaris and Minutemen; Atlas and Titans; and Thor and Jupiter IRBMs respectively replaced by advanced models; by solid-fuel missiles; and by ICBMs); or by ideology which proclaimed high-altitude aircraft obsolete, and therefore not worth defending against (Army Terrier, Air Force Talos, Nike-Ajax and Nike-Zeus); or by premature development (a rash of American cruise missiles before electronics had advanced enough to make them reliable). Proxmire believes that cruise missiles had been abandoned because "they were 'air-breathing' ... [and] incapable of leaving the earth's atmosphere" (page 66), once again tautologically obvious, by definition (space-going military ballistic missiles evade Proxmire's mania about civilian space religiosity). But he also theorizes that the military is incapable of abandoning failed projects, which supposedly "just keep rollin' along" (page 81), when he has already listed dozens that were, his word, "abandoned", "abandoned", "abandoned", "abandoned", "abandoned", "abandoned", "abandoned", "abandoned", "abandoned", "abandoned" and "abandoned" (pages 65-66) by the military, despite the presumed power of the munitions industry (Proxmire's prose merely summarized a chart "furnished by the Pentagon", according to Seymour Melman).

In the high-altitude missiles case, his own party had done most of the damage, so that the missiles had to be described as defective. But the Talos, Terrier and the Nike series, which also included the cancelled Nike-Hercules and Nike-X, were not only effective in shooting down aircraft, they even had an anti-ballistic missile capability. There are multiple chances for a defective or uneconomical weapon to be abandoned, because weapons procurement is hardly the on-going process Proxmire attempts to point it out to be. Peace-time production runs are limited to fleshing out the desired number of units, and sometimes fewer (as in 31 fewer C-5As, later necessitating expensive retooling for the Reagan-era C-5B). Nor are all weapons kept as additions to strength, because there isn't sufficient manpower (old prop cargo planes were recycled for their aluminum, for example). That is how we went from a 900-ship Navy to a 423-ship Navy in the supposed heyday of the military-industrial complex.

Contrary to Proxmire's proxy Schultze (page 94), we **have** cut down the number of planes as their size and power has increased, going from tens of thousands of prop models to thousands of early jet models to the high hundreds of early supersonic models to the low hundreds, or even lower, for the less dramatic jump to later supersonic aircraft. And if the number of carriers declined more slowly, due to their durability and the slower pace of ship improvements, their plane-loads decreased. The *Midway* started with 145 prop planes, had fewer with early jets, even when enlarged with an angled deck could handle only 85-90 of the large later jets, in 1979 carried only 54 aircraft on an extended Indian Ocean cruise (the last was due more to the absence of American bases in an area when the U.S. had old alliances, new enemies in Iran and a new perceived vulnerability in the Persian Gulf) and as a training carrier will carry none of its own planes.

But effectiveness, presumed or actual, is just a red herring, albeit an important one for deceiving the public. To slander successful aerospace projects, Proxmire, through a bureaucratic proxy named Stubbing, compares the reliability of their "High Risk" (page 61) electronics against contract specifications. As a result, General Dynamics, making planes that flew fast and reliably, with long range and large payloads before the Whiz Kid blight, is criticized for "seven dubious results out of seven starts" (page 63), because some minor electronic gizmos needed replacing more often than expected. Meanwhile, North American, builder of the dangerous F-100, gets higher marks because of reliable electronics (pages 62-63). Evidently, plane crashes did not count as failures or even as a "central fact" (page 64). In developing new items, specifications are no more than goals, hopes and prophecies; the odds of actually achieving all particulars are infinitesimal. More realistically, some goals will be met, some will be passed, and others will not. A lower level in some parameters might be more economical (we have had more recently the "scandal" of expensive and overly durable coffee urns for transport aircraft, for example). In the military, focusing on minutiae is called "gold-bricking", wasting time. If the vehicle has a flat tire, change it, don't blame the vehicle.

Through yet another proxy, Richard Goodwin, Proxmire presents what he calls the view from the Left (*i.e.*, a Kennedy Democrat), that military effectiveness is bad, because strength might cause us to overuse the military. (Some of Proxmire's confusion is just carelessness, with Goodwin described as a "former Kennedy White House aide" on page 127, and "a speechwriter for President Kennedy" on page 133; was he so important he has to be described twice, or so marginal that his previous intro was forgotten?) And the political alliance which was challenging American defense included all such leftists, people opposed to defense itself. Proxmire himself straddles this dichotomy, taking several sides as usual; through the proxy of another congressional committee, he affects being incensed at the military's failure to respond to North Korea's capture of an American ship and its shooting-down of an American plane (pages 5-6). His solution to this military weakness? Cut the military and its commitments -- "is it our responsibility to be able to fight *simultaneously* a NATO war, a major war in Asia such as a Red Chinese attack on Southeast Asia, and a minor *contretemps* [no pun intended, this was another decade] such as that which occurred in the Dominican Republic?" (page 95) Apparently not, for "[f]oreign policy should be returned to the province of the President and the State Department.... [so that the] annual posture statement [introduced by McNamara to Proxmire's praise, pages 127 and, via Clark Clifford, 203] should be presented to Congress by the Secretary of State" (pages 127 and 223, echoing a similar sentiment quoted from Schultze, page 117).

All foreign military commitments binding upon the U.S. under the Constitution (not the part quoted on page 110 by Proxmire) have been made by the President and/or the Secretary of State with the consent of Congress (the House through appropriations, and the Senate also through confirming treaties). The military is the means of meeting those commitments which are military in nature, and presenting the statement of military means through an official dealing with diplomatic ends is rather backward. It's the sort of thing we do with military "peace-keeping" listed under the State Department budget. The Pentagon makes no commitments, while State doesn't meet any.

But, of course, while Proxmire suggests the U.S. is over-extended, while denying his isolationism, there is no attack on Democratic verities -- the U.N., Yalta or Israel -- and the extent to which these have mediated American commitments (by the President, State and Congress, **not** by the military). Proxmire rages at the C-5A, but shortly afterward it was used to funnel arms to Israel when Nixon chose to honor a commitment from LBJ's stillborn re-election campaign. Proxmire also rages at foreign basing and the Navy's carrier and amphibious forces, but the decisions to divide Korea and to defend the South were political, Truman's response to the North's invasion, not naval (or even diplomatic, as both the State Department and the Republicans' diplomatic spokesman had written off defending the South before the invasion). The Navy's left-over rump in those areas was barely adequate to stem the first North Korean offensive, let alone to have handled major wars in Europe or Asia. Proxmire graciously admits, on page 4, that "we" cut the military too deeply after World War II, but he doesn't admit that some of the cutting was of money voted by the Republican "Do-Nothing" Congress and then impounded by the Democratic President Truman.

Obviously, improving bases and forces was necessary to meet later commitments, including such sudden ones as the North Korean provocations that Proxmire used, again by proxy, to woof at the military's inadequacy in meeting. Ships do not move at the speed of light, and the type of military force that Proxmire affects to favor, nuclear-tipped strategic missiles, are a limited option and one that invites retaliation in kind. In the case of the seizure of the *Pueblo* that Proxmire affects anger at (page 5), its sister ship's sinking in 1967 by the Israelis had been followed by a carrier-launched nuclear strike recalled by President Johnson, a political decision ruling out a response that the military had been prepared to finish carrying out. The extended political response was to mute such automatic military responses, making North Korea's otherwise lunatic games of chicken relatively risk-free, while endangering Americans, just as deeming South Korea outside of American defense commitments in early 1950 had encouraged the North's earlier adventurism.

Proxmire's own bias, to blame the military and selected bureaucratic and congressional villains while shielding his party and its national leaders, was aided by the advent of A. Ernest Fitzgerald. Fitzgerald came to Proxmire in early 1968 with tales of misfeasance on the C-5A project "since early 1966" (Fitzgerald, 1972, page 291); Proxmire sat on the information until his party lost control of the executive branch, and then began using it as part of the flowering of Modern Liberalism, partisan attacks on the Republicans for on-going Democratic boondoggles, such as Vietnam and the other Whiz Kid programs. Whiz Kids Cyrus Vance and Harold Brown, future cabineteers, were involved in overruns such as the C-5A's (Fitzgerald, 1972, page 151, has Vance approving one 9-figure TFX electronics overrun needing Brown's signature with a "CRV OK"). But with such high-profile stars, although responsible, inexpediently Democratic, Proxmire had to attack various Nixonites. According to Fitzgerald, Nixon defense minions Moot and Shillito told Proxmire in 1970 that $700 million had been diverted to the L-1011 (Fitzgerald, 1972, page 294).

Lockheed, building the C-5A in Georgia with GE engines and its civilian L-1011 in California with Rolls-Royce engines, was also billing the Air Force too much money for Fitzgerald's taste. But Fitzgerald also anomalously took GE to task (several dozen pages worth, 1972, the bulk of chapter "Five/The Big Issue"), but for a different engine and type (the magnificent J-79, which had powered the F-104, F-105, F-4 and B-58, not even a turbofan). Yet according to Proxmire's 1970 appendicized figures, GE's turbofans were only barely over cost (less than 1/17th the overrun of Lockheed's airframe, page 239).

The real engine trouble was with Rolls-Royce for the L-1011; with the British government's interest in that concern and its inability to keep a secret, blaming GE was explicable only for someone looking only to blame yet another large American military contractor when it was Rolls-Royce which nearly destroyed both Lockheed and itself. Fitzgerald, of course, was full of rancor for Lockheed, calling it one of the "dedicated boondoggle corporations" (Fitzgerald, 1989, page 133) unfit for "civilian enterprise" when Lockheed had been originally enlisted by various militaries precisely because of its fine civilian projects, first by the Japanese (license-built military transport version of the Lockheed Electra) and British governments (Hudson patrol bomber version of same), and then later by the U.S. government (Hudson, Harpoon, Ventura and Orion maritime patrol-bomber versions of various Lockheed airliners). Lockheed had also succeeded on contemporary purely military projects, the Lightning, the jet Shooting Star, the U-2, the Starfighter and the SR-71. Typically, the last superlative project was downgraded, by those usual suspects the Whiz Kids, to reconnaissance and limited procurement.

Failure came in with the Whiz Kids, and when the Whiz Kids went away, why, so did most of the failure. Government programs themselves were hardly the problem. Indeed, Lockheed and the two engine companies had been involved in cleaning up the American Army Air Corps' decision to adopt GM's mediocre Allison engine for fighters. Replacing the Allison with Roll-Royce's Merlin made the American Mustang formidable, even as souping up the Allison with GE superchargers had earlier made Lockheed's Lightning a useful plane. Fast and long-ranged, but too heavy for dogfighting, supercharging made the Lightning superior at high altitude, more able to effectively dive at more nimble enemies from height. More useful than Army Air allowed it to be, the high-altitude Lightning was not used to escort bombers misused at middle altitudes, which accordingly suffered horren-dous losses until upgraded Mustangs became available.

But the growth of socialism in Britain, as of Liberal Democracy in the U.S., had stifled creative industry with hare-brained top-down reforms. Instead of rewriting the 1959 restriction leaving the Army with helicopters, the Whiz Kids tried to put jet engines under the long-surpassed rigid rotor. An inexperienced helicopter builder, Lockheed won the contract for the Cheyenne, but it was simply an aerospace contractor bidding on available projects. Instead of getting an improved engine for a great design, Lockheed became involved in souping up a bad idea, and ended up with a dangerous craft. Meanwhile, trying to sell aircraft in a world crowded with government-owned national airlines, Lockheed had brought in Rolls-Royce, partnered by a British government which had gutted Britain's aerospace industry as it had defined away Britain's armed forces. A half-dozen firms which had survived Ramsay MacDonald's Great Depression to give sterling service in Mr. Churchill's war disappeared, victims not of their success but of political failure, the kind that sees the dole as the source of a nation's strength, and its armed forces as an anachronism. Fortunately, it can't happen here.

What can and does happen here is headline-hunting politicians and letterhead hustlers grabbing attention and funds with their bogus melodramas, public nuisances pretending to be doing good while grandstanding. If Proxmire was no slouch at that, Fitzgerald's public travails about his own career metamorphosed into the chairmanship of the National Taxpayers Union, and then membership in Seymour Melman's leftist agit-prop SANE. It is not politics, but bad faith in politics, which makes strange bedfellows. Fitzgerald claims that the association was partly "outreach" (whose?) and partly to remove Melman's purportedly overrosy view of defense contractors. Most appalling was that Nixon gave this Proxmire and Melman associate another defense job. Of course, Fitzgerald, while ostensibly resigning from the NTU, "kept in touch by reading the NTU newspaper ... and by talking frequently with the Washington staff" of that "lobbying organization" (page 127).

By virtue of showing just how much he had learned from his previous activities, Fitzgerald, who had devoted 63 pages of his 1972 opus (pages 109-172) to the *electronics* of the TFX, was in 1989 still moaning about the failure to adopt a lightweight TFX for both the Air Force and Navy. This precious nostalgia for failure-lite he used to toss some more vitriol on a defense contractor. "Northrop was still trying to become one of the big boys. It had scored a coup in persuading the Navy to buy its new F-18 fighter plane in apparent defiance of a congressional order that the Pentagon buy versions of the same 'lightweight/low-cost' fighter for both the Air Force and the Navy, so Northrop simply teamed up with McDonnell-[*sic*]Douglas, and sold the loser to the Navy." (Fitzgerald, 1989, pages 82-83). In fact, the Ford Administration, with congressional appropriations, had already gone forward with the single-engine F-16 for the land role. Northrop had entered its twin-engine land-based F-17 for that role, but the also carrier-incapable F-16 had been chosen.

Simple design, co-production and foreign sales of a land-plane recouped more than would have been saved with a combined services aircraft. Congress **had** approved by appropriating money for the land-based F-16, also saving money by waiting on a naval plane. It wasn't "the Navy" which was persuaded, it was **Congress**. The decision for a lightweight low-cost new naval fighter was left to the in-coming Carter Administration, whose Whiz Kid revival decided on a twin-engine multi-role project, middleweight and high-cost, for its own dyseconomy drive. Northrop's F-17, a landplane, was incapable of filling such carrier roles, so Northrop indeed teamed up with carrier-experienced McDonnell Douglas in a complete redesign, the F-18, not that old "loser" the F-17. The team's (not "its" for Northrop's) design was what Carter, his minions and his Congress wanted, even if it met no druthers of a previous Congress. It was their preferences which made the F-18 a goer, not Northrop's persuasiveness; if Carter's Whiz Kids had been less scatter-brained (they wouldn't have been working for Carter), they could have met the original lightweight low-cost criteria with a modest refurbishment of the Vought Crusaders that were instead left mouldering in reserve.

Northrop was a target only because it had been annoyingly punctilious in furnishing a list of guests at its duck-hunting lodge. While some rage at corruption in defense, it is amusing that they rage **more** at the public airing of possible improprieties, a passel of weekend Elmer Fudds zombie-ized into doing Northrop's sinister bidding. In the McCarthy-era phrase, if it looks like a duck and quacks like a duck, it's probably a decoy. Fitzgerald was also dismayed (1989, page 194) at General Dynamics' release of Electric Boats' records detailing the long list of extras demanded by Admiral Rickover. There, the situation was a little bit different, for Rickover was a publicity-humping media guy with a near-veto for decades over Electric Boat's business. Unlike Northrop's parade of minor functionaries, Rickover was a major power, and had demanded to be treated as one, publicly and, seamily, privately. A liberal hero (Proxmire, page 4, to wit) with feet of clay and hands of grab was hardly what was needed for a selective partisan attack upon the military and industry, especially one whose empire-building in the expensive and largely useless field of submarines was far more wasteful than all of the minor bugbears of self-styled reformers. Instead, General Dynamics, revealing that its new subsidiary had been shaken down for decades by Rickover, got the proverbial treatment of the messenger with bad news (accusations that it "wove a net", for example, straight out of Sophocles, when it had only recently bought the company and its records), as Congressmen frantically tried to deflect the story away from the old publicity-hound Rickover to the burning public issue of, for example, the "ordeal" of one "George Spanton" (1989, page 194). What the liberals and their allies affected to find important was some squeaky cog among scads of bureaucrats, you see, not the weapons process or its arbitrators, including the public trying to be distracted with the phony investigations, tantrums and revelations of turbulent careerists. Suddenly, Hyman Rickover **wasn't** big news, George Spanton was.

The minor remedies of the publicists opposing the fruits of government by publicity tend to resemble the minor foibles they rage against. Proxmire lists a number of Whiz Kid managerial crackpotisms, but, much like himself, they were largely products of a business school mentality, America's ivory towers affecting "can-do". Proxmire's own, which is say borrowed, numbskullisms for improvement were three-fold: an end to incremental budgeting (hardly a problem with massive discrete projects such as those of weapons procurement), uniform accounting and more prototypes. "Zero-based" or "zero base" (pages 80 and 226; or maybe it was zero-base and zero based) budgeting was the belief that things should be looked at anew. That is fine when bad things are being done, but rather silly when good things have to be rejustified. It would give government the continuity of an idiot, when lack of continuity is already a problem of democratic governments. Nominally practiced under that sanctimonious loony Jimmy Carter, the result was just a cate-chism to justify the usual increment for continuing programs, rather than a real look at their effectiveness and/or constitutionality. Paraphrasing Aaron Wildovsky, "the urge to justify everything is the path to inanity".

Nor did the implementation of uniform accounting, boomed by Proxmire (pages 3 and 82), make the Pentagon more frugal. Bureau-cratic reforms just mean more cost, not less, with more paper churned out to justify the reforms. Those smaller-scale inspirational early McNa-mara reforms of non-weapons procurement had just harvested publicity (such as Proxmire's praise, pages 123-126); budgets went up, not down, as the nation got less, not more, for its money. Even more pathetic was Fitzgerald, who after two stints in the bureaucracy still has trouble distinguishing auditing from financial or cost accounting. The man who sneers at accountants who "'plugged'" (1989, page 218 -- used known figures to calculate unknown residuals) is the man with a zero-based mentor. Quite obviously, the financial and cost accounting problems of a job-order contractor (of a few large discrete projects) are different from those of a more typical, and more continuous, long-run producer. Costs are incurred, and must be expensed to whatever sources of revenue the company has at the moment. Start-up costs of new projects are therefore frequently charged to revenue from on-going projects, even as the start-up costs of the old projects had been expensed to earlier proj-ects. If the government serially funds development, prototyping, tooling and production in pursuit of defense excellence, it must expect that over-head for a contractor's civilian projects, where the revenue is more downstream, will tend to be spread among its defense projects, with their more continuous revenue.

Proxmire's third reform was that "[m]ore prototypes can be built before rushing into volume production" and, simultaneously, "[a] minimum of $2 billion can be saved by not building the prototypes" for the B-1 project (page 237). In other words, build prototypes in general, but not specific prototypes -- reform projects by making them longer and more expensive, and then "save" money by cancelling the projects made more expensive. The B-1 was a project of North American, a company denounced by Proxmire as formerly a "98 per cent" (page 62) government supplier. But accounting difficulties, including failure to control expenses or outright fraud, occur mostly when there are different sources of funds -- a movie studio billing its entire overhead to each of several groups of film investors, for example -- not 98% from one source. There is less incentive to save, indeed an outright incentive to run up expenses, when different groups can be billed -- the same limo can be paid for several times over, so the most expensive limo is bought.

But then, of course, high-risk projects are also frequently cancelled before production; more prototyping would mean more abandonments and the consequent griping of Proxmire, Melman and kindred spirits. The problem with many Whiz Kid projects was that they were bad ideas *ab initio* (Cheyenne, DASH and TFX, to wit), and building more prototypes would have simply increased the cost of demonstrating the bloody obvious. Prototyping is not only expensive, it takes time. When the pace of technological advance is fast, lengthening the design and pre-production process would leave actual procurement of items with a reduced useful service life -- and prototyping already occurs at its fullest extent where the advances are most rapid. Aircraft carriers, etc. don't have, or need, prototypes. The government is already a slave to appropriations and political mood-swings, with its access to the marketplace accordingly disadvantaged, and such a slave is already overworked without the added burdens of bootless reforms. Fewer tasks, cutting away the post-constitutional ones, would be more fruitful.

Major Wars Graphic

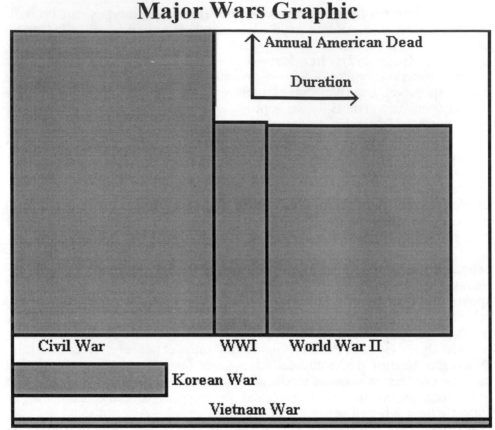

The above is the average annualized and total death tolls of America's five costliest wars. Note the relationship between blood spilled and nostalgia, the Civil War and World War II most, the Cold War Crusades least. World War I is usually not thought of as a nostalgia item, but compared to the Cold War Crusades, or such successful, and accordingly liberal-despised, wars as the Mexican, Spanish and Gulf, it is: Poppies, Billy Mitchell, Sergeant York, the Lafayette Escadrile and the other "aces". Guess from the graphic which of the "major" wars was most frequently described as "tearing this country apart". Hint: it wasn't the Civil War, where that actually happened.

HUNG OUT TO DIE:
American Wars and Defense Politics

Summary

Terminology. "Media", used as a singular item, denotes the American mass communications entities largely controlled by various left-wing factions. Liberal in the classical sense meant people opposed to intrusive government. As this movement gained its goals, however, some sought to prolong the phase of activism by arguing that government was needed for "true freedom", with themselves as the putative governors. John Stuart Mill, the bureaucrat running India, was one apostle of such an ideology, complete with the usual mental aberrations found in his American counterparts. These became socialists -- Mill himself in later life and his Utopian American counterparts -- and Progressives. World War I exacerbated a split in the American left between tinkering liberals and the more thorough leftist ideologues. Franklin Roosevelt's New Deal papered over this split until his death. The left attempted to oust Truman, and the old liberals became Cold War Liberals, casting the left out of leadership for twenty years while keeping it in a subordinate position through the device of blaming the Republican McCarthy (a former New Deal liberal before the casting-down of the left). In 1968, the left and the Cold War Liberals reformed their New Deal coalition as Modern Liberalism, this time with left-wing ideology taking the lead in the Democratic Party.

Typology and the American Civil War. The collective description of America's three costliest wars -- the Civil War, World War I and World War II -- as Liberal Crusades is the author's, although the description has been separately made for each (Eisenhower's *Crusade in Europe*) and by implication for all (Frank Freidel's *Over There ... America's First Great Overseas Crusade*, by a palace guard historian implying at least one domestic crusade and others overseas). The bad faith of liberal leadership, its backing and filling, and its solemn adoption of high-faluting goals compared to the massacre and sordid statesmanship are all common, although it is World War I which is most often disowned by liberal Americans as well as those further to the left. Of course, despite ritualistic denunciations of trench warfare and hide-bound generals (most nastily of *The General* by British navalist C.S. Forester), it was the war most technologically innovative, as well as the most well fought of the five wars of American liberalism. However, the post-World War I defeat of world Red Revolution and the postponement of American internationalism have given all segments of the American left a sour taste from the experience. Only pacifists profiteered via the disabusement. Nonetheless, Woodrow Wilson is reliably and solidly part of the liberal historians' pantheon of praised presidents, part of the Big Three along with Lincoln and Franklin Roosevelt.

And if the other two have a legacy of domestic programs which Wilson did not, despite his admirers, and if Lincoln advanced Black rights as Wilson marginally reversed them and Franklin Roosevelt disregarded them, the real common denominator is their death tolls (Lincoln's corpses, for example, would have stacked 43 miles high), and how they were achieved, with passive-aggressive war-mongering. It was as necessary for Lincoln to procure the Confederacy's firing of the first shots -- which did little damage -- as it was for Wilson and FDR to play the victims, which is to say it was not necessary at all. Lincoln had sufficient pretext with secession (which as a Whig he had defended in principle when the Democrats were in power) and confederacy, without the firing upon Fort Sumter.

Wilson could have ordered the convoying of American ships against all comers, and preserved American neutrality and freedom of the seas without contributing American blood to that spilled on the Western Front. FDR could have avoided disadvantageous war by less provocative diplomacy and still gotten it by his own aggressive plans. But they didn't. FDR and his minions were mesmerized by Lincoln's and Wilson's examples, although they neglected the *Maine* and the *Chesapeake*, probably because in those cases America **was** the honest victim. And topping the liberal historians' lists of underestimated presidents are Truman and Lyndon Johnson, whose programs, corruption and civil rights are in common along with their own smaller death tolls, not part of the Big Three, but part of the Big Five.

The left's varied illusions heavily weight purportedly mainstream history. This is clear in treatment of the American Civil War, hagiography of the icon Lincoln. Typically, most attempts at an accurate portrayal soft-peddled Lincoln's inconsistencies. Only from a further left perspective was the air allowed some temporary clearing, although only in service of a greater pollution. Richard Hofstadter indicted Lincoln as a typical politician not to score him for his opportune descents into radical rabble-rousing, but to denigrate him for not having been there all of the time. Certainly, the Lincoln who journeyed the length of Mississippi vainly trying to cut real estate deals with big slave-holders, or who endorsed the slave-holder Taylor, a hero of the Mexican War, after having denounced the war as a Democratic plot started through American aggression under Taylor's immediate command, is slimy enough to challenge any would-be iconizer. But when the death toll began mounting, the cosmetics had to be troweled on ever thicker. Lincoln, a common man save for rabid ambition and an absence of scruples, had proclaimed the certainty of civil war even as he sought the job of commander-in-chief, without bothering to inform himself of the nature of that job, then or subsequently. Between bouts of trying his untrained hand at strategy, "General" Lincoln was busy promoting various madcap miracle weapons that were unperfected by the end of that long war, or indeed ever. It was the foundering politician's response, find a gimmick.

After the Debauchs, the Desponds. The American Civil War provided not only the paradigm of a liberal war, pacifism and righteousness mutating into a bloody war and a massive military, but also the typical aftermath, as along with the abandonment of the excuse for war, the institution of the military is neglected, leading to various national weakness, insults and disasters. Evolving technology and the neglect left the U.S. Navy weaker after the Civil War's huge expansion that it had been before that war. The Navy which had fought pirates in the East Indies, sent gunboats to China and opened Japan, for better or worse, with Perry's expeditions was left with aging ships badly maintained. The most important later activity in the Pacific (Grant's attempt at grabbing Korea misfiring) was obtaining coaling stations, occupying uninhabited Midway Island in the Central Pacific and later dealing with the Samoans for a station at Pago Pago in the South Central Pacific. Both were important when Spain tried to keep its colonial empire and Germany tried to build its own.

Both European colonial efforts resulted in national humiliation for the disarmed U.S., with Spain's subjugation of rebellious Cuba including the removal of Americans from the *Virginius* on the high seas, along with their execution (during America's own rebellion, the Union Navy had removed two Confederate diplomats from the *Trent*, but the U.S. had released them after British protests). The U.S. was too weak to respond effectively, but the action showed the contempt with which a hard-line Spanish government would treat any revival of the traditional American interest in Cuba. The success of that Spanish government did not extend to holding power in Spain, however, as its opponents succeeded in turn to power but failed to exercise it by either mollifying or subjugating Cuba.

But before that happened, German and British agents and warships began seeking toeholds beside of the American station in Samoa. A series of comic opera incidents lasted more than a decade, with some minor skirmishing followed by the loss of three squadrons -- British, American and German -- from bad weather. Before that side show could blow up, the Cuba rebellion flared up again, but this time the U.S. Navy was small but capable and modernized. With the help of the fateful explosion of the *Maine*, deadlier than the previous generation's Spanish massacre of Americans if less emphatically official, the Spanish distraction was removed by American military might. The German Pacific squadron's appearance at Manila Bay failed to dissuade Dewey, and the shortness of the war left an armed America seeking some revenge against the interfering Germans, although not against the also-present Brits (along with the unsettled Philippines, German-bashing was a reason for the disastrously slow mustering-out at Yaphank).

In 1899, the U.S. and Britain jointly bombarded Germany's Samoan claim (with Germany the victim, such war-mongering aggression swiftly got the memory-hole treatment), before there was a four-party resolution the following year. Samoa was split between the U.S. and Germany, Britain had its title to Tonga and the fateful Solomons removed from dispute, Germany purchased three island groups from Spain, future bloody battlegrounds like the Philippines already were and would be again, and even French claims were confirmed. The U.S. in arms had proved willing to avenge past wrongs against itself, but the results of so doing left further grudges, and an extended geographical vulnerability. But the first three links in that chain had been a liberal bloodbath, followed by military neglect, followed by national humiliations -- in Samoa and in Cuba as at the Little Big Horn.

The next act of these recurring fiascos would be military reform, usually having extremely little to do with military effectiveness. The Spanish-American War's naval victories would be followed by a naval build-up of transient ship types, as well as a "reform" of the militia that would mutate into "Preparedness" (a hand-me-down of "Be Prepared!", British pre-war hysteria) and war, with the military virtually unprepared. Build-up of a more mature Navy would be followed by the Washington Treaty build-down and straitjacket and, as the long-looked-for war with Japan neared, thanks in large part to American policies, by the London Treaty vandalism. This could be summarized as militant Unpreparedness. More recently, after the major wars, World War II and the Cold War, military reform has focused on liberal racial and sexual concerns, along with their military fetishes, emphasizing the big bomber after World War II, and de-emphasizing it after the Cold War.

After the drawn-out conventional wars in Korea and Vietnam, by contrast, the liberal emphasis was on strategic atomic warfare along with a renewed conventional emphasis. In the post-Korean case, for example, Ike's emphasis on the atomic bomb led him to his throw-away executive order giving the Army its helicopter franchise, taken seriously mostly by such airborne generals as Ridgeway and Gavin. A Cold War Liberal administration fused these concepts into a giant waste machine. In a truncated replay after Vietnam, it was Trident, MX and Midgetman, along with the Rapid Deployment of armed forces that were substantially untrained and with broken or non-existent equipment. This was defense when liberals looked directly at it; when they were distracted or distracting the public for political advantage, the situation was even worse.

<u>Domestic Distractions and Their Reason</u>. Liberalism's obvious domestic political agenda is crowding out its opponent, constitutional government, with patronage. The Pentagon may be badly run, the courts might be slow and expensive, Congress may be corrupt and superficial about anything except its re-election or perks, the post office might be slow, expensive and unreliable (although it was Lenin's inspiration),

motor vehicle departments might be slow and surly and still license man-
iacs, but the answer is more government. Unfortunately, the question is
what provides the surest distraction from achieving the legitimate goals
of government. If liberalism were an electrician, and your lights were
flickering, it would be trying to sell you new appliances to plug in right
away. Constitutional organs and public attention have limited capacities;
to attempt everything is to achieve nothing.

But, of course, the goal of liberalism is not really to achieve
anything more than to maintain and extend its position. That is clearest,
to anyone not fooled by the hype, in the area of environmentalism,
where imaginary alarums are sounded to demonstrate the ability of
liberals to dominate the national agenda. And what clearer indication of
dominance can there be of an attitude-check based on triviality, or even
upon absurdity, such as the Chicken Littlisms of "Global Warming" and
"Ozone Layer Depletion"? One principal focus of arbitrary liberal power is the permanent poor, those whose habits unfailingly guarantee their
failure in the richest country around. The liberal leadership uses this
class both as an excuse for bureaucratic brigandage as well as a club with
which to threaten productive society, what Karl Marx described as the
natural alliance between the scoundrels (*lumpenproletariat*) at the top
and the scoundrels at the bottom. Marx rather unsympathetically described the conduct of such scum as regularly "lead[ing them] to brothels,
to workhouses and lunatic asylums, before the Bench, to bagnos and to
the scaffold" (and today, before the television cameras). There is nothing original in Marx that is valid, but his acid observations upon the
peregrinations of contemporary "national liberals" are pertinent today.
In American experience, the liberals at the top -- including the corporate
and foundation brass with their mania for "social work" (anti-social failure) -- have emptied the jails (both jails and reform schools were formerly used to penalize illegitimacy and failure to support such children by
their parents, for example) and the asylums and shut down the scaffolds,
and have replaced workhouses with public housing, food stamps, Medicaid, student loans, job-training, unemployment insurance, etc. etc. By
some additional perverse mentation, these steps are called being rational
and responsible. The responsible response when Los Angeles riff-raff
riot after some turbulent piece of garbage is clubbed by the police while
resisting arrest? Give the mob more tax money to replace what they've
burned and stolen. And how was the mob whipped up to its frenzy?
Unlike say the looting in 1977 New York, when the lights went out, or
the later flooded expressway in Chicago, when hundreds of motorists
were pulled from their cars and robbed and beaten or murdered, the Los
Angeles riot was preceded by a massive media barrage of hundreds of
millions of dollars of saturation time devoted to the "police beating" of a
"motorist", the violation of the "civil rights" of that "unemployed con-

struction worker". Civil rights means resisting arrest for drunk-driving your new car, if you are an out-on-parole convict. This time, the media didn't have to affect mindreading the mob, it had programmed the rioters itself. The police, castigated for using their issued clubs, were soon castigated for "not doing their job". Why does anyone believe either the mainstream media, whether its output, the people who own it or their employees, or the peculiar elite whose mouthpiece it is?

As to how this elite reaches its decisions and establishes its priorities, one should remember that it is in many ways the mirror image of the failures at the bottom of society, save for a slightly greater capacity for attaining personal advancement. The primary difference is that while most scum sinks to the bottom, some of the rest rises to the top, where its failures affect not just itself and its immediate environs, but also disaffect the entire society with sentimental outbursts to disguise its sly grabs at transient advantage or its other infantilisms of emotion, intellect and character. Obviously, a political persuasion that panders to rioting garbage has little interest in seeing to the proper functioning of society. With hysterical emotionalism the ways and means, the end product is mood-swings of policies and priorities. This is by far the main cause of America's wars and their largely unnecessary death-tolls.

Picture American military history as a simple chart, with war at the top and peace at the bottom, and events moving from left to right. There is a world-line which swings back and forth between those two states (this line is actually a composite, of course, and at least some of its components are always swinging into the war-zone), and there is a separate line for American policy. When this line is flat, American policy is rather settled, military waste is minimized (whether from a small military or from a constant large military) and war depends upon the "objective" situation, the subjective acts of other nations. This would be an isolationistic policy, liberals once having been emphatically isolationistic, preferring to see America war upon itself and denigrating stable patriots as "dough-faces". Liberal policy, by contrast, is mood-swings, with steep climbs toward war, vectoring the "world-line" downward to a bloody collision while wastefully building up neglected military muscle, leading toward large clashes and sloping sharply away to wasteful disengagement, foreign aid ballooning to keep wasting money while the military is precipitously pared until the next such episode. Part of the move toward peace is of course the embrace of distractions, beating swords into plowshares and wondering why agricultural surpluses follow war, as it were. Mood-swings aside, some long-term military economies are possible.

<u>How To Economize on the Military -- Basing</u>. Since military bases are not subject to local taxation, bases near prosperous cities should be closed. The federal government would get more money by

selling the land, and property tax rolls could be increased, with selective closures that would not damage local economies. Bases near distressed cities should be kept up where otherwise desirable, because housing for military families is cheaper in such places, and the local economy needs the civilian payroll of such bases. As usual, when liberals squawk, doing things in some way opposed is the best policy. Concentrating land-intensive bases near expensive cities would be the surest way of short-changing cities and nation.

Organization. Aside from inter-service rivalry, the main issue in American military organization has been the organization of the air. Deciding to form an independent Air Force merely increased the number of possible rivalries and the problems of co-operation. This pole of alleged reform flares into activity during periods of disarmament, when military efficiency is not at a premium. It also happens that strange alliances occur, with liberals treating Barry Goldwater as a savant instead of a maniac when he touts the Air Force. After all, liberals reason, if we ally ourselves with the Air Force to cut the Army and the Navy, we are in total cutting defense. Goldwater's jape that the U.S. has four air forces was only partly accurate. Actually, we have two, that of the maritime Navy and its Marines, and that of the land-based Air Force, along with Army Air, the helicopter force. Not much can be done about the fundamental difference between land-basing and maritime operations, but the Army helicopter force could be easily eliminated. The best way to achieve that would be to transfer the Tactical Air Force to the Army, leaving the present well integrated Navy/Marine air operation, a Strategic Air Force for the roles that the Air Force traditionally cares about (in spite of the ordered abolition of SAC) and Army Air for battlefield support without helicopter addiction. That would be three air forces, two integrated into the traditional services and a third free to pursue air for air's sake, a reduction from Goldwater's rhetorical four and a balancing of assets and organizations with tasks and responsibilities.

Procurement. Since many weapons have reached a plateau in their development, and the world situation is not particularly threatening, procurement can be expected to slow down. But there will be opportunity to ignore the unacknowledged lessons of the past (high-altitude reconnaissance being boomed while high-altitude bombing is declared impossible, the TFX approach of a compromise expected to do everything and capable of little, the cheap F-18-type weapon inflated into an overloaded second-rate plane at premium prices, the B-58-type premature scrappings, helicopter and submarine manias, the continued dependence on fossil fuels for surface warships, etc. etc.). There appears to be a fixed quotient of imbecility from the bureaucracy as well as from liberals and those further to the left in Congress. The obvious solution is to cut the civilian Pentagon and to vote the rascals out of Congress. Recent, and less well publicized earlier, episodes of congressional debauchery made some turnover in Congress occur; it was refreshing that congressmen posturing indignation about $200 ashtrays and $100 bolts were themselves victims of their own minor transgressions after having escaped responsibility for decades of grotesque waste and negligent stewardship. Off-year congressional elections are usually referenda on sitting presidents, and foundering Bill Clinton could conceivably take down Democratic control of the House, indispensable to defense waste since the Kennedy Administration.

Arms Trade. Clinton's anomalous endorsement of continued production of the *Seawolf* submarine (he opposed nuclear power in New Hampshire and Maine to a spavined harvest of votes, but more profitably favored it in Connecticut) illustrates the liberal approach to defense infrastructure. Liberals will handicap the arms industry by stymying its exports, crippling otherwise doted-upon "free trade" in the name of morality. Boycotts, embargoes and subsidies (to foreigners as well as to some American pets) are routine, although flagrant restraints upon trade. Liberals will also routinely favor cutting defense, although there again they will be frequently be seduced by high-tech glitz with little military utility. One such domestic favorite has been the submarine, at the same time as liberals have warred upon submarine exports. The result is that Americans pay for a swollen capacity to produce unnecessary large nuclear-powered submarines, instead of keeping manufacturers in business by allowing them to export smaller submarines. The nation loses an export, even while it is taxed for an over-grown submarine arm.

In the aerospace field, by contrast, the government, first by the Whiz Kids and later by a Republican-Congressional bailout, funnelled money to Lockheed through the C-5A program, propping up the civilian Tristar jumbo-jet for exports of that transnational extravaganza. Although nominally done to keep a key defense manufacturer in business, the subsidization ended up hurting Boeing and the Douglas portion of McDonnell Douglas by enabling Lockheed to go on with its foreign bribery. It is probably no accident that a company indulging in bribery had so many friends in Washington, even getting a bail-out without having really leaked. Keeping the civilian airliner-maker Douglas in operation had been the justification for allowing the pro-trust merger of defense contractors McDonnell and Douglas (helping keep up the cost of carrier aircraft, almost completely an American market), but the government's tender concern for the export of jets did not extend to McDonnell Douglas' superb fighters.

Twice, nominal adherents of high-tech in the abstract were joined by the Israel Lobby to prevent large sales to Saudi Arabia, giving export earnings to Europe and leaving McDonnell Douglas first in need of the ludicrous Apache contract and eventually in need of a bail-out. Liberals favor free trade only when they can't raid the Treasury or weigh down the Defense Department with overly elaborate versions of the wrong weapons. While some exports have been permitted, a few more F-15s to Israel and F-18s to Switzerland, good for McDonnell Douglas, these have not made up for the procurement recently forgone -- the cancelled A-12 and F-22, Grumman's A-6 and F-14 updates and the curtailled B-2 Stealth Bomber. Those are planes that can't be exported, and in many cases companies are leaving the aerospace business, meaning less capacity, less competition and fewer exports, and less revenue and more unproductive expenditure for social programs.

Liberal high-tech and anti-anti-trust imperatives combined to give us the VS-22 Osprey program, a short-takeoff-and-landing aircraft that crashes. Despite the obvious lesson from airplane history that the way to achieve lift is by raising the ratio of wing surface to weight, the Osprey's backers chose to achieve vertical lift by putting its huge engines out on its stubby wings, and swiveling them from vertical into horizontal flight. This approach had failed with a number of projects, and was abandoned in favor of vectoring the thrust -- not the thrusters! -- of more successful projects such as the Harrier. If a plane to fill the Osprey's planned role (deep amphibious penetration inland from carriers or from rudimentary airfields; the tacit mission seems to be rescuing hostages when American embassies are captured) is really needed, the way to achieve it is with an extra wing, extendible for short takeoffs and landings and retractable for less drag and longer range, not with stubby wings, off-axis engines and draggy rotor-props. Instead of backing stupidity, back performance, and get value and exports.

How To Reduce the Navy. The main problem in reducing the Navy is that the most useful ships tend to be the most expensive to operate, although not necessarily to have bought in the first place. Submarines are the least capable warships, but their biggest costs are upfront -- construction and nuclear reactors. To save money on submarines with the least effect on capabilities, first cut all new construction for domestic use, cut extra crews and cut the training establishment. To further cut basing and crew costs, mothball all pre-*Los Angeles* "attack" submarines. To economically cut the carrier force, demobilize several oil-fired carriers and keep their planes and pilots based in the Southern U.S. for occasional carrier practice in the Gulf of Mexico training area between rotations to active carriers. For surface warships, keep the battleships in commission in preference to a single extra oil-fired carrier; four battleships have a slightly smaller total crew, use very little aviation fuel and do not need constant steaming at high fuel usage -- they can optimize cheap dock-time instead of expensive cruising without sacrificing the edge necessary for carrier operations. To save on other surface warships, stop building conventionally powered ships (as the Eisenhower administration did with submarines), and demobilize many uneconomical oil-fired ships (*Belknap*, *Leahy*, *Coontz*, *Adams* and *Knox* class ships);

these have some hull life left but are expensive oil-burners and manpower-intensive (about twice the oil and manning requirements per ton as battleships). Sell some such ships to countries which have cash (if not credit), oil and cheap manpower -- Mexico, Indonesia and Iran, to name three. Close naval bases in Europe, the most expensive to operate, and not subsidized like those in Japan and Okinawa. Lastly, cut many officers and periodically mothball the rest by giving them mandatory five-year leaves at some point in their careers at quarter pay. If they cannot put the time to use, chances are that they are not very resourceful and therefore over-paid in the Navy. As noted many years ago by H.L. Mencken, naval officers tend to be socially sophisticated; now that the classes they hob-nob with are rotten, there is little point in further shielding naval officers from them, as there would be with Army or Air Force officers. Cutting the Army and Air Force in Europe and putting them back onto isolated American bases would reinforce such tradition-al, and beneficial, isolation.

The Army has been shorted herein, but for a reason. People are land animals, not birds or fish; armies can march and fight with low technology -- Napoleon could ignore innovations and tactics in favor of organization and massing troops at the battlefield and usually win. But navies and air forces cannot exist without ships and airplanes. As noted, the modern battleship and fighting aircraft were contemporaries, and even preceded World War I's tank (although radar, sonar, paratroops and the atom bomb awaited World War II, World War I balloonists had parachutes and Ernest Rutherford, working on early sonar, split the atom in his spare time). Even the methods used for developing them were similar -- the Wright Brothers used a wind tunnel to develop the airplane even as the Royal Navy's Directors of Naval Construction were using a similar device to refine its warships (the Soviets even combined their aero and hydro research facilities). The result was ships which were tapered, stable gun platforms and good in heavy weather, if at the expense of not being effectively armored or maneuverable.

For navies and air forces, technology is definitive, and organiz-ing it is key. As armies have become more technological -- helicopters, missiles and tanks -- the experiences of the more technical services have become more appropriate. By the same token, the Army's (and the Marines') examples of concentration and battlefield co-ordination should be absorbed by the two services which have seen submarine and bomber mania absorb their budgets while detracting from their efficiency.

HUNG OUT TO DIE:
American Wars and Defense Politics

Notes

Preface. The Pentagon was built under the direction of General Leslie Grove before he headed up the atomic bomb project. Most critical World War II decisions were made at other locations.

In 1993, *THE NEWSPAPER OF RECORD* took cognizance of the U.S. Army's helicopter Jones and found it a new and "reasonable" idea of General Colin Powell. It was neither. It was from 1959, and probably the decision of then Secretary of Defense Thomas Gates.

1. Intro and Typology. Pete Seeger describes himself orally as a Communist. The upper-casing is the author's guess. Seeger, a Harvard man in the John Reed-Michael Dukakis continuum, was accidently invited to perform by someone in the 1988 Dukakis campaign unable to distinguish him from the sought performer, Detroit/L.A. rocker Bob Seger, more popular and probably more politically palatable to the general electorate. The American destroyer *Reuben James*, sunk while guarding a Canada-to-Britain convoy on October 30, 1941, was an allowable object of Communist concern only insofar as it occurred after the invasion of Soviet Russia by Germany, when the Soviet Empire was at risk. By contrast, the attack by Communist torpedo boats in 1964 on the American destroyers *Maddox* and *Turner Joy* also resulted in a de-nunciation -- of the United States -- by the Unquestionably Patriotic. It was the same Navy, but at least Seeger mainly attacked the U.S. Army, resurrecting his shifting Communist-line attacks from before mid-1941 with post-1943 additions.

The truism that government is force has been attributed to George Washington.

Millis' musketry reference is from *Arms and Men* (N.Y., 1956 PB), page 17.

Amnesty International has moved from the embrace of future political mass murderers to past serial killers, trying to keep them away from execution and therefore potentially back in business. In the name of humanity, of course!

The description of Rome's tribunate is conservative. Its initiation co-incided with the earliest popular and agrarian agitation, and the early Senate had killed a consul siding with it. The Gracchi were merely re-viving an old tradition like that of the limited tribunate, one illustrating the reasons for the limitations. Caesar was an oily dissembler, and carried various implicit prejudices. Many Latin pupils remember little more than his statement about Gaul being divided into three parts, but what Caesar meant by Gaul was the part he conquered. Other parts had already been conquered by other Romans. Cable television's "Learning Channel", per British historian Geoffrey Barraclough, tells us that Caesar crossed the Rubicon "to invade Gaul", when in fact he was invading Italy from Cisalpine Gaul, now called Lombardy.

Why is classical Rome invoked? Because the dominating ethos of America is not Meso-American, East Asian, Hindu, Egyptian or Mesopotamian, save of the last in religion, it is Greek and Roman. That was a tradition where, at least in healthy stages, military affairs were a proper concern of the mass of citizens, rather than of a caste or of foreign conquerors. The terminology of government, however badly misunderstood, is also a product of the western tradition, rather than of the more archaic traditions of the east, with their melange of politics and religion or other ritual. But usage is frequently slovenly. People (and dictionaries) say dictator when they mean a tyrant; they think an autocrat is a tyrant, instead of someone who will not be tyrannized; they let posturing self-perpetuating oligarchs call themselves aristocrats (or the elite, or the nobility, even if only in the transparent exercise of *noblesse oblige*); they think that Plato actually used the Roman word republic and, although they may know that democracy can mean rule of the people, they usually don't know that it can also mean rule of the beef-fat, the tallow instead of the shallow. There is enough sloppiness in politics without exacerbating it with sloppy use of words.

The Diadochi were Alexander's Greek generals, who split his empire and founded a group of feuding dynasties. The longest lasting was Ptolemy's Egypt, with the last Greek power-wielder the Greek-named and Greek-descended Cleopatra. American Black ignoramuses pronouncing Cleopatra Black also find the Phoenecian aristocrat Hannibal with the same hue; not even **Elvis** is safe. They are humored by liberals.

The first colonial capture of Port Royal occurred before 1700, during King William's War. Abandoned to "peace", it was the target of three further colonial attempts, until at the end of Queen Anne's War the British kept it and the rest of Acadia, but returned St. Augustine to Spain and left the French with Cape Breton Island. In the third French and Indian War, King George's, the colonials captured the new bastion of Louisbourg on Cape Breton Island, but the British gave it up in return for another depot for the East India Company at Madras, setting up an enmity in Massachusetts for the East India Company that would fester up through the Boston Tea Party. In the fourth French and Indian War, the British were not heavily engaged in Europe except financially, and Clive early won a smashing victory at Plassy in India; this left Canada as their target. The prize was fully achieved -- by British regulars as well as colonials -- and kept. But the defeat of France left the British haughty and the Americans both insulted and without need for the British military aid so belatedly and expensively proffered. To Americans of the colonial era, Canada had been conquered by their blood. To Americans of the post-colonial era, Canada was the source of two British Empire vexations, the instigation of Indian raids and the maintenance of a chain of forts running onto American soil. With impressment, the third gripe, being done by the massive Royal Navy, Canada was not only the source of two grievances but the only area where the young U.S. could engage the British Empire on more equal terms. Liberal hindsight bleaches this geopolitical tableau into land hunger.

One glaring weakness of America's constitutional system is the vice presidency, usually the repository of a ticket-splitting (constitutionally mandated) nebbish. While Dan Quayle is considered the prototype, the Democrats have, as usual, been more at fault. Grover Cleveland's Veep, Adlai Stevenson, was such a nut that Cleveland had a cancer operation at sea, rather than risk stock market chaos -- compare that with the stock market rise on the day when George's Bush's health was briefly imperiled. Wilson's Thomas R. Marshall, he of the 5¢ cigar (what we still need is a no-scent cigar), was effectively negated during Wilson's prolonged incapacity by Mrs. Edith Wilson.

All major American war presidents have been affected in some degree by the vice presidency. The first two, Lincoln and Wilson, were killed or disabled after their wars. Franklin Roosevelt was progressively less functional over the lunatic Wallace and then died over the corrupt and inept Truman. As with LBJ, Truman's weakness led to insecurity, foreign probes leading to wars, stalemates or ultimate defeats. Gerald Ford's accession meant failure of the Vietnam War after its American conclusion; while Ford's presence in a weakened presidency was key to that, he still managed to get his party's nomination, crippling it against Jimmy Carter the Otherwise Unlikely. Consider if, as advocated herein, successive President Ford had been constitutionally ineligible for an elective term. The country might've had Reagan running against Carter in 1976; there are few Americans who would be adverse to the chance of either having not had Carter as a president or having Reagan's political career end before 1988, maybe even in 1976.

2. Prelude and Mr. Lincoln's War. The Mexican War diatribe is from Pete Hamill, Abe Lincoln idiot (*Village Voice* column, 1987), citing those unreliable old "Conscience" Whigs Abe Lincoln and Philip Hone (Lincoln's speech in the House of Representatives and Hone's published diary). Democratic partisans seem to have a code for permissible party disloyalty, finding it expedient to praise the proper ideology in rival parties; they also seem to enjoy reading other people's diaries.

The Marshal Tureen quip is usually attributed to Lord Ashburton, British Ambassador and a principal of the Baring Brothers' trading company. Ashburton was a financial support for "Conscience" Whig Daniel Webster, so that mocking Webster's Whig rival Winfield Scott was protecting an investment, not just Ney-saying. In 1842, Webster signed away northern Maine to his patron's Britain and the Baring Brothers' timber interests, with the U.S. receiving what became northeastern Minnesota in return. There is no evidence that either man recognized the value of the iron ore there. Previous exploration, survey and mapping of the area had been vexed by compass problems.

Lincoln's fall-guy for his military haste was Treasury Secretary Salmon P. Chase, whom Lincoln blamed for pressuring him about bond sales (the buck may stop in the White House, but the bonds get passed by the Treasury Department). Why Lincoln could not resist Chase's pressure is unclear, but bond sales were not helped by Lincoln's frequent military disasters, although fluctuations of previous bonds sold were certainly aided by the uneven war-effort, helping make profits for lucky speculators. Lincoln is usually saluted as a large-souled humanist, but his description of Chase as a carrion fly "laying his eggs at every sore point" is vintage Lincoln, ungenerously and ungraciously attributing his own folly, and its effects, to others. His back-handed compliment to Harriet Beecher Stowe for having started the Civil War is of similar kidney -- who had advanced himself more through such agitation than Lincoln?

The build-up to Civil War was the attempt to delegitimize the Union, most auspiciously on the part of abolitionists. Tolerance of slavery and of states' rights had been the price of Union, and Northern agitators wanted to withdraw that capital. Disunion was the result. Reconstruction was little more than a shoddy substitute, a forcibly Reconstituted Union, New and Improved.

Lincoln as the essential paradigm of liberal statecraft rests on five props. The first is the combination of paranoia with ideology. Some designated enemy is presented as all-evil, and about to descend upon us (slavery expanding into the North, instead of shrinking into the South, as it was in reality; Hitler about to invade America; the Junior Senator from Wisconsin terrorizing America, etc. etc.). The second prop is ambition, which illuminates the ideological paranoia and moves it forward. The third prop is war-mongering, usually disguised as pacifism ("the war is forced upon us") or disinterested internationalism (siding with Mexico, even liberal hindsight is defective). The fourth prop is sanctimoniousness (the Lincoln-Douglas debates restricted to a single issue having nothing to do with Illinois, with Lincoln alternating indignation and moderation, and Douglas' attempts to split the difference splitting his party for 1860). The fifth prop is ineptitude, as ambition and company find themselves in the saddle, propelled forward to unreconnoitered battlefields.

Descriptions of Gen. Wm. Farrar "Baldy" Smith are from Allan Nevins, *The War for the Union*, volume 4 (N.Y. 1971), pages 8-9 and 48. The same author's variable, and frequently unindexed, opinions of Kansas Gov. Lane are found in *Ordeal of the Union* and *The Emergence of Lincoln*. It is notable that Nevins, before becoming a history professor, had been a journalist, working under time pressure. That excuse is hardly available to a tenured professor working on a lengthy project (was to have been 10 volumes, including Reconstruction, ended as 8). But this episode was merely historical, the distortion of the dead by someone grinding an ideological axe some generations later. More obvious is the treatment of Admiral Theobald discussed in Section 4 below.

The description of Lincoln is from the Harold J. Laski-Felix Frankfurter correspondence, shortened from a blurb in an article by Harvard Prof. Martin Peretz, lately "chairman" of *The New Republic* ("Laski Redivivus", page 90, in Laqueur, Walter & Mosse, George (eds.), *Journal of Contemporary History: 2, The Left-Wing Intellectuals Between the Wars* (N.Y. 1966)).

The comparison of Lincoln to Nero is admittedly unfair, and the author apologizes to Nero and his partisans. After all, Nero's reign over a huge and populous empire was long and generally peaceful, and his later cruelties fell mainly upon his fellow patricians, the city of Rome and the cult of the Nazarene, whose later-day followers were so enthusiastic about the American Civil War. And, with Nero, the real bloodbath came after his assassination, civil war for which he cannot really be blamed, while the American Civil War came expressly because of Lincoln's accession and his qualities, actions and omissions.

John Wilkes Booth was a veteran before the Civil War. He had been wounded during Brown's rising at Harper's Ferry, and accordingly disliked the persuasion.

Thomas Carlyle was a friend of Ralph Waldo Emerson, a mainstay of Boston's Transcendentalist Club (1836) and its abolitionistic agitation. In his second volume of *The French Revolution* (1837), Carlyle says: "For a man, once committed headlong to republican or any other Transcendentalism, and fighting and fanaticizing amid a Nation of his like, becomes as it were enveloped in an ambient atmosphere of Transcendentalism and Delirium: his individual self is lost in something that is not himself, but foreign though inseparable from him. Strange to think of, the man's cloak still seems to hold the same man: and yet the man is not there, his volition is not there; nor the source of what he will do and devise; instead of the man and his volition there is a piece of Fanaticism and Fatalism incarnated in the shape of him. He, the hapless incarnated Fanaticism, goes his road; no man can help him, he himself least of all." (pages 246-7, Oxford 1989 PB).

Carlyle had lent the manuscript's first volume to John Stuart Mill, the archetypical liberal turning socialist, and consequently a rosy romanticist about the French Revolution and those whom it inspired; Mill "accidentally" burned the manuscript. A Freudian nightmare come to life, Mill's imbalance and lack of insight can be seen in his *Autobiography*, wherein his mysterious depression miraculously clears up when he learns of the death of his domineering father; his mother, one of the most accomplished women in England, is not mentioned. Consider Mill: one year, a senior East India Company bureaucrat; the next year, the Sepoy Mutiny; the next year, the Company dissolved; the next year, Mill the apostle of liberty (for India?); after that, Mill the apostle of government ownership, "true freedom". The mish-mashing of such demented rationalists is what liberalism is all about: principles, supposedly eternal but mutating, and destruction and corpses. In the American case abolitionism, civil war for union, and then reconstruction, the South thrown out and re-occupied. The connection beyond ideology? India was the major export market for clothing made from American cotton. The Sepoy War had disrupted the cotton trade, leading to a Southern depression and restiveness that preceded secession.

    3. Intervention. There is another reason for Spain to have blown up the *Maine* at the specific time. Spain's previous bellicosity during the Marti Rebellion had been with naval superiority, but in 1898 the U.S. had five more battleships under construction. Spanish militarists may have wanted to fight or to humiliate the U.S. while they still had a chance, a chance greatly increased by destroying 1/6 of America's battle squadron.

    Critics of America maintain that the *Maine* sank when one of its 6-inch shell magazines exploded, with the putative cause of this sudden and dramatic disaster left unexplained. But there is a recorded incident of what happened when a ship of similar fighting power, 2 9.2" guns and 6" secondary guns, did have an incident with its largest 6" shell magazine. In 1918, in port but raising steam (the *Maine* hadn't been), HMS *Glatton*'s under-insulated boilers (determined by later examining its sister ship; the *Maine* was unique) ignited the ship's nearest 6" shell magazine. Instead of blowing up and sinking with the main casualties being those drowned, the *Glatton* burned and exploded serially, for about four hours, with many burned but few drowned. The *Glatton* was sunk by repeated torpedoes (it was well bulged) to keep its fire from damaging nearby ships, including an ammunition freighter.

    The *Maine* was bang/blub, with few men burned; Barbara Tuchman expediently misdescribed it as an "armored cruiser" (*The Proud Tower*, N.Y. 1967, PB page 173). A bang/blub involving an armored cruiser was the biggest American naval disaster of World War I. The *San Diego* (the *California* until the nation mobilized available state names for Teddy Roosevelt's battleships) was mined off Long Island; few were burned but many drowned. Armored cruisers and their contemporary pre-modern battleships were extremely vulnerable to underwater blasts. Note that the *Maine*, a U.S. battleship **victimized**, is lyingly denigrated, while Mrs. Tuchman, an Office of War Information veteran, describes the old and even weaker *Texas* in **victory** as new and stronger, one of the "so-lately-built battleships" (*ibid.*, page 181). "Baldy" Smith, "Fuzzy" Theobald and *Newsday*'s F-14 get company.

The Czechs had invaded the two contiguous areas that are still "theirs". Bohemia and Moravia are corruptions of Boii-home and Marcomania, named after two German confederacies which had occupied the areas before invading the Roman Empire. The Czechs, of the Crown of St. Stephen, became part of Austria as a result of some 15th century dynastic dealings. Hungary possessed some Serbs as a result of its old military frontier with the Turkish European domain, which had expanded largely by its defeat of the 14th century Bulgarian and Serbian Empires (Constantinople in 1453 was in the rear of those earlier Turkish gains). As Hungary, by itself and then under the Hapsburgs, slowly rolled back the Turks, first Hungarians and then Serbs and Croats were liberated.

After the 1867 establishment of the Austro-Hungarian "Dual Monarchy" from Hungarian pressure, the Austrian realm occupied Bosnia-Hercegovina, with more Serbs, in 1878, but annexed the area only in 1908. 1878 also established Serbian and Bulgarian rumps, with their half-millenium-deferred rivalries; when Bulgaria grabbed its present middle third, "East Rumelia", from Turkey in 1884, Serbia soon attacked it, with Austrian aid. 1878 and the 1908 annexation were with the connivance of other Great Powers, although the latter did not sit well with newly bold Serbia. After Serbian expansion in the Balkan Wars of 1912 and 1913 against Turkey and Bulgaria, Serbian anti-Austrian animus found expression in the assassinations of 1914.

Russia possessed the core of traditional Poland, Warsaw and its environs, although Prussia had some Poles and Austria had Galicia and the last gasp, the independent city of Cracow (1831) and environs, the more vital part of Poland from the late Middle Ages. Re-constituting Poland with territory from its enemy Russia was a World War I German fetish. Poland and Czechoslovakia, particularly between the wars, and Yugoslavia were only smaller editions of the Austrian Empire which, as Austria-Hungary, had more than one domineering ethnic group.

As discussed in Chapters 5 and 14, German militarism, taking on a naval aspect, is falsely blamed as the root cause of World War I. Aside from the anti-German tradition, disguised as anti-militarism, there is the other ritual plunder and falsification of the past to enrich liberal dogma of the present. The U.S., then engulfed in a wave of Progressive hysteria, is forgiven its own naval build-ups, Cleveland/McKinley/Roosevelt's and Wilson's, because those were partisan idols, all except McKinley having been progressive for their time, no matter how embarrassing the specifics are in retrospect (imperialism, militarism, segregation, getting women out of the workplace). The lesson affected to be taught is that military strength produces war, and military innovation is self-defeating. That would leave the military stagnant, and hence vulnerable to more liberal carping on that score (note that the military manages, in liberal ideology anyway, to be both hidebound and too innovative).

In historical service, the fixation upon military build-up deflects attention away from the aggressive policy of Britain and its "Allies" to their militaries as well as those of the Central "Powers". The linkage was in fact quite solid. German diplomacy (the Zimmermann Note) contemplated carving up the U.S., for Mexico's bribe and benefit, in much the same way Woodrow Wilson contemplated dismantling the German and Austro-Hungarian Empires. The moral difference is slight, although large to liberals. The U.S. is conceded the right to meddle and the right to be itself left alone; designated enemies are conceded neither right, which is why they tend to become actual enemies.

It is probable that the *Lusitania*'s cargo of rifles was meant for training and use by British troops in Ireland. That would have freed up standard British rifles for use in France, although the Irish use would have been a political hot potato in the U.S., a possible additional, or even main, reason for official American coyness. Secrecy left the U.S. government, the venue of the rifles, open to blackmail.

The World War II German submarine atrocity canard is covered by William L. Shirer in *The Nightmare Years* (Volume 2 of *Twentieth Century Journey*), pages 465-66 (Boston 1984). The ship sunk was the *Royal Sceptre*, the transport spiriting the survivors to Brazil was the *Browning*, and the German submarine was the *U-48*, "the most successful submarine of the Second World War" (J. Rohwer and G. Hummelchen, *Chronology of the War at Sea*, Volume 1, page 110 (N.Y. 1972)). When a U.S. submarine torpedoed a relief ship granted safe passage in the Pacific, Admiral Nimitz first suggested a cover story of the ship striking a mine, later reprimanding the court-martial which only weakly treated the submarine captain (Buell, *Master of Sea Power* (Boston 1980), pages 327-8).

Wilson is frequently portrayed as aghast at submarine warfare, rather than anti-German, but in fact he greatly favored America's own submarine build-up, and permitted the export of 20 to belligerent Britain. And while it is true that Wilson's 14 Points included the usual bromide about freedom of the seas, Germany's submarine blockade was not fully effective, with the main disaffect on American freedom of the seas having been the Allied (British) blockade of Germany and its allies. So why didn't the U.S. convoy ships to Germany or declare war on Britain? Wilson's rancor was against Germany.

Leftists seeking to demonize Wilson without letting up on the Germans used Wilson's endorsement of the bombardment of Vera Cruz "for failing to salute the American flag" as an example of an atrocity. It went without saying that such American "atrocities" were decontextualized by the bowdlerization of Mexico's previous efforts in that direction.

Hoover was the only elected U.S. President without military command, congressional or gubernatorial experience, and brought us the Great Depression. The least experienced other elected U.S. President was Lincoln, with a single term in the House, who brought us our blood-iest war. Republicans look fondly upon Lincoln as the archetypical Republican President, although he was a leftist radical (in addition to his more acceptable corporate humanism), while Democrats are pleased to regard Herbert Hoover as the archetypical Republican President, al-though he too had more in common with modern Democrats than with Republicanism. Chester Alan Arthur is often regarded as the least ex-perienced American President, and he did give us the recurring national disaster of the civil service, but he did have previous military experience as a general, quartermaster-general of N.Y.'s scads of Civil War volunteers.

The Hoover-Roosevelt policy of delaying the fall of prices was not the only way to fail. While inflation is difficult to cause when demand is falling rapidly, deliberate deflation is the other extreme. This was tried in Weimar Germany, and to no good end; it simply does not help to create what would in normal circumstances be the appearance of bargains when prices are in total free-fall -- instead of greed overcoming fear, you simply have more fear than ever.

Aside from Sherlock Holmes, stamps and model ships, geogra-phy was FDR's hobby and, next to islands, rivers were his strong point. He was aware that the Rhine flowed mainly through Germany, and his statement baited Hitler more subtly than the usual abusive molasses oozing from his White House. Roosevelt's characterization of General MacArthur as the second most dangerous man in the country was a Sher-lock Holmes reference, to Colonel Sebastian Moran, Professor Mori-arty's henchman.

In between Japanese success in obtaining military concessions in northern Vietnam in 1940 and their full occupation of Vichy French In-dochina in mid-1941, Thailand tried to muscle into Cambodia. This led to the destruction of the Siamese fleet in a January 1941 attack by the Vichy French Indochinese squadron, showing the French would fight there against a beatable foe. This battle may have engaged FDR's symp-athies. Aside from the Japanese movement into Indochina beginning in December 1940, there had been two other developments not involving China which might have been critical for American policy. In Septem-ber 1940, Tokyo had joined the Berlin-Rome Axis, a paper diplomatic triumph for Japanese hard-liners that was more provocative to other countries -- a successful axis, after all, is linear and solid, not triangular paper. The other critical element was FDR's re-election, as critical for an active policy as Woodrow Wilson's had been in 1916. Although he was still fobbing off his wife's activism, with a new four-year lease, and still with an impeachment-proof Congress, FDR could take any of multi-ple belligerent actions to provoke war. That was the gravamen of subse-quent discussions with the British General Staff and in orders to the U.S. military.

Also present at Hawaii, and largely destroyed, were two squadrons of B-18 bombers, Douglas' failed twin-engine competition against the B-17. A few hundred had been bought when the early B-17s had production and high-altitude troubles, and most were later used as anti-submarine patrol bombers. Those in Hawaii were in active reserve for bombing (by the Army) in the event of an invasion or other attack, and were therefore not being used for patrol to supplement the inadequate numbers of Catalina flying boats (at the time the Navy was allowed only flying boats for patrol from shore, and it had the responsibility for patrol from Hawaii). This misuse was the only real malaprop of divided command, wherein the Navy, responsible for patrol, was not given use of an appropriate supplement for that mission, the B-18s, which were to have been used as bombers only because of the paucity of the more desired fixed-up B-17s, too few and being concentrated in the Philippines as they became serially available.

FDR's decisions to squander American scout planes abroad is especially ill-considered compared to the new Prime Minister Churchill's withholding of the RAF from the Battle of France. Churchill as warlord realized that charity, as with winning wars, begins at home.

Some Pearl Harbor commentators have examined foreign sources and found evidence of radio intercepts from the Pearl Harbor attack force, hinting darkly that the U.S. 'must have known' the ships were on their way. As has long been known, however, the Japanese had landed their carrier fleet's radio operators so that they could broadcast bogus radio traffic from Japan, individual operators being recognizable by their characteristic "fist", or touch, on the keys. Intercepts were not from the ships themselves, and their relative paucity was from the bad atmospherics of the day, with few messages picked up by the U.S. and direction-finding disrupted.

Among the latest works on Pearl Harbor is the bombastic *Pearl Harbor: Final Judgement* (N.Y. 1992) by former Army investigator Henry Clausen and Bruce Lee. Latest misjudgment would be the more appropriate title. For Clausen and Lee, Pearl Harbor, with its 2400 dead (or "3,300" lost, as they quote Nimitz, page 240) was "the greatest military defeat in American history" (page 22); evidently, the fall of the Philippines, with its eventual 55,000 American dead, didn't count.

Their list of the Pearl Harbor damage is "Three ... battleships ... sank on the bottom; a fourth capsized.... The target battleship, *Utah*, ... also sank. Also damaged beyond repair were three light cruisers, three destroyers and four auxiliary vessels. At a time when our Navy was frantically preparing to fight a two-ocean war, it lost eighteen of its more important and combat-ready warships (not including the *Utah*)." (page 9). First, there were five battleships, not four, on the bottom, and only one was "damaged beyond repair" (the *Oklahoma* was reparable, but only slowly and expensively so, and therefore wasn't). Second, of the ships "also damaged beyond repair", the cruisers, the destroyers and the seaplane tender *Curtiss* were repaired. Third, the *Utah*, counted twice and then left out once, was one of the four auxiliaries referred to, and both it and the old minelayer *Oglala* were sunk, not just damaged. Fourth, the damaged 33-year-old repair ship *Vestal*, the *Utah* and the *Oglala* were hardly "important and combat-ready"; the *Vestal*'s job had been to repair the *Utah* after it was damaged by practice bombing, an occupation rendered meaningless with the loss of that ship, and the ancient *Oglala*, a former liner, was so decrepit that it sank from hits on other ships. Fifth, four other damaged ships had been in drydock, and were hardly "combat-ready". Sixth, as noted here in text, the Navy's more combat-ready ships -- rebuilds, AA-ships and radar ships -- had at the time of Pearl Harbor been mostly siphoned off to the transiently more active Atlantic.

Similar malaprops abound. For example, in 1944, the authors have Patton penetrating the Maginot Line, instead of the Siegfried Line, and "the last of Japan's aircraft carriers" eliminated at Leyte Gulf (page 22). In fact, two more Japanese carriers were later sunk by submarines, several bombed into rubble at Kure and other bases, and several more captured. The authors also have us later creating an "independent [of whom?] National Security Agency to prevent similar disasters" (page 311); the nascent NSA was of course already operating, along with the OSS and the OWI, at the time of Pearl Harbor. If it don't work, institutionalize it. The object lesson being propounded is sideways-looking history, at intelligence about nuclear war (page 221); history is hindsight, and it is hard to accomplish with willful distractions.

Although Clausen's brief was to interview Army personnel on behalf of an Army investigation, a brief he managed to repeatedly exceed, he betrayed little curiosity about why the fleet was based at Pearl Harbor. Admiral Richardson, the former Pacific fleet commander, is quoted as saying the Japanese could have also attacked Puget Sound, as though that was where the fleet had been based (page 250), and as though he hadn't vociferously opposed the Pearl basing to the point of effectively ending his own career. Actually, of course, the fleet had earlier been based at San Diego, which was thousands of miles farther away from Japan, and would have necessitated nearly a week of exposure within shipping lanes for an attacking force, four thousand miles of steaming at high speeds which would have drained destroyers burning more than four tons of oil an hour and mandated two refuelings in enemy waters, two more than did the Pearl raid. Bear in mind that Japan started the Pacific War because of its oil shortage, and that most of its oil reserve and ships were involved in capturing the oil of the East Indies and the military threats near it.

Puget Sound was not really a big naval base, it was mostly a naval shipyard specializing in repair and rebuilding, something Pearl's "combat-ready" battleships urgently needed even before -- especially before! -- they were attacked. Clausen and Lee neglect their mandated rebuilding, continuing to play Clausen's accustomed game of protecting FDR and his minions. The book is fraught with references to "trials", "interrogations", "conspiracies" and allegations of attempted political profiteering by isolationists. Nonetheless, Clausen admits the sequence of Army activities and his part in them, which included the suppression of politically damaging information, including about enemy codes even 25 years after those enemies had been occupied. With such suppression of information, is it odd that other conspiracies are alleged? Even the authors admit the responsibility of Stimson and FDR (page 40) for American secrecy laws.

For Clausen and Lee, however, the real enemy was the Republican Party, the possibility that it might succeed in chalking up some of the disasters that occurred to Democratic leadership. For some, mud only sticks when Mr. Hoover's party is the target, even if the mud is self-inflicted. But the Democrats had been in absolute control; inter-service problems or inept officers were all Democratic omissions or appointments. Where should the buck have stopped, if not at the Commander-in-Chief's desk? FDR ordered the fleet to Pearl Harbor, he kept the battleships there despite their congressionally scheduled re-building and he adopted a Japanese-baiting foreign policy of progressive trade sanctions and military aid to China, all of which Clausen and Lee deny the existence of; **those** were the "proximate and contributory causes of the disaster at Pearl Harbor" (page 8).

However much FDR may have "loved the Navy", the assertion that "[h]e would never have allowed his precious ships and men to be sent to the bottom" (page 310) is fatuous. Before Pearl Harbor, Roosevelt was not only risking ships in the Atlantic war-zones, he had already lost one. He and his advisors wanted the U.S. in a "two-ocean war", albeit on the Germany First basis that even Clausen and Lee admit, and the loss of ships and men in war-time is rather a given. As for the Army's implication of its own men Short and Marshall, the authors admit that Marshall withheld evidence, although they do not admit his responsibility for those under his command. And the authors spread their own noisome theories.

For example, they fault Pearl Harbor commander Admiral Bloch for not passing on to the Army his intelligence that "at least one [Japanese] carrier division and one-third of the overall submarine fleet" "were located in the vicinity of the Marshall Islands." (page 232) But, of course, Bloch's information about the Japanese carriers was false -- the big three Japanese carrier divisions were about to leave Japan itself, another carrier division consisting of incomplete conversions was still in Japan and committed to a reserve role for the thrust to the south, a single carrier was in Japan for training and never saw combat until attacked in

1945, and the only Japanese carrier outside of Japan was at Palau, nearly two thousand miles on the other side of the Marshalls from Hawaii, and poised to move east, not west. A pair of seaplane carriers was anomalously classed as a "carrier division" at that time (and was eventually converted to aircraft carriers), but this "carrier" division was also at Palau. As for submarines, there were indeed three squadrons in the Marshalls (as opposed to four squadrons earmarked for the East Indies), but Bloch himself didn't believe in the submarine threat even when Japanese midget submarines were attacked at the entrance to Pearl Harbor itself, an action he tried to cancel, but would later, as a broken man, appropriate as proof of his vigilance.

The authors labor to point out that Kimmel did not tell Short of this information held by Bloch, but they admit several things that show the banality of that allegation. First, Short's orders were to protect the base, which Bloch commanded, not the fleet, which Kimmel commanded. Second, an appendix contains a Clausen letter wherein he describes three affidavits and other "proof previously reported" to show that Short **did** know of the alleged Marshalls build-up (page 404(h)). And third, the War Department had told Short on November 26, 1941 to send two armed B-24s to Jaluit in the Marshalls (pages 437-38); this was six months before that plane nominally entered active service, and an order for an armed violation of Japanese airspace should have told Short that something was up there. Note that the War Department was telling Short to violate the "Joint Air Operations Agreement" giving the Navy the responsibility for recon.

Did Short investigate and find no carriers? Had the headmen on Oahu directed their full attention to a phantom carrier threat in the Marshalls, west-southwest of Hawaii, a false alarm which distracted them from where the carrier raid came from, the northwest, and helped erode their confidence in American intelligence? Although Clausen and Lee do fault the Army on occasion, such as its anti-aircraft inadequacies (not land-locked on peaceful Hawaii, Navy ships could practice at sea and hence had ammunition on board), their main emphasis is the old inter-service bugaboo, for which the Navy is primarily blamed. For example, Kimmel is faulted for not having carried out his "Joint Air Operations" recon responsibility, although the Army was holding back about half of the patrol planes in Hawaii. The authors neglect to mention that such planes were only later placed under Navy control when the Army was relieved from generic maritime patrol.

Clausen and Lee's book is, in the fairest and also most pejorative sense of the word, revisionistic. It is part of a continuing effort to excuse America's leadership of the time for the policies it pursued and their consequences. Clausen is obsessed with the notion that he was some kind of primary source of information with regard to Pearl Harbor and that others are "second avenue historians", and many of those biased. In fact, Clausen was a primary source not for Pearl Harbor, but rather for the later apologias for it, biased to protect Stimson, Marshall and Roosevelt, including their roles in stymying earlier investigations. Almost inevitably, the book veers into a self-contradictory defense of General Marshall's post-war China policy ("pre[-]ordained to fail", page 252) and an attack upon its opponents, specifically Senator McCarthy. Why shouldn't someone oppose a policy that was "pre[-]ordained to fail"? Sounds like a stupid policy! Quite obviously, what was being protected was General Marshall, failed mediator and architect of foreign aid giveaways. Clausen and Stimson, Republican internationalists, were protecting their beliefs, the Army and the administration by scapegoating General Short, inter-service problems, and the Navy. Their mission was not the truth, something we should never expect from a bureaucracy anyway. But we should expect that a publishing house can always be "pursuaded" (page x) by one of its senior editors to publish such drivel.

The charge that gets FDR defenders angriest is the charge that he deliberately exposed the fleet at Pearl Harbor to Japanese attack in order to get the U.S. into war. There no evidence that he did not do so, and some evidence to suggest that he expected war. There is also the fact that he relieved a concerned commander on the spot, and that he failed to provide the base with adequate reconnaissance, preferring to divert the planes needed to other countries and their needs and to future U.S. offensive operations. There are also various statements on the record that FDR and his subordinates expected other American possessions to be the targets of surprise attack, and indeed to be overrun. They actually planned on it happening, absent the commencement of war at American initiative. Why they should have thought Pearl invulnerable, especially in view of its known inadequacies, is inexplicable at best. The problem for FDR's defenders is that there is no evidence in his favor, merely actions that at best, such as his stymying of legislated ship modernization, were criminally negligent. Absent a clear statement of intent regarding Pearl Harbor (as opposed to, say, the Philippines), we can only plumb Roosevelt's intent from his actions. When the U.S. is caught flat-footed and thousands killed after the commander-in-chief takes diplomatic actions that he believes will, or at least had previously stated would, cause such blows to take place, the burden should be on his defenders; they have avoided that burden precisely because they cannot meet it.

There is evidence that Roosevelt planned, for early 1942, to get the U.S. into war with Japan by launching a bombing raid on Japan by American "Flying Tigers" operating from China. Had this gimmick succeeded, the Pacific Fleet battleships would **still** have remained unmodernized, unnecessarily risking their later permanent lost at sea, instead of temporarily on a harbor bottom.

The command structure at Hawaii was scapegoated in 1941-2 and subsequently. In 1992, in a typical post-war "reform" economization, Navy and Air Force nuclear attack forces were placed under one command, "solving" the Pearl Harbor "flaw" of a divided command. Of course, the real flaw at Pearl Harbor, the restriction of the Navy to flying boats for maritime patrol, was addressed in mid-1942 by allowing the Navy to operate land-based patrol planes, removing Army Air from that mission. The modern analogy to the Navy's old restriction to flying boats is the Army's restriction, since 1959, to helicopters, in lieu of fixed-wing aircraft; that flaw has yet to be addressed.

The torpedoing of the *Saratoga* (page 39) occurred in January 1942, after the failure of the Wake relief mission, when it had resumed its voyage to the West Coast interrupted by the attack on Pearl Harbor.

The criticisms of General MacArthur for the parlous state of the Philippines, including the success of the Japanese air raid of December 8, are off-base primarily not because MacArthur won brilliant victories, but because he delayed and damaged the enemy more with the means available to him that did comparable Allied commanders in Hawaii, Malaya or the Dutch East Indies. His ground forces fought better and longer than did the British in Malaya or the Dutch in the East Indies, and his air force was far smaller (albeit with many B-17s) than either ally's or that equipping General Short and Admiral Kimmel in Hawaii. It is noteworthy that General MacArthur's Air Force, lacking radar, anti-aircraft artillery at Clark Field and visual reconnaissance forces, lost only 42 planes in the first onslaught by two Japanese naval air flotillas (about 200 attack bombers), while a single Japanese naval air flotilla (98 attack bombers, with 10 scouting for 61 carrying torpedoes and 27 carrying bombs) two days later sank two British battleships, each at sea, maneuvering, with radar and with more than a hundred anti-aircraft guns defending them. Similarly, MacArthur lost less than 1/3 of the aircraft lost in the Pearl Harbor raid, even though the Pearl Raiders' main target was the American fleet, not aircraft. MacArthur simply had no fleet to distract the Japanese set upon him. But MacArthur did come out best of the three early Allied aerial victims (or the best of four, counting the five later serial American air disasters in the East Indies, each as big a defeat as the Clark Field attack, as a single incident) as well as best of the three Allied field generals.

Morison's criticisms of Admiral Fletcher can be found in his *The Two-Ocean War* ("*TOW*")(Boston 1963) at pages 77 and 138n. That book was a late summation of his 15-volume *History of the United States Naval Operations in World War II*, in serial production from the late 1940s. Fletcher's relief does not appear to have been political, so that Morison's rancor was personal, the application of special standards to an accomplished individual. But Morison's evaluations could change, and for reasons other than personal.

For example, in 1948, Morison described the 1942 Admiral Theobald as "one of the most able and energetic flag officers in the Navy" (Morison, III, *Coral Sea, Midway and Submarine Actions, May 1942-August 1942* (Boston 1948), page 166), a group Morison mostly praised. Morison attributed Theobald's later relief from the North Pacific command at Dutch Harbor as resulting from friction with the Army, "[a]lthough Theobald was right" (VII, *Aleutians, Gilberts and Marshalls, June 1942-April 1944* (Boston 1951), page 17) in the specific incident. But after Theobald had gone public with his own book attacking Morison's patron FDR, Morison's tune changed in *The Two-Ocean War*: "'Fuzzy' Theobald thought he knew better.... The Japanese could have landed at Dutch Harbor, for all the protection it had from Theobald" (page 151), and Theobald's relief was limned as "Cincpac wanted Kincaid to command the North Pacific Force based on Dutch Harbor, where 'Fuzzy' Theobald was making a mess of things" (page 209). What reason for this flip-flop -- more extensive treatment in one volume than in 15 -- other than that Theobald had been "politically incorrect" in attempting to revise the so-called official history (contemporary public relations apologia, in Morison's case, mutating into the calculated and malicious falsification of history)?

It was Morison, elsewhere a fervent foe of such "revisionists" ("History through a Beard", by FDR's beard in *By Land and By Sea* (N.Y. 1953), the year before Theobald's book), who literally became a revisionist with a vengeance. "Fuzzy" Theobald was "Baldy" Smith all over again, an attempt to obscure the massive flaws of a politically correct icon, FDR instead of Lincoln, by deliberately disfiguring innocent bystanders. Describing one's opponents as "revisionists" is a sure sign not of the sober pursuit of truth but rather of orthodox ideology (Stalin allied with Trotsky, or Mao and the Red Guards, for examples), and the desire to maintain it; actual error would be dismissed as incompetence were reality, instead of some politically palatable worldview, at issue. Morison's publishers find such lines of enquiry "too academic", although they were glad enough to publish an academic.

One indication of the court historians' treatment of history is the different reception accorded the ultimata of McKinley and FDR. McKinley's is treated as having been imposed by a jingoistic press upon a passive president, who then provokes war with the blameless Spanish victims. The Spaniards' previous bloody malevolence and their own declaration of war has to be ignored to distort American resolve and competence into an unjustified aggression. Yet when FDR sent his ultimatum in November 1941, American newspapers at the time unblushingly referred to it as an "ultimatum" (the egregious *New York Post*, for example, which Roosevelt had partly owned); but after Pearl Harbor the characterization as an ultimatum was restricted for a generation to "revisionists". As usual, it was the apologists who did the revising.

Halsey was handicapped before and after the Battle of Midway by a rash. Usually just rash, he was relieved late in 1945 for unnecessarily exposing his ships to typhoons.

After Fletcher's "controversial" refueling before the failure to relieve Wake, the island was soon slated for the first American carrier raid, Admiral Wilson Brown in the *Lexington*, but his tanker was sunk. Such tankers were most important for the destroyers of a carrier's screens, light ships with large engines and small fuel capacity; their primary purpose was to shield from submarines such as the one which sank the tanker involved. Fletcher was also criticized for refueling in the Coral Sea after damaging the Japanese Solomons force; it is fortunate he did so, because his tanker was soon sunk by Japanese carrier aircraft.

Morison's anachronistic quote about a diversionary spectacular is from his volume III, page 389. The failed Rabaul raid is mentioned by Rohwer and Hummelchen, I, page 185. Morison says the raid happened in *TOW*, page 139; his "paled in comparison" sneer is on the same page.

The Japanese carrier fleet raided Java in 3/42.

In addition to the fustian written apologias for American muckings-about in World War II, there were contemporary newsreels and films and later documentaries, film and video. Almost all of these rely upon unattributed stock footage or outright fakery. Wars were fought and won before such idiocy; modern media as a political instrument simply meant one more source of lies and deceptions, one more technology to intercept any iota of truth trying to slip through. Is it really surprising that people viewing "documentaries" about Pearl Harbor, with sound effects added (synchronized with distant explosions, too!), close-ups of "Japanese" pilots from cameras on studio mock-ups, low-flying planes (special effects) disappearing into high clouds, cameras waiting all over Hawaii for the big fly-by, American dive-bombers and training planes tricked up in Japanese colors, etc. etc., should suspect they are being lied to? They were, and continue to be. Actor Monte Markham's effort said the Doolittle Raid "turned the tide of" the Pacific War. Morison lackey Henry Salomon gave us NBC's faked-up *Victory at Sea*. War by public relations meets fake history, the electronic Morison.

Japan's fiscal policies, the 1930 valuation of the yen at one per dollar, had cut trade with foreign nations except that at the government's direction. In the Pacific Nuremberg Trials, one alleged indication of Japanese aggression was its proliferation of automobile companies (six; although two were under control of the Fuji combine, these were functionally independent), so unlike the American trend toward merger and monopoly (six at the time, including Studebaker, Packard-Nash and American); another alleged indication was the size of Japanese industrial/finance combines, whose break-up was pursued by the occupation in the Jackson/Truman tradition of fighting the big banks, the "money pow-er". Japan's pursuit of rational financing and product competition was and remains under-appreciated in this country, which tries instead for bigness in itself, without market discipline, as an "industrial policy" to succeed the passing of anti-trust discipline. Such was the Pacific enemy.

Franklin Roosevelt followed in Cousin Theodore's footsteps as far as attitude, including the naval orientation and the fear and suspicion of Japan, generally justified. Although Roosevelt had signed onto a Germany First agenda at a time when the U.S. was officially at peace, it is noteworthy that both the U.S. and Britain planned to war upon Japan at a later date. Although the China War is usually accepted as the starting point for that hostility, the U.S. had treated Japan as its most likely future foe from the end of the Russo-Japanese War, 1905, when China had not been a target (the land war had been fought mainly in Manchuria, then ideologically allowed to be distinguished from China).

American peace mediation did succeed in expelling Japan from Manchuria for a generation, but it was Pyrrhic diplomacy. Keeping Japan off the mainland merely meant that its center of expansionary gravity, Formosa (Taiwan) and Chosen (Korea), was kept unnaturally near the American-possessed Philippines. The Taiwan seizure had come before the Open Door, and Japanese control of Korea, made official in 1908, had substantially occurred after Napoleon III's France and Grant's U.S. had failed in takeover bids there.

Marshall's conference notes quoted in James MacGregor Burns' widely available *Roosevelt*(Volume 2)*: The Soldier of Freedom* (N.Y. 1970), page 86. Stark's inflammatory description of the occupation of Iceland with "OK FDR" is *ibid.*, page 105. It is significant that such a sympathetic biographer as Burns, a Democratic historian in the Schlesinger Jr. tradition, should have so graciously conceded one charge of earlier so-called revisionists, although always with the proper deference to Roosevelt the icon.

4. <u>The Doolittle Raid</u>. The exchange of letters between the Roosevelts took place a week after his 1940 re-election. They have been repeatedly cited elsewhere. Aside from East Indian oil, Franklin fretted in his reply about Mexican oil, something the U.S. would have had more leverage over if FDR hadn't sat on his hands while it was being nationalized, and its Americans owners robbed.

Thomas B. Buell's Admiral King biography, *Master of Sea Power* (Boston 1980), describes Admiral King as the mainspring of the Doolittle Raid (page 178), although Buell also cites in an appendix (V, page 504) King's memo of Pacific strategy of the previous month in which King emphasized the importance of protecting Australia and New Zealand. Morison's statement about the Doolittle Raid and supposed Japanese over-extension is from his volume III, page 398. Morison's contrary implication that the Midway operation was to have followed the

Coral Sea attacks is from *TOW*, page 140. John B. Lundstrom, *The First South Pacific Campaign: Pacific Fleet Strategy December 1941-June 1942* (Annapolis 1976), outlines Japan's Southwest Pacific strategy at page 45; the possibility of removing Yamamoto at page 46, along with Lundstrom's belief that the Doolittle Raid "compelled ... adopting the whole Midway plan" although Yamamoto's assistants already "knew they would triumph" in getting the Midway Plan approved even before the Doolittle Raid; at page 44, however, Lundstrom states that previous American raids compelled the Midway operation; Lundstrom's testimony to the intelligence value of the Doolittle raid is at page 81, specifically submarine deployment, at page 44. The major damage to the U.S. at Midway, the sinking of the *Yorktown*, was done **after** the air battle by a Japanese submarine unaffected by radio intelligence, and radio intelligence could have been just as well gathered from less spectacular carrier raids as had already sparked futile and hasty Japanese pursuit, such as those on the Gilberts and Marshalls by Halsey and Fletcher (Rohwer and Hummelchen, I, page 183).

Brown's attempted raid on Rabaul was publicized because it led to the first significant air battle by American carrier planes. The publicity given to O'Hare and Thach overshadowed failure to make the raid.

Napalm was first used in the mid-1944 Marianas campaign, from Army fighter-bombers. It was also being used by 1945 from Marine fighter-bombers, so it was very possible that it was also used from Navy or Marine bombers in the January 1945 attack on the Japanese naval base in Central Vietnam.

5. <u>German-Bashing</u>. DeKalb would have seemed the obvious alternative to Steuben in the subtitle, except that he was one German who spent most of his military career in French service.

One piece of gibbering idiocy in German-bashing propaganda is the equation of modern Germans with the German barbarians invading the Roman Empire. Leaving aside Roman Imperialism, the attacks of the Romans upon Germany, and their later decadence, it is worth noting that many of the *non*-German states are descended from those early Germans. The Franks, Burgundians and Visigoths are ancestors of the modern French, Vandals, Goths and Suevi of Spaniards, Lombards, Goths and Vandals of Italians, Saxons and Angles of the English, etc. etc. The modern Germans are among the **least** related to those old wandering warriors; their ancestors are the ones who stayed home, who **didn't** go militaristically raiding.

One big American fan of Napoleon III had been travel book author Mark Twain, an admirer of France's big new avenues and efficient railroads. Twain was newspaper-editing in 1870 Buffalo when Napoleon III was overthrown, making him newly and vitriolically anti-French. This, along with his schemes for a civic clean-up of the Buffalo Creek shanty town, with its murders and epidemics, caused rival newspapermen to forge an old map of Buffalo, "proving" that the word Buffalo was "really" French for beautiful river, not the Niagara but Twain's local eyesore. Locals and visitors are still being taken in by this canard.

Dr. Jameson had been tried for his raid. He received a token sentence, including credit for his time on trial -- when he had been free and the toast of London society -- and a royal pardon on the ludicrous grounds of ill health. Returning to his strenuous life in South Africa, he lived another twenty-five years. His honor was the highest short of being ennobled, a baronetcy, a title with a bad reputation. It had been started by King James I as a purchased title for royal revenue. Europe had become choked with Mexican silver, causing inflation; expenses increased as old revenues became inadequate and Parliament wasn't voting more. The initial fee for a baronetcy was 1,095£, the birth of modern marketing, only ten ninety-five! After having roped in all who would pay 1,095£, James, still needing money, knocked the price down to 600£. This let in the riff-raff, while alienating those who had paid the top price. One of the latter was Sir Richard Greenfield, Bart., who tried to blow up Edinburgh Castle with James' son Charles in it.

Winston Churchill's nightmare of peaceful German control of Europe -- an early Master-Race Treaty, as it were -- is taken from his 1931 speculative essay "If Lee Had Not Won the Battle of Gettysburg" in J.C. Squire (ed.), *If It Had Not Happened Otherwise* (London 1931), reprinted in Benford, G. and Greenberg, M. (eds.), *What Might Have Been* (N.Y. 1991). Churchill's premise, that a disunited America would have obviated World War I, is a subtle hint of pre-World War I British fear of the burgeoning U.S. and its effect on British nerves, and therefore on subsequent British aggression against Germany.

Another extremely anti-German voice retrospectively admitting fear of peaceful Germany was G.M. Trevelyan: "Germany aimed at drawing first Russia and then France into her orbit. Britain would then be at her mercy. We were no longer in a position to defy a united Europe.... [T]he danger of such a European combination under German leadership was actual." (*History of England*, Volume III (N.Y. 1953 3rd Ed. PB), page 276). The "actual" event was that the other three nations drew into a common orbit and attacked Germany militarily.

The Anthrax citations can be seen in the (British) *Foreign Office Index* (London). The actual documents are on file at the Public Record Office, unless bowdlerized earlier or later for matters embarrassing to the British government, as have other such documents.

Mary McGrory column as carried in the *New York Post* (anathema to liberals during the first Rupert Murdoch ownership, many young liberals do not remember when the Post's flagrant sensationalism was leftist, and therefore welcome).

Belgium's initial essay into non-neutrality was within the decade of its establishment -- in part by Anglo-French blockade of the Netherlands, buttressed by German and Prussian diplomatic support. The early Belgium was smaller than that of today, not only lacking the German portion of the Ardennes annexed after World War I, but also with the Netherlands retaining all of greater Luxembourg and greater Limburg. With Britain and France distracted in 1839 by their quarrel over Egypt, Belgium and the German Confederation partitioned the two areas, with Belgium getting most of Luxembourg while the Dutch were fobbed off with the right to re-establish a branch of their royal family on the rump (which persists to this day alongside Belgium's Luxembourg province) and Belgium getting most of Limburg and the German Confederation a slice. Since all of greater Luxembourg had, even under Dutch rule, been part of the German Customs Union, this was by no means a unilateral German advance (three years later, in 1842, independent Luxembourg rejoined the German Customs Union). It is significant that neutral Belgium's first big splash on the international scene was a despoilation, in cahoots with Germany, of its Dutch uncle. Belgium the victimizer was a historical curiosity not allowed to infect the reams of Anglophilic and Francophilic propaganda, however. It that respect Belgium was to World War I what Poland and Soviet Russia were to World War II, three predatory states themselves preyed upon.

The response of France, during the prolonged Egyptian crisis, was in 1840 to demand the Rhine as a French frontier, reacting to the Belgian-German aggrandizement it had been left out of as well as conveniently sabre-rattling at the British and other powers opposing France in Egypt. The Rhine frontier would have meant France taking over Belgium, Luxembourg, Limburg, the Palatine, most of the Prussian Province of the Rhine and a large area of the Netherlands. The sponsoring French minister was Thiers, then and subsequently a major figure in France as tricked up as a German victim. Thiers' last significant acts were to organize the crushing of the French Communes in 1871 (France devastating itself) and then to organize the rapid repayment of French war indemnities to the new German Empire. This last minor achievement, by a country largely unmarked by war and with its trade and finances intact, was later used to justify the attempt to crush defeated Germany beneath the weight of the Versailles reparations, which many French sponsors hoped would leave the Germans forever prostrate and unable to pay.

Before British public opinion had been massaged over the German "rape" of Belgium, "in defiance of solemn diplomatic undertakings", British leadership had weaseled out of the various international guarantees of Moroccan neutrality. Planning to enlist France and its rivalry with Germany into the British scheme for invading an engaged Germany through neutral Danish water (internationalized for peaceful purposes), the British were soon egging on the French in their various schemes, such as seizing control of Morocco. Other guarantors -- Italy, Spain and Portugal -- were soon mollified with French bribes (made, as usual, with other peoples' countries), and only Germany proved obdurate in upholding the "scrap of paper" which guaranteed Moroccan neutrality. For this, Germany was promptly branded a war-monger. The time was not yet ripe in Eastern Europe for Russia to step into a war with Germany, so the opportunity for a big war was temporarily forgone. But the publicity build-up helped brand Germany as a trouble-maker, to the credulous and their descendants, so the Moroccan crises were not a total waste. Along with rancor against Germany distilled from Alsace-Lorraine and South Africa, the Moroccan vintage would be blended into alleged German atrocities in Belgium.

The three big Balkan Wars were 1877-78, 1912 and 1913. There were also the 1885-86 Serbian-Bulgarian War, the 1897 Greek-Turkish War and the 1911-12 War between Italy and Turkey (fought mostly in Libya), with Italy also bombarding the Dardanelles forts and occupying Rhodes and its neighbors, subsidiary actions in Asia Minor.

Events in 1908 tied together the earlier and later Balkan wars. Austria's 1878 occupation of Bosnia-Hercegovina was consummated by annexation in 1908, while Bulgaria and Serbia's 1885-86 falling-out and other Balkan rivalries were papered over by prospective plunder. Making those actions possible was the "Young Turk" Revolution of 1908, together with Greek revolts in Macedonia and Asia Minor, although recently defeated Russia's pressure on Turkey was successfully resisted with various foreign support. As in the next year British support of France became official, the priorities of those nations shifted to Western Europe and Germany; their roles as bulwarks of Turkey ended, they even cemented their relationship by planning a Turkish partition. The Balkan Wars of 1911-12, 1912, 1913 and 1914 impended, courtesy of the struggle for parts of the Ottomanless Empire.

The role of Bismarck as prototypical German warlord is a product of diseased minds. Bismarck was a civilian, a lawyer, politician, farmer and humorist, not a professional militarist -- he had less military experience than did Michael Dukakis. The state of Prussia, as later with the German Empire, operated with a separate structure for the military and the civilian governments. The military reported to the Emperor and, for appropriations, to the legislature. Bismarck had no control over the German military, and no professional politician voluntarily relies upon people not under his control. Furthermore, in Bismarck's ouster, the famed episode of "letting down the pilot", Wilhelm II's steady ally was the military chief of staff von Waldersee, who thought Bismarck's policy of friendship with Russia was wrong, that Russia would be a future opponent. With France in eclipse, that idea did have brief merit, but von Waldersee's successor, von Moltke, the son of his immediate predecessor, rated France as the most likely, and most vulnerable, foe (in 1914, the youngest von Moltke and the younger von Waldersee had break-downs on their fathers' respective emphasized fronts).

Britain's 6 1914 divisions do not include its Indian or Common-wealth "Territorial" forces, which would include Canada's, South Africa's and the Australian-New Zealand Corps (ANZAC).

Two French coinages which unfortunately didn't get into English were *oblos* for shells, meaning oblong and imparting the critical aero-dynamic aspect while negating the frequently misleading -- for smaller calibers anyway -- aspect of a complex shell, and *contre-torpilleurs* for destroyers, leaving clear the genesis of the class as opponents of torpedo boats, a sense lost in the dropping of torpedo boat as a modifier of de-stroyer; but then, the French would probably have been cut to *contres* if that expression had been adopted for English.

The valence of military words changes with technology. The grenade was originally named after the smooth pomegranate, but with shrapnel-inducing incisions in the fragmentation type it came to resemble a pineapple or, with a handle for those nations without a baseball-throw-ing or cricket-bowling tradition, it came to resemble a potato-masher. A mortar was originally a heavy bowl-shaped cannon resembling the pharmaceutical tool, until it was re-invented by Stokes into an elongated light tubular rocket-launcher, not mortar-like at all; the silly modifier "trench" was soon dropped. The torpedo was originally a torpid device named from the marine creature with torpid habits, a bottom-feeding ray, but kept the name when re-invented as a streamlined self-propelled vehicle, more like a shark, which happens to be a distant relative of the rays. Torpedoes were originally automobile torpedoes, until the horse-less carriage took the inappropriate name of automobile, or self-driven, for an object driven by a driver. With the name torpedo taken, mines of the nautical type got their definitive name, although pseudo-precisionists had attempted to call them submarine mines in counter-distinction to landmines, but the submarine took back that name. One opponent of the submarine in later years was the frigate, a small cheap escort taking its name, and nothing else, from the important sailing ship of the same name.

6. The Cold War. More actually traumatic for American Com-munists than the Truman-"McCarthy" episode was the Browder-Hall succession. Part of the obfuscation of people denying that they them-selves, or Mao and company, were Communists was the standard of ide-ology. Loyally disloyal Americans had their bona fides challenged not only by patriots, but also by each other. Some left the party with Trot-sky, some left "active work" with Browder's ouster, others ended on the Chinese side of the Sino-Soviet split.

Several "innocent victims of McCarthyism" turned up as long-term residents of Mao-land, for example (and as "revisionists" there when the Party line switched), even as the son of one Red China Hand who had denied the validity of Mao as a Communist ended up defending the Soviets for their downing of a Korean airliner (joining those other two apexes of the media Iron Triangle, an academic and a former investigative reporter for *THE NEWSPAPER OF RECORD*). After all, if Mao had been a real Communist, Stalin wouldn't have been trying so hard to correct him. Another tact has been to inflate, or to deflate, the "innocent victims". The point of the first is to magnify the accused and their accomplishments, what is generally known as the halo effect. Careerism becomes some sort of virtue, and dissembling becomes prophecy. The simultaneous, and opposite, tact is to emphasize the obscurity of those innocent victims, just some plain old joes doing their jobs, leaking a few secrets and then fleeing the country or staying behind to stonewall.

The usual bromide defending Communists is that they are idealists and humanists who got caught up in an activity that got corrupted. While Marx's wild and windy prose is hardly quotable, his clearer and earliest associate Engels was much more straight-forward. In *Scientific Socialism*, Engels called the title condition possible upon a technology new to him: barbed wire made real socialism possible, because people could be kept imprisoned in a socialist society, instead of being allowed to leave when conditions displeased them, as in the old "Utopian" communes of voluntary socialists. In a foreword to a collection of Marx's articles on the 1870-71 Paris Commune called *The Civil War In France* (3rd German edition), Engels called the Commune, with its taking and killing of hostages that Marx had variously denied, belittled and excused, an example of what Marx had meant by "the Dictatorship of the Proletariat" (Peking 1970 PB, page 18). If this is what is meant by idealism and humanity, we need less of them.

As with Chambers and McCarthy under attack, so did the Watergate and subsequent "scandals" have the Republicans in the weird position of being threatened with expulsion from office and jail for real or imagined wrongs, political vendettas used to undermine constitutional organs in the guise of legality. The first of these episodes was the Pentagon Papers and the wire-tapping of Morton Halperin, allegedly at the orders of Henry Kissinger. Given Mr. Halperin's later activities, it would seem that Kissinger's judgment on the particular matter was excellent; too bad his larger judgments were markedly duller.

After their initial euphoria over Kissinger's trip to China, liberal Democrats have delighted in blaming Republicans for Communist misdeeds there, constantly calling for trade sanctions. The time for such sanctions against the Communists was before they took over that country, for example when FDR was arming their ill-fated southern army. That accomplished nothing for the Chinese Communists, but Truman's long embargo against Chiang did. Without that particular sanction, there may have been no T'ien An Men Square Massacre, or any of its less publicized and far more massive predecessors.

7. Semantics and Secrecy. The treatment of the Lyme Bay episode as a 1984 media lesson was based on a long chain of assumptions, first, that the landing exercises had been secret; second, that they were a secret from the Germans; third, that the Germans had blundered into the area; fourth, that the nature of the damage and the nature of the landing ships was unknown to the Germans; fifth, that revelation of the exercises or the success of the attack would have jeopardized the Normandy invasion that later took place; sixth, that such successes by German small craft were not a scandal that should have been exposed for the better prosecution of the war; and seventh, that these episodes were news in 1984. Not only is there not a break in this chain, there is not even a single intact link. It was all media swill, from a media that dotes upon amnesia as a way of regurgitating old scoops, many of which are mysteries even to the six-bucks-an-hour "researchers" they employ. It was very appropriate for 1984, anyway.

On May 13, 1994, ABC's Nightline ran yet another Lyme Bay "secrecy" story. Instead of Dorothy Rabinowitz and submarines, this time an American, a British pilot and Garrick Utley find German "E-boats" responsible. E-boats were German motorboats armed with machine guns -- they were too small to carry torpedoes and they were not involved at all in the Lyme Bay episode. This time secrecy was blasted for having browbeaten Allied personnel; its lack of effect on the enemy was completely ignored.

As with the *Iowa* turret explosion, training activites were censured on the basis that the troops being trained were inexperienced, why they were being trained. But of course, those American troops in 1944 England included some who were experienced in North African, Sicilian and/or Italian fighting. The great mass of the rest had more than twice the training of World War I's American soldiers, who had a better combat record.

8. Liberal Distractions. Not only were Truman and Johnson each weak successors grasping at civil rights as an electoral gimmick, each was from a segregated area outside of the Deep South. This meant that each could spurn the Deep South in favor of votes in the liberal North, knowing that their own and various other border states could be carried in spite of the left move on civil rights.

Each had cozy ties with machines in their own states. Truman, from the suburbs of Kansas City of the Prendergast machine, had been brought on board the national ticket as part of the effort to secure the wavering swing-state of Missouri, then still an electoral college giant. FDR also had squared the St. Louis machine, with one alumnus starting a massive scam as head of the Internal Revenue Bureau during FDR's third term (in between White House visits about patronage and politics, the legitimate concerns of Internal Revenue at no point whatsoever); to further court Missouri, that factotum was made Democratic National Chairman for the FDR-Truman ticket, which with two large machines still barely carried off Missouri's electoral votes.

Johnson's machine pals helped him win the Texas Senatorial primary courtesy of a late reporting of some hundreds of voters, who had voted in alphabetical order, some from beyond the grave. The Kennedy-Johnson ticket never met a machine it didn't like, which stood it well in Texas, Illinois, Missouri, Michigan, Ohio, New Jersey and Pennsylvania, as the 1960 Democratic ticket swept the close states by margins congruent with the usual ballot-box stuffing. In 1964, Lyndon Johnson ran a national machine, dispensing enough subsidies and tax-breaks to assist even such lacklustre machines as Cleveland's and Newark's to carry their states. With his Highway Beautification Plan to nobble highway signs, their competitors in the print and broadcast media (including the Johnsons, of course) were soon tilting toward Johnson. How do we get into wars? We let sleazy vermin slime into office.

The modern equivalent of racial integration is sexual and homosexual integration. Does either promote military effectiveness? Or do the promoters have another agenda than military effectiveness? The questions are rhetorical.

A 1993 magazine article and follow-up newspaper column by George Mason University Professor Walter Williams mentioned the 3/5 clause accurately in print for the first time to the author's knowledge. Professor Williams found the author's supplementary comments on that clause and the 14th Amendment "valid" but mentioned his own lack of editorial space (letter to author). The problem is not an overall lack of editorial space, it is the people and attitudes taking up most of it.

The provisionality of the National Defense excuse for federal aid to higher education -- that more college grads would strengthen America's defense -- was emphasized not only by its rapid supersession, but by the hysterical keening of liberals at conservatives who had been to college. Among those scorned as draft-dodgers were Pat Buchanan and Dick Cheney. Buchanan, scorned as an equal-time Bill Clinton dodging the Vietnam War, had in fact been expelled from Georgetown in 1959, losing his ROTC scholarship long before the U.S. became embroiled in combat in Vietnam. And Cheney would appear to have been one college attendee who actually benefitted the nation's defense.

One well publicized critique of the America of yesteryear was Philip Wylie's 1942 *Generation of Vipers*. On page 77 (1955 revision; N.Y. 1958 PB), at the beginning of a diatribe on education of the time, Wylie found the schools were practicing "a sedulous care in teaching the basic principles of the physical sciences..... The school is an organism which teaches reading, writing, and arithmetic.... The next step in school procedure is to teach the child political geography." With an extended generation of more money, we have largely destroyed that level of performance. The bulk of Wylie's diatribe on education was directed at the indoctrination of pupils with pap. We now have an even more inferior grade of that, although our incompetence in the basics ironically prevents its effective absorption. For example, 93% of recent Harvard grads surveyed didn't know that seasonality is caused by the tilt of the earth's axis, and some of them probably didn't know about "our endangered planet".

As disgraceful as is Conkling on Madison Avenue, consider Times Square, where muggers, pickpockets, pimps and prostitutes are defamed by being linked with *THE NEWSPAPER OF RECORD*. Consider also the libelous record of that paper, which claims the right to tell lies about its opponents -- all [of] the libel that is expedient to print.

9. Radiation. The discussion of alpha and beta decay -- the former by heavier elements and causing further damage to atomic nuclei struck by the heavy alpha particles -- should not minimize the danger of fallout. Although both alpha and beta particles are easily shielded against -- merely remaining indoors is enough -- the light elements making up fallout are primarily beta emitters. But along with the easily shielded-against beta electron, the act of decay emits gamma radiation, which can be mutagenic in quantity, and is much more penetrating than either alpha or beta particles. It is this gamma radiation which makes fallout shelter underground or behind thick walls important. Fortunately, most fallout quickly destroys itself because of its short half-life, and does not result in further radioactive by-products, so that the time of shelter is relatively short.

One major whopper of the anti-nukes scare crowd is that a longer half-life is equated with greater danger. This is nonsense (and would make fallout a matter of little concern). First, all matter is somewhat radioactive, although much less so than that designated as specifically radioactive. The longer half-life canard would make ordinary matter more dangerous than highly radioactive matter. In fact, shorter half-life material is more radioactive and more dangerous, the chemical equivalent being nitro-glycerine.

Nor is the natural occurrence of a material any indication of its radioactive potency. Uranium-235 is almost exactly as radioactive as fissionable plutonium, the element that in commercial or military quantities is artificially produced, but U-235 is not a great enviro-bugbear. Both U-235 and plutonium have half-lives of about 25,000 years. Scare-mongers harp upon this to emphasize the longevity of their danger, but both are economically valuable and can be consumed -- made harmless -- to generate nuclear power. That is in fact the present limitation of simple nuclear power generation, that it would in a few centuries use up the earth's supply of fissionable uranium-235 as well as the production of plutonium from non-fissionable uranium-238.

By contrast, radon, with its violent radioactivity from a very short half-life, is being generated from scattered small radioactive pockets in the earth's crust. Thorium is more typically fissionable than uranium, but that apparently occurred naturally very early in the earth's history, dispersing it through spontaneous fission. This may have happened with uranium on a larger scale, but less violently, so that uranium had remained more concentrated (there was apparently some minor natural fission late in geologic time in West Africa, when erosion and sedimentation in streams reconcentrated uranium). Thorium is less valuable because of its dispersion, making its location difficult and its refining expensive. India's and Brazil's large deposits may remain economically unimportant.

There are three sources of heat for the earth. The lowest possible temperature is -459.67 degrees F., Absolute Zero. The first source, cosmic heat, apparently from the initial formation of the universe, would raise this by somewhat more than five degrees, to approximately -454 degrees F. The second source, geologic heat, although spectacular at a few discrete locations -- volcanoes and geysers -- is insufficient to raise the earth's base temperature beyond -450 degrees F. The third source of heat is solar, and raises the earth's temperature from -450 to an average of 60 degrees F., an increase of 510 degrees F. at one astronomical unit from the sun. The planet Venus, at .72 astronomical units from the sun, is accorded the status of an object lesson for the earth by such "peace" activists and "environmentalists" as famed television scientist Carl Sagan. Sagan denies that Venus' proximity to the sun is "significant" in causing its high temperature.

Under Newton's Inverse Square Law, of which Sagan may have heard (it is also a factor in the older bugbear of overkill from explosive atomic radiation), a patch of Venus at .72 AUs receives the reciprocal of the square of that distance, 1/.72 squared (the basis of the Inverse Square Law is simple geometry -- the sphere heated by the sun expands with greater distance, diluting the radiation). .72 squared is .5184, and that divided into 1 yields 1.929, so that a patch of Venus receives 192.9% as much heat as a similar-sized patch of the earth, or a 93% increase. This would in itself result in an average temperature rise of 474 degrees F., so that Venus' average temperature, assuming an earth-like atmosphere and hydrosphere, would be 534 degrees F. Plainly, there never was any possibility of normality for Venus or its atmosphere, the spoutings of television scientist ideologues notwithstanding.

Nor, as noted, is Venus' composition earth-like. The gas-giant planets were first obviously not earth-like, in spite of the attempts of television scientists to project carbon-containing methane and nitrogen-containing ammonia as their atmospheres. One flawed assumption was that there would be less oxygen in the gas-giants' atmospheres, enabling such fragile organic compounds to persist; but why such huge amounts expected (methane is also produced by volcanoes on earth, but the earth was never considered a fit comparison for the gassy planets)? And why so little of the cosmically abundant free hydrogen and helium? Evidence from meteors had also long revealed the presence elsewhere of differing composition, the comparative abundance of iridium, for example. Moon rocks proved to have similar discrepancies with earth, with the gas-giants and with meteors, featuring huge amounts of titanium, for example.

With those records, why would anyone possibly think Venus would be like earth? There is no water, and the only perceptible hydrogen is the trace presence of sulfuric acid (H_2SO_4) in its thick atmosphere. Liquified, this would give Venus possibly an inch-thick coating of a hydrogen compound, compared to earth's average of thousands of feet of water for its surface. There is abundant oxygen in Venus' atmosphere, albeit tied up with carbon, which may be more common on Venus than on earth (or there just may be more of it in the air around Venus because there is no biosphere there, with water traps to cause carbon to be concentrated). Carbon bombarded with solar particles tends to become radioactive carbon-14 (six protons and eight neutrons), which by emission from a neutron of a beta electron becomes ordinary nitrogen (one neutron having changed to a proton to yield seven protons and seven neutrons). Because of Venus' lack of a strong magnetic field and its proximity to the sun, it should have, with its atmospheric carbon, a small multiple of the earth's quantity of nitrogen; it does, with 3.6 times as much in its atmosphere. Another product of solar radiation is argon atoms produced by the bombardment of chlorine atoms by solar neutrinos (unaffected by magnetic fields and little else beside the occasional chlorine atom). Venus has extremely little argon, and thus would also have extremely little chlorine. The absence of argon and chlorine indicates that it is just not the light-weight hydrogen that is absent, but also more substantial atoms.

For evaluating the temperature of Venus, or any other planet, the energy-retaining characteristics of its constituent atoms is crucial (although heat is molecular motion, the energy for it comes and goes, on a planetary scale, from radiation, and there the atom is more important). Hydrogen and helium are the two atoms with their electron or electrons only at the closest possible orbit or orbits. As they circle the tiny nuclei at 670 million miles per hour, electrons appear to vibrate, and those in the inner shell of orbits, without the damping effect of outer shells possessed by larger atoms, have more possible energy states than do those of more complex atoms, with their more sedate outer electron orbits. (In a molecule where electrons are shared, of course, electrons orbiting the smaller atoms at a given instant would have more energy levels; how an electron could transmit this change in energy levels while passing to an orbit around another type of atom is unknown.) Helium and hydrogen atoms therefore sop up energy for a given temperature rise than do other atoms, making reactive hydrogen's compounds -- ammonia, CFCs, water, anti-freeze, etc. -- valuable as heat storers and temperature maintainers (helium doesn't form compounds and its tiny atoms are hard to store in their non-compounded state).

On a planetary scale, richness in helium and/or hydrogen tends to moderate temperature. Venus, with virtually none, sees its temperature rise beyond the 534 degree F. average it would expect with terrestrial amounts of hydrogen (and terrestrial rotation). This extra global warming occurs not because Venus is an object lesson for the earth, but rather because it is manifestly a different globe.

Such minor validity as there is to the ineptly named Greenhouse Effect arises from the tendency of some atoms and molecules to absorb some wavelengths of radiation, lengthening the radiation as it passes through and turning the energy into heat. The only major gas that does this in the earth's atmosphere is **oxygen**, which absorbs four fairly broad bands of radiation, two in the red spectrum and two in the ultraviolet band. There are two major reasons why carbon dioxide is not a real Greenhouse Threat. First, carbon dioxide is usually formed by the burning of carbon, combining with oxygen already in the air. The oxygen being absorbed into carbon dioxide was already as radiation-absorbent as it was going to get, and the added smaller carbon atom absorbs little additional radiation. Second, assuming the carbon dioxide were a total addition to the atmosphere (say the oxygen came from metal refining, for example), it is transient. Atmospheric carbon dioxide peaks during a hemisphere's winter, when there is little sunlight to be absorbed -- that is why it is winter. In warmer areas, sunlight, open water and growing plants prevent local carbon dioxide build-ups (although the tropics absorb very little carbon dioxide from temperate areas -- "tropical rain forests" are globally unimportant, reflecting climate more than affecting it). In short, the Greenhouse Effect is tripe, a typical left-liberal distraction.

Nuclear Winter is the global equivalent of a mother telling her child to put on clean underwear in case he is hit by a car. If you are hit by a car, there will probably be all sorts of new stains in your underwear, and nobody will notice the old ones. By the same token, bad weather would be overshadowed by a nuclear war.

Planetary chemistry and radiation problems are difficult even for professors. Physics Professor Benford, a more prolific science fiction writer than Carl Sagan, tells us that the presumed ammonia (NH_3) in Jupiter's atmosphere is household ammonia (NH_4OH, ammonium hydroxide), as though Jupiter's atmosphere is water able to dissolve the purported ammonia (*Jupiter Project*, N.Y. 1975; PB 1990, page 20). And he tells us that a carbon atom and an alpha particle come from the breakdown of a nitrogen atom (*Across the Sea of Suns*, N.Y. 1983-4, PB 1987, page 201), when the resulting eight protons and eight neutrons would have to come from an oxygen atom, not a nitrogen atom. Oxygen is the reactive stuff we need to live, nitrogen is the less reactive stuff that keeps us from burning up in the oxygen. Nit-picking? -- there is none without lousy mistakes. But then, as the prolific "Ted Sturgeon" (Edward Hamilton Waldo) used to say, 90% of everything is crud.

Aside from the British canard about depleted uranium, there was also a British canard about being able to detect American Stealth fighters with their Type 1022 naval radars, a fix-up for the Type 965 radars which couldn't find Exocet missiles in the Falklands War. That gives the British a two-to-one lead over the Israelis and their slander of the Patriot missiles in the race for purported friends we can do without.

10. Vietnam and Iraq. An additional parallel between Canada and South Vietnam was Catholicism, largely a remnant of French colonialism in both cases. In Canada, the Catholics were fairly well settled, and had long exasperated the American North, and the colonial West, as the focus of popery and the intrigues of the French king, most particularly as proselytizing and provoking the Indians. But Canadian Catholicism had been watered down by refugee Tories, mostly Protestants. In Vietnam, on the other hand, refugees fleeing to the South were largely Catholics, with their Northern opponents stirring up the Buddhists in the South.

Among The Best and the Brightest were Edsel-man McNamara and that corrupt old ballot box-stuffer and fixer LBJ. The State Department was headed by Southern Rhodes Scholar Dean Rusk (yes Virginia, there is a quota system for American Rhodes Scholars), who had gotten valuable experience for a Cold War Liberal during the Twenty Years of Treason. Rusk had ministered the creation and hand-over of North Korea to the Soviets. What worse experience to lead an Anti-Communist War in South Vietnam? If these were The Best and the Brightest, who were The Bunglers and the Climbers?

Much pre-1972 McGovern info is available in his candid "authorized" campaign biography *McGovern: A Biography*, by Robert Sam Anson (N.Y. 1972). Among the more embarrassing tidbits are that the author was thought well enough of by the Viet Cong and Khmer Rouge that they let him go, and McGovern's World War II habit of bombing farmhouses. Joining McGovern in voting for the Tonkin Gulf Resolution were Senators Eugene McCarthy, Edward Kennedy and 1972 peacenik Hubert Humphrey (Robert Kennedy was still a cabinet member). One of the two in opposition was that squalid old lefty Wayne Morse of Oregon, who had once on the Senate floor described Chiang Kai-shek's $700,000 lobbying expenditure as $700 million, leaving the scholarly opponents of Senator McCarthy's alleged inaccuracies a well used "official" citation that was off by a thousand times.

A phony atrocity story alleged that Iraqi soldiers had disconnected babies from respirators in Kuwaiti hospitals. Kuwait is a small country, with few people, no poor and no drug or alcohol problems. There simply weren't that many babies on respirators in Kuwait. The atrocity was invented for an American audience used to the socio-economic chaos of the permissive society. The media was glad to help circulate the lies when they were needed to whip up support for the Gulf War, and the Israel Lobby in Congress was glad to help. How about a grateful Kuwait waiving diplomatic immunity for the ambassador's daughter who perjured before Congress? No one is asking.

11. Bases. While the Jeffersonian experiment with cheap coastal gunboats is justifiably infamous, the Democrats' concentrations on state militias and fortifications proved invaluable in the War of 1812. Fortifications prevented attacks on most America cities, saved Baltimore and the American base on Lake Ontario and, with one exception lost at sea, even saved the Federalist frigates for their valuable later use against pirates. Typically, the frigates' presence in fortified ports was resented most in Boston, opposed to the first "Democrat War" and the center of American merchant shipping.

The French carriers for their phase of the Vietnam War were the old Washington Treaty convert *Béarn*, reworked into a fully fledged carrier after its modification into an aircraft ferry in the U.S. during World War II following its capture from occupation of the Vichy West Indies; the former late World War II British medium carrier *Colossus*, renamed *Arromanches* after a British D-Day beach; and the former HMS *Biter*, an old Lend-Lease jeep carrier renamed *Dixmunde*. The *Arromanches* operated Hellcats, an American type that had not been Lend-Leased because the British had used the earlier and smaller Wildcats from their jeep carriers and Avengers, Corsairs and navalized and old Fleet Air Arm compromise models from their larger carriers.

Yes, it was President Jimmy Carter, not Senator Sam Nunn, who got the Kings Bay submarine base for Georgia. A President is roughly 200 times as powerful as a Senator. If a buck stops at the President's desk, a ha'penny stops at a Senator's desk. Truman did what McCarthy was credited with; the buck got passed again. But wasn't it Truman's slogan? Yes, it was a slogan, and a deceptive one, nothing more.

12 & 13. Organization. The *Furious'* raid on the Tondern airship base came **after** the RAF's formation but **before** that re-organization had had time to disaffect British naval airpower.

An Austrian submarine torpedoed the French dreadnought *Jean Bart* on December 21, 1914, which did not sink on Christmas Eve (Cyril Falls, *The Great War*, N.Y. 1961 PB, page 92). Rather, it later intervened in the Russian Civil War, was taken out of service in the 1930s and renamed *Océan* as a hulk until scuttled at the death of the Vichy Navy in 1942 Toulon. The unfinished new *Jean Bart* unsuccessfully fought the U.S. *Massachusetts* in North Africa and later -- repaired, finished and modernized -- took part in the 1956 Suez invasion.

Reagan made the White House, if not *Casablanca.*

Comparable efficiency to the British Rolls-Royce Merlin (license-built in the U.S. by Packard) was achieved by Japan's Nakajima Sakae engine. This was efficient, but lighter and less capable of development. 150,000 Merlins powered 12 British aircraft models, Mustangs and very late Warhawks. By contrast, only about 10,000 Sakae engines powered only four Japanese models, all originally naval models with a genesis in the late 1930s. Used in Mitsubishi's famous Zero, the Sakae could take that light aerobatic airframe long distances at high speeds (to save weight, Zeros had only folding wing-**tips**, which were left off the middle Hamp variant); but, as war dragged on, even the Zeros needed larger, if less efficient, powerplants. The Sakae was also used on light scout planes, the single-engined Babs and the twin-engined Irving, but its most devastating use was on Nakajima's own Kate torpedo planes, powering those slowish planes with their specialized torpedoes and adapted battle-ship shells to Pearl Harbor's Battleship Row. Unable to be upgraded for higher performance in faster fighters or torpedo planes, the Sakae passed out of service except for a minor late-war splurge when the Irvings were adopted as high-altitude night-fighters against U.S. B-29s. They could still out-climb many heavier-engined Japanese fighters.

The startling helplessness of land-based air power alone, Billy Mitchell's fetish, was illustrated not only by Pearl Harbor but throughout World War II (as indeed it had been by the first carrier raid back in World War I). Burns (*Roosevelt*(II), page 223) quickly sums up the five disasters in the attempt to defend Java with P-40s in 1942, with successive reinforcements destroyed in the air by the enemy, in the air by bad weather, on the ground in Australia, by the sinking of the aircraft ferry *Langley* (not a "[s]eaplane tender" without a flight deck, as maintained by Morison (*TOW*, page 98), but a ship still with flying-off capability), and finally by the destruction of the last crated allotment by their dumping at sea to prevent their capture by the Japanese. Flying planes to the besieged base had failed so repeatedly, through Japanese air-shielded amphibious advances, that the expedient of shipping the planes crated was tried.

Although the Fleet Air Arm and other RAF Commands were later raided for fighter pilots because of losses in the Battle of Britain, the *Glorious* episode during the evacuation of Norway lost more than a hundred pilots -- and most of those already fighter pilots -- in a few minutes, about ¼ as many pilots as Britain lost in the many weeks of the Battle of Britain. Had the *Luftwaffe* persisted with its air control strategy, using its attack bombers, dive-bombers and twin-engined fighters against radar stations and fighter airfields and factories, that single loss of pilots, by "obsolete" battleships, might have proved decisive.

The incipient American division between Army Air and Strategic Air was illustrated by the division of bombers into light or attack (A) classification, for Army support or ocean patrol, and medium and heavy bombers (B) for strategic bombing of heavily defended targets. The principal difference between twin-engined attack and medium bombers was that the latter had larger crews devoted to serving the machine-gun positions throughout their fuselages, while attack bombers had smaller crews with defensive armament concentrated in the front. The lack of even real medium bombers showed the tactical military role planned for most Axis bombers compared to such authentically medium bombers as the British Wellington and the U.S. B-25 and the original B-26. The Germans just did not have the aircraft for the strategic bombing they eventually tried against Britain, and the British knew it. That is why they baited the Germans into it.

American blimps were pulled out of their short retirement to provide a radar watch of Cuba, inconveniently south of the DEW and other Northern lines. They continue that mission sporadically, along with anti-drug-smuggling patrol.

14. Types of Warships. Part of the misconception about Roman naval affairs stems from the over-valuation of their invention of the "corvus", yet another grappling device for boarding purposes. This did not make a Roman Navy practical, such had existed to fight the Greek city-states for several hundred years, and Roman ships continued to be equipped with rams and large missile-throwing engines. The provision that wealthy Romans subsidize naval equipment and manpower was separate and distinct from the similar military requirements.

Besides the *Chesapeake*, the other unlucky Federalist frigate was the *Philadelphia*, whose capture by Tripoli was thought redeemed by early liberals when Stephen Decatur succeeded in burning it. Although the ship was denied to an enemy, it was also confirmed in its denial to the U.S., which had built it.

The references to boxes are the parts of what are referred to by the pompous as a "weapons system". Before "tanks" was its code for landships, "boxes" was the Royal Navy's code for the seaplanes to be included as designed equipment in its belated provision of Baltic Plan monitors for World War I (Ian Buxton, *Big Gun Monitors* (Annapolis 1980), page 26).

One recent obscuration of the importance of Britain in the inception of the 20th century capital ship race are the figures given for capital ships at the start of World War I by Captain John Moore in his foreword to the compilation *Jane's Fighting Ships of World War I* (N.Y. 1990). Adopting the turbine as a defining feature of the then-modern capital ship, and lumping in some ships still with the semi-heavy guns already found wanting at Santiago and Tsushima and to be found further lacking in the World War I naval battles to come, Moore finds the U.S. with 10 modern capital ships in commission, tied with France and ahead of Japan, given 5.

But those figures are far more inaccurate than those of Millis, who had found the subject "peculiarly tricky" (*Arms and Men*, page 176). Moore's French figure apparently includes their last 6 pre-dreadnoughts and their first 4 dreadnoughts, although the former were unimportant and 2 of the latter were not finished until the following year (contemporary *Jane's* figures often erred); the proper French figure is 2 dreadnoughts available in 1914, not 10. The Japanese figure apparently includes 2 battleships, 2 super-dreadnought battle cruisers and 1 pre-dreadnought battleship with turbine engines, although not its reciprocating-engined sister ship. Yet both of those ships had mostly semi-heavy guns, which, although of the same caliber as the main batteries of the American "second-class" battleships of a generation earlier, were outmoded at the time. Neither ship should have been counted; the proper Japanese capital strength at the time was 4, not 5, or 6. But although Moore uses turbines to include ships, and apparently their absence to exclude a Japanese ship, 5 out of the 10 American ships included did not have turbines, nor did 8 of the German 18. Why make definitions only to ignore them?

The American ships got around, and were as battleworthy as any others of their type, and more so than others not of their type. 9 of them, 4 without turbines, managed to limp over to help Britain hold off the Germans (the turbined ship of one pair did not make it), and that at a time when the British fleet did not have enough heavy shells for a major battle, the greatest secret of World War I (but banal because of the second greatest secret, the German fleet's lack of range to fight that battle near Britain). The U.S. advantage was the conservatism of their ships' propulsion -- without turbines, there was less incentive for the ships to be oil-fired, and oil was in short supply during World War I; only 2 of those 9 American battleships were totally oil-fired. The German position was similar, a coal-rich country with even more advanced technology than Britain's opting for a conservative approach with turbines, and later seeking instead to use oil-conserving diesels.

Millis' quote on the *Dreadnought* making the Royal Navy's own ships obsolete is from *Arms and Men*, page 164. Yet on page 163, he characterized American pre-dreadnoughts as "already obsolete", while on three other pages intermediate positions are taken (*ibid.*, pages 168, 170, 175). Obsolete and outmoded are not the same.

Robert Massie, in *Dreadnought/Britain, Germany, and the Coming of the Great War* (N.Y. 1991), is the source for the quote (page 783) about the British 15-inch gun being 40% more powerful than its likely competitor, the unacknowledged American 14-inch gun. Former Rhodes Scholar Massie is reticent about the importance of the United States in the Two-Power Standard, the first of the Two when the *Dreadnought* was introduced and back to the second of the Two by the start of World War I. Massie is not reticent about when France and Russia were the Two; what except ideology would cause an American writer to neglect an American angle while pursuing a French and Russian angle? Only one contemporary naval gun fit Massie's nearly 40% description, the U.S. 14-inch gun, with the British 15-inch gun having a 37.8% greater shell weight. The British 15-inch gun was 29.6% heavier than the Vickers 1908 model 14-inch gun then being sold to Japan, and only 21.6% heavier than the 14-inch Vickers model 1913 would be, nominally sold to Chile, although the two ships to have been equipped with it were seized for the Royal Navy.

Massie's list of capital ships omits the British battle cruisers *Renown* and *Repulse*, the latter seeing battle alongside two of the also unmentioned Baltic cruisers in 1917, and incorrectly includes Germany's tenth and last armored cruiser, *Blucher*, as a battle cruiser (pages 910-11). Note that the U.S. had 50% more armored cruisers than did Germany and was the first of the Two-Powers in that regard. Were such errors random, there should be a 50% chance that they would exaggerate or denigrate both sides, and a 25% chance that they would denigrate German strength while exaggerating Britain's; instead, at 3-to-1 against randomness, the mistakes dovetail with Anglophilia, showing Britain weaker than it was and Germany stronger.

Similarly, British Vice Admiral Beatty is described as having five battle cruisers under his command at Jutland, when he had 9, along with four of the most powerful battleships then afloat. Beatty not only generally outranked the two Jutland battle cruiser and fast battleship Rear Admirals, he also headed the Royal Navy's Battle Cruiser Command, to which the fast battleships had been assigned. (Beatty was young and dashing, an insubordinate fop. Twitted by Admiral Jellicoe about wearing a six-button coat while the other admirals wore five-button coats, Beatty went about with his lowest coat button undone. This became a fashion statement in Britain after Jutland, when supporters of the impetuous Beatty started keeping their lowest coat button undone, a moronic habit that persists to this day.)

The battle cruiser action was not equal, the Germans won it against overwhelming odds. The German Jutland battlefleet was fleshed out with old battleships, something the British did not have to do; indeed, the massive new *Queen Elizabeth* was in the Mediterranean with many of Britain's old battleships, and the *Dreadnought* itself was with the rest in the Channel Fleet. Britain could commit some of its modern capital ships away from the purported threat, and battle cruiser *Australia* and battleship *Emperor of India* actually took the battle off.

There are also Massie's less willful misconceptions about battle cruisers in general. First, belt armor size was becoming less important during that era, as gun ranges opened up. What was more important was underwater protection -- against torpedoes and mines -- and deck armor -- against plunging shells at long range and, later, aircraft bombs. What disaffected British battle cruisers at Jutland was turret hits which, because of inadequate baffles, flared down into magazines. Second, battle cruisers never joined a battleline of dreadnoughts; rather, fast battleships later worked with battle cruisers. And, because of the torpedo, the battleline at Jutland and subsequently was always attended by unarmored destroyers and frequently also by cruisers, unarmored or armored (the British lost two such at Jutland); such ships were in far more peril in or near the battleline than were battle cruisers.

Massie's book leads off with a description of the 1805 Battle of Trafalgar as saving Britain from an invasion by a huge French army camped near the English Channel (page xiv). But it just wasn't so. At the time of Trafalgar, the French Army was heavily engaged in Central Europe, and the combined French-Spanish fleet wasn't headed for the English Channel, but rather to the Mediterranean, to help install Napoleon's brother Joseph as King of Naples. Admiral Nelson didn't save England; he didn't even save Naples.

A similar sentimentality pervades other views of the Royal Navy. In 1807, at the time of the British ban on the slave trade, it was mainly in the hands of ships operating from Spain, Denmark, and the Netherlands, all then blockaded by the British for trading with Napoleon; indeed, in 1807 Nelson destroyed the remnants of the Danish Navy he hadn't sunk in 1801. This was thuggery, not idealism. And the internal African slave trade continued under British, French and especially Belgian colonialism, with the main pockets of resistance to it -- Togo and the Ibo domain -- claimed, with native support, by Germany.

When France did attain naval parity with Britain, during the reign of Napoleon III (as noted by Massie, page 386, and denied by Massie, page 373), the British worked with him against Russia and encouraged French involvement in other wars. That combination sufficed, and Napoleon III was effectually overthrown by the Prussian Army. Only when the French fleet had been neglected and surpassed, and France had become again a colonial rival to Britain, was the Two-Power Standard promulgated. Although announced for "Europe", where the world's largest navies were at the time, Russia's Pacific fleet was part of the Two-Power calculus from the beginning, Japan was a factor and the U.S. soon became one. That was reflected in the positioning of Royal Navy battlefleets off Asia and North America.

In Massie's view, such positionings helped keep the peace and protect against piracy. But by the time of the Two-Power Standard, sailing ships were in heavy eclipse, along with piracy. The U.S. Navy was far more active against pirates worldwide than the Royal Navy ever was, including against the Barbary pirates. After one early dramatic raid against Tunis -- in the 17th century, the first victory of the institutionalized Royal Navy -- the British had neglected the Mediterranean until bases were won there. When the Mediterranean had become safer, due also to the decline of Turkey itself and the Italian city-states, Britain and other large merchant shippers paid off the North Africans with the cynical knowledge that smaller nations would find their trade adversely impacted by proportionately greater *baksheesh*. And, of course, Britain and some other European states were the major creditors of the Barbary pirates, so that the money was in fact flowing back to Europe, and there were financial interests to prevent the Royal Navy from chastising the Barbary pirates.

When the U.S. took the job in hand and dealt with Tripoli and Algeria, the big European governments and finance were miffed. It was only after the repeat performance against the Berbers by the U.S. in 1815 -- right after the War of 1812 and the Napoleonic Wars had ended -- that the smaller European navies chose bravery over being blackmailed. The Royal Navy took little part. Even more telling was the Falklands; there, a U.S. Navy ship drove out Argentine pirates, and then the Royal Navy scavenged the islands. The Royal Navy was not a charitable institution, and was itself long prone to steal ships, treasure and men, nearly 5,000 of the latter from American ships. Only when the British Empire, most of which had previously been parts of the Spanish, Portuguese, Dutch and French Empires, waxed enormous did the British begin to wallow in Victorian respectability, or rather hypocrisy.

Victoria's Opium War secured British trade, ensuring that Britain could import tea, with taxes which supported the Royal Navy along with what it could seize. Massie doesn't mention this, although he does opine that Britain stopped taxing imports in 1848 (page 326); it didn't, although it did largely stop taxing grain imports in 1846 (after smaller reductions in 1842), a buzz-date in British, and free trade, history.

Aside from helping destroy British agriculture, helping "free trade" mill-owners get cheaper labor and exacerbating a depression in doing so, while ensuring that British food production was low before the onset of the European potato famines -- things that helped make 1848 a famous year in Europe -- "free trade" co-incided with the institutionalization of 1842's income tax, the Inland Revenue. Such taxes would swell and swell, until they were far greater restraints upon "free trade" then customs duties ever were. But not ideologically so.

Massie mentions Royal Navy operations against a Chinese "pirate" fleet in 1857 and a Chinese fort in 1858 as part of a biography of Admiral Fisher (pages 411-12), but doesn't appear to have understood that the British were putting down a massive Rebellion, the Taiping, against the weak government they had intimidated, not an outburst of piracy. The later Boxer Rebellion, with the patronage of the Chinese Government, is weirdly chalked up to the Germans on the Shantung

Peninsula (page 276), although in fact Britain's own Shantung station, and Chinese Christians, were heavier targets. When one wants to write on the history of war and geopolitics, one should know something about geography, war and history.

In the European context, for example, the Hohenzollerns took over Nuremberg -- future home of Nazi rallies, laws and trials -- in 1415, not Stuttgart (page 50) (Stud-garden, a breeding station, the future home of Mercedes). Both Brandenburg and Nuremberg were invaded by the Czechs during the Hussite Wars (after the first wave of anti-German pogroms in Bohemia), with Hohenzollern resistance to this pre-Reformation leading eventually to a late position in the Teutonic Knights Order, picking up the pieces when it was dissolved.

Massie's misconceptions go worldwide when it comes to German colonialism (page 89). First, the German colonies were not primarily desert. German East Africa's driest area got about as much rainfall as did the Junker estates of the German Empire's east or as does the immensely fertile area around Des Moines, Iowa. Second, German East Africa was not modern Tanzania, it became Tanganyika, long British, and Rwanda and Burundi, both long Belgian. Tanzania came from the fusion of Tanganyika with Zanzibar, which was never a German area (pages 209-10, 813), but rather became a British bailiwick as Britain assumed control of its Arabian Omani overlords and then detached Zanzibar as an independent protectorate. Third, the Bismarck Archipelago was never part of the Solomons Islands; it was previously called the New British Archipelago by its Portuguese discoverer. Britain had undisputed control of the southern and central Solomons since 1893, and received some, not all (not Bougainville), of the northern Solomons in 1899 (*not* Guadalcanal, page 261, part of the 1893 protectorate brought in for an American angle so studiously absent from Massie's account of the naval arms race) from Germany in return for recognizing the Bismarck Archipelago and Bougainville as Germany's, the closest thing to a British gift in the entire German colonial empire. Fourth, the Germans did not get the Carolines in 1884; they bought them, along with the Palaus and the Northern Marianas, from Spain in 1900. Fifth, as noted, the non-deserts of Togo and Kamerun, eminently suitable plantation areas including the Ibo portion of modern Nigeria, were solicited as British protectorates, but were hostile to the slaving tribes already "protected" by Britain and France. That is why, when those countries carved up German Africa, the seeds of the Biafra War were sown by detaching the Ibo area from the Cameroons and attaching it to Nigeria.

15. Warships Limited. The treaty cruiser torpedoed twice, according to Morison, anyway, was the *Minneapolis*, hit at Tassafaronga in November 1942 (*TOW*, page 210). As Morison notes, and as is corroborated by the Japanese ships involved, the torpedoes would have been the heavy 24-inch Japanese Long Lance variety. The two trios were the

most borderline cases covered in S. Breyer's monumental *Battleships and Battle Cruisers 1905-1970* (Garden City 1973; German edition, Munich 1970). Morison, *Arkansas* at D-Day, *TOW* page 403; *West Virginia* at Leyte, page 446; a similar error appears in Clausen and Lee, picture following page 262, Kimmel and company, where the *Pennsylvania* is miscredited with 16-inch instead of 14-inch guns.

Aside from the "successful" Washington and London confabs and their Treaties, there were a series of failed 1930s' conferences at which French-Italian rivalry and Japanese ambitions were joined by Germany's re-emergence in negating further limits. National attention and finances already constrained warship engineering. Further constraints merely kept up the cost while negating the achievement of military value for the funds expended. The "failed" conferences prevented more such insanity.

16. <u>Troubled Minds and Troubled Waters</u>. Allied surface warship losses include "battleships" *Prince of Wales* and *Repulse* (a battle cruiser), lost off Malaya from air attack, 12/41; small "heavy" cruiser *Exeter*, small Dutch cruisers *Java* and *De Ruyter* and small Australian cruiser *Perth*, 2/42 East Indies surface battles; treaty heavy cruisers *Dorsetshire* and *Cornwall*, Bay of Bengal Raid air attack, 4/42; and Aussie sister *Canberra,* 8/42 Savo Island surface battle. The only big "light" (six-inch guns) cruiser lost was the American *Helena* in a July 1943 night surface battle.

During the Falklands crisis, there was a British production of Euripides' play about the Greek fleet headed for Troy being becalmed at a place called Aulis. King Agamemnon decides to sacrifice his daughter Iphigenia to the gods that the fleet can be sped on the way to its mission of regaining his faithless sister-in-law Helen. To many, this is a perfect paradigm of the cost of war, its fruitlessness. As Iphigenia was being pulled away to the sacrificial altar, an anguished British policeman in the audience, with a son on the fleet heading for the Falklands, stood up and cried "'Ere, what's Aulis then?"

The description of the *Iowa*s as fairly safe from atomic near-misses will cause even more troubled minds. It is noteworthy that the explosion of the *Arizona*'s forward magazine by a force equal to a respectable modern tactical nuclear weapon left even that old ship with such salvageable items as its two rear gun turrets. Moreover, look at the actual results of the earlier battleships tested by 1946 blasts "Able" and "Baker" compared to the stage of battleship construction represented by the *Iowa*s. The *Iowa*s were seven classes later than the newest U.S. atomic targets, and ten classes later than the *Arkansas*. Each class had seen improved armor and construction. The *Arkansas* was only a year younger than the *Ostfriesland*, Billy Mitchell's famous target, sunk like the Pearl Harbor victims by a surprise attack (Mitchell ignored test rules calling for damage assessment between bombs, converting the tests to a public relations stunt). What did in battleships in battle was conventional weapons accurately and repeatedly delivered. From the latest to the earliest classes of post-London Treaty American battleships:

Post-World War II U.S. Battleship Disposals:	
Iowa	Retained, modernized 1980s
Massachusetts	Retained until 1960s, scrapped or monumentalized
North Carolina	Same
(*South Dakota*)	(Unfinished, scrapped under Washington Treaty)
West Virginia	Retained until 1960s, 4th ship scrapped as above
Tennessee	Retained until 1960s
Idaho	Scrapped 1948, except test-bed *Mississippi*
Pennsylvania	Survived both atomic tests (sister *Arizona* sunk at Pearl Harbor); target until 1948
Nevada	Same except sister *Oklahoma* sunk at Pearl Harbor
New York	Same except sister *Texas* monumentalized
Arkansas	Sunk by second atomic blast, along with Japanese trophy battleship *Nagato* (and carrier/former battle cruiser *Saratoga*, carriers *Ranger, Enterprise, Independence*, etc.), damaged and less armored contemporary of *West Virginia* class

The modern battleship also saw brief splurges of two naval fads. Early modern battleships, in a 19th century hang-over, were still equipped with rams. Later, torpedoes came to equip British battle cruisers as well as *Nelson* class treaty battleships (one of which, the *Rodney*, was in close action against the German battleship *Bismarck* only **after** changing naval fashions had dictated the landing of the very powerful torpedoes it and its sister had carried for years); these were in side or centerline tubes, after the manner of pre-modern capital ships. Late in World War II, the Germans equipped their three surviving battleships with mountings salvaged from a destroyer (apparently in early 1942, judging from an RAF photo of the Bismarck's sister ship *Tirpitz*) and some (large) torpedo boats; these were intended for use against merchant convoys, but the three ships involved never again got close enough to a convoy to use them.

Two things made post-World War II battleships actually or potentially less vulnerable, rather than more vulnerable. The number of items specifically targeted at armored ships had decreased as the number of armored ships had decreased due to naval fashions. One minor fashion was the decline in aircraft and surface ships carrying torpedoes meant for use against surface ships -- they had been effective, but were largely abandoned as torpedoes aimed at combating submarines, another fashion, became the rage. Cruise missiles were also meant primarily for use against unarmored ships, especially flammable aluminum ones; heavy armor plate was less threatened by such than it had been by underwater explosions which would have destroyed the buoyancy necessary to support that armor's weight.

One opponent of the battleships' refurbishment was Admiral Bobby Ray Inman, a Jimmy Carter crony fuming that the tactical nuclear capabilities of the Tomahawk missiles would prevent a tactical nuclear arms control agreement. For such episodes of being flatly wrong, and opposed to American capability in the process, Inman was nominated as Bill Clinton's second Secretary of Defense before mothballing himself. Where else but in a left-wing Democratic Administration would being unpatriotic and stupid be qualifications for a position of trust?

Small anti-aircraft cruiser *Juneau* was sunk by torpedoes, with the fourth highest death toll of a World War II American warship (*Arizona* highest, then *Indianapolis*, *Franklin* (not sunk), *Juneau*, *Liscombe Bay*, *Princeton* and *Oklahoma*).

The intrigues of the Western Allies with the French recalled the smaller episode with the Yugoslavian *junta* used to undermine a more precarious political system and then themselves intrigued against and murdered. The Third Republic had a parliamentary system, which had been well respected by the anti-German coalitions when declaring or carrying on war. But when that republicanism, that representative democracy, became a threat to the fight against "the dictators" (except Stalin and Mao), why, then, "right-wing" military coups were sought by the liberals of that era as they have been decried by the liberals of our own. A temporary junior cabinet officer, General DeGaulle, was accepted by Churchill as his personal French government. Later, a more senior French general, Henri Girard, escaped from German captivity but failed to pass Churchill's muster. Even after the U.S. was in the war, it continued to treat with the Vichy government of Petain and Laval (Petain had replaced a resigned President of France by Parliamentary Act), even as American General Mark Wayne Clark swam ashore nude in North Africa to conspire with Vichy Army officers. Once Vichy North Africa had been occupied, former Vichy naval leader Admiral Darlan was put in charge there, until his assassination. Military intrigue continued, with the area and the meddlesome Girard fobbed off on each other.

The Vichy Navy may have been savaged several times by the British and the Americans, and in smaller ways by DeGaulle's troops fronting for the British, but it kept its word and scuttled its main surviving force when the Germans took over its Toulon base after the fall of Algeria and Morocco. Beforehand, the Vichy Navy had won three victories, defeating two strong British attacks on its base at Dakar in mid-1940 and the later Siamese Navy probe at Indochina. The most important weapon at Dakar had been the battleship *Richelieu*, which, having survived the two British onslaughts, went on to serve with the British in the Indian Ocean in 1944-45, with its big guns, its anti-aircraft guns and its speed, escorting carrier raids, bombarding Japanese positions and helping to trap a Japanese heavy cruiser. The record of the Vichy Navy stands in glowing contrast to the murderous treacheries of Churchill and FDR.

As battleships receded in fashion, restrictions upon them were not re-imposed. Such restrictions had previously minimized cheap protections against underwater explosions, keeping ships unpadded or underpadded -- bulges had been minimized in width, extent and nature (air transmitted shock less than water- or semi-solid-filled bulges) by tonnage limits, dooming such underbulged ships, and their crews, as the British *Royal Oak* and *Barham* and the Italian battleships (although generic and specific design flaws -- large compartments and the defective Pugliese within-hull protective system respectively -- had also contributed to their vulnerabilities). But the surviving battleships, France's *Jean Bart* of the 1950s, including the Suez landing, and the American *Iowa*s of several modern wars, were not so buffered. But then they were not usually exposed to sophisticated underwater threats in Korea, the Suez, Vietnam, Grenada or the Persian Gulf.

There was also the question, perhaps the major real question, of the battleship's effectiveness, essentially that of its big guns as against that of bombs or missiles. In World War II, American battleship bombardment had been largely against dug-in Japanese troops, and was largely ineffective against troops in caves and rock tunnels. With far fewer battleships (the 4 *Iowa* class) but more often used against mobile and vulnerable enemy troop concentrations, the report was better from Korea, also an advantageous peninsular war-zone. After Korea, those four were put into mothballs, with only the *New Jersey* re-activated for an effective year's service off Vietnam in 1968-69.

The last American warship lost was in the Carter Administration. Destroyer *John R. Craig* rolled over and sank at its pier.

17. Landships. The re-introduction of mobile armor courtesy of the tank made combat more complex, eventually. The key at first was not the conservatism of the generals, but rather the inefficiency of the engineers. Tanks were not built in the quantities achieved for early warplanes, but the main sticking point for both was quality, the lack of horsepower to put weight into the air or to put more armor, firepower and range on tracks.

As tanks became successively appreciated as threats -- most easily measured by the fatuously bombastic announcements of anti-tank breakthroughs -- the means of opposing them became more specialized. Anti-tank missiles displaced machine guns and mortars, or aircraft bombs. High-velocity anti-tank guns were less effective against unarmored targets than low-velocity artillery was, with anti-armor shells having less explosive power (more metal, less powder), little use for indirect, spotted fire (the safest and most common form of artillery fire) and often not exploding when not hitting hard targets. The effect was that of a matrix, with the diversion of effort directed specifically at armored targets leading to less concentration of resources against opposing infantry -- the artillery barrages of World War I were left unexceeded.

Despite some similarities, purpose-built anti-tank guns are cheaper than purpose-built anti-aircraft guns; tanks are easier targets.

A naval matrix resulted from armored ships and their nemesis the torpedo. The new ship types -- using various combinations of speed, protection and weapons -- were therefore less dangerous and bloody than previously experienced or subsequently expected. Jutland and its smaller brothers were more like the Sino-Japanese War or the last pre-torpedo war than they were to the decisive clashes of the Spanish-American War and the Russo-Japanese War; after a lapse, technology and organization had adjusted. Eventually, the unfashionability of armor simplified the naval matrix, but on land there was and is little alternative. Airmobile troops are extremely expensive and frequently ineffective, for example. Deadlock -- World War I, the later Korean War, American involvement in Vietnam and the Iran-Iraq War -- is also uneconomic, and mobile armor is the surest means of breaking it.

The Roebling Amphibian had a Japanese equivalent built by Daihatsu, the last of Japan's "aggressive" car companies to export.

19. The TFX. Martin, by abandoning the main airframe business no longer profitable for it, stayed in business, and eventually, in 1992, bought out the Vought, or aerospace component, of bankrupt LTV, as well as the California missile business of General Dynamics. In its last big spasm of activity, LTV had tried to buy Grumman, proclaiming, probably dishonestly, that it would be Martinizing its Vought operation while moving aircraft production totally to Grumman. Jimmy Ling became a partner in a brokerage house specializing in municipal bonds and political contributions. Unlike erstwhile associate Paul Thayer, Ling was more Democratic in his associations.

General Dynamics also left the airframe business after winning the new Air Force multi-role fighter in company with Lockheed and Boeing, where its political influence was probably not harmful, selling its Ft. Worth operation to Lockheed in late 1992. GD nuclear submarines were buoyed by campaign promises from Bill Clinton, while the F-22 was cancelled shortly after GD bailed out.

The two TFX investigations, 1963 and 1970, were by the Senate's McClellan Investigations Subcommittee, but in each case the cause was not investigation by the Arkansas Chairman, but rather re-electioneering by the ranking member, Washington Senator Henry "Scoop" Jackson, for his 1964 and 1970 poses of having slaved for Boeing, his state's biggest employer. The hearings were thus heavily loaded as an apologia for Jackson supporters, to demonstrate that poor little Boeing had been euchred by the Pentagon, bureaucrats and those corrupt other aerospace concerns who didn't have a Senator cagy enough to call himself a crass name like Scoop.

The Navy's first "jet" fighter was the Ryan Fireball, a deceptively typical World War II-like fighter with an extra engine, jet, in its tail.

Along with early jet projects, NACA (NASA's predecessor) and the Navy had worked with Vought on two prototypes of a naval project, the short take-off "Flying Pancake".

Before Bell faded out of the fixed-wing business, it had adopted a twin-engine proposal even more radical -- pusher-powered -- than McDonnell's P-67 into an early jet. But McDonnell had not had the problems with its naval projects that Bell had had with Army Air with its Cobras, so it stayed in the fixed-wing business.

Bell moved mainly to helicopters, but with Boeing it has developed the V-22 Osprey project from its Carter-era V-15 project, which had moved the engines, instead of just the rotor/props, to the wing-tips. Curtiss had earlier attempted a come-back with wing-tip rotors in a Whiz Kid mobility project culminating in a series of crashes.

The six main TFX bidders were General Dynamics, Boeing, North American, Lockheed, McDonnell and Republic (smaller Northrop, prospering with its F-5/T-38 model tapping both the Air Force trainer and cheap export markets, was not a bidder). The traditional naval aircraft builders -- Grumman, Douglas and Vought -- were not involved as main bidders (although Grumman, for example, was a junior partner to General Dynamics when the contract was finally let) for what was purportedly a bi-service project.

It was here that the shake-out attempt had its greatest success, as two firms were merged and another, Grumman, was a take-over target. The two most recent successful naval aircraft builders, North American with its Vigilante and McDonnell with its Phantom, were quickly shut out in early 1962 by the TFX "Source Selection Board", which had only a single naval member. Follow the verbiage: the program was selecting a contractor, not a design.

If navalized planes were so mediocre and slow to perfect, why is there a Seafire, navalized Spitfire, still on the racing circuit? There are few land-based Spitfires around precisely because they had become militarily outmoded while the Seafires were still being tinkered into the ability to be used from carriers, albeit long after they were outmoded. But that extended development meant there were more in surplus when planes of that era began to be sought for preservation.

John Stack, a mainstay of the NASA swing-wing project, joined Republic after its rejection from the bid. In 1963, he said Republic "competed but the design was no good. That is, it was no good in comparison to what the competitors had." (*1963 Hearings*, page 21). Although Stack's testimony generally supported Boeing, it is noteworthy that he describes more than one superior competitor. Aside from telling of its advantages, Stack described Boeing's back scoop as having "some special problems ... such as high angle of attack and this sort of thing." (page 33). That is, a steep loop might cut air intake. By the same token, a steep turn by a side-scoop might cut air intake -- although this has not been reported -- but that would be on the inner engine and would cut power where it was not needed, if it did indeed occur.

Aside from the usual security deletions in the Hearings, there was the usual pomposity, with Stack dilating upon the boundary air problem (lift and aerial maneuvers mean drag), dealt with theoretically in 1904 by one Prandtl, and practically in 1903 by two Wrights, and earlier by curveballers with raised-seam baseballs. The witness droned on, while Senator Jackson kept trying to edge in for his cameo (it would've been inappropriate for a witness to highlight the Senator's co-incidental appearance, so his entrance had to occur when a Senator had the floor).

McNamara's 1963 "dual" statement is quoted in the *1970 Hearings*, page 2.

Senator Proxmire's proxy, A. Ernest Fitzgerald, later called Northrop peculiarly corrupt. The F-5 fighter was a variant of the T-38 trainer, and won the Freedom Fighter competition. Its improved version, the F-5E, won a similar competition against simplified export versions of Lockheed's Starfighter, McDonnell Douglas' Phantom and LTV's Crusader, three excellent aircraft, two by companies with their own raffish activities (the Lockheed C-5A/Tristar funding and bribery scams, and LTV with Ling and Thayer). The Phantom was too heavy and the other two had single large engines where two smaller ones were more desirable (for easier field maintenance). Other such competitions had been held in the past. Lockheed, for example, had beaten out Douglas, Boeing and Fairchild for the C-130, Douglas and Boeing for the C-141, and Boeing for the C-5A. The factor in the number of competitors was the size of the project versus the size of the company. Fairchild was too small for the C-141 and Douglas for the C-5A -- and for its own DC-10. Indeed, even giant Lockheed ran into trouble with the Georgia C-5A and the California L-1011. With those two huge projects, Lockheed was not greatly discomfitted when its TFX bid lost out in the first round of evaluations.

NASA's wind-tunnel tested a swing-wing model of the Vigilante, or A5J. This was miscalled the A3J in the 1963 TFX Hearings (page 21); there was no "J" model of the A3D-for-Douglas-Skywarrior, J at the time referring to North America, the Vigilante builder. The Vigilante was then replacing the Skywarrior.

The Vigilante as the paradigmatic high-wing side-scoop high-performer has been superseded by the later trend toward more pancake-like bodies, with less room for side scoops. The Stealth planes, the B-2 Bomber and the F-117 Fighter, use scoops that are more on the back, the B-2's on its wings and the F-117's on its wing roots. The Stealth planes are not designed to be greatly dependent upon maneuverability, and so the opportunity to shield the scoops completely from ground-based radar is maximized at the cost of disrupting the airflow over the control surfaces; neither plane is meant for looping-the-loop, the maneuver which was felt to most imperil engine performance of back scoops on earlier designs. Planes more high-performing in the traditional sense have been more inclined toward bottom scoops, although unlike the F-16 these have not been of single-engine planes, and they have tended to be on flatter, and less tubular, bodies, and therefore not as low-hanging.

Following the cancelled B-70 with its six-engine belly-pack, the delayed giant B-1 bomber has its engine pods slung under its low wings' roots. But the B-1 is not meant to be extremely maneuverable, and because of its length its landing gear is long-strutted, to prevent its tail from scraping the runway on take-off. Those features respectively prevent the shielding of the scoops during maneuvers and the sucking-up of runway debris. Five more maneuverable planes from three countries have dual scoops on their undersides. Dassault's naval/land French Rafele's near-belly scoops are tucked under a low-middle wing, giving more ground clearance than the F-16's scoop. Like the B-1's intakes and those of the modern fighters, the Rafele's are not centered behind a debris-churning nosewheel (the F-16's nosewheel actually extends from the underside of its belly scoop, not from the more dangerous position in front of the scoop, from the nose proper). Similar are the Russian Su-27 and MiG-29 and the American Lockheed (, Boeing & General Dynamics) F-22 and its earlier failed competitor the Northrop (& McDonnell Douglas) F-23.

In all of these projects, the boxy lifting-body characteristic of the Vigilante and its clones (and of the Space Shuttle) has been merged with the airframe, making a more saucer-like object (including more rounded wings). The rejected F-23 went further in this direction than the more conservative F-22. The last was Northrop's fourth important project in co-operation with "Douglas" -- the DC-3's wings, the World War II Dauntless and the F-18 were the others.

Northrop's B-2 is currently planned to be produced in a lot of 20 for the multi-billion dollars spent on development. Its predecessors were the two Flying Wing projects, the twin-engined pusher prop B-35 and the multi-jet B-49.

20. Merchants of Political Merchandise. The phallic imagery of guns is misplaced; most jibes are directed at collectors of guns or trophy heads, and collecting is more an anal trait than a phallic one. Observe the art gallery scene, where art collectors, money-grubbing gallery-owners and "creative" artists mix, anal infantilism given a weird patina of sexuality by a credulous media; phallicism would be a step or two up.

People go inside supposedly "phallic" skyscrapers; more womb-like than phallic, skyscrapers are really sypmtoms of an edifice complex.

Feminists and authoritarian conservatives join in the mystification; a malignant example is the tawdry misuse of the term "sex object". Mystifiers use sex object as though it meant people as inanimate objects rather than as the mental renunciation of infantile self-infatuation, seeking pleasure outside of one's self. Inward infantilism is good for a political movement's cohesion, enabling ideology to remain unchallenged by such abstruse concepts as intellectual integrity.

In May 1994, Rush Limbaugh's television program mentioned a 7-year-old Boston schoolgirl suspended from school for three days and ordered to get a psychiatric evaluation, for bringing a squirt-gun to school. Mr. Limbaugh asked rhetorically what kind of idiots would ban squirt-guns. Aside from Boston school authorities, it's the Swedish legislature.

The liberal gun thing extends to the Second Amendment. To liberals, of course, the Bill of Rights is "really" the Bill of Further Government Powers. But the word people refers to individuals, not to governments. The Constitution is in English, and doesn't need "interpretation" (quote the 28-word 2nd Amendment to newspapers, and they will invariably **alter** it). Amendments are changes to a document, and must legally be so read; the federal powers over militias had already been set forth, along with the reserved militia powers of the states, in Article I, Section 8. The new part of the 2nd Amendment was the addition of a right of the people: that is why it is a "shall" clause, while the retention of government militia powers is a "being" -- already in place -- sub-clause. Liberals point to the holdings of their satraps on the federal bench as "precedents", but the problem there is that Congress has long since stopped removing such loonies (and lawyers are barred from criticizing them!). Liberals were **hostile** to precedent when the *Plessy* case upheld segregation, or when FDR's early programs were being declared unconstitutional before the Supreme Court lost its backbone. Unchecked authorities tend toward increasing authoritarianism; what we need is judicial term limits to substitute for a distracted Congress's negligence.

One liberal canard is that individuals are constitutionally banned from owning so-called militia weapons, such as artillery. Yet privately owned artillery was a fixture on American shipping for generations after the Bill of Rights, and privateering was specifically permissible under the Constitution. Such activities were **not** militias.

The left's infantilism and intellectual incompetence is exemplified by its obligatory portentous references to Heisenberg's Uncertainty Principle, that glum and barren re-affirmation of Newton's Third Law wherein light's photons disturb the electrons of an atom, thereby preventing us from pinpointing an electron (as though something that small whipping around an atom at the speed of light were susceptible of being pinpointed -- the main point of quantum mechanics). This innocuous truism becomes the excuse for fatuous meditation upon the hoary observer/subject canard. In the atomic case, light falls anyway, and its effects occur **regardless** of whether anyone is watching. Reactions and reflections occur whether an observer sees them or not; if a tree falls in the woods, environmentalists panic. In the social case, the subjects of liberal tinkering are conscious and try to avoid its disaffects, even as the tinkerers stoutly try to avoid any accurate data. Those who moon about atoms -- the fragility of the continuum and its contents -- end up supporting social engineering, from misconception to stillborn ineptitude. Perhaps they should consider the metaphor of the Pauli Exclusion Principle, limited capacity, or meaningless semantic profundity crowding out simple truth.

In action, the main differences between American liberals and conservatives are that liberals say we and conservatives say they; liberals start crusades which conservatives turn into inquisitions (for example, the move into World War II spawning the Jewish-inspired (Adolph Sabath and Sam Dickstein) House Un-American Activities Committee, or Cold War Liberalism spawning the Truman purges, joining as "McCarthyism"); and conservative photo ops feature stereotyped back-drops while liberals back-drops are a mob of fellow lunatics trying to look serious. And a photo op is as serious as these people get. The generic photo op is a ribbon-cutting or ground-breaking ceremony at a construction site by a group of dignitaries usually notable for distancing themselves from actual work (such events preceded the camera, however). If scrambling to mug for a camera makes one a "dignitary" or a "VIP", one hesitates to speculate what would make someone an indignitary, a Very Inane Person or even a posturing clown (PC).

In the service of corporate PR, Northrop's dud F-20 Tigershark was briefly replaced by the F-22 (including for a video game claiming a carrier capability for it) before it crashed and was cancelled. American high-tech glamor, media-style, is today portrayed by a surplus Swedish fighter from the late 1950s, the Saab Draken. The American consumer picks up the reality check for such excesses. A contemporary of the boxy archetype Vigilante, the Draken was, however, indeed the early first of the more saucer-like post-Vigilante configurations, including, strangely enough, the F-20 and F-22. Score one for Madison Avenue.

The two *Idaho*s sold to Greece in 1914 had been small even for pre-modern battleships, at the insistence of Senator Eugene Hale, long-time Navy Committee Chairman (a Maine Republican in era when that state's long-standing delegation dominated Congress as Southerners would do during Democratic control). Hale thought any ship would always be sunk by a torpedo, so he didn't want any big or expensive ones that could survive. This self-fulfilling prophecy led to a natural desire to be rid of the two small potatoes, particularly after the quick advent of the dreadnought era. Germany's failure to deliver its contracted dreadnought to Greece led Greece, satisfied by the American effort on the guns and turrets for the aborted project, to buy the available *Idaho*s. The proceeds were used by the newly Hale-less, and Democratic, Congress to finance a new modern battleship, the new *Idaho* making a third ship in its class when U.S. construction had been proceeding by twos. By virtue of their place in the sequence of American battleships, the *Idaho*s ended up the only modified under the more advantageous London Treaty, with a long hiatus before such rebuildings came to be restricted by aggressive diplomacy and war instead of treaties.

21. <u>Proxmire at Length</u>. Aside from Congresswomen Rankin and Vietnam dove Mike Mansfield, Montana also gave us acerbic America Firster Senator Burton K. Wheeler. Senator Wheeler compared FDR's foreign and agricultural policies with the acid observation that Roosevelt would plow under every third American boy. That was an exaggeration, as **only** 400,000 odd were lost.

The sixty references from Proxmire's "1970 opus" are from *Report from Wasteland/America's Military-Industrial Complex* (N.Y. 1970). The calculation of GE's C-5A overruns as less than 1/17th of Lockheed's are from adding GE overruns for its engines from R&D, Run A and Run B (43.2, 20.7 and 44.9 million dollars = \$108.8 million) and dividing it into the non-GE overruns of \$1,850.3 million, yielding 17.0006433. To those who might say that a further GE overrun of 'only \$700,001' would have put it over 1/17th, send the author \$700,001 and he'll consider it significant. Proxmire calls the original cost figures "independent" (page 239) rather than Lockheed's.

While the FB-111 was only a marginal strategic bomber, small rather than medium due to its semi-fighter genesis, the TU-26 Backfire bomber was at least a medium bomber (35% larger than the old American B-47 and about 60% bigger than the B-58), 2.7 times as big as the FB-111. Not only did it have 50% more range than Proxmire credited it with, the Soviets had tried to get British computerized fuel-flow technology for their SST, which used the same engines as the Backfire; with Atlee dead, they failed. The Soviets did eventually build an F-111 clone with the Su-24, which was given the same role as the F-111, an intruder ground-attack plane. Note that the Soviets usually assigned even numbers to bombers, but Proxmire still dismissed the Backfire as a bomber, even as NATO coders classed the Su-24 as an "F"-for-fighter-Fencer, because it, not the "B"-for-Bomber-Backfire, was like that alleged American fighter, the F-111.

For 1970, Senator Proxmire was faced with the dilemma of reelection in a closely contested state, one with an isolationistic antigovernment tradition, a big government tradition and an anti-Communist tradition (strongest in Milwaukee's key Democratic wards) and strong anti-Vietnam War feelings. Democrats in simpler liberal areas could come out openly against the war; although it was their party which had bungled it in the first place, it was "Nixon's War" they wanted to bug out of. Proxmire's solution was to run against the Defense Department rather than against the war. Obviously, his own party had done most of the wasting, but, as were other Democrats, Proxmire was happy to run against the mess in Washington, at least in the form of faceless bureaucrats and a newly Republican presidency. His gambit was successful in Wisconsin, and for later re-elections he extended his vendetta to "waste" in government, although never against the spoilsmen of his own party. The closest he came was in retirement, twenty years after *Wasteland*, when he attacked the results of the Kennedy-Quayle job-training bill as maladministered, wasting more than 90% of the $20 billion spent, rather than as a fools' errand from the start. Proxmire himself had advocated federal job-training, of course. That made three rich heels promoting themselves by wasting taxpayers' money on nebulous schemes.

Proxmire also proudly boosted himself as the only MBA (Me Big ?) in the Senate, although he was a skeptic about many business school nostrums. His zero-based phantasy was little more than similar "radical" academic fads, however, echoing such bombastic leftist cant as Reconstruction, Lenin's "Ruthless Criticism of Everything Existing" or even that New Frontier bromide of "an agonizing re-appraisal", an exhaustive flawed analysis followed by some minor reform or major waste. Zero-basing and sunset legislation were boosted by arch-boob Jimmy Carter on the curious assumption that legislatures passing pork barrel budgets would not repass pork barrel legislation. They did, as "entitlements".

The Fitzgerald references, five each to 1972 and 1989, are to his *The High Priests of Waste* (N.Y. 1972) and *The Pentagonists/An Insider's View of Waste, Mismanagement, and Fraud in Defense Spending* (Boston 1989). The latter describes the Reagan Defense Department as part of "Poor Richard's Network" (Richard Stubbing, one of Proxmire's exemplars, not Richard Nixon). Although speculation about Fitzgerald's politics has been as variable as his free spirit/cheapskate personality, who else except a leftist would think of linking someone to Founding Father Benjamin Franklin's Poor Richard as derogatory? The Fitzgerald phrase about General Dynamics weaving a net echoes a line from a prominent Greek tragedy wherein the beset king accuses a messenger of plotting against him; actually, it was the playwright.

Fitzgerald in turn has combined with ABC News to bring forth Dina Rasor, who portentously tells us that "it is no accident" that the B-1 bomber was made in 48 states. No, it wasn't an accident, it was a press release pointing out a banality of a national economy to help Congressmen support defense for local appeal rather than for national reasons, cycling credulity and viciousness. Boeing's civilian 747 is also subcontracted in 48 states, and the Hostess Twinkie probably is, but neither is pork barrel politics. But then again, nor was the B-1, which was merely merchandised, by friends and foes alike, as such. It is natural for Modern Liberals to confuse marketing and a product; having no product except themselves, they naturally obsess upon marketing.

The Seymour Melman quote is from page 177, and the referenced chart is from pages 177-79, of *Pentagon Capitalism/The Political Economy of War* (N.Y. 1970). Political Economy was the old name for Economics before it became so heavily larded with political ideology that the word political had to be dropped. Economy in the original sense meant efficiency in managing a household in ancient Greece. While some dictionaries will tell us that political comes from the Greek *polis* for city, that begs a question, for those cities and their names came from marketplaces, where polists, or sellers, would attract buyers from the surrounding countryside. The sense of macro-economics, of markets, was in politics from the beginning, and abstracting it out led the brash to proclaim it a new discovery, with tail-fins, from time to time. Adam Smith and Karl Marx were two such offenders.

Summary. The Marx quotation is from *Class Struggles in France 1848-1850* (N.Y. 1964 PB), page 37. A "bagno" is probably a bagnio, meaning either a brothel or, more restrictively, a prison. Since Marx had already used brothel in the cited passage, and "bagnos" appears between bench and scaffold, evidently it meant prisons in the specific case. Both Marx and Hitler, crackpots with ramshackle systems, succeeded through a shrewd understanding of their opponents, in particular the "National Liberals". National liberals American-style champion so-called free trade and the "world market" (higher taxes and unemployment), which call forth social programs and more of the same, and an active foreign policy of interference and wars.

Of Marx's claimed original contributions, the first was lifted from the ancient Greeks, and the other two were false (letter to Weydemeyer, March 5, 1852, quoted in the second edition of Lenin's 1918 *State and Revolution* (N.Y. 1974 PB), page 29; Lenin's homily to civil service bureaucracy: "To organise the *whole* national economy like the postal system ... is our immediate aim." (page 44)). Lenin is miscredited with coining the phrase "fellow-traveller", which was in fact Carlyle's (*The French Revolution*, 1989 PB, volume 2, page 337) to describe the associates of young Louis Philippe, Republican turned King of France by the time Carlyle's book came out. The Communists were of course close readers of accounts of all of those French Revolutions.

The Rodney King riot was preceded by his violent arrest, the media barrage and the initial acquittal of the arresting officers. After the riots began, there was some comparison with Los Angeles' 1964 Watts riot. Note that the Watts riot was set off, without a prepatory media barrage, when a Black woman got a traffic ticket. She was not beaten, and there was still a riot. The media's conclusion about that and similar episodes? We needed more "social programs" to "rebuild" the "ghettos".